AN OBEDIENT & PATIENT FAITH

ROBERT LEIGHTON

D1282682

Calvary Press
Amityville, New York

An OBEDIENT & PATIENT FAITH

First Printing in May 1995

CALVARY PRESS
P.O. Box 805
Amityville, NY 11701
1-800-789-8175

ISBN 1-879737-15-9

2 4 6 8 10 9 7 5 3 1

Cover design by Michael Rotolo

This edition is a photolithograph of
the 1853 edition by
Henry G. Bohn, London
Formerly titled:
A Practical Commentary on the First Epistle of St. Peter

PRINTED AND BOUND IN THE UNITED STATES OF AMERICA

Publisher's Preface

"In an age when the study of Theology was the universal and leading pursuit, and amounted almost to a passion, Robert Leighton was a preeminent Theologian." With these words James Aikman began his brief biographical sketch of the author of this commentary about which has been said: "Perhaps there is no expository work in the English language equal to this exposition of St. Peter."

Robert Leighton was born in London in 1611, as a young man he was sent by his father to Scotland to receive his education. He was trained for the ministry at the University of Edinburgh. Became the minister of the parish at Newbattle in 1641. Later became principal and professor of divinity at the University of Edinburgh where he held this position for ten years. He then became the bishop of Dunblane about 1662 and archbishop of Glasgow in 1670. Retiring from that post in 1674 he died ten years later in London in 1684.

Leighton is noted as a striking example of extensive learning and un-bounded liberality. "He had," said Bishop Burnet, "a sublime strain in preaching, with so great a gesture and such a majesty, both of thought, of language and of pronunciation, that I never once saw a wandering eye where he preached and have seen whole assemblies often melt in tears before him."

Brought back into print for you here is the volume originally titled *A Practical Commentary of the First Epistle of St. Peter* but we've entitled it *An Obedient and Patient Faith* because Leighton summarized the Epistle with these words; "The heads of doctrine contained in it are many, *(p. 9)* but the main that are most insisted on, are these three, *faith, obedience,* and *patience;* to establish them in believing, to direct them in doing, and to comfort them in suffering."

Leighton labored to present for us a banquet of precious and delightful truths to be savored by every reader. Each and every page is full of the flavor and aroma of deep and genuine piety, mingled with sound and judicious instruction. No Christian's library, especially that of a minister's, should be without a copy. "Great light is poured on many very difficult passages, in a very masterly manner, and often by a few weighty words" was Philip Doddridge's praise for this classic work.

In a day of *fluffy* books that seek to gratify some immediate "felt" need, this gem distinguishes itself from the crowd. It was not written to be read quickly, but rather to be digested slowly and carefully. We invite you to sit at the feast which Leighton has spread and enjoy it... one bite at a time.

your friends at Calvary Press

FIRST PETER

CHAPTER 1

Ver. 1. Peter, an apostle of Jesus Christ, to the strangers scattered throughout
Pontus, Galatia, Cappadocia, Asia, and Bithynia.

THE grace of God in the heart of man, is a tender plant in a strange,
unkindly soil ; and therefore cannot well prosper and grow, without
much care and pains, and that of a skilful hand, and which hath the art
of cherishing it : for this end hath God given the constant ministry
of the word to his Church, not only for the first work of conversion,
but also for confirming and increasing of his grace in the hearts of his
children.

And though the extraordinary ministers of the Gospel, the Apostles,
had principally the former for their charge—the converting of unbelievers, Jews and Gentiles, and so the planting of churches, to be after
kept and watered by others, (as the Apostle intimates, 1 Cor. iii. 6,)
yet did they not neglect the other work of strengthening the grace of
God begun in the new converts of those times, both by revisiting them,
and exhorting them in person, as they could, and by the supply of their
writing to them when absent.

And the benefit of this extends (not by accident, but by the purpose
and good providence of God) to the Church of God in all succeeding
ages.

This excellent Epistle (full of evangelical doctrine and apostolical
authority) is a brief, and yet very clear summary both of the consolations and instructions needful for the encouragement and direction of a
Christian in his journey to heaven, elevating his thoughts and desires
to that happiness, and strengthening him against all opposition in the
way, both that of corruption within, and temptations and afflictions
from without.

The heads of doctrine contained in it are many, but the main that
are most insisted on, are these three, *faith, obedience,* and *patience ;*
to establish them in believing, to direct them in doing, and to comfort

9

them in suffering. And because the first is the ground-work and support of the other two, this first chapter is much occupied with persuading them of the truth of the mystery which they had received and did believe, *viz.*, their redemption and salvation by Christ Jesus ; that inheritance of immortality bought by his blood for them, and the evidence and stability of their right and title to it.

And then he uses this belief, this assurance of the glory to come, as the great persuasive to the other two, both to holy obedience, and constant patience, since nothing can be too much either to forego or undergo, either to do or to suffer, for the attainment of that blessed state.

And as, from the consideration of that object and matter of the hope of believers, he encourages to patience, and exhorteth to holiness in this chapter in general, so, in the following chapters, he expresses more particularly, both the universal and special duties of Christians, both in doing and suffering, often setting before those to whom he wrote, the matchless example of the Lord Jesus, and the greatness of their engagement to follow him.

In the first two verses, we have the *Inscription* and *Salutation*, in the usual style of the Apostolic Epistles.

The *Inscription* hath the *author* and the *address*,—from whom, and to whom. The *author* of this *Epistle* is designated by his *name*— Peter ; and his *calling*—an Apostle.

We shall not insist upon his name, that it was imposed by Christ, or what is its signification : this the Evangelists teach us, John i. 42 ; Matt. xvi. 18.

By that which is spoken of him in divers passages of the Gospel, he is very remarkable amongst the Apostles, both for his graces, and his failings ; eminent in zeal and courage, and yet stumbling oft in his forwardness, and once grossly falling. And these by the providence of God being recorded in Scripture, give a check to the excess of Rome's conceit concerning this Apostle. Their extolling and exalting him above the rest, is not for his cause, much less to the honour of his Lord and Master Jesus Christ, for he is injured and dishonoured by it ; but it is in favour of themselves. As Alexander distinguished his two friends, that the one was a friend of Alexander, the other a friend of the *king*, the preferment which they give this Apostle, is not in goodwill to Peter, but in the desire of *primacy*. But whatsoever he was, they would be much in pain to prove Rome's right to it by succession. And if ever it had any such right, we may confidently say, it has forfeited it long ·ago, by departing from St. Peter's footsteps, and from his faith, and retaining too much those things wherein he was faulty : namely,

His unwillingness to hear of, and consent to, Christ's sufferings,— his *Master, spare thyself*, or, *Far be it from thee*,—in those they are like him ; for thus they would disburden and exempt the Church from the cross, from the real cross or afflictions, and, instead of that, have nothing but painted, or carved, or gilded crosses ; these they are content to embrace, and worship too, but cannot endure to hear of the other. Instead of the cross of affliction, they make the *crown* or *mitre* the badge of their Church, and will have it known by prosperity, and outward pomp ; and so turn the Church militant into the Church triumphant, not considering that it is Babylon's voice, not the Church's, *I sit as a queen, and shall see no sorrow.*

Again, they are like him in his saying on the mount at Christ's transfiguration, when he knew not what he said, *It is good to be here:* so they have little of the true glory of Christ, but the false glory of that monarchy on their seven hills : *It is good to be here,* say they.

Again, in their undue striking with the sword, not the enemies, as he, but the faithful friends and servants of Jesus Christ. But to proceed.

We see here Peter's office or title,—*an Apostle;* not *chief bishop.* Some in their glossing have been so impudent as to add that beside the text ; though in chap. v. ver. 4, he gives that title to Christ alone, and to himself only *fellow elder;* and here, not *prince of the Apostles,* but *an Apostle,* restored and re-established after his fall, by repentance, and by Christ himself after his own death and resurrection. (See John xxi.) Thus we have in our Apostle a singular instance of human frailty on the one side, and of the sweetness of Divine grace on the other. Free and rich grace it is indeed, that forgives and swallows up multitudes of sins, of the greatest sins ; not only sins before conversion, as to St. Paul, but foul offences committed after conversion, as to David, and to this Apostle ; not only once raising them from the dead, but when they fall, stretching out the same hand, and raising them again, and restoring them to their station, and comforting them in it by his *free Spirit,* as David prays ; not only to cleanse polluted clay, but to work it into vessels of honour, yea, of the most defiled shape to make the most refined vessels, not vessels of honour of the lowest sort, but for the highest and most honourable services, vessels to bear his own precious name to the nations ; making the most unworthy and the most unfit, fit by his grace to be his messengers.

Of Jesus Christ.] Both as the beginning and the end of his apostleship, as Christ is called *Alpha* and *Omega;* chosen and called by him, and called to this—to preach him, and salvation wrought by him.

Apostle of Jesus Christ.] Sent by him and the message no other than his name, to make that known. And what this apostleship was then, after some extraordinary way, befitting these first times of the Gospel, the ministry of the word in ordinary is now, and therefore an employment of more difficulty and excellency than is usually conceived by many, not only of those who look upon it, but even of those who are exercised in it ;—to be ambassadors for the greatest of kings, and upon no mean employment, that great treaty of peace and reconcilement betwixt him and mankind. See 2 Cor. v. 20.

This Epistle is directed to the *Elect,* who are described here, by their *temporal* and by their *spiritual* conditions. The one hath very much dignity and comfort in it ; the other hath neither, but rather the contrary of both ; and therefore the Apostle, intending their comfort, mentions the one but in passing, to signify to whom particularly he sent his Epistle ; but the other is that which he would have their thoughts dwell upon, and therefore he prosecutes it in his following discourse. And if we look to the order of the words, their temporal condition is but interjected ; for it is said, *To the Elect,* first, and then,

To the Strangers scattered, &c. And he would have this as it were drowned in the other — *According to the foreknowledge of God the Father.*

That those dispersed strangers who dwelt in the countries here named, were Jews, appears, if we look to the foregoing Epistle, where the same word is used, and expressly appropriated to the Jews. James i. 1. St. Peter in Gal. ii. is called *an Apostle of the circumcision,* as exercising his apostleship most towards them ; and there is in some passages of this Epistle, somewhat which, though belonging to all Christians, yet hath, in the strain and way of expression, a particular fitness to the believing Jews, as being particularly verified in them, which was spoken of their nation, chap. ii. ver. 9, 10.

Some argue from the name, Strangers, that the Gentiles are here meant, which seems not to be ; for proselyte Gentiles were indeed called strangers in Jerusalem, and by the Jews ; but were not the Jews strangers in these places — Pontus, Galatia, Cappadocia, Asia, and Bithynia ? — Not strangers dwelling together in a prosperous, flourishing condition, as a well-planted colony, but *strangers of the dispersion,* scattered to and fro. *Their dispersion* was partly, first by the Assyrian captivity, and after that by the Babylonish, and by the invasion of the Romans ; and it might be in these very times increased by the believing Jews flying from the hatred and persecution raised against them at home.

The places here mentioned, through which they were dispersed, are all in Asia. So Asia here, is Asia the *lesser.* Where it is to be observed, that some of those who heard St. Peter, Acts ii. 9, are said to be of those regions. And if any of the number then converted were amongst these dispersed, the comfort was no doubt the more grateful from the hand of the same Apostle by whom they were first converted ; but this is only conjecture. Though divine truths are to be received equally from every minister alike, yet it must be acknowledged, that there is something (we know not what to call it) of a more acceptable reception of those who at first were the means of bringing men to God, than of others ; like the opinion some have of physicians whom they love.

The Apostle comforts these strangers of this dispersion, by the spiritual union which they obtained by *effectual calling ;* and so calls off their eyes from their outward, dispersed, and despised condition, to look above that, as high as the spring of their happiness, the *free love* and *election* of God. *Scattered* in the countries, and yet gathered in God's election, chosen or picked out ; strangers to men amongst whom they dwelt, but *known* and *foreknown* to God ; removed from their own country, to which men have naturally an unalterable affection, but *heirs* made of a better, (as follows, ver. 3, 4,) and having within them the evidence both of eternal election and of that expected salvation, the *Spirit of holiness.* (Ver. 2.) At the best, a Christian is but a stranger here, set him where you will, as our Apostle teacheth after ; and it is his privilege that he is so ; and when he thinks not so, he forgets and disparages himself: he descends far below his quality, when he is much taken with any thing in this place of his exile.

But this is the wisdom of a Christian, when he can solace himself against the meanness of his outward condition, and any kind of discomfort attending it, with the comfortable assurance of the love of God, that he hath called him to holiness, given him some measure of it, and an endeavour after more ; and by this may he conclude, that he hath ordained him unto salvation. If either he is a stranger where he lives, or as a stranger deserted of his friends, and very near stripped of all outward comforts, yet may he rejoice in this, that the eternal, unchangeable love of God, which is from everlasting to everlasting, is sealed to his soul. And oh what will it avail a man to be compassed about with the favour of the world, to sit unmolested in his own home and possessions, and to have them very great and pleasant, to be well monied, and landed, and befriended, and yet estranged and severed from God, not having any token of his special love ?

To the Elect.] The Apostle here denominates all the Christians to whom he writes, by the condition of true believers, calling them *Elect* and *Sanctified*, &c. ; and the Apostle St. Paul writes in the same style in his Epistles to the churches. Not that all in these churches were such indeed, but because they professed to be such, and, by that their profession and calling as Christians, they were obliged to be such : and as many of them as were in any measure true to that their calling and profession were really such. Besides, it would seem not unworthy of consideration, that in all probability there would be fewer false Christians, and the number of true believers would be usually greater, in the churches in those primitive times, than now in the best reformed churches : because there could not then be many of them that were from their infancy bred in the Christian faith, but the greatest part were such as, being of years of discretion, were, by the hearing of the Gospel, converted from Paganism and Judaism to the Christian religion first, and made a deliberate choice of it ; to which there were at that time no great outward encouragements, and therefore the less danger of multitudes of hypocrites, which, as vermin in summer, breed most in the time of the Church's prosperity. Though no nation or kingdom had then universally received the faith, but rather hated and persecuted it, yet, were there even then amongst them, as the writings of the Apostles testify, false brethren, and inordinate walkers, and men of corrupt minds, earthly-minded, and led with a spirit of envy and contention and vain-glory.

Although the question that is moved concerning the necessary qualifications of all the members of a true visible church can no way (as I conceive) be decided from the inscriptions of the Epistles, yet certainly they are useful to teach Christians and Christian churches what they ought to be, and what their holy profession requires of them, and sharply to reprove the gross unlikeness and inconformity that is in the most part of men to the description of Christians. As there be some that are too strait in their judgment concerning the being and nature of the visible Church, so certainly the greatest part of churches are too loose in their practice.

From the dissimilitude betwixt our churches and those we may make this use of reproof, that if an Apostolical Epistle were to be directed to us, it ought to be inscribed, to the ignorant, profane, malicious, &c. As he who, at the hearing of the Gospel read, said,

"Either this is not the Gospel, or we are not Christians;" so, either these characters, given in the inscription of these Epistles, are not true characters, or we are not true Christians.

Ver. 2. Elect, according to the foreknowledge of God the Father, through sanctification of the Spirit, unto obedience, and sprinkling of the blood of Jesus Christ.

In this verse we have their *condition* and the *causes* of it.—Their condition, *sanctified* and *justified;* the former expressed by *obedience*, the
latter by *sprinkling of the blood of Christ*. The causes, 1. *Eternal
election*, 2. *The execution of that decree*, their *effectual calling*, which
(I conceive) is meant by *Election* here, the selecting them out of the
world, and joining them to the fellowship of the children of God.
So John xv. 19. The former, *Election*, is particularly ascribed to
God the Father, the latter to the Holy Spirit; and the *blood of Jesus
Christ*, the Son of God, is here assigned as the cause of their *justification;* and so the whole Trinity concurring dignify them with this
their spiritual and happy estate.

First, I shall discourse of these separately, and then of their connexion.

1. Of the State itself, and 1. of *Justification*, though named last.

This *sprinkling* has respect to the rite of the legal purification by
the sprinkling of blood; and that appositely, for these rites of
sprinkling and blood did all point out this blood and this sprinkling,
and exhibited this true ransom of souls, which was only shadowed by
them.

The use and end of sprinkling were *purification* and *expiation*,
because sin merited death, and the pollutions and stains of human
nature were by sin. Such is the pollution, that it can be no manner
of way washed off but by blood. (Heb. ix. 22.) Neither is there
any blood able to purge from sin except the most precious blood of
Jesus Christ, which is called (Acts xx. 28) the *blood of God.*

That the stain of sin can be washed off only by blood intimates
that it merits death; and that no blood, but that of the Son of God,
can do it intimates that this stain merits eternal death; and it had
been our portion, except the death of the eternal Lord of life had freed
us from it.

Filthiness needs sprinkling; *guiltiness* (such as deserves death)
needs sprinkling of blood; and the death it deserves being everlasting
death, the blood must be the blood of Christ, the eternal Lord of life,
dying to free us from the sentence of death.

The soul (as the body) hath its life, its health, its purity, and the contrary of these,—its death, diseases, deformities, and impurity,—which
belong to it as to their first subject, and to the body by participation.

The soul and body of all mankind are stained by the pollution of
sin. The impure leprosy of the soul is not a spot outwardly, but
wholly inward; hence, as the corporal leprosy was purified by the
sprinkling of blood, so is this. Then, by reflecting, we see how all
this that the Apostle St. Peter expresseth is necessary to justification.
1. Christ, the Mediator betwixt God and man, is God and man.
2. A Mediator not only interceding, but also satisfying. Eph. ii. 16.

3. This satisfaction doth not reconcile us, unless it be applied : therefore there is not only mention of blood, but the *sprinkling* of it.   The
Spirit by faith sprinkleth the soul, as with hyssop, wherewith the
sprinkling was made : this is it of which the Prophet speaks, (Isa. lii.
15,) *So shall he sprinkle many nations;* and which the Apostle to the
Hebrews prefers above all legal sprinklings, (chap. ix. 12, 13, 14,) both
as to its duration and as to the excellency of its effects.

Men are not easily convinced and persuaded of the deep stain of
sin, and that no other laver can fetch it out but the sprinkling of the
blood of Jesus Christ.   Some who have moral resolutions of amendment, dislike, at least, gross sins, and purpose to avoid them, and it is
to them cleanness enough to reform in those things ; but they consider
not what becomes of the guiltiness they have contracted already, and
how that shall be purged, how their natural pollution shall be taken
away.   Be not deceived in this, it is not a transient sigh, or a light
word, or a wish of *God forgive me;* no, nor the highest current of
repentance, nor that which is the truest evidence of repentance, amendment ; it is none of these that purify in the sight of God, and expiate
wrath ; they are all imperfect and stained in themselves, cannot stand
and answer for themselves, much less be of value to counterpoise the
former guilt of sin.   The very tears of the purest repentance, unless
they be sprinkled with this blood, are impure ; all our washings without this are but washings of the blackmoor—it is labour in vain.   Jer.
ii. 22 ; Job ix. 30, 31.   There are none truly purified by the blood of
Christ who do not endeavour after purity of heart and conversation ;
but yet it is the blood of Christ by which they are all made fair, and
there is no spot in them.   Here it is said, *Elect to obedience;* but because that obedience is not perfect, there must be sprinkling of the
blood too.   There is nothing in religion further out of nature's reach,
and out of its liking and believing, than the doctrine of redemption by
a Saviour, and a crucified Saviour,—by Christ, and by his blood, first
shed on the cross in his suffering, and then sprinkled on the soul by his
Spirit.   It is easier to make men sensible of the necessity of repentance
and amendment of life, (though that is very difficult,) than of this purging
by the sprinkling of this precious blood.   Did we see how needful
Christ is to us, we should esteem and love him more.

It is not by the hearing of Christ and of his blood in the doctrine
of the Gospel ; it is not by the sprinkling of water, even that water
which is the sign of his blood, without the blood itself and the sprinkling of it.   Many are present where it is sprinkled, and yet have no
portion in it.   Look to this, that this blood be sprinkled on your souls,
that the destroying angel may pass by you.   *There is a generation*
(not some few, but a generation) deceived in this ; they are their own
deceivers, *pure in their own eyes.* (Prov. xxx. 12.)   How earnestly
doth David pray, *Wash me, purge me with hyssop!*   Though bathed
in tears, (Psal. vi. 6,) that satisfied not :—*Wash thou me.*   This is the
honourable condition of the saints, that they are purified and consecrated unto God by this sprinkling ; yea, they have on *long white
robes washed in the blood of the Lamb.*   There is mention indeed of
great tribulation, but there is a double comfort joined with it.   1. They
come out of it ; that tribulation hath an end.   And, 2. They pass from

that to glory ; for they have on the robe of *candidates, long white robes washed in the blood of the Lamb,* washed white in blood.   As for this blood, it is nothing but purity and spotlessness, being stained with no sin, and besides hath that virtue to take away the stain of sin, where it is sprinkled.   *My well-beloved is white and ruddy,* saith the spouse ; thus in his death, ruddy by bloodshed, white by innocence and purity of that blood.

Shall they then, who are purified by this blood, return to live among the swine, and tumble with them in the puddle ?   What gross injury were this to themselves, and to that blood by which they are cleansed ! They who are chosen to this *sprinkling,* are likewise chosen to *obedience.* This blood purifieth the heart ; yea, this blood *purgeth our consciences from dead works to serve the living God.*   Heb. ix. 14.

2. Of their Sanctification.   *Elect unto obedience.*]   It is easily understood to whom.   When obedience to God is expressed by the simple absolute name of obedience, it teacheth us that to him alone belongs absolute and unlimited obedience, all obedience by all creatures.   It is the shame and misery of man, that he hath departed from this obedience, that we are become *sons of disobedience;* but Grace, renewing the hearts of believers, changeth their natures, and so their names, and makes them *children of obedience* (as afterwards in this chapter).   As this obedience consists in the receiving Christ as our Redeemer, so also at the same time as our Lord or King ; there is an entire rendering up of the whole man to his obedience.   This obedience, then, of the only begotten Jesus Christ, may well be understood not as *his actively,* as Beza interprets it, but *objectively,* as 2 Cor. x. 5.   I think here it is contained, yea, chiefly understood to signify that *obedience* which the Apostle in the Epistle to the Romans calls the *obedience of faith,* by which the doctrine of Christ is received, (and so Christ himself,) which uniteth the believing soul to Christ,—he sprinkles it with his blood, to the remission of sin,—and which is the root and spring of all future obedience in the Christian life.

By *obedience,* sanctification is here intimated ; it signifies, then, both habitual and active obedience, renovation of heart, and conformity to the Divine will.   The mind is illuminated by the Holy Ghost, to know and believe the Divine will ; yea, this faith is the great and chief part of obedience.   (See Rom. i. 8.)   The truth of the doctrine is first impressed on the mind ; hence flows out pleasant obedience, and full of love ; hence all the affections, and the whole body, with its members, learn to give a willing obedience, and submit unto God ; whereas before they resisted him, being under the standard of Satan.

This obedience, though imperfect, yet hath a certain (if I may so say) *imperfect perfection.*   It is universal in three manner of ways. 1. In the subject.   2. In the object.   3. In the duration : the whole man is subjected to the whole law, and that constantly and perseveringly.

The first universality is the cause of the other : because it is not in the tongue alone, or in the hand, &c., but has its root in the heart ; therefore it doth not wither as the grass or flower lying on the surface of the earth, but it flourishes, because rooted.   And it embraces the whole law, because it arises from a reverence it has for the Lawgiver himself. Reverence, I say, but tempered with love; hence, it accounts no law nor command little, or of small value, which is from God, because he is great and highly esteemed by the pious heart; no command hard, (though contrary to the flesh,) because all things are easy to love. There is the same authority in all, as St. James divinely argues; and this authority is the golden chain of all the commandments, which if broken in any link, all falls to pieces.

That this three-fold perfection of obedience is not a picture drawn by fancy, is evident in David, Psal. cxix., where he subjects himself to the whole law; his feet, ver. 105; his mouth, ver. 13; his heart, ver. 11; the whole tenor of his life, ver. 24. He subjects himself to the whole law, ver. 6, and he professes his constancy therein, in verses 16 and 33: *Teach me the way of thy statutes, and I shall keep it unto the end.*

II. We have the causes of the condition above described.

According to the foreknowledge of God the Father.] The exactest knowledge of things is, to know them in their causes; it is then an excellent thing, and worthy of their endeavours who are most desirous of knowledge, to know the best things in their highest causes; and the happiest way of attaining to this knowledge, is, to possess those things, and to know them in experience. To such persons the Apostle here speaks, and sets before them the excellency of their spiritual condition, and leads them to the causes of it.

Their state is, that they are *sanctified* and *justified:* the nearest cause of both these is, Jesus Christ. He is made unto them both *righteousness* and *sanctification:* the sprinkling of his blood purifies them from guiltiness, and quickens them to obedience.

The appropriating or applying cause comes next under consideration, which is the *Holy,* and *holy-making* or *sanctifying Spirit,* the author of their selection from the world, and effectual calling unto grace.

The source of all the appointing or decreeing cause, is *God the Father:* for though they all work equally in all, yet, in order of working, we are taught thus to distinguish and particularly to ascribe the first work of eternal election to the first person of the blessed Trinity.

In or through sanctification.] For to render it, *elect to the sanctification,* is strained: so then I conceive this election is their effectual calling, which is by the working of the Holy Spirit: see 1 Cor. i. 26—28, where *vocation* and *election* are used in the same sense: *Ye see your calling, brethren, how that not many wise men after the flesh,* &c.; *but God hath chosen the foolish things of the world to confound the wise.* It is the first act of decree of election; the beginning of its performance in those that are elected; and it is in itself a real separating of men from the profane and miserable condition of the world, and an appropriating and consecrating of a man unto God; and therefore, both in regard of its relation to election, and in regard of its own nature, it well bears that name. See Rom. viii. 28, 30; Acts ii. 47, and xiii. 48; John xv. 19.

Sanctification in the narrower sense, as distinguished from *justification,* signifieth the inherent holiness of a Christian, or his being inclined and enabled to perform the *obedience* mentioned in this verse;

but it has here a sense more large, and is co-extended with the whole work of renovation ; it is the severing or separating of men to God, by his Holy Spirit drawing them unto him ; and so it comprehends justification (as here) and the first working of faith, by which the soul is justified, through its apprehending and applying the righteousness of Jesus Christ.

Of the Spirit.] The word calls men externally, and by that external calling prevails with many to an external receiving and professing of religion ; but if it be left alone it goes no farther.   It is indeed the means of sanctification and effectual calling, as John xvii. 17, *Sanctify them through thy truth ;* but this it doth when the Spirit, which speaks in the word, works in the heart, and causes it to hear and obey. The spirit or soul of a man is the chief and the first subject of this work, and it is but slight, false work that begins not there ; but the *spirit* here is to be taken for the Spirit of God, the efficient, rather than for the spirit of man, the subject of this sanctification.   And therefore our Saviour in that place prays to the Father, *that he would sanctify his own by that truth ;* and this he doth by the concurrence of his Spirit with that word of truth which is the life and vigour of it, and makes it prove *the power of God unto salvation to them that believe.*   It is a fit means in itself, but it is a prevailing means only when the Spirit of God brings it into the heart.   It is a sword, and *sharper than a two-edged sword,* fit to divide, yea, *even to the dividing of soul and spirit ;* but this it doth not, unless it be in the Spirit's hand, and he apply it to this cutting and dividing.   The word calls, but the Spirit draws, not severed from that word, but working in it, and by it.

It is very difficult work to draw a soul out of the hands and strong chains of Satan, and out of the pleasing entanglements of the world, and out of its own natural perverseness, to yield up itself unto God,— to deny itself, and live to him, and in so doing, to run against the main stream, and the current of the ungodly world without, and corruption within.

The strongest rhetoric, the most moving and persuasive way of discourse, is all too weak ; the tongue of men or angels cannot prevail with the soul to free itself, and shake off all that detains it.   Although it be convinced of the truth of those things that are represented to it, yet still it can and will hold out against it, and say, *Non persuadebis etiamsi persuaseris.*

The hand of man is too weak to pluck any soul out of the crowd of the world, and to set it in amongst the select number of believers. Only the Father of spirits hath absolute command of spirits, *viz.*, the souls of men, to work on them as he pleaseth, and where he will. This powerful, this sanctifying Spirit knows no resistance ; works sweetly, and yet strongly ; it can come into the heart, whereas all other speakers are forced to stand without.   That still voice within persuades more than all the loud crying without ; as he that is within the house, though he speaks low, is better heard and understood, than he that shouts without-doors.

When the Lord himself speaks by this his Spirit to a man, selecting and calling him out of the lost world, he can no more disobey than Abraham did, when the Lord spoke to him after an extraordinary manner, to depart from his own country and kindred : *Abraham departed as the Lord had spoken to him.* Gen. xii. 4.   There is a secret, but very powerful, virtue in a word, or look, or touch of this Spirit upon the soul, by which it is forced, not with a harsh, but a pleasing violence, and cannot choose but follow it, not unlike that of Elijah's mantle upon Elisha.   How easily did the disciples forsake their callings and their dwellings to follow Christ !

The Spirit of God draws a man out of the world by a sanctified light sent into his mind, 1. Discovering to him, how base and false the sweetness of sin is, which withholds men and amuses them, that they return not ; and how true and sad the bitterness is that will follow upon it ; 2. Setting before his eyes the free and happy condition, *the glorious liberty of the sons of God,* the riches of their present enjoyment, and their far larger and assured hopes for hereafter ; 3. Making the beauty of Jesus Christ visible to the soul ; which straightway takes it so, that it cannot be stayed from coming to him though its most beloved friends, most beloved sins, lie in the way, and hang about it, and cry, Will you leave us so ?   It will tread upon all to come within the embraces of Jesus Christ, and say with St. Paul, *I was not disobedient to (or unpersuaded by) the heavenly vision.*

It is no wonder that the godly are by some called singular and precise ; they are so, singular, a few selected ones picked out by God's own hand, for himself : *Know that the Lord hath set apart him that is godly for himself.* Psal. iv. 3.   *Therefore,* saith our Saviour, *the world hates you, because I have chosen you out of the world.*   For the world lies in unholiness and wickedness—is buried in it ; and as living men can have no pleasure among the dead, neither can these elected ones amongst the ungodly ; they walk in the world as warily as a man or woman neatly apparelled would do amongst a multitude that are all sullied and bemired.

Endeavour to have this sanctifying Spirit in yourselves ; pray much for it ; for his promise is passed to us, that *He will give this Holy Spirit to them that ask it.*   And shall we be such fools as to want it, for want of asking ?   When we find heavy fetters on our souls, and much weakness, yea averseness to follow the voice of God calling us to his obedience, then let us pray with the spouse, *Draw me.*   She cannot go nor stir without that drawing ; and yet, with it, not only goes, but runs.   *We will run after thee.*

Think it not enough that you hear the word, and use the outward ordinances of God, and profess his name ; for many are thus called, and yet but a few of them are chosen.   There is but small part of the world outwardly called, in comparison of the rest that is not so, and yet the number of the true elect is so small, that it gains the number of these that are called, the name of *many.*   They who are in the visible Church, and partake of external vocation, are but like a large list of names, (as in civil elections is usual,) out of which a small number is chosen to the dignity of true Christians, and invested into their privilege.   Some men in nomination to offices or employments, think it a worse disappointment and disgrace to have been in the list, and yet not chosen, than if their names had not been mentioned at all.   Certainly, it is a greater unhappiness to have been *not far from the kingdom of God,* (as our Saviour speaks,) and miss of it, than still to have remained in the farthest distance; to have been at the mouth of the haven, (the fair havens indeed,) and yet driven back and shipwrecked. Your labour is most preposterous; you seek to ascertain and make sure things that cannot be made sure, and that which is both more worth, and may be made surer than them all, you will not endeavour to make sure. Hearken to the Apostle's advice, and at length set about this in earnest, *to make your calling and election sure.* Make sure this election, as it is here, (for that is the order,) your effectual calling sure, and that will bring with it assurance of the other, the eternal election and love of God towards you, which follows to be considered.

According to the foreknowledge of God the Father.] *Known unto God are all his works from the beginning,* saith the Apostle James. Acts xv. 18. He sees all things from the beginning of time to the end of it, and beyond to all eternity, and from all eternity he did foresee them. But this foreknowledge here relates peculiarly to the elect. *Verba sensus in sacra scriptura denotant affectus,* as the Rabbins remark. So in man, Psal. lxvi., *If I see iniquity;* and in God, Psal. i. 6, *For the Lord knoweth the way of the righteous,* &c. And again, Amos iii. 2, *You only have I known of all the families of the earth,* &c. And in that speech of our Saviour, relating it as the terrible doom of reprobates at the last day, *Depart,* &c., *I know you not, I never knew you.* So St. Paul, Rom. vii. 15, *For that which I do, I allow* [Gr. *know*] *not.* And Beza observes that γινώσκειν is by the Greeks sometimes taken for *decernere, judicare;* thus some speak, to *cognosce* upon a business. So then this foreknowledge is no other than that eternal love of God, or decree of election, by which some are appointed unto life, and being foreknown or elected to that end, they are predestinate to the way to it. *For whom he did foreknow, he also did predestinate to be conformed to the image of his Son, that he might be the firstborn among many brethren.* Rom. viii. 29.

It is most vain to imagine a foresight of faith in men, and that God in the view of that faith, as the condition of election itself, as it is called, has chosen them: for, 1. Nothing at all is *futurum,* or can have that imagined futurition, but as it is, and because it is decreed by God to be; and, therefore, (as says the Apostle St. James, in the passage before cited,) *Known unto God are all his works,* because they are his works in time, and his purpose from eternity. 2. It is most absurd to give any reason of Divine will without Himself. 3. This supposition easily solves all the difficulty which the Apostle speaks of; and yet he never thought of such a solution, but runs high for an answer, not to satisfy cavilling reason, but to silence it, and stop its mouth: for thus the Apostle argues, Rom. ix. 19, 20: *Thou wilt say then unto me, Why doth he yet find fault; for who hath resisted his will? Nay, but, O man, who art thou that repliest against God?* Who can conceive whence this should be, that any man should believe, unless it be given him of God? And if given him, then it was His purpose to give it him; and if so, then it is evident that He had a purpose to save him; and for that end He gives faith: not therefore purposes to save, because man shall believe. 4. This seems cross to these Scriptures, where they speak of the subordination, or rather coordination, of those two : as here, *foreknown* and *elect*, not because of obedience, or sprinkling, or any such thing, but to obedience and sprinkling which is by faith. So God predestinated, not because he foresaw men would be conformed to Christ, but that they might be so. Rom. viii. 29, *For whom he did foreknow he also did predestinate.* And the same order is observable, Acts ii. 47, *And the Lord added to the Church daily such as should be saved.* Also xiii. 48, *And as many as were ordained to eternal life believed.*

This foreknowledge, then, is His eternal and unchangeable love ; and that thus he chooseth some, and rejecteth others, is for that great end, to manifest and magnify his mercy and justice : but why he appointed this man for the one, and that man for the other, made Peter a vessel of this mercy, and Judas of wrath, this is even so, because it seemed good to Him. This, if it be harsh, yet is Apostolic doctrine. *Hath not the potter* (saith St. Paul) *power over the same lump, to make one vessel unto honour and another unto dishonour?* This deep we must admire, and always, in considering it, close with this : *O the depth of the riches both of the wisdom and knowledge of God!*

III. The connexion of these we are now for our profit to take notice of ; that *effectual calling* is inseparably tied to this eternal *foreknowledge* or *election* on the one side, and to *salvation* on the other. These two links of the chain are up in heaven in God's own hand ; but this middle one is let down to earth into the hearts of his children, and they, laying hold on it, have sure hold on the other two, for no power can sever them. If, therefore, they can read the characters of God's image in their own souls, those are the counterpart of the golden characters of His love, in which their names are written in the book of life. Their believing writes their names under the promises of the revealed book of life,—the Scriptures, and so ascertains them, that the same names are in the secret book of life which God hath by himself from eternity. So that finding the stream of grace in their hearts, though they see not the fountain whence it flows, nor the ocean into which it returns, yet they know that it hath its source, and shall return to that ocean which ariseth from their eternal election, and shall empty itself into that eternity of happiness and salvation.

Hence much joy ariseth to the believer ; this tie is indissoluble, as the agents are, the Father, the Son, and the Spirit : so are *election*, and *vocation*, and *sanctification*, and *justification*, and *glory*. Therefore, in all conditions, believers may, from a sense of the working of the Spirit in them, look back to that election, and forward to that salvation ; but they that remain unholy and disobedient, have as yet no evidence of this love ; and therefore cannot, without vain presumption and self-delusion, judge thus of themselves, that they are within the peculiar love of God. But in this *let the righteous be glad, and let them shout for joy, all that are upright in heart.*

It is one main point of happiness, that he that is happy doth know and judge himself to be so ; this being the peculiar good of a reasonable creature, it is to be enjoyed in a reasonable way : it is not as the dull resting of a stone, or any other natural body, in its natural place ; but the knowledge and consideration of it is the fruition of it, the very relishing and tasting its sweetness.

The perfect blessedness of the saints is awaiting them above ; but even their present condition is truly happy, though incompletely, and but a small beginning of that which they expect. And this their present happiness is so much the greater the more clear knowledge and firm persuasion they have of it. It is one of the pleasant fruits of the godly, *to know the things that are freely given them of God*, 1 Cor. ii. 12. Therefore the Apostle, to comfort his dispersed brethren, sets before them a description of that excellent spiritual condition to which they are called.

If *election, effectual calling*, and *salvation* be inseparably linked together, then, by any one of them a man may lay hold upon all the rest, and may know that his hold is sure ; and this is that way wherein we may attain, and ought to seek, that comfortable assurance of the love of God. Therefore *make your calling sure*, and by that, your *election ;* for that being done, this follows of itself. We are not to pry immediately into the decree, but to read it in the performance. Though the mariner sees not the pole-star, yet the needle of the compass which points to it, tells him which way he sails : thus the heart that is touched with the loadstone of Divine love, trembling with godly fear, and yet still looking towards God by fixed believing, points at the love of election, and tells the soul that its course is heavenward, towards the haven of eternal rest. He that loves may be sure he was loved first ; and he that chooses God for his delight and portion may conclude confidently that God hath chosen him to be one of those that shall enjoy him, and be happy in him for ever ; for that our love and electing of him is but the return and repercussion of the beams of his love shining upon us.

Find thou but within thee sanctification by the Spirit, and this argues, necessarily, both justification by the Son, and the election of God the Father. *Hereby know we that we dwell in him, and he in us, because he has given us of his Spirit.* 1 John iv. 13. It is a most strange demonstration, *ab effectu reciproco :* he called those he hath elected ; he *elected* those he called. Where this sanctifying Spirit is not, there can be no persuasion of this eternal love of God : they that are *children of disobedience* can conclude no otherwise of themselves but that they are the *children of wrath.* Although, from present unsanctification, a man cannot infer that he is not elected ; for the decree may, for a part of man's life, run (as it were) under ground ; yet this is sure, that the estate leads to death, and unless it be broken, will prove the black line of reprobation. A man hath no portion amongst the children of God, nor can read one word of comfort in all the promises that belong to them, while he remains unholy. Men may please themselves in profane scoffing at the holy Spirit of grace, but let them withal know this, that that holy Spirit, whom they mock and despise, is that Spirit *who seals men to the day of redemption.* Eph. iv. 30.

If any pretend that they have the Spirit, and so turn away from the straight rule of the Holy Scriptures, they have a spirit indeed, but it is a fanatical spirit, the spirit of delusion and giddiness ; but the Spirit of God, that leads his children in the way of truth, and is for that purpose sent them from heaven to guide them thither, squares their thoughts and ways to that rule whereof it is author, and that word which was inspired by it, and sanctifies them to obedience. *He that saith, I know him, and keepeth not his commandments, is a liar, and the truth is not in him.* 1 John ii. 5.

Now this Spirit which sanctifieth, and sanctifieth to obedience, is within us the evidence of our election, and the earnest of our salvation. And whoso are not sanctified and led by this Spirit, the Apostle tells us what is their condition. Rom. viii. 9. *If any man have not the Spirit of Christ, he is none of his.*

Let us not delude ourselves : this is a truth, if there be any in religion ; they who are not made saints in the state of grace shall never be saints in glory.

The stones which are appointed for that glorious temple above are hewn and polished, and prepared for it here ; as the stones were wrought and prepared in the mountains for building the temple at Jerusalem.　　(v. 11)

This is God's order. Psalm lxxxiv. 12. He gives *grace* and *glory.* Moralists can tell us, that the way to the temple of honour is through the temple of virtue. They that think they are bound for heaven in the ways of sin, have either found a new way untrodden by all that are gone thither, or will find themselves deceived in the end. We need not then that poor shift for the pressing of holiness and obedience upon men, to represent it to them as the meriting cause of salvation. This is not at all to the purpose, seeing that without it the necessity of holiness to salvation is pressing enough ; for holiness is no less necessary to salvation, than if it were the meriting cause of it ; it is as inseparably tied to it in the purpose of God. And in the order of performance, godliness is as certainly before salvation as if salvation did wholly and altogether depend upon it, and were in point of justice deserved by it. Seeing, then, there is no other way to happiness but by holiness, no assurance of the love of God without it, take the Apostle's advice ; study it, seek it, follow earnestly after holiness, *without which no man shall see the Lord.*

Grace unto you and peace be multiplied.] It hath always been a civil custom amongst men, to season their intercourse with good wishes one for another ; this the Apostles use in their Epistles in a spiritual, divine way, suitable to their holy writings. It well becomes the messengers of *grace* and *peace*, to wish both, and to make their salutation conform to the main scope and subject of their discourse. The Hebrew word of salutation we have here—*Peace*, and that which is the spring both of this and all good things, in the other word of salutation used by the Greeks—*Grace.* All right rejoicing, and prosperity, and happiness, flow from this source, and from this alone, and are sought elsewhere in vain.

In general, this is the character of a Christian spirit, to have a heart filled with *blessing*, with this sweet good-will and good-wishing to all, especially to those who are their brethren in the same profession of religion. And this charity is a precious balm, diffusing itself in the wise and seasonable expressions of it, upon fit occasions ; and those expressions must be cordial and sincere, not like what you call court holy-water, in which there is nothing else but falsehood, or vanity at the best. This manifests men to be the sons of blessing, and of the ever-blessed God, the Father of all blessing, when in his name they bless one another : yea, our Saviour's rule goes higher, to *bless those that curse them*, and urges it by that relation to God as their Father, that in this they may resemble him : *That ye may be the children of your Father which is in heaven.*

But in a more eminent way it is the duty of pastors to bless their people, not only by their public and solemn benediction, but by daily and instant prayers for them in secret. And the great *Father, who seeth in secret, will reward them openly.*

They are to be ever both endeavouring and wishing their increase of knowledge and all spiritual grace, in which they have in St. Paul a frequent pattern.

They who are messengers of this *grace,* if they have experience of it, it is the oil of gladness that will dilate their heart, and make it large in love and spiritual desires for others, especially their own flocks.

Let us consider, 1. The matter of the Apostle's desire for them,— *grace and peace.* 2. The measure of it,—that it may *be multiplied.*

1*st.* The matter of the Apostle's desire, *Grace.* We need not make a noise with the many school-distinctions of *Grace,* and describe in what sense it is here to be taken : for no doubt it is all *saving Grace* to those dispersed brethren, so that in the largest notion which it can have that way, we may safely here take it.

What are *preventing grace, assisting grace, working* and *co-working grace,* (as we may admit these differences in a sound sense,) but divers names of the same effectual saving grace, in relation to our different estate? as the same sea receives different names from the different parts of the shore it beats upon. First it prevents and works ; then it assists and prosecutes what it hath wrought : *He worketh in us to will and to do.* But the whole sense of saving grace, I conceive, is comprehended in these two. 1. Grace in the fountain, that is, the peculiar love and favour of God. 2. Grace in the streams, the fruits of this love, (for it is not unempty, but a most rich and liberal love,) *viz.,* all the grace and spiritual blessings of God bestowed upon them whom he hath freely chosen. The love of God in itself can neither diminish or increase, but it is multiplied, or abounds in the manifestation and effects of it. So then, to desire grace to be multiplied to them, is to wish to them the living spring of it, that love which cannot be exhausted, but is ever flowing forth, and instead of abating, makes each day richer than the preceding.

And this is that which should be the top and sum of Christian desires,—to have, or want any other thing indifferently, but to be resolved and resolute in this, to seek a share in this grace, the free love of God, and the sure evidences of it within you, the fruit of holiness, and the graces of his Spirit. But the most of us are otherwise taken up : we will not be convinced how basely and foolishly we are busied, though in the best and most respected employments of the world, so long as we neglect our noblest trade of growing rich in grace, and the comfortable enjoyment of the love of God. Our Saviour tells us of *one thing needful,* importing that all other things are comparatively unnecessary, by-works, and mere impertinencies ; and yet in these we lavish out our short and uncertain time ; we let the other stand by till we find leisure. Men who are altogether profane, think not on it at all. Some others possibly deceive themselves thus, and say, When I have done with such a business in which I am engaged, then I will sit down seriously to this, and bestow more time and pains on these things, which are undeniably greater and better, and more worthy of it. But this is a slight that is in danger to undo us. What if we attain not to the end of that business, but end ourselves before it ? Or if we do not, yet some other business may step in after that. Oh then, say we, that must be despatched also. Thus, by such delays, we may lose the present opportunity, and in the end, our own souls.

Oh ! be persuaded it deserves your diligence, and that without delay, to seek somewhat that may be constant enough to abide with you, and strong enough to uphold you in all conditions, and that is alone this free grace and love of God. While many say, *Who will show us any good?* set you in with David in his choice, *Lord, lift thou up the light of thy countenance upon me, and this shall rejoice my heart more than the abundance of corn and wine.* Psal. iv. 6, 7.

This is that light which can break into the darkest dungeons, from which all other lights and comforts are shut out ; and without this, all other enjoyments are, what the world would be without the sun, nothing but darkness. Happy they who have this light of Divine favour and grace shining into their souls, for by it they shall be led to that city, where the sun and moon are needless ; for *The glory of God doth lighten it, and the Lamb is the light thereof.* Rev. xxi. 23.

Godliness is profitable for all things, saith the apostle, *having the promises of this life and that which is to come;* all other blessings are the attendants of grace, and follow upon it. This blessing which the Apostle here (as St. Paul also in his Epistles) joins with Grace, was, with the Jews, of so large a sense, as to comprehend all that they could desire ; when they wished Peace, they meant all kind of good, all welfare and prosperity. And thus we may take it here, for all kind of peace ; yea, and for all other blessings, but especially that spiritual peace which is the proper fruit of grace, and doth so intrinsically flow from it.

We may and ought to wish to the Church of God outward blessings, and particularly outward peace, as one of the greatest, and one of the most valuable favours of God: thus prayed the Psalmist, *Peace be within thy walls, and prosperity within thy palaces.*

That Wisdom which doth what he will, by what means he will, and works one contrariety out of another, brings light out of darkness, good out of evil,—can and doth turn tears and troubles to the advantage of his Church ; but certainly, in itself, peace is more suitable to its increase, and, if not abused, it proves so too. Thus in the Apostolic times, it is said, Acts ix. 31, *The Church had peace, and increased exceedingly.*

We ought also to wish for ecclesiastical peace to the Church, that she may be free from dissensions and divisions. These readily arise, more or less, as we see, in all times, and haunt religion, and the reformation of it, as a *malus genius.* St. Paul had this to say to his

Corinthians, 1 Ep. i. 5, though he had given them this testimony, that they were enriched in all utterance and knowledge, and were wanting in no gift, yet presently after, ver. 13, *I hear that there are divisions and contentions among you.* *The enemy had done this,* as our Saviour speaks ; and this enemy is no fool, for, by Divine permission, he works to his own end very wisely ; there is not one thing that doth on all hands choke the seed of religion so much, as thorny debates and differences about itself. So, in succeeding ages, and at the breaking forth of the light in Germany, in Luther's time, multitudes of sects arose.

Profane men do not only stumble, but fall and break their necks upon these divisions. We see, (think they, and some of them possibly say it out,) that they who mind religion most, cannot agree upon it : our easiest way is, not to embroil ourselves, not at all to be troubled with the business. Many are of Gallio's temper ; they *will care for none of those things.* Thus these offences prove a mischief to the profane world, as our Saviour says, *Woe to the world because of offences!*

Then those on the erring side, who are taken with new opinions and fancies, are altogether taken up with them, their main thoughts are spent upon them ; and thus the sap is drawn from that which should nourish and prosper in their hearts, *sanctified useful knowledge* and *saving grace.* The other are as weeds, which divert the nourishment in gardens from the plants and flowers ; and certainly these weeds, *viz.,* men's own conceits, cannot but grow more with them, when they give way to them, than solid religion doth ; for their hearts (as one said of the earth) are mother to those, and but step-mother to this.

It is also a loss even to those that oppose errors and divisions, that they are forced to be busied in that way ; for the wisest and godliest of them find (and such are sensible of it) that disputes in religion are no friends to that which is far sweeter in it ; but hinders and abates it, *viz.,* those pious and devout thoughts, that are both the more useful and truly delightful.

As grace is a choice blessing, so this is the choicest peace, and is the peculiar inseparable effect of this grace with which it is here jointly wished,—*Grace* and *Peace ;* the flower of peace growing upon the root of grace. This spiritual peace hath two things in it. 1. Reconciliation with God. 2. Tranquillity of spirit. The quarrel and matter of enmity, you know, betwixt God and man, is, the rebellion, the sin of man ; and he being naturally altogether sinful, there can proceed nothing from him, but what foments and increases the hostility. It is grace alone, the most free grace of God, that contrives, and offers, and makes the peace, else it had never been ; we had universally perished without it. Now in this consists the wonder of Divine grace, that the Almighty God seeks agreement, and entreats for it, with sinful clay, which he could wholly destroy in a moment.

Jesus Christ, the Mediator and purchaser of this peace, bought it with his blood, killed the enmity by his own death. Eph. ii. 15. And therefore the tenor of it in the Gospel runs still in his name, (Rom.

v. 1,) *We have peace with God through Jesus Christ our Lord;* and St. Paul expresses it in his salutations, which are the same with this, *Grace and peace from God the Father, and our Lord Jesus Christ.*

As the free love and grace of God appointed this means and way of our peace, and offered it,—so the same grace applies it, and makes it ours, and gives us faith to apprehend it.

And from our sense of this peace, or reconcilement with God, arises that which is our inward peace, a calm and quiet temper of mind. This peace which we have with God in Christ, is inviolable ; but because the sense and persuasion of it may be interrupted, the soul that is truly at peace with God may for a time be disquieted in itself, through weakness of faith, or the strength of temptation, or the darkness of desertion, losing sight of that grace, that love and light of God's countenance, on which its tranquillity and joy depend. *Thou didst hide thy face,* saith David, *and I was troubled.* But when these eclipses are over, the soul is revived with new consolation, as the face of the earth is renewed and made to smile with the return of the sun in the spring : and this ought always to uphold Christians in the saddest times, *viz.,* that the grace and love of God towards them depend not on their sense, nor upon any thing in them, but is still in itself incapable of the smallest alteration.

It is natural to men to desire their own peace, the quietness and contentment of their minds : but most men miss the way to it, and therefore find it not ; for there is no way to it, indeed, but this one, wherein few seek it, *viz.,* reconcilement and peace with God. The persuasion of that alone makes the mind clear and serene, like your fairest summer days. *My peace I give you,* saith Christ, *not as the world. Let not your hearts be troubled.* All the peace and favour of the world cannot calm a troubled heart ; but where this peace is which Christ gives, all the trouble and disquiet of the world cannot disturb it. *When he giveth quietness, who then can make trouble? and when he hideth his face, who then can behold him? whether it be done against a nation or against a man only.* (See also for this, Psalms xlvi., cxxiii.) All outward distress to a mind thus at peace, is but as the rattling of the hail upon the tiles, to him that sits within the house at a sumptuous feast. A good conscience is styled a feast, and with an advantage which no other feast can have, nor, were it possible, could men endure it. A few hours of feasting will weary the most professed epicure ; but a conscience thus at peace, is a *continual feast,* with continual, unwearied delight. What makes the world take up such a prejudice against religion as a sour, unpleasant thing ? They see the afflictions and griefs of Christians, but they do not see their joys, the inward pleasure of mind that they can possess in a very hard estate. Have you not tried other ways enough ? Hath not he tried them who had more ability and skill for it than you, and found them not only *vanity* but *vexation of spirit?* If you have any belief of holy truth, put but this once upon the trial, seek peace in the way of grace. This inward peace is too precious a liquor to be poured into a filthy vessel. A holy heart, that gladly entertains grace, shall find that it and peace cannot dwell asunder.

An ungodly man may sleep to death in the lethargy of carnal presumption and impenitency ; but a true, lively, solid peace, he cannot have. *There is no peace to the wicked, saith my God.* Isa. lvii. 21. And if He say there is none, speak peace who will, if all the world with one voice should speak it, it shall prove none.

2dly. Consider the *measure* of the Apostle's desire for his scattered brethren, that this *Grace* and *Peace* may be *multiplied.* This the Apostle wishes for them, knowing the imperfection of the graces and peace of the saints while they are here below ; and this they themselves, under a sense of that imperfection, ardently desire. They that have tasted the sweetness of this grace and peace, call incessantly for more. This is a disease in earthly desires, and a disease incurable by all the things desired ; there is no satisfaction attainable by them ; but this avarice of spiritual things is a virtue, and by our Saviour is called *Blessedness,* because it tends to fulness and satisfaction. *Blessed are they that hunger and thirst after righteousness, for they shall be filled.*

Ver. 3. Blessed be the God and Father of our Lord Jesus Christ, who, according to his abundant mercy, hath begotten us again unto a lively hope, by the resurrection of Jesus Christ from the dead,
4. To an inheritance incorruptible, and undefiled, and that fadeth not away.

IT is a cold, lifeless thing to speak of spiritual things upon mere report : but they that speak of them as their own, as having share and interest in them, and some experience of their sweetness, their discourse of them is enlivened with firm belief, and ardent affection ; they cannot mention them, but their hearts are straight taken with such gladness, as they are forced to vent in praises. Thus our Apostle here, and St. Paul, and often elsewhere, when they considered these things wherewith they were about to comfort the godly to whom they wrote, they were suddenly elevated with the joy of them, and broke forth into thanksgiving ; so teaching us, by their example, what real joy there is in the consolations of the Gospel, and what praise is due from all the saints to the God of those consolations. This is such an inheritance, that the very thoughts and hopes of it are able to sweeten the greatest griefs and afflictions. What then shall the possession of it be, wherein there shall be no rupture, nor the least drop of any grief at all ? The main subject of these verses is, that which is the main comfort that supports the spirits of the godly in all conditions.

1st, Their *after inheritance,* as in the 4th verse. 2dly, Their *present title* to it, and *assured hope* of it, ver. 3. 3rdly, The *immediate cause* of both assigned, viz., *Jesus Christ.* 4thly, All this derived from the *free mercy of God,* as the first and highest cause, and returned to his praise and glory, as the last and highest end of it.

For the *first :* The *inheritance.* [But because the 4th verse, which describes it, is linked with the subsequent, we will not go so far off to return back again, but first speak to this 3rd verse, and in it,]

Consider, 1. Their *Title* to this *inheritance, Begotten again.* 2. Their *Assurance* of it, viz., *a holy or lively hope.*

The *title* which the saints have to their rich inheritance is of the validest and most unquestionable kind, *viz.,* by birth. Not by their first natural birth; by that we are all born indeed, but we find what it is, (Eph. ii. 3,) *Children of wrath*, heirs-apparent of eternal flames. It is an everlasting inheritance too, but so much the more fearful, being of everlasting misery, or (so to speak) of immortal death; and we are made sure to it, they who remain in that condition cannot lose their right, although they gladly would escape it; they shall be forced to enter possession. But it is by a new and supernatural birth that men are both freed from their engagement to that woeful inheritance, and invested into the rights of this other here mentioned, which is as full of happiness as the former is miserable : therefore are they said here to be begotten again to that lively hope. God, the Father of our Lord Jesus Christ, hath begotten us again. And thus the regenerate are the children of an immortal Father, and, as such, entitled to an inheritance of immortality : *If children, then heirs, heirs of God :* and this sonship is by adoption in Christ; therefore it is added, *joint heirs with Christ.* Rom. viii. 17. We adopted children, and He the only begotten Son of God by an eternal, ineffable generation.

And yet, this our adoption is not a mere extrinsical denomination, as is adoption amongst men; but is accompanied with a real change in those that are adopted, a new nature and spirit being infused into them, by reason of which, as they are adopted to this their inheritance in Christ, they are likewise begotten of God, and born again to it, by the supernatural work of regeneration. They are like their heavenly Father; they have his image renewed on their souls, and their Father's Spirit; they have it, and are actuated and led by it. This is that great mystery of the kingdom of God which puzzled Nicodemus; it was darkness to him at first, till he was instructed in that night, under the covert whereof he came to Christ.

Nature cannot conceive of any generation or birth, but that which is within its own compass : only they who are partakers of this spiritual birth understand what it means; to others it is a riddle, an unsavoury, unpleasant subject.

It is sometimes ascribed to the subordinate means ;—to Baptism, called therefore the *laver of regeneration,* Tit. iii. 5 ; to the word of God, James i. 18 ; it is that immortal seed, whereby we are born again ; to the ministers of this word, and the seals of it, as 1 Cor. iv. 15, *For though you have ten thousand instructors in Christ, yet have ye not many fathers ; for in Christ Jesus have I begotten you through the Gospel;* as also, Gal. iv. 19. But all these means have their vigour and efficacy in this great work from the Father of spirits, who is their Father in their first creation, and infusion, and in this their regeneration, which is a new and second creation, *If any man be in Christ he is a new creature.* 2 Cor. v. 17.

Divines have reason to infer from the nature of conversion thus expressed, that man doth not bring any thing to this work himself. It is true he hath a will, as his natural faculty; but that this will embraces the offer of grace, and turns to him that offers it, is from renewing grace, which sweetly and yet strongly, strongly yet sweetly, inclines it.

1. Nature cannot raise itself to this any more than a man can give natural being to himself. 2. It is not a superficial change ; it is a new life and being. A moral man in his changes and reformations of

himself, is still the same man.   Though he reform so far, as that men, in their ordinary phrase, shall call him quite another man, yet, in truth, till he be born again, there is no new nature in him.   *The slug-gard turns on his bed as the door on the hinges,* says Solomon.   Thus the natural man turns from one custom and posture to another, but never turns off.   But the Christian, by virtue of this new birth, can say indeed, *Ego non sum ego,* I am not the same man I was.

You that are nobles, aspire to this honourable condition ; add this nobleness to the other, for it far surpasses it ; make it the crown of all your honours and advantages.   And you that are of mean birth, or if you have any stain on your birth, the only way to make up and repair all, and truly to ennoble you, is this—to be the sons of a King, yea, of the King of kings, and *this honour have all his saints.   To as many as received him, he gave this privilege to be the sons of God,* John i. 12.

Unto a lively hope.] *Now are we the sons of God,* saith the Apostle, (1 John iii. 2,) *but it doth not yet appear what we shall be.*   These sons are heirs, but all this lifetime is their minority ; yet, even now, being partakers of this new birth and sonship, they have a right to it, and in the assurance of that right, this *living hope ;* as an heir, when he is capable of those thoughts, hath not only right of inherit-ance, but may rejoice in the hope he hath of it, and please himself in thinking of it.   But hope is said to be only in respect of an uncertain good : true, in the world's phrase, it is so ; for *their* hope is convers-ant in uncertain things, or in things that may be certain, after an uncertain manner ; all their worldly hopes are tottering, built upon sand, and their hopes of heaven are but blind and groundless conjec-tures ; but the hope of the sons of the living God is a living hope. That which Alexander said when he dealt liberally about him, that he *left hope to himself,* the children of God may more wisely and happily say, when they leave the hot pursuit of the world to others, and despise it ; their portion is hope.   The thread of Alexander's life was cut off in the midst of his victories, and so all his hopes vanished ; but their hope cannot die nor disappoint them.

But then it is said to be *lively* not only *objectively,* but *effectively ;* enlivening and comforting the children of God in all distresses, en-abling them to encounter and surmount all difficulties in the way. And then it is *formally* so ; it cannot fail—dies not before accomplish-ment.   Worldly hopes often mock men, and so cause them to be ashamed ; and men take it as a great blot, and are most of all ashamed of those things that discover weakness of judgment in them.   Now worldly hopes do thus—they put the fool upon a man : when he hath judged himself sure, and laid so much weight and expectation on them, then they break and foil him : they are not living, but lying hopes, and dying hopes ; they die often before us, and we live to bury them, and see our own folly and infelicity in trusting to them ; but at the utmost, they die with us when we die, and can accompany us no further.   But this hope answers expectation to the full, and much be-yond it, and deceives no way but in that happy way of far exceeding it.

A *living hope*—living in death itself !   The world dares say no more for its device, than *Dum spiro spero ;* but the children of God can add by virtue of this living hope, *Dum exspiro spero.*   It is a fearful thing when a man and all his hopes die together.   Thus saith Solomon of the wicked, Prov. xi. 7 : When he dieth, then die his hopes ; (many of them *before*, but at the utmost *then*, all of them ;) but the *righteous hath hope in his death*, Prov. xiv. 32.   Death, which cuts the sinews of all other hopes, and turns men out of all other inheritances, alone fulfils this hope, and ends it in fruition ; as a messenger sent to bring the children of God home to the possession of their inheritance.

By the resurrection of Jesus Christ from the dead.] This refers both to *begotten again* by his resurrection, and having this *living hope* by his resurrection : and well suits both, it being the proper cause of both in this order.   First, then, of the *birth ;* next, of the hope.

The image of God is renewed in us by our union with Him who is *the express image of his Father's person*, Heb. i. 3.   Therefore this new birth in the conception, is expressed by the *forming of Christ in the soul*, Gal. iv. 19 ; and his resurrection particularly is assigned as the cause of our new life.   This new birth is called our *resurrection*, and that in conformity to Christ, yea, by the virtue and influence of his.   His resurrection is called a *birth*, he, the *first begotten from the dead*, Rev. i. 5 ; and that prophecy, *Thou art my Son, this day have I begotten thee*, Psal. ii. 7, is applied to his resurrection as fulfilled in it, Acts xiii. 33 : *God hath fulfilled the same unto us their children, in that he hath raised up Jesus again ; as it is also written in the second Psalm, Thou art my Son, this day have I begotten thee.*   Not only is it the exemplar, but the efficient cause of our new birth.   Thus, in the sixth chapter of Romans, at large, and often elsewhere.

And thus likewise it is the cause of our *living hope*,—that which indeed inspires and maintains life in it.   Because he hath conquered death, and is risen again, and that is implied which followeth, he is *set down at the right hand of God*, hath entered into possession of that inheritance ;—this gives us a living hope, that, according to his own request, *where he is there we may be also.*   Thus this hope is strongly underset, on the one side, by the resurrection of Christ ; on the other, by the abundant mercy of God the Father.   Our hope depends not on our own strength or wisdom, nor on any thing in us ; (for if it did, it would be short-lived, would die, and die quickly ;) but on his resurrection who can die no more : for *in that he died, he died unto sin once ; but in that he liveth, he liveth unto God*, Rom. vi. 10.   This makes this hope not to imply, in the notion of it, uncertainty, as worldly hopes do ; but it is a firm, stable, inviolable hope, *an anchor fixed within the vail.*

According to his abundant mercy.] Mercy is the spring of all this ; yea, great mercy, and manifold mercy : " for (as St. Bernard saith) " great sins and great miseries need great mercy, and many sins and " miseries need many mercies."   And is not this great mercy, to make of Satan's slaves, sons of the Most High ?   Well may the Apostle say, *Behold what manner of love, and how great love the Father hath showed us, that we should be called the sons of God !*—The world knows us not because it knew not Him.   They that have not seen the father of a child cannot know that it resembles him ; thus the world knows not God, and therefore discerns not his image in his children so as to esteem them for it.   But whatever be their opinion, this we must say ourselves, Behold what manner of love is this ! to take firebrands of hell, and to appoint them to be one day brighter than the sun in the firmament ; to *raise the poor out of the dunghill, and set them with princes.* Psal. cxiii. 7, 8.

Blessed be the God and Father of our Lord Jesus Christ.] Here, lastly, we see it stirs up the Apostle to praise the God and Father of our Lord Jesus Christ. This is the style of the Gospel,—as formerly, under the Law, it was *The God of Abraham, Isaac, and Jacob,* and *The God that brought thee up out of the land of Egypt,* &c. This now is the order of the government of grace, that it holds first with Christ our Head, and in him with us. So he says, *I go to my Father and your Father, and my God and your God;* which, as St. Cyril of Jerusalem, in his Catechism, observes, shows us not only our communion with him,—that might have been expressed thus, *I go to my God and Father,*—but the order of the covenant, first my Father and my God, and then yours. Thus ought we, in our consideration of the mercies of God, still to take in Christ, for in him they are conveyed to us : thus, (Eph. i. 3,) *With all spiritual blessings in Christ Jesus.*

Blessed.] He blesseth us really : *benefaciendo benedicit.* We bless Him by acknowledging his goodness. And this we ought to do at all times, Psal. xxxiv. 1 : *I will bless the Lord at all times, his praise shall continually be in my mouth.* All this is far below Him and his mercies. What are our lame praises in comparison of his love ? Nothing, and less than nothing ; but love will stammer, rather than be dumb. They who are amongst his children *begotten again,* have, in the resurrection of Christ, a lively hope of glory : as it is, Col. i. 27, *Which is Christ in you, the hope of glory.* This leads them to observe and admire that rich mercy whence it flows ; and this consideration awakes them, and constrains them to break forth into praises.

To an inheritance incorruptible.] *As he that taketh away a garment in cold weather, and as vinegar upon nitre, so is he that singeth songs to a heavy heart.* Prov. xxv. 20. Worldly mirth is so far from curing spiritual grief, that even worldly grief, where it is great and takes deep root, is not allayed but increased by it. A man who is full of inward heaviness, the more he is encompassed about with mirth, it exasperates and enrages his grief the more ; like ineffectual weak physic, which removes not the humour, but stirs it and makes it more unquiet. But spiritual joy is seasonable for all estates : in prosperity, it is pertinent to crown and sanctify all other enjoyments, with this which so far surpasses them ; and in distress, it is the only *Nepenthe,* the cordial of fainting spirits : so, Psal. iv. 7, *He hath put joy into my heart.* This mirth makes way for itself, which other mirth cannot do. These songs are sweetest in the night of distress. Therefore the Apostle, writing to his scattered, afflicted brethren, begins his Epistle with this song of praise, *Blessed be the God and Father of our Lord Jesus Christ.*

The matter of this joy is, the joyful remembrance of the happiness laid up for them, under the name of *inheritance.* Now this inheritance is described by the singular qualities of it, *viz.,* 1. The excellency of its nature ; 2. The certainty of its attainment. The former is conveyed in these three, *Incorruptible, undefiled, and that fadeth not away;* the latter, in the last words of this verse, and in the verse following : *Reserved in heaven for you,* &c.

God is bountiful to all—gives to all men all that they have, health, riches, honour, strength, beauty, and wit ; but these things he scatters (as it were) with an indifferent hand.   Upon others he looks as well as upon his beloved children ; but the *inheritance* is peculiarly *theirs.* Inheritance is convertible with sonship ; Abraham gave gifts to Keturah's sons, and dismissed them, Gen. xxv. 5 ; but the inheritance was for the Son of the Promise.   When we see a man rising in preferment or estate, or admired for excellent gifts and endowments of mind, we think there is a happy man ; but we consider not that none of all those things are matter of inheritance ; within awhile he is to be turned out of all, and if he have not somewhat beyond all those to look to, he is but a miserable man, and so much the more miserable, that once he seemed and was reputed happy.   There is a certain time wherein heirs come to possess : thus it is with this inheritance too.   There is mention made by the Apostle of *a perfect man,—unto the measure of the stature of the fulness of Christ,* Eph. iv. 13.   And though the inheritance is rich and honourable, yet the heir, being young, is held under discipline, and is more strictly dealt with, possibly, than the servants,— sharply corrected for that which is let pass in them ; but still, even then, in regard of that which he is born to, his condition is much better than theirs, and all the correction he suffers prejudices him not, but fits him for inheriting.   The love of our heavenly Father is beyond the love of mothers in tenderness, and yet beyond the love of fathers (who are usually said to love more wisely) in point of wisdom. He will not undo his children, his heirs, with too much indulgence. It is one of his heavy judgments upon the foolish children of disobedience, that *Ease shall slay them, and their prosperity shall prove their destruction.*

While the children of God are childish and weak in faith, they are like some great heirs before they come to years of understanding : they consider not their inheritance, and what they are to come to, have not their spirits elevated to thoughts worthy of their estate, and their behaviour conformed to it ; but as they grow up in years, they come, by little and little, to be sensible of those things, and the nearer they come to possession, the more apprehensive they are of their quality, and of what doth answerably become them to do.   And this is the duty of such as are indeed heirs of glory ;—to grow in the understanding and consideration of that which is prepared for them, and to suit themselves, as they are able, to those great hopes.   This is what the Apostle St. Paul prays for, on behalf of his Ephesians, ch. i. ver. 18 : *The eyes of your understanding being enlightened, that ye may know what is the hope of his calling, and what the riches of the glory of his inheritance in the saints.*   This would make them holy and heavenly, to *have their conversation in heaven, from whence they look for a Saviour.*   That we may, then, the better know somewhat of the dignity and riches of this inheritance, let us consider the description which is here given us of it.   And, first, It is

Incorruptible.]   Although this seems to be much the same with the *third* quality, *that fadeth not away,* (which is a borrowed expression for the illustrating of its incorruptibleness,) yet, I conceive that there is some difference, and that in these three qualities there is a gradation. Thus it is called *incorruptible;* that is, it perisheth not, cannot come to nothing, is an estate that cannot be spent : but though it were abiding, yet it might be such as that the continuance of it were not very desirable ; it would be but a .misery at best, to continue always in this life. *Plotinus* thanked God that his soul was not tied to an immortal body. Then, *undefiled;* it is not stained with the least spot : *this* signifies the purity and perfection of it, as *that* the perpetuity of it. It doth not only abide, and is pure, but both together, it abideth always in its integrity. And lastly, *it fadeth not away;* it doth not fade nor wither at all, is not sometimes more, sometimes less pleasant, but ever the same, still like itself ; and this constitutes the immutability of it.

As it is *incorruptible,* it carries away the palm from all earthly possessions and inheritances ; for all those epithets are intended to signify its opposition to the things of this world, and to show how far it excels them all ; and in this comparative light we are to consider it. For as divines say of the knowledge of God which we have here, that the negative notion makes up a great part of it—we know rather what He is not than what He is, infinite, incomprehensible, immutable, &c.; so it is of this happiness, this inheritance ; and indeed it is no other than God. We cannot tell you what it is, but we can say so far what it is not, as declares it is unspeakably above all the most excellent things of the inferior world and this present life. It is by privatives, by removing imperfections from it, that we describe it, and we can go no farther than this,—*incorruptible, undefiled, and that fadeth not away.*

All things that we see, being compounded, may be dissolved again. The very visible heavens, which are the purest piece of the material world, (notwithstanding the pains the philosopher takes to exempt them,) the Scriptures teach us that they are *corruptible,* Psal. cii. 26 : *They shall perish, but thou shalt endure ; yea, all of them shall wax old like a garment; as a vesture shalt thou change them, and they shall be changed.* And from thence the Apostle to the *Hebrews,* ch. i. ver. 10, and our Apostle, in his other Epistle, ch. iii. ver. 11, use the same expression. But it is needless to fetch too great a compass, to evince the corruptibleness of all inheritances. Besides what they are in themselves, it is a shorter way to prove them corruptible in relation to us and our possessing them, by our own corruptibleness and corruption, or perishing out of this life in which we enjoy them. We are here *inter peritura perituri;* the things are passing which we enjoy, and we are passing who enjoy them. An earthly inheritance is so called in regard of succession ; but to every one it is at the most but for term of life. As one of the kings of Spain replied to one of his courtiers, who, thinking to please his master, wished that kings were immortal ; *If that had been,* said he, *I should never have been king.* When death comes, that removes a man out of all his possessions to give place to another ; therefore are these inheritances decaying and dying in relation to us, because we decay and die ; and when a man dies, his inheritances and honours, and all· things here, are at an end, in respect of him ; yea, we may say the world ends to him.

Thus Solomon reasons, that a man's happiness cannot be upon this earth ; because it must be some durable, abiding thing that must make him happy—abiding, to wit, in his enjoyment. Now, though the earth abide, yet, because man abides not on the earth to possess it, but one age drives out another, one generation passeth and another cometh, *velut unda impellitur unda*, therefore, his rest and his happiness cannot be here.

Undefiled.] All possessions here are defiled and stained with many other defects and failings—still somewhat wanting, some damp on them or crack in them ; fair houses, but sad cares flying about the gilded and ceiled roofs ; stately and soft beds, and a full table, but a sickly body and queasy stomach. As the fairest face has some mole or wart in it, so all possessions are stained with sin, either in acquiring or in using them, and therefore they are called, *mammon of unrighteousness*, Luke xvi. 9. Iniquity is so involved in the notion of riches, that it can very hardly be separated from them. St. Jerome says, *Verum mihi videtur illud, dives aut iniquus est, aut iniqui hæres :* To me it appears, that he who is rich is either himself an unjust man or the heir of one. Foul hands pollute all they touch ; it is our sin that defiles what we possess ; it is sin that burdens the whole creation, and presses groans out of the very frame of the world, Rom. viii. 22, *For we know that the whole creation groaneth and travaileth in pain together until now.* This our leprosy defiles our houses, the very walls and floors, our meat and drink and all we touch, polluted when alone, and polluted in society, our meetings and conversations together being for the greatest part nothing but a commerce and interchange of sin and vanity.

We breathe up and down in an infected air, and are very receptive of the infection by our own corruption within us. We readily turn the things we possess here to occasions and instruments of sin, and think there is no liberty nor delight in their use without abusing them. How few are they who can carry (as they say) a full cup even ; who can have digestion strong enough for the right use of great places and estates ; who can bear preferment without pride, and riches without covetousness, and ease without wantonness !

Then, as these earthly inheritances are stained with sin in their use, so what grief, and strife, and contentions about obtaining or retaining them ! Doth not the matter of possession, this same *meum* and *tuum*, divide many times the affections of those who are knit together in nature, or other strict ties, and prove the very apple of strife betwixt nearest friends ?

If we trace great estates to their first original, how few will be found that owe not their beginning either to fraud, or rapine, or oppression ! and the greatest empires and kingdoms in the world have had their foundations laid in blood. Are not these defiled inheritances ?

That withereth not.] A borrowed phrase, alluding to the decaying of plants and flowers, which bud and flourish at a certain time of the year, and then fade and wither, and in winter are as if they were dead.

And this is the third disadvantage of possessions and all things worldly, that they abide not in one estate, but are in a more uncertain and irregular inconstancy than either the flowers and plants of the field, or the moon, from which they are called *sublunary;* like Nebu-chadnezzar's image, degenerating by degrees into baser metals, and, in the end, into a mixture of iron and clay.

The excellency, then, of this inheritance, is, that it is free from all those evils. It falls not under the stroke of time, comes not within the compass of its scythe, which hath so large a compass, and cuts down all other things.

There is nothing in it weighing it towards corruption. It is immortal, everlasting; for it is the fruition of the immortal, everlasting God, by immortal souls; and the body joined with it, shall likewise be immortal, having *put on incorruption,* as the Apostle speaks, 1 Cor. xv. 54.

It *fadeth not away.*] No spot of sin nor sorrow there; all pollution wiped away, and all tears with it; no envy nor strife; not as here among men, one supplanting another, one pleading and fighting against another, dividing this point of earth with fire and sword;—no, this inheritance is not the less by division, by being parted amongst so many brethren, every one hath it all, each his crown, and all agreeing in casting them down before his throne, from whom they have received them, and in the harmony of his praises.

This inheritance is often called a kingdom, and a crown of glory. This last word may allude to those garlands of the ancients; and this is its property, that the flowers in it are all *Amaranthes,* (as a certain plant is named,) and so it is called, (1 Pet. v. 4,) *A crown of glory that fadeth not away.*

No change at all there, no winter and summer; not like the poor comforts here, but a bliss always flourishing. The grief of the saints here, is not so much for the changes of outward things, as of their inward comforts. *Suavis hora, sed brevis mora.* Sweet presences of God they sometimes have, but they are short, and often interrupted; but *there* no cloud shall come betwixt them and their Sun; they shall behold him in his full brightness for ever. As there shall be no change in their beholding, so no weariness nor abatement of their delight in beholding. They sing a new song, always the same, and yet always new. The sweetest of our music, if it were to be heard but for one whole day, would weary them who are most delighted with it. What we have here cloys, but satisfies not; the joys above never cloy, and yet always satisfy.

We should here consider the last property of this inheritance, namely, the *certainty* of it—*reserved in heaven for you;* but that is connected with the following verse, and so will be fitly joined with it. Now for some use of all this.

If these things were believed, they would persuade for themselves; we should not need add any entreaties to move you to seek after this inheritance. Have we not experience enough of the vanity and misery of things corruptible? and are not a great part of our days already spent amongst them? Is it not time to consider whether we be pro-vided with any thing surer and better than what we have here; whether we have any inheritance to go home to after our wandering? or can say with the Apostle, (2 Cor. v. 1,) *We know that if our earthly house of this tabernacle were dissolved, we have a building of God, an house not made with hands, eternal in the heavens*

If these things gain our assent while we hear them, yet it dies soon. Scarcely any retire within themselves afterwards to pursue those thoughts, and to make a work indeed of them ; they busy their heads rather another way, building castles in the air, and spinning out their thoughts in vain contrivances.—Happy are they whose hearts the Spirit of God sets and fixes upon this inheritance : they may join in with the Apostle, and say, as here, *Blessed be the God and Father of our Lord Jesus Christ, who hath begotten us again unto this lively hope, to this inheritance incorruptible, undefiled, and that fadeth not away.*

Ver. 5. Who are kept by the power of God, through faith, unto salvation, ready to be revealed in the last time.

It is doubtless a great contentment to the children of God, to hear of the excellencies of the life to come ; they do not use to become weary of that subject ; yet there is one doubt, which, if it be not removed, may damp their delight in hearing and considering of all the rest. The richer the estate is, it will the more kindle the malice and diligence of their enemies to deprive them of it, and to cut them short of possessing it. And this they know, that those spiritual powers who seek to ruin them, do overmatch them far, both in craft and force.

Against the fears of this, the Apostle comforts the heirs of salvation, assuring them, that, as the estate they look for is excellent, so it is certain and safe, laid up where it is out of the reach of all adverse powers, *reserved in heaven for you.* Besides that this is a further evidence of the worth and excellency of this inheritance, it makes it sure. It confirms what was said of its excellency ; for it must be a thing of greatest worth, that is laid up in the highest and best place of the world, namely, in heaven for you, where nothing that is impure once enters, much less is laid up and kept. Thus the land where this inheritance lies, makes good all that hath been spoken of the dignity and riches of it.

But further, as it is a rich and pleasant country where it lieth, it hath also this privilege, to be the only land of rest and peace, free from all possibility of invasion. There is no spoiling of it, and laying it waste, and defacing its beauty, by leading armies into it, and making it the seat of war ; no noise of drums or trumpets, no inundations of one people driving out another and sitting down in their possessions. In a word, there is nothing there subject to decay of itself, so neither is it in danger of fraud or violence. When our Saviour speaks of this same happiness, in a like term, Matt. vi. 20, what is here called an *inheritance,* is there called a *treasure.* He expresses the permanency of it by these two, that it *hath neither moth nor rust* in itself to *corrupt* it, nor can *thieves break through and steal it.* There is a worm at the root of all our enjoyments here, corrupting causes within themselves ; and besides that, they are exposed to injury from without, which may deprive us of them. How many stately palaces, which have been possibly divers years in building, hath fire upon a very small beginning destroyed in a few hours ! What great hopes of gain by traffic hath one tempest mocked and disappointed ! How many who have thought their possessions very sure, yet have lost them by some trick of law, and others (as in time of war) been driven from them by the sword !

Nothing free from all danger but this *inheritance,* which is laid up in the hands of God, and kept in heaven for us. The highest stations in the world, namely, the estate of kings, they are but mountains of prey, one robbing and spoiling another ; but in that holy mountain above, there is none to hurt, or spoil, or offer violence. What the Prophet speaks of the Church here, is more perfectly and eminently true of it above, Isaiah lxv. 25.

This is, indeed, a necessary condition of our joy in the thoughts of this happy estate, that we have some persuasion of our propriety, that it is *ours;* that we do not speak and hear of it, as travellers passing by a pleasant place do behold and discourse of its fair structure, the sweetness of the seat, the planting, the gardens, the meadows that are about it, and so pass on ; having no further interest in it. But when we hear of this glorious inheritance, this treasure, this kingdom that is pure, and rich, and lasting, we may add, It is mine, it is reserved in heaven, and reserved for me ; I have received the evidences and the earnest of it ; and, as it is kept safe for me, so I shall likewise be preserved to it, and that is the other part of the certainty that completes the comforts of it. Eph. i. 14.

The salvation which Christ hath purchased is, indeed, laid up in heaven, but we who seek after it, are on earth, compassed about with dangers and temptations. What avails it us, that our salvation is in heaven, in the place of safety and quietness, while we ourselves are tossed upon the stormy seas of this world, amidst rocks and shelves, every hour in danger of shipwreck ? Our inheritance is in a sure hand indeed, our enemies cannot come at it ; but they may overrun and destroy us at their pleasure, for we are in the midst of them. Thus might we think and complain, and lose the sweetness of all our other thoughts concerning heaven, if there were not as firm a promise for our own safety in the midst of our dangers, as there is of the safety of our inheritance that is out of danger.

The assurance is full, thus ; it is *kept* for us in heaven, and we kept on earth for it : as it is *reserved* for us, we are no less surely *preserved* to it. There is here, 1. The estate itself, *salvation.* 2. The preservation, or securing, of those that expect it, *kept.* 3. The time of full possession, *in the last time.*

1. The estate—*Unto salvation.* Before it is called an *inheritance;* here we are more particularly told what is meant by that, namely, *salvation.* This is more expressly sure, being a deliverance from misery, and it imports, withal, the possession of perfect happiness. The first part of our happiness is, to be freed from those miseries to which we are subject by our guiltiness ; to be set free, 1. From the curse of the law, and the wrath of God, from everlasting death. 2. From all kind of mortality and decaying. 3. From all power and stain of sin. 4. From all temptation. 5. From all the griefs and afflictions of this life. To have the perfection of grace in the fulness of holiness, and the perfection of bliss in the fulness of joy, in the continual vision of God !— but how little we are able to say of this, our Apostle here teacheth us, in that it is vailed to us ; only so much shines through, as we are capable of here ; but the revealed knowledge of it is only in the possession ; it is *to be revealed in the last time.*

2dly, Their preservation, with the causes of it. *Kept by the power of God through faith.* The inheritance is kept not only in safety, but in quietness. The children of God, for whom it is kept, while they are here, are kept safe indeed, but not unmolested and unassaulted; they have enemies, and such as are stirring, and cunning, and powerful; but, in the midst of them, they are guarded and defended; they perish not, according to the prayer of our Saviour poured out for them, John xvii. 16, *I pray not that thou shouldest take them out of the world; but that thou shouldest keep them from the evil.*

They have the prince of the power of the air, and all his armies, all the forces he can make, against them. Though his power is nothing but tyranny and usurpation, yet because once they were under his yoke, he bestirs himself to pursue them, when they are led forth from their captivity, as Pharaoh, with all his chariots and horses and horsemen, pursues after the Israelites going out of Egypt.

The word in the original (φρουρουμενοι) here translated *kept*, is a military term, used for those who are *kept* as in a fort or garrison-town besieged. So Satan is still raising batteries against this fort, using all ways to take it, by strength or stratagem, unwearied in his assaults, and very skilful to know his advantages, and where we are weakest, there to set on. And besides all this, he hath intelligence with a party within us, ready to betray us to him; so that it were impossible for us to hold out, were there not another watch and guard than our own, and other walls and bulwarks than any that our skill and industry can raise for our own defence. In this, then, is our safety, that there is a power above our own, yea, and above all our enemies, that guards us, *salvation* itself *our walls and bulwarks.* We ought to watch, but when we do so in obedience to our commander, the Captain of our salvation, yet it is His own watching, who *sleeps* not, nor so much as *slumbers*, it is that preserves us, and makes ours not to be in vain. Psal. cxxvi. 1; Isa. xxvii. 3. And therefore those two are jointly commanded, *Watch and pray, that ye enter not into temptation.* *Watch*, there is the necessity of our diligence; *Pray*, there is the insufficiency of it, and the necessity of His watching, by whose power we are effectually preserved, and that power is our fort. Isa. xxvi. 1, *Salvation hath God appointed for walls and bulwarks.* What more safe than to be walled with *Salvation* itself. So, Prov. xviii. 10, *The name of the Lord is a strong tower; the righteous fly into it and are safe.*

Now the causes of our preservation are two : 1. Supreme, *The power of God.* 2. Subordinate, *Faith.* The supreme *power of God*, is that on which depend our stability and perseverance. When we consider how weak we are in ourselves, yea, the very strongest among us, and how assaulted, we wonder, and justly we may, that any can continue one day in the state of grace: but when we look on the strength by which we are guarded, the power of God, then we see the reason of our stability to the end; for Omnipotency supports us, and the everlasting arms are under us.

Then *Faith* is the second cause of our preservation; because it applies the first cause, the *power of God.* Our faith lays hold upon this power, and this power strengthens faith, and so we are preserved; it puts us within those walls, sets the soul within the guard of the power of God, which, by self-confidence and vain presuming in its own strength, is exposed to all kind of danger. Faith is an humble, self-denying grace; it makes the Christian nothing in himself and all in God.

The weakest persons who are within a strong place, women and children, though they were not able to resist the enemy if they were alone, yet so long as the place wherein they are is of sufficient strength, and well manned, and every way accommodate to hold out, they are in safety; thus the weakest believer is safe, because by believing he is within the strongest of all defences. Faith is the victory, and Christ sets his strength against Satan's; and when the Christian is hard beset with some temptation, too strong for himself, then he looks up to Him who is the great conqueror of the powers of darkness, and calls to him, "Now, Lord, assist thy servant in this encounter, and put to thy "strength, that the glory may be thine." Thus, faith is such an engine as draws in the power of God and his Son Jesus into the works and conflicts that it hath in hand. *This is our victory, even our faith.* 1 John v. 4.

It is the property of *a good Christian* to magnify the power of God, and to have high thoughts of it, and therefore it is his privilege to find safety in that power. David cannot satisfy himself with one or two expressions of it, but delights in multiplying them. Psalm xviii. 1, *The Lord is my rock, and my fortress, and my deliverer; my God, my strength, in whom I will trust; my buckler, and the horn of my salvation, and my high tower.* Faith looks above all, both that which the soul hath, and that which it wants, and answers all doubts and fears with this almighty power upon which it rests.

3dly, The time of full possession—*Ready to be revealed in the last time.* This salvation is that great work wherein God intended to manifest the glory of his grace, contrived before time, and in the several ages of the world brought forward, after the decreed manner; and the full accomplishment of it is reserved for the end of time.

The souls of the faithful do enter into the possession of it, when they remove from their houses of clay; yet is not their happiness complete till that great day of the appearing of Jesus Christ. They are naturally imperfect till their bodies be raised and rejoined to their souls, to partake together of their bliss; and they are mystically imperfect, till all the rest of the members of Jesus Christ be added to them.

But then shall their joy be absolutely full, when both their own bodies and the mystical body of Christ shall be glorified; when all the children of that glorious family shall meet, and sit down to that great marriage supper at their Father's table. Then shall the music of that new song be full, when there is not one wanting of those that are appointed to sing it for eternity. In that day shall our Lord Jesus *be glorified in his saints, and admired in all them that believe,* 2 Thess. i. 10.

You see what it is that the Gospel offers you, and you may gather how great both your folly and your guiltiness will be, if you neglect and slight so great salvation when it is brought to you, and you are entreated to receive it. This is all that the preaching of the word aims at, and yet, who hearkens to it ? How few lay hold on this eternal life, this inheritance, this crown that is held forth to all that hear of it !

Oh ! that you could be persuaded to be saved, that you would be willing to embrace salvation ! You think you would ; but if it be so, then I may say, though you would be saved, yet your custom of sin, your love to sin, and love to the world, will not suffer you ; and these will still hinder you, unless you put on holy resolutions to break through them, and trample them under foot, and take this kingdom by a hand of violence, which God is so well pleased with. He is willingly overcome by that force, and gives this kingdom most willingly, where it is so taken ; it is not attained by slothfulness, and sitting still with folded hands ; it must be invaded with strength of faith, with armies of prayers and tears ; and they who set upon it thus are sure to take it.

Consider what we are doing, how we misplace our diligence on things that abide not, or we abide not to enjoy them. *We have no abiding city here,* saith the Apostle ; but he adds that which comforts the citizens of the New Jerusalem, *We look for one to come, whose builder and maker is God.* Hear not these things idly, as if they concerned you not, but let them move you to resolution and actions. Say, as they said of *Canaan, It is a good land, let us go up and possess it.* Learn to use what you have here as travellers, and let your home, your inheritance, your treasure be on high, which is by far the richest and the safest ; and if it be so with you, then, *where your treasure is, there will your hearts be also.*

Ver. 6. Wherein ye greatly rejoice, though now for a season (if need be) ye are in heaviness through manifold temptations.

THE same motives cannot beget contrary passions in the soul ; therefore, the Apostle reduces the mixture of sorrowing and rejoicing that is usual in the heart of a Christian to the different causes of both, and shows which of the two hath the stronger cause, and is therefore always predominant in him who entertains and considers it aright.

His scope is, to stir up and strengthen spiritual joy in his afflicted brethren ; and therefore having set the matter of it before them in the preceding verses, he now applies it, and expressly opposes it to their distresses.

Some read these words exhortatively, *In which rejoice ye.* It is so intended, but I conceive it serves that end better indicatively, as we now read it, *In which ye rejoice.* It exhorts in a more insinuating and persuasive manner, that it may be so, to urge it on them, that it is so. Thus St. Paul, Acts xxvi. 27, *King Agrippa, believest thou the prophets ? I know that thou believest.* And straight he answered, *Thou almost persuadest me to be a Christian.* This implies how just and how reasonable it is, that the things spoken of should make them glad ; in these they will rejoice, yea, do rejoice. Certainly, if you know and consider what the causes of your joy are, ye cannot choose but find it within you, and in such a measure as to swallow up all your temporary sorrows, how great and how many soever their causes be.

We are then to consider severally these bitter waters and the sweet, this sorrow and this joy. 1. In their springs ; 2. In their streams.

And first, they are called *temptations,* and *manifold temptations.*

The habits of Divine supernatural grace are not acquirable by human study, or by industry, or by exercise; they are of immediate infusion from Heaven; yet are they infused to the end that they may act and exercise themselves in the several conditions and occurrences of a Christian's life, and by that they grow stronger. Whatsoever oppositions or difficulties grace meets with in its acting, go under this general name of *temptations*. It is not necessary to reckon up the variety of senses of this word, in its full latitude; how God is said to tempt man, and how it is said that He tempts him not; how man tempts God, and how it is said that God is not tempted; how Satan tempts men, and men one another, and a man himself: all these are several acceptations of this word; but the *temptations* here meant, are the things by which men are tempted, and particularly the saints of God. And though there is nothing in the words, that may not agree to all sorts of temptations which the godly are subject to; yet I conceive it is particularly meant of their afflictions and distresses, as the Apostle James likewise uses it, chap. i. ver. 2.

And they are so called, because they give particular and notable proof of the temper of a Christian's spirit, and draw forth evidence both of the truth and the measure of the grace that is in them. If they fail and are foiled, as sometimes they are, this convinces them of that human frailty and weakness which are in them, and so humbles them, and drives them out of themselves to depend upon Another for more strength and better success in after-encounters. If they acquit themselves like Christians indeed, (the Lord managing and assisting that grace which he hath given them,) then all their valour, and strength, and victories turn to his praise, from whom they have received all.

A man is not only unknown to others, but to himself, that hath never met with such difficulties as require faith, and Christian fortitude, and patience to surmount them. How shall a man know whether his meekness and calmness of spirit be real or not, while he meets with no provocation, nothing that contradicts or crosses him? But when somewhat sets upon him, that is in itself very unpleasant and grievous to him, and yet, if in that case he retains his moderation of spirit, and flies not out into impatience, either against God or men, this gives experiment of the truth and soundness of that grace within him; whereas standing water which is clear at top while it is untouched, yet if it have mud at the bottom, stir it a little, and it rises presently.

It is not altogether unprofitable; yea, it is great wisdom in Christians to be arming themselves against such temptations as may befall them hereafter, though they have not as yet met with them; to labour to overcome them beforehand; to suppose the hardest things that may be incident to them; and to put on the strongest resolutions they can attain unto. Yet all that is but an imaginary effort; and therefore there is no assurance that the victory is any more than imaginary too, till it come to action, and then, they that have spoken and thought very confidently, may prove but (as one said of the Athenians) *fortes in tabula*, patient and courageous in picture or fancy; and notwithstanding all their arms, and dexterity in handling them by way of exercise, may be foully defeated when they are to fight in earnest. The children of Ephraim being armed, and carrying bows, (says the Psalmist, Psal. lxxviii. 9,) *yet turned back in the day of battle.* It is the battle that tries the soldier, and the storm the pilot. How would it appear that Christians can be themselves, not only patient, but cheerful in poverty, in disgrace, and temptations, and persecutions, if it were not often their lot to meet with them ? He who framed the heart, knows it to be but deceitful, and He who gives grace, knows the weakness and strength of it exactly ; yet he is pleased to speak thus, that by afflictions and hard tasks he tries what is in the hearts of his children. For the word of God speaks to men, and therefore it speaks the language of the children of men : thus, Gen. xxii. 12, *Now I know that thou fearest God, seeing thou hast not withheld thy son, thine only son from me.*

God delights to call forth his champions to meet with great temptations, to make them bear crosses of more than ordinary weight ; as commanders in war put men of most valour and skill upon the hardest services. God sets some strong, furious trial upon a strong Christian, made strong by his own grace, and by his victory makes it appear to the world, that though there is a great deal of the counterfeit coin of profession in religion, yet some there are, who have the power, the reality of it, and that it is not an invention, but there is truth in it ; that the invincible grace, the very Spirit of God, dwells in the hearts of true believers ; that he hath a number who do not only speak big, but do indeed and in good earnest despise the world, and overcome it by His strength. Some men take delight to see some kind of beasts fight together ; but to see a Christian mind encountering some great affliction, and conquering it, to see his valour in not sinking at the hardest distresses of this life, nor the most frightful end of it, the cruellest kinds of death, for His sake,—this is (as one said) *dignum Deo spectaculum;* this is a combat which God delights to look upon ; and He is not a mere beholder in it, for it is the power of His own grace that enables and supports the Christian in all those conflicts and temptations.

Through manifold temptations.] This expresses a multitude of temptations, and those too of divers kinds, many and manifold. It were no hard condition to have a trial now and then, with long ease and prosperity betwixt ; but to be plied with one affliction at the heels of another, to have them come thronging in by multitudes and of different kinds, uncouth, unaccustomed evils, such as a man hath not been acquainted with before, this is that which is often the portion of those who are the beloved of God. Psal. xlii. 7, *Deep calleth unto deep at the noise of thy water-spouts ; all thy waves and thy billows are gone over me.*

Ye are in heaviness.] This the Apostle blames not, but aims at the moderating of it. Seek not altogether to dry up this stream, but to bound it, and keep it within its banks. Grace doth not destroy the life of nature, but adds to it a life more excellent ; yea, grace doth not only permit, but requires some feeling of afflictions. There is an affected pride of spirit in some men, instead of patience, suitable only to the doctrine of the Stoics as it is usually taken : they strive not to feel at all the afflictions that are on them ; but this is to *despise the cor-*

rection of the Lord, which is alike forbidden with fainting under it.
Heb. xii. 5.   We should not stop our ears, but *hear the rod, and him
that hath appointed it,* as the Prophet speaks, Mic. vi. 9.   Where there
is no feeling at all, there can be no patience.   Consider it as the hand
of God, and thence argue the soul into submission : Psal. xxxix. 9, *I
was dumb, I opened not my mouth, because thou didst it.*   But this
heaviness is mitigated, and set, as it were, within its banks, betwixt
these two considerations, 1. The *utility,* 2. The *brevity* of it : the pro-
fitableness—and the shortness of it.

To a worldly man, great gain sweetens the hardest labour ; and to
a Christian, spiritual profit and advantage may do much to move him
to take those afflictions well which are otherwise very unpleasant.
Though *they are not joyous for the present,* yet this allays the sorrow
of them, the fruit that grows out of them, *that peaceable fruit of righteousness.*   Heb. xii. 11.

*A bundle of folly is in the heart of a child, but the rod of correction
shall beat it out,* saith Solomon.   Though the children of God are
truly (as our Saviour calls them) the children of wisdom, yet, being
renewed only in part, they are not altogether free from those follies
that call for this rod to beat them out, and sometimes have such a bundle of follies as require a bundle of rods to be spent upon it—*many and
manifold afflictions.*

It is not an easy matter to be drawn from, nor to be beaten from,
the love of this world, and this is what God mainly requires of his
children, that they be not in love with the world, nor the things of it ;
for that is contrary to the love of God, and so far as that is entertained,
this is wanting.   And if in the midst of afflictions they are sometimes
subject to this disease, how would it grow upon them with ease and
prosperity !   When they are beaten from one worldly folly or delight,
they are ready, through nature's corruption, to lay hold upon some
other,—being thrust out from it at one door, to enter at some other ; as
children unwilling to be weaned, if one breast be imbittered, they seek
to the other ;   and therefore there must be somewhat to drive them
from that too.   Thus it is clear there is need, great need of afflictions,
yea, of many afflictions, that the saints be *chastened by the Lord, that
they may not be condemned with the world.*   1 Cor. xi. 32.

Many resemblances there are for illustration of this truth, in things
both of nature and of art, some common, and others choicer ; but
these are not needful.   The experience of Christians tells them, how
easily they grow proud, and secure, and carnal, with a little ease, and
when outward things go smoothly with them ; and therefore what unhappiness were it for them to be very happy that way !

Let us learn, then, that in regard of our present frailty there is need
of afflictions, and so not promise ourselves exemption, how calm
soever our seas are for the present ; and then for the number, and
measure, and weight of them, to resign that wholly into the hands of
our wise Father and Physician, who perfectly knows our mould and
our maladies, and what kind and quantity of chastisement is needful
for our cure.

Though now for a season (if need be) ye are in heaviness.]   The
other consideration which moderates this heaviness, is its shortness.

Because we willingly forget eternity, therefore this moment seems much in our eyes : but if we could look upon it aright, of how little concernment is it what be our condition here ! If it were as prosperous as we could wish or imagine, it is but for a *little season.* The rich man in the Gospel talked of many years, but, *Thou fool, this night shall thy soul be required of thee,* was the longest period. The many years are quickly drawn to a very great abatement, and if full of pains and griefs, those do help to put an end to themselves, and hasten to it. Well then might St. Austin say, *Hic ure, cæde, modò ibi parcas,* Use me here as pleaseth thee, so that hereafter it may be well with me.

Wherein.] This word, though it cannot fall amiss, being referred to any particular to which interpreters have appropriated it, yet it is rather to be taken as relative to the whole complex sense of the preceding verses, concerning the hope of glory. In this thing ye rejoice, that ye are begotten again,—that there is such an inheritance, and that you are made heirs of it,—that it is kept for you, and you for it,—that nothing can come betwixt you and it, to disappoint you of possessing and enjoying it,—that though there be many deserts, and mountains, and seas in the way, yet you are ascertained, that you shall come safe thither.

This is but one thing, while the cause of your grief is, *temptations,* and *manifold temptations,* yet this one thing weighs down all that multitude. The heart being grieved in one thing, naturally looks out for its ease to some other ; and there is usually somewhat that is a man's great comfort, that he turns his thoughts to, when he is crossed and afflicted in other things : but herein lies the folly of the world, that the things they choose for their refuge and comfort are such as may change themselves, and turn into discomfort and sorrow ; but the godly man, who is the fool in the natural man's eyes, goes beyond all the rest in his wise choice in this. He rises above all that is subject to change, casts his anchor within the vail. That in which he rejoiceth is still matter of joy unmovable and unalterable ; although not only his estate, but the whole world were turned upside down, yet this is the same, or rather, in the Psalmist's words, *Though the earth were removed, and the greatest mountains cast into the sea, yet will not we fear.* Psal. xlvi. 2. When we shall receive that rich, and pure, and abiding inheritance, that salvation which shall be revealed in the last time, and when time itself shall cease to be, then there shall be no more reckoning of our joys by days and hours, but they shall run parallel with eternity. Then all our love, that is now scattered and parcelled out upon the vanities amongst which we are here, shall be united and gathered into one, and fixed upon God, and the soul filled with the delight of his presence.

The sorrow was limited and bounded by the considerations we spoke of ; but this joy, this exultation, and leaping for joy, (for so it is,) is not bounded, it cannot be too much ; its measure is, to know no measure. The afflictions, the matter of heaviness, are but a transient touch of pain ; but that whereon this joy is built is most permanent, the measure of it cannot exceed, for the matter of it is infinite and eternal, beyond all hyperbole. There is no expression we have which can reach it, much less go beyond it ; itself is the hyperbole, still surpassing all that can be said of it. Even in the midst of heaviness itself, such is this joy that it can maintain itself in the depth of sorrow ; this oil of gladness still swims above, and cannot be drowned by all the floods of affliction, yea, it is often most sweet in the greatest distress. The soul relishes spiritual joy best, when it is not glutted with worldly delights, but finds them turned into bitterness.

For application. In that we profess ourselves Christians, we all pretend to be the sons of God, and so heirs of this glory ; and if each man were individually asked, he would say, he hoped to attain it : but were there nothing else, this might abundantly convince us, that the greatest part of us delude ourselves, and are deceived in this ; for how few are there who do really find this height of joy, of gladness and exultation, in their thoughts and hopes of it, who do daily refresh and glad themselves with the consideration of what is laid up for them above, more than with all their enjoyments here below !

Consider how the news of some small outward advantage that is to come to us raises our light, vain hearts, and makes them leap within us ; and yet this news of a kingdom prepared for us, (if we be indeed believers,) stirs us not ; our hearts are as little affected with it as if it concerned us not at all : and this is too clear an evidence against us, that indeed it concerns us not, that our portion as yet is not in it.

In what a fool's paradise will men be with the thoughts of worthless things, and such things too as they shall never obtain, nor ever shall have any further being than what they have in their fancy ! And how will men frequently roll over in their minds the thoughts of any pleasing good they hope for ! And yet we, who say we have hopes of the glory to come, can pass many days without one hour spent in the rejoicing thought of the happiness we look for ! If any person of a mean condition for the present were made sure to become very rich and be advanced to great honour within a week, and after that to live to a great age in that high estate, enjoying health and all imaginable pleasures, judge ye, whether in the few days betwixt the knowledge of those news and the enjoying of them, the thoughts of what he were to attain to would not be frequent with him, and be always welcome. There is no comparison betwixt all we can imagine this way and the hopes we speak of ; and yet, how seldom are our thoughts upon those things, and how faint and slender is our rejoicing in them ! Can we deny that it is unbelief of these things that causeth this neglect and forgetting of them ? The discourse, the tongue of men and angels cannot beget divine belief of the happiness to come ; only He who gives it, gives faith likewise to apprehend it, and lay hold upon it, and, upon our believing, to be filled with joy in the hopes of it.

Ver. 7. That the trial of your faith, being much more precious than of gold that perisheth, though it be tried with fire, might be found unto praise, and honour, and glory at the appearing of Jesus Christ.

The way of the just (saith *Solomon*) *is as the shining light, that shineth more and more to the perfect day.* Still making forward, and ascending towards perfection, moving as fast when they are clouded with affliction as at any time else ; yea, all that seems to work against them, furthers them. Those graces that would possibly grow heavy and unwieldy, by too much ease, are held in breath, and increase their activity and strength by conflict. Divine grace, even in the heart of weak and sinful man, is an invincible thing. Drown it in the waters of adversity, it rises more beautiful, as not being drowned indeed, but only washed; throw it into the furnace of fiery trials, it comes out purer, and loses nothing but the dross which our corrupt nature mixes with it. Thus the Apostle here expounds the *if need be* of the former verse, and so justifies the joy in afflictions, which there he speaks of, by their utility and the advantage faith derives from them : it is so tried that it shall appear in its full brightness at the revelation of Jesus Christ.

The peculiar treasure of a Christian being the grace which he receives from Heaven, and particularly that sovereign grace of Faith, whatsoever he can be assured will better him any way in this he will not only bear patiently, but gladly embrace it. See Rom. v. 3. Therefore the Apostle sets this before his brethren in those words of this verse which express, 1. The worth and excellency of faith ; 2. The usefulness of temptations in relation to it.

1*st*, The worth and excellency of faith. The trial of faith is called *more precious*, a work of more worth than the trial of gold, because faith itself is of more value than gold. The Apostle chooses this comparison, as fitting his purpose for the illustration of both,—the worth of faith, and likewise the use of temptations, representing the one by gold, and the other by the trying of gold in the fire.

The worth of gold is, 1. Real, the purest and most precious of all metals, having many excellent properties beyond them, as they who write of the nature of gold observe. 2. Far greater in the esteem and opinion of men. See how men hurry up and down, over sea and land, unwearied in their pursuit, with hazard of life, and often with the loss of uprightness and a good conscience ; and not only thus esteem it in itself, but make it the rule of their esteem one of another, valuing men less or more as they are more or less furnished with it. And we see at what a height this is ; for things we would commend much, we borrow its name to describe them, e. g., *Golden mediocrity;* and that age which they would call the best of all, they name it the *Golden Age;* and as Seneca observes, describing heavenly things, (as *Ovid* the sun's palace and chariot,) still *Gold* is the word for all.

And the Holy Scriptures, descending to our reach, do set forth the riches of the new Jerusalem by it, Rev. xxi., and the excellency of Christ, Cant. v. 11, 14. And here the preciousness of faith, whereof Christ is the object, is said to be *more precious than gold.*

I will not insist in the parallel of faith with gold in the other qualities of it, as that it is pure and solid as gold, and that it is most ductile and malleable as gold ; beyond all other metals, it plies any way with the will of God. But then faith truly enriches the soul ; and as gold answers all things, so faith gives the soul propriety in all the rich consolations of the Gospel, in all the promises of life and salvation, in all needful blessings ; it draws virtue from Christ to strengthen itself, and all other graces.

And thus it is not only precious as gold, but goes far above the comparison ; it is *more precious,* yea, *much more precious,* 1. In its original : the other is digged out of the bowels of the earth ; but the mine of this gold is above, it comes from heaven. 2. In its nature, answerable to its original, it is immaterial, spiritual, and pure. We refine gold and make it purer, but when we receive faith pure in itself, we mix dross with it, and make it impure by the alloy of unbelief. 3. In its endurance, flowing from the former ; it perisheth not. Gold is a thing in itself corruptible and perishing, and to particular owners it perisheth in their loss of it, they being deprived of it in any way.

Other graces are likewise tried in the same furnace ; but Faith is named as the root of all the rest. Sharp afflictions give a Christian a trial of his love to God, whether it be single and for himself or not ; for then it will be the same when he strikes as when he embraces, and in the fire of affliction will rather grow the hotter, and be more taken off from the world, and set upon him. Again, the grace of patience is put particularly upon trial in distresses. But both these spring from Faith ; for love rises from a right and strong belief of the goodness of God, and patience from a persuasion of the wisdom and love of God, and the truth of his promises. He hath said, *I will not fail thee,* and that we shall not be tempted above our strength, and he will give the issue. Now the belief of these things causes patience. *The trial of faith worketh patience.* James i. 3. For therefore doth the Christian resign up himself, and all that concerns him, his trials, the measure and length of them all, unto God's disposal, because he knows that he is in the hands of a wise and loving Father. Thus the trial of these and other particular graces doth still resolve into this, and is comprised under the trial of faith. This brings us,

2dly, To the usefulness of temptations in relation to it.

This trial (as that of gold) may be for a two-fold end. 1. For experiment of the truth and pureness of a Christian's faith. 2. To refine it yet more, and to raise it to a higher pitch or degree of pureness.

1. The furnace of afflictions shows upright, real faith to be such indeed, remaining still the same even in the fire, the same that it was, undiminished, as good gold loses none of its quantity in the fire. Doubtless many are deceived in time of ease and prosperity, with imaginary faith and fortitude : so that there may be still some doubt, while a man is unders t with outward helps, as riches, friends, esteem, &c., whether he leans upon those or upon God, who is an invisible support, though stronger than all that are visible, and is the peculiar and alone stay of faith in all conditions. But when all these outward props are plucked away from a man, then it will be manifest, whether something else upholds him or not ; for if there be nothing else, then he falls ; but if his mind stands firm and unremoved as before, then it is evident he laid not his weight upon these things which he had then about him, but was built upon a foundation, though not seen, which is able alone to stay him, although he be not only frustrated of all other supports, but beaten upon with storms and tempests ; as our Saviour says *the house fell not, because it was founded on a rock.* Matt. vii. 25.

This testified the truth of *David's* faith, who found it stay his mind upon God, when there was nothing else near that could do it : *I had*

fainted, unless I had believed. Psal. xxvii. 13. So in his strait,
1 Sam. xxx. 6, where it is said that *David was greatly distressed; but
he encouraged himself in the Lord his God.* Thus Psal. lxxxiii. 26,
*My flesh and my heart faileth; but God is the strength of my heart
and my portion for ever.* The heart's natural strength of spirit and
resolution may bear up under outward weakness, or the failing of the
flesh; but when the heart itself fails, which is the strength of the flesh,
what shall strengthen it? nothing but God, *who is the strength of the
heart and its portion for ever.* Thus faith worketh alone, when the
case suits that of the Prophet's, Hab. iii. 17 : *Although the fig tree
shall not blossom, neither shall fruit be in the vine,* &c., *yet I will rejoice
in the Lord, I will joy in the God of my salvation.*

In spiritual trials, which are the sharpest and most fiery of all, when
the furnace is within a man, when God doth not only shut up his loving-
kindness from his feeling, but seems to shut it up in hot displeasure ;
when he writes bitter things against him; yet then to depend upon him,
and wait for his salvation, and the more he smites the more he cleaves
to him,—this is not only a true, but a strong and very refined faith
indeed. Well might *he* say, *When I am tried I shall come forth as
gold,* who could say that word, *Though he slay me, yet will I trust in
him :* though I saw, as it were, his hand lifted up to destroy me, yet
from that same hand would I expect salvation.

2. As the furnace shows faith to be what it is, so also it betters it,
and makes it more precious and purer than it was.

The graces of the Spirit, as they come from the hand of God who
infuses them, are nothing but pureness; but being put into a heart
where sin dwells, (which, till the body be dissolved and taken to pieces,
cannot be fully purged out,) there they are mixed with corruption and
dross : and particularly faith is mixed with unbelief, and love of earthly
things, and dependence upon the creature, if not more than God, yet
together with him ; and for this is the furnace needful, that the soul
may be purified from this dross, and made more sublime and spiritual
in believing. It is a hard task, and many times comes but slowly forward, to teach the heart, by discourse and speculation, to sit loose from
the world at all sides, not to cleave to the best things in it, though we
be compassed about with them, *though riches do increase,* yet, *not
to set our hearts on them,* Psal. lxxii. 10; not to trust in such *uncertain things,* as they are, as the Apostle speaks, 1 Tim. vi. 17. Therefore
God is pleased to choose the more effectual way to teach his own the
right and pure exercise of faith, either by withholding or withdrawing
those things from them. He makes them relish the sweetness of
spiritual comfort, by depriving them of those outward comforts whereon they were in most danger to have doted to excess, and so to have
forgotten themselves and him. When they are reduced to necessity,
and experimentally trained up easily to let go their hold of any thing
earthly, and to stay themselves only upon their Rock, this is the very
refining of their faith, by those losses and afflictions wherewith they
are exercised. They who learn bodily exercises, as fencing, &c., are
not taught by sitting still, and hearing rules, or seeing others practise, but they learn by exercising themselves. The way to profit in
the art of believing, or of coming to this spiritual activity of faith,

is, to be often put to that work in the most difficult way, to make up all wants and losses in God, and to sweeten the bitterest griefs with his loving-kindness.

Might be found unto praise, and honour, and glory.] This is the end that is intended, and shall be certainly obtained by all these hot trials. Faith shall come through them all, and *shall be found unto praise*, &c. An unskilful beholder may think it strange to see gold thrown into the fire, and left there for a time; but he that puts it there, would be loth to lose it; his purpose is to make some costly piece of work of it. Every believer gives himself to Christ, and he undertakes to present them blameless to the Father; not one of them shall be lost, nor one drachm of their faith; they shall be found, and their faith shall be found, when He appears. That faith which is here in the furnace, shall be then made up into a crown of pure gold: *it shall be found unto praise, and honour, and glory.*

This praise, and honour, and glory may be referred, either to believers themselves, according to the Apostle St. Paul's expression, Rom. ii. 7, or to Christ who appears: but the two will agree well together, that it be both to their praise, and to the praise of Christ; for certainly, all their praise and glory shall terminate in the glory of their Head —Christ, who is God, blessed for ever. They have each their crown, but their honour is, to cast them all down before his throne. *He shall be glorified in his saints, and admired in them that believe.* They shall be glorious in him; and therefore in all their glory he shall be glorified; for as they have derived their glory from him, it shall all return back to him again.

At the appearance of Jesus Christ.] This denotes the time when this shall come to pass; for Christ is faithful and true; he hath promised to come again, and to judge the world in righteousness, and he will come and will not tarry. He shall judge righteously in that day, who was himself unrighteously judged here on earth. It is called the *revelation;* all other things shall be revealed in that day, the most hidden things, good and evil, shall be unvailed; but it is eminently the day of *His revelation:* it shall be by his light, by the brightness of his coming, that all other things shall be revealed; but he himself shall be the worthiest sight of all. All eyes shall behold him. He shall then gloriously appear before all men and angels, and shall by all be acknowledged to be the Son of God and Judge of the world: some shall with joy know him, and acknowledge him to be so; others to their horror and amazement. How beautiful shall he be to those who love him, when he as the glorious Head shall appear with his whole body mystical together with him!

Then, the glory and praise which all the saints shall be honoured with, shall recompense fully all the scorns and ignominies and distresses they have met with here. And they shall shine the brighter for them. Oh! if we considered often that solemn day, how light should we set by the opinions of men, and all outward hardships that can befall us! How easily should we digest dispraise and dishonour here, and pass through all cheerfully, provided we may be then found in him, and so partakers of *praise, and glory, and honour, in that day of his appearing!*

Ver. 8. Whom having not seen, ye love; in whom, though now ye see him not, yet
   believing, ye rejoice with joy unspeakable and full of glory :
9. Receiving the end of your faith, even the salvation of your souls.

It is a paradox to͜ the world which the Apostle hath asserted, that
there is a joy which can subsist in the midst of sorrow ; therefore he
insists in confirmation of it, and in all these words proves it to the full,
yea, with advantage, that the saints have not only some measure of
joy in the griefs that abound upon them here, but excellent and eminent joy, such as makes good all that can be said of it, such as cannot
be spoken too much of, for it is *unspeakable*, nor too much magnified,
for it is *glorious*.

To evidence the truth of this, and to confirm his brethren in the
experienced knowledge of it, he expresses here more particularly and
distinctly the causes of this their joy, which are,

1. The *object* or *matter* of it ; 2. The *apprehension* and *appropria-
tion* of that *object:* which two conjoined, are the entire cause of all
rejoicing.

1. The *object* is Jesus Christ, ver. 8, and the salvation purchased
by him, ver. 9.   For these two cannot be severed, and these two
verses which speak of them, require (as is evident by their connexion)
to be considered together.

2. The apprehension of these is set forth, first, negatively, not by
bodily sight; secondly, positively : whereas it might seem to abate
the certainty and liveliness of their rejoicing, that it is of things they
had not seen, nor do yet see ; this is abundantly made up by three for
one, each of them more excellent than the mere bodily sight of Christ
in the flesh, which many had who were never the better by it : the
three things are, those three prime Christian graces, faith, love, and
hope ; the two former in ver. 8, the third in ver. 9.—Faith in Christ
begetting love to him, and both these giving assured hope of salvation
by him, making it as certain to them, as if it were already in their
hand, and they in possession of it.   And from all these together results
this exultation, or leaping for joy, *joy unspeakable, and full of glory.*

This is that *one thing* that so much concerns us ; and therefore we
mistake very far, and forget our own highest interest too much, when
we either speak or hear of it slightly, and apply not our hearts to it.
What is it that all our thoughts and endeavours drive at ?   What
means all that we are doing in the world ?   Though we take several
ways to it, and wrong ways for the most part, yea, such ways as lead
not to it, but set us further off from it ; yet what we all seek after by
all our labour under the sun, is something that may be matter of contentment and rejoicing to us when we have attained it.   Now here it
is, and in vain is it sought for elsewhere.   And for this end it is represented to you, that it may be yours, if ye will entertain it ; not only
that you may know this to be a truth, that in Jesus Christ is laid up
true consolation and rejoicing, that he is the magazine and treasury of
it, but that you may know how to bring him home into your hearts,
and lodge him there, and so to have the spring of joy within you.

That which gives full joy to the soul, must be something that is
higher and better than itself.   In a word, He who made it, can alone
make it glad after this manner, with *unspeakable and glorious joy.*

But the soul, while remaining guilty of rebellion against Him, and unreconciled, cannot behold him but as an enemy; any belief that it can have of him while it is in that posture, is not such as can fetch *love*, and *hope*, and so *rejoicing*, but what the faith of devils produceth, only begetting terror and trembling. But the light of his countenance, shining in the face of his Son the Mediator, gladdens the heart; and it is the looking upon him so that causeth the soul to *believe*, and *love*, and *hope*, and *rejoice*. Therefore the Apostle, in his description of the estate of the Gentiles before Christ was preached to them, Eph. ii., joins these together: *Without Christ,*—that was the cause of all the rest,—therefore, without comfort in the promises, *without hope, and without God in the world.* So he is here by our Apostle expressed, as the object. In all these, therefore, he is the matter of our joy, because our *faith*, and *love*, and *hope of salvation* do centre in him.

The Apostle writing to the dispersed Jews, many of whom had not known or seen Christ in the flesh, commends their love and faith, for this reason, that it did not depend upon bodily sight, but was pure, and spiritual, and made them of the number of those whom our Saviour himself pronounces *blessed, who have not seen, and yet believe.* You saw him not when he dwelt amongst men, and walked to and fro, preaching and working miracles. Many of those who did then hear and see him believed not; yea, they scoffed, and hated, and persecuted him, and in the end crucified him; you have seen none of all those things, yet having heard the Gospel which declares him, *you have believed.*

Thus *observe*, the working or not working of faith doth not depend upon the difference of the external ministry and gifts of men; for what greater difference can there be that way than betwixt the Master and the servants, betwixt the great Prophet himself and his weak, sinful messengers? and yet many of those who saw and heard him in person were not converted, believed not in him; and thousands who never saw him were converted by his Apostles, and, as it seems, even some of those who were some way accessory to his death, yet were brought to repentance by this same Apostle's sermon. See Acts ii.

Learn, then, to look above the outward ministry, and any difference that in God's dispensation can be there; and know, that if Jesus Christ himself were on earth, and now preaching amongst us, yet might his incomparable words be unprofitable to us, not being mixed with faith in the hearers. But where that is, the meanest and the most despicable conveyance of his message, received with humility and affection, will work blessed effects.

Whom not seeing, yet believing.] Faith elevates the soul not only above sense, and sensible things, but above reason itself. As reason corrects the errors which sense might occasion, so, supernatural faith corrects the errors of natural reason, judging according to sense.

The sun seems less than the wheel of a chariot, but reason teaches the philosopher, that it is much bigger than the whole earth, and the cause that it seems so little, is, its great distance. The naturally wise man is equally deceived by this carnal reason, in his estimate of Jesus Christ *the Sun of righteousness*, and the cause is the same, his great distance from him; as the Psalmist speaks of the wicked, Psal. x. 5,

Thy judgments are far above out of his sight. He accounts Christ and his glory a smaller matter than his own gain, honour, or pleasure; for these are near him, and he sees their quantity to the full, and counts them bigger, yea, far more worth than they are indeed. But the Apostle St. Paul, and all who are enlightened by the same Spirit, they know by faith, which is divine reason, that the excellency of Jesus Christ far surpasses the worth of the whole earth, and all things earthly. Phil. iii. 7, 8.

To give a right assent to the Gospel of Christ is impossible, without divine and saving faith infused in the soul. To believe that the eternal Son of God clothed himself with human flesh, and dwelt amongst men in a tabernacle like theirs, and suffered death in the flesh; that he who was Lord of life, hath freed us from the sentence of eternal death; that he broke the bars and chains of death and rose again; that he went up into heaven, and there at the Father's right hand sits in our flesh, and that glorified above the angels; this is the *great mystery of godliness.* And a part of this mystery is, that *he is believed on in the world.* 1 Tim. ii. 16. This natural men may discourse of, and that very knowingly, and give a kind of natural credit to it, as to a history that may be true; but firmly to believe that there is *Divine truth* in all these things, and to have a persuasion of it stronger than of the very things we see with our eyes,—such an assent as this is the peculiar work of the Spirit of God, and is certainly saving faith.

The soul that so believes cannot choose but love. It is commonly true, that the eye is the ordinary door by which love enters into the soul, and it is true in respect of this love; though it is denied of the eye of sense, yet (you see) it is ascribed to the eye of faith, *though you have not seen him, you love him, because you believe:* which is to see him spiritually. Faith, indeed, is distinguished from that vision which shall be in glory; but it is the vision of the kingdom of grace, it is the eye of the new creature, that quick-sighted eye which pierces all the visible heavens, and sees above them; which *looks to things that are not seen,* 2 Cor. iv. 18, *and is the evidence of things not seen,* Heb. xi. 1, and *sees him who is invisible,* ver. 27. It is possible that a person may be much beloved upon the report of his worth and virtues, and upon a picture of him lively drawn, before sight of the party so commended and represented; but certainly when he is seen, and found answerable to the former, it raises the affection already begun to a far greater height. We have the report of the perfections of Jesus Christ in the Gospel; yea, so clear a description of him, that it gives a picture of him, and that, together with the sacraments, is the only lawful, and the only lively picture of our Saviour. Gal. iii. 1. Now faith believes this report, and beholds this picture, and so lets in the love of Christ to the soul. But further, it gives a particular experimental knowledge of Christ and acquaintance with him; it causes the soul to find all that is spoken of him in the word, and his beauty there represented, to be abundantly true: makes it really taste of his sweetness, and by that possesses the heart more strongly with his love, persuading it of the truth of those things, not by reasons and arguments, but by an inexpressible kind of evidence, which they only know who have it. Faith persuades a Christian of these two things which the philosopher gives as the causes of all love, *beauty* and *propriety*, the loveliness of Christ in himself, and our interest in him.

The former it effectuates not only by the first apprehending and believing of those his excellencies and beauty, but by frequent beholding of him, and eyeing him in whom all perfection dwells; and it looks so oft on him, till it sets the very impression of his image (as it were) upon the soul, so that it can never be blotted out and forgotten. The latter it doth by that particular *uniting* act which makes him our God and our Saviour.

Ye love.] The distinctions which some make in *love*, need not be taken as importing different kinds, but different actings of the same love, by which we may try our so much pretended love of Christ, which in truth is so rarely found. There will then be in this love, if it be genuine, these three qualities, *good-will, delight,* and *desire.*

1st, *Good-will,* earnest wishing, and (as we can) promoting God's glory, and stirring up others so to do. They who *seek more their own things than the things of Jesus Christ,* more their own praise and esteem than his, are strangers to this divine love; for *she seeks not her own things.* The bitter root of self-love is most hard to pluck up; this strongest and sweetest love of Christ alone doth it actually, though gradually. This love makes the soul like the lower heaven, slow in its own motion, most swift in the motion of that first which wheels it about; so, the higher degree of love, the more swift. It loves the hardest tasks and greatest difficulties, where it may perform God service, either in doing or in suffering for him. *It is strong as death, and many waters cannot quench it.* Eccles. viii. 6, 7. The greater the task is, the more real are the testimony and expression of love, and therefore the more acceptable to God.

2dly, There is in true love, a complacency and *delight* in God; a conformity to his will; a loving what he loves: it is studious of his will, ever seeking to know more clearly what it is that is most pleasing to him, contracting a likeness to God in all his actions, by conversing with him, by frequent contemplation of God, and looking on his beauty. As the eye lets in this affection, so it serves it constantly, and readily looks that way which love directs it. Thus the soul possessed with this love of Jesus Christ, the soul which hath its eye much upon him, often thinking on his former sufferings and present glory, the more it looks upon Christ, the more it loves; and still the more it loves, the more it delights to look upon him.

3dly, There is in true love a *desire;* for it is but small beginnings and tastes of his goodness which the soul hath here; therefore it is still looking out and longing for the day of marriage. The time is sad and wearisome, and seems much longer than it is, while it is detained here. *I desire to be dissolved* (saith St. Paul) *and to be with Christ.* Phil. i. 23.

God is the sum of all things lovely. Thus excellently Gregory Nazianzen expresseth himself, Orat. 1. "If I have any possessions, "health, credit, learning, this is all the contentment I have of them, "that I have somewhat I may despise for Christ, who is *totus deside-* "*rabilis, et totum desiderabile* (the all-desirable one, the every thing "desirable)." And this love is the sum of all he requires of us; it is that which makes all our meanest services acceptable, and without which all we offer to him is distasteful. God doth deserve our love not only by his matchless excellency and beauty, but by his matchless love to us, and that is the strongest loadstone of love. *He hath loved me*, saith the Apostle, Gal. ii. 20. How appears that? In no less than this, *He hath given himself for me.* Certainly, then, there is no clearer character of our love than this, to give ourselves to him who hath so loved us, and given himself for us.

This affection must be bestowed some where : there is no man but hath some prime choice, somewhat that is the predominant delight of his soul ; will it not then be our wisdom to make the worthiest choice? seeing it is offered us, it is extreme folly to reject it.

Grace doth not pluck up by the roots and wholly destroy the natural passions of the mind, because they are distempered by sin ; that were an extreme remedy, to cure by killing, and heal by cutting off : no, but it corrects the distemper in them ; it dries not up this main stream of love, but purifies it from the mud which it is full of in its wrong course, or turns it into its right channel, by which it may run into happiness, and empty itself into the ocean of goodness. The Holy Spirit turns the love of the soul towards God in Christ, for in that way only can it apprehend His love ; so then Jesus Christ is the first *object* of this Divine love ; he is *medium unionis*, through whom God conveys the sense of his love to the soul, and receives back its love to Himself.

And if we will consider his incomparable beauty, we may look on it in the Holy Scriptures, particularly in that Divine song of loves, wherein Solomon borrows all the beauties of the creatures, dips his pencil in all their several excellencies, to set him forth unto us, who is the *chief of ten thousands.* There is an inseparable intermixture of love with belief and a pious affection, in receiving Divine truth ; so that in effect, as we distinguish them, they are mutually strengthened, the one by the other, and so, though it seem a circle, it is a Divine one, and falls not under censure of the school's pedantry. If you ask, How shall I do to *love?* I answer, *Believe.* If you ask, How shall I *believe?* I answer, *Love.* Although the expressions to a carnal mind are altogether unsavoury, by grossly mistaking them, yet to a soul taught to read and hear them, by any measure of that same spirit of love wherewith they were penned, they are full of heavenly and unutterable sweetness.

Many directions as to the means of begetting and increasing this love of Christ may be here offered, and they who delight in number may multiply them ; but surely this one will comprehend the greatest and best part, if not all of them ; *Believe, and you shall love; believe much, and you shall love much;* labour for strong and deep persuasions of the glorious things which are spoken of Christ, and this will command love. Certainly, did men indeed believe his worth, they would accordingly love him ; for the reasonable creature cannot but affect that most which it firmly believes to be worthiest of affection. Oh ! this mischievous unbelief is that which makes the heart cold and dead towards God. Seek then to believe Christ's excellency in himself, and his love to us, and our interest in him, and this will kindle such a fire in the heart, as will make it ascend in a sacrifice of love to him.

The signs likewise of this love may be multiplied, according to the many fruits and workings of it ; but in them all, itself is its own most infallible evidence.   When the soul finds that all its obedience and endeavour to keep the commands of Jesus Christ, which himself makes its character, do flow from love, then it is true and sincere ; for do or suffer what you will, without love all passes for nothing ; all are ciphers without it, they signify nothing.   1 Cor. xiii.

This is the message of the Gospel, and that which the ministry aims at ; and therefore the ministers ought to be suitors, not for themselves, but for Christ, to espouse souls to him, and to bring in many hearts to love him.   And certainly, this is the most compendious way to persuade to all other Christian duties, for this is to converse with Jesus Christ, and where his love is, no other incentive will be needful ; for love delights in the presence and converse of the party loved.   If we are to persuade to duties of the second table, the sum of those is, love to our brethren, resulting from the love of Christ, which diffuseth such a sweetness into the soul, that it is all love, and meekness, and gentleness, and long-suffering.

If times be for suffering, love will make the soul not only bear, but welcome the bitterest afflictions of life, and the hardest kinds of death, for his sake.   In a word, there is in love a sweet constraint, or tying of the heart to all obedience and duty.

The love of God is requisite in ministers for their preaching of the word ; so our Saviour to St. Peter, John xxi. 15, *Peter, lovest thou me? then feed my lambs.*   It is requisite for the people that they receive the truth in the love of it, and that Christ preached may be entertained in the soul, and embraced by faith and love.

You that have made choice of Christ for your love, let not your hearts slip out, to renew your wonted base familiarity with sin ; for that will bring new bitterness to your souls, and at least for some time deprive you of the sensible favour of your beloved Jesus.   Delight always in God, and give him your whole heart ; for he deserves it all, and is a satisfying good to it.   The largest heart is all of it too strait for the riches of consolation which he brings with him. Seek to increase in this love ; and though it is at first weak, yet labour to find it daily rise higher, and burn hotter and clearer, and consume the dross of earthly desires.

Receiving the end of your faith.]   Although the soul that believes and loves, is put in present possession of God, as far as it is capable in its sojourning here, yet it desires a full enjoyment, which it cannot attain to without removing hence.   *While we are present in the body, we are absent from the Lord,* saith the Apostle.   And because they are assured of that happy exchange, that being untied and freed of this body, they shall be present with the Lord, having his own word for it, that *where he is they shall be also;* this begets such an assured hope, as bears the name of *Possession.*   Therefore it is said here, *Receiving the end of your faith.*

This receiving likewise flows from faith.   Faith apprehends the present truth of the Divine promises, and so makes the things to come, present : and hope looks out to their after-accomplishment, which, if the promises be true, as faith avers, then hope hath good reason firmly to expect.   This desire and hope are the very wheels of the soul which carry it on, and faith is the common axis on which they rest.

In these words there are two things : 1. The good hoped for in Christ so believed on and loved : 2. The assuredness of the hope itself : yea, it is as sure as if it were already accomplished.

I. As for the good hoped for, it consists, 1. In the nature of it, *viz.*, the *salvation of their soul;* 2. In a relative property of it, *the end of their faith.*

1st, The nature of it is, *salvation, and salvation of the soul:* it imports full deliverance from all kinds of misery, and the safe possession of perfect happiness, when the soul shall be out of the reach of all adversaries, and adverse accidents, no more subjected to those evils which are properly its own, namely, the conscience of sin, and fear of wrath, and sad defections ; nor yet subject to those other evils which it endured by society with the body—outward distresses and afflictions, persecutions, poverty, diseases, *&c.*

It is called *salvation of the soul:* not excluding the body from the society of that glory, when it shall be raised and reunited to the soul ; but because the soul is of itself an immortal substance, and both the more noble part of man, and the prime subject both of grace and glory, and because it arrives first at that blessedness, and for a time leaves the body in the dust to do homage to its original ; therefore it is alone named here.   But Jesus is the Saviour of the body too, and he shall, at his coming, *change our vile bodies, and make them like his glorious body.*

2dly, We have the relative property of this hope,—*The end of your faith,* the *end* or *reward;* for it is both.   It is the *end,* either at which faith aims, or wherein it ceaseth.   It is the *reward,* not of their works, nor of faith, as a work deserving it, but as the condition of the new covenant, which God, according to the tenor of that covenant, first works in his own, and then rewards as if it were their work.   And this salvation, or fruition of Christ, is the proper reward of faith, which believes in him unseen, and so obtains that happy sight.   It is the proper work of faith to believe what thou seest not, and the reward of faith, to see what thou hast believed.

II. This is the certainty of their hope, that it is as if they had already received it.   If the promise of God and the merit of Christ hold good, then they who believe in him, and love him, are made sure of salvation.   The promises of God in Christ *are not yea and nay ; but they are in him yea, and in him amen.*   Sooner may the rivers run backward, and the course of the heavens change, and the frame of nature be dissolved, than any one soul that is united to Christ Jesus by faith and love, can be severed from him, and so fall short of the salvation hoped for in him ; and this is the matter of their rejoicing.

Ye rejoice with joy unspeakable.]   *The natural man,* says the Apostle, *receiveth not the things of God, for they are foolishness unto him;* and he adds the reason why he cannot know them, *for they are spiritually discerned.*   He hath none of that faculty by which they are discerned.   There is a vast disproportion betwixt those things and nature's highest capacity ; it cannot work beyond its sphere.   Speak to the natural man, of the matter of spiritual grief, the sense of guiltiness, and the apprehension of God's displeasure, or the hiding of his favour and the light of his countenance from the soul ; these things stir not him, he knows not what they mean. Speak to him again of the peace of conscience, and sense of God's love, and the joy that arises hence ; he is no less a stranger to that. *Mourn to him, and he laments not; pipe to him, and he dances not*, as our Saviour speaks, Matt. xi. 17. But as it there follows, ver. 19, there is a wisdom in these things, though they seem folly and nonsense to the foolish world, and this *wisdom is justified of her own children.*

Having said somewhat already of the Causes of this spiritual joy, which the Apostle here speaks of, it remains that we consider these two things : 1. How joy ariseth from these causes ; 2. The excellency of this joy, as it is here expressed.

There is here a solid, sufficient good, and the heart made sure of it, being partly put in present possession of it, and having a most certain hope of all the rest. And what more can be required to make it joyful ? Jesus Christ, the treasure of all blessings, received and united to the soul, by faith, and love, and hope !

Is not Christ the light and joy of the nations ? such a light as Abraham, at the distance of many ages, of more than two thousand years, yet saw by faith, and seeing, rejoiced in. Besides this brightness, which makes light a joyful object, light is often in Scripture put for joy. Christ, who is this light, brings salvation with him : he is the *Sun of righteousness*, and there is *healing under his wings. I bring you*, said the angel, *good tidings of great joy, that shall be to all people.* And their song hath in it the matter of that joy, *Glory to God in the highest, peace on earth, and good-will toward men.* Luke ii. 10, 14.

But to the end we may rejoice in Christ, we must find him ours ; otherwise, the more excellent he is, the more cause hath the heart to be sad, while it hath no portion in him. *My spirit hath rejoiced* (said the blessed Virgin) *in God my Saviour.* Luke i. 47.

Thus, having spoken of our communion with Christ, the Apostle adds, 1 John i. 7, *These things I write, that your joy may be full.* Faith worketh this joy by uniting the soul to Christ, and applying his merits, from the application of which arises the pardon of sin ; and so that load of misery, which was the great cause of sorrow, is removed ; and so soon as the soul finds itself lightened and unloaded of that burden which was sinking it to hell, it cannot choose but leap for joy, in the ease and refreshment it finds. Therefore that Psalm which David begins with the doctrine of the pardon of sin, he ends with an exhortation to *rejoicing. Blessed is the man whose transgression is forgiven, whose sin is covered :* Psal. xxxii. 1 : thus he begins, but he ends, *Be glad in the Lord and rejoice, ye righteous, and shout for joy, all ye that are upright in heart.* St. Peter speaks to his hearers of the remission of sins, Acts ii. 38, and at ver. 41, it is added, *They received his words gladly.* And our Saviour joins these two together, *Be of good comfort, thy sins are forgiven thee.* Thus, Isaiah lxi. 1, good tidings of liberty to captives are proclaimed, and a notable change there is of their estate *who mourn in Zion, giving them beauty for ashes, the oil of joy for mourning, and the garment of praise for the spirit of heaviness.* Think with what joy the long-imprisoned debtor, drowned in debt, receives a full discharge, and his liberty ; or a condemned malefactor the news of his pardon ; and this will somewhat resemble it, but yet fall far short of the joy which faith brings, by bringing Christ to the soul, and so forgiveness of sins in him.

But this is not all. This believing soul is not only a debtor acquitted and set free, but enriched besides with a new and great estate ; not only a pardoned malefactor, but withal highly preferred and advanced to honour, having a right, by the promises, *to the unsearchable riches of Christ,* as the Apostle speaks, and is received into favour with God, and unto the dignity of sonship, taken *from the dunghill, and set with princes.* Psal. cxiii. 8.

As there is joy from Faith, so also from Love. Though this is in itself the most sweet and delightful passion of the soul, yet, as we foolishly misplace it, it proveth often full of bitterness ; but being set upon Jesus Christ, the only right and worthy object, it causeth this unspeakable delight and rejoicing.

First, It is matter of joy to have bestowed our love so worthily. When our Saviour seems to withdraw himself, and sometimes saddens the soul that loves him, with *absences,* in regard of sense, yet even in those sad times, the soul delights to love him, and there is a pleasure in the very pains it hath in seeking after him. And this it knows, that his mercies are everlasting, and that he cannot be long unkind, but will return and speak comfortably unto it.

Secondly, Our love to Christ gives us assurance of His to us, so that we have not only chosen worthily, but shall not be frustrated and disappointed ; and it assures us of his, not as following, but as preceding and causing ours ; for our love to Jesus Christ is no other than the reflex of his on us. *Wine maketh glad the heart,* but *thy love is better than wine,* saith the spouse. And having this persuasion, that he *hath loved us and washed us in his blood,* and forgets us not in our conflicts, that though he himself is in his glory, yet that he intercedes for us there, and will bring us thither, what condition can befall us so hard, but we may rejoice in it, and in them, so far as we are sure to arrive at that full salvation and the fruition of him who hath purchased it ?

Then there is the third cause of our rejoicing, *viz.,* our *Hope.* Now hope is our *anchor fixed within the vail,* which stays us against all the storms that beat upon us in this troublesome sea that we are tossed upon. The soul which strongly believes and loves, may confidently hope to see what it believes, and to enjoy what it loves, and in that it may rejoice. It may say, whatsoever hazards, whether outward or inward, whatsoever afflictions and temptations I endure, yet this one thing puts me out of hazard, and in that I will rejoice, that the salvation of my soul depends not upon my own strength, but is in my Saviour's hand : *My life is hid with Christ in God ; and when he who is my life shall appear, I likewise shall appear with him in glory.* The childish world are hunting shadows, and gaping and hoping after they know not what ; but the believer can say, *I know whom I have trusted, and am persuaded that he is able to keep that which I have committed to him against that day.* Now we must have not only a right to these things, but withal there must be frequent consideration of them to produce joy. The soul must often view them, and so rejoice. *My meditation of him shall be sweet,* saith David. *I will be glad in the Lord,* Psal. civ. 34. The godly, failing in this, deprive themselves of much of that joy they might have; and they who are most in these sublime thoughts have the highest and truest joy.

The excellency of this joy, the Apostle here expresseth by these two words, *Unspeakable* and *Full of glory.*

That it is *unspeakable,* no wonder, seeing the matter of it is inconceivable; it is an infinite good. God reconciled in Jesus Christ, and testifying and sealing his love unto the soul, and giving assured hope of that blessed vision of eternity,—what more unspeakable than this? And for the same reason it is *glorious,* or glorified joy, having the highest and most glorious object; for it derives all its excellency from thence.

Unspeakable.] The best worldly joys are easily speakable; they may be expressed to the utmost, yea, usually more is spoken of them than they are indeed. Their name is beyond their worth; they are very seldom found, upon experience, equal to the opinion and expectation that men have of them. But this spiritual joy is above the report any can make of it: say what they can of it who are of happiest expression, yet when a man comes to know it in his own breast, he will say, (as that queen said of Solomon's wisdom,) *the half was not told me of it.*

Again, earthly joys are inglorious; many of which men are ashamed of, and those that seem most plausible, yet are below the excellency of the soul, and cannot fill it: but the joys which arise from union with Christ, as they are most avowable, a man needs not blush to own them,—so they are truly contenting and satisfying, and that is their glory, and the cause why we may glory in them. *My soul shall make her boast in God,* says David. Psal. xxxiv. 2.

For *Application* of all this. If these things were believed, we should hearken no more to the foolish prejudice which the world hath taken up against religion, and wherewith Satan endeavours to possess men's hearts, that they may be scared from the ways of holiness: they think it a sour, melancholy life, which hath nothing but sadness and mourning in it. But, to remove this prejudice,

Consider, 1. Religion debars not from the lawful delights which are taken in natural things, but teaches the moderate and regular use of them, which is far the sweeter; for things lawful in themselves are in their excess sinful, and so prove bitterness in the end. And if in some cases it requires the forsaking of lawful enjoyments, as of pleasure, or profits, or honour, for God and for his glory, it is generous and more truly delightful to deny them for this reason, than to enjoy them. Men have done much this way for the love of their country, and by a principle of moral virtue; but to lose any delight, or to suffer any hardship, for that highest end—the glory of God, and by the strength of love to him, is far more excellent, and truly pleasant.

2. The delights and pleasures of sin religion indeed banishes, but it is to change them for this joy that is unspeakably beyond them. It calls men from sordid and base delights to those that are pure delights indeed: it calls to men, Drink ye no longer of the puddle, here are the crystal streams of a living fountain. There is a delight in the very despising of impure delights; as St. Augustine exclaims, *Quàm suave*

est istis suavitatibus carere! How pleasant is it to want these pleasures! But for such a change, to have in their stead such delights, as that in comparison the other deserve not the name ; to have such spiritual joy as shall end in eternal joy ; it is a wonder we hasten not all to choose this joy, but it is indeed because we believe it not.

3. It is true, the godly are subject to great distresses and afflictions ; but their joy is not extinguished by them, no, nor diminished neither, but often sensibly increased. When they have least of the world's joy, they abound most in spiritual consolations, and then relish them best. They find them sweetest, when their taste is not depraved by earthly enjoyments. *We rejoice in tribulation,* says St. Paul : and here our Apostle insists on that, to verify the substance of this joy in the midst of the greatest afflictions.

4. Spiritual grief, which seems most opposite to this spiritual joy, excludeth it not, for there is a secret delight and sweetness in the tears of repentance, a balm in them that refreshes the soul ; and even their saddest kind of mourning, *viz.,* the dark times of desertion, hath this in it, which is someway sweet, that those mournings after their Beloved, who absents himself, are a mark of their love to him, and a true evidence of it. And then all these spiritual sorrows, of what nature soever, are turned into spiritual joy ; that is the proper end of them ; they have a natural tendency that way.

5. But the natural man still doubts of this joy we speak of ; because he sees and hears so little of it from them who profess to have it, and seem to have the best right to it. If we consider the wretchedness of this life, and especially the abundance of sin that is in the world, what wonder though this their joy retire much inward, and appear little abroad, where all things are so contrary to it, and so few are capable of it, to whom it were pertinent to vent it ? Again, we see here, it is *unspeakable;* it were a poor thing if he that hath it could tell it all out. *Pauperis est numerare pecus.* And when the soul hath most of it, then it remains most within itself, and is so inwardly taken up with it, that possibly it can then least of all express it. It is with joys, as they say of cares and griefs, *Leves loquuntur ingentes stupent.* The deepest waters run stillest. *Res severa est verum gaudium,* says Seneca. True joy is a solid, grave thing, dwells more in the heart than in the countenance : whereas, on the contrary, base and false joys are but superficial, skin-deep (as we say) ; they are all in the face.

Think not that it is with the godly, as the Prophet says of the wicked, that *there is no peace* to them. The *Septuagint* reads it, *no joy;* certainly it is true ; there is no true joy to the wicked : they may revel and make a noise, but they rejoice not ; *The laughter of the fool is as the crackling of thorns under the pot,* a great noise but little heat, and soon at an end. There is no continuing feast, but that of *a good conscience.* Wickedness and real joy cannot dwell together, as the very moralist Seneca hath it often, and at large. But he that can say, The righteousness of Jesus Christ is mine, and in him the favour of God, and the hope of eternal happiness, hath such a light as can shine in the darkest dungeon, yea, in the *dark valley of the shadow of death itself.*

Say not thou, If I betake myself to the way of godliness, I must bid farewell to gladness, never a merry day more ; no, on the contrary, never a truly joyful day till then, yea, no days at all, but night to the soul, till it entertain Jesus Christ and his kingdom, which consists in *righteousness, peace,* and *joy in the Holy Ghost.* Thou dost not sacrifice Isaac, which signifies laughter, (as St. Bernard has it,) but a ram ; not your joy, but filthy, sinful delights which end in sorrow.

Oh ! seek to know in your experience what those joys mean ; for all describing and commending them to you will not make you understand them ; but *taste, and see that the Lord is good: Lauda mellis dulcedinem quantum potes, qui non gustaverit, non intelliget,* says Augustine ; *Praise the sweetness of honey to the utmost, he who has never tasted it, cannot understand it.* You cannot see and know this goodness, but by tasting it ; and having tasted it, all those poor joys you thought sweet before, will then be bitter and distasteful to you.

And you that have Christ yours by believing, know your happiness, and rejoice, and glory in it. Whatsoever is your outward condition, *rejoice always, and again I say rejoice,* for *light is sown to the righteous, and gladness for the upright in heart.* Phil. iv. 4 ; Psal. xcvii. 11.

Ver. 10. Of which salvation the prophets have inquired and searched diligently, who prophesied of the grace that should come unto you :

11. Searching what, or what manner of time the Spirit of Christ which was in them did signify, when it testified beforehand the sufferings of Christ, and the glory that should follow.

12. Unto whom it was revealed, that not unto themselves, but unto us they did minister the things, which are now reported unto you by them that have preached the Gospel unto you with the Holy Ghost sent down from heaven ; which things the angels desire to look into.

IT is the ignorance, or at least the inconsideration of Divine things, that makes earthly things, whether good or evil, appear great in our eyes ; therefore the Apostle's great aim is, by representing the certainty and excellency of the belief and hope of Christians to his afflicted brethren, to strengthen their minds against all discouragements and oppositions ; that they may account nothing too hard to do or suffer for so high a cause and so happy an end. It is the low and mean thoughts, and the shallow persuasion we have of things that are spiritual, that is the cause of all our remissness and coldness in them. The doctrine of salvation, mentioned in the former verse as the end of our Christian faith, is illustrated in these words, from its antiquity, dignity, and infallible truth.

It is no modern invention ; for the Prophets inquired after it, and foretold it in former ages from the beginning. Thus the prejudice of novelty is removed, which usually meets the most ancient truth in its new discoveries.

Again, it is no mean thing that such men as were of unquestioned eminency in wisdom and holiness, did so much study and search after, and having found it out, were careful not only to publish it in their own times, but to record it to posterity ; and this not by the private motion of their own spirits, but by the acting and guidance of the Spirit of God ; which likewise sets the truth of their testimony above all doubtfulness and uncertainty.

But taking the three verses entirely together, we have in them these three things, testifying how excellent the doctrine of the Gospel is. 1. We have the principal author of it. 2. The matter of it. 3. The worth of those who are exercised about it, *viz.*, the best of men, the Prophets and Apostles, in administering it, and the best of all the creatures, the Angels, in admiring it.

1. The first author is the absolutely *first*, the Spirit of God in the prophets, ver. 11, in the apostles, ver. 12. But the Spirit of Christ, in ver. 11, is the same Spirit that he sent down on his disciples after his ascending to glory, and which spoke in his prophets before his descending to the earth. It is the Spirit of Christ, proceeding jointly from him with the Father, as he is the Son of God, and dwelling most richly and fully in him as the Son of man.

The Holy Ghost is in himself holiness, and the source and worker of holiness, and author of this holy doctrine which breathes nothing but holiness, and urges it most pressingly upon all that receive it.

This is the very life of divine faith, touching the mysteries of salvation, firmly to believe their *revelation* by the Spirit of God. This the word itself testifies, as we see; and it is really manifest in it; it carries the lively stamp of Divine inspiration, but there must be a spiritual eye to discern it. He that is blind, knows not that the sun shines at noon, but by the report of others; but they that see, are assured they see it, and assured by no other thing but its own light. To ask one who is a true believer, How know you the Scriptures to be Divine? is the same as to ask him, How know you light to be light?

The soul is nothing but darkness and blindness within, till that same Spirit that shines without in the word, shines likewise within it, and effectually makes it light; but that once done, then is the word read with some measure of the same Spirit by which it was written, and the soul is ascertained that it is Divine; as in bodily sight, there must be a meeting of inward light, *viz.*, the visual spirits with the outward *object*.

The Spirit of God within, brings evidence with it, and makes itself discernible in the word; this all arguments, all books and study, cannot attain unto. *It is given to believe*, Phil. i. 29.

No man knows the things of a man but the spirit of man, 1 Cor. ii. 11. But how holds that here? For if a man speak out the things that are in his spirit, then others may know them; but the Apostle's aim there, is, to conclude that the things of God, even such as were revealed in his word, could not be known but by his own Spirit; so that though revealed, yet they remain still unrevealed, till the Spirit teach within as well as without; because they are intelligible by none, but by those who are the private scholars and hearers of the Holy Ghost, the author of them; and because there are so few of these, therefore there is so little real believing amidst all the noise and profession that we make of it. Who is there (if you will believe them) that believes not? And yet truly there is too much cause to continue the Prophet's regret, Isa. liii. 1, *Who hath believed our report?*

Learn, then, to suspect yourselves, and to find out your own unbelief, that you may desire this Spirit to teach you inwardly those great mysteries which he outwardly reveals and teaches by his word. Make use of that promise, and press the Lord with it, *They shall be all taught of God,* Isaiah liv. 13 ; and John vi. 45.

But, II. There is here the *matter* of this doctrine, which we have in three several expressions : 1. That which is repeated from the foregoing verse ; it is the *Doctrine of Salvation,* that is the end of it. 2. The *Doctrine of the sufferings and glory of Christ,* as the means. And, 3. The *Doctrine of Grace,* the spring of both.

1. It is the doctrine of *Salvation,* the only true doctrine of true happiness, which the wisest of natural men have groped and sought after with much earnestness, but with no success ; they had no other than the dark moonlight of nature, and that is not sufficient to find it out ; only the Sun of righteousness shining in the sphere of the Gospel, *brings life and immortality to light,* 2 Tim. i. 10. No wonder that natural wisdom, the deepest of it, is far from finding out the true method and way of cure, seeing it cannot discover the disease of miserable mankind, *viz.,* the sinful and wretched condition of nature by the first disobedience.

Salvation expresses not only that which is negative, but implies likewise positive and perfect happiness ; thus forgiveness of sins is put for the whole nature of Justification frequently in Scripture. It is more easy to say of this unspeakable happiness, what it is not, than what it is. There is in it a full and final freedom from all annoyance ; all tears are wiped away, and their fountain is dried up ; all feeling and fear, or danger, of any the least evil, either of sin or punishment, is banished for ever ; there are no invasions of enemies, no robbing or destroying in all this holy mountain, no voice of complaining in the streets of the new Jerusalem. Here it is at the best but interchanges of mornings of joy, with sad evenings of weeping ; but there, there shall be no light, no need of sun nor moon, *For the glory of the Lord shall lighten it, and the Lamb shall be the light thereof,* Rev. xxi. 23.

Well may the Apostle (as he doth here throughout this Chapter) lay this salvation to counterbalance all sorrows and persecutions, and whatsoever hardships can be in the way to it. The soul that is persuaded of this, in the midst of storms and tempests enjoys a calm, triumphs in disgraces, grows richer by all its losses, and by death itself attains this immortal life.

Happy are they who have their eye fixed upon this salvation, and are longing and waiting for it ; who see so much of that brightness and glory, as darkens all the lustre of earthly things to them, and makes them trample upon those things which formerly they admired and doted on with the rest of the foolish world. Those things we account so much of, are but as rotten wood, or glow-worms, that shine only in the night of our ignorance and vanity : so soon as the light-beam of this salvation enters into the soul, it cannot much esteem or affect any thing below it ; and if those glances of it which shine in the word, and in the soul of a Christian, be so bright and powerful, what then shall the full sight and real possession of it be ?

2. The Gospel is represented as the *Doctrine of the sufferings and glory of Christ, as the means of salvation.* The worker of this salvation, whom the Prophets and Apostles make the sum of all their doctrine, is Jesus Christ, and the sum of that work of redemption, (as we have it here,) is his humiliation and exaltation ; his sufferings,

and the glory that followed thereupon. Now, though this serve as an encouragement to Christians in their sufferings, that this is the way by which their Lord went into his glory, and is true also of Christ mystical, the Head with the members, as the Scriptures often teach us, yet I conceive it is here mainly intended as a summary of the work of our redemption by Jesus Christ, relating to the salvation mentioned ver. 10, and as the cause for the effect, so it is put for it here. The Prophets inquired, and prophesied of that salvation. How? By searching out, and foretelling the sufferings and glory of Christ. His sufferings, then, and his after-glories are our salvation. His suffering is the purchase of our salvation, and his glory is our assurance of it; he as our Head having triumphed, and being crowned, makes us likewise sure of victory and triumph. His having entered on the possession of glory, makes our hope certain. This is his prayer, *That where he is, there we may be also;* and this is his own assertion, *The glory which thou gavest me, I have given them,* John xvii. 22, 24. This is his promise, *Because I live, ye shall live also,* John xiv. 19. Christ and the believer are one; this is that great mystery the Apostle speaks of, Eph. v. 30. Though it is a common known truth, the words and outside of it obvious to all, yet none can understand it but they who indeed partake of it. By virtue of that union, their sins were accounted his, and Christ's sufferings are accounted theirs, and by consequence, his glory, the consequent of his sufferings, is likewise theirs. There is an indissoluble connexion betwixt the life of Christ, and of a believer. *Our life is hid with Christ in God;* and therefore, while we remain there, our life is there, though hid, *and when he who is our life shall appear, we likewise shall appear with him in glory,* Col. iii. 3, 4. Seeing the sufferings and glory of our Redeemer are the main subject of the Gospel, and the causes of our salvation, and of our comfortable persuasion of it, it is a wonder that they are not more the matter of our thoughts. Ought we not daily to consider the bitterness of that cup of wrath he drank for us, and be wrought to repentance and hatred of sin, to have sin imbittered to us by that consideration, and find the sweetness of his love in that he did drink it, and by that, be deeply possessed with love to him? These things we now and then speak of, but they sink not into our minds, as our Saviour exhorts, where he is speaking of those same sufferings. Oh that they were engraven on our hearts, and that sin were crucified in us, and *the world crucified to us, and we unto the world,* by the cross of Christ! Gal. vi. 14.

And let us be frequently considering the glory wherein he is, and have our eye often upon that, and our hearts solacing and refreshing themselves frequently with the thoughts of that place and condition wherein Christ is, and where our hopes are, ere long, to behold him; both to see his glory, and to be glorified with him. Is it not reason? yea, it is necessary, it cannot be otherwise, if our treasure and Head be there, that our hearts be there likewise, Matt. vi. 21; Col. iii. 1, 2.

The third expression here of the Gospel, is, That *it is the Doctrine of Grace.* The work of redemption itself, and the several parts of it, and the doctrine revealing it, have all the name of Grace; because they all flow from Free Grace; that is their spring and first cause.

And it is this wherein the doctrine of salvation is mainly comfortable, that it is free: *Ye are saved by grace*, Eph. ii. 8.   It is true, God
requires faith, it is *through faith;* but he that requires that, gives it
too: *That it is not of yourselves, it is the gift of God*, Eph. ii. 8.   It is
wonderful grace to save upon believing ; believe in Jesus for salvation,
and live accordingly, and it is done ; there is no more required to thy
pardon, but that thou receive it by faith.   But truly nature cannot do
this ; it is as impossible for us of ourselves to believe, as to do.   This,
then, is that which makes it all grace from beginning to end, that God
not only saves upon believing, but gives believing itself.   Christ is
called not only the *Author and Finisher* of our salvation, but even *of
our faith*, Heb. xii. 2.

Free Grace being rightly apprehended, is that which stays the heart
in all estates, and keeps it from fainting, even in its saddest times.
What though there is nothing in myself but matter of sorrow and discomfort, it cannot be otherwise ; it is not from myself that I look for
comfort at any time, but from my God and his free grace.   Here is
comfort enough for all times : when I am at the best, I ought not, I dare
not, rely upon myself; when I am at the worst, I may, and should, rely
upon Christ, and his sufficient grace.   Though I be the vilest sinner that
ever came to him, yet I know that he is more gracious than I am sinful ; yea, the more my sin is, the more glory will it be to his grace to
pardon it ; it will appear the richer.   Doth not David argue thus, Psal.
xxv. 11 ? *For thy name's sake, O Lord, pardon mine iniquity, for it is
very great.*   But it is an empty, fruitless notion of grace, to consider it
only in the general, and in a wandering way : we are to look upon it
particularly, as addressed to us ; and it is not enough that it comes to
us, in the message of him that brings it only to our ear, but, that we
may know what it is, it must come into us ; then it is ours indeed.   But
if it come to us in the message only, and we send it away again, if it
shall so depart, we had better never have heard of it ; it will leave a
guiltiness behind it, that shall make all our sins weigh much heavier
than before.

Inquire whether you have entertained this grace or not ; whether it
be come to you, and into you, or not ; whether the *kingdom of God is
within you*, as our Saviour speaks, Luke xvii. 21.   It is the most
woeful condition that can be, not to be far from the kingdom of God, and
yet to fall short, and miss of it.   The grace of God revealed in the Gospel
is entreating you daily to receive it, is willing to become yours, if you reject it not.   Were your eyes open to behold the beauty and excellency of
this grace, there would need no deliberation ; yea, you would endure none.
Desire your eyes to be opened, and enlightened from above, that you may
know it, and your hearts opened, that you may be happy by receiving it.

The Apostle, speaking of Jesus Christ as the foundation of our faith,
calls him *The same, yesterday, to-day, and for ever.*   Heb. xiii. 8.
Yesterday, under the Law ; *to-day*, in those primitive times, nearest
his incarnation ; and *for ever*, in all succeeding ages.   And the resemblance holds good between the two cherubim over the mercy-seat, and
the two Testaments : *those* had their faces toward one another, and both
toward the mercy-seat ; and *these* look to one another in their doctrine,
agreeing perfectly, and both look to Christ, the true mercy-seat, and

the great subject of the Scriptures. Thus we see here ; the things which the Prophets foretold as to come, and the Apostles reported were accomplished, were the same, and from the same Spirit ; they were the *sufferings of Christ*, and *his after-glory*, and in them our salvation by free grace. The prophecies look forward to the times of the Gospel ; and the things then fulfilled look back to the prophecies ; and each confirms the other, meeting all in Christ, who is their truth and centre.

We have spoken already of the Author, and Subject of this salvation. Now we come to say something, III. Concerning the worth of those who are employed about it, as well in administering to it, as in admiring it. And these are the Prophets and the Apostles : the first foretold what was to come, the second preached them when they came to pass.

In the Prophets, there are three things here remarked. 1. Their diligence. 2. The success of it. 3. The extent of its usefulness.

1. This their diligence disparages not their extraordinary visions and revelations, and that which is added, that the Spirit of Christ was in them, and did foretell the things to come.

It was their constant duty, and they, being sensible of their duty, made it their constant exercise, to search into Divine mysteries by meditation and prayer ; yea, and by reading such holy writers as were already extant in their times, as Daniel ix. 3 ; x. 11. For which cause, some, taking the word actively, conceive Daniel to be called there a *man of desires*, because of his great desire, and diligent search after the knowledge of those high things. And in this diligent way they constantly waited for those revelations which sometimes, when it seemed good unto the Spirit of God, were imparted unto them.

" Prophecy resideth not (say the Hebrew doctors) but in a man " who is great in wisdom and virtue, whose affections overcome him " not in any worldly things, but by his knowledge he overcometh his " affections continually : on such a man the Holy Spirit cometh down, " and his soul is associated to the angels, and he is changed to another " man." Thus Maimonides.

It was the way of the prince of darkness amongst the idolatrous Gentiles, to speak either through senseless statues, or, where he uttered his oracles by such profane prophets as he had, to cause them in a fury to mumble forth words which they understood not, and knew not what they said. But the Spirit of God, being *Light*, and the holy prophets inspired with it, they being diligent attendants on its motions, and searchers of the mysteries of salvation, understood well what their business was, and to what purpose those things of the kingdom of Christ tended, which they by inspiration did foretell ; and therefore bended their thoughts this way, praying, and searching, and waiting for answers, studying to keep the passage, as it were, open for the beams of those Divine revelations to come in at ; not to have their spirits clogged and stopped with earthly and sinful affections, endeavouring for that calm and quiet composure of spirit, in which the voice of God's Spirit might be the better heard. See Psal. lxxx. 8, and Hab. ii. 1 ; in both which places follows an excellent prophecy concerning Christ and that salvation which he wrought for his people.

Were the prophets not exempted from the pains of search and inquiry, who had the Spirit of God not only in a high measure, but after a singular manner ? How unbeseeming, then, are slothfulness and idleness in us ! Whether is it, that we judge ourselves advantaged with more of the Spirit than those holy men, or that we esteem the doctrine and mysteries of salvation, on which they bestowed so much of their labour, unworthy of ours ? These are both so gross, that we shall be loth to own either of them ; and yet, our laziness and negligence in searching after these things, seems to charge us with some such thought as one of those.

You will say, This concerns those who succeed to the work of the Prophets and Apostles in ordinary, — the ministers of the Gospel. And it doth indeed fall first upon them. It is their task indeed to be diligent, and, as the Apostle exhorts his Timothy, *to attend on reading,* 1 Tim. iv. 13 ; but, above all, to study to have much experimental knowledge of God and his Son Jesus Christ, and for this end, to disentangle and free themselves, as much as is possible, from lower things, in order to the search of heavenly mysteries. Prov. xviii. 1. As they are called *angels,* so ought they to be, as much as they can attain to it, in a constant nearness unto God, and attendance on him, like unto the angels, and to look much into these things, as the angels here are said to do ; to endeavour to have their souls purified from the affections of sin, that the light of Divine truth may shine clear in them, and not be fogged and misted with filthy vapours ; to have the impressions of God clearly written in their breasts, not mixed and blurred with earthly characters ; seasoning all their readings and common studies with much prayer, and divine meditation. They who converse most with the king, and are inward with him, know most of the affairs of state, and even the secrets of them, which are hid from others : and certainly those of God's messengers who are oftenest with himself, cannot but understand their business best, and know most of his meaning, and the affairs of his kingdom ; and to that end it is confessed, that singular diligence is required in them. But seeing the Lord hath said without exception, that *His secret is with them that fear him,* Psal. xxv. 14, and that he will reveal Himself and his saving truths to those that humbly seek them ; do not any of you to yourselves so much injury, as to debar yourselves from sharing in your measure of the search of these things, which were the study of the Prophets, and which by their study and publishing them, are made the more accessible and easy to us. Consider that they do concern us universally, if we would be saved ; for it is salvation here that they studied. *Search the Scriptures,* says our Saviour, John v. 39, and that is the motive, if there can be any that may be thought in reason pressing enough, or if we do indeed think so, *For in them ye think to have eternal life.* And it is there to be found : Christ is this *salvation* and this *eternal life.* And he adds further, *It is they* (these Scriptures) *that testify of me.* These are the golden mines in which alone the abiding treasures of eternity are to be found, and therefore worthy all the digging and pains we can bestow on them.

Besides their *industry* in this inquiry and *search,* there are here expressed their ardent affection to the thing they prophesied of, and their longings and wishes for its accomplishment, *viz.,* the coming of

Jesus Christ, the promised Messiah, the top of all their desires, the great Hope and the Light of Israel. No wonder they *desired his day*, who had so much joy in the seeing it so far off, as over the head almost of two thousand years. Faith overlooking them, and foreseeing it so in Abraham, his heart danced for joy. John viii. 56, *Abraham saw my day, and rejoiced.*

And this is conceived to be the meaning of those expressions in that mystical Song, as they suit those times of the Jewish Church, breathing out her longings for the coming of her Beloved. His speaking by the Prophets was his voice as afar off; but his incarnation was his coming near, and kissing his Church *with the kisses of his mouth.* Cant. i. 1. And to omit other expressions throughout the Song, the last chapter, ver. 1, is tender and pathetical, *O that thou wert as my brother*, &c. ; and the last words of it, *Make haste, my beloved, and be thou like a roe or a young hart upon the mountains of spices.* And when this salvation came in the fulness of time, we see how joyfully good old Simeon embraces it, and thought he had seen enough, and therefore upon the sight desired to have his eyes closed : *Now let thy servant depart in peace, for mine eyes have seen thy salvation.* Luke ii. 29. Therefore our Saviour says to his Apostles, Matt. xiii. 16, *Blessed are your eyes, for they see : for many prophets and righteous men have desired to see those things which ye see, and have not seen them.* This is He, whom we disesteem and make so small account of, being now so clearly revealed, whom they studied, and sought, and wished so much for, so many ages before.

2ndly, The *success* of their search is remarked ; in seeking they found the certainty, and the time of his coming ; they sought out till they found, and then they prophesied of that salvation and grace ; *they searched what*, and *what manner of time*, and the Spirit did manifestly foretell it them.

They sought to know *what manner of time* it should come to pass, *viz.*, in a time of great distress, and bad estate of the people, as all the Prophets testify : and particularly that place, Gen. xlix. 10, gives an express character of the time ; though there be some diversity of exposition of the particular words, yet the main sense is agreed on by all sound interpreters, and the Chaldee paraphrase hath it expressly, that that Shiloh is the Messiah.

And of his sufferings and after-glories they prophesied very clearly, as Psal. xxii., Isa. liii., &c. And our Saviour himself makes use of their testimony in both these points, Luke xxiv. 25—27.

3rdly, There is the benefit of their search and finding, in the *extent* of it, verse 12, to the believers in the Apostle's times, and to the succeeding Christian Church, and so to us in these days ; but in some peculiar sense the Prophets ministered to the people of those times wherein Christ did suffer and enter into glory, inasmuch as they were the first who enjoyed the accomplishment of those prophecies, they being fulfilled in their own days.

The Prophets knew well that the things they prophesied were not to be fulfilled in their own times, and therefore in their prophesying concerning them, though both themselves and the people of God who were contemporary with them did reap the comfort of that doctrine, and were by faith partakers of the same salvation, and so it was to themselves as well as to us, yet in regard of the accomplishment, they knew it was not to themselves, it was not to be brought to pass in their days ; and therefore, speaking of the glory of Christ's kingdom, they often foretell it for *the latter days,* as their phrase is. And as we have the things they prophesied of, so we have this peculiar benefit of their prophecies, that their suiting so perfectly with the event and performance, serves much to confirm our Christian faith.

There is a foolish and miserable way of verifying this expression,— men ministering the doctrine of salvation to others and *not to themselves;* carrying it all in their heads and tongues, and none of it in their hearts ; not hearing it even while they preach it ; extending the bread of life to others, and eating none of it themselves. And this the Apostle says that he was most careful to avoid, and therefore dealt severely with his body, that it might not in this way endanger his soul. *I beat down my body,* says he, *and keep it in subjection, lest when I have preached to others, I myself should be a cast-away,* 1 Cor. ix. 27. It is not in this sense that the Prophets ministered to others, and not to themselves. No, they had joy and comfort in the very hopes of the Redeemer to come, and in the belief of the things which any others had spoken, and which themselves spake concerning him. And thus the true preachers of the Gospel, though their ministerial gifts are for the use of others, yet that salvation which they preach, they lay hold on and partake of themselves ; as your boxes, wherein perfumes are kept for garments and other uses, are themselves perfumed by keeping them.

We see how the Prophets ministered it as the never-failing consolation of the Church in those days, in all their distresses. It is wonderful when they are foretelling either the sorrows and afflictions, or the temporal restoration and deliverances of that people of the Jews, what sudden outleaps they will make, to speak of the kingdom of Jesus Christ and the days of the Gospel, insomuch that he who considers not the spirit they were moved by, would think it were incoherence and impertinency ; but they knew well what they meant, that *those news* were never unseasonable, nor beside the purpose ; that the sweetness of those thoughts, *viz.,* the consideration of the Messiah, was able (to such as believed) to allay the bitterest distresses, and that the great deliverance He was to work, was the top and sum of all deliverances. Thus their prophecies of Him were present comfort to themselves and other believers then : and further, were to serve for a clear evidence of the Divine truth of those mysteries in the days of the Gospel, in and after their fulfilment.

This sweet stream of their doctrine did, as the rivers, make its own banks fertile and pleasant as it ran by, and flowed still forward to after-ages, and by the confluence of more such prophecies, grew greater as it went, till it fell in with the main current of the Gospel in the New Testament, both acted and preached by the Great Prophet himself whom they foretold as *to come,* and recorded by his Apostles and Evangelists, and thus united into one river, clear as crystal. This doctrine of salvation in the Scriptures hath still refreshed the city of God, his Church under the Gospel, and still shall do so, till it empty itself into the ocean of eternity.

The first discovery we have of this stream nearest its source, the eternal purpose of Divine mercy, is in that promise which the Lord himself preached in few words to our first parents, who had newly made themselves and their race miserable ; *The seed of the woman shall break the head of the serpent*, Gen. iii. 15.

The agreement of the predictions of the Prophets with the things themselves, and the preaching of the Apostles following, (the other kind of men employed in this salvation,) make up one organ or great instrument, tuned by the same hand, and sounding by the same breath of the Spirit of God ; and that is expressed here, as the common authority of the doctrine in both, and the cause of their harmony and agreement in it.

All these extraordinary *gifts of the Holy Ghost*, the calling *of prophets and apostles and evangelists*, and the ordinary ministry of the Gospel by *pastors and teachers*, tend to that great design which God hath in *building his Church*, in making up that great assembly of all the elect, to enjoy and praise him for all eternity, Eph. iv. 11. For this end he sent his Son, out of his bosom, and for this end he sends forth his messengers to divulge that salvation which his Son hath wrought, and sends down his Spirit upon them, that they may be fitted for so high a service. Those cherubim wonder how guilty man escapes their flaming swords, and re-enters paradise. The angels see that their companions who fell are not restored, but behold their room filled up with the spirits of just men, and they envy it not : *Which mystery the angels desire to look into;* and this is added in the close of these words for the extolling of it.

The angels look upon what they have seen already fulfilled, with delight and admiration, and what remains, namely, the full accomplishment of this great work in the end of time, they look upon with desire to see it finished ; it is not a slight glance they take of it, but they fix their eyes and look stedfastly on it, *viz.*, that mystery of godliness, *God manifested in the flesh ;* and it is added, *seen of angels*, 1 Tim. iii. 16.

The Word made flesh, draws the eyes of those glorious spirits, and possesses them with wonder to see the Almighty Godhead joined with the weakness of a man, yea, of an infant ; He that stretcheth forth the heavens bound up in swaddling clothes ! And to surpass all the wonders of his life, this is beyond all admiration, that the Lord of life was subject to death, and that his love to rebellious mankind moved him both to take on and lay down that life.

It is no wonder that angels admire these things, and delight to look upon them ; but it is strange that we do not so. They view them stedfastly, and we neglect them : either we consider them not at all, or give them but a transient look, half an eye. That which was the great business of the Prophets and Apostles, both for their own times, and to convey them to us, we regard not ; and turn our eyes to foolish wandering thoughts, which angels are ashamed at. They are not so concerned in this great mystery as we are ; they are but mere beholders, in comparison of us, yea, they seem rather to be losers some way, in that our nature, in itself inferior to theirs, is in Jesus Christ exalted above theirs, Heb. ii. 16. We bow down to the earth, and study, and grovel in it, rake into the very bowels of it, and content ourselves with the outside of *the unsearchable riches of Christ,* and look not within it; but they, having no will nor desire but for the glory of God, being pure flames of fire burning only in love to him, are no less delighted than amazed with the bottomless wonders of his wisdom and goodness shining in the work of our redemption.

It is our shame and folly, that we lose ourselves and our thoughts in poor childish things, and trifle away our days we know not how, and let these rich mysteries lie unregarded. They look up upon the Deity in itself with continual admiration; but then they look down to this mystery as another wonder. We give them an ear in public, and in a cold, formal way stop conscience's mouth with some religious performances in private, and no more; but to have deep and frequent thoughts, and to be ravished in the meditation of our Lord Jesus, once on the cross, and now in glory,—how few of us are acquainted with this!

We see here excellent company, and examples not only of the best of men that have been,—we have them for fellow servants and fellow students,—but, if that can persuade us, we may all study the same lesson with the very angels, and have the same thoughts with them. This the soul doth, which often entertains itself with the delightful admiration of Jesus Christ, and the redemption he hath wrought for us.

Ver. 13. Wherefore gird up the loins of your mind, be sober, and hope to the end for the grace that is to be brought unto you at the revelation of Jesus Christ.

THE great error of man's mind, and the cause of all his errors of life, is the diverting of the soul from God, and turning downward to inferior confidences and comforts; and this mischoice is the very root of all our miseries: therefore the main end of the holy word of God, is to untie the hearts of men from the world, and reduce them to God as their only rest and solid comfort; and this is here the Apostle's mark at which all the preceding discourse aims; it all meets and terminates in this exhortation, *Wherefore gird up the loins of your mind.*

In the words are these *three* things: 1*st,* The great stay and comfort of the soul, which the Apostle repeats, and represents to his afflicted brethren. 2*ndly,* His exciting them to the right apprehension and confident expectation of it. 3*rdly,* The inference of that exhortation.

1. The great matter of their comfort is, *The grace which is to be brought to them at the revelation of Jesus Christ.* Some for *grace* read *joy,* having, as it seems, for χάριν read χαρὰν: the words are not more near one to another, than the things they signify, *grace* and *joy;* but it is most commonly thus read.

The estate of grace and that of glory are not only so inseparably connected, but so like one to the other, yea, so essentially the same, that the same expressions in Scripture do often fit both of them; and so fit them, that it is doubtful for which of the two to understand them: but the hazard is not great, seeing they are so near, and so one, grace being glory begun, and glory grace completed, and both are often called *the kingdom of God.* So the *grace* here said to be *brought to them,* is either the *Doctrine of grace* in the Gospel wherein Jesus Christ is revealed, and that grace in him; (for the whole tenor of the covenant of grace, every clause of it, holds in him ; His precious name runs through it all ;) or, it is the *Grace of salvation* which is to be fully perfected at the last and clearest revelation of Jesus Christ. And for this rather I take it here, inasmuch as the Apostle's nearest forego-ing words were concerning it, and it is set up here as the object of hope, which, though often put for faith, yet, in its proper notion, looks out to that which is to come.

This is the last act of Grace, and yet still it is called by its own name, and not turned into the name of merit, notwithstanding all the obedience and all the sufferings of the saints that have gone before it ; yea, *even the salvation to be revealed* to them, is called Grace. But it is needless to insist on this, for certainly none who partake of grace, will be of another mind, or ever admit the mixture of the least notion of self-deserving.

Though much dispute hath been bestowed on this, and questions have been multiplying in the disputant's hands, (as is usual in contro-versies,) one growing out of another, yet truly I think the debate in this matter to be but waste ; it is not only against the voice of the Scriptures, and of grace itself in the soul, but even against sound reason, to imagine any meriting, properly taken, in any mere creature at his Creator's hand, who hath given him his being ; of which gift all his services and obedience fall short, so that he can never come to be upon even disengaged terms, much less to oblige anew, and deserve somewhat further. Besides, that same grace by which any one serves and obeys God, is likewise his own gift, as it is said, 1 Chron. xxix. 14, *All things come of thee, and of thine own have I given thee.* Both the ability and the will of giving to him, are from him ; so that in these respects, not angels, nor man in innocency, could properly merit at the hands of God, much less man lost, redeemed again, and so coming under the new obligation of infinite mercy. And this is so evident a truth, that the most learned and most ingenious Jesuits and schoolmen have, in divers passages of their writings, acknowledged it, that there cannot be any compensation, and much less merit, from the creature to God, but only in relation to his own free purpose, and the tenor of his word and covenant, which is inviolable, because he is unchangeable, and truth itself.

His first grace he gives freely, and no less freely the increases of it, and with the same gracious hand sets the crown of glory upon all the grace that he hath given before. It is but the following forth of his own work, and fulfilling his own thoughts of free love, which love hath no cause but in himself, and finds none worthy, but gives them all the worthiness they have, and accepts of their love, not as worthy in itself to be accepted, but because he himself hath wrought it in them. Not only the first tastes, but the full draught of the waters of life is freely given, Rev. xxii. 17 ; nothing is brought with them but *thirst.*

That is to be brought.] Not *that is brought*, or, *that shall be brought*, but if we will render it strictly, it is, *that is a bringing to you.* That blessedness, that consummation of grace the saints are hastening for-ward to, walking on in their way wheresoever it lies indifferently, *through honour and dishonour, through evil report and good report,* 2 Cor. vi. 8.

And as they are hastening to it, it is hastening to them in the course of time; every day brings it nearer to them than before; and notwithstanding all difficulties and dangers in the way, they who have their eye and hopes upon it, shall arrive at it, and it shall be brought safe to their hand; all the malice of men and devils shall not be able to cut them short of this grace that is a bringing to them against the day of the *revelation of Jesus Christ.*

At the revelation of Jesus Christ.] This is repeated from the 7th verse. And it is termed *a day of revelation, a revelation of the just judgment of God*, Rom. ii. 5. And thus it would be to all, were it not that it is withal the *revelation of Jesus Christ;* therefore is it a day of grace, all light and blessedness to them who are in him, because they shall appear in him, and if he be glorious, they shall not be inglorious and ashamed. Indeed were our secret sins then to be set before our own eyes, in their most affrighted visage, and to be set open to the view of angels and men, and to the eye of Divine justice, and we left alone so revealed, who is there that could gather any comfort, and would not rather have their thoughts filled with horror at the remembrance and expectation of that day? And thus indeed all unbelieving and ungodly men may look upon it, and find it terrible; but to those who are shadowed under the robe of righteous Jesus, yea, who are made one with him, and shall partake of his glory in his appearing, it is the sweetest, the most comfortable thought that their souls can be entertained and possessed withal, to remember this glorious revelation of their Redeemer.

It is their great grief here, not that themselves are hated and vilified, but that their Lord Jesus is so little known, and therefore so much despised in the world. He is vailed and hid from the world. Many nations acknowledge him not at all; and many of those that do in word confess, yet in deed deny him. Many that have a form of godliness, do not only want, but mock and scoff at the power of it; and to such Christ is not known, his excellencies are hid from their eyes. Now this glory of their Lord being precious to them that love him, they rejoice much in the consideration of this, that there is a day at hand, wherein he shall appear in his brightness and full of glory to all nations, and all shall be forced to acknowledge him; it shall be without doubt and unquestioned to all, that he is *the Messiah, the Redeemer, the Judge of the World.*

And as it is the day of His revelation, it is also the revelation of all the adopted sons of God in him. See Rom. viii. 9. They are now accounted the refuse of the world, exposed to all kinds of contempt; but then the beams of Christ's glory shall beautify them, and they shall be known for his. See 1 John iii. 2; Col. iii. 4.

Next, there is, II. The exhortation, by which the Apostle excites them to the right apprehension and confident expectation of this grace —*Hope to the end.* The difference of these two graces, *faith* and *hope,* is so small, that the one is often taken for the other in Scripture; it is but a different aspect of the same confidence, *faith* apprehending the infallible truth of those Divine promises of which *hope* doth assuredly expect the accomplishment, and that is their truth; so that this immediately results from the other. This is the anchor fixed within the vail, which keeps the soul firm against all the tossings on these swelling seas, and the winds and tempests that arise upon them. The firmest thing in this inferior world is a believing soul.

Faith establishes the heart on Jesus Christ, and hope lifts it up, being on that rock, over the head of all intervenient dangers, crosses, and temptations, and sees the glory and happiness that follow after them.

To the end.] Or perfectly : and therefore the Christian seeks most earnestly, and yet waits most patiently. Psal. cxxx. 6. Indeed, this hope is perfect in continuance, it is a *hope unto the end*, because it is perfect in its nature, although imperfect in degree. Sometimes doubtings are intermixed with it in the souls of Christians, yet *this is their infirmity*, as the Psalmist speaks, (Psal. lxxvii. 10,) not the infirmity and insufficiency of the object of their hope. Worldly hopes are in their own nature imperfect ; they do imply, in their very being, doubtfulness and wavering, because the things whereon they are built are inconstant and uncertain, and full of deceit and disappointments. How can that hope be immovable which is built upon moving sands or quagmire ? That which is itself unfixed cannot give stability to any other thing resting upon it ; but because the truth and goodness of the immutable God are the foundation of spiritual hope, therefore it is assured, and *like Mount Zion that cannot be removed:* (Psal. cxxv. 1 :) and this is its perfection.

Now the apostle exhorts his brethren to endeavour to have their hearts possessed with as high a measure and degree of this hope as may be ; seeing in itself it is so perfect and firm, so assured an hope, he would have them aspire to all the assurance and perfection of it they can attain.

This exercise of hope, as I conceive, is not only to have the habit of it strong in the soul, but to act it often, to be often turning that way, to view that approaching day of liberty : *Lift up your heads, for the day of your redemption draweth nigh.* Luke xxi. 28. Where this hope is often acted, it will grow strong, as all habits do ; and where it is strong, it will work much, and delight to act often, and will control both the doubtings and the other many impertinent thoughts of the mind, and force them to yield the place to it. Certainly they who long much for that coming of Christ, will often look up to it. We are usually hoping after other things, which do but offer themselves to draw us after them, and to scorn us. What are the breasts of most of us, but so many nests of foolish hopes and fears intermixed, which entertain us day and night, and steal away our precious hours from us, that might be laid out so gainfully upon the wise and sweet thoughts of eternity, and upon the blessed and assured hope of the coming of our beloved Saviour !

The other words of exhortation here used, are subservient to this end, that this hope may be the more perfect and firm ; a similar exhortation is much after the same manner joined by our Saviour (Luke xii. 35) with the expectance and waiting for his coming ; and in this posture the Israelites, eating the passover, were expecting their deliverance ; so we our full and final freedom.

If you would have much of this, call off your affections from other things, that they may be capable of much of it. The same eye cannot both look up to heaven and down to earth at the same time. The more your affections are trussed up and disentangled from the world, the more expedite and active will they be in this hope: the more sober they are, the less will they fill themselves with the coarse delights of earth, the more room will there be in them, and the more they shall be filled with this hope. It is great folly in our spiritual warfare to charge ourselves superfluously. The fulness of one thing hinders the receiving and admittance of any other, especially of things so opposite as these fulnesses are. *Be not drunk with wine, wherein is excess, but be ye filled with the Holy Ghost,* saith the Apostle, Eph. v. 18. *That is a* brutish fulness, which makes a man no man; *this* divine fulness makes him more than a man; it were happy to be so filled with this, as that it might be called a kind of drunkenness, as it was with the Apostles, Acts ii.

Be sober.] Or *watch.* The same word signifies both, and with good reason; for you know the unsober cannot watch. Now though one main part of sobriety, and that which more properly and particularly bears this name, viz., *temperance* in meat and drink, is here intended; and though against the opposite to this, not only the purity and spirituality of religion, but even moral virtue inveighs as its special enemy, yea, nature itself; and they that only naturally consider the body and its interest of life and health, find reason enough to cry down this base intemperance, which is so hateful by its own deformity, and withal carries its punishment along with it; although (I say) this sobriety is indeed most necessary for the preservation of grace and of the spiritual temper of the soul, and is here intended, yet, I conceive, it is not all that is here meant; the word is more general, comprehending the moderate and sober use of all things worldly. As the Apostle says, *Gird up the loins of your mind,* so it is to be understood, let your *minds* be sober, all your affections inwardly attempered to your spiritual condition, not glutting yourselves with fleshly and perishing delights of any kind; for the more you take in of these, the less you shall have of spiritual comfort and of this perfect hope. They that pour out themselves upon present delights, look not like strangers here, and hopeful expectants of another life and better pleasures.

And certainly, the Captain of our salvation will not own them for his followers, who lie down to drink of these waters, but only such as in passing take of them with their hand. As excessive eating or drinking both makes the body sickly and lazy, fit for nothing but sleep, and besots the mind, as it cloys up with filthy crudities the ways through which the spirit should pass, bemiring them, and making them move heavily, as a coach in a deep way; thus doth all immoderate use of the world, and its delights, wrong the soul in its spiritual condition, makes it sickly and feeble, full of spiritual distempers and inactivity, benumbs the graces of the Spirit, and fills the soul with sleepy vapours, makes it grow secure and heavy in spiritual exercises, and obstructs the way and motion of the Spirit of God in the soul. Therefore, if you would be spiritual, healthful, and vigorous, and enjoy much of the consolations of heaven, be sparing and sober in those of the earth, and what you abate of the one, shall be certainly made up in the other. Health, with a good constitution of body, is a more constant, permanent pleasure, than that of excess and a momentary pleasing of the palate : thus the comfort of this hope is a more refined and more abiding contentment than any that is to be found in the passing enjoyments of this world ; and it is a foolish bargain to exchange a drachm of the one for many pounds of the other. Consider how pressingly the Apostle St. Paul reasons, 1 Cor. ix. 25, *And every man that striveth for the mastery is temperate in all things.* And take withal our Saviour's exhortation, *Be sober and watch, for ye know not at what hour your Lord will come.* Matt. xxv. 13.

The double-minded man (says St. James) *is unstable in all his ways,* Jam. i. 8. Although the word usually signifies deceitfulness and dissimulation of mind,—answering to the Hebrew phrase, *a heart and a heart,*—yet here I conceive it hath another sense, agreeable to the Apostle's present discourse and scope ; it implies doubtfulness and unsettled wavering of mind.

It is impossible that the course of life can be any other than uneven and incomposed, if the spring of it, *the heart,* whence *are the issues of life,* be so. A man that is not agreed within, not of one mind with himself, although there were nothing to trouble or alter him from without, that inward commotion is a sufficient principle and cause of inconstancy. How much more then must he waver, when he is assaulted and beat upon by outward oppositions ! He is *like the waves of the sea,* of himself ever fluctuating to and fro, according to the natural instability of that element, and at the same time exposed to the tossings of all the waves that arise.

It is, therefore, in religion, a main thing, to have the heart established and fixed in the belief and hope of the great things we look for : this will beget strength of resolution, and constancy in action, and in suffering too. And this is here our Apostle's great intent, to ballast the souls of his brethren with this firm belief, that they might sail even and steady in those seas of trouble. Wherefore, (says he,) if these things we have spoken be thus, if there is indeed truth in them, and you believe it to be so, what remains then, but to resolve for it upon any terms, to fit out for the journey, whatsoever be the difficulties, and amid them all to keep up the soul by that certain hope that will not disappoint us ?

What he hath said before, is, as it were, showing them some fruits, some clusters of grapes, of that promised land ; and this exhortation is answerable to Caleb's words, Numb. xiii. 30, *Seeing it so good a land, let us go up and possess it.* Though there be fleshly objects, *sons of Anak,* giants of temptations, and afflictions, and sins to be overcome, ere it be ours, yet it is well worth all our labour, and our God hath ascertained us of the victory, and given us, by his own word, undoubted hope of possessing it.

That which he principally exhorts unto in this verse is the right placing and firm continuing of our hope. When we consider how much of our life is taken up this way, in hoping for things we have not, and that even they who have most of what others are desiring and pursuing are still hoping for somewhat further ; that when men have attained one thing, though it be something they promised themselves to rest contented withal, yet presently upon obtaining it, hope begins

to find out some new matter for itself ; I say, considering the incessant working of this passion throughout our life, it is of very much
concernment for us to give it a right object, and not still to be living
in vanity and uncertainty.   Here is, then, that for our hope to apply
itself to, after which it needs not change, nor can change without the
greatest loss.   *Hope for the grace that is coming at the revelation of
Jesus Christ;* bestow all your hope on this and recall it not.   *Hope
perfectly, and to the end.*

The other part of the exhortation relates to this as the main end,
and in the original runs in this form :   *Wherefore, girding up the loins
of your mind, being sober, hope.*   And to the end that hope may be the
more perfect and endure to the end, and be more like itself, *i. e.*, heavenly, your minds must be freed from the earth, that they may·set for
heaven.   And this is expressed in two several words, but both meaning much the same thing :   that temper of *sobriety*, and that posture of
being *girt*, are no other than the same removal of earthly-mindedness
and encumbering cares and desires of earthly things.

Gird up the loins.]   The custom of those countries was, that, wearing long garments, they trussed them up for work or a journey.
Chastity is indeed a Christian grace, and a great part of the soul's
freedom and spiritualness, and fits it much for Divine things, yet I
think it is not so particularly and entirely intended in this expression,
as St. Jerome and others take it ; for though the girding of the loins
seemed to them to favour that sense, it is only an allusion to the manner of girding up which was then used : and besides, the Apostle here
makes it clear that he meant somewhat else ; for he says, *the loins of
your minds.*   Gather up your affections, that they hang not down to
hinder you in your race, and so, in your hopes of obtaining ; and do
not only gather them up, but tie them up, that they fall not down
again, or if they do, be sure to gird them straiter than before.   Thus
be still as men prepared for a journey, tending to another place.   This
is not our home, nor the place of our rest : therefore our loins must be
still girt up, our affections kept from training and dragging down upon
the earth.

Men who are altogether earthly and profane, are so far from girding
up the loins of their mind, that they set them wholly downwards.   The
very highest part of their soul is glued to the earth, and they are daily
partakers of the serpent's curse, they go on their belly and eat the dust:
they mind earthly things.   Phil. iii. 19.   Now this disposition is inconsistent with grace ; but they that are in some measure truly godly,
though they grovel not so, yet may be somewhat guilty of suffering
their affections to fall too low, that is, to be too much conversant with
vanity, and further engaged than is meet to some things that are
worldly ; and by this means they may abate of their heavenly hopes,
and render them less perfect, less clear and sensible to their souls.

And because they are most subject to take this liberty in the fair and
calm weather of prosperity, God doth often wisely and mercifully cause
rough blasts of affliction to arise upon them, to make them gather their
loose garments nearer to them, and gird them closer.

Let us then remember our way, and where we are, and keep our
garments girt up, for we walk amidst thorns and briers which, if we

let them down, will entangle and stop us, and possibly tear our garments. We walk through a world where there is much mire of sinful pollutions, and therefore it cannot but defile them ; and the crowd we are among will be ready to tread on them, yea, our own feet may be entangled in them, and so make us stumble, and possibly fall. Our only safest way is to gird up our affections wholly.

This perfect hope is enforced by the whole strain of it ; for well may we fix our hope on that happiness to which we are appointed in the eternal election of God, ver. 2, and born to it by our new birth, ver. 3, 4, and preserved to it by his almighty power, ver. 5, and cannot be cut short of it by all the afflictions and oppositions in the way ; no, nor so much as deprived by them of our present joy and comfort in the assurance of it, ver. 6, 7, 8, 9. And then, being taught the greatness and excellency of that blessed salvation, by the doctrine of the Prophets and Apostles, and the admiration of Angels, all these conspire to confirm our hope, to make it perfect and persevering to the end.

And we may also learn by the foregoing doctrine, that this is the place of our trial and conflict, but the place of our rest is above. We must here have *our loins girt*, but when we come there, we may wear our long white robes at their full length without disturbance, for there is nothing there but peace, and without danger of defilement, for *no unclean thing is there*, yea, the streets of that new Jerusalem are paved with gold. To Him, then, who hath prepared that city for us, let us ever give praise.

Ver. 14. As obedient children, not fashioning yourselves according to the former lusts in your ignorance :
15. But as he which hath called you is holy, so be ye holy in all manner of conversation ;
16. Because it is written, Be ye holy; for I am holy.

Thy word is a lamp unto my feet, says David, *and a light unto my paths,* Psal. cxix. 105 ; not only comfortable, as light is to the eyes, but withal directive, as a lamp to his feet. Thus here the Apostle doth not only furnish consolation against distress, but exhorts and directs his brethren in the way of holiness, without which, the apprehension and feeling of those comforts cannot subsist.

This is no other than a clearer and fuller expression, and further pressing of that sobriety and spiritualness of mind and life, which he jointly exhorted unto, with that duty of perfect hope, ver. 13, as inseparably connected with it. If you would enjoy this hope, be not conformed to the lusts of your former ignorance, but *be holy.*

There is no doctrine in the world either so pleasant or so pure as that of Christianity : it is matchless, both in sweetness and holiness. The faith and hope of a Christian have in them an abiding precious balm of comfort ; but this is never to be so lavished away, as to be poured into the puddle of an impure conscience : no, that were to lose it unworthily. *As many as have this hope purify themselves, even as He is pure.* 1 John iii. 3. Here they are commanded to *be holy as He is holy.* Faith first purifies the heart, (Acts xv. 9,) empties it of the love of sin, and then fills it with the consolation of Christ and the hope of glory.

It is a foolish, misgrounded fear, and such as argues inexperience of the nature and workings of Divine grace, to imagine that the assured hope of salvation will beget unholiness and presumptuous boldness in sin, and that therefore the doctrine of that assurance is a doctrine of licentiousness. Our Apostle, we see, is not so sharp-sighted as these men think themselves ; he apprehends no such matter, but indeed supposes the contrary as unquestionable ; he takes not assured hope and holiness as enemies, but joins them as nearest friends : *hope perfectly* and *be holy.*

They are mutually strengthened and increased each by the other. The more assurance of salvation, the more holiness, the more delight in it, and study of it as the only way to that end. And as labour is most pleasant when we are made surest it shall not be lost, nothing doth make the soul so nimble and active in obedience as this *oil of gladness,* this assured hope of glory. Again, the more holiness there is in the soul, the clearer always is this assurance ; as we see the face of the heavens best, when there are fewest clouds. The greatest affliction doth not damp this hope so much as the smallest sin ; yea, it may be the more lively and sensible to the soul by affliction ; but by sin it always suffers loss, as the experience of all Christians does certainly teach them.

The Apostle exhorts to obedience, and enforceth it by a most persuasive reason. His exhortation is, 1. Negative, *Not fashioning yourselves.* 2. Positive, *Be ye holy.*

I. For the negative part of the exhortation. That from which he would remove and separate them is *Lusts:* this is in Scripture the usual name of all the irregular and sinful desires of the heart, both the polluted habits of them and their corrupt streams, both as they exist within and as they outwardly vent themselves in the lives of men. The Apostle St. John (1 John ii. 17) calls it the *Lust of the world,* and (verse 15) *Love of the world ;* and then (verse 16) branches it into those three, which are, indeed, the base anti-trinity that the world worships, *The lust of the eyes, the lust of the flesh, and the pride of life.*

The soul of man unconverted is no other than a den of impure lusts, wherein dwell pride, uncleanness, avarice, malice, &c., just as Babylon is described, Rev. xviii. 2, or as Isa. xiii. 21. Were a man's eyes opened, he would as much abhor to remain with himself in that condition as to dwell in a house full of snakes and serpents, as St. Austin says. And the first part of conversion is at once to rid the soul of these noisome inhabitants ; for there is no one at all found naturally vacant and free from them. Thus the Apostle here expresses of the believers to whom he wrote, that these lusts were theirs before, *in their ignorance.*

There is a truth implied in it, *viz.,* that all sin arises from some kind of ignorance, or, at least, from present inadvertence and inconsideration, turning away the mind from the light ; which therefore, for the time, is as if it were not, and is all one with ignorance in the effect, and therefore the works of sin are all called *works of darkness ;* for were the true visage of sin seen by a full light, undressed and unpainted, it were impossible, while it so appeared, that any one soul could be in love with it ; it would rather fly it, as hideous and abominable. But because the soul unrenewed is all darkness, therefore it is all lust and love of sin ; there is no order in it, because no light. As at the first in the world, confusion and darkness went together, and *darkness was upon the face of the deep,* it is so in the soul ; the more ignorance, the more abundance of lusts.

That light which frees the soul, and rescues it from the very kingdom of darkness, must be somewhat beyond that which nature can attain to. All the light of philosophy, natural and moral, is not sufficient, yea, the very knowledge of the law, severed from Christ, serves not so to enlighten and renew the soul, as to free it from the darkness or ignorance here spoken of ; for our Apostle writes to Jews who knew the law, and were instructed in it before their conversion, yet he calls those times, wherein Christ was unknown to them, the *times of their ignorance.* Though the stars shine never so bright, and the moon with them in its full, yet they do not altogether make it day ; still it is night till the sun appear. Therefore the Hebrew doctors, upon that word of Solomon's, *Vanity of vanities, all is vanity,* say, *Vana etiam lex, donec venerit Messias:* Vain even the law, until Messiah come. Therefore of him Zacharias says, *The day-spring from on high hath visited us, to give light to them that sit in darkness and in the shadow of death, and to guide our feet into the way of peace,* Luke i. 78, 79.

A natural man may attain to very much acquired knowledge of the doctrine of Christ, and may discourse excellently of it, and yet still his soul be in the *chains of darkness,* fast locked up under the ignorance here mentioned ; and so he may be still of a *carnal mind,* in subjection to these lusts of ignorance.

The saving light of faith is a beam of the *Sun of righteousness* himself, that he sends into the soul, by which he makes it discern his incomparable beauties, and by that sight alienates it from all those lusts and desires, which do then appear to be what indeed they are, vileness and filthiness itself, making the soul wonder at itself, how it could love such base trash so long, and fully resolve now on the choice of Jesus Christ, *the chief among ten thousands,* Cant. v. 10 ; yea, *the fairest of the children of men,* Psal. xlv. 2 ; for that he is withal the only begotten Son of God, *the brightness of his Father's glory, and the express image of his person,* Heb. i. 3.

The soul once acquainted with him, can, with disdain, turn off all the base solicitations and importunities of sin, and command them away that formerly had command over it, though they plead former familiarities, and the interest they once had in the heart of the Christian before it was enlightened and renewed. He can well tell them, after his sight of Christ, that it is true, while he knew no better pleasures than they were, he thought them lovely and pleasing, but that one glance of the face of Jesus Christ hath turned them all into extreme blackness and deformity ; that so soon as ever Christ appeared to him, they straightway lost all their credit and esteem in his heart, and have lost it for ever ; they need never look to recover it any more.

And it is by this that the Apostle enforceth this dehortation. It is true, that the lusts and vanities that are in request in the world were so with you, but it was when you were blind, they were the lusts of your ignorance; but now you know how ill they will suit with the light of that Gospel which you profess, and that inward light of faith which is in the souls of such as be really believers.

Therefore, seeing you have renounced them, keep them still at that distance; not only never admit them more to lodge within you; that surely you cannot do; but do not so much as for custom' sake, and in compliance with the world about you, outwardly conform yourselves to any of them, or make semblance to partake of them: as St. Paul says, *Have no more fellowship with the unfruitful works of darkness, but rather reprove them,* Eph. v. 11; reprove them by your carriage, and let the light of your holy lives discover their foulness.

II. We have the positive part of the Apostle's exhortation, *Be ye holy.* This includes the former, the renouncing of the lusts and pollutions of the world, both in heart and life; and adds to it, further, the filling of their room, being cast out, with the beautifying graces of the Spirit of God, and the acting of those graces in their whole conversation, both in private and abroad, in conversing with themselves, and conversing with others, whether good or bad, in a constant, even course, still like themselves, and like Him who hath called them: for it is a most unseemly and unpleasant thing to see a man's life full of ups and downs, one step like a Christian, and another like a worldling; it cannot choose but both pain himself and mar the edification of others.

But as he which hath called you is holy.] Consider whose you are, and you cannot deny that it becomes you to be holy. Consider your near relation to the holy God; this is expressed two ways, namely, *As children,* and *As he which hath called you;* which is all one as if he had said, hath begotten you again. The very outward vocation of those who profess Christ, presseth holiness upon them, but the inward vocation far more. You were running to destruction in the way of sin, and there was a voice which, together with the Gospel preached to your ear, spake into your heart, and called you back from that path of death to the way of holiness, which is the only way of life. He hath severed you from the mass of the profane world, and picked you out to be jewels for himself. He hath set you apart for this end, that you may be *holy to Him* (as the Hebrew word, which signifies *holiness,* imports *setting apart,* or fitting for a peculiar use); be not then untrue to his design. *He hath not called you unto uncleanness, but unto holiness,* 1 Thess. iv. 7; therefore *be ye holy.* It is sacrilege for you to dispose of yourselves after the impure manner of the world, and to apply yourselves to any profane use, whom God hath consecrated to himself.

As children.] This is, no doubt, relative to that which he spoke, verse 3, by way of thanksgiving; and that *Wherefore* in the 13th verse, draws it down hither by way of exhortation. Seeing you are, by a spiritual and new birth, the children of so great and good a Father, who commands you to holiness, be obedient children, in being holy; and seeing he himself is most holy, be like him as his children, *Be ye holy, as he is holy.*

As obedient children.] Opposed to that expression, Eph. ii. 2, *Sons of disobedience,* or *unbelief,* as the word may be rendered, and that is always the spring of disobedience; sons of mispersuasibleness, who will not be drawn and persuaded by the tenderest mercies of God.

Now, though this Hebrew manner of speech, *Sons of obedience* or *disobedience,* signifies no more than obedient or disobedient persons, yet it doth signify them most emphatically, and means a high degree of obedience or disobedience ; these *sons of disobedience* (verse 2) are likewise *sons of wrath* (verse 3).

Of all children, the children of God are the most obliged to obedience, for he is both the wisest and the most loving of fathers. And the sum of all his commands is that which is their glory and happiness, that they endeavour to be like him, to resemble their heavenly Father. *Be ye perfect, as your heavenly Father is perfect,* says our Saviour, Matt. v. 48. And here the Apostle is citing out of the Law : *Be ye holy, for I am holy,* Levit. xi. 44. Law and Gospel agree in this. Again : children who resemble their fathers, as they grow up in years, they grow the more like to them ; thus the children of God do increase in their resemblance, and are daily more and more renewed after his image. There is in them an innate likeness by reason of his image impressed on them in their first renovation, and his Spirit dwelling within them ; and there is a continual increase of it arising from their pious imitation and study of conformity, which is here exhorted to.

The imitation of vicious men and the corrupt world is here forbidden. The imitation of men's indifferent customs is base and servile; the imitation of the virtues of good men is commendable ; but the imitation of this highest pattern, this primitive goodness, the most holy God, is the top of excellency. It is well said, *Summa religionis est imitari quem colis:* The essence of religion consists in the imitation of Him we worship. All of us offer Him some kind of worship, but few seriously study and endeavour this blessed conformity.

There is, unquestionably, among those who profess themselves the people of God, a select number who are indeed his children, and bear his image both in their hearts and in their lives ; this impression of holiness is on their souls and their conversation ; but with the most, a name and a form of godliness are all they have for religion. Alas ! we speak of holiness, and we hear of it, and it may be we commend it, but we act it not ; or, if we do, it is but an acting of it, in the sense in which the word is often taken for a personated acting, as on a stage in the sight of men ; not as in the sight of our lovely God, lodging it in our hearts, and from thence diffusing it into all our actions. A child is truly like his father, when not only his visage resembles him, but still more so his mind and inward disposition ; thus are the true children of God like their heavenly Father in their words and in their actions, but most of all in heart.

It is no matter though the profane world (which so hates God that it cannot endure his image) do mock and revile ; it is thy honour to be, as David said, (2 Sam. vi. 22,) thus *more vile,* in growing still more like unto Him in holiness. What though the polite man count thy fashion a little odd and too precise, it is because he knows nothing above that model of goodness which he hath set himself, and therefore approves of nothing beyond it : he knows not God, and therefore doth not discern and esteem what is most like him. When courtiers come down into the country, the common homebred people possibly think

their habit strange, but they care not for that, it is the fashion at court.
What need then that the godly should be so tender-foreheaded, as to
be put out of countenance because the world looks on holiness as a singularity ? it is the only fashion in the highest court, yea, of the King
of kings himself.

For I am holy.] As it will raise our endeavour high to look on the
highest pattern, so it will lay our thoughts low concerning ourselves.
Men compare themselves with men, and readily with the worst, and
flatter themselves with that comparative betterness. This is not the
way to see our spots, to look into the muddy streams of profane men's
lives ; but look into the clear fountain of the word, and there we may
both discern and wash them. Consider the infinite holiness of God,
and this will humble us to the dust. When Isaiah saw the glory of
the Lord, and heard the Seraphim cry, *Holy, holy, holy,* he cried out
of his own and the people's unholiness, *Woe is me, for I am undone,
for I am a man of unclean lips, and I dwell in the midst of a people of
unclean lips; for mine eyes have seen the King, the Lord of hosts.*
Chap. vi. 3, 4.

Ver. 17. And if ye call on the Father, who without respect of persons judgeth according to every man's work, pass the time of your sojourning here in fear.

THE temptations which meet a Christian in the world, to turn him
aside from the straight way of obedience and holiness, are either such
as present the hope of some apparent good, to draw him from that
way, or the fear of some evil, to drive and affright him from it : and
therefore the word of God is much in strengthening the Christian
mind against these two ; and it doth it especially, by possessing it both
with hopes and fears of a higher nature, that do by far weigh down
the other.

The most frequent assaults of temptation are upon these two passions of the mind : therefore they are chiefly to be fortified and defended by a hope and fear opposite to those that do assault us, and sufficiently strong to resist and repel them.

These two, therefore, our Apostle here urges : 1. The *hope* of that
glory which the Gospel propounds, and so outbids all the proffers of
the world, both in the greatness and the certainty of its promises.
2. The *fear* of God, the greatest and justest Judge, alone worthy to be
feared and reverenced ; the highest anger and enmity of all the world
being less than nothing, in comparison of his smallest displeasure. We
have here,

I. This fear. II. The reason enforcing it. III. The term or continuance of it.

I. The fear itself, *In fear.* But how suits this with the high discourse that went before, of perfect assured hope, of faith, and love, and
joy, yea, joy unspeakable and glorious, arising out of these ? How are all
those excellencies fallen, as it were, into a dungeon, when fear is mentioned after them ! Doth not the Apostle St. John say, that *True love
casteth out fear?* 1 John iv. 18. And it is not more clearly opposite
to perfect or assured hope, and to faith and joy ?

If ye understand it aright, this is such a fear as doth not prejudice,
but preserve those other graces, and the comfort and joy that arise

from them : and they all agree so well with it, that they are naturally helps to each other.

It were superfluous to insist on the defining of this passion of fear, and the manifold distinctions of it, either with philosophers or divines. The fear here recommended is, out of question, a holy self-suspicion and fear of offending God, which may not only consist with assured hope of salvation, and with faith, and love, and spiritual joy, but is their inseparable companion ; as all divine graces are linked together, (as the heathens said of their three graces,) and, as they dwell together, they grow or decrease together. The more a Christian believes, and loves, and rejoices in the love of God, the more unwilling surely he is to displease him, and if in danger of displeasing him, the more afraid of it ; and, on the other side, this fear being the true principle of a wary and holy conversation, fleeing sin, and the occasions of sin, and temptations to it, and resisting them when they make an assault, is as a watch or guard that keeps out the enemies and disturbers of the soul, and so preserves its inward peace, keeps the assurance of faith and hope unmolested, and that joy which they cause, and the intercourse and societies of love betwixt the soul and her Beloved, uninterrupted ; all which are most in danger when this fear abates and falls to slumbering ; for then, some notable sin or other is ready to break in and put all into disorder, and for a time make those graces, and the comfort of them to present feeling, as much to seek as if they were not there at all.

No wonder, then, that the Apostle, having stirred up his Christian brethren, whatsoever be their estate in the world, to seek to be rich in those jewels of faith, and hope, and love, and spiritual joy, and then, considering that they travel amongst a world of thieves and robbers,— no wonder, I say, that he adds this, advises them to give those their jewels in custody, under God, to this trusty and watchful grace of godly fear ; and having earnestly exhorted them to holiness, he is very fitly particular in this fear, which makes up so great a part of that holiness, that it is often in Scripture named for it all.

Solomon calls it the *beginning* or the *top of wisdom*, Prov. xv. 33 : the word signifies both, and it is both. The beginning of it is the beginning of wisdom, and the progress and increase of it is the increase of wisdom. That hardy rashness which many account valour is the companion of ignorance ; and of all rashness, boldness to sin is the most witless and foolish. There is in this, as in all fear, an apprehension of an evil whereof we are in danger. The evil is sin, and the displeasure of God and punishment following upon sin. The godly man judgeth wisely, as the truth is, that sin is the greatest of evils, and the cause of all other evils ; it is a transgression of the just law of God, and so a provocation of his just anger, and the cause of those punishments, temporal, spiritual, and eternal, which he inflicts. And then, considering how mighty He is to punish, considering both the power and the reach of his hand, that it is both most heavy and unavoidable ; all these things may and should concur to the working of this fear.

There is, no doubt, a great difference betwixt those two kinds of fear that are usually differenced by the names of *servile* and *filial* fear ; but certainly, the most genuine fear of the sons of God, who call him Father, doth not exclude the consideration of his justice, and of the punishment of sin which his justice inflicts. We see here, it is used as the great motive of this fear, that He *judgeth every man according to his works.* And David, in that Psalm wherein he so much breathes forth those other sweet affections of love, and hope, and delight in God and in his word, yet expresseth this fear even of the justice of God : *My flesh trembleth for fear of thee, and I am afraid of thy judgments.* Psal. cxix. 120. The flesh is to be awed by Divine judgments, though the higher and surer part of the soul is strongly and freely tied with the cords of love. Temporal corrections, indeed, they fear not so much in themselves, as that impression of wrath that may be upon them for their sins. Psal. vi. 1. That is the main matter of their fear, because their happiness is in His love, and the light of His countenance, that is their life. They regard not how the world looks upon them ; they care not who frown, so He smile on them ; because no other enemy nor evil in the world can deprive them of this but their own sin, therefore that is what they fear most.

As the evil is great, so the Christian hath great reason to fear in regard of his danger of it, considering the multitude, strength, and craft of his enemies, and his own weakness and unskilfulness to resist them. And his sad experience in being often foiled, teacheth him that it is thus ; he cannot be ignorant of it ; he finds how often his own resolutions and purposes deceive him. Certainly, a godly man is some- times driven to wonder at his own frailty and inconstancy. What strange differences will be betwixt him and himself : how high and how delightful at some times are his thoughts of God and the glory of the life to come ; and yet, how easily at another time base temptations will bemire him, or, at the least, molest and vex him ! And this keeps him in a continual fear, and that fear in continual vigilancy and cir- cumspectness. When he looks up to God, and considers the truth of his promises, and the sufficiency of his grace and protection, and the almighty strength of his Redeemer, these things fill his soul with con- fidence and assurance ; but when he turns his eye downward again upon himself, and finds so much remaining corruption within, and so many temptations, and dangers, and adversaries without, this forces him not only to fear, but to despair of himself ; and it should do so, that his trust in God may be the purer and more entire. That con- fidence in God will not make him secure and presumptuous in himself, nor that fear of himself make him diffident of God. This fear is not opposite to faith, but high-mindedness and presumption are. See Rom. xi. 20. To a natural man, it would seem an odd kind of reasoning, that of the apostle, Phil. ii. 12, 13, *It is God that worketh in you to will and to do of his good pleasure :* therefore (would he think) you may save labour, you may sit still, and not work, or, if you work, you may work fearlessly, being so sure of His help : but the apostle is of another mind ; his inference is, Therefore, *work out your own salva- tion,* and work it *with fear and trembling.*

But he that hath assurance of salvation, why should he fear ? If there is truth in his assurance, nothing can disappoint him, not sin itself. It is true ; but it is no less true, that if he do not fear to sin, there is no truth in his assurance: it is not the assurance of faith, but the mispersuasion of a secure and profane mind. Suppose it so, that the sins of a godly man cannot be such as to cut him short of that salvation whereof he is assured; yet they may be such as for a time will deprive him of that assurance, and not only remove the comfort he hath in that, but let in horrors and anguish of conscience in its stead. Though a believer is freed from hell, (and we may overstrain this assurance, in our doctrine, beyond what the soberest and devoutest men in the world can ever find in themselves, though they will not trouble themselves to contest and dispute with them that say they have it,) so that his soul cannot come there; yet some sins may bring as it were a hell into his soul for a time, and this is reason enough for any Christian in his right wits to be afraid of sin. No man would willingly hazard himself upon a fall that may break his leg, or some other bone; though he could be made sure that he should not break his neck, or that his life were not at all in danger, and that he should be perfectly cured, yet, the pain and trouble of such a hurt would terrify him, and make him wary and fearful when he walks in danger. The broken bones that David complains of after his fall, may work fear and wariness in those that hear him, though they were ascertained of a like recovery.

This fear is not cowardice: it doth not debase, but elevates the mind; for it drowns all lower fears, and begets true fortitude and courage to encounter all dangers, for the sake of a good conscience and the obeying of God. *The righteous is bold as a lion.* Prov. xxviii. 1. He dares do any thing but offend God; and to dare to do that is the greatest folly, and weakness, and baseness in the world. From this fear have sprung all the generous resolutions and patient sufferings of the saints and martyrs of God; because they durst not sin against Him, therefore they durst be imprisoned, and impoverished, and tortured, and die for Him. Thus the Prophet sets carnal and godly fear as opposite, and the one expelling the other, Isa. viii. 12, 13. And our Saviour, Luke xii. 4, *Fear not them that kill the body; but fear Him which, after he hath killed, hath power to cast into hell; yea, I say unto you, fear Him.* Fear not, but fear; and therefore fear, that you may not fear. This fear is like the trembling that hath been observed in some of great courage before battles. Moses was bold and fearless in dealing with a proud and wicked king, but when God appeared, he said, (as the Apostle informs us,) *I exceedingly fear and quake.* Heb. xii. 21.

II. The reason we have here to persuade to this fear is twofold. (1.) Their relation to God. (2.) Their relation to the world.

(1.) To God as their Father, and as their Judge. Because you do call him Father, and profess yourselves his children, *begotten again* by Him, (for this verse looks back to that expression,) it becomes you, as obedient children, to stand in awe, and fear to offend him your Father, and a Father so full of goodness and tender love. But as he is the best Father, so consider that he is withal the greatest and justest Judge: *He judges every man according to his work.*

God always sees and discerns men, and all their works, and *judgeth,* that is, accounteth of them, as they are, and sometimes in this life declares this his judgment of them to their own consciences, and in some to the view of others, in visible punishments and rewards ; but the most solemn judgment of all is reserved to that great day which he hath appointed, *wherein he will judge the world in righteousness by his Son Jesus.* Acts xvii. 32.

There is here, the *sovereignty* of this Judge, the *universality* of his judgment, and the *equity* of it. All must answer at His great court ; He is supreme Judge of the world. He made it, and hath therefore unquestionable right to judge it. *He judgeth every man ;* and it is a most righteous judgment, which hath these two in it : 1. An exact and perfect knowledge of all men's works ; 2. Impartial judgment of them so known. This second is expressed negatively, by removing the crooked rule which man's judgment often follows ; it is without consideration of those personal differences which men eye so much. And the first is according to the work itself. Job xxxiv. 19, *He accepteth not the person of princes, nor regardeth the rich more than the poor ;* and the reason is added there, *For they are all the work of his hands.* He made all the persons, and he makes all those differences Himself as it pleaseth Him ; therefore He doth not admire them as we do, no, nor at all regard them. We find very great odds betwixt stately palaces and poor cottages, betwixt a prince's robes and a beggar's cloak ; but to God they are all one ; all these petty differences vanish in comparison of his own greatness. Men are great and small, compared with one another ; but they altogether amount to just nothing in respect of Him. We find high mountains and low valleys on this earth ; but compared with the vast compass of the heavens, it is all but as a point, and hath no sensible greatness at all.

Nor regards he any other differences to bias his judgment, from the works of men, to their persons. You profess the true religion, and call him Father ; but if you live devoid of his fear, and be disobedient children, he will not spare you because of that relation, but rather punish you the more severely. Because you pretended to be His children, and yet obeyed him not, therefore you shall find him your Judge, and an impartial Judge of your works. Remember, therefore, that your Father is this Judge, and fear to offend him. But then, indeed, a believer may look back to the other comfort, who abuses it not to a sinful security. He resolves thus willingly ; " I will not sin, because my Father is this just Judge : but for my frailties I will hope for mercy, because the Judge is my Father."

Their works.] This comprehends all actions and words, yea, thoughts , and each work entirely, taken outside and inside together ; for he sees all alike, and judgeth according to all together. He looks on the wheels and paces within, as well as on the handle without, and therefore ought we to fear the least crookedness of our intentions in the best works ; for if we entertain any such, and study not singleness of heart, this will cast all, though we pray and hear the word, and preach it, and live outwardly unblamably. And in that great judgment, all secret things shall be manifest ; as they are always open to the eye of this Judge, so He shall then open them before men and angels : therefore let the remembrance and frequent consideration of this all-seeing Judge, and of that great judgment, waken our hearts, and beget in us this fear. 2 Cor. v. 10, 11. If you would have confidence in that day, and not fear it when it comes, fear it now, so as to avoid sin ; for they that now tremble at it, shall then, when it comes, lift up their faces with joy ; and they that will not fear it now, shall then be overwhelmed with fears and terror ; they shall have such a burden of fear then as that they shall account the hills and mountains lighter than it.

Pass the time of your sojourning here in fear.] In this I conceive is implied another persuasive of this fear, arising, (2.) from their relation to this world. You are *sojourners* and *strangers*, (as here the word signifies,) and a wary, circumspect carriage becomes strangers, because they are most exposed to wrongs and hard accidents. You are encompassed with enemies and snares ; how can you be secure in the midst of them ? This is not your rest ; watchful fear becomes this your sojourning. Perfect peace and security are reserved for you at home, and that is the last term of this fear ; it continues all the time of this sojourning life, dies not before us ; we and it shall expire together.

III. This, then, is the term or continuance of this fear.

Blessed is he that feareth always, says Solomon, Prov. xxviii. 14 ; in secret and in society, in his own house and in God's. We must hear the word with fear, and preach it with fear, afraid to miscarry in our intentions and manners. *Serve the Lord with fear,* yea, in times of inward comfort and joy, yet *rejoice with trembling.* Psal. ii. 11. Not only when a man feels most his own weakness, but when he finds himself strongest. None are so high advanced in grace here below, as to be out of need of this grace ; but when their sojourning shall be done, and they are come home to their Father's house above, then no more fearing. No entrance for dangers there, and therefore no fear. A holy reverence of the majesty of God they shall indeed have then most of all, as the angels still have, because they shall see Him most clearly, and because the more he is known the more he is reverenced ; but this fear that relates to danger shall then vanish, for in that world there is neither sin, nor sorrow for sin, nor temptation to sin ; no more conflicts, but after a full and final victory, an eternal peace, an everlasting triumph. Not only fear, but faith, and hope, do imply some imperfection not consistent with that blessed estate ; and therefore all of them, having obtained their end, shall end ; *faith* in *sight, hope* in *possession,* and *fear* in *perfect safety;* and everlasting love and delight shall fill the whole soul in the vision of God.

Ver. 18. Forasmuch as ye know that ye were not redeemed with corruptible things, as silver and gold, from your vain conversation received by tradition from your fathers ;

19. But with the precious blood of Christ, as of a lamb without blemish and without spot.

It is impossible for a Christian to give himself to conform to the world's ungodliness, unless first he forgets who he is, and by what means he attained to be what he is. Therefore the Apostle, persuading his brethren to holiness, puts them in mind of this, as the strongest incentive. Not only have you the example of God set before you, as your Father, to beget in you the love of holiness, as being your liveliest resemblance of him ; and the justice of God, as your Judge, to argue you into a pious fear of offending him ; but consider this, that he is your Redeemer ; He hath bought out your liberty from sin and the world, to be altogether His ; and think on the price laid down in this ransom ; and these out of question will prevail with you.

We have here, 1. The evil dissuaded from, *viz.*, *A vain conversation.* 2. The dissuasion itself.

1. It is called *their vain conversation.*   2. *Received by tradition from their fathers.*   By this I conceive is to be understood not only the superstitions and vain devices in religion, which abounded amongst the Jews by tradition, for which our Saviour often reproved them while he was conversant among them, as we find in the Gospel ; (and all this was meant, ver. 14, *by the lusts of their former ignorance ;*) but generally, all the corrupt and sinful customs of their lives ; for it seems not so pertinent to his purpose when exhorting to holiness of life, to speak of their superstitious traditions, as of their other sinful habitudes, which are no less hereditary, and by the power of example, traditional ; which by reason of their common root in man's sinful nature, do so easily pass from parents to children, nature making their example powerful, and the corruption of nature giving it most power in that which is evil.   And this is the rather mentioned to take away the force of it, and cut off that influence which it might have had in their minds. There is a kind of conversation that the authority of your father pleads for ; but remember, that it is that very thing from which you are delivered, and you are called to a new state and form of life, and have a new pattern set before you, instead of that corrupt example.

It is one great error, not only in religion and manners, but even in human science, that men are ready to take things upon trust, unexamined, from those that went before them, partly out of easiness and sparing the pains of trial, partly out of a superstitious over-esteem of their authority ; but the chief reason why corruptions in religion, and in the practice of preceding ages, take so much with posterity, is that before mentioned, the universal sympathy and agreement which those evils have with the corrupt nature of man.

The prophet Ezekiel observes this particularly in the Jews, chap. xx. ver. 24, *That their eyes were after their fathers' idols,* contrary to God's express forewarning, ver. 18.   This was the great quarrel of the Heathens against the Christian religion in the primitive times, that it was new and unknown to their fathers ; and the ancient writers of those times are frequent in showing the vanity of this exception, particularly *Lactantius, Instit. lib. 2. cap.* 7, 8.   The same prejudice doth the Church of Rome sing over continually against the reformed religion : Where was it before Luther ? *&c.*   But this is a foolish and unreasonable diversion from the search of truth, because error is more at hand ; or from the entertaining it, being found, because falsehood is in possession.

As in religion, so in the course and practice of men's lives, the stream of sin runs from one age into another, and every age makes it greater, adding somewhat to what it receives, as rivers grow in their course by the accession of brooks that fall into them ; and every man when he is born falls like a drop into this main current of corruption, and so is carried down with it, and this by reason of its strength, and his own nature, which willingly dissolves into it, and runs along with it. In this is manifest the power of Divine grace in a man's conversion, that it severs him so powerfully from the profane world, and gives him strength to run contrary to the great current of wickedness that is round about him, in his parents possibly, and in his kindred and friends, and in the most of men that he meets withal. The voice of God, that powerful word of effectual calling which he speaks into the heart, makes a man break through all, and leave all to follow God, as Abraham did, being called out from his kindred and father's house, to journey towards the land that God had promised him. And this is that which was spoken to the Church and to each believing soul by the Spirit of God, *Forget also thine own people and thy father's house, so shall the king greatly delight in thy beauty,* Psal. xlv. 10, 11. Regard not what others think, though they be thy nearest friends, but study only to please Him, and then thou shalt please Him indeed. Do not deform thy face with looking out asquint to the custom of the world, but look straightforward on Him, and so thou shalt be beautiful in His eyes. When God calls a man in a remarkable manner, his profane friends are all in a tumult ; what needs this to be more precise than we and all your neighbours ? But all this is a confused noise, that works nothing on the heart which the Lord hath touched : it must follow Him, though by trampling upon friends and kindred, if they lie in the way. We see how powerfully a word from Christ drew his disciples to leave all and follow him.

The *exhortation* is against all sinful and unholy conversation, by what authority and example soever recommended to us. The Apostle's reasons in these words are strong and pressing ; there is one expressed in the very name he gives it ; *it is vain conversation.*

The mind of man, the guide and source of his actions, while it is estranged from God, is nothing but a forge of vanities. The Apostle St. Paul speaks this of the Gentiles, that *they became vain in their imaginations, and their foolish heart was darkened,* Rom. i. 21, their great naturalists and philosophers not excepted ; and the more they strove to play the wise men, the more they befooled themselves. Thus likewise, Eph. iv. 17. And thus the Lord complains by his prophet Isaiah, of the extreme folly of his people, ch. xliv. 20, and by Jeremy, that *their hearts are lodges of vain thoughts,* ch. iv. 14 : and these are the true cause of a *vain conversation.*

The whole course of a man's life out of Christ, is nothing but a continual trading in vanity, running a circle of toil and labour, and reaping no profit at all. This is the vanity of every natural man's conversation, that not only others are not benefited by it, but it is fruitless to himself ; there arises to him no solid good out of it. That is most truly vain, which attains not its proper end ; now, since all a man's endeavours aim at his satisfaction and contentment, that conversation which gives him nothing of that, but removes him further from it, is justly called *vain conversation.* *What fruit had ye,* says the Apostle, *in those things whereof ye are now ashamed?* Rom. vi. 21. Either count that shame which at the best grows out of them, their fruit, or confess they have none ; therefore they are called *the unfruitful works of darkness,* Eph. v. 11.

Let the voluptuous person say it out upon his death-bed, what pleasure or profit doth then abide with him of all his former sinful delights. Let him tell if there remain any thing of them all, but that which he would gladly not have to remain, the sting of an accusing conscience, which is as lasting as the delight of sin was short and vanishing. Let the covetous and ambitious declare freely, even those of them who have prospered most in their pursuit of riches and honour, what ease all their possessions or titles do then help them to ; whether their pains are the less because their chests are full, or their houses stately, or a multitude of friends and servants waiting on them with hat and knee. And if all these things cannot ease their body, how much less can they quiet the mind ! And therefore is it not true, that all pains in these things, and the uneven ways into which they sometimes stepped aside to serve those ends, and generally, that all the ways of sin wherein they have wearied themselves, were vain rollings and tossings up and down, not tending to a certain haven of peace and happiness ? It is a lamentable thing to be deluded a whole lifetime with a false dream. See Isaiah ii. 8.

You that are going on in the common road of sin, although many, and possibly your own parents, have trodden it before you, and the greatest part of those you now know are in it with you, and keep you company in it, yet, be persuaded to stop a little, and ask yourselves what is it you seek, or expect in the end of it. Would it not grieve any labouring man, to work hard all the day, and have no wages to look for at night ? It is a greater loss to wear out our whole life, and in the evening of our days find nothing but anguish and vexation. Let us then think this, that so much of our life as is spent in the ways of sin is all lost, fruitless, and *vain conversation*.

And in so far as the Apostle says here, *You are redeemed from this conversation*, this imports it to be a servile, slavish condition, as the other word, *vain*, expresses it to be fruitless. And this is the madness of a sinner, that he fancies liberty in that which is the basest thraldom ; as those poor frantic persons that are lying ragged and bound in chains, yet imagine that they are kings, that their irons are chains of gold, their rags robes, and their filthy lodge a palace. As it is misery to be liable to the sentence of death, so it is slavery to be subject to the dominion of sin ; and he that is delivered from the one, is likewise set free from the other. There is one redemption from both. He that is redeemed from destruction by the blood of Christ, is likewise redeemed from that vain and unholy conversation that leads to it. So, Tit. ii. 14. Our Redeemer was anointed for this purpose, not to free the captives from the sentence of death, and yet leave them still in prison, but to *proclaim liberty to them, and the opening of the prison to them that are bound.* Isa. lxi. 1.

You easily persuade yourselves that Christ hath died for you, and redeemed you from hell ; but you consider not, that if it be so, he hath likewise redeemed you from your vain conversation, and hath set you free from the service of sin. Certainly, while you find not that, you can have no assurance of the other : if the chains of sin continue still upon you, for any thing you can know, these chains do bind you over to the other *chains of darkness* the Apostle speaks of, 2 Pet. ii. 4.

Let us not delude ourselves; if we find the love of sin and of the world work stronger in our hearts than the love of Christ, we are not as yet partakers of his redemption.

But if we have indeed laid hold upon him as our Redeemer, then are we redeemed from the service of sin; not only from the grossest profaneness, but even from all kind of fruitless and *vain conversation*. And therefore ought we to *stand fast in that liberty, and not to entangle ourselves again to any of our former vanities*. Gal. v. 1.

Not redeemed with corruptible things.] From the high price of our redemption, the Apostle doth mainly enforce our esteem of it, and urge the preservation of that liberty so dearly bought, and the avoiding all that unholiness and vain conversation, from which we are freed by that redemption. First, he expresseth it negatively, *not with corruptible things;* (oh! foolish we, who hunt them, as if they were incorruptible and everlasting treasures!) no, not the best of them, those that are in highest account with men, *not with silver and gold;* these are not of any value at all towards the ransom of souls, they cannot buy off the death of the body, nor purchase the continuance of temporal life, much less can they reach to the worth of spiritual and eternal life. The precious soul could not be redeemed but by blood, and by no blood but that of this spotless Lamb, Jesus Christ, who is God equal with the Father; and therefore his blood is called *The blood of God*, Acts xx. So that the Apostle may well call it here *precious*, exceeding the whole world and all things in it in value. Therefore frustrate not the sufferings of Christ: if he shed his blood to redeem you from sin, be not false to his purpose.

As a Lamb without blemish.] He is that great and everlasting sacrifice which gave value and virtue to all the sacrifices under the Law: their blood was of no worth to the purging away of sin, but by relation to his blood; and the laws concerning the choice of the Paschal Lamb, or other lambs for sacrifice, were but obscure and imperfect shadows of His purity and perfections, who is the undefiled *Lamb of God that taketh away the sins of the world*. John i. 29. A lamb in meekness and silence, *he opened not his mouth*. Isa. liii. 7. And in purity here *without spot or blemish*. *My well-beloved*, says the spouse, *is white and ruddy*, Cant. v. 10;—white in spotless innocency, and red in suffering a bloody death.

For as much as ye know.] It is that must make all this effectual, the right knowledge and due consideration of it. Ye do know it already, but I would have you know it better, more deeply and practically: turn it often over, be more in the study and meditation of it. There is work enough in it still for the most discerning mind; it is a mystery so deep, that you shall never reach the bottom of it, and withal so useful, that you shall find always new profit by it. Our folly is, we gape after new things, and yet are in effect ignorant of the things we think we know best. That learned Apostle who knew so much, and spoke so many tongues, yet says, *I determined to know nothing among you, save Jesus Christ, and him crucified*. 1 Cor. ii. 2. And again he expresses this as the top of his ambition, *That I may know him, and the power of his resurrection, and the fellowship of his sufferings, being made conformable unto his death*. Phil. iii. 10. That con formity is this only knowledge. He that hath his lusts unmortified, and a heart unweaned from the world, though he know all the history of the death and sufferings of Jesus Christ, and can discourse well of them, yet indeed he knows them not.

If you would increase much in holiness, and be strong against the temptations to sin, this is the only art of it ; view much, and so seek to know much of the death of Jesus Christ. Consider often at how high a rate we were redeemed from sin, and provide this answer for all the enticements of sin and the world: "Except you can offer my soul "something beyond that price that was given for it on the cross, I "cannot hearken to you."—"Far be it from me," will a Christian say, who considers this redemption, "that ever I should prefer a base lust, "or any thing in this world, or it all, to Him who gave himself to death "for me, and paid my ransom with his blood. His matchless love hath "freed me from the miserable captivity of sin, and hath for ever fast-"ened me to the sweet yoke of his obedience. Let him alone to dwell "and rule within me, and never let him go forth from my heart; who "for my sake refused to come down from the cross."

Ver. 20. Who verily was foreordained before the foundation of the world, but was manifest in these last times for you.

OF all those considerations (and there are many) that may move men to obedience, there is no one that persuades both more sweetly and strongly, than the sense of God's goodness and mercy towards men; and amongst all the evidences of that, there is none like the sending and giving of his Son for man's redemption ; therefore the Apostle, having mentioned that, insists further on it ; and in these words expresses, 1. The purpose ; 2. The performance ; and, 3. The application of it.

1. The purpose or *decree foreknown;* but it is well rendered, *fore-ordained,* for this knowing is decreeing, and there is little either solid truth or profit in the distinguishing them.

We say, usually, that where there is little wisdom there is much chance ; and comparatively amongst men, some are far more fore-sighted, and of further reach than others ; yet the wisest and most provident men, both wanting skill to design all things aright, and power to act as they contrive, meet with many unexpected casualties and frequent disappointments in their undertakings. But with God, where both wisdom and power are infinite, there can be neither any chance nor resistance from without, nor any imperfection at all in the contrivance of things within Himself, that can give cause to add, or abate, or alter any thing in the frame of His purposes. The model of the whole world, and of all the course of time, was with Him one and the same from all eternity, and whatsoever is brought to pass is ex-actly answerable to that pattern, for with Him *there is no change nor shadow of turning.* Jam. i. 17. There is nothing dark to *the Father of lights:* He sees at one view through all things, and all ages, from the beginning of time to the end of it, yea, from eternity to eternity. And this incomprehensible wisdom is too wonderful for us ; we do but childishly stammer when we offer to speak of it.

It is no wonder that men beat their own brains, and knock their heads one against another, in the contest of their opinions, to little purpose, in their several mouldings of God's decree. Is not this to cut and square God's thoughts to ours, and examine his sovereign purposes by the low principles of human wisdom? How much more learned than all such knowledge, is the Apostle's ignorance, when he cries out, *O the depth of the riches both of the wisdom and knowledge of God! how unsearchable are his judgments, and his ways past finding out!* Rom. xi. 33. Why then should any man debate what place, in the series of God's decrees, is to be assigned to this purpose of sending his Son in the flesh! Let us rather (seeing it is manifest that it was for the redemption of lost mankind) admire that same love of God to mankind, which appears in that purpose of our recovery by the *Word made flesh;* that before man had made himself miserable, yea, before either he or the world was made, this thought of boundless love was in the bosom of God; to send his Son forth from thence, to bring fallen man out of misery, and restore him to happiness; and to do this, not only by taking on his nature, but the curse; to shift it off from us that were sunk under it, and to bear it himself, and by bearing to take it away. *He laid on him the iniquity of us all.* And to this he was appointed, says the Apostle, Heb. iii. 2.

Before the foundation of the world.] This we understand by faith, *that the world was framed by the word of God.* Heb. xi. 3. Although the learned probably think it evincible by human reason, yet some of those who have gloried most in that, and are reputed generally masters of reason, have not seen it by that light. Therefore, that we may have a divine belief of it, we must learn it from the word of God, and be persuaded of its truth by the Spirit of God, that the whole world, and all things in it, were drawn out of nothing by his Almighty power, who is the only eternal and increated Being, and therefore the fountain and source of being to all things.

Foundation.] In this word is plainly intimated the resemblance of the world to a building; and such a building it is, as doth evidence the greatness of Him who framed it; so spacious, rich, and comely, so firm a foundation, raised to so high and stately a roof, and set with variety of stars, as with jewels, therefore called, as some conceive it, *the work of his fingers,* Psal. viii., to express the curious artifice that appears in them. Though naturalists have attempted to give the reason of the earth's stability from its heaviness, which stays it necessarily in the lowest part of the world, yet that abates not our admiring the wisdom and power of God, in laying its foundation so, and establishing it; for it is His will that is the first cause of that, its nature, and hath appointed that to be the property of its heaviness, to fix it there; and therefore Job alleges this amongst the wonderful works of God, and evidences of his power, that *He hangeth the earth upon nothing.* Job xxvi. 7.

Before there was time, or place, or any creature, God, the blessed Trinity, was in Himself, and, as the Prophet speaks, *inhabiting eternity,* completely happy in Himself: but intending to manifest and communicate His goodness, He gave being to the world, and to time with it; made all to set forth His goodness, and the most excellent of his creatures to contemplate and enjoy it. But amongst all the works he intended before time, and in time effected, this is the masterpiece, which is here said to be foreordained, the manifesting of God in the flesh for man's redemption, and that by his Son Jesus Christ, as *the first-born amongst many brethren*, in order that those appointed for salvation should be rescued from the common misery, and be made one mystical body, whereof Christ is the Head, and so entitled to that everlasting glory and happiness that he hath purchased for them.

This, I say, is the great work, wherein all those glorious attributes shine jointly, the wisdom, and power, and goodness, justice, and mercy of God. As in great maps, or pictures, you will see the border decorated with meadows, and fountains, and flowers, &c., represented in it, but in the middle you have the main design; thus is this foreordained redemption amongst the works of God; all His other works in the world, all the beauty of the creatures, and the succession of ages, and things that come to pass in them, are but as the border to this as the main-piece. But as a foolish, unskilful beholder, not discerning the excellency of the principal piece in such maps or pictures, gazes only on the fair border, and goes no further, thus do the greatest part of us: our eyes are taken with the goodly show of the world and appearance of earthly things; but as for this great work of God, Christ *fore-ordained*, and in time sent for our redemption, though it most deserves our attentive regard, yet we do not view and consider it as we ought.

2. We have the performance of that purpose, *Was manifested in these last times for you.* He was manifested both by his incarnation, according to that word of the Apostle St. Paul, *manifested in the flesh*, 1 Tim. iii. 16, and manifested by his marvellous works and doctrine; by his sufferings and death, resurrection and ascension, by the sending down of the Holy Ghost according to his promise, and by the preaching of the Gospel, in the fulness of time that God had appointed, wherein all the prophecies that foretold his coming, and all the types and ceremonies that prefigured him, had their accomplishment.

The times of the Gospel are often called *the last times* by the prophets; for that the Jewish priesthood and ceremonies being abolished, that which succeeded was appointed by God to remain the same to the end of the world. Besides this, the time of our Saviour's incarnation may be called *the last times*, because, although it were not near the end of time by many ages, yet in all probability it is much nearer the end of time than the beginning of it. Some resemble the time of his sufferings in the end of the world, to the Paschal Lamb which was slain in the evening.

It was doubtless the fit time; but notwithstanding the schoolmen offer at reasons to prove the fitness of it, as their humour is to prove all things, none dare, I think, conclude, but if God had so appointed, it might have been either sooner or later. And our safest way is to rest in this, that it was the fit time, because so it pleased Him, and to seek no other reason why, having promised the Messiah so quickly after man's fall, He deferred his coming about four thousand years, and a great part of that time shut up the knowledge of Himself and the true religion, within the narrow compass of that one nation of which Christ was to be born; of these and such like things, we can give no other reason than that which he teacheth us in a like case, *Even so, Father, because it seemeth good unto thee.* Matt. xi. 26.

3. The application of this manifestation, *For you.*] The Apostle represents these things to those he writes to, particularly for their use; therefore he applies it to them, but without prejudice of the believers who went before, or of those who were to follow in after-ages. He who is here said to be *foreappointed* before the foundation of the world, is therefore called *A Lamb slain from the foundation of the world.* Rev. xiii. 8. And as the virtue of his death looks backward to all preceding ages, whose faith and sacrifices looked forward to it; so the same death is of force and perpetual value to the end of the world. *After he had offered one sacrifice for sins,* says the author of the Epistle to the Hebrews, ch. x. ver. 12, 14, *he sat down for ever on the right hand of God; for by one offering he hath perfected for ever them that are sanctified.* The cross on which he was extended, points, in the length of it, to heaven and earth, reconciling them together, and in the breadth of it, to former and following ages, as being equally salvation to both.

In this appropriating and peculiar interest in Jesus Christ lies our happiness, without which it avails not that he was ordained from eternity, and in time manifested. It is not the general contemplation, but the peculiar possession of Christ, that gives both solid comfort and strong persuasion to obedience and holiness, which is here the Apostle's particular scope.

Ver. 21. Who by him do believe in God, that raised him up from the dead, and gave him glory; that your faith and hope might be in God.

Now, because it is faith that gives the soul this particular title to Jesus Christ, the Apostle adds this, to declare whom he meant by *you.* *For you,* says he, *who by him do believe in God,* &c.

Where we have, 1. The complete object of faith. 2. The ground or warrant of it. The object, *God in Christ.* The ground or warrant, *In that he raised him up from the dead, and gave him glory.*

A man may have, while living out of Christ, yea, he must, he cannot choose but have a conviction within him, that there is a God; and further he may have, even out of Christ, some kind of belief of those things that are spoken concerning God; but to repose on God as his God and his salvation, which is indeed to believe in Him, this cannot be but where Christ is the *medium* through which we look upon God; for so long as we look upon God through our own guiltiness, we can see nothing but His wrath, and apprehend Him as an armed enemy; and therefore are so far from resting on Him as our happiness, that the more we view it, it puts us upon the more speed to fly from Him, and to cry out, *Who can dwell with everlasting burnings, and abide with a consuming fire?* But our Saviour, taking sin out of the way, puts himself betwixt our sins and God, and so makes a wonderful change of our apprehension of Him. When you look through a red glass, the whole heavens seem bloody; but through pure uncoloured glass, you receive the clear light that is so refreshing and comfortable to behold. When sin unpardoned is betwixt, and we look on God through that, we can perceive nothing but anger and enmity in his countenance; but make Christ once the *medium*, our pure Redeemer, and through him, as clear, transparent glass, the beams of God's favourable countenance shine in upon the soul. The Father cannot look upon his well-beloved Son, but graciously and pleasingly. God looks on us out of Christ, sees us rebels, and fit to be condemned : we look on God as being just and powerful to punish us ; but when Christ is betwixt, God looks on us in him as justified, and we look on God in him as pacified, and see the smiles of His favourable countenance. Take Christ out, all is terrible ; interpose him, all is full of peace ; therefore set him always betwixt, and by him we shall believe in God.

The warrant and ground of believing in God by Christ is this, that God *raised him from the dead, and gave him glory*, which evidences the full satisfaction of his death ; and in all that work, both in his humiliation and exaltation, standing in our room, we may repute it his as ours. If all is paid that could be exacted of him, and therefore he set free from death, then are we acquitted, and have nothing to pay. If he was raised from the dead, and exalted to glory, then so shall we ; He hath taken possession of that glory for us, and we may judge ourselves possessed of it already, because He, our Head, possesseth it.

And this the last words of the verse confirm to us, implying this to be the very purpose and end for which God, having given him to death, *raised him up and gave him glory:* it is for this end, expressly, that *our faith and hope might be in God.* The last end is, that we may have life and glory through him ; the nearer end, that in the mean while, till we attain them, we may have firm belief and hope of them, and rest on God as the giver of them, and so in part enjoy them beforehand, and be upheld in our joy and conflicts by the comfort of them. And as St. Stephen in his vision, Faith doth, in a spiritual way, look through all the visible heavens, and see Christ at the Father's right hand, and is comforted by that in the greatest troubles, though it were amidst a shower of stones, as St. Stephen was. The comfort is no less than this, that being by faith made one with Christ, his present glory wherein he sits at the Father's right hand, is an assurance to us, that *where he is we shall be also.* John xiv. 3.

Ver. 22. Seeing ye have purified your souls in obeying the truth through the Spirit unto unfeigned love of the brethren, see that ye love one another with a pure heart fervently.

JESUS CHRIST is made unto us of God, *wisdom, righteousness, sanctification, and redemption,* 1 Cor. i. 30. It is a known truth, and yet very needful to be often represented to us, that redemption and holiness are undivided companions, yea, that we are redeemed on purpose for this end, that we should be holy. The pressing of this, we see, is here the Apostle's scope ; and having by that reason enforced it in the general, he now takes that as concluded and confessed, and so makes use of it particularly to exhort to the exercise of that main Christian grace of *brotherly love.*

The obedience and holiness mentioned in the foregoing verses, comprehend the whole duties and frame of a Christian life towards God and men : and, having urged that in the general, he specifies this grace of mutual Christian love, as the great evidence of their sincerity and the truth of their love to God ; for men are subject to much hypocrisy this way, and deceive themselves ; if they find themselves diligent in religious exercises, they scarcely once ask their hearts how they stand affected this way, namely, in love to their brethren.   They can come constantly to the church, and pray, it may be, at home too, and yet cannot find in their hearts to forgive an injury.

As forgiving injuries argues the truth of piety, so it is that which makes all converse both sweet and profitable, and besides, it graces and commends men in their holy profession, to such as are without and strangers to it, yea, even to their enemies.

Therefore is it that our Saviour doth so much recommend this to his disciples, and they to others, as we see in all their Epistles.   He gives it them as the very badge and livery by which they should be known for his followers, *By this shall all men know that you are my disciples, if ye love one another*, John xiii. 35.   And St. Paul is frequent in exhorting to, and extolling this grace.   See Rom. xii. 10, and xiii. 8 ; 1 Cor. i. 13 ; Gal. v. 13 ; Eph. iv. 2 ; and in many other places.   He calls it *the bond of perfectness*, Col. iii. 14,—that grace which unites and binds all together.   So doth our Apostle here, and often in this and the other Epistle ; and that beloved disciple St. John, who leaned on our Saviour's breast, drank deep of that spring of love that was here, and therefore it streams forth so abundantly in his writings : they contain nothing so much as this divine doctrine of love.

We have here, 1. The due qualifications of it.   2. A Christian's obligation to it.

The *qualifications* are three ; namely, *sincerity, purity,* and *fervency.* The *sincerity* is expressed in the former clause of the verse, *unfeigned love;* and repeated again in the latter part, that it be *with a pure heart,* as the *purity* is included in *fervency.*

1. Love must be *unfeigned.*   It appears that this dissimulation is a disease that is very incident in this particular.   The Apostle St. Paul hath the same word, Rom. xii. 9, and the Apostle St. John to the same sense, 1 John iii. 18.   That it have that double reality which is opposed to double-dissembled love ; that it be cordial and effectual ; that the professing of it arise from truth of affection, and, as much as may be, be seconded with action ; that both the heart and the hand may be the seal of it rather than the tongue ; not court holy-water and empty noise of service and affection, that fears nothing more than to be put upon trial.   Although thy brother, with whom thou conversest, cannot, it may be, see through thy false appearances, He who commands this love looks chiefly within, seeks it there, and, if he find it not there, hates them most who most pretend it ; so that the art of dissembling, though never so well studied, cannot pass in this King's court, to whom all hearts are open, and all desires known.   When, after variances, men are brought to an agreement, they are much subject to this, rather to cover their remaining malices with superficial verbal forgiveness, than to dislodge them, and free the heart of them.   This is a poor self-deceit.   As the philosopher said to him, who being ashamed that he was espied by him in a tavern in the outer room, withdrew himself to the inner, he called after him, "That is not the way out ; the more you go that way, you will be the further within it:" so when hatreds are upon admonition

not thrown out, but retire inward to hide themselves, they grow deeper and stronger than before ; and those constrained semblances of reconcilement are but a false healing, do but skin the wound over, and therefore it usually breaks forth worse again.

How few there are that have truly maliceless hearts, and find this entire upright affection towards their brethren meeting them in their whole conversation, this *law of love* deeply impressed on their hearts, and from thence expressed in their words and actions, and that is *unfeigned love*, as real to their brethren as to themselves.

2. It must be *pure*, from a pure heart. This is not all one with the former, as some take it. It is true, doubleness or hypocrisy is an impurity, and a great one ; but all impurity is not doubleness : one may really mean that friendship and affection he expresses, and yet it may be most contrary to that which is here required, because *impure;* such a *brotherly love* as that of Simeon and Levi, brethren in iniquity, as the expressing them *brethren*, Gen. xlix., is taken to mean. When hearts are cemented together by impurity itself, by ungodly conversation and society in sin, as in uncleanness or drunkenness, &c., this is a swinish fraternity, a friendship which is contracted, as it were, by wallowing in the same mire. Call it good fellowship, or what you will, all the fruit that in the end can be expected out of unholy friendliness and fellowship in sinning together, is, to be tormented together, and to add each to the torment of another.

The mutual love of Christians must be pure, arising from such causes as are pure and spiritual, from the sense of our Saviour's command and of his example ; for he himself joins that with it, *A new commandment give I you,* saith he, *that as I have loved you, so you also love one another,* John xiii. 34. They that are indeed lovers of God are united, by that their hearts meet in Him, as in one centre : they cannot but love one another. Where a godly man sees his Father's image, he is forced to love it ; he loves those whom he perceives godly, so as to delight in them, because that image is in them ; and those that appear destitute of it, he loves them so as to wish them partakers of that image. And this is all for God : he loves *amicum in Deo, et inimicum propter Deum :* that is, he loves a friend in God, and an enemy for God. And as the Christian's love is pure in its cause, so in its effects and exercise. His society and converse with any, tends mainly to this, that he may mutually help and be helped in the knowledge and love of God ; he desires most that he and his brethren may jointly mind their journey heavenwards, and further one another in their way to the full enjoyment of God. And this is truly the love of a pure heart, which both begins and ends in God.

3. We must love *fervently*, not after a cold, indifferent manner. Let the love of your brethren be as a fire within you, consuming that selfishness which is so contrary to it, and is so natural to men ; let it set your thoughts on work to study how to do others good ; let your love be an active love, intense within you, and extending itself in doing good to the souls and bodies of your brethren as they need, and you are able : *Alium re, alium consilio, alium gratiâ :* (Seneca *de Beneficiis*, lib. i. c. 2 :) One by money, another by counsel, another by kindness.

It is self-love that contracts the heart, and shuts out all other love, both of God and man, save only so far as our own interest carries, and that is still self-love : but the love of God dilates the heart, purifies love, and extends it to all men, but after a special manner directs it to those who are more peculiarly beloved of him, and that is here the particular love required.

Love of the brethren.] In this is implied our obligation after a special manner to love those of *the household of faith*, because they are our *brethren*. This includes not only, as Abraham saith, *that there ought to be no strife*, (Gen. xiii. 8,) but it binds most strongly to this sincere, and pure, and fervent love ; and therefore the Apostle in the next verse repeats expressly the doctrine of the mysterious new birth, and explains it more fully, which he had mentioned in the entrance of the Epistle, and again referred to, ver. 14, 17.

There is in this fervent love, sympathy with the griefs of our brethren, desire and endeavour to help them, bearing their infirmities, and recovering them too, if it may be ; raising them when they fall, admonishing and reproving them as is needful, sometimes sharply, and yet still in love ; rejoicing in their good, in their gifts and graces, so far from envying them, that we be glad as if they were our own. There is the same blood running in their veins : you have the same Father, and the same Spirit within you, and the same Jesus Christ, the Head of that glorious fraternity, *The first-born among many brethren*, Rom. viii. 29 ; of whom the Apostle saith, that *He hath re-collected into one, all things in heaven and in earth*, Eph. i. 10. The word is, *gathered them into one head;* and so suits very fitly to express our union in him. *In whom*, says he in the same Epistle, Eph. iv. 16, *the whole body is fitly compacted together;* and he adds that which agrees to our purpose, that this body *grows up and edifies itself in love.* All the members receive spirits from the same head, and are useful and serviceable one to another, and to the whole body. Thus, these brethren, receiving of the same Spirit from their Head, Christ, are most strongly bent to the good of one another. If there be but a thorn in the foot, the back boweth, the head stoops down, the eyes look, the hands reach to it, and endeavour its help and ease : in a word, all the members partake of the good and evil, one of another. Now, by how much this body is more spiritual and lively, so much the stronger must the union and love of the parts of it be each to every other. You are brethren by the same new birth, and born to the same inheritance, and such an one as shall not be an apple of strife amongst you, to beget debates and contentions : no, it is enough for all, and none shall prejudge another, but you shall have joy in the happiness one of another ; seeing you shall then be perfect in love ; all harmony, no difference in judgment or in affection, all your harps tuned to the same new song, which you shall sing for ever. Let that love begin here, which shall never end.

And this same union, I conceive, is likewise expressed in the first words of the verse. Seeing you are partakers of that work of sanctification by the same word, and the same Spirit, that works it in all the faithful, and are by that called and incorporated into that fraternity, therefore live in it and like it. You are purified to it ; therefore love one another after that same manner purely. Let the profane world scoff at that name of *brethren;* you will not be so foolish as to be scorned out of it, being so honourable and happy; and the day is at hand wherein those that scoff you, would give much more than all that the best of them ever possessed in the world, to be admitted into your number.

Seeing you have purified your souls in obeying the truth through the Spirit.] Here is, 1. The chief seat, or subject of the work of sanctification, *the soul.* 2. The subordinate means, *truth.* 3. The nature of it, *obeying of truth.* 4. The chief worker of it, *the Holy Spirit.*

For the *first*, the chief seat of sanctification, *the soul:* it is no doubt a work that goes through the whole man, renews and purifies all. Heb. x. 22; 2 Cor. vii. 1. But because it purifies the soul, therefore it is that it does purify all. There impurity begins, Matt. xv. 18; not only evil thoughts, but all evil actions come forth from the heart, which is there all one with the soul; and therefore this purifying begins there, *makes the tree good that the fruit may be good.* It is not so much external performances that make the difference between men, as their inward temper. We meet here in the same place, and all partake of the same word and prayer; but how wide a difference is there, in God's eye, betwixt an unwashed, profane heart in the same exercise, and a soul purified in some measure *in obeying the truth*, and desirous to be further purified by further obeying it!

Secondly, That which is the subordinate means of this purity, is, *the Truth,* or the word of God. It is truth, pure in itself, and it begets truth and purity in the heart, by teaching it concerning the holy and pure nature of God, showing it and his holy will, which is to us the rule of purity; and by representing Jesus Christ unto us as the fountain of our purity and renovation, from whose fulness we may *receive grace for grace.* John i. 16.

Thirdly, The nature of this work, that wherein the very being of this purifying consists, is, *the receiving or obeying of this truth.* So Gal. iii. 1, where it is put for right believing. The chief point of obedience is believing; the proper obedience to truth is to give credit to it; and this divine belief doth necessarily bring the whole soul into obedience and conformity to that pure truth which is in the word; and so the very purifying and renewing of the soul is this obedience of faith, as unbelief is its chief impurity and disobedience; therefore, Acts xv. 9, Faith is said to *purify the heart.*

Fourthly, The chief worker of this sanctification, is, *the Holy Spirit of God.* They are said here to *purify themselves,* for it is certain and undeniable, that the soul itself doth act in believing or obeying the truth; but not of itself, it is not the first principle of motion. They purify their souls, but it is *by the Spirit.* They do it by His enlivening power, and a purifying virtue received from Him. Faith, or obeying the truth, works this purity, but the Holy Ghost works that faith; as in the forecited place, God is said to *purify their hearts by faith,* ver. 8. He doth that by giving them the Holy Ghost. The truth is pure and purifying, yet can it not of itself purify the soul, but by the obeying or believing of it; and the soul cannot obey or believe but by the Spirit which works in it that faith, and by that faith purifies it, and works love in it. The impurity and earthliness of men's minds, is the great cause of disunion and disaffection amongst them, and of all their strifes. James iv. 1.

This Spirit is that fire which refines and purifies the soul from the dross of earthly desires that possess it, and which sublimates it to the love of God and of his saints, because they are his, and are purified by the same Spirit. It is the property of fire to draw together things of the same kind: the outward fire of enmities and persecution that are kindled against the godly by the world, doth somewhat, and if it were more considered by them, would do more, in this knitting their hearts closer one to another; but it is this inward pure and purifying fire of the Holy Ghost, that doth most powerfully unite them.

The true reason why there is so little truth of this Christian mutual love amongst those that are called Christians, is, because there is so little of this purifying obedience to the truth whence it flows. Faith unfeigned would beget this love unfeigned. Men may exhort to them both, but they require the hand of God to work them in the heart.

Ver. 23. Being born again, not of corruptible seed, but of incorruptible, by the word of God, which liveth and abideth for ever.

THE two things which make up the Apostle's exhortation, are the very sum of a Christian's duty; to walk as obedient children towards God, and as loving brethren one towards another: and that it may yet have the deeper impression, he here represents to them anew that new birth he mentioned before, by which they are the children of God, and so brethren.

We shall first speak of this Regeneration; and then of the Seed. 1st, Of the regeneration itself. This is the great dignity of believers, that they are the sons of God, John i. 12, as it is the great evidence of the love of God, that He hath bestowed this dignity on them, 1 John iii. 1. For they are no way needful to Him: He had from eternity a Son perfectly like Himself, *the character of His person*, Heb. i. 3, and one Spirit proceeding from both; and there is no creation, neither the first nor the second, can add any thing to Those and Their happiness. It is most true of that Blessed Trinity, *Satis amplum alter alteri theatrum sumus*. But the gracious purpose of God to impart his goodness appears in this, that he hath made himself such a multitude of sons, not only angels that are so called, but man, a little lower than they in nature, yet dignified with this name in his creation: Luke iii. 38, *Which was the Son of Adam, which was the Son of God*. He had not only the impression of God's footsteps, (as they speak,) which all the creatures have, but of his image. And most of all in this is His rich grace magnified, that sin having defaced that image, and so degraded man from his honour, and divested him of that title of sonship, and stamped our polluted nature with the marks of vileness and bondage, yea, with the very image of Satan, rebellion and enmity against God; that out of mankind thus ruined and degenerated, God should raise to himself a new race and generation of Sons.

For this design was the *Word made flesh*, John i. 12, the Son made man, to make men the sons of God. And it is by him alone we are restored to this; they who receive him, receive with him, and in him, this privilege, ver. 12. And therefore it is a sonship by adoption, and is so called in Scripture, in difference from his eternal and ineffable generation, who is, and was, *the only begotten Son of God.* Yet, that we may know that this Divine adoption is not a mere outward relative name, as that of men, the sonship of the saints is here, and often elsewhere in Scripture, expressed by *new generation,* and *new birth.* They are *begotten of God.* John i. 13 ; 1 John ii. 29. A new being, a spiritual life, is communicated to them ; they have in them of their Father's Spirit ; and this is derived to them through Christ, and therefore called his Spirit. Gal. iv. 6. They are not only accounted of the family of God by adoption, but by this new birth they are indeed his children, partakers of the Divine nature, as our Apostle expresseth it.

Now though it be easy to speak and hear the words of this doctrine, yet the truth itself that is in it, is so high and mysterious, that it is altogether impossible, without a portion of this new nature, to conceive of it. Corrupt nature cannot understand it. What wonder that there is nothing of it in the subtilest schools of philosophers, when a very *doctor of Israel* mistook it grossly ! John iii. 10. It is indeed a great mystery, and he that was the sublimest of all the Evangelists, and therefore called the divine, the soaring eagle, (as they compare him,) he is more abundant in this subject than the rest.

And the most profitable way of considering this regeneration and sonship, is certainly to follow the light of those holy writings, and not to jangle in disputes about the order and manner of it, of which, though somewhat may be profitably said, and safely, namely, so much as the Scripture speaks, yet much that is spoken of it, and debated by many, is but a useless expense of time and pains. What those previous dispositions are, and how far they go, and where is the mark or point of difference betwixt them and the infusion of spiritual life, I conceive not so easily determinable.

If naturalists and physicians cannot agree upon the order of formation of the parts of the human body in the womb, how much less can we be peremptory in the other ! If there be so many wonders (as indeed there be) in the natural structure and frame of man, how much richer in wonders must this Divine and supernatural generation be ! See how David speaks of the former, Psal. xiv. 15. Things spiritual being more refined than material things, their workmanship must be far more wonderful and curious. But then, it must be viewed with a spiritual eye. There is an unspeakable lustre and beauty of the new creature, by the mixture of all Divine graces, each setting off another, as so many rich several colours in embroidery ; but who can trace that Invisible Hand that works it, so as to determine of the order, and to say which was first, which second, and so on ; whether faith, or repentance, and all graces, &c. ? This is certain, that these and all graces do inseparably make up the same work, and are all in the new formation of every soul that is born again.

If the ways of God's universal providence be untraceable, then most of all the workings of his grace are conducted in a secret, unperceivable way in this new birth. He gives this spiritual being as the dew, which is silently and insensibly formed, and this generation of the Sons of God is compared to it by the Psalmist, Psal. cx. 3 : they have this original from heaven as the dew. *Except a man be born from above, he cannot enter into the kingdom of God.* John iii. 3. And it is the peculiar work of the Spirit of God ; as He himself speaks of the dew to Job, Job xxxviii. 28, *Hath the rain a father, or who hath begotten the drops of the dew?* The sharpest wits are to seek in the knowledge and discovery of it, as Job speaketh of a way that no fowl knoweth, and *which the vulture's eye hath not seen.* Ch. xxviii. ver. 7.

To contest much, how in this regeneration He works upon the will, and renews it, is to little purpose, provided this be granted, that it is in his power to regenerate and renew a man at his pleasure : and how is it possible not to grant this, unless we will run into that error, to think that God hath made a creature too hard for himself to rule, or hath willingly exempted it ? And shall the works of the Almighty, especially this work, wherein most of all others He glories, fail in His hand, and remain imperfect ? Shall there be any abortive births whereof God is the Father ? *Shall I bring to the birth, and not cause to bring forth?* Isa. lxvi. 9. No ; no sinner so dead, but there is virtue in His hand to revive out of the very stones. Though the most impenitent hearts are as stones within them, yet He *can make of them children to Abraham.* Luke iii. 8. He can dig out *the heart of stone, and put a heart of flesh* in its place, Ezek. xxvi. 26 ; otherwise, He would not have made such a promise. *Not of flesh, nor of the will of man, but of God.* John i. 13. If his sovereign will is not a sufficient principle of this regeneration, why then says the Apostle St. James, *Of his own will begat he us?* And he adds the subordinate cause, *By the word of truth,* James i. 18, which is here called the immortal seed of this new birth.

Therefore it is that the Lord hath appointed the continuance of the ministry of this word, to the end that his Church may be still fruitful, bringing forth sons unto him ; that the assemblies of his people may be like *flocks of sheep coming up from the washing, none barren amongst them.* Cant. iv. 2.

Though the ministers of this word, by reason of their employment in dispensing it, have, by the Scriptures, the relation of parents imparted to them ; (which is an exceeding great dignity for them, as they are called *co-workers* with God ; and the same Apostle that writes so, calls the Galatians his *little children, of whom he travailed in birth again till Christ were formed in them ;* and the ministers of God have often very much pain in this travail ;) yet the privilege of the Father of spirits remains untouched, which is, effectually to beget again those same spirits which he creates, and to make that seed of the word fruitful in the way and at the season that it may please Him. The preacher of the word, be he never so powerful, can cast this seed only into the ear ; his hand reaches no farther ; and the hearer, by his attention, may convey it into his head ; but it is the supreme Father and Teacher above, who carries it into the heart, the only soil wherein it proves lively and fruitful. One man cannot reach the heart of another ; how should he then renew its fruitfulness ? If natural births have been always acknowledged to belong to God's prerogative, (Psal. cxxvii. 3, *Lo, children are an heritage of the Lord, and the fruit of the womb is his reward;* and so Jacob answered wisely to his wife's foolish passion, Gen. xxx. 2, *Am I in God's stead?*) how much more is this new birth wholly dependent on His hand!

But though this word cannot beget without Him, yet it is by this word that He begets, and ordinarily not without it. It is true that the substantial Eternal Word is to us (as we said) the spring of this new birth and life, the Head from whom the spirits of this super-natural life flow; but that by *the word* here, is meant the Gospel, the Apostle puts out of doubt, *verse* the last, *And this is the word which by the Gospel is preached unto you.* Therefore thus is this word really the seed of this new birth, because it contains and declares that other Word, the Son of God, as our life. The word is spoken in common, and so is the same to all hearers; but then, all hearts being naturally shut against it, God doth by his own hand open some to receive it, and mixes it with faith; and those it renews, and restoreth in them the image of God, draws the traces of it anew, and makes them the sons of God. *My doctrine shall drop as the dew,* says Moses, Deut. xxxii. 2. The word, as a heavenly dew, not falling beside, but dropped into the heart by the hand of God's own Spirit, makes it all become spiritual and heavenly, and turns it into one of those drops of dew that the children of God are compared to, Psal. cx. 3, *Thou hast the dew of thy youth.*

The natural estate of the soul is darkness, and the word, as a Divine light shining into it, transforms the soul into its own nature; so that as the word is called light, so is the soul that is renewed by it. *Ye were darkness, but now are ye,* not only enlightened, but *light in the Lord,* Eph. v. 8. All the evils of the natural mind are often com-prised under the name of darkness and error, and therefore is the whole work of conversion likewise signified by light and truth: *He begat us by the word of truth,* Jam. i. 18. So 2 Cor. iv. 16, alluding to the first *Fiat lux,* or, *Let there be light,* in the creation. The word brought within the soul by the Spirit, lets it see its own necessity, and Christ's sufficiency convinceth it thoroughly, and causeth it to cast over itself upon him for life; and this is the very begetting of it again to eternal life.

So that this efficacy of the word to prove successful seed, doth not hang upon the different abilities of the preachers, their having more or less rhetoric or learning. It is true, eloquence hath a great advan-tage in civil and moral things to persuade, and to draw the hearers by the ears, almost which way it will; but in this spiritual work, to revive a soul, to beget it anew, the influence of Heaven is the main thing requisite. There is no way so common and plain, (being war-ranted by God in the delivery of saving truth,) but the Spirit of God can revive the soul by it; and the most skilful and authorita-tive way, yea, being withal very spiritual, yet may effect nothing, because left alone to itself. One word of Holy Scripture, or of truth conformable to it, may be the principle of regeneration to him that hath heard multitudes of excellent sermons, and hath often read the whole Bible, and hath still continued unchanged. If the Spirit of God preach that one or any such word to the soul, *God so loved the world, that he gave his only begotten Son, that whosoever should believe in him should not perish, but have everlasting life,* John iii. 15, it will be cast down with the fear of perishing, and driven out of itself by that, and raised up and drawn to Jesus Christ by the hope of everlasting life ; it will believe on him that it may have life, and be inflamed with the love of God, and give itself to Him who so loved the world, as to give His only begotten Son to purchase for us that everlasting life.   Thus may that word prove this immortal seed, which, though very often read and heard before, was but a dead letter.   A drop of those liquors which are called spirits operates more than large draughts of other waters : one word spoken by the Lord to the heart is all spirit, and doth that which whole streams of man's eloquence could never effect.

In hearing of the word, men look usually too much upon men, and forget from what spring the word hath its power ; they observe too narrowly the different hand of the sowers, and too little depend on His hand, who is great Lord of both seed-time and harvest.   Be it sown by a weak hand, or a stronger, the immortal seed is still the same ; yea, suppose the worst, that it be a foul hand that sows it, that the preacher himself be not so sanctified and of so edifying a life as you would wish, yet, the seed itself, being good, contracts no defilement, and may be effectual to regeneration in some, and to the strengthening of others ; although he that is not renewed by it himself, cannot have much hope of success, nor reap much comfort by it, and usually doth not seek nor regard it much ; but all instruments are alike in an Almighty hand.

Hence learn, 1. That true conversion is not so slight a work as we commonly account it.   It is not the outward change of some bad customs, which gains the name of a reformed man, in the ordinary dialect ; it is a new birth and being, and elsewhere called *a new creation*.   Though it be but a change in qualities, yet it is such a one, and the qualities are so far different, that it bears the name of the most substantial productions : from *children of disobedience*, and that which is linked with it, *heirs of wrath*, to be *sons of God, and heirs of glory !*   They have a new spirit given them, a free, princely, noble spirit, as the word is, Psal. li. 10, and this spirit acts in their life and actions.

2. Consider this dignity, and be kindled with an ambition worthy of it.   How doth a Christian pity that poor vanity which men make so much noise about, of their kindred and extraction !   This is worth glorying in indeed, to be of the highest blood-royal, sons of the King of kings by this new birth, and in the nearest relation to Him !   This adds matchless honour to that birth which is so honourable in the esteem of the world.

But we all pretend to be of this number.   Would we not study to cozen ourselves, the discovery whether we are, or not, would not be so hard.

In many, their false confidence is too evident ; there is no appearance in them of the Spirit of God, not a footstep like His leading, nor any trace of that character, Rom. viii. 14, *As many as are led by the Spirit of God, they are the children of God ;* not a lineament of God's visage, as their Father.   *If ye know that He is righteous,* (says St. John, chap. ii. ver. 29,) *ye know then that every one that doth righteous-*

ness is born of Him. And so, on the other hand, how contrary to the most holy God, the lover and fountain of holiness, are they who swinishly love to wallow in the mire of unholiness ! Is swearing and cursing the accent of the regenerate, the children of God ? No ; it is the language of hell. Do children delight to indignify and dishonour their father's name ? No ; earthly-mindedness is a countersign. Shall the king's children, *they that were brought up in scarlet,* (as Jeremiah laments,) embrace *the dunghill ?* Lam. iv. 5. Princes, by their high birth, and education, have usually their hearts filled with far higher thoughts than mean persons : the children of the poorest sort being pinched that way, their greatest thoughts, as they grow up, are ordinerily, how they shall shift to live, how they shall get their bread : but princes think either of the conquest or governing of kingdoms. Are you not born to a better inheritance, if indeed you are born again : why then do you vilify yourselves ? Why are you not more in prayer ? There are no dumb children among those that are born of God ; they have all that Spirit of prayer by which they not only speak, but *cry, Abba, Father.*

2ndly, We come to consider the seed of this regeneration, *the word of God.* The most part of us esteem the preaching of the word, as a transient discourse that amuses us for an hour. We look for no more, and therefore we find no more. We receive it not as the immortal seed of our regeneration, as *the ingrafted word that is able to save our souls.* Jam. i. 21. Oh ! learn to reverence this holy and happy ordinance of God, this word of life, and know, that they who are not regenerated, and so saved by it, shall be judged by it.

Not of corruptible seed.] It is a main cause of the unsuitable and unworthy behaviour of Christians, (those that profess themselves such,) that a great part of them either do not know, or at least do not seriously and frequently consider, what is indeed the estate and quality of Christians, how excellent and of what descent their new nature is ; therefore they are often to be reminded of this. Our Apostle here doth so, and by it binds on all his exhortations.

Of this new being we have here these two things specified : 1. Its high original, from God, *Begotten again of His word :* 2. That which so much commends good things, its duration. And this follows from the other ; for if the principle of this be *incorruptible,* itself must be so too. The word of God is not only a living and ever-abiding word in itself, but likewise in reference to this new birth and spiritual life of a Christian ; and in this sense that which is here spoken of it, is intended : it is therefore called, not only an abiding word, but *incorruptible seed,* which expressly relates to regeneration. And because we are most sensible of the good and evil of things by comparison, the everlastingness of the word, and of that spiritual life which it begets, is set off by the frailty and shortness of natural life, and of all the good that concerns it. This the Apostle expresseth in the words of Isaiah, in the next verse.

Ver. 24. For all flesh is as grass, and all the glory of man as the flower of grass. The grass withereth, and the flower thereof falleth away.

IN expressing the vanity and frailty of the natural life of man, it agrees very well with the subject to call him *flesh,* giving to the whole man the name of his corruptible part, both to make the wretched and perishing condition of this life more sensible, and man the more humble by it ; for though by providing all for the flesh, and bestowing his whole time in the endeavours which are of the flesh's concernment, he remembers it too much, and forgets his spiritual and immortal part ; yet, in that over-eager care for the flesh, he seems, in some sense, to forget that he is flesh, or, at least, that flesh is perishing because flesh ; extending his desires and projects so far for the flesh, as if it were immortal, and should always abide to enjoy and use these things. As the philosopher said of his countrymen, upbraiding at once their surfeitings and excess in feasting, and their sumptuousness in building, " That they ate as if they meant to die to-morrow, and yet built as if they were never to die :" thus, in men's immoderate pursuits of earth, they seem both to forget they are any thing else beside flesh, and in this sense, too, to forget that they are flesh, that is, mortal and perishing ; they rightly remember neither their immortality nor their mortality. If we consider what it is to be flesh, the naming of that were sufficient to the purpose : All man is flesh ; but it is plainer thus, *All flesh is grass.* Thus, in the lxxviiith Psalm, *He remembered that they were but flesh ;* that speaks their frailty enough ; but it is added, to make the vanity of their estate the clearer—*a wind that passeth and cometh not again.* So Psal. ciii. 15, *As for man, his days are as grass, as a flower of the field so he flourisheth. For the wind passeth over it and it is gone, and the place thereof shall know it no more.*

This natural life is compared, even by natural men, to the vainest things, and scarcely find they things light enough to express its *vanity ;* as it is here called *grass,* so they have compared the generations of men to the leaves of trees. But the light of Scripture doth most discover this, and it is a lesson that requires the Spirit of God to teach it aright. *Teach us* (says Moses, Psal. xc. 12) *so to number our days that we may apply our hearts unto wisdom.* And David, (Psal. xxxix. 4,) *Make me to know my life, how frail I am.* So James iv. 14, *What is your life ? it is even a vapour.* And here it is called *grass.* So Job xiv. 1, 2, *Man that is born of a woman, is of few days and full of trouble. He cometh forth like a flower, and is cut down.*

Grass hath its root in the earth, and is fed by the moisture of it for a while ; but besides that, it is under the hazard of such weather as favours it not, or of the scythe that cuts it down : give it all the forbearance that may be, let it be free from both those, yet how quickly will it wither of itself ! Set aside those many accidents, the smallest of which is able to destroy our natural life, the diseases of our own bodies, and outward violences, and casualties that cut down many in their greenness, in the flower of their youth, the utmost term is not long ; in the course of nature it will wither. Our life indeed is a lighted torch, either blown out by some stroke or some wind, or, if spared, yet within a while it burns away, and will die out of itself.

And all the glory of man.] This is elegantly added. There is indeed a great deal of seeming difference betwixt the outward conditions of life amongst men. Shall the rich, and honourable, and beautiful, and healthful go in together, under the same name, with the baser and unhappier part, the poor, wretched sort of the world, who seem to be born for nothing but sufferings and miseries ? At least, hath the wise no advantage beyond the fools ? Is all grass ? Make you no distinction ? No ; *all is grass,* or if you will have some other name, be it so : once, this is true, that all flesh is grass ; and if that glory which shines so much in your eyes, must have a difference, then this is all it can have,—it is but *the flower* of that same grass ; somewhat above the common grass in gayness, a little comelier and better apparelled than it, but partaker of its frail and fading nature ; it hath no privilege nor immunity that way ; yea, of the two, is the less durable, and usually shorter lived ; at the best it decays with it : *The grass withereth, and the flower thereof falleth away.*

How easily and quickly hath the highest splendour of a man's prosperity been blasted, either by men's power, or by the immediate hand of God ! The Spirit of the Lord blows upon it, (as Isaiah there says,) and by that, not only withers the grass, but the flower fades though never so fair. *When thou correctest man for iniquity,* says David, *thou makest his beauty to consume away like a moth.* Psal. xxxix. 11. How many have the casualties of fire, or war, or shipwreck, in one day, or in one night, or in a small part of either, turned out of great riches into extreme poverty ! And the instances are not few, of those who have on a sudden fallen from the top of honour into the foulest disgraces, not by degrees coming down the stair they went up, but tumbled down headlong. And the most vigorous beauty and strength of body, how doth a few days' sickness, or if it escape that, a few years' time, blast that flower ! Yea, those higher advantages which have somewhat both of truer and more lasting beauty in them, the endowments of wit, and learning, and eloquence, yea, and of moral goodness and virtue, yet they cannot rise above this word, they are still, in all their glory, but the *flower of grass;* their root is in the earth. Natural ornaments are of some use in this present life, but they reach no further. When men have wasted their strength, and endured the toil of study night and day, it is but a small parcel of knowledge they can attain to, and they are forced to lie down in the dust in the midst of their pursuit of it : that head that lodges most sciences shall within a while be disfurnished of them all ; and the tongue that speaks most languages be silenced.

The great projects of kings and princes, and they also themselves, come under this same notion ; all the vast designs that are framing in their heads fall to the ground in a moment ; *They return to their dust, and in that day all their thoughts perish.* Psal. cxlvi. 4. Archimedes was killed in the midst of his demonstration.

If they themselves did consider this in the heat of their affairs, it would much allay the swelling and loftiness of their minds ; and if they who live upon their favour would consider it, they would not value it at so high a rate, and buy it so dear as often they do. *Men of low degree are vanity,* says the Psalmist, (Psal. lxii. 9,) but he adds, *Men of high degree are a lie.* From base, mean persons we expect nothing ; but the estate of great persons promises fair, and often keeps not ; therefore they are a lie, although they can least endure that word.

They are, in respect of mean persons, as the flower to the grass; a somewhat fairer lustre they have, but no more endurance, nor exemption from decaying. Thus, then, it is a universal and undeniable truth : it begins here with διότι, and is as sure a conclusion as the surest of those in their best demonstrations, which they call διότι. And as particular men, so whole states and kingdoms, have thus their budding, flourishing, and withering, and it is in both as with flowers— when they are fullest spread, then they are near their declining and withering. And thus it is with all whole generations of men upon earth : as Solomon says, *One goeth, and another cometh,* Eccl. i. 4 ; but not a word of abiding at all. We, in our thoughts, shut up death into a very narrow compass, namely, into the moment of our expiring ; but the truth is, as the moralist observes, it goes through all our life : for we are still losing and spending life as we enjoy it, yea, our very enjoying of it is the spending of it. Yesterday's life is dead to-day, and so shall this day's life be to-morrow. *We spend our years,* says Moses, *as a tale,* (Psal. xc. 8,) or as a thought, so swift and vanishing is it. Every word helps a tale towards its end; while it lasts, it is generally vanity, and when it is done, it vanishes as a sound in the air. What is become of all the pompous solemnities of kings and princes at their births and marriages, coronations and triumphs? They are now as a dream ; as St. Luke (Acts xxv. 23) calls the pomp of Agrippa and Bernice, φαντασία, a mere phantasy.

Hence, learn the folly and pride of man, who can glory and please himself in the frail and wretched being he hath here, who dotes on this poor natural life, and cannot be persuaded to think on one higher and more abiding, although the course of time, and his daily experience, tell him this truth, that *all flesh is grass.* Yea, the Prophet prefixes to these words a command of crying ; they must be shouted aloud in our ears, ere we will hear them, and by that time the sound of the cry is done, we have forgotten it again. Would we consider this, in the midst of those vanities that toss our light minds to and fro, it would give us wiser thoughts, and ballast our hearts ; make them more solid and stedfast in those spiritual endeavours which concern a durable condition, a being that abides for ever ; in comparison of which, the longest term of natural life is less than a moment, and the happiest estate of it but a heap of miseries. Were all of us more constantly prosperous than any one of us is, yet that one thing were enough to cry down the price we put upon this life, that it continues not. As he answered to one who had a mind to flatter him in the midst of a pompous triumph, by saying, What is wanting here ? *Continuance,* said he. It was wisely said at any time, but wisest of all, to have so sober a thought in such a solemnity, in which weak heads cannot escape either to be wholly drunk, or somewhat giddy at least. Surely we forget this, when we grow vain upon any human glory or advantage.; the colour of it pleases us, and we forget that it is but a flower, and foolishly over-esteem it. This is like that madness upon flowers, which is some where prevalent, where they will give as much for one flower as would buy a good dwelling-house. Is it not a most foolish bargain, to bestow continual pains and diligence upon the purchasing of great possessions or honours, if we believe this, that the best of them is no other than a short-lived flower, and to neglect the purchase of those glorious mansions of eternity, a garland of such flowers as wither not, an unfading crown, that everlasting life, and those everlasting pleasures that are at the right hand of God?

Now, that life which shall never end must begin here; it is the new spiritual life, whereof the word of God is the immortal seed; and in opposition to corruptible seed and the corruptible life of flesh, it is here said to endure for ever. And for this end is the frailty of natural life mentioned, that our affections may be drawn off from it to this spiritual life, which is not subject unto death.

Ver. 25. But the word of the Lord endureth for ever. And this is the word which by the Gospel is preached unto you.

THE word of God is so like Himself, and carries so plainly the image and impression of his power and wisdom, that where they are spoken of together, it is sometimes doubtful whether the expressions are to be referred to Himself or to His word: (as Heb. iv. 12; and so here:) but there is no hazard in referring them either way, seeing there is truth in both, and pertinency too; for they who refer them to God, affirm that they are intended for the extolling of His word, being the subject in hand, and that we may know it to be like Him. But I rather think here that the Apostle speaks of the word; it is said to be quick or living ($\zeta \tilde{\omega} \nu$) in the forecited text, as well as in the passage before us; and the phrase, *abiding for ever*, is expressly repeated of it here, in the Prophet's words. And (with respect to those learned men that apply them to God) I remember not that this *abiding for ever* is used to express God's eternity in Himself. Howsoever, this incorruptible seed is the living and everlasting word of the living and everlasting God, and is therefore such, because He, whose it is, is such.

Now, this is not to be taken in an abstract sense of the word only in its nature, but as the principle of regeneration, the seed of this new life; because the word is enlivening and living, therefore they with whom it is effectual, and into whose hearts it is received, are begotten again and made alive by it; and because the word is incorruptible, and endureth for ever, therefore that life begotten by it is such too, cannot perish or be cut down, as the natural life; no, this spiritual life of grace is the certain beginning of that eternal life of glory, and shall issue in it, and therefore hath no end.

As the word of God in itself cannot be abolished, but surpasses the permanence of heaven and earth, as our Saviour teaches; and all the attempts of men against the Divine truth of that word to undo it are as vain as if they should consult to pluck the sun out of the firmament; so, likewise, in the heart of a Christian, it is immortal and incorruptible. Where it is once received by faith, it cannot be obliterated again: all the powers of darkness cannot destroy it, although they be never so diligent in their attempts that way. And this is the comfort of the Saints, that though the life, which God by His word hath breathed into their souls, have many and strong enemies, such as they themselves could never hold out against, yet for His own glory, and His promise sake, He will maintain that life, and bring it to its perfection; *God will perfect that which concerneth me,* saith the Psalmist,

Psal. cxxxviii. 8. It is grossly contrary to the truth of the Scriptures to imagine, that they who are thus renewed can be unborn again. This new birth is but once, of one kind : though they are subject to frailties and weaknesses here in this spiritual life, yet not to death any more, nor to such way of sinning as would extinguish this life. This is that which the Apostle John says, *He that is born of God sinneth not;* and the reason he adds, is the same that is here given, the permanence and incorruptibleness of this word, *The seed of God abideth in him.* John iii. 9.

This is the word which by the Gospel is preached unto you.] It is not sufficient to have these thoughts of the word of God in a general way, and not to know what that word is ; but we must be persuaded, that that word which is *preached to us* is this very word of so excellent virtue, and of which these high things are spoken ; that it is *incorruptible* and *abideth for ever,* and therefore surpasses all the world, and all the excellencies and glory of it. Although delivered by weak men— the Apostles, and by far weaker than they in the constant ministry of it, yet it loseth none of its own virtue ; for that depends upon the first Owner and Author of it, the ever-living GOD, who by it begets his chosen unto life eternal.

This, therefore, is that which we should learn thus to hear, and thus to receive, esteem, and love, this holy, this living word ; to despise all the glittering vanities of this perishing life, all outward pomp, yea, all inward worth, all wisdom and natural endowments of mind, in comparison of the heavenly light of the Gospel preached unto us : rather to hazard all than lose that, and banish all other things from the place that is due to it ; to lodge it alone in our hearts, as our only treasure here, and the certain pledge of that treasure of glory laid up for us in heaven. To which blessed state may God of his infinite mercy bring us ! *Amen.*

FIRST PETER
CHAPTER 2

Ver. 1. Wherefore laying aside all malice, and all guile, and hypocrisies, and envies, and all evil speakings,

2. As new-born babes, desire the sincere milk of the word, that ye may grow thereby.

THE same power and goodness of God that manifests itself in giving being to His creatures, appears likewise in sustaining and preserving them. To give being is the first, and to support it is the continued effect of that power and goodness. Thus it is both in the first creation, and in the second. In the first, the creatures to which He gave life, He provided with convenient nourishment to uphold that life (Gen. i. 11) : so here, in the close of the former chapter, we find the doctrine of the new birth and life of a Christian, and in the beginning of this, the proper food of that life. And it is the same word by which we there find it to be begotten, that is here the nourishment of it ; and therefore Christians are here exhorted by the Apostle so to esteem and so to use it ; and that is the main scope of the words.

Observe in general : The word, the principle, and the support of our spiritual being, is both the *incorruptible seed* and the *incorruptible food* of that new life of grace, which must therefore be an incorruptible life ; and this may convince us, that the ordinary thoughts, even of us who hear this word, are far below the true excellency and worth of it. The stream of custom and our profession bring us hither, and we sit out our hour under the sound of this word ; but how few consider and prize it as the great ordinance of God for the salvation of souls, the beginner and the sustainer of the Divine life of grace within us ! And certainly, until we have these thoughts of it, and seek to feel it thus ourselves, although we hear it most frequently, and let slip no occasion, yea, hear it with attention and some present delight, yet still we miss the right use of it, and turn it from its true end, while we take it not as *that ingrafted word which is able to save our souls.* James i. 21.

Thus ought they who preach to speak it ; to endeavour their utmost to accommodate it to this end, that sinners may be converted, begotten again, and believers nourished and strengthened in their spiritual life ; to regard no lower end, but aim steadily at that mark. Their hearts and tongues ought to be set on fire with holy zeal for God and love to souls, kindled by the Holy Ghost, that came down on the Apostles in the shape of fiery tongues.

And those that hear should remember this as the end of their hearing, that they may receive spiritual life and strength by the word. For though it seems a poor, despicable business, that a frail, sinful man like yourselves should speak a few words in your hearing, yet, look upon it as the way wherein God communicates happiness to those who believe, and works that believing unto happiness, alters the whole frame of the soul, and makes a new creation, as it begets it again to the inheritance of glory. Consider it thus, which is its true notion ; and then what can be so precious ? Let the world disesteem it as they will, know ye, that *it is the power of God unto salvation. The preaching of the cross is to them that perish foolishness; but unto them that are saved, it is the power of God,* says the Apostle, 1 Cor. i. 18. And if you would have the experience of this, if you would have life and growth by it, you must look above the poor worthless messenger, and call in His almighty help, who is the Lord of life. As the philosophers affirm, that if the heavens should stand still, there would be no generation or flourishing of any thing here below, so it is the moving and influence of the Spirit that makes the Church fruitful. Would you but do this before you come here, present the blindness of your minds and the deadness of your hearts to God, and say, " Lord, " here is an opportunity for Thee to show the power of thy word. I " would find life and strength in it ; but neither can I who hear, nor " he that speaks, make it thus unto me : that is thy prerogative ; say " Thou the word, and it shall be done." *God said, Let there be light, and it was light.*

In this exhortation to the due use of the word, the Apostle continues the resemblance of that new birth he mentioned in the preceding chapter.

As new-born babes.] Be not satisfied with yourselves, till you find some evidence of this new, this supernatural life. There be delights and comforts in this life, in its lowest condition, that would persuade us to look after it, if we knew them ; but as the most cannot be made sensible of these, consider therefore the end of it.   Better never to have been than not to have been partaker of this new being.   *Except a man be born again*, says our Saviour, *he cannot enter into the kingdom of God*, John iii. 3.   Surely they that are not born again, shall one day wish they had never been born.   What a poor wretched thing is the life that we have here ! a very heap of follies and miseries ! Now if we would share in a happier being after it, in that life which ends not, it must begin here.   Grace and glory are one and the same life, only with this difference, that the one is the beginning, and the other the perfection of it ; or, if we do call them two several lives, yet the one is the undoubted pledge of the other.   It was a strange word for a heathen to say, that that day of death we fear so, *æterni natalis est, is the birth-day of eternity*.   Thus it is indeed to those who are here born again : this new birth of grace is the sure earnest and pledge of that birth-day of glory.   Why do we not then labour to make this certain by the former ?   Is it not a fearful thing to spend our days in vanity, and then lie down in darkness and sorrow for ever ; to disregard the life of our soul, while we may and should be provident for it, and then, when it is going out, cry, *Quò nunc abibis ?* Whither art thou going, O my soul ?

But this new life puts us out of the danger and fear of that eternal death.   *We are passed from death to life*, says St. John, (1 John iii. 14,) speaking of those who are born again ; and being passed, there is no re-passing, no going back from this life to death again.

This new birth is the same that St. John calls the *first resurrection*, and he pronounces them blessed who partake of it : *Blessed are they that have part in the first resurrection; the second death shall have no power over them.* Rev. xx. 6.

The weak beginnings of grace, weak in comparison of the further strength attainable even in this life, are sometimes expressed as the infancy of it ; and so believers ought not to continue infants ; if they do, it is reprovable in them, as we see, Eph. iv. 14 ; 1 Cor. ii. 2 ; xiv. 20 ; Heb. v. 12.   Though the Apostle writes to new converts, and so may possibly imply the tenderness of their beginnings of grace, yet I conceive that infancy is here to be taken in such a sense as agrees to a Christian in the whole course and best estate of his spiritual life here below.   So, likewise, the *milk* here recommended is answerable to infancy, taken in this sense, and not in the former ; (as it is in some of those cited places, where it means the easiest and first principles of religion, and so is opposed to the higher mysteries of it, as to strong meat ;) but here it signifies the whole word of God, and all its wholesome and saving truths, as the proper nourishment of the children of God.   And so the Apostle's words are a standing exhortation for all Christians of all degrees.

And the whole estate and course of their spiritual life here is called their *infancy*, not only as opposed to the corruption and wickedness of the old man, but likewise as signifying the weakness and imperfection of it, at its best in this life, compared with the perfection of the life to come ; for the weakest beginnings of grace are by no means so far below the highest degree of it possible in this life, as that highest degree falls short of the state of glory; so that, if one measure of grace is called infancy in respect of another, much more is all grace infancy in respect of glory. And surely, as for duration, the time of our present life is far less compared to eternity, than the time of our natural infancy is to the rest of our life; so that we may be still called but *new or lately born.* Our best pace and strongest walking in obedience here, is but as the stepping of children when they begin to go by hold, in comparison of the perfect obedience in glory when *we shall follow the Lamb wheresoever he goes.* All our knowledge here is but as the ignorance of infants, and all our expressions of God and of his praises but as the first stammerings of children, in comparison of the knowledge we shall have of Him hereafter, when *we shall know as we are known,* and of the praises we shall then offer him, when that new song shall be taught us. A child hath in it a reasonable soul, and yet, by the indisposedness of the body, and abundance of moisture, it is so bound up, that its difference from the beasts in partaking of a rational life, is not so apparent as afterwards; and thus the spiritual life that is from above infused into a Christian, though it doth act and work in some degree, yet it is so clogged with the natural corruption still remaining in him, that the excellency of it is much clouded and obscured; but in the life to come, it shall have nothing at all encumbering and indisposing it. And this is the Apostle St. Paul's doctrine, 1 Cor. xiii. 9—12.

And this is the wonder of Divine grace, that brings so small beginnings to that height of perfection that we are not able to conceive of; that a little spark of true grace, which is not only indiscernible to others, but often to the Christian himself, should yet be the beginning of that condition wherein they shall shine brighter than the sun in the firmament. The difference is great in our natural life, in some persons especially; that they who in infancy were so feeble, and wrapped up as others in swaddling clothes, yet afterwards come to excel in wisdom and in the knowledge of sciences, or to be commanders of great armies, or to be kings: but the distance is far greater and more admirable betwixt the weakness of these *new-born babes,* the small beginnings of grace, and our after-perfection, that fulness of knowledge that we look for, and that crown of immortality which all they are born to who are born of God.

But as in the faces or actions of children, characters and presages of their after-greatness have appeared, (as a singular beauty in Moses's face, as they write of him, and as Cyrus was made king among the shepherds' children with whom he was brought up, &c.,) so also, certainly, in these children of God, there be some characters and evidences that they are born for heaven by their new birth. That holiness and meekness, that patience and faith, which shine in the actions and sufferings of the saints, are characters of their Father's image, and show their high original, and foretell their glory to come; such a glory as doth not only surpass the world's thoughts, but the thoughts of the children of God themselves. 1 John iii. 2.

Now that the children of God may grow by the word of God, the Apostle requires these two things of them: 1. The innocency of children; 2. The appetite of children. For this expression, as I conceive, is relative not only to the desiring of *the milk of the word*, ver. 2, but to the former verse, the *putting off malice*. So, the Apostle Paul exhorts, 1 Cor. xiv. 20, *As concerning malice, be ye children.*

Wherefore laying aside.] This imports that we are naturally prepossessed with these evils, and therefore we are exhorted to put them off. Our hearts are by nature no other than cages of those unclean birds, malice, envy, hypocrisy, &c. The Apostle sometimes names some of these evils, and sometimes others of them, but they are inseparable,—all one garment, and all comprehended under that one word, Eph. iv. 22, *the old man,* which the Apostle there exhorts Christians to put off: and here it is pressed as a necessary evidence of their new birth, as well as for the furtherance of their spiritual growth, that these base habits be thrown away; ragged, filthy habits, unbeseeming the children of God. They are the proper marks of an unrenewed mind, the very characters of the children of Satan, for they constitute his image. He hath his names from enmity, and envy, and slandering; and he is that grand hypocrite and deceiver, who can *transform himself into an angel of light,* 2 Cor. xi. 14.

So, on the contrary, the Spirit of God that dwells in his children is the spirit of meekness, and love, and truth. That dove-like Spirit which descended on our Saviour, is from him communicated to believers. It is the grossest impudence to pretend to be Christians, and yet to entertain hatred and envyings upon whatsoever occasion; for there is nothing more frequently recommended to them by our Saviour's own doctrine, nothing more impressed upon their hearts by his Spirit, than love. Κακία may be taken generally, but I conceive it intends that which we particularly call *malice.*

Malice and envy are but two branches growing out of the same bitter root; self-love and evil speakings are the fruit they bear. Malice is properly the procuring or wishing another's evil; envy, the repining at his good; and both these vent themselves by evil speaking. This infernal fire within smokes and flashes out by the tongue, which, St. James says, *is set on fire of hell,* (ch. iii. 6,) and fires all about it; censuring the actions of those they hate or envy, aggravating their failings, and detracting from their virtues, taking all things by the left ear; for (as Epictetus says) *every thing hath two handles.* The art of taking things by the better side, which charity always doth, would save much of those janglings and heart-burnings that so abound in the world. But folly and perverseness possess the hearts of the most, and therefore their discourses are usually the vent of these; *For out of the abundance of the heart the mouth must speak,* Matt. xii. 34. The unsavoury breaths of men argue their inward corruption. Where shall a man come, almost, in societies, but his ears shall be beaten with the unpleasant noise (surely it is so to a Christian mind) of one detracting and disparaging another? And yet this is extreme baseness, and the practice only of false, counterfeit goodness, to make up one's own reputation out of the ruins of the good name of others. Real virtue neither needs nor can endure this dishonest shift; it can subsist of itself, and therefore ingenuously commends and acknowledges what good exists in others, and loves to hear it acknowledged; and neither readily speaks nor hears evil of any, but rather, where duty and conscience require not discovery, casts a veil upon men's failings to hide them : this is the true temper of the children of God.

These evils of *malice*, and *envy*, and *evil speakings*, and such like, are not to be dissembled by us, in ourselves, and conveyed under better appearances, but to be cast away ; not to be covered, but put off ; and therefore that which is the upper garment and cloak of all other evils, the Apostle here commands us to cast that off too, namely, *hypocrisy*.

What avails it to wear this mask ? A man may indeed in the sight of men act his part handsomely under it, and pass so for a time ; but know we not that there is an Eye that sees through it, and a Hand that, if we will not put off this mask, will pull it off to our shame, either here in the sight of men, or, if we should escape all our life, and go fair off the stage under it, yet that there is a day appointed wherein all hypocrites shall be unveiled, and appear what they are indeed before men and angels ? It is a poor thing, to be approved and applauded by men, while God condemns, to whose sentence all men must stand or fall. Oh ! seek to be approved and justified by Him, and then, *who shall condemn ?* Rom. viii. 34. It is no matter who do. How easily may we bear the mistakes and dislikes of all the world, if He declare himself well pleased with us ! *It is a small thing for me to be judged of man, or man's day : he that judgeth me is the Lord*, saith the Apostle, 1 Cor. iv. 3.

But these evils are here particularly to be put off, as contrary to the right and profitable receiving of the word of God ; for this part of the exhortation *(Laying aside)* looks to that which follows, *(Desire,* &c.,) and is specially so to be considered.

There is this double task in religion : when a man enters upon it, he is not only to be taught true wisdom, but he is withal, yea, first of all, to be untaught the errors and wickedness that are deep-rooted in his mind, which he hath not only learned by the corrupt conversation of the world, but brought the seeds of them into the world with him. They do indeed improve and grow by the favour of that example that is round about a man, but they are originally in our nature as it is now ; they are connatural to us, besides being strengthened by continual custom, which is another nature. There is no one comes to the school of Christ suiting the philosopher's word, *ut tabula rasa*, as blank paper, to receive his doctrine ; but, on the contrary, all scribbled and blurred with such base habits as these, *malice, hypocrisy, envy*, &c.

Therefore, the first work is, to rase out these, to cleanse and purify the heart from these blots, these foul characters, that it may receive the impression of the image of God. And because it is the word of God that both begins and advances this work, and perfects the lineaments of that Divine image on the soul, therefore, to the receiving of this word aright, and to this proper effect by means of it, the conforming of the soul to Jesus Christ, which is the true growth of the spiritual life, this is pre-required, that the hearts of those who hear it be purged of these and such like impurities.

These dispositions are so opposite to the profitable receiving of the word of God, that while they possess and rule the soul, it cannot at all embrace these Divine truths ; while it is filled with such guests, there is no room to entertain the word.

They cannot dwell together, by reason of their contrary nature : the word will not mix with these. The saving mixture of the word of God in the soul is what the Apostle speaks of, and he assigns the want of it as the cause of unprofitable hearing of the word, Heb. iv. 2, *not mixing of it with faith.* For by that the word is concocted into the nourishment of the life of grace, united to the soul, and mixed with it, by being mixed with faith, as the Apostle's expression imports : that is the proper mixture it requires. But with the qualities here mentioned it will not mix ; there is a natural antipathy betwixt them, as strong as in those things in nature, that cannot be brought by any means to agree and mingle together.

Can there be any thing more contrary than the *good word of God,* as the Apostle calls it, and those *evil speakings?* than the word that is of such excellent sweetness and the bitter words of a malignant tongue ? than the word of life and words *full of deadly poison?* For so slanders and defamings of our brethren are termed. And is not all *malice* and *envy* most opposite to the word, that is the message of *peace* and *love?* How can the gall of *malice* and this *milk* of the word agree ? Hypocrisy and guile stand in direct opposition to the name of this word, which is called the *word of truth ;* and here the very words show this contrariety, *sincere milk,* and a *double, unsincere mind.*

These two are necessary conditions of good nourishment : 1*st*, That the food be good and wholesome ; 2*dly*, That the inward constitution of them who use it be so too. And if this fail, the other profits not. This sincere milk is the only proper nourishment of spiritual life, and there is no defect or undue quality in it ; but the greatest part of hearers are inwardly unwholesome, diseased with the evils here mentioned, and others of the like nature ; and therefore, either have no kind of appetite to the word at all, but rather feed upon such trash as suits with their distemper, (as some kind of diseases incline those that have them to eat coals or lime, &c.,) or, if they be any ways desirous to hear the word, and seem to feed on it, yet the noxious humours that abound in them, make it altogether unprofitable, and they are not nourished by it. This evil of malice and envying, so ordinary among men, (and, which is most strange, amongst Christians,) like an overflowing of the gall, possesses their whole minds ; so that they not only fail of being nourished by the word they hear, but are made the worse by it ; their disease is fed by it, as an unwholesome stomach turns the best meat it receives into that humour that abounds in it. Do not they thus, who observe what the word says, that they may be the better enabled to discover the failings of others, and speak maliciously and uncharitably of them, and vent themselves, as is too common ? *This word met well with such a one's fault, and this with another's :*—Is not this to feed these diseases of *malice, envy,* and *evil speakings,* with this *pure milk,* and make *them* grow, instead of growing by it ourselves in grace and holiness ?

Thus, likewise, the hypocrite turns all that he hears of this word, not to the inward renovation of his mind, and redressing what is amiss there, but only to the composing of his outward carriage, and to enable himself to act his part better : to be cunninger in his own faculty, a more refined and expert hypocrite ; not to grow more a

Christian indeed, but more such in appearance only, and in the opinion of others.

Therefore it is a very needful advertisement, seeing these evils are so natural to men, and so contrary to the nature of the word of God, that they be purged out, to the end it may be profitably received. A very like exhortation to this hath the Apostle St. James, and some of the same words, but in another metaphor : Jam. i. 21, *Wherefore lay apart all filthiness, and superfluity of naughtiness, and receive with meekness the ingrafted word.* He compares the word to a plant of excellent virtue, the very tree of life, the word that is able to save your souls ; but the only soil wherein it will grow is a heart full of meekness, a heart that is purged of those luxuriant weeds that grow so rank in it by nature ; they must be plucked up and thrown out to make place for this word.

And there is such a necessity for this, that the most approved teachers of wisdom, in a human way, have required of their scholars that, to the end their minds might be capable of it, they should be purified from vice and wickedness. For this reason, the philosopher judges young men unfit hearers of moral philosophy, because of the abounding and untamedness of their passions, granting that, if those were composed and ordered, they might be admitted. And it was Socrates' custom, when any one asked him a question, seeking to be informed by him, before he would answer them, he asked them concerning their own qualities and course of life.

Now, if men require a calm and purified disposition of mind to make it capable of *their* doctrine, how much more is it suitable and necessary for learning the doctrine of God, and those deep mysteries that His word opens up ! It is well expressed in that Apocryphal book of Wisdom, that *Froward thoughts separate from God, and wisdom enters not into a malicious soul :* no, indeed, that is a very unfit dwelling for it ; and even a heathen (Seneca) could say, *The mind that is impure is not capable of God and divine things.* Therefore we see the strain of that book of Proverbs that speaks so much of this wisdom ; it requires, in the first chapter, that they who would hear it do retire themselves from all ungodly customs and practices. And, indeed, how can the soul apprehend spiritual things, that is not in some measure refined from the love of sin, which abuses and bemires the minds of men, and makes them unable to arise to heavenly thoughts ? *Blessed are the pure in heart, for they shall see God,* says our Saviour (Matt. v. 8) : not only shall they see him perfectly hereafter, but so far as they can receive him, He will impart and make Himself known unto them here. *If any man love me, he will keep my words, and my Father will love him, and we will come unto him, and make our abode with him.* (John xiv. 23.) What makes the word obscure is the filthy mists within ; whereas, on the contrary, He will in just judgment hide himself, and the saving truth of His word, from those that entertain and delight in sin : the very sins wherein they delight shall obscure and darken the light of the Gospel to them, so that though it shine clear as the sun at noon-day, they shall be as those that live in a dungeon, they shall not discern it.

And as they receive no benefit by the word, who have the evils here mentioned reigning and in full strength within them, so they that are indeed born again, the more they retain of these, the less shall they find the influence and profit of the word ; for this exhortation concerns them. They may possibly some of them have a great remainder of these corruptions unmortified ; therefore are they exhorted to lay aside entirely those evils, *all malice, all hypocrisy*, &c., else, though they hear the word often, yet they will be in a spiritual atrophy ; they will eat much, but grow nothing by it ; they will find no increase of grace and spiritual strength.

Would we know the main cause of our fruitless hearing of the word, here it is : men bring not meek and guileless spirits to it, not minds emptied and purified to receive it, but stuffed with *malice*, and *hypocrisy*, and *pride*, and other such evils : and where should the word enter, when all is so taken up ? And if it did enter, how should it prosper amongst so many enemies, or at all abide amongst them ? Either they will turn it out again, or choke and kill the power of it. We think religion and our own lusts and secret heart-idols should agree together, because we would have it so ; but this is not possible. Therefore labour to entertain the word of truth in the love of it, and lodge the mystery of faith *in a pure conscience*, as the Apostle St. Paul speaks, 1 Tim. iii. 9. Join those together with David, (Psal. cxix. 113,) *I hate vain thoughts, but thy law do I love.* And as here our Apostle, *Lay aside all malice, and hypocrisy, and envy, and evil speakings*, and so receive the word, or else look for no benefit by it here, nor for salvation by it hereafter ; but be prevailed upon to cast out all impurity, and give your whole heart to it ; so desire it, that *you may grow*, and then, as you desire, *you shall grow by it.*

Every real believer hath received a life from Heaven, far more excelling our natural life than that excels the life of the beasts. And this life hath its own peculiar desires and delights, which are the proper actings, and the certain characters and evidence of it : amongst others this is one, and a main one, answerable to the like desire in natural life, namely, a desire of food ; and because it is here still imperfect, therefore the natural end of this is not only nourishment, but growth, as it is here expressed.

The sincere milk of the word.] The life of grace is the proper life of a reasonable soul, and without it, the soul is dead, as the body is without the soul ; so that this may be truly rendered, *reasonable milk*, as some read it ; but certainly, that reasonable milk is the word of God, *The milk of the word.*

It was before called *the immortal seed*, and here it is *the milk* of those that are born again, and thus it is nourishment very agreeable to that spiritual life, according to their saying, *Iisdem alimur ex quibus constamus*, We are nourished by that of which we consist. As the milk that infants draw from the breast, is the most connatural food to them, being of that same substance that nourished them in the womb ; so, when they are brought forth, that food follows them as it were for their supply, in the way that is provided in nature for it ; by certain veins it ascends into the breasts, and is there fitted for them, and they are by nature directed to find it there. Thus, as a Christian begins to live by the power of the word, so he is by the nature of that spiritual life directed to that same word as its nourishment. To follow the resemblance further in the qualities of milk, after the monkish way, that runs itself out of breath in allegory, I conceive is neither solid nor profitable ; and to speak freely, the curious searching of the similitude in other qualities of milk seems to wrong the quality here given it by the Apostle, in which it is so well resembled by milk, namely, the simple pureness and sincerity of the word ; besides that the pressing of comparisons of this kind too far, proves often so constrained ere they have done with it, that by too much drawing, they bring forth blood instead of milk.

Pure and unmixed, as milk drawn immediately from the breast ; the pure word of God without the mixture, not only of error, but of all other composition of vain, unprofitable subtleties, or affected human eloquence, such as become not the majesty and gravity of God's word. *If any man speak,* says our Apostle, (ch. iv. ver. 11,) *let him speak as the oracles of God.* Light conceits and flowers of rhetoric wrong the word more than they can please the hearers ; the weeds among the corn make it look gay, but it were all the better they were not amongst it. Nor can those mixtures be pleasing to any but carnal minds. They who are indeed the children of God, as infants who like their breast-milk best pure, do love the word best so, and wheresoever they find it so, they relish it well ; whereas natural men cannot love spiritual things for themselves, desire not the word for its own sweetness, but would have it sauced with such conceits as possibly spoil the simplicity of it ; or at the best, love to hear it for the wit and learning which, without any wrongful mixture of it, they find in one person's delivering it more than another's. But the natural and genuine appetite of the children of God is to the word for itself, and only as milk, *sincere milk :* and where they find it so, from whomsoever or in what way soever delivered unto them, they feed upon it with delight. Before conversion, wit or eloquence may draw a man to the word, and possibly prove a happy bait to catch him (as St. Augustine reports of his hearing St. Ambrose) ; but when once he is born again, then it is the milk itself that he desires for itself.

Desire the sincere milk.] Not only hear it because it is your custom, but desire it because it is your food. And it is, 1. A *natural* desire, as the infant's desire of milk ; not upon any external respect or inducement, but from an inward principle and bent of nature. And because natural, therefore, 2. *Earnest;* not a cold, indifferent willing, that cares not whether it obtain or not, but a vehement desire, as the word signifies, and as the resemblance clearly bears ; as a child that will not be stilled till it have the breast ; offer it what you will, silver, gold, or jewels, it regards them not, these answer not its desire, and that must be answered. Thus David, (Psal. cxix. 20,) *My soul breaketh for the longing it hath to thy judgments ;* as a child like to break its heart with crying for want of the breast. And again, because natural, it is, 3. *Constant.* The infant is not cloyed nor wearied with daily feeding on the breast, but desires it every day, as if it had never had it before : so the child of God hath an unchangeable appetite for the word : it is daily new to him ; he finds still fresh delight in it. Thus David, as before cited, *My soul breaketh for the longing it hath for thy judgments at all times.* And then, Psal. i., this law was his *meditation day and night.* Whereas, a natural man is easily surfeited of it, and the very commonness and cheapness of it makes it contemptible to him. And this is our case; that wherein we should wonder at God's singular goodness to us, and therefore prize his word the more, that very thing makes us despise it : while others, our brethren, have bought this milk with their own blood, we have it upon the easiest terms that can be wished, only for the desiring, without the hazard of bleeding for it, and scarcely need we be at the pains of sweating for it.

That ye may grow thereby.] This is not only the end for which God hath provided His children with the word, and moves them to desire it, but that which they are to intend in their desire and use of it ; and, answerable to God's purpose, they are therefore to desire it, because it is proper for this end, and that by it they may attain this end, *to grow thereby.* And herein, indeed, these children differ from infants in the natural life, who are directed to their food beside their knowledge, and without intention of its end ; but this *rational milk* is to be desired by the children of God in a rational way, knowing and intending its end, having the use of natural reason renewed and sanctified by supernatural grace.

Now the end of this desire is, growth. Desire the word, not that you may only hear it ; that is to fall very far short of its true end ; yea, it is to take the beginning of the work for the end of it. The ear is indeed the mouth of the mind, by which it receives the word, (as Elihu compares it, Job xxxiv. 2,) but meat that goes no farther than the mouth, you know cannot nourish. Neither ought this desire of the word to be, only to satisfy a custom ; it were an exceeding folly to make so superficial a thing the end of so serious a work. Again, to hear it only to stop the mouth of conscience, that it may not clamour more for the gross impiety of contemning it, this is to hear it, not out of desire, but out of fear. To desire it only for some present pleasure and delight that a man may find in it, is not the due use and end of it : that there is delight in it, may help to commend it to those that find it so, and so be a mean to advance the end ; but the end it is not. To seek no more than a present delight, that evanisheth with the sound of the words that die in the air, is not to desire the word as meat, but as music, as God tells the prophet Ezekiel of his people, Ezek. xxxiii. 32 : *And lo, thou art unto them as a very lovely song of one that hath a pleasant voice, and can play well upon an instrument; for they hear thy words, and they do them not.* To desire the word for the increase of knowledge, although this is necessary and commendable, and, being rightly qualified, is a part of spiritual accretion, yet, taking it as going no further, it is not the true end of the word. Nor is the vesting of that knowledge in speech and frequent discourse of the word and the Divine truths that are in it ; which, where it is governed with Christian prudence, is not to be despised, but commended ; yet, certainly, the highest knowledge, and the most frequent and skilful speaking of the word, severed from the growth here mentioned, misses the true end of the word. If any one's head or tongue should grow apace, and all the rest stand at a stay, it would certainly make him a monster ; and they are no other, who are knowing and discoursing Christians, and grow daily in that respect, but not at all in holiness of heart and life, which is the proper growth of the children of God. Apposite to their case is Epictetus's comparison of the sheep ; they re-

turn not what they eat in grass, but in wool. David, in that cxixth
Psalm, which is wholly spent upon this subject, the excellency and use
of the word of God, expresseth, ver. 15, 16, 24, his delight in it, his
earnest desire to be further taught, and to know more of it ; his readiness to speak of it, ver. 13, 27 ; but withal, you know he joins his desire and care *to keep it, to hide it in his heart,* &c., ver. 5, 11 ; to make
it *the man of his counsel,* to let it be as the whole assembly of his privy
counsellors, and to be ruled and guided by it ; and, with him, to use it
so, is indeed to grow by it.

If we know what this spiritual life is, and wherein the nature of it
consists, we may easily know what is the growth of it. When holiness
increases, when the sanctifying graces of the Spirit grow stronger in
the soul, and consequently act more strongly in the life of a Christian,
then he grows spiritually.

And as the word is the mean of begetting this spiritual life, so likewise of its increase.

1. This will appear, if we consider the nature of the word in general,
that it is spiritual and Divine, treats of the highest things, and therefore hath in it a fitness to elevate men's minds from the earth, and
to assimilate to itself such as are often conversant with it ; as all kind
of doctrine readily doth to those who are much in it, and apply their
minds to study it. Doubtless, such kind of things as are frequent with
men, have an influence into the disposition of their souls. The Gospel
is called *light,* and the children of God are likewise called *light,* as being
transformed into its nature ; and thus they become still the more, by
more hearing of it, and so they grow.

2. If we look more particularly unto the strain and tenor of the
word, it will appear most fit for increasing the graces of the Spirit
in a Christian ; for there be in it particular truths relative to them,
that are apt to excite them, and set them on work, and so to make
them grow, as all habits do, by acting. It doth (as the Apostle's
word may be translated) *stir up the sparks,* and blow them into a
greater flame, make them burn clearer and hotter. This it doth both
by particular exhortation to the study and exercise of those graces,
sometimes pressing one, and sometimes another ; and by right representing to them their objects. The word feeds *faith,* by setting before
it the free grace of God, His rich promises, and His power and truth
to perform them all ; shows it the strength of the new covenant, not
depending upon itself, but holding in Christ, in whom all the promises
of God are *yea* and *amen;* and drawing faith still to rest more entirely
upon his righteousness. It feeds *repentance,* by making the vileness
and deformity of sin daily more clear and visible. Still as more of the
word hath admission into the soul, the more it hates sin, sin being the
more discovered and the better known in its own native colour : as the
more light there is in a house, the more any thing that is uncleanly or
deformed is seen and disliked. Likewise it increaseth *love to God,* by
opening up still more and more of His infinite excellency and loveliness. As it borrows the resemblance of the vilest things in nature, to
express the foulness and hatefulness of sin, so all the beauties and dignities that are in all the creatures are called together in the word, to
give us some small scantling of that Uncreated Beauty that alone

deserves to be loved. Thus might its fitness be instanced in respect to all other graces.

But above all other considerations, this is observable in the word as the increaser of grace, that it holds forth Jesus Christ to our view to look upon, not only as the perfect pattern, but as the full fountain of all grace, from *whose fulness we all receive*. The contemplating of Him as the perfect image of God, and then drawing from Him as having in himself a treasure for us, these give the soul more of that image in which consists truly spiritual growth. This the Apostle expresseth excellently, 2 Cor. iii. *ult.*, speaking of the ministry of the Gospel revealing Christ, that *beholding in him* (as it is, ch. iv. ver. 6, *in his face) the glory of the Lord, we are changed into the same image from glory to glory, as by the Spirit of the Lord :* not only that we may take the copy of his graces, but have a share of them.

There may be many things that might be said of this spiritual growth, but I will add only a few.

First, on the one hand, in the judging of this growth, some persons conclude too rigidly against themselves, that they grow not by the word, because their growth is not so sensible to them as they desire. But, 1. It is well known, that in all things that grow, this principle is not discerned *in motu, sed in termino*, not in the growing, but when they are grown. 2. Besides, other things are to be considered in this : although other graces seem not to advance, yet if thou growest more self-denying and humble in the sense of thy slowness, all is not lost ; although the branches shoot not up so fast as thou wishest, yet, if the root grow deeper, and fasten more, it is a useful growth. He that is still learning to be more in Jesus Christ, and less in himself, to have all his dependence and comfort in Him, is doubtless a growing believer.

On the other side, a far greater number conclude wrong in their own favour, imagining that they do grow, if they gain ground in some of those things we mentioned above ; namely, more knowledge and more faculty of discoursing, if they find often some present stirrings of joy or sorrow in hearing of the word, if they reform their life, grow more civil and blameless, &c. ; yet all these, and many such things, may be in a natural man, who notwithstanding grows not, for that is impossible ; he is not, in that state, a subject capable of this growth, for he is dead, he hath none of the new life to which this growth relates. *Herod heard gladly, and obeyed many things*, Mark vi. 20.

Consider, then, what true delight we might have in this. You find a pleasure when you see your children grow, when they begin to stand and walk, and so forth ; you love well to perceive your estate or your honour grow : but for the soul to be growing liker God, and nearer heaven, if we know it, is a pleasure far beyond them all : to find pride, earthliness, and vanity abating, and faith, love, and spiritual-mindedness increasing ; especially if we reflect that this growth is not as our natural life, which is often cut off before it has attained full age, as we call it, and, if it attain that, falls again to move downwards, and decays, as the sun, being at its meridian, begins to decline again ; but this life shall grow on in whomsoever it is, and come certainly to its fulness ; after which, there is no more need of this word, either for growth or nourishment, no death, no decay, no old age, but perpetual youth, and a perpetual spring, *ver æternum ; fulness of joy in the presence of God, and everlasting pleasures at His right hand.*

Ver. 3. If so be ye have tasted that the Lord is gracious.

OUR natural desire of food arises principally from its necessity for that end which nature seeks, *viz.,* the growth, or at least the nourishment of our bodies.   But there is besides, a present sweetness and pleasantness in the use of it, that serves to sharpen our desire, and is placed in our nature for that purpose.   Thus the children of God, in their spiritual life, are naturally carried to desire the means of their nourishment and of their growth, being always here in a growing state ; but withal there is a spiritual delight and sweetness in the word, in that which it reveals concerning God, and this adds to their desire, stirs up their appetite towards it.   The former idea is expressed in the foregoing verse, the latter in this.   Nature disposes the infant to the breast ; but when it hath once tasted of it, that is a new superadded attractive, and makes it desire after it the more earnestly.   So here,

The word is fully recommended to us by these two, usefulness and pleasantness : like milk, (as it is compared here,) which is a nourishing food, and withal sweet and delightful to the taste : *by* it we grow, and *in* it we taste the graciousness of God.   David, in that psalm which he dedicates wholly to this subject, gives both these as the reason of his appetite.   His love to it he expresses pathetically, (cxix. 97,) *O how love I thy law !*   It follows, that by it he was *made wiser than his enemies,—than his teachers,—*and *than the ancients ;* taught to refrain *from every evil way,* ver. 101 ; taught by the Author of that word, the Lord himself, to grow wiser, and warier, and holier in the divine ways ; and then, ver. 103, he adds this other reason, *How sweet are thy words unto my taste ! yea, sweeter than honey to my mouth !*

We shall speak, I. Of the goodness or graciousness of the Lord ; II. Of this taste ; and, III. Of the inference from both.

I. The goodness of God : *The Lord is gracious ;* or, of a bountiful, kind disposition.   The Hebrew word in Psal. xxxiv. 8, whence this is taken, signifies *good.*   The Septuagint render it by the same word as is used here by our Apostle.   Both the words signify a benignity and kindness of nature.   It is given as one of love's attributes, 1 Cor. xiii. 4, that it is *kind,* χρηστεύεται, ever compassionate, and helpful as it can be in straits and distresses, still ready to forget and pass by evil, and to do good.   In the largest and most comprehensive sense must we take the expression here, and yet still we shall speak and think infinitely below what His goodness is.   He is naturally good, yea, goodness is His nature ; He is goodness and love itself.   *He that loveth not, knoweth not God ; for God is love,* 1 John iv. 8.   He is primitively good ; all goodness is derived from Him, and all that is in the creature comes forth from no other than that ocean ; and his graciousness is still larger than them all.

There is a common bounty of God, wherein he doth good to all, and so *the whole earth is full of his goodness,* Psal. xxxiii. 5.   But the goodness that the Gospel is full of,—the particular stream that runs in that channel, is his peculiar graciousness and love to his own children, that by which they are first enlivened, and then refreshed and sustained in their spiritual being. It is this that is here spoken of. He is gracious to them in freely forgiving their sins, in giving no less than Himself unto them ; He frees them from all evils, and fills them with all good. He *satisfies thy mouth with good things,* Psal. ciii. 3—5 : and so it follows with good reason, ver. 8, that he is *merciful and gracious ;* and his graciousness is there further expressed in his gentleness and *slowness to anger,* His bearing with the frailties of His own, and pitying them *as a father pitieth his children,* ver. 13.

No friend is so kind and friendly, (as this word signifies,) and none so powerful. He is *a present help in trouble,* ready to be found : whereas others may be far off, He is always at hand, and his presence is always comfortable.

They that know God, still find Him a real, useful good. Some things and some persons are useful at one time, and others at another, but God at all times. A well-furnished table may please a man while he hath health and appetite, but offer it to him in the height of a fever, how unpleasant would it be then ! Though never so richly decked, it is then not only useless, but hateful to him : but the kindness and love of God is then as seasonable and refreshing to him, as in health, and possibly more ; he can find sweetness in that, even on his sick bed. The choler abounding in the mouth, in a fever, doth not disrelish this sweetness ; it transcends and goes above it. Thus all earthly enjoyments have but some time (as meats) when they are in season, but the graciousness of God is always sweet ; the taste of that is never out of season. See how old age spoils the relish of outward delights, in the example of Barzillai, 2 Sam. xix. 35 ; but it makes not this distasteful. Therefore the Psalmist prays, that when other comforts forsake him and wear out, when they ebb from him and leave him on the sand, this may not ; that still he may feed on the goodness of God : Psal. lxxi. 9, *Cast me not off in old age, forsake me not when my strength faileth.* It is the continual influence of His graciousness that makes them still grow like *cedars in Lebanon,* Psal. xcii. 14, 15, that makes them *bring forth fruit in old age, and to be still fat and flourishing; to show that the Lord is upright,* as it is there added, that he is (as the word imports) *still like Himself,* and his goodness ever the same.

Full chests or large possessions may seem sweet to a man, till death present itself ; but then (as the Prophet speaks of *throwing away their idols of silver and gold to the bats and moles, in the day of calamity,* Isa. ii. 20)—then, he is forced to throw away all he possesses, with disdain of it and of his former folly in doting on it ; then, the kindness of friends, and wife, and children, can do nothing but increase his grief and their own ; but then is the love of God the good indeed and abiding sweetness, and it best relisheth when all other things are most unsavoury and uncomfortable.

God is gracious, but it is God in Christ ; otherwise we cannot find Him so ; therefore this is here spoken in particular of Jesus Christ, (as it appears by that which followeth,) through whom all the peculiar kindness and love of God is conveyed to the soul, for it can come no other way ; and the word here mentioned is the Gospel, (see ch. i.

ver. *ult.,)* whereof Christ is the subject. Though God is mercy and goodness in Himself, yet we cannot find or apprehend him so to us, but as we are looking through that *medium,* the Mediator. That main point of the goodness of God in the Gospel, which is so sweet to a humbled sinner, the forgiveness of sins, we know we cannot taste of, but in Christ, *In whom we have redemption,* Eph. i. 7. And all the favour that shines on us, all the grace we receive, is *of his fulness;* all our acceptance with God, our being taken into grace and kindness again, is in him. *He made us accepted in the Beloved,* ver. 6. His grace appears in both, as it is there expressed, but it is all in Christ. Let us therefore never leave him out in our desires of tasting the graciousness and love of God ; for otherwise, we shall but dishonour him, and disappoint ourselves.

The free grace of God was given to be tasted, in the promises, before the coming of Christ in the flesh ; but being accomplished in his coming, then was the sweetness of grace made more sensible ; then was it more fully broached, and let out to the elect world, when he was pierced on the cross, and his blood poured out for our redemption. *Through those holes of his wounds may we draw, and taste that the Lord is gracious,* says St. Augustine.

II. As to this taste : *Ye have tasted.*] There is a tasting exercised by temporary believers, spoken of Heb. vi. 4. Their highest sense of spiritual things, (and it will be in some far higher than we easily think,) yet is but a taste, and is called so in comparison of the truer, fuller sense that true believers have of the grace and goodness of God, which, compared with a temporary taste, is more than tasting. The former is merely tasting ; rather an imaginary taste than real ; but this is a true feeding on the graciousness of God, yet it is called but a taste in respect of the fulness to come. Though it is more than a taste, as distinguishable from the hypocrite's sense, yet it is no more than a taste, compared with the great marriage-feast we look for.

Jesus Christ being *all in all* unto the soul, faith apprehending him, is all the spiritual sense. Faith is the eye that beholds his matchless beauty, and so kindles love in the soul, and can speak of him as having seen him and taken particular notice of him, Cant. v. 9. It is the ear that discerns his voice, Cant. ii. 8. It is faith that smells *his name poured forth as ointment;* faith that touches him, and draws virtue from him ; and faith that tastes him, Cant. ii. 3 : and so here, *If ye have tasted.*

In order to this, there must be, 1. A firm believing of the truth of the promises, wherein the free grace of God is expressed and exhibited to us. 2. A particular application or attraction of that grace to ourselves, which is the drawing of those *breasts of consolation,* Isa. lxvi. 11, namely, the promises contained in the Old and New Testaments. 3. A sense of the sweetness of that grace, being applied or drawn into the soul, and that constitutes properly this taste. No unrenewed man hath any of these in truth, not the highest kind of temporary believer ; he cannot have so much as a real lively assent to the general truth of the promises ; for had he that, the rest would follow. But as he cannot have the least of these in truth, he may have the counterfeit of them all ; not only of assent but of application : yea, and a false spiritual joy arising from it ; and all these so drawn to the life, that they may resemble much of the reality : to give clear characters of difference is not so easy as most persons imagine ; but doubtless, the true living faith of a Christian hath in itself such a particular stamp, as brings with it its own evidence, when the soul is clear and the light of God's face shines upon it.   Indeed, in the dark we cannot read, nor distinguish one mark from another ; but when a Christian hath light to look upon the work of God in his own soul, although he cannot make another sensible of that by which he knows it, yet he himself is ascertained, and can say confidently in himself, " This I know, that this faith and taste of God I have is true ; the seal of the Spirit of God is upon it ;" and this is the reading of that *new name in the white stone, which no man knows but he that hath it,* Rev. ii. 17.   There is, in a true believer, such a constant love to God for Himself, and such a continual desire after Him simply for His own excellency and goodness, as no other can have.   On the other side, would a hypocrite deal truly and impartially by himself, he would readily find out something that would discover him, more or less, to himself.   But the truth is, men are willing to deceive themselves, and thence arises the difficulty.

One man cannot make another sensible of the sweetness of Divine grace : he may speak to him of it very excellently, but all he says in that kind, is an unknown language to a natural man ; he heareth many good words, but he cannot tell what they mean.   *The natural man tastes not the things of God, for they are spiritually discerned.*   1 Cor. ii. 14.

A spiritual man himself doth not fully conceive this sweetness that he tastes of ; it is an infinite goodness, and he hath but a taste of it.   The *peace of God,* which is a main fruit of this His goodness, *passeth all understanding,* says the Apostle, Phil. iv. 7 : not only all natural understanding, (as some modify it,) but all understanding, even the supernatural understanding of those who enjoy it.   And as the godly man cannot conceive it all, so, as to that which he conceives, he cannot express it all, and that which he doth express, the carnal mind cannot conceive of by his expression.

But he that hath indeed tasted of this goodness, oh how tasteless are those things to him that the world call sweet !   As when you have tasted somewhat that is very sweet, it disrelishes other things after it.   Therefore can a Christian so easily either want, or use with disregard the delights of this earth.   His heart is not upon them : for the delight that he finds in God carrieth it unspeakably away from all the rest, and makes them in comparison seem sapless to his taste.

Solomon tasted of all the delicacies, the choicest dishes that are in such esteem amongst men, and not only tasted, but ate largely of them, and yet, see how he goes over them, to let us know what they are, and passes from one dish to another.   *This also is vanity,* and of the next, *This also is vanity,* and so through all, and of all in general, *All is vanity and vexation of spirit,* or *feeding on the wind,* as the word may be rendered.

III. We come in the third place to the *inference: If ye have tasted,* &c., then, *lay aside all malice, and guile, and hypocrisies, and envies, and all evil speakings,* ver. 1 ; for it looks back to the whole exhortation.   Surely, if you have tasted of that kindness and sweetness of

God in Christ, it will compose your spirits, and conform them to Him ; it will diffuse such a sweetness through your soul, that there will be no place for *malice and guile;* there will be nothing but love, and meekness, and singleness of heart. Therefore, they who have bitter, malicious spirits, evidence they have not tasted of the love of God. As the Lord is good, so they who taste of His goodness are made like Him. *Be ye kind one to another, tender-hearted, forgiving one another, even as God, for Christ's sake, hath forgiven you.* Eph. iv. 32.

Again, if ye have tasted, then desire more. And this will be the truest sign of it : he that is in a continual hunger and thirst after this graciousness of God, has surely tasted of it. *My soul thirsteth for God,* saith David, Psal. xlii. 2. He had tasted before ; he remembers, ver. 4, that he *went to the house of God, with the voice of joy.*

This is that happy circle wherein the soul of the believer moves : the more they love it, the more they shall taste of this goodness ; and the more they taste, the more they shall still love and desire it.

But observe, *if ye have tasted that the Lord is gracious,* then, *desire the milk of the word.* This is the sweetness of the *word,* that it hath in it the Lord's graciousness, gives us the knowledge of his love. This they find in it, who have spiritual life and senses, and those senses exercised to discern good and evil ; and this engages a Christian to further desire of the word. They are fantastical, deluding tastes, that draw men from the written word, and make them expect other revelations. This graciousness is first conveyed to us by the *word;* there first we taste it, and therefore, there still we are to seek it ; to hang upon those breasts that cannot be drawn dry ; there the love of God in Christ streams forth in the several promises. The heart that cleaves to the word of God, and delights in it, cannot but find in it, daily, new tastes of His goodness ; there it reads His love, and by that stirs up its own to Him, and so grows and loves, every day more than the former, and thus is tending from tastes to fulness. It is but little we can receive here, some drops of joy that enter into us ; but there we shall enter into joy, as vessels put into a sea of happiness.

Ver. 4. To whom coming, as unto a living stone, disallowed indeed of men, but chosen of God, and precious,
5. Ye also, as lively stones, are built up a spiritual house, an holy priesthood, to offer up spiritual sacrifices, acceptable to God by Jesus Christ.

THE spring of all the dignities of a Christian, which is therefore the great motive of all his duties, is, his near relation to Jesus Christ. Thence it is, that the Apostle makes that the great subject of his doctrine, both to represent to his distressed brethren their dignity in that respect, and to press by it the necessary duties he exhorts unto. Having spoken of their spiritual life and growth in him, under the resemblance of natural life, he prosecutes it here by another comparison very frequent in the Scriptures, and therefore makes use in it of some passages of these Scriptures, that were prophetical of Christ and his Church. Though there be here two different similitudes, yet they have so near a relation one to another, and meet so well in the same subject, that he joins them together, and then illustrates them severally in the following verses ; a *temple*, and a *priesthood*, comparing the saints to both : the former in these words of this verse.

We have in it, 1. The nature of the building : 2. The materials of it : 3. The structure or way of building it.

1. The *nature* of it is, *a spiritual building.* Time and place, we know, received their being from God, and He was eternally before both ; He is therefore styled by the prophet, *The high and lofty One that inhabiteth eternity*, Isaiah lvii. 15. But having made the world, He fills it, though not as contained in it, and so, the whole frame of it is His palace or temple, but after a more special manner, the higher and statelier part of it, the highest heaven ; therefore it is called His *holy place*, and *the habitation of His holiness and glory.* And on earth, the houses of His public worship are called *His houses;* especially the Jewish temple in its time, having in it such a relative typical holiness, which others have not. But besides all these, and beyond them all in excellency, He hath a house wherein he dwells more peculiarly than in any of the rest, even more than in Heaven, taken for the place only, and that is this *spiritual building.* And this is most suitable to the nature of God. As our Saviour says of the necessary conformity of his worship to Himself, *God is a Spirit, and therefore will be worshipped in spirit and in truth,* John iv. 24 : so, it holds of his house ; he must have a spiritual one, because He is a Spirit ; so God's temple is, His people.

And for this purpose chiefly did He make the world, the heaven and the earth, that in it He might raise this spiritual building for Himself to dwell in for ever, to have a number of His reasonable creatures to enjoy Him, and glorify Him in eternity. And from that eternity He knew what the dimensions, and frame, and materials of it should be. The continuance of this present world, as now it is, is but for the service of this work, like the scaffolding about it ; and therefore, when this spiritual building shall be fully completed, all the present frame of things in the world, and in the Church itself, shall be taken away, and appear no more.

This building is, as the particular designation of its materials will teach us, *the whole invisible Church of God*, and each good man is a stone of this building. But as the nature of it is spiritual, it hath this privilege, (as they speak of the soul,) that it is *tota in toto, et tota in qualibet parte:* the whole Church is the spouse of Christ, and each believing soul hath the same title and dignity to be called so : thus each of these stones is called a whole temple, *temples of the Holy Ghost,* 1 Cor. vi. 19 ; though, taking the Temple or Building in a completer sense, they are but each one a part, or a stone of it, as here it is expressed.

The whole excellency of this building is comprised in this, that it is *spiritual*, a term distinguishing it from all other buildings, and preferring it above them. And inasmuch as the Apostle speaks immediately after of a priesthood and sacrifices, it seems to be called a *spiritual building*, particularly in opposition to that material temple wherein the Jews gloried, which was now null, in regard of its former use, and was quickly after entirely destroyed. But while it stood, and the legal use of it stood in its fullest vigour, yet, in this respect, still it was inferior, that it was not a *spiritual house* made up of *living stones*, as this, but of a like matter with other earthly buildings.

This spiritual house is the palace of the Great King, or his temple. The Hebrew word for *palace* and *temple* is one. God's temple is a palace, and therefore must be full of the richest beauty and magnificence, but such as agrees with the nature of it, a spiritual beauty. In that Psalm that wishes so many prosperities, one is, that *their daughters may be as corner-stones, polished after the similitude of a palace*, Psal. cxliv. 12. Thus is the Church : she is called the *King's daughter*, Psal. xlv. 13 ; but her comeliness is invisible to the world, *she is all glorious within.* Through sorrows and persecutions, she may be smoky and black to the world's eye, as the *tents of Kedar ;* but in regard of spiritual beauty, she *is comely as the curtains of Solomon.* And in this the Jewish temple resembles it aright, which had most of its riches and beauty in the inside. Holiness is the gold of this spiritual house, and it is inwardly enriched with that.

The glory of the Church of God consists not in stately buildings of temples, and rich furniture, and pompous ceremonies ; these agree not with its spiritual nature. Its true and genuine beauty is, to grow in spirituality, and so to be liker itself, and to have more of the presence of God, and His glory filling it as a cloud. And it hath been observed, that the more the Church grew in outward riches and state, the less she grew, or rather the more sensibly she abated in spiritual excellencies. But the spiritualness of this Building will better appear in considering particularly,

2dly, The *materials* of it, as here expressed : *To whom coming,* &c., *ye also, as lively stones, are,* &c. Now the whole building is Christ mystical, Christ together with the entire body of the elect : He as the foundation, and they as the stones built upon him ; He, the living stone, and they likewise, by union with him, living stones ; He, *having life in himself,* as he speaks, John vi., and they deriving it from him ; He, primitively living, and they, by participation. For therefore is he called here a *living stone,* not only because of his immortality and glorious resurrection, being *a Lamb that was slain, and is alive again for ever,* but because he is the principle of spiritual and eternal life unto us, a living foundation that transfuses this life into the whole building, and every stone of it, *In whom* (says the Apostle, Eph. ii. 21) *all the building is fitly framed together.* It is the Spirit that flows from Him, which enlivens it, and knits it together, as a living body ; for the same word, συναρμολογούμενον, is used, ch. iv. 16, for the Church under the similitude of a body. When it is said, ch. ii. 20, *to be built upon the foundation of the Prophets and Apostles,* it only refers to their doctrine concerning Christ ; and therefore it is added, that He, as being the subject of their doctrine, is the *chief Corner-stone.* The foundation, then, of the Church, lies not in *Rome*, but in Heaven, and therefore is out of the reach of all enemies, and above the power of *the gates of hell.* Fear not, then, when you see the storms arise, and the winds blow against this spiritual Building, for *it shall stand ; it is built upon an* invisible, immovable *Rock ;* and that great *Babylon,* Rome itself, that, under the false title and pretence of supporting this

Building is working to overthrow it, shall be utterly overthrown, and laid equal with the ground, and never be rebuilt again.

But this *Foundation-stone*, as it is commended by its quality, that it is a *living* and enlivening stone, having life and giving life to those that are built on it, so it is also further described by God's choosing it, and by its own worth ; in both opposed to men's disesteem, and therefore it is said here to be *chosen of God and precious*. God did indeed from eternity contrive this Building, and choose this same foundation, and accordingly, in the fulness of time, did perform His purpose ; so the thing being one, we may take it either for His purpose, or the performance of it, or both ; yet it seems most suitable to the strain of the words, and to the place after alleged, in respect to *laying him in Sion* in opposition to the rejection of men, that we take it for God's actual employing of Jesus Christ in the work of our redemption. He alone was fit for that work ; it was utterly impossible that any other should bear the weight of that service (and so of this building) than He who was Almighty. Therefore the spouse calls him *the select*, or *choice of ten thousand*, yet he was *rejected of men*. There is an antipathy (if we may so speak) betwixt the mind of God and corrupt nature ; the things that are highly esteemed with men, are abomination to God ; and thus we see here, that which is highly esteemed with God, is cast out and *disallowed by men*. But surely there is no comparison ; the choosing and esteem of God stands ; and by that, (judge men of Christ as they will,) he is the foundation of this Building. And he is in true value answerable to this esteem : he is *precious*, which seems to signify a kind of inward worth, hidden from the eyes of men, blind, unbelieving men, but well known to God, and to those to whom He reveals him. And this is the very cause of his rejection by the most, the ignorance of his worth and excellency ; as a precious stone that the skilful lapidary esteems of great value, an ignorant beholder makes little or no account of.

These things hold likewise in the other stones of this Building ; they, too, are *chosen* before time : all that should be of this Building, foreordained in God's purpose, all written in that book beforehand, and then, in due time, they are chosen, by actual calling, according to that purpose, hewed out and severed by God's own hand, out of the quarry of corrupt nature ; dead stones in themselves, as the rest, but made living, by his bringing them to Christ, and so made truly *precious*, and accounted precious by Him who hath made them so. All the stones in this Building are called *God's jewels*, Mal. iii. 17. Though they be vilified, and scoffed at, and despised by men, though they pass for fools and the refuse of the world, yet they may easily digest all that, in the comfort of this, if they are chosen of God, and precious in His eyes. This is the very lot of Christ, and therefore by that the more welcome, that it conforms them to Him,—suits these stones to their Foundation.

And if we consider it aright, what a poor despicable thing is the esteem of men ! How soon is it past ! *It is a small thing for me*, says the Apostle Paul, *to be judged of men*, 1 Cor. iv. 3. Now that God often chooses for this building such stones as men cast away as good for nothing, see 1 Cor. i. 26. And where he says, Isa. lvii. 15, that He *dwells in the high and holy place*, what is His other dwelling ? His habitation on earth, is it in great palaces and courts ? No ; but *with him also that is of a contrite and humble spirit.* Now, these are the basest in men's account ; yet *He* chooses them, and prefers them to all other palaces and temples. Isa. lxvi. 1, 2, *Thus saith the Lord, The Heaven is my throne, and the earth is my footstool : where is the house that ye build unto me ? and where is the place of my rest ? For all those things hath mine hand made, and all those things have been, saith the Lord : but to this man will I look, even to him that is poor, and of a contrite spirit, and trembleth at my word.* q. d. You cannot gratify me with any dwelling, for I myself have made all, and a surer house than any you can make me ; *The Heaven is my throne, and the earth my footstool :* but I, who am so high, am pleased to regard the lowly.

3rdly, We have the *structure,* or way of building. *To whom coming.*] First, *coming,* then, *built up.* They that come unto Christ, come not only from *the world that lieth in wickedness,* but out of themselves. Of a great many that seem to come to Christ, it may be said, that they are not come to Him, *because they have not left themselves.* This is believing on him, which is the very resigning of the soul to Christ, and living by him. *Ye will not come unto me that ye may have life,* says Christ, John v. 40. He complains of it as a wrong done to him ; but the loss is ours. It is his glory to give us life who were dead ; but it is our happiness to receive that life from him. Now these stones come unto their foundation ; which imports the moving of the soul to Christ, being moved by his Spirit, and that the will acts, and willingly, (for it cannot act otherwise,) but still as being actuated and drawn by the Father : John vi. 65, *No man can come to me except the Father draw him.* And the outward mean of drawing is, by the word ; it is the sound of that harp that brings the stones of this spiritual building together. And then, being united to Christ, they are built up ; that is, as St. Paul expresses it, Eph. ii. 21, *they grow up unto a holy temple in the Lord.*

In times of peace, the Church may dilate more, and build as it were into breadth, but in times of trouble, it arises more in height ; it is then built upwards : as in cities where men are straitened, they build usually higher than in the country. Notwithstanding the Church's afflictions, yet still the building is going forward ; it is built, as Daniel speaks of Jerusalem, *in troublous times.* And it is this which the Apostle intends, as suiting with his foregoing exhortation : this passage may be read exhortatively too ; but taking it rather as asserting their condition, it is for this end, that they may remember to be like it, and grow up. For this end he expressly calls them *living stones;* an adjunct root not usual for stones, but here inseparable ; and therefore, though the Apostle changes the similitude, from infants to stones, yet he will not let go this quality of living, as making chiefly for his purpose.

To teach us the necessity of growth in believers, they are therefore often compared to things that grow, to *trees planted* in fruitful growing places, as *by the rivers of water ;* to *cedars in Lebanon,* where they are tallest ; to *the morning light;* to infants on the breast ; and here, where the word seems to refuse it, to *stones;* yet (it must, and well doth admit this unwonted epithet) they are called *living* and *growing stones.*

If, then, you would have the comfortable persuasion of this union with Christ, see whether you find your souls established upon Jesus Christ, finding him as your strong foundation; not resting on yourselves, nor on any other thing, either within you or without you, but supported by him alone; drawing life from him, by virtue of that union, as from a living foundation, so as to say with the Apostle, *I live by faith in the Son of God, who loved me, and gave himself for me.* Gal. ii. 20.

As these stones are built on Christ by faith, so they are cemented one to another by love; and, therefore, where that is not, it is but a delusion for persons to think themselves parts of this Building. As it is knit to him, it is knit together in itself through him; and if dead stones in a building support and mutually strengthen one another, how much more ought *living stones* in an active, lively way so to do! The stones of this Building keep their place: the lower rise not up to be in the place of the higher. As the Apostle speaks of the parts of the body, so the stones of this building in humility and love keep their station, and grow up in it, *edifying in love,* saith the Apostle, Eph. iv. 16; importing, that the want of this much prejudices edification.

These stones, because they are living, therefore grow in the life of grace and spiritualness, being a *spiritual building;* so that if we find not this, but our hearts are still carnal, and glued to the earth, *minding earthly things,* wiser in those than in spirituals, this evidences strongly against us, that we are not of this Building. How few of us have that spiritualness that becomes the temples of the Holy Ghost, or the stones of that Building! Base lusts are still lodging and ruling within us, and so our hearts are as cages of unclean birds and filthy spirits.

Consider this as your happiness, to form part of this Building, and consider the unsolidness of other comforts and privileges. If some have called those stones happy, that were taken for the building of temples or altars, beyond those in common houses, how true is it here! Happy indeed the stones that God chooses to be living stones in this spiritual temple, though they be hammered and hewed to be polished for it, by afflictions and the inward work of mortification and repentance. It is worth the enduring of all, to be fitted for this Building. Happy they, beyond all the rest of men, though they be set in never so great honours, as prime parts of politic buildings, (states and kingdoms,) in the courts of kings, yea, or kings themselves. For all other buildings, and all the parts of them, shall be demolished and come to nothing, from the foundation to the cope-stone; all your houses, both cottages and palaces; *the elements shall melt away, and the earth, with all the works in it, shall be consumed,* as our Apostle hath it, 2 Pet. iii. 10. But this spiritual building shall grow up to heaven; and being come to perfection, shall abide for ever in perfection of beauty and glory. In it shall be found *no unclean thing,* nor unclean person, but only they *that are written in the Lamb's book of life.*

An holy priesthood.] For the worship and ceremonies of the Jewish Church were all shadows of Jesus Christ, and have their accomplishment in him, not only after a singular manner in his own person, but in a derived way, in his mystical body, his Church. The Priesthood of the Law represented him as the great High Priest that *offered up himself for our sins*, and that is a priesthood altogether incommunicable ; neither is there any peculiar office of priesthood for offering sacrifice in the Christian Church, but his alone who is Head of it. But this dignity that is here mentioned, of a *spiritual priesthood,* offering up *spiritual sacrifices,* is common to all those who are in Christ. As they are living stones built on him into a spiritual temple, so, they are priests of that same temple made by him. (Rev. i. 6.) As he was, after a transcendent manner, temple, and priest, and sacrifice, so, in their kind, are Christians all these three through him ; and by his Spirit that is in them, their offerings through him are made acceptable.

We have here, 1. The office ; 2. The service of that office ; 3. The success of that service.

1. The Office. The death of Jesus Christ, as being every way powerful for reconcilement and union, did not only break down the partition-wall of guiltiness that stood betwixt God and man, but the wall of ceremonies that stood betwixt the Jews and the Gentiles : it made all that believe one with God, *and made of both one,* as the Apostle speaks — united them one to another. The way of salvation was made known, not to one nation only, but to all people : so that whereas the knowledge of God was before confined to one little corner, it is now diffused through the nations ; and whereas the dignity of their priesthood staid in a few persons, all they who believe are now thus dignified to be priests unto God the Father. And this was sig-nified by the rending of the vail of the Temple at his death ; not only that those ceremonies and sacrifices were to cease, as being all fulfilled in him, but that the people of God, who were before by that vail held out in the outer court, were to be admitted into the Holy Place, as being all of them priests, and fitted to offer sacrifices.

The Priesthood of the Law was holy, and its holiness was signified by many outward things suitable to their manner, by *anointings,* and *washings,* and *vestments ;* but in this spiritual priesthood of the Gospel, holiness itself is instead of all those, as being the substance of all. The children of God are all anointed, and purified, and clothed with holiness. But then,

2. There is here the service of this office, namely, *to offer.* There is no priesthood without sacrifice, for these terms are correlative, and offering sacrifices was the chief employment of the legal priests. Now, because the priesthood here spoken of is altogether spiritual, therefore the sacrifices must be so too, as the Apostle here expresses it.

We are saved the pains and cost of bringing bullocks and rams, and other such sacrifices ; and these are in their stead. As the Apostle speaks (Heb. vii. 12) of the high priesthood of Christ, that *the Priest-hood being changed, there followed of necessity a change of the law;* so, in this priesthood of Christians, there is a change of the kind of sacrifice from the other. All sacrifice is not taken away, but it is changed from the offering of those things formerly in use to spiritual sacrifices.

Now these are every way preferable ; they are easier and cheaper to us, and yet more precious and acceptable to God ; as it follows here in the text. Even in the time when the other sacrifices were in request, these spiritual offerings had ever the precedence in God's account, and without them he hated and despised all burnt-offerings and the largest sacrifices, though they were then according to His own appointment. How much more should we abound in spiritual sacrifice, who are eased of the other ! How much more holds that answer now, that was given even in those times to the inquiry, *Wherewith shall I come before the Lord ?* &c. (Mic. vi. 6.) You need not all that trouble and expense, *thousands of rams*, &c. : that is at hand which God requires most of all, namely, *to do justly, and to love mercy, and to walk humbly with thy God.* So, Psal. l. 23 : *Whoso offereth praise, glorifieth me.* That which is peculiarly spoken of Christ, holds in Christians by conformity with him.

But though the spiritual sacrificing is easier in its own nature, yet to the corrupt nature of man it is by far the harder. He would rather choose still all the toil and cost of the former way, if it were in his option. This was the sin of the Jews in those times, that they leaned the soul upon the body's service too much, and would have done enough of that, to be dispensed from this spiritual service. Hence are the Lord's frequent reproofs and complaints of this, Psalm l., Isaiah i., &c. Hence the willingness in Popery for outward work, for penances and satisfactions of bodies and purses, — any thing of that kind, if it might serve, rather than the inward work of repentance and mortification, the spiritual service and sacrifices of the soul. But the answer to all those from God, is that of the Prophet, *Who hath required these things at your hands?*

Indeed the sacred writers press works of charity, if they be done with a right hand, and the left hand not so much as acquainted with the business, as our Saviour speaks, *Let not thy left hand know what thy right hand doth.* (Matt. vi. 3.) They must be done with a right and single intention, and from a right principle moving to them, without any vain opinion of meriting by them with God, or any vain desire of gaining applause with men, but merely out of love to God, and to man for his sake. Thus they become one of these spiritual sacrifices, and therefore ought by no means to be neglected by Christian priests, that is, by any who are Christians.

Another spiritual sacrifice is, *the prayers of the saints,* Rev. v. 8.— Psal. cxli. 2, *Let my prayer be set forth before thee as incense, and the lifting up of my hands as the evening sacrifice.* It is not the composition of prayer, or the eloquence of expression, that is the sweetness of it in God's account, and makes it a sacrifice of a pleasing smell or sweet odour to Him, but the breathing forth of the desire of the heart ; that is what makes it a spiritual sacrifice, otherwise, it is as carnal, and dead, and worthless in God's account, as the carcasses of beasts. Incense can neither smell nor ascend without fire ; no more doth prayer, unless it arises from a bent of spiritual affection ; it is that which both makes it smell, and sends it heavenwards, makes it never leave moving upwards till it come before God, and smell sweet in His nostrils, which few, too few, of our prayers do.

Praise also is a *sacrifice ;* to make respectful and honourable mention of the name of God, and of His goodness ; to bless Him humbly and heartily. See Heb. xiii. 15, and Psal. l. 14, 23. *Offer unto God thanksgiving. Whoso offereth praise glorifieth me.* And this is that sacrifice that shall never end, but continues in heaven to eternity.

Then, *a holy course of life* is called the *sacrifice of righteousness,* Psal. iv. 6, and Phil. iv. 18. So also Heb. xiii. 16, where the Apostle shows what sacrifices succeed to those which, as he hath taught at large, are abolished. Christ was sacrificed for us, and that offering alone was powerful to take away sin ; but our gratulatory sacrifices, praise and alms, are as incense burnt to God, of which as the standers-by find the sweet smell, so, the holy life of Christians smells sweet to those with whom they live. But the wicked, as putrified carcasses, are of a noisome smell to God and man. *They are corrupt: they have done abominable works.* Psal. xiv. 4.

In a word, that sacrifice of ours which includes all these, and with-out which none of these can be rightly offered, is *Ourselves,* our whole selves. Our *bodies* are to be presented *a living sacrifice,* Rom. xii. 1 ; and they are not that without our souls. It is our heart given, that gives all the rest, for that commands all. *My son, give me thy heart,* and then the other will follow, *thine eyes will delight in my ways.* This makes the eyes, ears, tongue, and hands, and all, to be holy, as God's peculiar property ; and being once given and consecrated to Him, it becomes sacrilege to turn them to any unholy use. This makes a man delight to hear and speak of things that concern God, and to think on him frequently, to be holy in his secret thoughts, and in all his ways. In every thing we bring Him, every thanksgiving and prayer we offer, His eye is upon the heart : He looks if it be along with our offering, and if He miss it, He cares not for all the rest, but throws it back again.

The heart must be offered withal, and the whole heart, all of it en-tirely given to Him. *Se totum obtulit Christus pro nobis:* Christ offer-ed up his whole self for us. In another sense, which crosses not this, thy heart must not be *whole,* but *broken.* Psal. li. 17. But if thou find it unbroken, yet give it Him, with a desire that it may be broken. And if it be broken, and if, when thou hast given it Him, He break it more, yea, and melt it too, yet thou shalt not repent thy gift ; for He breaks and melts it, that He may refine it, and make it up a new and excellent frame, and may impress His own image on it, and make it holy, and so like to Himself.

Let us then give Him ourselves, or nothing ; and to give ourselves to Him, is not his advantage, but ours. As the philosopher said to his poor scholar, who, when others gave him great gifts, told him, *He had nothing but Himself to give: It is well,* said he, *and I will endeavour to give thee back to thyself, better than I received thee;*—thus doth God with us, and thus doth a Christian make himself his daily sacrifice : he renews this gift of himself every day to God, and receiving it every day bettered again, still he hath the more delight in giving it as being fitter for God, the more it is sanctified by former sacrificing.

Now that whereby we offer all other spiritual sacrifices, and even ourselves, is love. That is the holy fire that burns up all, sends up our prayers, and our hearts, and our whole selves a whole burnt offer-ing to God ; and, as the fire of the altar, it is originally from Heaven, being kindled by God's own love to us ; and by this the Church (and so, each believer) ascends like a *straight pillar of smoke*, (as the word is, Cant. iii. 6,) going even up to God *perfumed with aloes and all the spices*, all the graces of the Spirit received from Christ, but above all, with his own merits.

How far from this are the common multitude of us, though professing to be Christians ! Who considers his holy calling ? As the peculiar holiness of the ministry should be much in their eye and thoughts who are called to it, as *they* should study to be answerably eminent in holiness, so, all you that are Christians, consider, you are priests unto God ; being called a *holy priesthood*, thus you ought to be. But if we speak what we are indeed, we must say rather, we are an unholy priesthood, a shame to that name and holy profession. Instead of the sacrifice of a godly life, and the incense of prayer and praise, in families and alone, what is there with many, but the filthy vapours of profane speaking and a profane life, as a noisome smell arising out of a dunghill ?

But you that have once offered up yourselves unto God, and are still doing so with all the services you can reach, continue to do so, and be assured, that how unworthy soever yourselves and all your offerings be, yet they shall not be rejected.

The 3rd thing here observable is, the Success of that service : *Acceptable to God by Jesus Christ*, Heb. xiii. 16. The children of God do delight in offering sacrifices to Him ; but if they might not know that they were well taken at their hands, this would discourage them much ; therefore this is added. How often do the godly find it in their sweet experience, that when they come to pray, He welcomes them, and gives them such evidences of His love, as they would not exchange for all worldly pleasures ! And when this doth not so presently appear at other times, yet they ought to believe it. He accepts themselves and their ways when offered in sincerity, though never so mean ; though they sometimes have no more than a sigh or a groan, it is most properly a spiritual sacrifice.

Stay not away because thou, and the gifts thou offerest, are inferior to the offering of others. No, none are excluded for that ; only give what thou hast, and act with affection, for that he regards most. Under the Law, they who had not a lamb, were welcome with a pair of pigeons. So that the Christian may say : *What I am, Lord, I offer myself unto Thee, to be wholly Thine; and had I a thousand times more of outward or inward gifts, all should be Thine ; had I a greater estate, or wit, or learning, or power, I would endeavour to serve Thee with all. What I have, I offer Thee, and it is most truly Thine ; it is but of Thy own that I give Thee.* No one needs forbear sacrifice for poverty, for what God desires, is, the heart, and there is none so poor, but hath a heart to give him.

But meanness is not all ; there is guiltiness on ourselves and on all we offer ;. our prayers and services are polluted. But this hinders not neither ; for our acceptance is not for ourselves, but for the sake of One who hath no guiltiness at all : *Acceptable by Jesus Christ.* In Him, our persons are clothed with righteousness, and in His clothing we are, as Isaac said of Jacob in his brother's garments, *as the smell of a field that the Lord hath blessed,* Gen. xxvii. 27. And all our other sacrifices, our prayers, and services, if we offer them by Him, and put them into His hand, to offer to the Father, then doubt not they will be accepted in Him ; for this *By Jesus Christ,* is relative both to our offering and our acceptance. We ought not to offer any thing but *by Him,* Heb. xiii. 15 ; and so, we are well-pleasing to the Father. For he is His well-beloved Son, in whom His soul is delighted ; not only delighted and pleased with himself, but *in him,* with all things and persons that appear in him, and are presented by him.

And this alone answers all our doubts. For we ourselves, as little as we see that way, yet may see so much in our best services, so many wanderings in prayer, so much deadness, &c., as would make us still doubtful of acceptance : so that we might say with Job, *Although he had answered me, yet would I not believe that he had hearkened to me:* were it not for this, that our prayers and all our sacrifices pass through Christ's hand. He is that *Angel that hath much sweet odours,* to mingle with *the prayers of the saints,* Rev. viii. 3, 4. He purifies them with his own merits and intercession, and so makes them pleasing unto the Father. How ought our hearts to be knit to Him, by whom we are brought into favour with God, and kept in favour with Him, in whom we obtain all the good we receive, and in whom all we offer is accepted ! In Him are all our supplies of grace, and our hopes of glory.

Ver. 6. Wherefore also it is contained in the Scripture, Behold, I lay in Sion a chief corner-stone, elect, precious : and he that believeth on him shall not be confounded.

That which is the chief of the works of God, is therefore very reasonably the chief subject of his word, as both most excellent in itself, and of most concernment for us to know ; and this is, the saving of lost mankind by his Son. Therefore is *his name as precious ointment,* or perfume, diffused through the whole Scriptures : all these holy leaves smell of it, not only those that were written after his coming, but those that were written before. *Search the Scriptures,* says he himself, *for they testify of me,* (John v. 39,) namely, the Scriptures of the Old Testament, which were alone then written ; and to evidence this, both Himself and his Apostles make so frequent use of their testimony, and we find so much of them inserted into the New, as being both one in substance ; their lines meeting in the same Jesus Christ as their centre.

The Apostle having, in the foregoing verse, expressed the happy estate and dignity of Christians under the double notion, 1. of a spiritual house or temple, 2. of a spiritual priesthood,—here amplifies and confirms both from the writings of the Prophets ; the former, verses 6, 7, 8 ; the latter, verse 9. The places that he cites touching this Building, are most pertinent, for they have clearly in them all that he spoke of it, both concerning the foundation and the edifice ; as the first, in these words of Isaiah, (chap. xxviii. 16,) *Behold, I lay in Sion a chief corner-stone,* &c.

Let this commend the Scriptures much to our diligence and affection, that their great theme is, our Redeemer, and redemption wrought by Him ; that they contain the doctrine of his excellencies,—are the lively picture of his matchless beauty. Were we more in them, we should daily see more of him in them, and so of necessity love him more. But we must look within them : the letter is but the case ; the spiritual sense is what we should desire to see. We usually huddle them over, and see no further than their outside, and therefore find so little sweetness in them : we read them, but we *search* them not, as he requires. Would we dig into those golden mines, we should find treasures of comfort that cannot be spent, but which would furnish us in the hardest times.

The prophecy here cited, if we look upon it in its own place, we shall find inserted in the middle of a very sad denunciation of judgment against the Jews. And this is usual with the Prophets, particularly with this evangelical Prophet Isaiah, to uphold the spirits of the godly, in the worst times, with this one great consolation, the promise of the Messiah, as weighing down all, alike temporal distresses and deliverances. Hence are those sudden ascents (so frequent in the Prophets) from their present subject to this great *Hope of Israel.* And if this expectation of a Saviour was so pertinent a comfort in all estates, so many ages before the accomplishment of it, how wrongfully do we undervalue it being accomplished, if we cannot live upon it, and answer all with it, and sweeten all our griefs, with this advantage, that there *is a foundation-stone laid in Sion,* on which they that are builded shall be sure not to be ashamed !

In these words there are five things : 1. This Foundation-stone ; 2. The laying of it ; 3. The building on it ; 4. The firmness of this building ; and, 5. The greatness and excellency of the work.

1st, For the *Foundation,* called here, a *chief corner-stone.* Though the Prophet's words are not precisely rendered, yet the substance and sense of them are the same. In Isaiah, both expressions, *a foundation* and *a corner-stone,* are employed, (chap. xxviii. 16,) the corner-stone in the foundation being the main support of the building, and throughout, the corner-stones uniting and knitting the building together ; and therefore this same word, *a corner,* is frequently taken in Scripture for *princes,* or heads of people, (see Judg. xx. 2 ; 1 Sam. xiv. 38,) because good governors and government are that which upholds and unites the societies of people in states or kingdoms as one building. And Jesus Christ is indeed the alone Head and King of his Church, who gives it laws, and rules it in wisdom and righteousness ; the alone Rock on which his Church is built ; not Peter, (if we will believe St. Peter himself, as here he teacheth us,) much less his pretended successors ; He is the foundation and corner-stone that knits together the walls of Jews and Gentiles, *having made of both one,* as St. Paul speaks, (Eph. ii. 14,) and unites the whole number of believers into one everlasting temple, and bears the weight of the whole fabric.

Elected] or chosen out for the purpose, and altogether fit for it. Isaiah hath it, *A stone of trial,* or *a tried stone,* as things amongst men are best chosen after trial. So, Jesus Christ was certainly known by the Father, as most fit for that work to which he chose him, before he tried him, as after, upon trial in his life, and death, and resurrection, he proved fully answerable to his Father's purpose, in all that was appointed him.

All the strength of angels combined, had not sufficed for that business ; but the wise Architect of this Building knew both what it would cost, and what a foundation was needful to bear so great and so lasting a structure as He intended.   Sin having defaced and demolished the first building of man in the integrity of his creation, it was God's design, out of the very ruins of fallen man, to raise a more lasting edifice than the former, one that should not be subject to decay, and therefore He fitted for it a Foundation that might be everlasting.   The sure founding is the main thing requisite in order to a lasting building ; therefore, that it might stand for the true honour of His majesty, (which Nebuchadnezzar vainly boasted of his Babel,) He chose His own Son, *made flesh.*   He was God, that he might be a strong foundation ; he was Man, that he might be suitable to the nature of the stones whereof the building was to consist, that they might join the cement together.

Precious.]   Inestimably precious, by all the conditions that can give worth to any ; by rareness, and by inward excellency, and by useful virtues.   *Rare* He is, out of doubt ; there is not such a person in the world again ; therefore He is called by the same Prophet, (Isa. ix. 6,) *Wonderful,* full of wonders :—the power of God and the frailty of man dwelling together in His person ; *the Ancient of days* becoming an infant ; He that *stretched forth the Heavens,* bound up in swaddling clothes in that his infancy, and in his full age stretched forth on the cross ; altogether *spotless* and *innocent,* and yet suffering not only the unjust cruelties of men, but the just wrath of God his Father ; *the Lord of life,* and yet dying ; His *excellency* appears in the same things, in that he is the Lord of life, *God blessed for ever,* equal with the Father : the sparkling brightness of this precious stone is no less than this, that he is *the brightness of the Father's glory ;* (Heb. i. 3 ;) so bright, that men could not have beheld him appearing in himself ; therefore he vailed it with our flesh ; and yet, through that it shined and sparkled so, that the Apostle St. John says of himself and of those others who had their eyes opened, and looked right upon him, *He dwelt amongst us,* and he had a tent like ours, and yet, through that *we saw his glory, as the glory of the only begotten Son of God, full of grace and truth,* (John i. 14,)—the Deity filling his human nature with all manner of grace in its highest perfection.   And Christ is not only thus excellent in himself, but of precious *virtue,* which he lets forth and imparts to others ; of such virtue, that a touch of him is the only cure of spiritual diseases.   Men tell of strange virtues of some stones ; but it is certain that this Precious Stone hath not only virtue to heal the sick, but even to raise the dead.   Dead bodies he raised in the days of his abode on earth, and dead souls he still doth raise by the power of his word.   The prophet Malachi calls him *the Sun of righteousness,* (ch. iv. 2,) which includes in it the rareness and excellency we speak of : he is singular ; as there is but one sun in the world, so but one Saviour : and his lustre is such a stone as outshines the sun in its fullest brightness.   And then, for his useful virtue, the Prophet adds, that *He hath healing under his wings.*   This his worth is unspeakable, and remains infinitely beyond all these resemblances.

2dly, There is here *the laying* of this Foundation : it is said to be laid in *Sion;* that is, it is laid in the Church of God. And it was first laid in *Sion,* literally, that being then the seat of the Church and of the true religion : he was laid there, in his manifestation in the flesh, and suffering and dying, and rising again ; and afterwards, being preached through the world, he became the foundation of his Church in all places where his name was received ; and so was a stone growing great, till it *filled the whole earth,* as Daniel hath it, ch. ii. 35.

He saith, *I lay;* by which the Lord expresseth this to be His own proper work, as the Psalmist speaks of the same subject, (Psal. cxviii. 23,) *This is the Lord's doing; and it is marvellous in our eyes.* So Isaiah, speaking of this promised Messiah, *The zeal of the Lord of Hosts will perform this,* ch. ix. 7.

And it is not only said, *I lay,* because God the Father had the first thought of this great work,—the model of it was in His mind from eternity, and the accomplishment of it was by His almighty power in the morning of his Son's birth, and his life, and death, and resurrection ; but also to signify the freeness of His grace, in giving His Son to be a foundation of happiness to man, without the least motion from man, or motive in man to draw Him to it. And this seems to be signified by the unexpected inserting of these prophetical promises of the Messiah, in the midst of complaints of the people's wickedness, and threatening them with punishment ; to intimate that there is no connexion betwixt this work and any thing on man's part to procure it: *q. d.* Although you do thus provoke me to destroy you, yet, of myself I have other thoughts, there is another purpose in my mind. And it is observable to this purpose, that that clearest promise of the virgin's Son is given, not only unrequired, but being refused by that profane king Ahaz, Isa. vii. 10—13.

This, again, that the Lord himself is the Layer of this Corner-stone, teaches us the firmness of it ; which is likewise expressed in the Prophet's words, very emphatically, by redoubling the same word, *Musad, Musad; fundamentum, fundamentum.*

So, Psal. ii. 6, *I have set my king upon my holy hill of Sion:*—who then shall dethrone him ? *I have given him the heathen for his inheritance, and the ends of the earth for his possession;* and who will hinder him to take possession of his right ? If any offer to do so, what shall they be, but a number of earthen vessels fighting against an iron sceptre, and so, certainly breaking themselves in pieces ? Thus here, *I lay this foundation-stone;* and if I lay it, who shall remove it ? and what I build upon it, who shall be able to cast down ? For it is the glory of this great Master-builder, that the whole fabric which is of His building cannot be ruined ; and for that end hath He laid an unmovable foundation, and for that end are we taught and reminded of its firmness, that we may have this confidence concerning the Church of God that is built upon it. To the eye of nature, the Church seems to have no foundation ; as Job speaks of the earth, that *it is hung upon nothing,* and yet, as the earth remaineth firm, being established in its place by the word and power of God, the Church is most firmly founded upon the *Word made flesh*—Jesus Christ as its *chief cornerstone.* And as all the winds that blow cannot remove the earth out of its place, so neither can all the attempts of men, no, nor of *the gates*

of hell, prevail against the Church, Matt. xvi. 18. It may be beaten
with very boisterous storms, *but it cannot fall, because it is founded
upon this Rock*, Matt. vii. 25. Thus it is with the whole house, and
thus with every stone in it ; as here it follows, *He that believeth shall
not be confounded.*

3rdly, There is next, *the building on this Foundation.* To be built
on Christ, is plainly to believe in him. But in this they most deceive
themselves ; they hear of great privileges and happiness in Christ, and
presently imagine it as all theirs, without any more ado ; as that mad-
man of Athens, who wrote up all the ships that came into the
haven for his own. We consider not what it is to believe in him, nor
what is the necessity of this believing, in order that we may be partakers of the salvation that he hath wrought. It is not they that have
heard of him, or that have some common knowledge of him, or that
are able to discourse of him, and speak of his person and nature
aright, but *they that believe in him.* Much of our knowledge is like
that of the poor philosopher, who defineth riches exactly, and dis-
courseth of their nature, but possesseth none ; or we are as a geome-
trician, who can measure land exactly in all its dimensions, but possesseth not a foot thereof. And truly it is but a lifeless, unsavoury
knowledge that men have of Christ by all books and study, till he
reveal himself and persuade the heart to *believe in him.* Then, indeed,
when it sees him, and is made one with him, it says of all the reports
it heard, I heard much, yet *the half was not told me.* There is in
lively faith, when it is infused into the soul, a clearer knowledge of
Christ and his excellency than before, and with it, a recumbency of
the soul upon him as the foundation of its life and comfort ; a resolving to rest on him, and not to depart from him upon any terms.
Though I be beset on all hands, be accused by the Law, and by mine
own conscience, and by Satan, and have nothing to answer for myself,
yet, here I will stay, for I am sure in him there is salvation, and no
where else. All other refuges are but lies, (as it is expressed in the
words before these in the Prophet,) poor base shifts that will do no
good. God hath laid this Precious Stone in Sion, for this very purpose, that weary souls may rest upon it ; and why should not I make
use of it according to his intention ? He hath not forbid any, how
wretched soever, to believe, but commands it, and Himself works it
where he will, even in the vilest sinners.

Think it not enough that you know this Stone is laid, but see
whether you are built on it by faith. The multitude of imaginary
believers lie round about it, but they are never the better nor the surer
for that, any more than stones that lie loose in heaps near unto a
foundation, but are not joined to it.—There is no benefit to us by
Christ, without union with him ; no comfort in his riches, without an
interest in them, and a title to them, by virtue of that union. Then is
the soul right, when it can say, *He is altogether lovely,* and as the
spouse, (Cant. iii. 16,) *He is mine, my well-beloved.* This union is
the spring of all spiritual consolations. And faith, by which we are
thus united, is a Divine work. He that laid this Foundation in Sion
with His own hand, works likewise, with the same hand, faith in the
heart, by which it is knit to this corner-stone. It is not so easy as we

imagine, to believe. See Eph. i. 19. Many that think they believe, are, on the contrary, like those of whom the Prophet there speaks, as *hardened in sin* and carnally secure, whom he represents as in covenant with hell and death, walking in sin, and yet promising themselves impunity.

4thly, There is *the firmness* of this Building, namely, *He that believeth on him shall not be confounded.* This firmness is answerable to the nature of the foundation. Not only the whole frame, but every stone of it abideth sure. It is a simple mistake, to judge the persuasion of perseverance to be self-presumption : they that have it, are far from building it on themselves, but their foundation is that which makes them sure ; because it doth not only remain firm itself, but indissolubly supports all that are once built on it. In the Prophet, whence this is cited, it is, *Shall not make haste,* but the sense is one : they that are disappointed and ashamed in their hopes, run to and fro, and seek after some new resource ; this they shall not need to do, who come to Christ. The believing soul makes haste to Christ, but it never finds cause to hasten from him ; and though the comfort it expects and longs for, be for a time deferred, yet it gives not over, knowing that in due time it shall rejoice, and shall not have cause to blush and think shame of its confidence in him. David expresseth this distrust, by *making haste,* Psal. xxxi. 22 ; and cxvi. 11, *I was too hasty when I said so.* Hopes frustrated, especially where they have been raised high, and continued long, do reproach men with folly, and so shame them. And thus do all earthly hopes serve us when we lean much upon them. We find usually those things that have promised us most content pay us with vexation ; and they not only prove broken reeds, deceiving our trust, but hurtful, running their broken splinters into our hand who leaned on them. This sure Foundation is laid for us, that our souls may be established on it, and be as *Mount Sion, that cannot be removed,* Psal. cxxv. 1. Such times may come as will shake all other supports, but this holds out against all : Psal. xlvi. 2, *Though the earth be removed, yet will not we fear.* Though the frame of the world were cracking about a man's ears, he may hear it unaffrighted who is built on this Foundation. Why then do we choose to *build upon the sand?* Believe it, wheresoever we lay our confidence and affection besides Christ, it shall sooner or later repent us and shame us ; either happily in time, while we may yet change them for him, and have recourse to him ; or miserably, when it is too late. Remember that we must die and *must appear before the judgment-seat of God,* and that the things we dote on here, have neither power to stay us here, nor have we power to take them along with us, nor, if we could, would they at all profit us there ; and therefore, when we look back upon them all at parting, we shall wonder what fools we were to make so poor a choice. And in *that great day wherein all faces shall gather blackness,* (Joel ii. 6,) and be filled with confusion, that have neglected to make Christ their stay when he was offered them, then it shall appear how happy they are who have trusted in him ; *They shall not be confounded,* but shall *lift up their faces,* and be acquitted in him. In their present estate they may be exercised, but then *they shall not be confounded*, nor ashamed,—there is a double negation in the original,—*by no means ;* they shall *be more than conquerors through him who hath loved them.* Rom. viii. 37.

5thly, The last thing observable is, the greatness and excellency of the work, intimated in that first word, *Behold,* which imports this work to be very remarkable, and calls the eyes to fix upon it.

The Lord is marvellous in the least of his works ; but in this he hath manifested more of his wisdom and power, and let out more of his love to mankind, than in all the rest. Yet we are foolish, and childishly gaze about us upon trifles, and let this great work pass unregarded ; we scarcely afford it half an eye. Turn your wandering eyes this way ; look upon this *Precious Stone,* and behold him, not in mere speculation, but so behold him, as to lay hold on him. For we see he is therefore here set forth, that we may *believe on him, and so not be confounded ;* that we may attain this blessed union, that cannot be dissolved. All other unions are dissoluble : a man may be plucked from his dwelling-house and lands, or they from him, though he have never so good a title to them ; may be removed from his dearest friends, the husband from the wife, if not by other accidents in their lifetime, yet sure by death, the great dissolver of all those unions, and of that straitest one, of the soul with the body ; but it can do nothing against this union, but, on the contrary, perfects it. *For I am persuaded,* says St. Paul, *that neither death, nor life, nor angels, nor principalities, nor powers, nor things present, nor things to come, nor height, nor depth, nor any other creature, shall be able to separate us from the love of God, which is in Christ Jesus our Lord.* Rom. viii. 38, 39.

There is a twofold mistake concerning faith : on the one side, they that are altogether void of it, abusing and flattering themselves in a vain opinion that they have it ; and, on the other side, they that have it, misjudging their own condition, and so depriving themselves of much comfort and sweetness that they might find in their believing.

The former is the worse, and yet by far the commoner evil. What one says of wisdom, is true of faith : *Many would seek after it, and attain it, if they did not falsely imagine that they have attained it already.** There is nothing more contrary to the lively nature of faith, than for the soul not to be at all busied with the thoughts of its own spiritual condition, and yet this very character of unbelief passes with a great many for believing. They doubt not, that is, indeed they consider not what they are ; their minds are not at all on these things—are not awakened to seek diligently after Jesus, so as not to rest till they find him. They are well enough without him ; it suffices them to hear there is such a one ; but they ask not themselves, Is he mine, or no ? Surely, if that be all—not to doubt, the brutes believe as well as they. It were better, out of all question, to be labouring under doubtings, if it be a more hopeful condition, to find a man groaning and complaining, than speechless, and breathless, and not stirring at all.

There be in spiritual doubtings two things ; there is a solicitous care

---

* Puto multos potuisse ad sapientiam pervenire, nisi putassent se jam pervenisse. Seneca, *De Tranquillitate.*

of the soul concerning its own estate, and a diligent inquiry into it, and that is laudable, being a true work of the Spirit of God; but the other thing in them, is perplexity and distrust arising from darkness and weakness in the soul. Where there is a great deal of smoke, and no clear flame, it argues much moisture in the matter, yet it witnesseth certainly that there is fire there; and therefore, dubious questioning of a man concerning himself, is a much better evidence, than that senseless deadness which most take for believing. Men that know nothing in sciences, have no doubts. He never truly believed, who was not made first sensible and convinced of unbelief. This is the Spirit's first errand in the world, to *convince it of sin;* and the sin is this, that *they believe not,* John xvi. 8, 9. If the faith that thou hast, grew out of thy natural heart of itself, be assured it is but a weed. The right plant of faith is always set by God's own hand, and it is watered and preserved by Him; because exposed to many hazards, He watches it night and day. Isa. xxvii. 3, *I the Lord do keep it, I will water it every moment; lest any hurt it, I will keep it night and day.*

Again, how impudent is it in the most, to pretend they believe, while they wallow in profaneness! If faith unite the soul unto Christ, certainly it puts it into participation of his Spirit; *for if any man have not the Spirit of Christ, he is none of his,* says St. Paul. This faith in Christ brings us into communion with God. Now, *God is light,* says St. John, and he therefore infers, *If we say we have fellowship with God, and walk in darkness, we lie, and do not the truth,* 1 John i. 6. The lie appears in our practice, an unsuitableness in our carriage; as one said of him that signed his verse wrong, *Fecit solæcismum manu.*

But there be imaginary believers who are a little more refined, who live after a blameless, yea, and a religious manner, as to their outward behaviour, and yet are but appearances of Christians, have not the living work of faith within, and all these exercises are *dead works* in their hands. Amongst these, some may have such motions within them as may deceive themselves, while their external deportment deceives others; they may have some transient touches of desire to Christ, upon the unfolding of his excellencies in the preaching of the word, and upon some conviction of their own necessity, and may conceive some joy upon thoughts of apprehending him; and yet, all this proves but a vanishing fancy, an embracing of a shadow. And because men who are thus deluded, meet not with Christ indeed, do not really find his sweetness, therefore, within a while, they return to the pleasures of sin, and *their latter end proves worse than their beginning,* 1 Pet. ii. 20. Their hearts could not possibly be stedfast, because there was nothing to fix them on, in all that work wherein Christ himself was wanting.

But the truly believing soul that is brought unto Jesus Christ, and fastened upon him by God's own hand, abides stayed on him, and departs not. And in these persons, the very belief of the things that are spoken concerning Christ in the Gospel, the persuasion of Divine truth, is of a higher nature than the common consent that is called historical; they have another knowledge and evidence of *the mysteries of the kingdom,* than natural men can have. This is indeed the ground of all, the very thing that causes a man to rest upon Christ, when he hath a persuasion wrought in his heart by the Spirit of God, that Christ is an able Redeemer, a sufficient Saviour, *able to save all that come to him*, Heb. vii. 25. Then, upon this, the heart resolves upon that course : Seeing I am persuaded of this, that *whoso believes in him shall not perish, but have everlasting life*, (or as it is here, *shall not be confounded,*) I am to deliberate no longer ; this is the thing I must do, I must lay my soul upon him, upon one who is an Almighty Redeemer : and it does so. Now, these first actings of faith have in themselves an evidence that distinguishes them from all that is counterfeit, a light of their own, by which the soul, wherein they are, may discern them and say, This is the right work of faith ; especially when God shines upon the soul, and clears it in the discovery of His own work within it.

And further, they may find the influence of faith upon the affections, *purifying* them, as our Apostle says of it, Acts xv. 9. Faith knits the heart to a holy Head, a pure Lord, the Spring of purity, and therefore cannot choose but make it pure ; it is a beam from Heaven, that raises the mind to a heavenly temper. Although there are remains of sin in a believing soul, yet it is a hated, wearisome guest there. It exists there, not as its delight, but as its greatest grief and malady, which it is still lamenting and complaining of ; it had rather be rid of it than gain a world. Thus the soul is purified from the love of sin.

So then, where these are—a spiritual apprehension of the promises, a cleaving of the soul unto Christ, and such a delight in him as makes sin vile and distasteful, so that the heart is set against it, and, as the needle touched with the loadstone, is still turned towards Christ, and looks at him in all estates,—the soul that is thus disposed, hath certainly interest in him ; and, therefore, ought not to affect an humour of doubting, but to conclude, that how unworthy soever in itself, yet being in Him, *it shall not be ashamed:* not only it shall never have cause to think shame of Him, but all its just cause of shame in itself shall be taken away ; it shall be covered with His righteousness, and appear so before the Father. Who must not think, If my sins were to be set in order, and appear against me, how would my face be filled with shame ! Though there were no more, if some thoughts that I am guilty of were laid to my charge, I were utterly ashamed and undone. Oh ! there is nothing in myself but matter of shame, but yet, in Christ there is more matter of glorying, who endured shame, that we might not be ashamed. We cannot distrust ourselves enough, nor trust enough in Him. Let it be right faith, and there can be no excess in believing. Though I have sinned against Him, and abused His goodness, yet I will not leave Him ; for *whither should I go?* He, and none but He, *hath the words of eternal life.* Yea, though He, being so often offended, should threaten to leave me to the shame of my own follies, yet I will stay by Him, and wait for a better answer, and I know I shall obtain it ; this assurance being given me for my comfort, that *whosoever believes in him shall not be ashamed.*

Ver. 7. Unto you therefore which believe he is precious : but unto them which be disobedient, the stone which the builders disallowed, the same is made the head of the corner,
8. And a stone of stumbling, and a rock of offence, even to them which stumble at the word, being disobedient: whereunto also they were appointed.

BESIDES all the opposition that meets faith within, in our hearts, it hath this without, that it rows against the great stream of the world's opinion ; and therefore hath need, especially where it is very tender and weak, to be strengthened against that. The multitude of unbe- lievers, and the considerable quality of many of them in the world, are continuing causes of that very multitude ; and the fewness of them that truly believe, doth much to the keeping of them still few. And as this prejudice prevails with them that believe not, so it may some- times assault the mind of a believer, when he thinks how many, and many of them wise men in the world, reject Christ. Whence can this be ? Particularly the believing Jews, to whom this Epistle is ad- dressed, might think it strange, that not only the Gentiles, who were strangers to true religion, but their own nation, that was the select people of God, and had the light of His oracles kept in amongst them only, should yet, so many of them, yea, and the chief of them, be despisers and haters of Jesus Christ ; and that they who were best versed in the Law, and so seemed best able to judge of the Messiah foretold, should have persecuted Christ all his life, and at last put him to a shameful death.

That they may know that this makes nothing against Him, nor ought to invalidate their faith at all, but that it rather indeed testifies with Christ, and so serves to confirm them in believing, the Apostle makes use of those prophetical Scriptures, which foretell the unbelief and contempt with which the most would entertain Christ withal ; as old Simeon speaks of him, when he was come, agreeably to those former predictions, that he should be a *sign of contradiction*, Luke ii. 34 ; that, as he was the promised sign of salvation to believers, so he should be a very mark of enmities and contradictions to the unbeliev- ing world. The passages the Apostle here useth suit with his present discourse, and with the words cited from Isaiah in the former verse, continuing the resemblance of *a corner-stone :* they are taken partly from the one hundred and eighteenth Psalm, partly out of the eighth chapter of Isaiah.

Unto you, &c.] Wonder not that others refuse Him, but believe the more for that, because you see the word to be true even in their not believing of it ; it is fulfilled and verified by their very rejecting of it as false.

And whatsoever are the world's thoughts concerning Christ, that imports not, for they know him not ; but you that do indeed believe, I dare appeal to yourselves, to your own faith that you have of him, whether he is not precious to you, whether you do not really find him fully answerable to all that is spoken of him in the word, and to all that you have accordingly believed concerning him.

We are here to consider, I. The opposition of the persons : and then, II. The opposition of the things spoken of them.

I. The persons are opposed under the names of *believers* and *disobedient*, or unbelievers ; for the word is so near, that it may be taken for unbelief, and it is by some so rendered : and the things are fully as near to each other as the words that signify them—*disobedience* and *unbelief.*

1. Unbelief is itself the grand disobedience. For *this is the work of God*, that which the Gospel mainly commands, *that ye believe*, John vi. 29 ; therefore the Apostle calls it *the obedience of faith*, Rom. i. 5. And there is nothing indeed more worthy of the name of obedience, than the subjection of the mind to receive and to believe those supernatural truths which the Gospel teaches concerning Jesus Christ ; to obey, so as to have, as the Apostle speaks, the *impression* of that Divine pattern stamped upon the heart ; to have the heart delivered up, as the word there is, and laid under it to receive it, Rom. vi. 17. The word here used for disobedience signifies properly *unpersuasion ;* and nothing can more properly express the nature of unbelief than that ; and it is the very nature of our corrupt hearts ; we are *children of disobedience*, or *unpersuasibleness*, Eph. ii. 2, altogether incredulous towards God, who is Truth itself, and pliable as wax in Satan's hand, who works in such persons what he will, as there the Apostle expresses. They are most easy of belief to him, who is *the very father of lies*, as our Saviour calls him, John viii. 44, *a liar and a murderer from the beginning*, murdering by lies, as he did in the beginning.

2. Unbelief is radically all other disobedience ; for all flows from unbelief. This we least of all are ready to suspect ; but it is the bitter root of all that ungodliness that abounds amongst us. A right and lively persuasion of the heart concerning Jesus Christ, alters the whole frame of it, *casts down its high, lofty imaginations, and brings*, not only the outward actions, but the very *thoughts unto the obedience of Christ.* 2 Cor. x. 5.

II. As for the things spoken concerning these disobedient unbelievers, these two testimonies taken together have in them these three things : 1. Their rejection of Christ ; 2. Their folly ; 3. Their misery in so doing.

1. Their rejection of Christ ; they did not receive him, as the Father appointed and designed him, as the Foundation and *chief corner-stone*, but slighted him, and threw him by, as unfit for the building ; and this did not only the ignorant multitude, but the *builders*, they that professed to have the skill and the office, or power, of building—the doctors of the law, the scribes and Pharisees, and chief priests—who thought to carry the matter by the weight of their authority, as overbalancing the belief of those that followed Christ. *Have any of the rulers believed in him? But this people who know not the law are cursed*, John vii. 48, 49.

We need not wonder, then, that not only the powers of the world are usually enemies to Christ, and that the contrivers of policies, those builders, leave out Christ in their building, but that the pretended builders of the Church of God, though they use the name of Christ, and serve their turn with that, yet reject Himself, and oppose the power of his spiritual kingdom. There may be wit and learning, and much knowledge of the Scriptures, amongst those that are haters of the Lord Christ, and of the power of godliness, and corrupters of the worship of God. It is the spirit of humility and obedience, and saving faith, that teach men to esteem Christ, and build upon him.

2. But the vanity and folly of those builders' opinion appears in this, that they are overpowered by the great Architect of the Church : His purpose stands. Notwithstanding their rejection of Christ, he is still made the head corner-stone. They cast him away by their miscensures and reproaches put upon him, and by giving him up to be crucified and then cast into the grave, causing a stone to be rolled upon this *Stone* which they had so rejected, that it might appear no more, and so thought themselves sure. But even from thence did he arise, and *became the head of the corner.* The disciples themselves spake, you know, very doubtfully of their former hopes : *We believed this had been he that would have delivered Israel ;* but he corrected their mistake, first by his word, showing them the true method of that great work, *Ought not Christ to suffer first these things, and so enter into glory?* and then really, by making himself known to them as risen from the dead. When he was by these rejected, and lay lowest, then was he nearest his exaltation ; as Joseph in the prison was nearest his preferment. And thus is it with the Church of Christ : when it is brought to the lowest and most desperate condition, then is deliverance at hand ; it prospers and gains in the event, by all the practices of men against it. And as this Corner-stone was fitted to be such, by the very rejection of it, even so is it with the whole building ; it rises the higher the more men seek to demolish it.

3. The unhappiness of them that believe not is expressed in the other word, *He is to them a stone of stumbling, and a rock of offence.* Because they will not be saved by him, they shall stumble and fall, and be broken to pieces on him, as it is in Isaiah, and in the Evangelists. But how is this ? Is He who came to save, become a destroyer of men ? He whose name is Salvation, proves He destruction to any ? Not He himself : His primary and proper use is the former, to be a foundation for souls to build and rest upon ; but they who, instead of building upon him, will stumble and fall on him, what wonder, being so firm a stone, though they be broken by their fall ! Thus we see the mischief of unbelief, that as other sins disable the Law, this disables the very Gospel to save us, and turns life into death to us. And this is the misery, not of a few, but of many in Israel. Many that hear of Christ by the preaching of the Gospel, shall lament that ever they heard that sound, and shall wish to have lived and died without it, finding so great an accession to their misery, by the *neglect of so great salvation.* They are said to *stumble at the word*, because the things that are therein testified concerning Christ, they labour not to understand and prize aright ; but either altogether slight them, and account them foolishness, or misconceive and pervert them.

The Jews stumbled at the meanness of Christ's birth and life, and the ignominy of his death, not judging of him according to the Scriptures ; and we, in another way, think we have some kind of belief that he is the Saviour of the world, yet, not making the Scripture the rule of our thoughts concerning him, many of us undo ourselves, and stumble and break our necks upon this rock, mistaking Christ and the way of believing ; looking on him as a Saviour at large, and judging that enough ; not endeavouring to make him ours, and to embrace him upon the terms of that new covenant whereof he is Mediator.

Whereunto also they were appointed.] This the Apostle adds, for the further satisfaction of believers in this point, how it is that so many reject Christ, and stumble at him ; telling them plainly, that the secret purpose of God is accomplished in this. God having determined to glorify his justice on impenitent sinners, as He shows His rich mercy in them that believe. Here it were easier to lead you into a deep, than to lead you forth again. I will rather stand on the shore, and silently admire it, than enter into it. This is certain, that the thoughts of God are all not less just in themselves, than deep and unsoundable by us. His justice appears clear, in that man's destruction is always the fruit of his own sin. But to give causes of God's decrees without Himself, is neither agreeable with the primitive being of the nature of God, nor with the doctrine of the Scriptures. This is sure, that God is not bound to give us further account of these things, and we are bound not to ask it. Let these two words, as St. Augustine says, answer all, *What art thou, O man?* and, *O the depth!* Rom. ix. 20 ; xi. 33.

Our only sure way to know that our names are not in that black line, and to be persuaded that he hath chosen us to be saved by His Son, is this, to find that we have chosen Him, and are built on Him by faith, which is the fruit of His love, who first chooseth us ; and that we may read in our esteem of Him.

He is precious.] Or, *your honour.* The difference is small. You account him your glory and your gain ; he is not only *precious* to you, but *preciousness* itself. He is the thing that you make account of, your jewel, which if you keep, though you be robbed of all besides, you know yourselves to be rich enough.

To you that believe.] Faith is absolutely necessary to make this due estimate of Christ.

1. The most excellent things, while their worth is undiscerned and unknown, affect us not. Now, Faith is the proper seeing faculty of the soul, in relation to Christ : that inward light must be infused from above, to make Christ visible to us ; without it, though he is beautiful, yet we are blind ; and therefore cannot love him for that beauty. But by Faith, we are enabled to see Him who is *fairer than the children of men*, Psal. xlv. 2, yea, to see in Him *the glory of the only begotten Son of God*, John i. 14 ; and then, it is not possible but to account Him *precious*, and to bestow the entire affection of our hearts upon Him. And if any one say to the soul, *What is thy beloved more than another?* (Cant. iii. 9,) it willingly lays hold on the question, and is glad of an opportunity to extol Him.

2. Faith, as it is that which discerns Christ, so it alone appropriates him, makes him our own. And these are the two reasons of our esteeming and affecting any thing, its own worth, and our interest in it. Faith begets this esteem of Christ by both : first it discovers to us

His excellencies, which we could not see before ; and then, it makes Him ours, gives us possession of whole Christ, all that He hath, and is. As it is Faith that commends Christ so much, and describes his comeliness in that Song, so that word is the voice of Faith, that expresses propriety. *My well-beloved is mine, and I am His.* Cant. ii. 16. And these together make Him most precious to the soul. Having once possession of Him, then it looks upon all his sufferings as endured particularly for it, and the benefit of them all as belonging to itself. Sure, it will say, can I choose but account Him precious who suffered shame that I might not be ashamed, and suffered death that I might not die ; who took that bitter cup of the Father's wrath, and drank it out, that I might be free from it ?

Think not that you believe, if your hearts be not taken up with Christ, if his love do not possess your soul, so that nothing is precious to you in respect of him ; if you cannot despise and trample upon all advantages that either you have or would have, for Christ, and count them, with the great Apostle, *loss and dung in comparison of Him,* Phil. iii. 8. And if you do esteem Him, labour for increase of faith, that you may esteem him more ; for as faith grows, so will He still be more precious to you. And if you would have it grow, turn that spiritual eye frequently to Him, who is the proper object of it. For even they who are believers, may possibly abate of their love and esteem of Christ, by suffering faith to lie dead within them, and not using it in beholding and applying of Christ ; and the world, or some particular vanities, may insensibly creep in, and get into the heart, and cause them much pains ere they can be thrust out again. But when they are daily reviewing those excellencies that are in Christ, which first persuaded their hearts to love Him, and are discovering still more and more of them, His love will certainly grow, and will chase away those follies that the world dotes upon, as unworthy to be taken notice of.

Ver. 9. But ye are a chosen generation, a royal priesthood, an holy nation, a peculiar people ; ·that ye should show forth the praises of Him who hath called you out of darkness into his marvellous light.

IT is a matter of very much consolation and instruction to Christians to know their own estate—what they are as they are Christians. This *Epistle* is much and often upon this point for both those ends ; that the reflecting upon their dignities in Christ, may uphold them with comfort under suffering for Him ; and also, that it may lead them in doing and walking as becomes such a condition. Here it hath been represented to us by a building, a spiritual temple, and by a priesthood conformable to it.

The former is confirmed and illustrated by testimonies of Scripture in the preceding verses ; the latter in this verse, in which, though it is not expressly cited, yet it is clear that the Apostle hath reference to Exod. xix. 5, 6, where this dignity of priesthood, together with the other titles here expressed, is ascribed to all the chosen people of God. It is there a promise made to the nation of the Jews, but under the condition of obedience, and therefore it is most fitly here applied, by the Apostle, to the believing Jews, to whom particularly he writes.

It is true, that the external priesthood of the Law is abolished by the coming of this great High Priest, Jesus Christ being the body of all those shadows ; but this promised dignity of spiritual priesthood is so far from being annulled by Christ, that it is altogether dependent on him, and therefore fails in those that reject Christ, although they be of that nation to which this promise was made.   But it holds good in all, of all nations, that believe, and particularly, says the Apostle, *it is verified in you.*   You that are believing Jews, by receiving Christ, receive withal this dignity.

As the Legal priesthood was removed by Christ's fulfilling all that is prefigured, so, he was rejected by them that were, at his coming, in possession of that office : as the standing of that their priesthood was inconsistent with the revealing of Jesus Christ, so, they who were then in it, being ungodly men, their carnal minds' had a kind of antipathy against him.   Though they pretended themselves builders of the Church, and by their calling ought to have been so, yet they threw away the Foundation-stone that God had chosen and designed, and in rejecting it, manifested that they themselves were rejected of God. But, on the contrary, you who have laid your souls on Christ by believing, have this your choosing him as a certain evidence that God hath chosen you to be his *peculiar people,* yea, to be so dignified as to be a *kingly priesthood,* through Christ.

We have here to consider, 1. The estate of Christians, in the words that here describe it ; 2. The opposition of it to the state of unbelievers ; 3. The end of it.

First, The state of Christians, *A chosen generation.*   So, in Psalm xxiv.   The Psalmist there speaks first of God's universal sovereignty, then of His peculiar choice.   *The earth is the Lord's,* (ver. 1,) but there is a select company appointed for His *holy mountain,* there described ; and the description is closed thus, *This is the generation of them that seek him.*   Thus, Deut. x. 14, 15, and Exod. xix. 5, whence this passage is taken, *For all the earth is mine,* and that nation which is a figure of the elect of all nations, God's *peculiar,* beyond all others in the world.   As men who have great variety of possessions, yet have usually their special delight in some one beyond all the rest, and choose to reside most in it, and bestow most expense on it to make it pleasant ; so doth the Lord of the whole earth choose out to Himself from the rest of the world, a number that are *a chosen generation.*

Choosing, here, is the work of effectual calling, or the severing of believers from the rest ; for it signifies a difference in their present estate, as do likewise the other words joined with it.   But this election is altogether conformable to that of God's eternal decree, and is no other than the execution or performance of it ; God's framing of this His building being just according to the idea of it which was in His mind and purpose before all time : it is the drawing forth and investing of those into this Christian, this kingly priesthood, whose names were expressly written up for it in the book of life.

Generation.]   This imports them to be of one race or stock.   As the Israelites, who were by outward calling the children of God, were all the *seed of Abraham according to the flesh;* so, they that believe in the Lord Jesus, are *children of the promise,* Gal. iv. 28 ; and all of them are, by their new birth, one people or generation.   They are of one nation, belonging to the same blessed land of promise, all citizens of the New Jerusalem, yea, all children of the same family, whereof Jesus Christ, the *root of Jesse*, is the stock, who is the great *King*, and the *great High Priest.* And thus they are a *royal priesthood.* There is no devolving of His royalty or priesthood on any other, as it is in Himself; for His proper dignity is supreme and incommunicable, and there is no succession in His order : He *lives for ever*, and *is priest for ever*, Psal. cx. 4 ; and *king for ever* too, Psal. xlv. 6. But they that are descended from Him, do derive from Him, by that new original, this double dignity, in that way that they are capable of it, to be likewise kings and priests, as He is both. They are of the seed-royal, and of the holy seed of the priesthood, inasmuch as they partake of a new life from Christ. Thus, in Rev. i. 5, 6, first, there is His own dignity expressed, then, his dignifying us : *Who is* Himself *the first begotten among the dead, and the prince of the kings of the earth ;* and then it follows, *And hath made us kings and priests unto God and his Father.*

A royal priesthood.] That the dignity of believers is expressed by these two together, by *priesthood* and *royalty*, teaches us the worth and excellency of that holy function taken properly, and so, by analogy, the dignity of the Ministry of the Gospel, which God hath placed in his Church, instead of the Priesthood of the Law ; for therefore doth this title of spiritual priesthood fitly signify a great privilege and honour that Christians are promoted to, and it is joined with that of kings, because the proper office of priesthood was so honourable. Before it was established in one family, the chief, the first-born of each family, had a right to this, as a special honour ; and amongst the heathens, in some places, their princes and greatest men, yea, their kings, were their priests ; and, universally, the performing of their holy things was an employment of great honour and esteem amongst them. Though human ambition hath strained this consideration too high, to the favouring and founding a monarchical prelacy in the Christian world, yet that abuse of it ought not to prejudge us of this due and just consequence from it, that the holy functions of God's house have very much honour and dignity in them. And the Apostle, we see, 2 Cor. iii., prefers the ministry of the Gospel to the priesthood of the Law. So then, they mistake much, who think it a disparagement to men that have some advantages of birth or wit more than ordinary, to bestow them thus, and who judge the meanest persons and things good enough for this high calling. Surely this conceit cannot have place, but in an unholy, irreligious mind, that hath either no thoughts, or very mean thoughts of God. If they who are called to this holy service would themselves consider this aright, it would not puff them up, but humble them : comparing their own worthlessness with this great work, they would wonder at God's dispensation, that should thus have honoured them. As St. Paul speaks of himself, Eph. iii. 8, *Unto me who am less than the least of all saints is this grace given*, &c., so, the more a man rightly extols this his calling, the more he humbles himself under the weight of it ; and this would make him very careful to walk more suitably to it in eminency of holiness, for in that consists its true dignity.

There is no doubt that this Kingly Priesthood is the common dignity of all believers : *this honour have all the saints.* They are kings, have victory and dominion given them over the powers of darkness and the lusts of their own hearts, that held them captive, and domineered over them before. Base, slavish lusts, not born to command, yet are the hard taskmasters of unrenewed minds ; and there is no true subduing of them, but by the power and Spirit of Christ. They may be quiet for a while in a natural man, but they are then but asleep ; as soon as they awake again, they return to hurry and drive him with their wonted violence. Now this is the benefit of receiving the kingdom of Christ into a man's heart, that it makes him a king himself. All the subjects of Christ are kings, not only in regard of that pure crown of glory they hope for, and shall certainly attain, but in the present, they have a kingdom which is the pledge of that other, overcoming the world, and Satan, and themselves, by the power of faith. *Mens bona regnum possidet,* A good mind is a kingdom in itself, it is true ; but there is no mind truly good, but that wherein Christ dwells. There is not any kind of spirit in the world, so noble as that spirit that is in a Christian, the very Spirit of Jesus Christ, that great King, the *Spirit of Glory,* as our Apostle calls it below, ch. iv. This is a sure way to ennoble the basest and poorest among us. This royalty takes away all attainders, and leaves nothing of all that is passed to be laid to our charge, or to dishonour us.

Believers are not shut out from God, as they were before, but, being in Christ, are brought near unto Him, and have free access to the throne of His grace, Heb. x. 21, 22. They resemble, in their spiritual state, the Legal priesthood very clearly, I. In their consecration ; II. In their service ; and, III. In their laws of living.

I. In their consecration. The Levitical priests were, 1. Washed ; therefore this is expressed, Rev. i. 5, *He hath washed us in his blood,* and then follows, *and hath made us kings and priests.* There would have been no coming near unto God in his holy services as his priests, unless we had been cleansed from the guiltiness and pollution of our sins. This that pure and purifying blood doth ; and it alone. No other laver can do it ; no water but that *fountain opened for sin and for uncleanness.* Zech. xiii. 1. No blood, none of all that blood of Legal sacrifices, (Heb. ix. 12,) but only the blood of that spotless Lamb that *takes away the sins of the world,* John i. 29. So with this, 2. We have that other ceremony of the priest's con-secration, which was by sacrifice, as well as by washing ; for Christ at once offered up himself as our sacrifice, and let out his blood for our washing. With good reason is that prefixed there, Rev. i. 5, *He hath loved us,* and then it follows, *washed us in his blood.* That precious stream of his heart-blood, that flowed for our washing, told clearly that it was a heart full of unspeakable love that was the source of it. 3. There is anointing, namely, the graces of the Spirit, conferred upon believers, flowing unto them from Christ. For *it is of His fulness that we all receive grace for grace* (John i. 16) ; and the Apostle St. Paul says, (2 Cor. i. 16,) that *we are established and anointed in Christ.* It was poured on Him as our head, and runs down from Him unto us ; He the *Christ,* and we *Christians,* as partakers of his anointing. The consecrating oil of the priests was made of the

richest ointments and spices, to show the preciousness of the graces of
God's Spirit, which are bestowed on these spiritual priests ; and as
that holy oil was not for common use, nor for any other persons to be
anointed withal, save the priests only, so is the Spirit of grace a peculiar gift to believers.   Others might have costly ointments amongst the
Jews, but none of that same sort with the consecration-oil.   Natural
men may have very great gifts of judgment, and learning, and eloquence, and moral virtues, but they have none of this precious oil,
namely, the Spirit of Christ communicated to them ; no, all their endowments are but common and profane.   That holy oil signified particularly, eminency of light and knowledge in the priests ; therefore, in
Christians there must be light.   They that are grossly ignorant of spiritual things are surely not of this order ; this anointing is said *to teach
us all things*, 1 John ii. 27.   That holy oil was of a most fragrant, sweet
smell, by reason of its precious composition ; but much more sweet is
the smell of that Spirit wherewith believers are anointed, those several
odoriferous graces, which are the ingredients of their anointing oil,
that heavenly-mindedness, and meekness, and patience, and humility,
and the rest, that diffuse a pleasant scent into the places and societies
where they come ; their words, their actions, and their deportment
smelling sweet of them.   4. The garments wherein the priests were
inaugurate, and which they were after to wear in their services, are
outshined by that purity and holiness wherewith all the saints are
adorned ; but still more by that imputed righteousness of Christ, *those
pure robes* that are put upon them, wherein they appear before the
Lord and are accepted in His sight.   These priests are indeed *clothed
with righteousness*, according to that of the Psalmist, Psal. cxxxii. 9.
5. The priests were to have the offerings put into their hands ; from
thence, *filling of the hand*, signifies consecrating to the priesthood.
And thus doth Jesus Christ, who is the consecrator of these priests,
put into their hands, by his Spirit, the offerings they are to present unto God.   He furnishes them with prayers, and praises, and all other
oblations, that are to be offered by them ; he gives them themselves,
which they are to offer a living sacrifice, rescuing them from the
usurped possession of Satan and sin.

Let us consider their services, which were divers.   To name the
chief, 1. They had charge of the sanctuary, and the vessels of it, and
the lights, and were to keep the lamps burning.   Thus the heart of
every Christian is made a temple to the Holy Ghost, and he himself, as
a priest consecrated unto God, is to keep it diligently, and the furniture of Divine Grace in it ; to have the light of spiritual knowledge
within him, and to nourish it by drawing continually new supplies from
Jesus Christ. 2. The priests were to bless the people.   And truly it
is this spiritual priesthood, *the Elect*, that procure blessings upon the
rest of the world, and particularly on the places where they live.
They are daily to offer the incense of prayer, and other spiritual sacrifices unto God, as the Apostle expresseth it above, verse 5, not to
neglect those holy exercises together or apart.   And as the priests
offered it not only for themselves, but for the people, so Christians are
to extend their prayers, and to entreat the blessings of God for others,
especially for the public estate of the Church.   As the Lord's priests,

they are to offer up those praises to God, that are His due from the other creatures, which praise Him indeed, yet cannot do it after the manner in which these priests do; therefore they are to offer, as it were, their sacrifices for them, as the priests did for the people. And because the most of men neglect to do this, and cannot do it indeed because they are unholy, and are not of this priesthood, therefore should they be so much the more careful of it, and diligent in it. How few of ,those, whom the heavens call to by their light and revolution, that they enjoy, do offer that sacrifice which becomes them, by acknowledging *the glory of God which the heavens declare!* This, therefore, is as it were put into the hands of these priests, namely, the godly, to do.

III. Let us consider their course of life. We shall find rules given to the legal priests, stricter than to others, of avoiding legal pollutions, &c. And from these, this spiritual priesthood must learn an exact, holy conversation, keeping themselves from the pollutions of the world; as here it follows : *A holy nation,* and that of necessity; if a priesthood, then holy. They are purchased indeed to be *a peculiar treasure* to God, (Exod. xix. 5,) purchased at a very high rate. He spared not His only Son, nor did the Son spare himself; so that these priests ought to be the Lord's peculiar portion. All believers are His *clergy;* and as they are His portion, so He is theirs. The priests had no assigned inheritance among their brethren, and the reason is added, for *the Lord is their portion;* and truly so they needed not envy any of the rest, they had the choicest of all, the Lord of all. Whatsoever a Christian possesses in the world, yet, being of this spiritual priesthood, he is *as if he possessed it not,* (1 Cor. vii. 30,) lays little account on it. That which his mind is set upon, is, how he may enjoy God, and find clear assurance that he hath Him for his portion.

It is not so mean a thing to be a Christian as we think ; it is a holy, an honourable, a happy state. Few of us can esteem it, or do labour to find it so. No, we know not these things, our hearts are not on them, to make this dignity and happiness sure to our souls. Where is that true greatness of mind, and that holiness to be found, that become those who are *kings* and *priests* unto God ? that contempt of earthly things, and minding of heaven, that should be in such ? But surely, as many as find themselves indeed partakers of these dignities, will study to live agreeably to them, and will not fail to love that Lord Jesus who hath purchased all this for them, and exalted them to it ; yea, humbled himself to exalt them.

Now, as to the opposition of the estate of Christians to that of unbelievers. We best discern, and are most sensible of the evil or good of things by comparison. In respect of outward condition, how many be there that are vexing themselves with causeless murmurings and discontents, who, if they would look upon the many in the world that are in a far meaner condition than they, would be cured of that evil! It would make them not only content, but cheerful and thankful. But the difference here expressed, is far greater and more considerable than any that can be in outward things. Though the estate of a Christian is very excellent and precious, and, when rightly valued, hath enough in itself to commend it, yet it doth and ought to raise our

esteem of it the higher, when we compare it both with the misery of
our former condition, and with the continuing misery of those that
abide still, and are left to perish in that woeful estate. We have here
both these parallels. The happiness and dignity to which they are
chosen and called, is opposed to the rejection and misery of them that
continue unbelievers and rejecters of Christ.

Not only natural men, but even they that have a spiritual life in
them, when they forget themselves, are subject to look upon the things
that are before them with a natural eye, and to think hardly, or at least
doubtfully, concerning God's dispensations, beholding the flourishing
and prosperities of the ungodly, together with their own sufferings
and distresses. Thus, Psal. lxxxiii. But when they turn the other side
of the medal, and view them with a right eye, and by a true light,
they are no longer abused with those appearances. When they consider unbelievers *as strangers,* yea, *enemies to God,* and slaves to Satan,
held fast in the chains of their own impenitency and unbelief, and by
these bound over to eternal death, and then see themselves called to the
liberties and dignities of the sons of God, partakers of the honour of the
only begotten Son, on whom they have believed, made by him *kings and
priests unto God the Father,* then, surely, they have other thoughts. It
makes them no more envy, but pity the ungodly, and account all their
pomp, and all their possessions, what they are indeed, no other than
a glistening misery, and account themselves happy in all estates. It
makes them say with David, *The lines have fallen to me in a pleasant
place, I have a goodly heritage.* It makes them digest all their sufferings and disgraces with patience, yea, with joy, and think more of
praising than complaining, more of showing forth His honour who
hath so honoured them ; especially when they consider the freeness
of His grace, that it was that alone which made the difference, calling
them altogether undeservedly from that same darkness and misery in
which unbelievers are deservedly left.

Now the third thing here to be spoken to, is, the *End* of their calling, *to show forth His praise,* &c. And that we may the more prize
the reasonableness of that happy estate to which God hath exalted
them, it is expressed in other terms ; which therefore we will first consider, and then the end.

To magnify the grace of God the more, we have here, 1. Both the
terms of this motion or change,—*from whence* and *to what* it is ; 2.
The principle of it, the calling of God.

1. For the terms of this motion : *From darkness.* There is nothing
more usual, not only in Divine, but in human writings, than to borrow
outward sensible things, to express things intellectual ; and amongst
such expressions there is none more frequent than that of *light* and *darkness* transferred, to signify the good and the evil estate of man, as sometimes for his outward prosperity or adversity, but especially for things
proper to his mind. The mind is called *light,* because the seat of truth,
and truth is most fitly called *light,* being the chief beauty and ornament
of the rational world, as light is of the visible. And as the light, because
of that its beauty, is a thing very refreshing and comfortable to them
that behold it, (as Solomon says, *It is a pleasant thing to see the sun,*)
so is truth a most delightful thing to the soul that rightly apprehends it.

This may help us to conceive of the spiritual sense in which it is here taken. The estate of lost mankind is indeed nothing but darkness, being destitute of all spiritual truth and comfort, and tending to utter and everlasting darkness.

And it is so, because by sin the soul is separate from God, who is the first and highest light, the primitive truth. As He is light in himself, (as the Apostle St. John tells us, *God is light, and in Him there is no darkness at all*, expressing the excellency and purity of his nature,) so He is light relatively to the soul of man: *The Lord is my light*, says David, Psal. xxvii. 1.

And the soul being made capable of Divine light, cannot be happy without it. Give it what other light you will, still it is in darkness, so long as it is without God, He being the peculiar light and life of the soul. And as truth is united with the soul in apprehending it, and light with the visive faculty, so, in order that the soul may have God as its light, it must of necessity be in union with God. Now sin hath broken that union, and so cut off the soul from its light, and plunged it into spiritual darkness.

Hence all that confusion and disorder in the soul, which is ever the companion of darkness :—*Tohu vabohu,* as it was at first, when *darkness was on the face of the deep*, Gen. i. 2. Being ignorant of God and of ourselves, it follows that we love not God, *because we know him not;* yea, (though we think it a hard word,) we are *haters of God ;* for not only doth our darkness import ignorance of Him, but an enmity to Him, because He is light, and we are darkness. And being ignorant of ourselves, not seeing our own vileness, because we are in the dark, we are pleased with ourselves, and having left God, do love ourselves instead of God. Hence arise all the wickednesses of our hearts and lives, which are no other than, instead of obeying and pleasing God, a continual sacrificing to those *Gillulim,* those base dunghill-gods, our own lusts. For this the Apostle Paul gives as the root of all evil dispositions, 2 Tim. iii. 2 ; because, in the first place, *lovers of themselves,* therefore *covetous, boasters, proud,* &c., and *lovers of pleasures more than of God.* And this self-love cannot subsist without gross ignorance, by which our minds are so darkened that we cannot withal see what we are; for if we did, it were not possible but we should be far of another mind, very far out of loving and liking with ourselves. Thus our souls being filled with darkness, are likewise full of uncleanness, as that goes along too with darkness ; they are not only dark as dungeons, but withal filthy as dungeons used to be. So Eph. iv. 18, *Understandings darkened, alienated from the life of God;* and therefore it is added, ver. 19, *they give themselves over unto lasciviousness, to work all uncleanness with greediness.* Again, in this state they have no light of solid comfort. Our great comfort here, is not in any thing present, but in hope ; now, being *without Christ, and without God,* we are *without hope.* Eph. ii. 12.

And as the estate from whence we are called by grace, is worthily called *darkness,* so that, to which it calls us, deserves as well the name of *light.* Christ, likewise, who came to work our deliverance, is frequently so called in Scripture ; as John i. 9, *That was the true light,* and elsewhere ; not only in regard of his own nature, being God equal with the Father, and therefore light, as he is *God of God*, and therefore *Light of Light;* but relatively to men, as John i. 4, *That life was the light of men.* So he is styled *The Word*, and *the Wisdom of the Father*, not only in regard of his own knowledge, but as revealing Him unto us. See John i. 18, and 1 Cor. i. 18, compared with v. 30. And he is styled by Malachi, (ch. iv. 2,) *The Sun of righteousness*. Now, the sun is not only a luminous body, but a luminary, giving light unto the world. Gen. i.1 5.

He is our *light*, opposed to all kind of darkness. He is so, in opposition to the dark shadows of the ceremonial law, which possibly are here meant, as part of that darkness from which the Apostle writes that these Jews were delivered also by the knowledge of Christ : when he came, *the day broke and the shadows flew away.* He is our light, as opposed likewise to the darkness of the Gentile superstitions and idolatries ; therefore these two are joined by old Simeon, *A light to lighten the Gentiles, and the glory of his people Israel,* Luke ii. 34. And to all who believe among either, he is light as opposed to the ignorance, slavery, and misery of their natural estate, teaching them by his Spirit the things of God, and reuniting them with God, who is the light of the soul. *I am*, says he, *the light of the world; he that followeth me shall not walk in darkness.* John viii. 12.

And it is that mysterious union of the soul with God in Christ, which a natural man so little understands, that is the cause of all that spiritual light of grace, that a believer does enjoy. There is no right knowledge of God, to man once fallen from it, but in his Son ; no comfort in beholding God, but through Him ; nothing but just anger and wrath to be seen in God's looks, but through Him, *in whom He is well pleased.* The Gospel shows us *the light of the knowledge of the Glory of God*, but it is *in the face of Jesus Christ.* 2 Cor. iv. 6. Therefore, the kingdom of light, as opposed to that of darkness, is called *the kingdom of his dear Son*, or, the *Son of his love.* Col. i. 13.

There is a spirit of light and knowledge flows from Jesus Christ into the souls of believers, that acquaints them with the *mysteries of the kingdom of God*, which cannot otherwise be known. And this spirit of knowledge is withal a spirit *of holiness;* for purity and holiness are likewise signified by this *light.* He removed that huge dark body of sin that was betwixt us and the Father, and eclipsed Him from us. The light of his countenance *sanctifieth by truth;* it is a light that hath heat with it, and hath influence upon the affections, warms them towards God and Divine things. This darkness here is indeed the shadow of death, and they that are without Christ, are said, till he visit them, *to sit in darkness and in the shadow of death*, Luke i. 79 ; so, this *Light* is life, John i. 4 ; it doth enlighten and enliven, begets new actions and motions in the soul. The right notion that a man hath of things as they are, works upon him, and stirs him accordingly ; thus this light discovers a man to himself, and lets him see his own natural filthiness, makes him loathe himself, and fly from himself, —run out of himself. And the excellency he sees in God and his Son Jesus Christ, by this new light, inflames his heart with their love, fills him with estimation of the Lord Jesus, and makes the world, and all things in it that he esteemed before, base and mean in his eyes. Then from this light arise *spiritual joy* and *comfort*, which are frequently signified by this expression, as in that verse of the Psalmist, (the latter clause expounds the former,) *Light is sown for the righteous, and joy for the upright in heart.* Psal. xcvii. 11. As this *kingdom of God's dear Son,* that is, this kingdom of *light,* hath righteousness in it, so it hath *peace and joy in the Holy Ghost.* Rom. xiv. 17. It is a false prejudice the world hath taken up against religion, that it is a sour, melancholy thing : there is no truly lightsome, comfortable life but it. All others, have they what they will, live in darkness : and is not that truly sad and comfortless ? Would you think it a pleasant life, though you had fine clothes, and good diet, never to see the sun, but still to be kept in a dungeon with them ? Thus are they who live in worldly honour and plenty, but still without God ; they are in continual darkness, with all their enjoyments.

It is true the light of believers is not here perfect, and therefore neither is their joy perfect : it is sometimes overclouded ; but the comfort is this, that it is an everlasting light, it shall never go out in darkness, as it is said in Job xviii. 5, *the light of the wicked shall;* and it shall within awhile be perfected : there is a bright morning without a cloud that shall arise. The saints have not only light to lead them in their journey, but much purer light at home, *an inheritance in light.* Col. i. 12. The land where their inheritance lieth is full of light, and their inheritance itself is light ; for the vision of God for ever is that inheritance. That city hath no need of the sun, nor of the moon, to shine in it, *for the glory of the Lord doth lighten it, and the Lamb is the light thereof.* Rev. xxi. 23. As we said, that Increated Light is the happiness of the soul, the beginnings of it are our happiness begun ; they are beams of it sent from above, to lead us to the fountain and fulness of it. *With Thee,* says David, *is the fountain of life, and in Thy light shall we see light.* Psal. xxxvi. 9.

There are two things spoken of this Light, to commend it—*His marvellous light;* that it is after a peculiar manner *God's,* and then, that it is *marvellous.*

All light is from Him, the light of sense, and that of reason ; therefore He is called the *Father of lights,* Jam. i. 17. But this *light of grace* is after a peculiar manner His, being a light above the reach of nature, infused into the soul in a supernatural way, the light of the elect world, where God specially and graciously resides. Natural men may know very much in natural things, and, it may be, may know much in supernatural things, after a natural manner. They may be full of school-divinity, and be able to discourse of God and his Son Christ, and the mystery of redemption, &c., and yet, they want this peculiar light, by which Christ is made known to believers. They may speak of him, but it is in the dark ; they see him not, and therefore they love him not. The light they have is as the light of some things that shine only in the night, a cold glow-worm light that hath no heat with it at all. Whereas a soul that hath some of *this* light, God's peculiar light, communicated to it, sees Jesus Christ, and loves and delights in him, and walks with him. A little of this light is worth a great deal, yea, more worth than all that other common, speculative, and discoursing knowledge that the greatest doctors can attain unto. It is of a more excellent kind and original : it is from

Heaven, and you know that one beam of the sun is of more worth than the light of ten thousand torches together. It is a pure, undecaying, heavenly light, whereas the other is gross and earthly, (be it never so great,) and lasts but a while. Let us not therefore think it incredible, that a poor unlettered Christian may know more of God in the best kind of knowledge, than any the wisest and most learned natural man can do ; for the one knows God only by man's light, the other knows him by His own light, and that is the only right knowledge. As the sun cannot be seen but by its own light, so neither can God be savingly known but by His own revealing.

Now this light being so peculiarly *God's*, no wonder if it be *marvellous*. The common light of the world is so, though, because of its commonness, we think not so of it. The Lord is marvellous in wisdom and in power, in all His works of creation and providence ; but above all, in the workings of His grace. This light is unknown to the world, and so *marvellous* in the rareness of beholding it, that there be but a few that partake of it. And to them that see, it is *marvellous;* because in it they see so many excellent things that they knew not before : as if a man were born and brought up, till he came to the years of understanding, in a dungeon, where he had never seen light, and were brought forth on a sudden ; or, not to need that imagination, take the man that was born blind, at his first sight, after Christ had cured him,—what wonder, think we, would seize upon him, to behold on a sudden the beauty of this visible world, especially of that sun, and that light that makes it both visible and beautiful ! But much more matter of admiration is there in this light, to the soul that is brought newly from the darkness of corrupt nature ! Such persons see as it were a new world, and in it such wonders of the rich grace and love of God, such matchless worth in Jesus Christ the Sun of righteousness, that their souls are filled with admiration. And if this light of *grace* be so *marvellous*, how much more *marvellous* shall the light of *glory* be in which it ends !

Hence, 1. Learn to esteem highly of the Gospel, in which this light shines unto us : the Apostle calls it, therefore, *The glorious Gospel*, 2 Cor. iv. 4. Surely we have no cause to be ashamed of it, but of ourselves, that we are so unlike it.

2. Think not, you who are grossly ignorant of God, and his Son Christ, and the mysteries of salvation, that you have any portion as yet in His grace ; for the first character of His renewed image in the soul, as it was His first work in the material world, is light. What avails it us to live in the noonday light of the Gospel, if our hearts be still shut against it, and so within we be nothing but darkness ?—as a house that is close shut up, and hath no entry for light, though it is day without, still it is night within.

3. Consider your delight in the works of darkness, and be afraid of that great condemnation, *This is the condemnation of the world, that light is come into it, and men love darkness rather than light.* John iii. 19.

4. You that are indeed partakers of this happy change, let your hearts be habitations of light. *Have no fellowship with the unfruitful works of darkness, but rather reprove them.* Eph. v. 11. Study

much to increase in spiritual light and knowledge, and withal in holiness and obedience ; if your light be this light of God, truly spiritual light, these will accompany it. Consider the rich love of God, and account His light *marvellous,* as in itself, so in this respect, that He hath bestowed it on you. And seeing *you were once darkness, but now are light in the Lord,* I beseech you,—nay, the Apostle, and in him the Spirit of God, beseeches you, *Walk as children of the light.* Eph. v. 8.

But to proceed to speak to the other parts of this verse, as to the Principle of this change, *the calling of God.*

It is known and confessed to be a chief point of wisdom in a man, to consider what he is, from whom he hath that his being, and to what end. When a Christian hath thought on this in his natural being, as he is a man, he hath the same to consider over again of his spiritual being, as he is a Christian, and so a new creature. And in this notion, all the three are very clearly represented to him in these words : 1. What he is, first, by these titles of dignity in the first words of this verse ; and again, by an estate of light in the last clause of it. 2. Whence a Christian hath this excellent being is very clearly expressed here, *He hath called you.* That God who is the author of all kind of being, hath given you this, *called you from darkness to his marvellous light.* If you be *a chosen generation,* it is He that hath *chosen you.* (Ch. i. 2.) If you be a *royal priesthood,* you know that it is He that hath anointed you. If *a holy nation,* He hath sanctified you. (John xvii. 17.) If *a peculiar* or *purchased people,* it is He that hath bought you. (1 Cor. vi. 20.) All are included in this calling, and they are all one thing. 3. To what end,—to *show forth His praises.* Of the first of these, in all the several expressions of it, we have spoken before ; now are to be considered the other two.

He hath called you.] Those who live in the society, and profess the faith of Christians, are called unto *light,* the light of the Gospel that shines in the Church of God. Now, this is no small favour and privilege, while many people are left in *darkness and in the shadow of death,* to have this light arise upon us, and to be in the region of it, the Church, the *Goshen* of the world ; for by this outward light we are invited to this happy state of saving inward light, and the former is here to be understood as the means of the latter. These Jews who were called to the profession of the Christian faith, to whom our Apostle writes, were even in that respect called unto a light hidden from the rest of their nation, and from many other nations in the world : but because the Apostle doth undoubtedly describe here the lively spiritual state of true believers, therefore this Calling doth further import the effectual work of conversion, making the daylight of salvation, not only without, but within them, *the day-star to arise in their hearts,* as he speaks, 2 Ep. i. 19. When the sun is arisen, yet if a man be lying fast in a dark prison, and in a deep sleep too, it is not day to him ; he is not *called to light,* till some one open the doors and awake him, and bring him forth to it. This God doth, in the calling here meant. That which is here termed *Calling,* in regard of the way of God's working with the soul, is, in regard of the power of it, called a *rescuing* and *bringing forth* of the soul : so the Apostle St. Paul speaks of it, Col. i. 13 : *Delivered from the power of darkness, and translated to the kingdom of his dear Son.* That delivering and translating is this *calling,* and it is *from the power of darkness*— a forcible power—that detains the soul captive. As there are chains of eternal darkness upon damned spirits, which shall never be taken off, wherein they are *said to be reserved to the judgment of the great day,* so there are chains of spiritual darkness upon the unconverted soul, that can be taken off by no other hand but the powerful hand of God. He calls the sinner to *come forth,* and withal causes, by the power of that His voice, the bolts and fetters to fall off, and enables the soul to *come forth* into the light. It is an operative word that effects what it bids, as that in the creation, *He said, Let there be light, and it was light,* to which the Apostle hath reference, 2 Cor. iv. 6, when he says, *God, who commanded the light to shine out of darkness, hath shined into your hearts.* God calls man. He works with him indeed as with a reasonable creature, but surely, He likewise works as Himself, as an Almighty Creator. He works strongly and sweetly, with an Almighty easiness. One man may call another to this light, and if there be no more, he may call long enough to no purpose ; as they tell of Mahomet's miracle that misgave,—he called a mountain to come to him, but it stirred not. But His call that shakes and removes the mountains, doth, in a way known to Himself, turn and wind the heart which way He pleaseth. *The voice of the Lord is powerful and full of majesty.* Psal. xxix. 4. If He speaks once to the heart, it cannot choose but follow Him, and yet most willingly chooses that. The workings of grace, (as oil, to which it is often compared,) do insensibly and silently penetrate and sink into the soul, and dilate themselves through it. That word of His own calling, disentangles the heart from all its nets, as it did the disciples from theirs, to follow Christ. That call which brought St. Matthew presently from his receipt of custom, puts off the heart from all its customs, and receipts too ; makes it reject gains and pleasures, and all that hinders it, to go after Christ. And it is a call that touches the soul so as the touch of Elijah's mantle, that made Elisha follow him. *Go back,* said he, *for what have I done unto thee?* Yet he had done so much, as made him forsake all to go with him. 1 Kings xix. 20. And this every believer is most ready to acknowledge, who knows what the rebellion of his heart was, and what his miserable love of darkness was, that the gracious, yet mighty call of God, was what drew him out of it ; and therefore he willingly assents to that which is the *Third* thing to be spoken of, that it becomes him, as being the End of his Calling, to *show forth His praise,* who hath so mercifully and so powerfully called him from so miserable to so happy an estate.

For, 1. This is God's end in calling us, to communicate His goodness to us, that so the glory of it may return to Himself. The highest Agent cannot work but for the highest end ; so that, as the Apostle speaks, when God would confirm his covenant by an oath, *He sware by Himself,* because He could swear by no greater, so, in all things, He must be the end of His own actions, because there is no greater nor better end, yea, none by infinite odds so great, or good. Particularly in the calling and exalting of a number of lost mankind to so great honour and happiness, both in designing that great work, and in performing it, He aims at the opening up and declaring of His *rich grace*, for the glory of it, as the Apostle St. Paul tells us, once and again, Eph. i. 6, 12.

2. As this is God's end, it ought to be ours, and therefore ours because it is His. And for this very purpose, both here and elsewhere, are we put in mind of it, that we may be true to His end, and intend it with Him. This is His purpose in calling us, and therefore it is our great duty, being so called—to declare His praises. All things and persons shall pay this tribute, even those who are most unwilling ; but the happiness of His chosen is, that they are active in it, others are passive only. Whereas the rest have His praise wrested from them, they do declare it cheerfully, as the glorious angels do. As the Gospel brings them glad tidings of peace from God, and declares to them that love and mercy that is in Him, they smother it not, but answer it ; they declare it, and set forth the glory of it, with their utmost power and skill.

There be in this two things : 1. Not only that they speak upon all occasions to the advantage of His grace, but that the frame of their actions be such as doth tend to the exalting of God. And, 2. That in those actions they do intend this end, or set up this for their aim.

1. Their words and actions being conformable to that high and holy estate to which they are called, do commend and praise their Lord, who hath called them to it. The virtues which are in them, tell us of His virtues, as brooks lead us to their springs. When a Christian can quietly repose his trust on God, in a matter of very great difficulty, wherein there is no other thing to stay him, but God alone, this declares that there is strength enough in God that bears him up, that there must be in Him that real abundance of goodness and truth that the word speaks of him. *Abraham believed, and gave glory to God :* (Rom. iv. 20 :) this is what a believer can do, to declare the truth of God ; he relies on it. *He that believes sets to his seal that God is true.* John iii. 33. So, also, their *holiness* is for His praise. Men hear that there is a God who is infinitely holy, but they can see neither Him nor His holiness ; yet, when they perceive some lineaments of it in the faces of His children, which are in no others, this may convince them that its perfection, which must be some where, can be no where else than in their heavenly Father. When these, which are His peculiar plants, bring forth the fruits of holiness, which naturally they yielded not, it testifies a supernatural work of His hand who planted them, and the more they are fruitful, the greater is His praise. *Herein,* says our Saviour, *is your heavenly Father glorified, that ye bring forth much fruit.* John xv. 8. Were it not for the conscience of this duty to God, and possibly the necessity of their station and calling, it may be, some Christian had rather altogether lock up and keep within himself any grace he hath, than let it appear at all, considering some hazards which he and it run in the discovery ; and, it may be, could take some pleasure in the world's mistakes and disesteem of him. But seeing both piety and charity require the acting of graces in converse with men, that which hypocrisy doth for itself, a real Christian may and should do for God.

2. The other thing mentioned as making up this rule, will give the

difference ; that not only what we speak and do should be such as agrees with this end, but that so speaking and doing, our eye be upon this end; that all our Christian conversation be directly intended by us, not to cry up our own virtues, but to glorify God, and His virtues,—*to declare His praises who hath called us.*

Let your light, says our Saviour, (Matt. v. 16,) *shine,* and *shine before men* too; that is not forbidden ; yea, it is commanded, but it is thus commanded, *Let your light so shine before men, that they seeing your good works*—yourselves as little as may be, your works more than yourselves, (as the sun gives us its light, and will scarce suffer us to look upon itself,)—*may glorify*—Whom ? You ? No, but—*your Father whch is in heaven. Let your light shine,* it is given for that purpose, but let it shine always to the glory of the *Father of lights.* Men that seek themselves, may share in the same public kind of actions with you ; but let your secret intention (which God eyes most) sever you. This is the impress that a sincere and humble Christian sets upon all his actions, *To the glory of God.* He useth all he hath, especially all his graces, to His praise who gives all, and is sorry he hath no more for this use, and is daily seeking after more, not to bring more esteem to himself, but more honour to God. It is a poor booty to hunt after that, namely, an airy, vain breath of men : the best things in them, their solidest good, is altogether vanity ; how much more that which is lightest and vainest in them ! This is the mind that is in every Christian, in all his ways to deny himself, and to be willing to abase himself to exalt his Master : to be of St. Paul's temper, who regarded not himself at all, honour or dishonour, prison or liberty, life or death, content he was with any thing, so *Christ might be magnified.* Phil. i. 20.

And as every godly mind must be thus affected, so especially the ministers of the Gospel, they who are not only called with others to partake of this *marvellous light,* but are in a special manner to hold it forth to others. How do pure affections become them, and ardent desires to promote His glory who hath so called them ! A rush for your praise or dispraise of us ; only receive Jesus Christ, and esteem highly of him, and it is enough. *We preach not ourselves,* says the Apostle, *but Christ Jesus the Lord.* 2 Cor. iv. 5. That is our errand, not to catch either at base gain or vain applause for ourselves, but to exalt our Lord Jesus in the hearts of men. And to those who are so minded, there is a reward abiding them, of such riches and honour as they would be very loth to exchange for any thing to be had amongst men.

But, in his station, this is the mind of every one who loves the Lord Jesus, most heartily to make a sacrifice of himself, and all he is and hath,—means, and esteem, and life, and all, to His glory who humbled himself so low, to exalt us to these dignities, to *make us kings and priests unto God.*

It is most just, seeing we have our crowns from Him, and that He hath set them on our heads, that we take them in our hands, and throw them down *before His throne.* All our graces (if we have any) are His free gift, and are given as the rich garments of this spiritual priesthood, only to attire us suitably for this spiritual sacrifice of His praises ; as the costly vesture of the high priest under the Law was not appointed to make him gay for himself, but to decorate him for his holy service, and to commend, as a figure of it, the perfect holiness wherewith our great High Priest, Jesus Christ, was clothed. What good thing have we that is not from the hand of our good God ? And receiving all from Him, and after a special manner spiritual blessings, is it not reasonable that all we have, but those spiritual gifts especially, should declare His praise, and His only ? David doth not grow big with vain thoughts, and lift up himself, because God had lifted him up, but exclaims, *I will extol Thee, because thou hast lifted me up.* Psal. xxx. 1. The visible heavens, and all the beauty and the lights in them, speak nothing but His glory who framed them ; (as the Psalmist teacheth us, Psal. xix. 1 ;) and shall not these spiritual lights, *His called ones,* whom he hath made lights so peculiarly for that purpose, these *stars in His right hand,* do it much more ? Oh ! let it be thus with us ! The more He gives, be still the more humble, and let Him have the return of more glory, and let it go entire to Him ; it is all His due ; and in doing thus, we shall still grow richer ; for where He sees the most faithful servant, who purloins nothing, but improves all to his Master's advantage, surely him He will trust with most.

And as it is thus both most due to God, and most profitable for ourselves, in all things to seek His praises, so it is the most excellent and generous intent, to have the same thought with God, the same purpose as His, and to aim no lower than at His glory : whereas it is a base, poor thing for a man to seek himself far below that royal dignity that is here put upon Christians, and that priesthood joined with it. Under the Law, those who were squint-eyed were incapable of the priesthood ; truly, this squinting out to our own interest, the looking aside to that, in God's affairs especially, so deforms the face of the soul, that it makes it altogether unworthy the honour of the spiritual priesthood. Oh ! this is a large task, an infinite task. The several creatures bear their part in this ; the sun says somewhat, and moon and stars, yea, the lowest have some share in it ; the very plants and herbs of the field speak of God ; and yet, the very highest and best, yea, all of them together, the whole concert of heaven and earth, cannot show forth all His praise to the full. No ; it is but a part, the smallest part of that glory which they can reach.

We all pretend to these dignities, in that we profess ourselves Christians ; but if we have a mind to be resolved of the truth in this, (for many, many are deceived in it !) we may, by asking ourselves seriously, and answering truly to these questions : 1*st,* Whether are my actions and the course of my life such as give evidence of the grace of God, and so speak His praise ? If not, surely I am not of this number that God hath thus called and dignified. And this test, I fear, would degrade many. 2*ndly,* If my life be somewhat regular and Christian-like, yet, whether do I in it all, singly and constantly, without any selfish or sinister end, desire and seek the glory of God alone ? Otherwise, I may be like this *chosen generation,* but I am not one of them. And this, out of doubt, would make the number yet far less. Well, think on it ; it is a miserable condition, for men either to be grossly staining and dishonouring the holy religion they profess, or, in seeming to serve and honour God, to be serving and seeking themselves; it is the way to lose themselves for ever. Oh! it is a comfortable thing to have an upright mind, and to love God for Himself: and *love seeks not its own things.* 1 Cor. xiii. 5. They are truly happy, who make this their work sincerely, though weakly, to advance the praises of their God in all things, and who, finding the great imperfection of their best diligence in this work here, are still longing to be in that state where they shall do it better.

Ver. 10. Which in time past were not a people, but are now the people of God: which had not obtained mercy, but now have obtained mercy.

THE love of God to His children is the great subject both of His word and of their thoughts, and therefore is it that His word (the rule of their thoughts and their whole lives) speaks so much of that love, to the very end that they may think much, and esteem highly of it, and walk answerably to it. This is the scope of St. Paul's doctrine to the Ephesians, and the top of his desires for them. (See chap. iii. 17.) And this is our Apostle's aim here. As he began the Epistle with opposing their election in heaven to their dispersion on earth, the same consideration runs through the whole of it. Here he is representing to them the great fruit of that love, the happy and high estate to which they are called in Christ; that the choosing of Christ and of believers is as one act, and they as one entire object of it,—one glorious Temple, He the foundation and head corner-stone, and they the edifice;—one honourable fraternity, He the King of kings and great High Priest, and they likewise through him made kings and priests unto God the Father, *a royal priesthood;* He the *light of the world,* and they through Him the *children of light.* Now that this their dignity, which shines so bright in its own innate worth, may yet appear the more, the Apostle here sets it off by a double opposition, *first,* of the misery under which others are, and *secondly,* of that misery under which they themselves were before their calling. And this being set on both sides, is as a dark shadowing round about their happiness here described, setting off the lustre of it.

Their former misery, expressed in the former verse by *darkness,* is here more fully and plainly set before their view in these words. They are borrowed from the Prophet Hosea, chap. ii. 23, where (as is usual with the Prophets) he is raised up by the Spirit of God, from the temporal troubles and deliverances of the Israelites, to consider and foretell that great restoration wrought by Jesus Christ, in purchasing a new people to Himself, made up both of Jews and Gentiles who believe; and therefore the prophecy is fit and applicable to both. So that the debate is altogether needless, whether it concerns the Jews or Gentiles; for in its spiritual sense, as relating to the kingdom of Christ, it foretells the making of the Gentiles, who were not before so, *the people of God,* and the recovery of the Jews likewise, who, by their apostacies, and the captivities and dispersions which came upon them as just punishments of those apostacies, were degraded from the outward dignities they had as the people of God, and withal were spiritually miserable and captives by nature, and so in both respects laid equal with the Gentiles, and stood as much in need of this restitution as they.   St. Paul useth the passage concerning the calling of the Gentiles, Rom. ix. 25.   And here, St. Peter writing, as is most probable, particularly to the dispersed Jews, applies it to them, as being, in the very reference it bears to the Jews, truly fulfilled in those alone who were believers, faith making them a part of the true Israel of God, to which the promises do peculiarly belong ; as the Apostle St. Paul argues at large, in the ninth chapter of his Epistle to the Romans.

Their former misery and their present happiness we have here under a double expression ; they were, 1. *not a people*, 2. *destitute of mercy.   Not the people of God*, says the Prophet ; *not a people*, says our Apostle : being not God's people, they were so base and miserable as not to be worthy of the name of a people at all ; as it is taken, Deut. xxxii. 21.

There is a kind of being, a life that a soul hath by a peculiar union with God, and therefore, in that sense, the soul without God is dead, as the body is without the soul.   Eph. ii. 1.   Yea, as the body separated from the soul is not only a lifeless lump, but putrefies, and becomes noisome and abominable, thus the soul separated from God is subject to a more loathsome and vile putrefaction.   See Psal. xiv. 3. So that men who are yet unbelievers, *are not*, as the Hebrews expressed death.   Multitudes of them *are not a people*, but a heap of filthy carcasses.   Again ; take our natural misery in the notion of a captivity, which was the judgment threatened against the Jews, to make them in this sense *not a people ;* therefore their captivity is often spoken of by the Prophets as a death, and their restoration as their resurrection, as Ezek. xxxvii.   And as a captive people is civilly dead, (as they speak,) so a soul captive to sin and the Prince of Darkness is spiritually dead, wanting happiness and well-being, which if it never attain, it had better, for itself, not be at all.   There is nothing but disorder and confusion in the soul without God, the affections hurrying it away tumultuously.

Thus, captive sinners *are not ; they are dead ;* they want that happy being that flows from God to the souls which are united to Himself, and, consequently, they must want that society and union one with another which results from the former, results from the same union that believers have with God, and the same being that they have in Him ; which makes them truly worthy to be called a people, and particularly the people of God.   His people are the only people in the world worthy to be called *a people ;* the rest are but refuse and dross. Although in the world's esteem, which judges by its own rules in favour of itself, the people of God be as no body, no people, a company of silly creatures : yea, *we are made*, says the great Apostle, *as the filth of the world, and the offscouring of all things* (1 Cor. iv. 13) ; yet in His account who hath chosen them, who alone knows the true value of things, His people are *the only people*, and all the rest of the world as *nothing* in His eyes.   He dignifies and beautifies them, and loves in them that beauty which He hath given them.

But under that term is comprised, not only that new being of believers in each one of them apart, but that tie and union that is amongst them as *one people*, being incorporated together, and living under the same government and laws, without which a people are but as the beasts of the field, or the *fishes of the sea, and the creeping things that have no ruler over them*, as the Prophet speaks, Habak. i. 14. That regular living in society and union in laws and policy makes many men to be one people ; but the civil union of men in states and kingdoms is nothing comparable to the mysterious union of the people of God with him, and one with another. That commonwealth hath a firmer union than all others. Believers are knit together in Christ as their Head, not merely as a civil or political head ruling them, but as a natural head enlivening them, giving them all one life. Men in other societies, though well ordered, yet are but as a multitude of trees, regularly planted indeed, but each hath its own root ; but the faithful are all branches of one root. Their union is so mysterious, that it is compared to the very union of Christ with his Father, as it is indeed the product of it, John xvii. 21.

People of God.] *I will say to them, Thou art my people, and they shall say, Thou art my God.* Hos. ii. 23. That mutual interest and possession is the very foundation of all our comfort. He is the first chooser ; He first says, *My people;* calls them so, and makes them to be so ; and then they say, *My God.* It is therefore a relation that shall hold, and shall not break, because it is founded upon His choice who changes not. The tenor of an external covenant with a people, (as the Jews particularly found,) is such as may be broken by man's unfaithfulness, though God remain faithful and true ; but the New Covenant of grace makes all sure on all hands, and cannot be broken ; the Lord not only keeping His own part, but likewise performing ours in us, and for us, and establishing us, that as He departs not from us first, so we shall not depart from Him. *I will betroth thee to me for ever.* It is an indissoluble marriage, that is not in danger of being broken either by divorce or death.

My people.] There is a treasure of instruction and comfort wrapped up in that word, not only more than the profane world can imagine, (for they indeed know nothing at all of it,) but more than they who are of the number of his people, are able to conceive,—a deep unfathomable. *My people;* they His portion, and He theirs ! He accounts nothing of all the world beside them, and they of nothing at all beside Him. For them he continues the world. Many and great are the privileges of His people, contained in that great charter, the Holy Scriptures, and rich is that land where their inheritance lies ; but all is in this reciprocal, that *He is their God.* All his power and wisdom are engaged for their good. How great and many soever are their enemies, they may well oppose this to all, *He is their God.* They are sure to be protected and prospered, and in the end to have full victory. *Happy then is that people whose God is the Lord.*

Which had not obtained mercy.] *The mercies of the Lord* to His chosen *are from everlasting;* yet, so long as His decree of mercy runs hid, and is not discovered to them in the effects of it, they are said *not to have* received, or *obtained mercy.* When it begins to act and work in their effectual calling, then they find it to be theirs. It was in a secret way moving forward towards them before, as the sun after midnight is still coming nearer to us, though we perceive not its approach till the dawning of the day.

Mercy.] The former word, *the people of God*, teaches us how *great* the change is that is wrought by the calling of God: this teaches us, 1. how *free* it is. *The people of God*, that is the good attained in the change: *Obtained mercy*, that is the spring whence it flows. This is indeed implied in the words of the change; of *no people*—such as have no right to such a dignity at all, and in themselves no disposition for it—to be made *His people*, can be owing to nothing but free grace, such mercy as supposes nothing, and seeks nothing, but misery in us, and works upon that. As it is expressed to have been very free to this people of the Jews, in choosing them before the rest of the world, Deut. vii. 7, 8, so it is to the spiritual Israel of God, and to every one particularly belonging to that company. Why is it, that He chooseth one of a family, and leaves another, but because it pleaseth Him? *He blots out their transgressions for his own name's sake.* Isa. xliii. 25. And, 2. as it is free mercy, so it is *tender mercy*. The word in the Prophet, signifies *tenderness*, or bowels of compassion; and such are the mercies of our God towards us. See Jer. xxxi. 20; the bowels of a father, as it is Psal. ciii. 13; and if you think not that tenderness enough, those of a mother, yea, more than a mother, Isa. xlix. 15. 3. It is *rich mercy;* it delights to glorify itself in the greatest misery; it pardons as easily the greatest as the smallest of debts. 4. It is a *constant, unalterable mercy*, a stream still running.

Now in both these expressions the Apostle draws the eyes of believers to reflect on their former misery, and to view it together with their present state. This is very frequent in the Scriptures. See Ezek. xvi.; Eph. ii. 12; 1 Cor. vi. 11, &c. And it is of very great use; it works the soul of a Christian to much humility, and love, and thankfulness, and obedience. It cannot choose but force him to abase himself, and to magnify the free grace and love of God. And this may be one reason why it pleaseth the Lord to suspend the conversion of some persons for many years of their life, yea, to suffer them to stain those years with grievous and gross sins, in order that the riches and glory of His grace, and the freeness of His choice, may be the more legible both to themselves and others. Likewise, those apprehensions of the wrath due to sin, and the sights of hell, as it were, which He brings some unto, either at or after their conversion, make for this same end. That glorious description of the *New Jerusalem*, Rev. xxi. 16, is abundantly delightful in itself; and yet, the fiery lake spoken of there makes all that is spoken of the other sound much the sweeter.

But, universally, all the godly have this to consider, that they *were strangers and enemies to God*, and to think, Whence was it that I, a lump of the same polluted clay with those that perish, should be taken, and purified, and moulded by the Lord's own hand for a vessel of glory? Nothing but free grace makes the difference; and where can there be love, and praises, and service found to answer this? All is to be ascribed to the mercy, gifts, and calling of Christ. And his ministers, with St. Paul, acknowledge that because they *have received mercy they faint not.* 2 Cor. iv. 1.

But alas! we neither enjoy the comfort of this mercy as obtained, nor are grieved for wanting it, nor stirred up to seek after it, if not yet obtained. What do we think ? Seems it a small thing in your eyes to be shut out from the presence of God, and to bear the weight of His wrath for ever, that you thus slight His mercy, and let it pass by you unregarded ? Or shall an imagined obtaining divert you from the real pursuit of it ? Will you be willingly deceived, and be your own deceivers in a matter of so great importance ? You cannot think too highly of the riches of Divine mercy ; it is above all your thoughts ; but remember and consider this, that there is a *peculiar people* of His own, to whom alone all the riches of it do belong. And therefore, how great soever it is, unless you find yourselves of that number, you cannot lay claim to the smallest share of it.

And you are not ignorant what is their character, what a kind of people they are, who have such a knowledge of God as Himself gives. *They are all taught of God*, enlightened and sanctified by His Spirit, a holy people, as He is a holy God : such as have the riches of that Grace by which they are saved in most precious esteem, and have their hearts by it inflamed with His love, and therefore their thoughts taken up with nothing so much as studying how they may obey and honour Him ; rather choosing to displease all the world than offend Him, and accounting nothing too dear, yea, nothing good enough to do Him service. If it be thus with you, then you have indeed *obtained mercy*.

But if you be such as can wallow in the same puddle with the profane world, and take a share of their ungodly ways, or if, though your outward carriage be somewhat more smooth, you *regard iniquity in your hearts*, have your hearts ardent in the love and pursuit of the world, but frozen to God ; if you have some bosom idol that you hide and entertain, and cannot find in your heart to part with some one beloved sin, whatsoever it is, for all the love that God hath manifested to man in the *Son of His love, Jesus Christ;* in a word, if you can please and delight yourself in any way displeasing unto God, (though his people, while they are here, have spots, yet these are not the spots of his people that I am now speaking of,) I can give you no assurance that as yet you have obtained mercy : on the contrary, it is certain that *the wrath of God is yet abiding on you*, and if you continue in this state, you are in apparent danger of perishing under it. You are yet children of spiritual darkness, and in the way to utter and everlasting darkness. Know ye what it is to be destitute of this mercy ? It is a woeful state, though you had all worldly enjoyments, and were at the top of outward prosperity, to be shut out from the mercy and love of God.

There is nothing doth so kindly work repentance, as the right apprehension of the mercy and love of God. The beams of that love are more powerful to melt the heart than all the flames of Mount Sinai— all the threatenings and terrors of the Law. Sin is the root of our misery ; and therefore it is the proper work of this mercy, to rescue the soul from it, both from the guilt and the power of it at once. Can you think there is any suitableness in it, that the peculiar people of God should despise His laws, and practise nothing but rebellions ? that those in whom He hath magnified His mercy, should take pleasure in abusing it ? or that He hath washed any with the blood of His Son, to the end that they may still *wallow again in the mire?* As if we were redeemed not *from* sin, but *to* sin ; as if we should say, *We are delivered to do all these abominations,* as the Prophet speaks, Jer. vii. 10. Oh ! let us not dare thus abuse and affront the free grace of God, if we mean to be saved by it ; but let as many as would be found amongst those that obtain mercy walk as His people, whose peculiar inheritance is His mercy. And seeing this *grace of God hath appeared unto us,* let us embrace it, and let it effectually *teach us to deny ungodliness and worldly lusts.* Tit. ii. 11, 12.

And if you be persuaded to be earnest suitors for this mercy, and to fly unto Jesus, who is the *true mercy-seat,* then be assured it is yours. Let not the greatest guiltiness scare you and drive you from it, but rather drive you the more to it ; for the greater the weight of that misery is under which you lie, the more need you have of this mercy, and the more will be the glory of it in you. It is a strange kind of argument used by the Psalmist, and yet a sure one,—it concludes well and strongly, Psal. xxv. 7 : *Lord, pardon my iniquity, for it is great.* The soul oppressed with the greatness of its sin lying heavy upon it, may, by that very greatness of it pressing upon it, urge the forgiveness of it at the hands of Free Mercy. It is *for thy name's sake,*—that makes it strong ; the force of the inference lies in that. Thou art nothing, and worse than nothing ? True ; but all that ever obtained this mercy were once so ; they were *nothing* of all that which it hath made them to be ; they were *not a people,* had no interest in God, were strangers to mercy, yea, *heirs of wrath;* yea, they had not so much as a desire after God, until this mercy prevented them, and showed itself to them, and them to themselves, and so moved them to desire it, and caused them to find it, caught hold on them and plucked them out of the dungeon. And it is unquestionably still the same mercy, and fails not ; ever expending, and yet never all spent, yea, not so much as at all diminished ; flowing, as the rivers, from one age to another, serving each age in the present, and yet no whit the less to those that come after. He who exercises it is *The Lord, forgiving iniquity, transgression, and sin,* to all that come unto Him, and yet, still *keeping mercy for thousands* that come after.

You who have obtained this mercy, and have the seal of it within you, it will certainly conform your hearts to its own nature ; it will work you to a merciful, compassionate temper of mind to the souls of others who have not yet obtained it. You will indeed, as the Lord doth, hate sin ; but, as He doth, likewise, you will pity the sinner. You will be so far from misconstruing and grumbling at the long-suffering of God, (as if you would have the bridge cut because you are over, as St. Augustine speaks,) that, on the contrary, your great desire will be to draw others to partake of the same mercy with you, knowing it to be rich enough ; and you will, in your station, use your best diligence to bring in many to it, from love both to the souls of men and to the glory of God.

And withal, you will be still admiring and extolling this mercy, as it is manifested unto yourselves, considering what it is, and what you were before it visited you. The Israelites confessed, (at the offering of the first-fruits,) to set off the bounty of God, *A Syrian ready to perish was my father;* they confessed their captivity in Egypt: but far poorer and baser is our natural condition, and far more precious is that land, to the possession of which this free mercy bringeth us.

Do but call back your thoughts, you that have indeed escaped it, and look but into that pit of misery whence the hand of the Lord hath drawn you out, and you cannot fail to love Him highly, and still kiss that gracious hand, even while it is scourging you with any affliction whatsoever; because it hath once done this for you, namely, plucked you out of everlasting destruction. So David, Psal. xl. 23, as the thoughts of this change will teach us to praise, *He hath brought me up out of an horrible pit:* then follows,—*He hath put a new song in my mouth, even praise unto our God;* not only *redeemed me from destruction,* but withal *crowned me with glory and honour.* Psal. ciii. 4. He not only doth forgive all our debts, and let us out of prison, but enriches us with an estate that cannot be spent, and dignifies us with a crown that cannot wither, made up of nothing of ours. These two considerations will stretch and tune the heart very high, namely, from what a low estate Grace brings a man, and how high it doth exalt him; in what a beggarly, vile condition the Lord finds us, and yet, that He doth not only free us thence, but puts such dignities on us. *He raises up the poor out of the dust, and lifts the needy out of the dunghill, that he may set him with princes, even with the princes of his people.* Psal. cxiii. 7. Or, as Joshua the priest was stripped of his filthy garments, and had a fair mitre set upon his head, (Zech. iii. 3—5,) so those of this Priesthood are dealt withal.

Now, that we may be the deeper in the sense and admiration of this mercy, it is indeed our duty to seek earnestly after the evidence and strong assurance of it; for things work on us according to our notice and apprehensions of them, and therefore, the more right assurance we have of mercy, the more love, and thankfulness, and obedience will spring from it. Therefore it is, that the Apostle here represents this great and happy change of estate to Christians as a thing that they may know concerning themselves, and that they ought to seek the knowledge of, that so they may be duly affected with it. And it is indeed a happy thing, to have in the soul an extract of that great archive and act of grace towards it, that hath stood in heaven from eternity. It is surely both a very comfortable and very profitable thing to find and to read clearly the seal of mercy upon the soul, which is holiness, that by which a man is marked by God, as a part of his peculiar possession that He hath chosen out of the world. And when we perceive any thing of this, let us look back, as here the Apostle would have us to do, and reflect how God has *called us from darkness to His marvellous light.*

Ver. 11. Dearly beloved, I beseech you as strangers and pilgrims, abstain from fleshly lusts, which war against the soul.

THE right spiritual knowledge that a Christian hath of God and of himself, differenceth itself from whatsoever is likest to it, by the power and influence it hath upon the heart and life. And in this, it hath the lively impression of that doctrine of the Holy Scriptures that teaches it; wherein we still find throughout, that the high mysteries of religion are accompanied with practical truths, which not only agree with them, but are drawn out of them, and not violently drawn, but naturally flowing from them, as pure streams from a pure spring. Thus, in this Epistle, we find the Apostle intermixing his divine doctrine with most useful and practical exhortations, ch. i. 13, 22 : and in the beginning of this chapter again : and now in these words.

And upon this model ought both the ministers of the Gospel to form their preaching, and the hearers their ear. Ministers are not to instruct only, or to exhort only, but to do both. To exhort men to holiness and the duties of a Christian life, without instructing them in the doctrine of faith, and bringing them to Jesus Christ, is to build a house without a foundation. And, on the other side, to instruct the mind in the knowledge of Divine things, and neglect the pressing of that practice and power of godliness which is the undivided companion of true faith, is to forget the building that ought to be raised upon that foundation once laid, which is likewise a point of very great folly. Or, if men, after laying that right foundation, do proceed to the superstructure of vain and empty speculations, it is but to *build hay and stubble*, instead of those solid truths that direct the soul in the way to happiness, which are of more solidity and worth than *gold, and silver, and precious stones.* 1 Cor. iii. 12. Christ, and the doctrine that reveals him, is called by St. Paul, *the mystery of the faith*, 1 Tim. iii. 9, and ver. 16, *the mystery of godliness :* as Christ is the object of faith, so is he the spring and fountain of godliness. The Apostle having, we see, in his foregoing discourse unfolded the excellency of Christ in him, proceeds here to exhort them to that pure and spiritual temper of mind and course of life that becomes them as Christians.

Those hearers are to blame, and do prejudice themselves, who are attentive only to such words and discourse as stir the affections for the present, and find no relish in the doctrine of faith, and the unfolding of those mysteries that bear the whole weight of religion, being the ground both of all Christian obedience, and all exhortations and persuasives to it. Those temporary, sudden stirrings of the affections, without a rightly informed mind, and some measure of due knowledge of God in Christ, do no good. It is the wind of a word of exhortation that stirs them for the time against their lusts, but the first wind of temptation that comes carries them away; and thus the mind is but tossed to and fro, like a wave of the sea, with all kinds of winds, not being *rooted and grounded in the faith of Christ*, (as it is Col. ii. 7,) and so, not *rooted in the love of Christ*, (Eph. iii. 17,) which are the conquering graces that subdue unto a Christian his lusts and the world. See 1 John v. 4 ; 2 Cor. v. 14, 15. Love makes a man to be dead to himself, and to the world, and to *live to Christ who died for him.*

On the other part, they are no less, yea, more to blame, who are glad to have their minds instructed in the mysteries of the Christian faith, and out of a mere natural desire to know, are curious to hear such things as inform them ; but when it comes to the urging of holiness and mortifying their lusts, *these are hard sayings,*—they had rather there were some way to receive Christ and retain their lusts too, and to bring them to agreement. To hear of the mercies of God, and the dignities of his people in Christ, is very pleasing ; but to have this follow upon it, *Abstain from fleshly lusts,* this is an importune, trouble-some discourse.   But it must be so for all that: those who will share in that mercy and happiness must *abstain from fleshly lusts.*

Dearly beloved, I beseech you.]   There is a faculty of reproving re-quired in the ministry, and sometimes a necessity of very sharp rebukes —cutting ones.   They who have much of the *spirit of meekness,* may have *a rod* by them too, to use upon necessity.   1 Cor. iv. 21.   But surely the way of meekness is that they use most willingly, as the Apostle there implies ; and out of all question, with ingenuous minds, the mild way of sweet entreaties is very forcible ; as oil that penetrates and sinks in insensibly, or, (to use that known resemblance,) they prevail as the sun-beams, which, without any noise, made the traveller cast his cloak, which all the blustering of the wind could not do, but made him rather gather it closer, and bind it faster about him.   We see the Apostles are frequent in this strain of entreaties, *I beseech you,* as Rom. xii. 1.   Now this word of entreaty is strengthened much by the other, *Dearly beloved.*   Scarcely can the harshest reproofs, much less gentle reproofs, be thrown back, that have upon them the stamp of love.   That which is known to come from love cannot readily but be so received too.   And it is thus expressed for that very purpose, that the request may be the more welcome : *Beloved.*   It is the advice of a friend, one that truly loves you, and aims at nothing in it but your good.   It is because I love you, that I entreat you, and entreat you as you love yourselves, *to abstain from fleshly lusts that war against your souls.*   And what is our purpose when we exhort you to believe and repent, but that you may be happy in the forgiveness of your sins ?   Why do we desire you to embrace Christ, but that through Him ye may have everlasting life ?   Howsoever you take these things, it is our duty incessantly to put you in mind of them ; and to do it with much love and tenderness of affection to your souls ; not only pressing you by frequent warnings and exhortings, but also by frequent prayers and tears for your salvation.

Abstain.]   It was a very wise abridgement that Epictetus made of philosophy, into those two words, *Bear and forbear.*   These are truly the two main duties that our Apostle recommends to his Christian brethren in this Epistle.   It is one and the same strength of spirit, that raises a man above both the troubles and pleasures of the world, and makes him despise and trample upon both.

We have, first, briefly to explain what these *fleshly lusts* mean ; then, to consider the exhortation of *abstaining* from them.

Unchaste desires are particularly called by this name indeed, but to take it for these only in this place is doubtless too narrow.   That which seems to be the true sense of it here, takes in all undue desires and use of earthly things, and all the corrupt affections of our carnal minds.

Now, in that sense, these *fleshly lusts* comprehend a great part of the body of sin.   All those three which St. John speaks of, 1 Epis. ii. 16, the world's accursed trinity, are included under this name here of *fleshly lusts.*   A crew of base, imperious masters they are, to which the natural man is a slave ; *serving divers lusts.*   Tit. iii. 3.   Some are more addicted to the service of one kind of lust, some to that of another ; but all are in this unhappy, that they are strangers, yea, enemies to God, and, as the brute creatures, servants to their flesh ;— either covetous, like the beasts of the field, with their eyes still upon the earth, or voluptuous, swimming in pleasures, as fishes in the sea, or like the fowls of the air, soaring in vain ambition. All the *strifes* that are raised about these things, all *malice* and *envyings*, all *bitterness* and *evil-speaking*, (Eph. iv. 31,) which are *works of the flesh*, and tend to the satisfying of its wicked desires, we are here entreated to abstain from.

To abstain from these lusts is to hate and fly from the very thoughts and first motions of them ; and if surprised by these, yet to kill them there, that they bring not forth ; and to suspect ourselves even in those things that are not sinful, and to keep afar off from all inducements to those polluted ways of sin.

In a word, we are to abstain not only from the serving of our flesh in things forbidden, as unjust gain or unlawful pleasures, but also from immoderate desire of, and delighting in, any earthly thing, although it may be in itself lawfully, yea, necessarily in some degree, desired and used. Yea, to have any feverish, pressing thirst after gain, even just gain, or after earthly delights, though lawful, is to be guilty of those fleshly lusts, and a thing very unbeseeming the dignity of a Christian. To see them that are *clothed in scarlet embracing a dunghill* (Lam. iv. 4) is a strange sight.   Therefore the Apostle, having so cleared that immediately before, hath the better reason to require this of them, that they *abstain from fleshly lusts.*

Let their own slaves serve them : you are redeemed and delivered from them, a free people, yea, kings ; and suits it with royal dignity to obey vile lusts? You are priests consecrated to God, and will you tumble yourselves and your precious garments in the mire ? It was a high speech of a heathen, *That he was greater, and born to greater things, than to be a servant to his body.* How much more ought he that is born again to say so, being born heir to *a crown that fadeth not away!*

Again, as the honour of a Christian's estate is far above this baseness of serving his lusts, so the happiness and pleasantness of his estate set him above the need of the pleasures of sin.   The Apostle said before, *If ye have tasted that the Lord is gracious, desire the sincere milk of the word*—desire that word wherein ye may taste more of His graciousness.   And as that exhortation fitly urgeth the appetite's desire of the word, so it strongly persuades to this abstinence from fleshly lusts ; yea, to the disdain and loathing of them. If you have the least experience of the sweetness of His love, if you have but tasted of the crystal river of His pleasures, the muddy puddle-pleasures of sin will be hateful and loathsome to you ; yea, the very best earthly delights will be disrelished, and will seem unsavoury to your taste. The imbittering of the breasts of the world to the godly by afflictions doth something, indeed, towards weaning them from them ; but the *breasts of consolation* that are given them in their stead wean much more effectually.

The true reason why we remain servants to these lusts, some to one, some to another, is, because we are still strangers to the love of God.

and those pure pleasures that are in Him. Though the pleasures of this earth be poor and low, and most unworthy our pursuit, yet so long as men know no better, they will stick by those they have, such as they are. The philosopher gives this as the reason why men are so much set upon sensual delights, because they know not the higher pleasures that are proper to the soul; and they must have it some way. It is too often in vain to speak to men in this strain, to follow them with the Apostle's entreaty, *I beseech you, abstain from fleshly lusts,* unless they who are spoken to be such as he speaks of in the former words, such as *have obtained mercy,* and *have tasted of the graciousness* and love of Christ, *whose loves are better than wine.* Cant. i. 2. Oh that we would seek the knowledge of this love! for, *seeking it, we should find it;* and finding it, there would need no force to pull the delights of sin out of our hands; we should throw them away of our own accord.

Thus a carnal mind prejudices itself against religion, when it hears that it requires an abstinence from fleshly lusts, and bereaves men of their mirth and delight in sin; but they know not that it is to make way for more refined and precious delights. There is nothing of this kind taken from us, but by a very advantageous exchange it is made up. *In the world ye shall have affliction, but in me ye shall have peace.* Is not want of the world's peace abundantly paid with peace in Christ? Thus, fleshly lusts are cast out of the hearts of believers as rubbish and trash, to make room for spiritual comforts. We are barred *fellowship* with *the unfruitful works of darkness,* to the end that *we may have fellowship with God and his Son Jesus Christ.* 1 John i. 3, 7. This is to make men *eat angels' food* indeed, as was said of the manna. The serving of the flesh sets man below himself, down amongst the beasts; but the consolations of the Spirit, and communion with God, raise him above himself, and associate him with the angels. But let us speak to the Apostle's own dissuasives from these lusts, taken, 1. From the condition of Christians; 2. From the condition of those lusts.

1. From the condition of Christians: *As strangers.* These dispersed Jews were strangers scattered in divers countries, ch. i. ver. 1, but that is not intended here; they are called strangers in that spiritual sense which applies in common to all the saints. Possibly, in calling them thus, he alludes to the outward dispersion, but means, by the allusion, to express their spiritual alienation from the world, and interest in the New Jerusalem.

And this he uses as a very pertinent enforcement of his exhortation. Whatsoever others do, the serving of the flesh and love of the world are most incongruous and unseemly in you. Consider what you are. If you were citizens of this world, then you might drive the same trade with them, and follow the same lusts; but seeing you are chosen and called out of this world, and invested into a new society, made free of another city, and are therefore here but travellers passing through to your own country, it is very reasonable that there be this difference betwixt you and the world, and while they live as at home, your carriage be such as becomes strangers; not glutting yourselves with their pleasures, not surfeiting upon their delicious fruits, as some unwary travellers do abroad, but as wise strangers, living warily and soberly, and still minding most of all your journey homewards, suspecting dangers and snares in your way, and so walking with holy fear (as the Hebrew word for *stranger* imports).

There is, indeed, a miserable party even within a Christian—the remainder of corruption—that is no *stranger* here, and therefore keeps friendship and correspondence with the world, and will readily betray him if he watch not the more. So that he is not only to fly *the pollutions of the world* that are round about him, and to choose his steps that he be not insnared from without, but he is to be upon a continual guard against the lusts and corruption that are yet within himself, to curb and control them, and give them resolute and flat refusals when they solicit him, and to stop up their essays and opportunities of intercourse with the world, and such things as nourish them, and so to do what he can to starve them out of the holds they keep within him, and to strengthen that new nature which is in him ; to live and act according to it, though, in doing so, he shall be sure to live as a stranger here, and a despised, mocked, and hated stranger.

And it is not, on the whole, the worse that it should be so. If men in foreign countries be subject to forget their own at any time, it is surely when they are most kindly used abroad, and are most at their ease : and thus a Christian may be in some danger when he is best accommodated, and hath most of the smiles and caresses of the world ; so that though he can never wholly forget his home that is above, yet his thoughts of it will be less frequent, and his desires of it less earnest, and, it may be, he may insensibly slide into its customs and habits, as men will do that are well seated in some other country. But by the troubles and unfriendliness of the world he gains this, that when they abound most upon him he then feels himself a stranger, and remembers to behave as such, and thinks often with much delight and strong desires on his own country, and the rich and sure inheritance that lies there, and the ease and rest he shall have when he comes thither.

And this will persuade him strongly to fly all polluted ways and lusts as fast as the world follows them. It will make him abhor *the pleasures of sin,* and use the allowable enjoyments of this earth warily and moderately, never engaging his heart to them as worldlings do, but always keeping that free,—free from that earnest desire in the pursuit of worldly things, and that deep delight in the enjoyment of them, which the men of the earth bestow upon them. There is a diligence in his calling, and a prudent regard of his affairs, not only permitted to a Christian, but required of him. But yet, in comparison of his great and *high calling,* (as the Apostle terms it,) he follows all his other business with a kind of coldness and indifferency, as not caring very much which way they go ; his heart is elsewhere. The traveller provides himself as he can with entertainment and lodging where he comes ; if it be commodious, it is well ; but if not, it is no great matter. If he find but necessaries, he can abate delicacies very well ; for where he finds them in his way, he neither can, nor, if he could, would choose to stay there. Though his inn were dressed with the richest hangings and furniture, yet it is not his home: he must and would leave it. This is the character of ungodly men, *they mind earthly things,* Phil. iii. 19 ; they are drowned in them over head and ears, as we say.

If Christians would consider how little, and for how little a while, they are concerned in any thing here, they would go through any state, and any changes of state, either to the better or the worse, with very composed, equal minds, always moderate in·their necessary cares, and never taking any care at all for the flesh, *to fulfil the lusts of it.* Rom. xiii. 14.

Let them that have no better home than this world to lay claim to, live here as at home, and serve their lusts ; they that have all *their portion in this life*—no more good to look for than what they can catch here—let them take their time of the poor profits and pleasures that are here ; but you that have your whole estate, all your riches and pleasures, laid up in heaven, and *reserved* there *for you,* let your hearts be there, and your *conversation* there.   This is not the place of your rest, nor of your delights, unless you would be willing to change, and to have *your good things here,* as some foolish travellers, who spend the estate they should live on at home, in a little while, braving it abroad amongst strangers.   Will you, with *profane Esau, sell your birthright for a mess of pottage,*—sell eternity for a moment, and, for a moment, sell such pleasures as a moment of them is more worth than an eternity of the other.

2. The Apostle argues from the condition of those lusts.   It were quarrel enough against *fleshly lusts, which war against the soul,* that they are so far below the soul, that they cannot content, no, nor at all reach the soul ; they are not a suitable, much less a satisfying good to it.   Although sin hath unspeakably abused the soul of man, yet its excellent nature and original does still cause a vast disproportion betwixt it and all those gross, base things of the earth which concern the flesh, and go no further.   But this is not all : these fleshly lusts are not only of no benefit to the soul, but they are its pernicious enemies—*they war against it.*   And their war against it is all made up of stratagem and sleight ; for they cannot hurt the soul but by itself. They promise it some contentment, and so gain its consent to serve them, and undo itself.   They embrace the soul that they may strangle it.   The soul is too much diverted from its own proper business by the inevitable and incessant necessities of the body ; and therefore it is the height of injustice and cruelty to make it likewise serve the extravagant and sinful desires of the flesh : so much time for sleep, and so much for eating and drinking, and dressing and undressing ; and by many, the greatest part of the time that remains, is spent in labouring and providing for these.   Look on the employments of most men : all the labour of the husbandmen in the country, and of tradesmen in the city, the multitude of shops and callings, what is the end of them all, but the interest and service of the body ?   And in all these the immortal soul is drawn down to drudge for the mortal body, the house of clay wherein it dwells.   And in the sense of this, those souls that truly know and consider themselves in this condition, do often groan under the burden, and desire the day of their deliverance.   But the service of the flesh in the *inordinate lusts* of it is a point of far baser slavery and indignity to the soul, and doth not only divert it

from spiritual things for the time, but habitually indisposes it to every spiritual work, and makes it earthly and sensual, and so unfits it for heavenly things. Where these lusts, or any one of them, have dominion, the soul cannot at all perform any good; can neither pray, nor hear, nor read the word aright; and in so far as any of them prevail upon the soul of a child of God, they do disjoint and disable it for holy things. Although they be not of the grossest kind of lusts, but such things as are scarcely taken notice of in a man, either by others or by his own conscience, some irregular desires or entanglements of the heart, yet, *these little foxes will destroy the vines* (Cant. ii. 15); they will prey upon the graces of a Christian, and keep them very low. Therefore it concerns us much to study our hearts, and to be exact in calling to account the several affections that are in them; otherwise, even such as *are called of God,* and *have obtained mercy,* (for such the Apostle speaks to,) may have such lusts within them as will much abate the flourishing of their graces and the spiritual beauty of the soul.

The godly know it well in their sad experience, that their own hearts do often deceive them, harbouring and hiding such things as deprive them much of that liveliness of grace, and those comforts of the Holy Ghost, that otherwise they would be very likely to attain unto.

This *warring against the soul,* which means their mischievous and hurtful nature, hath this also included under it, that these lusts, as breaches of God's law, do subject the soul to His wrath. So that by this, the Apostle might well urge his point, Besides that these lusts are unworthy of you, the truth is, if you Christians serve your lusts, you kill your souls. So Romans viii. 13.

Consider, when men are on their death-beds, and near their entering into eternity, what they then think of all their toiling in the earth, and serving of their own hearts and lusts in any kind; when they see that of all these ways nothing remains to them but the guiltiness of their sin, and the accusations of conscience, and the wrath of God.

Oh! that you would be persuaded to esteem your precious souls, and not wound them as you do, but war for them, against all those lusts that war against them. The soul of a Christian is doubly precious, being, besides its natural excellency, ennobled by grace, and so twice descended of heaven; and therefore it deserves better usage than to be turned into a scullion to serve the flesh. The service of Jesus Christ is that which alone is fitting to it: it is alone honourable for the soul to serve so high a Lord, and its service is due only to Him who bought it at so high a rate.

Ver. 12. Having your conversation honest among the Gentiles : that, whereas they speak against you as evil-doers, they may by your good works, which they shall behold, glorify God in the day of visitation.

THESE two things that a natural man makes least account of are of all things in highest regard with a Christian, his own soul and God's glory: so that there be no stronger persuasives to him in any thing than the interest of these two. And by these the Apostle urgeth his present exhortation to holiness and blamelessness of life. For the substance of his advice or request in this and the former verse is the same : a truly *honest conversation* is that only which is spiritual, not defiled with *the carnal lusts and pollutions of the world.*

The abstaining from those lusts doth indeed comprehend, not only the rule of outward carriage, but the inward temper of the mind ; whereas this *honest conversation* doth more expressly concern our external deportment amongst men ; as it is added, *honest among the Gentiles,* and so tending to the glory of God.   So that these two are inseparably to be regarded, the inward disposition of our hearts, and the outward conversation and course of our lives.

I shall speak to the former first, as the spring of the latter.   *Keep thine heart with all diligence,*—all depends upon that—*for from thence are the issues of life.*   Prov. iv. 23.   And if so, then the regulating of the tongue, and eyes, and feet, and all will follow, as there it follows, ver. 24, *Put away from thee a froward mouth.*   That the impure streams may cease from running, the corrupt spring must be dried up. Men may convey them in a close and concealed manner, making them run, as it were, under ground, as they do filth under vaults and in ditches *(sentinas et cloacas)* ; but till the heart be renewed and purged from base lusts, it will still be sending forth, some way or other, the streams of iniquity.   *As a fountain swelleth out,* or casteth forth her waters incessantly, *so she casteth out her wickedness,* says the Prophet, of that very people and city that were called *holy,* by reason of the ordinances of God and the profession of the true religion that were amongst them : and therefore it is the same Prophet's advice from the Lord, *Wash thine heart, O Jerusalem.   How long shall thy vain thoughts lodge within thee ?*   Jer. vi. 7, and iv. 14.

This is the true method according to our Saviour's doctrine : *Make the tree good, and then the fruits will be good ;* not till then ; for *who can gather grapes of thorns, or figs of thistles ?*   Matt. vii. 16, 17. Some good outward actions avail nothing, the soul being unrenewed ; as you may stick some figs or hang some clusters of grapes upon a thorn-bush, but they cannot grow upon it.

In this men deceive themselves, even such as have some thoughts of amendment ; when they fall into sin, and are reproved for it, they say, (and possibly think so too,) " I will take heed to myself, I will be guilty of this no more."   And because they go no deeper, they are many of them insnared in the same kind again ; but however, if they do never commit that same sin, they do but change it for some other : as a current of waters, if you stop their passage one way, they rest not till they find another.   The conversation can never be uniformly and entirely good till the frame of the heart, the affections and desires that lodge in it, be changed.   It is naturally *an evil treasure* of impure lusts, and must in some way vent and spend what it hath within. It is to begin with the wrong end of your work, to rectify the outside first, to smooth the conversation, and not first of all purge the heart. Evil affections are the source of evil speeches and actions.   *Whence are strifes and fightings ?* says St. James ; *Are they not from your lusts which war in your members ?*   James iv. 1.   Unquiet, unruly lusts within, are the cause of the unquietnesses and contentions abroad in the world.   One man will have his corrupt will, and another his, and thus they shock and justle one another ; and by the cross encounters of their purposes, as flints meeting, they strike out those sparks that set all on fire.

So then, according to the order of the Apostle's exhortation, the only true principle of all good and Christian conversation in the world is the mortifying of all earthly and sinful lusts in the heart. While they have possession of the heart, they do so clog it, and straiten it towards God and His ways, that it cannot walk constantly in them ; but when the heart is freed from them, it is enlarged, and so, as David speaks, the man is fitted not only to walk, but to *run the way of God's commandments.* Psal. cxix. 32.   And without this *freeing of the heart,* a man will be at the best very uneven and incongruous in his ways,—in one step like a Christian, and in another like a worldling ; which is an unpleasant and unprofitable way, not according to that word, Psal. xviii. 32, *Thou hast set my feet as hinds' feet,*—set them *even,* as the word is, not only swift, but straight and even ; and that is the thing here required, that the whole course and revolution of a Christian's life be like himself.   And that it may be so, the whole body of sin, and all the members of it, *all the deceitful lusts, must be crucified.*

In the words there are three things : 1. One point of a Christian's ordinary entertainment in the world is *to be evil spoken of.*   2. Their good use of that evil is *to do the better for it.*   3. The good end and the certain effect of their so doing is *the glory of God.*

1. *Whereas they speak against you as evil-doers.*]   This is in general the disease of man's corrupt nature, and argues much the baseness and depravedness of it,—this propension to evil speaking one of another, either blotting the best actions with misconstructions, or taking doubtful things by the left ear ; not choosing the most favourable, but, on the contrary, the very harshest sense that can be put upon them.   Some men take more pleasure in the narrow eyeing of the true and real faults of men, and then speak of them with a kind of delight. All these kinds of evil speakings are such fruits as spring from that bitter root of pride and self-love which is naturally deep fastened in every man's heart.   But, besides this general bent to evil speaking, there is a particular malice in the world against those that are *born of God,* which must have vent in calumnies and reproaches.   If this evil speaking be the hissing that is natural to the serpent's seed, surely, by reason of their natural antipathy, it must be breathed forth most against the *seed of the woman,* those that are one with Jesus Christ. If the *tongues* of the ungodly be *sharp swords* even to one another, they will *whet them* sharper than ordinary when they are to use them against the righteous, to wound their name.   The evil tongue must be always burning, that *is set on fire of hell,* as St. James speaks ; but against the godly, it will be sure to be heated seven times hotter than it is for others.   The reasons for this are, 1. Being naturally haters of God, and yet unable to reach Him, what wonder is it if their malice vent itself against His image in His children, and labour to blot and stain that, all they can, with the foulest calumnies ?   2. Because they are neither able nor willing themselves to attain unto the spotless, holy life of Christians, they bemire them, and would make them like themselves, by false aspersions : they cannot rise to the estate of the

godly, and therefore they endeavour to draw them down to theirs by detraction. 3. The reproaches they cast upon the professors of pure religion they mean mainly against religion itself, and intend by them to reflect upon it.

These evil speakings of the world against pious men professing religion are partly gross falsehoods, invented without the least ground or appearance of truth ; for the world being ever credulous of evil, especially upon so deep a prejudice as it hath against the godly, the falsest and most absurd calumnies will always find so much belief as to make them odious, or very suspected at least, to such as know them not. This is the world's maxim, *Lie confidently, and it will always do something;* as a stone taken out of the mire and thrown against a white wall, though it stick not there, but rebound presently back again, yet it leaves a spot behind it. And with this kind of evil speakings were the primitive Christians surcharged, even with gross and horrible falsehoods, as all know who know any thing of the history of those times ; even such things were reported of them as the worst of wicked men would scarcely be guilty of. The Devil, as crafty as he is, makes use, again and again, of his old inventions, and makes them serve in several ages ; for so were the *Waldenses* accused of inhuman banquetings and beastly promiscuous uncleanness, and divers things *not once to be named among Christians,* much less to be practised by them. So that it is no new thing to meet with the impurest, vilest slanders, as the world's reward of holiness and the practice of pure religion.

Then again consider, how much more will the wicked insult upon the least *real blemishes* that they can espy amongst the professors of godliness. And in this there is a threefold injury very ordinary ; 1. Strictly to pry into, and maliciously to object against Christians, the smallest imperfections and frailties of their lives, as if they pretended to and promised absolute perfection. They do indeed *exercise themselves,* (such as are Christians indeed,) with St. Paul, *to keep a good conscience in all things towards God and men;* (Acts xxiv. 16 ;) they have a *regard unto all God's commandments,* as David speaks ; they have a sincere love to God, which makes them study the exactest obedience they can reach : and this is an imperfect kind of perfection ; it is evangelical, but not angelical. 2. Men are apt to impute the scandalous falls of some particular Christians to the whole number. It is a very short, incompetent rule, to make judgment of any one man himself by one action, much more to measure all the rest of the same profession by it. And they yet proceed further in this way of misjudging. 3. They impute the personal failings of men to their religion, and disparage it because of the faults of those that profess it ; which, as the ancients plead well, is the greatest injustice, and such as they would not be guilty of against their own philosophers. They could well distinguish betwixt their doctrine and the manners of some of their followers, and thus ought they to have dealt with Christians too. They ought to have considered their religion in itself, and the doctrine that it teacheth, and had they found it vicious, the blame had been just ; but if it taught nothing but holiness and righteousness, then the blame of any unholiness or unrighteousness found amongst Christians ought to rest upon the persons themselves who were guilty of it, and not to be stretched to the whole number of professors, much less to the religion that they professed. And yet this is still the custom of the world upon the least failing they can espy in the godly, or such as seem to be so ; much more with open mouth do they revile religion upon any gross sin in any of its professors.

But seeing this is the very character of a profane mind, and the badge of the enemies of religion, beware of sharing in the least with them in it. Give not easy entertainment to the reports of profane or of mere civil men against the professors of religion ; they are undoubtedly partial, and their testimony may be justly suspected. Lend them not a ready ear to receive their evil speakings, much less your tongue to divulge them, and set them further going ; yea, take heed that you take not pleasure in any the least kind of scoffs against the sincerity and power of religion. And, all of you who desire to walk as Christians, be very wary that you wrong not one another, and help not the wicked against you, by your mutual misconstructions and miscensures one of another. Far be it from you to take pleasure in hearing others evil spoken of ; whether unjustly or though it be some way deservedly, yet let it be alway grievous to you, and no way pleasing to hear such things, much less to speak of them. It is the Devil's delight to be pleased with evil speakings. The Syrian calls him an *Akal Kartza, Eater of slanders or calumnies.* They are a dish that pleases his palate, and men are naturally fond of this diet. In Psal. xxxv. 16, there is a word that is rendered *mockers at feasts,* or *feasting-mockers* — persons who feasted men's ears at their meetings with speaking of the faults of others scoffingly, and therefore shared with them of their cakes, or feasts, as the word is. But to a renewed Christian mind, which hath a new taste, and all its senses new, there is nothing more unsavoury than to hear the defaming of others, especially of such as profess religion. Did *the law of love* possess our hearts, it would regulate both the ear and tongue, and make them most tender of the name of our brethren : it would teach us the faculty of covering their infirmities, and judging favourably, taking always the best side and most charitable sense of their actions : it would teach us to blunt the edge of our censures upon ourselves, our own hard hearts and rebellious wills within, that they might remain no more sharp against others than is needful for their good.

And this would cut short those that are without from a great deal of provisions of evil speaking against Christians that they many times are furnished with by Christians themselves, through their uncharitable carriage one towards another. However, this being the hard measure that they always find in the world, it is their wisdom to consider it aright, and to study that good which, according to the Apostle's advice, may be extracted out of it, and that is the second thing to be spoken to.

Having your conversation honest among the Gentiles.] As the sovereign power of drawing good out of evil resides in God, and argues His primitive goodness, so He teacheth his own children some faculty this way, that they may resemble Him in it. He teacheth them to draw sweetness out of their bitterest afflictions, and increase of inward peace from their outward troubles. And as these buffetings of the tongue are no small part of their sufferings, so they reap no small benefit by them many ways : particularly in this one, that they order their conversation the better, and walk the more exactly for it.

And this, no doubt, in Divine providence, is intended and ordered for their good, as are all their other trials. The sharp censures and evil speakings that a Christian is encompassed with in the world, is no other than a hedge of thorns set on every side, that he go not out of his way, but keep straight on in it betwixt them, not declining to the right hand nor to the left ; whereas, if they found nothing but the favour and good opinion of the world, they might, as in a way unhedged, be subject to expatiate and wander out into the meadows of carnal pleasures that are about them, which would call and allure them, and often divert them from their journey.

And thus it might fall out, that Christians would deserve censure and evil speakings the more, if they did not usually suffer them undeserved. This then turns into a great advantage to them, making their conduct more answerable to those two things that our Saviour joins, *watch and pray;* causing them to be the more vigilant over themselves, and the more earnest with God for His watching over them and conducting of them. *Make my ways straight,* says David, *because of mine enemies,* Psal. v. 8 : the word is, *my observers,* or those that scan my ways, every foot of them ; that examine them as a verse, or as a song of music ; if there be but a wrong measure in them, they will not let it slip, but will be sure to mark it.

And if the enemies of the godly wait for their halting, shall not they scan their own paths themselves, that they may not halt ? Shall they not examine them to order them, as the wicked do to censure them ; still depending wholly upon the Spirit of God as their guide, *to lead them into all truth,* and to teach them how *to order their conversation aright,* that it may be all of a piece, holy and blameless, and still like itself ?

Honest.] Fair or beautiful : the same word doth fitly signify goodness and beauty, for that which is the truest and most lasting beauty grows fresher in old age, as the Psalmist speaks of the righteous, *those that be planted in the house of God,* Psal. xcii. 12—14. Could the beauty of virtue be seen, said a philosopher, it would draw all to love it. A Christian, holy conversation hath such a beauty, that when they who are strangers to it begin to discern it all aright, they cannot choose but love it ; and where it begets not love, yet it silences calumny, or at least evinces its falsehood.

The goodness or beauty of a Christian's conversation consisting in symmetry and conformity to the word of God as its rule, he ought diligently to study that rule, and to square his ways by it ; not to walk at random, but to apply that rule to every step at home and abroad, and to be as careful to keep the beauty of his ways unspotted, as those women are of their faces and attire who are most studious of comeliness.

But so far are we who call ourselves Christians from this exact regard of our conversation, that the most part not only have many foul spots, but they themselves, and all their ways, are nothing but defilement, all one spot ;—as our Apostle calls them, *blots are they and spots*, 2 Pet. ii. 13. And even they who are Christians indeed, yet are not so watchful and accurate in all their ways as becomes them, but stain their *holy profession* either with pride, or covetousness, or contentions, or some other such like uncomeliness.

Let us all, therefore, resolve more to study this good and comely conversation the Apostle here exhorts to, that it may be such as *becometh the Gospel of Christ*, as St. Paul desires his Philippians, ch. i. ver. 27. And if you live amongst profane .persons, who will be to you as the unbelieving Gentiles were to these believing Jews who lived amongst them, traducers of you, and given to speak evil of you, and of religion in you, trouble not yourselves with many apologies and clearings when you are evil spoken of, but let the track of your life answer for you, your *honest* and *blameless conversation :* that will be the shortest and most real and effectual way of confuting all obloquies ; as when one in the schools was proving by a sophistical argument, that there could be no motion, the philosopher answered it fully and shortly by rising up and walking. If thou wouldst pay them home, this is a kind of revenge not only allowed thee, but recommended to thee ; be avenged on evil speakings by well-doing, shame them from it. It was a king that said, *It was kingly to do well and be ill spoken of.* Well may Christians acknowledge it to be true, when they consider that it was the lot of their King, Jesus Christ ; and well may they be content, seeing he hath made them likewise *kings,* (as we heard, ver. 9,) to be conformable to him in this too, this kingly way of suffering, to be unjustly evil spoken of, and still to go on in doing the more good ; always aiming in so doing (as our Lord did) at the glory of our Heavenly Father. This is the third thing.

That they may glorify God in the day of their visitation. He says not, they shall praise or commend you, but *shall glorify God.* In what way soever this time, this *day of visitation,* be taken, the effect itself is this, *They shall glorify God.* It is this the Apostle still holds before their eye, as that upon which a Christian doth willingly set his eye, and keep it fixed in all his ways. He doth not teach them to be sensible of their own esteem as it concerns themselves, but only as the glory of their God is interested in it. Were it not for this, a generous-minded Christian could set a very light rate upon all the thoughts and speeches of men concerning him, whether good or bad ; and could easily drown all their mistakes in the conscience of the favour and approbation of his God. *It is a very small thing for me to be judged of you, or of the day of man : he that judgeth me is the Lord.* 1 Cor. iv. 3. Man hath a day of judging, but it, and his judgment with it, soon passes away ; but God hath *His day,* and it, together with His sentence, abideth for ever, as the Apostle there adds. As if he should say, *I appeal to God ;* but considering that the religion he professes, and the God whom he worships in that religion, are wronged by those reproaches, and that the calumnies cast upon Christians reflect upon their Lord,—this is the thing that makes him sensible ; he feels on that side only. *The reproaches of them that reproached thee are fallen upon me,* says the Psalmist : and this makes a Christian desirous to vindicate, even to men, his religion and his God, without regard to himself; because he may say, *The reproaches of them that reproach* only *me, have fallen upon Thee.* Psal. lxix. 9.

This is his intent in the holiness and integrity of his life, that God may be glorified; this is the axis about which all *this good conversation* moves and turns continually.

And he that forgets this, let his conversation be never so plausible and spotless, knows not what it is to be a Christian. As they say of the eagles, who try their young ones whether they be of the right kind or not, by holding them before the sun, and if they can look stedfastly upon it, they own them, if not, they throw them away: this is the true evidence of an upright and real Christian, to have a stedfast eye on the glory of God, the *Father of lights.* In all, let God be glorified, says the Christian, and that suffices: that is the sum of his desires. He is far from glorying in himself, or seeking to raise himself, for he knows that of himself he is nothing, but by the *free grace of God he is what he is.* "Whence any glorying to thee, rottenness and dust?" says St. Bernard. "Whence is it to thee if thou art holy? Is it not the Holy Spirit that hath sanctified thee? If thou couldst work miracles, though they were done by thy hand, yet it were not by thy power, but by the power of God."

To the end that my glory may sing praise unto thee, says David, Psal. xxx. 12. Whether his tongue, or his soul, or both be meant, what he calls *his glory,* he shows us, and what use he hath for it, namely, to give the Lord glory, to sing his praises, and that then it was truly David's glory when it was so employed, in giving glory to Him whose peculiar due glory is. What have we to do in the world as His creatures, once and again His creatures, His new creatures, *created unto good works,* but to exercise ourselves in those, and by those to advance His glory, that all may return to Him from whom all is, as the rivers run back to the sea from whence they came? *Of Him, and through Him,* and therefore, *for Him are all things,* says the Apostle, Rom. xi. 36. They that serve base gods, seek how to advance and aggrandize them. The covetous man studies to make his *Mammon* as great as he can, all his thoughts and pains run upon that service, and so do the voluptuous and ambitious for theirs; and shall not they who profess themselves to be the servants of the Only Great and the Only True God, have their hearts much more, at least as much possessed with desires of honouring and exalting *Him?* Should not this be their predominant design and thought?—What way shall I most advance the glory of my God? How shall I, who am under stronger obligations than they all, set in with the heavens and the earth, and the other creatures, to declare His excellency, His greatness, and His goodness?

In the day of visitation.] The beholding of your good works may work this in them, that they may be gained to acknowledge and embrace that religion, and that God, which for the present they reject; but that it may be thus, they must be visited with that same light and grace from above, which hath sanctified you. This, I conceive, is the sense of this word, though it may be and is taken divers other ways by interpreters. Possibly, in this *day of visitation* is implied the clearer preaching of the Gospel amongst those Gentiles, where the dispersed Jews dwelt; and that when they should compare the light of that doctrine with the light of their lives, and find the agreement betwixt them, that might be helpful to their effectual calling, and so they might glorify God. But to the end that they might do thus indeed, there must be, along with the word of God, and the good works of his people, a particular visiting of their souls by the Spirit of God. Your good conversation may be one good mean of their conversion; therefore this may be a motive to that; but to make it an effectual mean, this day of gracious visitation must dawn upon them; *the dayspring from on high* must visit them, as it is Luke i. 7, 8.

Ver. 13. Submit yourselves to every ordinance of man for the Lord's sake : whether it be to the king, as supreme ;
14. Or unto governors, as unto them that are sent by him for the punishment of evil-doers, and for the praise of them that do well.

It is one of the falsest, and yet one of the commonest prejudices that the world hath always entertained against true religion, that it is an enemy to civil power and government. The adversaries of the Jews charged this fault upon their city, the then seat of the true worship of God, Ezra iv. 15. The Jews charged it upon the preachers of the Christian religion, Acts xvii. 7, as they pretended the same quarrel against Christ himself. And generally, the enemies of the Christians of primitive times loaded them with the slander of rebellion and contempt of authority. Therefore our Apostle, descending to particular rules of Christian life, by which it may be blameless, and silence calumny, begins with this, not only as a thing of prime importance in itself, but as particularly fit for those he wrote to, being at once both Jews and Christians, for the clearing of themselves and their religion : *Submit yourselves,* &c.

There are in the words divers particulars to be considered, all concurring to press this main duty of obedience to magistrates, not only as well consistent with true religion, but as indeed inseparable from it. Not to parcel out the words into many pieces, they may, I conceive, be all not unfitly comprised under these two : 1. The extent of this duty ; 2. The ground of it.

1. The extent of the duty, viz., *To all civil power,* of what kind soever, for the time received and authorized ; there being no need of questioning what was the rise and original of civil power, either in the nature of it, or in the persons of those that are in possession of it. For if you will trace them quite through in the succession of ages, and narrowly eye their whole circle, there be few crowns in the world, in which there will not be found some crack or other, more or less. If you look on those great monarchies in Daniel's vision, you see one of them built up upon the ruins of another ; and all of them represented by terrible devouring beasts of monstrous shape. And whether the Roman empire be the fourth there, as many take it, or not, yet, in the things spoken of that fourth, as well as of the rest, it is inferior to none of them, enlarging itself by conquests in all parts of the world. And under it were the provinces to which this Epistle is addressed : yet the Apostle enjoins his brethren subjection and obedience to its authority.

Nor is it a question so to be moved as to suspend, or at all abate, our obedience to that which possesses in the present where we live, what form of government is most just and commodious.

God hath indeed been more express in the officers and government of his own house, his Church ; but civil societies He hath left at liberty in the choosing and modelling of civil government, though always, indeed, over-ruling their choice and changes in that, by the secret hand of His wise and powerful providence. Yet He hath set them no particular rule touching the frame of it ; only, the common rule of equity and justice ought to be regarded, both in the contriving and managing of government. Nevertheless, though it be some way defective in both, those that are subject to it, are in all things lawful to submit to its authority, whether supreme or subordinate ; as we have it here expressly, *Whether to the king as supreme,* (namely, to the emperor,) or *to the governors sent by him;*—which though a judicious interpreter refers to God, and will not admit of any other sense, yet it seems most suitable both to the words and to the nature of the government of those provinces, to take that word *To him,* as relating to the king ; for the expression *them that are sent,* answers to the other, *the king as supreme,* and so is a very clear designation of the inferior governors of those times and places. And whatsoever was their end who sent them, and their carriage who were sent, that which the Apostle adds, expresses the end for which they should be sent to govern, and at which they should aim in governing, as the true end of all government. And though they were not fully true to that end in their deportment, but possibly did many things unjustly, yet, as God hath ordained authority for this end, there is always so much justice in the most depraved government, as renders it a public good, and therefore puts upon inferiors an obligation to obedience : and this leads us to consider,

2. The ground of this duty. The main ground of submitting to human authority, is the interest that Divine authority hath in it, God having both appointed civil government as a common good amongst men, and particularly commanded his people obedience to it, as a particular good to them, and a thing very suitable with their profession : it is *for the Lord's sake.* This word carries the whole weight of the duty, and is a counterbalance to the former, which seems to be therefore on purpose so expressed, that this may answer it. Although civil authority, in regard of particular forms of government, and the choice of particular persons to govern, is but a human ordinance, or *man's creature,* as the word is, yet, both the good of government, and the duty of subjection to it, are God's ordinance ; and therefore, *for His sake submit yourselves.*

[1.] God hath in general instituted civil government for the good of human society, and still there is good in it. Tyranny is better than anarchy. [2.] It is by His providence that men are advanced to places of authority. See Psal. lxxv. 6, 7 ; Dan. iv. 25 ; John xix. 11. [3.] It is His command, that obedience be yielded to them. Rom. xiii. 1 ; Tit. iii. 1, &c. And the consideration of this, ties a Christian to all loyalty and due obedience, which, being still *for the Lord's sake,* cannot hold in any thing that is against the Lord's own command ; for kings and rulers, in such case, leave their station. Now the subjection here enjoined is, ὑποτάγητε, *Be subject* to them, as it were in your rank, still in subordination to God; but if they go out of that even line, follow them not. They that obey the unlawful commands of kings do it in regard to *their god,* no question, but that *their god is their belly,* or their ambition, or their avarice.

But not only ought the exercise of authority, and submission to it, to be confined to things just and lawful in themselves, but the very purpose of the heart, both in command and obedience, should be in *the Lord,* and *for His sake.* This is the only straight, and the only safe rule, both for rulers and for people to walk by. Would kings, and the other powers of the world, consider the supremacy and greatness of that King of whom they hold all their crowns and dignities, they would be no less careful of their submission and homage to Him, than they are desirous of their people's submission to themselves.

I will not speak at all of their civil obligations to their people, and the covenant of justice that with good reason is betwixt them in the fundamental constitutions of all well-ordered kingdoms ; nor meddle with that point—the dependence that human authority hath upon the societies of men over whom it is, according to which it is here called *man's ordinance,* or *creature,* ἀνθρωπίνη κτίσει. This is a thing that the greatest and most absolute of princes cannot deny, that all their authority is dependent upon the great God, both as the Author of it in the general, and the sovereign Disposer of it to particular men, *giving the kingdoms of the earth to whom He will.* Dan. iv. 25. And therefore He may most justly require obedience and fealty of them, that they *serve the Lord in fear ;* and if they rejoice in their dignities over men, yet that they do it with *trembling,* under a sense of their duty to God, and that they throw down their crowns at the feet of Christ, *the Lord's anointed.*

And to this they are the more obliged, considering that religion and the Gospel of Christ do so much press the duty of their people's obedience to them ; so that they wrong both Christianity and themselves very far, in mistaking it as an enemy to their authority, when it is so far from prejudicing it, that it confirms it, and pleads for it. Surely they do most ungratefully requite the Lord and His Christ, when they say, (as Psal. ii.,) *Let us break their bands asunder, and cast away their cords from us.* Whereas the Lord binds the cords of kings and their authority fast upon their people ; not the cords of tyranny indeed, to bind the subjects as beasts to be sacrifices to the passion of their rulers, but the cords of just and due obedience to their kings and governors. The Lord doth (as you see here) bind it upon all that profess His name, and strengthens it by the respect His people carry to Himself, enjoining them that, *for His sake,* they would obey their rulers. So that kings need not fear true religion, that it will ever favour any thing that can justly be called rebellion ; on the contrary, it still urges loyalty and obedience : so that as they ought in duty, they may in true policy and wisdom, befriend true religion, as a special friend to their authority, and hate that religion of *Rome* which is indeed rebellion, and that *mother of abominations,* who makes the *kings of the earth drunk with her cup,* and makes them dream of increase of authority while they are truly on the losing hand. But besides that they owe their power to the advancement of Christ's kingdom, by so employing themselves as to strengthen it, they do themselves good; they confirm their own thrones, when they erect His : as it was said of Cæsar, that by setting up Pompey's statue, he settled and fastened his own.

But it is an evil too natural to men, to forget the true end and use of any good the Lord confers on them. And thus kings and rulers too often consider not for what they are exalted ; they think it is for themselves, to honour and please themselves, and not to honour God, and benefit their people, to encourage and reward the good, (as here it is,) and to punish the wicked. They are set on high for the good of those that are below them, that they may be refreshed with their light and influence ; as the lights of heaven are set there in the highest parts of the world, for the use and benefit of the very lowest. God set them in the firmament of heaven, but to what end ? *To give light upon the earth.* Gen. i. 15. And the mountains are raised above the rest of the earth, not to be places of prey and robbery, as sometimes they are turned to be, but to send forth streams from their springs into the valleys, and make them fertile ; these mountains and hills (greater and lesser rulers, higher and lower) are to send forth to the people the *streams of righteousness and peace.* Psal. lxxii. 31.

But it is the corruption and misery of man's nature, that he doth not know, and can hardly be persuaded to learn, either how to command aright, or how to obey ; and no doubt many of those that can see and blame the injustice of others in authority, would be more guilty that way themselves, if they had the same power.

It is the pride and self-love of our nature, that begets disobedience in inferiors, and violence and injustice in superiors ; that depraved humour which ties to every kind of government a propension to a particular disease ; which makes royalty easily degenerate into tyranny, the government of nobles into faction, and popular government into confusion.

As civil authority, and subjection to it, are the institution of God, so, the peaceable correspondence of these two, just government and due obedience, is the special gift of God's own hand, and a prime blessing to states and kingdoms ; and the troubling and interruption of their course is one of the highest public judgments by which the Lord punishes oftentimes the other sins both of rulers and people. And whatsoever be the cause, and on which side soever be the justice of the cause, it cannot be looked upon but as a heavy plague, and the fruit of many and great provocations, when kings and their people, who should be a mutual blessing and honour to each other, are turned into scourges one to another, or into a devouring fire ; as it is in the parable, Judg. ix. 20, *Fire going forth from Abimelech to devour the men of Shechem, and fire from Shechem to devour Abimelech.*

Ver. 15. For so is the will of God, that with well doing ye may put to silence the ignorance of foolish men :
16. As free, and not using your liberty for a cloak of maliciousness, but as the servants of God.

THIS continues the same reason of the same Christian duty : if they will obey the Lord, then they must obey civil powers, for that is His will, and they will not deny their obligation to Him, for they are His servants, ver. 16. The words, indeed, are more general than the former, but they relate chiefly, in this place, to the particular in hand, implying that neither in that kind nor in any other, Christians should dishonour their profession, and abuse their liberty, mistaking it as an exemption from those duties to which it doth more straitly tie them. So then, the point of civil obedience and all other good conversation amongst men, is here recommended to Christians, as conformable to the will of God, and the most effectual clearing of their profession, and very agreeable to their Christian liberty.

The will of God.] This is the strongest and most binding reason that can be used to a Christian mind, which hath resigned itself to be governed by that rule, to have *the will of God* for its law. Whatsoever is required of it upon that warrant, it cannot refuse. Although it cross a man's own humour, or his private interest, yet if his heart be subjected to the will of God, he will not stand with Him in any thing. One word from God, *I will have it so,* silences all, and carries it against all opposition.

It were a great point, if we could be persuaded to esteem duly of this : it were indeed all. It would make light and easy work in those things that go so hardly on with us, though we are daily exhorted to them. Is it the will of God that I should live soberly ? Then, though my own corrupt will and my companions be against it, yet it must be so. Wills He that I forbear cursing and oaths, though it is my custom to use them ? Yet I must offer violence to my custom, and go against the stream of all their customs that are round about me, to obey His will, who wills all things justly and holily. Will He have my charity not only liberal in giving, but in forgiving, and real and hearty in both ? Will He have me *bless them that curse me, and do good to them that hate me, and love mine enemies?* Though the world counts it a hard task, and my own corrupt heart possibly finds it so, yet it shall be done ; and not as upon unpleasant necessity, but willingly, and cheerfully, and with the more delight because it is difficult ; for so it proves my obedience the more, and my love to Him whose will it is. Though mine enemies deserve not my love, yet He who bids me love them, does ; and if He will have this the touchstone to try the uprightness of my love to Him, shall it fail there ? No, His will commands me so absolutely, and He himself is so lovely, that there can be nobody so unlovely in themselves, or to me, but I can love them upon His command, and for His sake.

But that it may be thus, there must be a renewed frame of mind, by which a man may renounce the world, and the forms of it, and himself, and his own sinful heart, and its way, to study and follow the only *good, and acceptable, and perfect will of God,* (Rom. xii. 2,) to move most in that line, not willingly declining to either hand, to have his whole mind taken up in searching it, and his whole heart in embracing it. *Be ye not unwise, but understanding what the will of the Lord is,* says the Apostle Paul, Eph. v. 17, being about to exhort to particular duties, as our Apostle here is doing.

This is the task of a Christian, to understand his Lord's will, and with a practical understanding, that he may walk in all well pleasing unto God. Thus the Apostle likewise exhorts the Thessalonians pathetically, (1 Ep. iv. 1,) and adds, *This is the will of God, even your sanctification.* And he then proceeds particularly against uncleanness and deceit, &c.

Let this, then, be your endeavour, to have your wills crucified to whatsoever is sinful, yea, to all outward indifferent things with a kind of indifferency. The most things that men are so stiff in, are not worth an earnest willing. In a word, it were the only happy and truly spiritual temper, to have our will quite rooted out, and the will of God placed in its stead ; to have no other will than His, that it might constantly, yea, (so to speak,) identically follow it in all things. This is the will of God, therefore it is mine.

That with well doing ye may put to silence the ignorance of foolish men.] The duties of the Second Table, or of well doing towards men, are more obvious to men devoid of religion, than those that have an immediate relation to God : and therefore (as in other Epistles) the Apostle is here particular in these, for the vindicating of religion to them that are without. Ignorance usually is loud and prattling, making a mighty noise, and so hath need of a *muzzle to silence it,* as the word φιμουν imports. They that were ready to speak evil of religion, are called *witless* or foolish men ; there was perverseness in their ignorance, as the word ἀφόνων intimates. And generally, all kinds of evil speakings and uncharitable censurings do argue a foolish, worthless mind, whence they proceed ; and yet, they are the usual divertisement of the greatest part of mankind, and take up very much of their converse and discourse ; which is an evidence of the baseness and perverseness of their minds. For, whereas those that have most real goodness, delight most to observe what is good and commendable in others, and to pass by their blemishes, it is the true character of vile, unworthy persons, (as scurvy flies sit upon sores,) to skip over all the good that is in men, and fasten upon their infirmities.

But especially doth it discover *ignorance and folly,* to turn the failings of men to the disadvantage of religion. None can be such enemies to it, but they that know it not, and see not the beauty that is in it. However, the way to silence them, we see, is by *well doing;* that silences them more than whole volumes of Apologies. When a Christian walks irreprovably, his enemies have no where to fasten their teeth on him, but are forced to gnaw their own malignant tongues. As it secures the godly, thus to stop the lying mouths of foolish men, so it is as painful to them to be thus stopped, as muzzling is to beasts, and it punishes their malice.

And this is a wise Christian's way, instead of impatiently fretting at the mistakes or wilful miscensures of men, to keep still on his calm temper of mind, and upright course of life, and silent innocence ; this, as a rock, breaks the waves into foam that roar about it.

As free.] This the Apostle adds, lest any should so far mistake the nature of their Christian liberty, as to dream of an exemption from obedience either to God, or to men for His sake, and according to His appointment. Their freedom he grants, but would have them understand aright what it is. I cannot here insist at large on the spiritual freedom of Christians ; nor is it here needful, being mentioned only for the clearing of it in this point ; but free they are, and they only, who are partakers of this liberty. *If the Son make you free, you shall be free indeed.* John viii. 36. The rest are slaves to Satan and the world, and their own lusts ; as the Israelites in Egypt, working in the clay under hard task-masters.

Much discourse hath been spent, and much ink hath been spilt upon the debate of *free-will,* but truly, all the liberty it hath till the Son and His Spirit free it, is that miserable freedom the Apostle speaks of, Rom. vi. 20: *While ye were servants to sin, ye were free from righteousness.*

And as we are naturally subject to the vile drudgery of sin, so we are condemned to the proper *wages of sin,* which the Apostle there tells us is *death,* according to the just sentence of the Law. But our Lord Christ was anointed for this purpose, *to set us free,*both to work and to publish liberty, to *proclaim liberty to captives, and the opening of the prison doors to them that are bound.* Isa. lxi. 1. Having paid our complete ransom, He sends His word as the message, and His Spirit, to perform it effectually, to set us free, to let us know it, and to bring us out of prison. He was bound and scourged, as a slave or malefactor, to purchase us this liberty ; therefore ought it to be our special care, first, to have part in it, and then to be like it, and *stand fast in it,* in all points.

But that we deceive not ourselves, as too many do who have no portion in this liberty, we ought to know that it is not *to* inordinate walking and licentiousness, as our liberty, that we are called, but *from* them, as our thraldom ; we are not called from obedience, but to it. Therefore beware that you shuffle in, under this specious name of *liberty,* nothing that belongs not to it. Make it not *a cloak of maliciousness ;* it is too precious a garment for so base a use. Liberty is indeed Christ's livery that he gives to all his followers ; but to live suitably to it, is not to live in wickedness or disobedience of any kind, but in obedience and holiness. You are called to be *the servants of God,* and that is your dignity and your liberty.

The Apostles of this Gospel of liberty gloried in this title, *The servants of Jesus Christ.* David, before that Psalm of praise for his victories and exaltations, being now settled on his throne, prefixes, as more honour than all these, *A Psalm of David, the servant of the Lord,* Psal. xviii. 1. It is the only true happiness both of kings and their subjects, to be His subjects. It is the glory of the angels to be His *ministering spirits.* The more we attain unto the faculty of serving him cheerfully and diligently, the more still we find of this spiritual liberty, and have the more joy in it. As it is the most honourable, it is likewise the most comfortable and most gainful service ; and they that once know it, will never change it for any other in the world. Oh ! that we could live as his servants, employing all our industry to do Him service in the condition and place wherein He hath set us, whatsoever it is, and as faithful servants, more careful of his affairs than of our own, accounting it our main business to seek the advancement of his glory. *Happy is the servant whom the master, when he cometh, shall find so doing.* Matt. xxiv. 46.

Ver. 17. Honour all men. Love the brotherhood. Fear God. Honour the king.

THIS is a precious cluster of Divine precepts. The whole face of the heavens is adorned with stars, but they are of different magnitudes, and in some parts they are thicker set than in others : thus is it likewise in the Holy Scriptures. And these are the two books that the Psalmist sets open before us, Psal. xix. ; the heavens as a choice piece of the works of God instructing us, and the word of God more full and clear than they. Here is a constellation of very bright stars near together. These words have very briefly, and yet not obscured by briefness, but withal very plainly, the sum of our duty towards God and men ; to men both in general, *Honour all men*, and in special relations,—in their Christian or religious relation, *Love the brotherhood*, and in a chief civil relation, *Honour the king*. And our whole duty to God, comprised under the name of *His fear*, is set in the middle betwixt these, as the common spring of all duty to men, and of all due observance of it, and the sovereign rule by which it is to be regulated.

I shall speak of them as they lie in the text. We need not labour about the connexion ; for in such variety of brief practical directions, it hath not such places as in doctrinal discourses. The Apostle having spoken of one particular wherein he would have his brethren to clear and commend their Christian profession, now accumulates these directions as most necessary, and afterwards goes on to particular duties of servants, &c. But first, observe in general, how plain and easy, and how few are those things that are the rule of our life ; no dark sentences to puzzle the understanding, nor large discourses and long periods to burden the memory ; they are all plain ; there *is nothing wreathed* nor distorted in them, as Wisdom speaks of her instructions, Prov. viii. 8.

And this gives check to a double folly amongst men, contrary the one to the other, but both agreeing in mistaking and wronging the word of God ; the one is of those that despise the word, and that doctrine and preaching that is conformable to it, for its plainness and simplicity ; the other of those that complain of its difficulty and darkness. As for the first, they certainly do not take the true end for which the word is designed, that it is the law of our life : (and it is mainly requisite in laws, that they be both brief and clear :) that it is our guide and light to happiness ; and if that which ought to be our *light, be darkness, how great will that darkness be!*

It is true, (but I am not now to insist on this point,) that there be dark and deep passages in Scripture, for the exercise, yea, for the humbling, yea, for the amazing and astonishing of the sharpest-sighted readers. But this argues much the pride and vanity of men's minds, when they busy themselves only in those, and throw aside altogether the most necessary, which are therefore the easiest and plainest truths in it. As in nature, the commodities that are of greatest necessity, God hath made most common and easiest to be had, so, in religion, such instructions as these now in our hands, are given us to live and walk by ; and in the search of things that are more obscure, and less useful, men evidence that they had rather be learned than holy, and have still more mind to the *tree of knowledge* than the *tree of life*. And in hearing of the word, are not they who are any whit more knowing than ordinary, still gaping after new notions, after something to add to the stock of their speculative and discoursing knowledge, loathing this daily manna, these profitable exhortations, and *requiring meat for their lust?* There is an intemperance of the mind, as well as of the mouth. You would think it, and, may be, not spare to call it, a poor cold sermon, that were made up of such plain precepts as these : *Honour all men; love the brotherhood; fear God; honour the king;* and yet, this is the language of God, it is His way, this foolish, despicable way by which He guides, and brings to heaven them that believe.

Again ; we have others that are still complaining of the *difficulty and darkness* of the word of God and Divine truths ; to say nothing of Rome's doctrine, who talks thus, in order to excuse her sacrilege of stealing away the word from the people of God ; (a senseless pretext though it were true : because the word is dark of itself, should it therefore be made darker, by locking it up in an unknown tongue ?) but we speak of the common, vulgar excuse, which the gross, ignorant profaneness of many seeks to shroud itself under, that they are not learned, and cannot reach the doctrine of the Scriptures. There be deep mysteries there indeed : but what say you to these things, such rules as these, *Honour all men,* &c. ? Are such as these riddles, that you cannot know their meaning ? Rather, do not all understand them, and all neglect them ? Why set you not on to do these ? and then you should understand more. *A good understanding have all they that do His commandments,* says the Psalmist, Psal. cxi. 10. As one said well, " The best way to understand the mysterious and high discourse in the beginning of St. Paul's Epistles, is, to begin at the practice of those rules and precepts that are in the latter end of them." The way to attain to know more is to *receive the truth in the love of it,* and to obey what you know. The truth is, such truths as these will leave you inexcusable, even the most ignorant of you. You cannot but know, you hear often, that you ought to *love one another,* and to *fear God,* &c., and yet you never apply yourselves in earnest to the practice of these things, as will appear to your own consciences, if they deal honestly with you in the particulars.

Honour all men.] Honour, in a narrower sense, is not a universal due to all, but peculiar to some kinds of persons. Of this the Apostle speaks, Rom. xiii. 7, *Honour to whom honour is due,* and that in different degrees, to parents, to masters, and other superiors. There is an honour that hath, as it were, Cæsar's image and superscription on it, and so is particularly due to him ; as here it follows, *Honour the king.* But there is something that goes not unfitly under the name of honour, generally due to every man without exception; and it consists, as all honour doth, partly in inward esteem of them, partly in outward behaviour towards them. And the former must be the ground and cause of the latter.

We owe not the same measure of esteem to all. We may, yea, we ought to take notice of the different outward quality, or inward graces and gifts of men ; nor is it a fault to perceive the shallowness and weakness of men with whom we converse, and to esteem more highly those on whom God hath conferred more of such things as are truly worthy of esteem. But unto the meanest we do owe some measure of esteem, 1st, Negatively. We are not to entertain despising, disdainful thoughts of any, how worthless and mean soever. As the admiring of men, the very best, is a foolish excess on the one hand, so, the total contemning of any, the very poorest, is against this rule on the other; for that *contemning of vile persons,* the Psalmist speaks of, Psal. xv. 3, and commends, is the dislike and hatred of their sin, which is their vileness, and the not accounting them, for outward respects, worthy of such esteem as their wickedness does, as it were, strip them of. 2ndly, We are to observe and respect the smallest good that is in any. Although a Christian be never so base in his outward condition, in body or mind, of very mean intellectuals and natural endowments, yet, they who know the worth of spiritual things, will esteem the grace of God that is in him, in the midst of all those disadvantages, as a pearl in a rough shell. Grace carries still its own worth, though under a deformed body and ragged garments, yea, though they have but a small measure of that neither—the very lowest degree of grace; as a pearl of the least size, or a small piece of gold, yet men will not throw it away, but, as they say, the least shavings of gold are worth the keeping. The Jews would not willingly tread upon the smallest piece of paper in their way, but took it up; for possibly, said they, the name of God may be on it. Though there was a little superstition in this, yet truly there is nothing but good religion in it, if we apply it to men. Trample not on any; there may be some work of grace there, that thou knowest not of. The name of God may be written upon that soul thou treadest on; it may be a soul that Christ thought so much of, as to give His precious blood for it; therefore despise it not. Much more, I say, if thou canst perceive any appearance that it is such a one, oughtest thou to esteem it. Wheresoever thou findest the least trait of Christ's image, if thou lovest Him, thou wilt honour it; or if there be nothing of this to be found in him thou lookest on, yet observe what common gift of any kind God hath bestowed on him, judgment, or memory, or faculty in his calling, or any such thing, for these in their degree are to be esteemed, and the person for them. And as there is no man so complete as to have the advantage in every thing, so there is no man so low and unworthy but he hath something wherein he is preferable even to those that in other respects are much more excellent. Or imagine thou canst find nothing else in some men, yet honour thy own nature; esteem humanity in them, especially since humanity is exalted in Christ to be one with the Deity: account of the individual as a man. And, along with this esteem goes, 3rdly, that general good-will and affection due to men: whereas there are many who do not only outwardly express, but inwardly bear more regard to some dog or horse that they love, than to poor distressed men, and in so doing, do reflect dishonour upon themselves, and upon mankind.

The outward behaviour wherein we owe honour to all, is nothing but a conformity to this inward temper of mind; for he that inwardly despiseth none, but esteemeth the good that is in the lowest, or at least esteemeth them in that they are men, and loves them as such, will accordingly use no outward sign of disdain of any; he will not have a scornful eye, **nor a** reproachful tongue to move at any, not the meanest of his servants, nor the worst of his enemies; but, on the contrary, will acknowledge the good that is in every man, and give unto all that outward respect that is convenient for them, and that they are capable of, and will be ready to do them good as he hath opportunity and ability.

But instead of walking by this rule of *honouring all men*, what is there almost to be found amongst men, but a perverse proneness to dishonour one another, and every man ready to dishonour all men, that he may honour himself, reckoning that what he gives to others is lost to himself, and taking what he detracts from others, as good booty to make up himself? Set aside men's own interest, and that common civility which for their own credit they use one with another, and truly there will be found very little of this real respect to others, proceeding from obedience to God and love to men,—little disposition to be tender of their reputation and good name, and their welfare, as of our own, (for so the rule is,) but we shall find mutual disesteem and defamation filling almost all societies.

And the bitter root of this iniquity is, that wicked, accursed self-love which dwells in us. Every man is naturally his own grand idol, would be esteemed and honoured by any means, and to magnify that idol *self*, kills the good name and esteem of others in sacrifice to it. Hence, the narrow-observing eye and broad-speaking tongue, upon any thing that tends to the dishonouring of others; and where other things fail, the disdainful upbraiding of their birth, or calling, or any thing that comes next to hand, serves for a reproach. And hence arises a great part of the jars and strifes amongst men, the most part being drunk with an overweening opinion of themselves, and the unworthiest the most so; *The sluggard*, says Solomon, *is wiser in his own conceit than seven men that can render a reason*, Prov. xxvi. 16: and not finding others of their mind, this frets and troubles them. They take the ready course to deceive themselves; for they look with both eyes on the failings and defects of others, and scarcely give their good qualities half an eye; while, on the contrary, in themselves, they study to the full their own advantages, and their weaknesses and defects (as one says) they skip over, as children do the hard words in their lesson, that are troublesome to read; and making this uneven parallel, what wonder if the result be a gross mistake of themselves! Men overrate themselves at home: they reckon that they ought to be regarded, and that their mind should carry it; and when they come abroad, and are crossed in this, this puts them out of all temper.

But the humble man, as he is more conformable to this Divine rule, so he hath more peace by it; for he sets so low a rate upon himself in his own thoughts, that it is scarcely possible for any to go lower in judging of him; and therefore, as he pays due respect to others to the full, and gives no ground of quarrel that way, so he challenges no such debt to himself, and thus avoids the usual contests that arise in this. *Only by pride comes contention*, says Solomon, Prov. xiii. 10. A man that will walk abroad in a crowded street, cannot choose but be often jostled; but he that contracts himself, passes through more easily.

Study, therefore, this excellent grace of humility; not the personated acting of it in appearance, which may be a chief agent for pride, but true lowliness of mind, which will make you to be nothing in your own eyes, and content to be so in the eyes of others. Then will you obey this word; you will esteem all men as is meet, and not be troubled though all men disesteem you. As this humility is a precious grace, so it is the preserver of all other graces, and without it, (if they could be without it,) they were but as a box of precious powder carried in the wind without a cover, in danger of being scattered and blown away. If you would have honour, there is an ambition both allowed you, and worthy of you, whosoever you are; φιλοτιμούμεθα, Rom. ii. 7; 2 Cor. v. 9: other honour, though it have its Hebrew name from *weight*, is all too light, and weighs only with cares and troubles.

Love the brotherhood.] There is a love, as we said, due to all, included under that word of *honouring all*, but a peculiar love to our Christian brethren, whom the Apostle Paul calls by a like word, *the household of faith*, Gal. vi. 10.

Christian brethren are united by a three-fold cord; two of them are common to other men, but the third is the strongest, and theirs peculiarly. Their bodies are descended of the same man, and their souls of the same God; but their new life, by which they are most entirely brethren, is derived from the same God-man, Jesus Christ; yea, in Him they are all one body, receiving life from Him their glorious Head, who is called *the first-born among many brethren*, Rom. viii. 29. And as His unspeakable love was the source of this new being and fraternity, so, doubtless, it cannot but produce indissoluble love amongst them that are partakers of it. The spirit of love and concord is that precious ointment that runs down from the head of our great High Priest, to the skirts of His garment. The life of Christ and this law of love are combined, and cannot be severed. Can there be enmity betwixt those hearts that meet in Him? Why do you pretend yourselves Christians, and yet remain not only strangers to this love, but most contrary to it, *biters and devourers* one of another, and will not be convinced of the great guiltiness and uncomeliness of strifes and envyings amongst you? Is this the badge that Christ hath left his brethren, to wrangle and malign one another? Do you not know, on the contrary, that they are to be known by mutual love? *By this shall all men know that you are my disciples, if ye love one another.* John xiii. 35. How often doth that beloved disciple press this! He drank deep of that well-spring of love that was in the breast on which he leaned, and (if they relate aright) he died exhorting this, *Love one another.* Oh that there were more of this love of Christ in our hearts, arising from the sense of His love to us! That would teach this mutual love more effectually, which the preaching of it may set before us, but, without that other teaching, cannot work within us. Why do we still hear these things in vain? Do we believe what the love of Christ did to us, and suffered for us? And will we do nothing for Him,—not forgive a shadow, a fancy of injury, much less a real one, for His sake, and love him that wronged us, whoever he be, but especially being one of our brethren in this spiritual sense?

Many are the duties of this peculiar fraternal love ; that mutual converse, and admonition, and reproof, and comforting, and other duties which are fallen into neglect, not only amongst formal, but even amongst real Christians. Let us entreat more of His Spirit who is love, and that will remedy this evil.

Fear God.] All the rules of equity and charity amongst men flow from a higher principle, and depend upon it ; and there is no right observing of them without due regard to that : therefore this word, which expresses that principle of obedience, is fitly inserted amongst these rules ; the first obligation of man being to the sovereign majesty of God who made him, and all the mutual duties of one to another being derived from that. A man may indeed, from moral principles, be of a mild, inoffensive carriage, and do civil right to all men ; but this answers not the Divine rule even in these same things, after the way that it requires them. The spiritual and religious observance of these duties towards men, springs from a respect to God, and terminates there too ; it begins and ends in Him. And generally, all obedience to His commands, both such as regulate our behaviour towards Himself immediately, and such as relate to man, doth arise from a holy fear of His name. Therefore, this *fear of God*, upon which follows necessarily *the keeping of His commandments*, is given us by Solomon as the total sum of man's business and duty, Eccl. xii. *ult.*, and so, the way to solid happiness : he pronounces it *totum hominis, the whole of man.* After he had made his discoveries of all things besides under the sun, gone the whole circuit, and made an exact valuation, he found all besides this to amount to nothing *but vanity and vexation of spirit.* The account he gives of all other things, was only for this purpose, to illustrate and establish this truth the more, and to make it the more acceptable ; to be a repose after so much weariness, and such a tedious journey, and so, as he speaks there, ver. 10, a word of delight as well as a word of truth ; that the mind might sit down and quiet itself in this, from the turmoil and pursuit of vanity, that keep it busy to no purpose in all other things. But whereas there was emptiness and vanity, that is, just nothing, in all other things, there was not only something to be found, but every thing in this one, this *fear of God*, and that *keeping of his commandments*, which is the proper fruit of that fear. All the repeated declaring of vanity in other things, both severally and all together in that book, are but so many strokes to drive and fasten this nail, (as it is there, ver. 11,) this word of wisdom, which is the sum of all, and contains all the rest. So Job, after a large inquest for wisdom, searching for its vein, as men do for mines of silver and gold, hath the return of a *Non inventum est,* from all the creatures : *The sea says, It is not in me,* &c. But in the close, he finds it in this, *The fear of the Lord, that is wisdom, and to depart from evil, that is understanding.* Job xxviii. *ult.*

Under this fear is comprehended all religion, both inward and outward, all the worship and service of God, and all the observance of His commandments, which is there (Eccl. xii.) and elsewhere expressly joined with it, and therefore is included in it when it is not expressed. So Job xxviii., as above, *To depart from evil is understanding,* repeating in effect the former words by these. So Psal. cxi.

10. It hath in it all holiness and obedience ; they grow all out of it. It is the *beginning*, and it is the top or consummation of *wisdom*, for the word signifies both.

Think it not, then, a trivial, common matter to speak or hear of this subject ; but take it as our great lesson and business here on earth. The best proficients in it have yet need to learn it better, and it requires our incessant diligence and study all our days.

This fear hath in it chiefly these things : 1. A reverential esteem of the majesty of God, which is a main, fundamental thing in religion, and moulds the heart most powerfully to the obedience of His will. 2. A firm belief of the purity of God, and of his power and justice, that He loves holiness, and hates all sin, and can and will punish it. 3. A right apprehension of the bitterness of His wrath, and the sweetness of His love ; that His incensed anger is the most terrible and intolerable thing in the world, absolutely the most fearful of all evils, and, on the other side, His love, of all good things the best, the most blessed and delightful, yea, the only blessedness. Life is the name of the sweetest good we know, and yet, His *loving-kindness is better than life*, says David, Psal. lxiii. 3.   4. It supposes, likewise, sovereign love to God, for His own infinite excellency and goodness. 5. From all these springs a most earnest desire to please Him in all things, and an unwillingness to offend Him in the least, and, because of our danger through the multitude and strength of temptations, and our own weakness, a continual self-suspicion, a holy fear lest we should sin, a care and watchfulness that we sin not, and deep sorrow, and speedy returning and humbling before Him, when we have sinned.

There is, indeed, a base kind of fear, which, in the usual distinction, they call *servile fear ;* but to account all fear of the judgments and wrath of God a servile fear, or, (not to stand upon words,) to account such a fear improper to the children of God, I conceive is a wide mistake.   Indeed, to fear the punishments of sin, without regard to God and His justice as the inflicter of them, or to forbear to sin only because of those punishments, so that if a man can be secured from those, he hath no other respect to God that would make him fear to offend,—this is the character of a slavish and base mind.

Again, for a man so to apprehend wrath in relation to himself, as to be still under the horror of it in that notion, and not to apprehend redemption and deliverance by Jesus Christ, is to be under that spirit of bondage, which the Apostle speaks of, Rom. viii. 15.   And though a child of God may for a time be under such fear, yet the lively actings of faith and persuasion of God's love, and the feeling of reflex love to Him in the soul, do cast it out, according to that word of the Apostle, 1 John iv. 18, *True* (or *perfect*) *love casteth out fear.*   But to apprehend the punishments which the Lord threatens against sin, as certain and true, and to consider the greatness and fearfulness of them, especially the terror of the Lord's anger and hot displeasure, above all punishments, and (though not only, no, nor chiefly for these, yet) in contemplation of these, as very great and weighty, to be afraid to offend that God who hath threatened such things as the just reward of sin ; this, I say, is not incongruous with the estate of the sons of God, yea, it is their duty and their property even thus to fear.

1st, This is the very end for which God hath published these intimations of His justice, and hath threatened to punish men if they transgress, to the end that they may fear and not transgress: so that not to look upon them thus, and not to be affected with them answerably to their design, were a very grievous sin ; a slight and disregard put upon the words of the great God.

2ndly, Above all others, the children of God have the rightest and clearest knowledge of God, and the deepest belief of His word, and therefore they cannot choose but be afraid, and more afraid than all others, to fall under the stroke of His hand. They know more of the greatness, and truth, and justice of God than others, and therefore they fear when he threatens. *My flesh trembleth for fear of Thee*, (says David,) *and I am afraid of Thy judgments.* Psa. cxix. 120. Yea, they tremble when they hear the sentence against others, or see it executed upon them ; it moves them when they see public executions ; *Knowing the terror of the Lord, we persuade men,* says St. Paul, 2 Cor. v. 11 ; and they cry out with Moses, Psal. xc. 11, *Who knows the power of Thine anger? Even according to Thy fear, so is Thy wrath!* It is not an imagination or invention, that makes men fear more than they need. His wrath is as terrible as any, that fear it most, can apprehend, and beyond that. So that this doth not only consist with the estate of the saints, but is their very character, *to tremble at the word* of their Lord. The rest neglect what He says, till death and judgment seize on them ; but the godly know and believe, that *it is a fearful thing to fall into the hands of the living God.* Heb. x. 31.

And though they have firm promises, and a *kingdom that cannot be shaken*, yet, they have still this *grace by which they serve God acceptably with reverence and godly fear;* even in this consideration, that *our God*, even he that is ours by peculiar covenant, *is a consuming fire.* Heb. xii. 28, 29.

But indeed, together with this, yea, more than by this, they are persuaded to fear the Lord, by the sense of His great love to them, and by the power of that love that works in them towards Him, and is wrought in them by His. *They shall fear the Lord and His goodness in their latter days.* Hos. iii. 5. In those days, His goodness shall manifest itself more than before ; the beams of His love shall break forth more abundantly in the days of the Gospel, and shall beat more direct and hotter on the hearts of men ; and then, they shall fear Him more, because they shall love Him more.

This fear agrees well both with faith and love, yea, they work this fear. Compare Psalm xxxi. 23, with Psalm xxxiv. 9, and that same Psalm xxxiv. ver. 8, with ver. 9, and Psalm cxii. ver. 1, with ver. 7. The heart touched with the load-stone of Divine love, ever trembles with this godly fear, and still looks fixedly by faith to that star of Jacob, Jesus Christ, who guides it to the haven of happiness.

The looking upon God in the face of Jesus Christ, takes off that terror of His countenance that drives men from Him ; and in the smiles of His love that appear through Christ, there is such a power as unites their hearts to Him, but *unites* them so, as to *fear His name*, as the Psalmist's prayer is, Psalm lxxxvi. 11. He puts such a fear in their hearts as will not cause them to depart from, yea, causes that they *shall not depart from Him.* Jer. xxxii. 40.

And this is the purest and highest kind of godly fear, that springs from love : and though it excludes not the consideration of wrath, as terrible in itself, and even some fear of it, yet it may surmount it ; and doubtless, where much of that love possesses the heart, it will sometimes drown the other consideration, so that it shall scarcely be perceptible at all, and will constantly set it aside, and will persuade a man purely for the goodness and loveliness of God, to fear to offend Him, though there were no interest at all in it of a man's own *personal misery or happiness.

But do we thus fear the Lord our God ? What mean, then, our oaths, and excesses, and uncleanness, our covetousness, and generally our unholy and unchristian conversation ? This fear would make men tremble, so as to shake them out of their profane customs, and to shake their beloved sins out of their bosoms. The knowledge of the holy one causes fear of Him. Prov. ix. 10.

But alas ! we know Him not, and therefore we fear Him not. Knew we but a little of the great majesty of God, how holy He is, and how powerful a punisher of unholiness, we should not dare provoke Him thus, who *can kill both body and soul, and cast them into hell,* as our Saviour tells us, Matt. x. 28. And He will do so with both, if we will not fear Him, because he can do so ; and it is told us that we may fear, and so not feel, this heavy wrath. A little lively, spiritual knowledge would go far, and work much, which a great deal, such as ours is, doth not. Some such word as that of Joseph, would do much, being engraven on the heart : *Shall I do this evil and sin against God?* Gen. xxxix. 9. It would make a man be at no more liberty to sin in secret than in public ; no, not to dispense with the sin of his thoughts, more than of the openest words or actions. If some grave wise man did see our secret behaviour and our thoughts, should we not look more narrowly to them, and not suffer such rovings and follies in ourselves ? Surely, therefore, we forget God's eye, which we could not, if we thought of it aright, but should respect it more than if all men did see within us.

Nor is this the main point to be pressed upon the ungodly only, but the children of God themselves have much need to be put in mind of this fear, and to increase in it. How often do they abuse the indulgence of so loving a Father ! They have not their thoughts so constantly full of Him, are not *in His fear* (as Solomon advises) *all the day long,* Prov. xxiii. 17, but many times slip out of His directing hand, and wander from Him, and do not so deeply fear His displeasure, and so watch over all their ways, as becomes them : they do not keep close by Him, and wait on his voice, and obey it constantly, and are not so humbled and afflicted in their repentings for sin, as this fear requires, but only in a slight and superficial degree. They offer much lip-labour, which is but dead service to the living God. These are things, my beloved, that concern us much, and that we ought seriously to lay to heart ; for even they who are freed from condemnation, yet if they will walk fearlessly and carelessly at any time, He hath ways enough to make them smart for it. And if there were nothing more, should it not wound them deeply, to think how they requite so great, so unspeakable love ?

Honour the king.] This was the particular that the Apostle pressed and insisted on before ; and here he repeats it as a special duty of the Second Table, and a vindication of religion, which is wrongfully blamed in this point; but of this before.

This is out of question in the general ; only in the measure and rule of it is the difference. And surely they cannot possibly be satisfied, who are so drunk with power as to admit of none at all,—no measure nor rate for it, no banks nor channel for those rivers, the hearts and wills of kings, to run in, but think that if they like to run over all they may.

This is such a wild conceit as destroys both all law of reason in human societies, and all religious obligation to the laws of God. For the qualification and measure, I shall mention no other than that in the text, that it be always regulated by what here goes before it, *the fear of God;* that we never think of any such obedience and honour due to kings, as crosseth that *fear* which is due to God. Let kings, and subjects, and all know that they are absolutely bound to this. It is spoken to kings, Psal. ii. 11, *Serve the Lord in fear;* and to all men, Psal. xcvi. 4, 9, *Fear before Him, all the earth, for he is great, and greatly to be praised; He is to be feared above all gods.* What is man in respect of Him ? Shall a worm, *whose breath is in his nostrils,* stand in competition with the ever-living God ? Shall an earthen *potsherd strive with his Maker? Let the potsherds strive with the potsherds of the earth ;*—let them work one against another, and try which is hardest, and so they shall often break each other ;—but, *Woe to him that striveth with his Maker !* Isa. xlv. 9. There is nothing here but certain perishing. As we conclude in the question with the Church of Rome, of the honour due to saints and angels, honour let them have, with good reason, but not Divine honour, not God's peculiar ; so, in this, *Give to Cæsar the things that are Cæsar's,* but withal, still *Give to God the things that are God's.*

But it is a miserable estate of a kingdom, when debates on this head arise and increase ; and their happiness is, when kings and people concur to honour God : *For those that honour Him, He will honour, and whosoever despises Him, shall be lightly esteemed.* 1 Sam. ii. 30.

Ver. 18. Servants, be subject to your masters with all fear ; not only to the good and gentle, but also to the froward.
19. For this is thank-worthy, if a man for conscience toward God endure grief, suffering wrongfully.
20. For what glory is it, if, when ye be buffeted for your faults, ye shall take it patiently ? but if, when ye do well, and suffer for it, ye take it patiently, this is acceptable with God.

Thy word (says the Psalmist) *is a light to my feet and a lamp to my paths,* Psal. cxix. 105 ;—not only a light to please his eyes, by the excellent truths and comforts that are in it, but withal a lamp to direct his feet, in the precepts and rules of life that it gives : not only to inform and delight his mind, but also to order his course. That philosopher was deservedly commended, who drew knowledge most this way, and therefore was said to have brought philosophy from the clouds to dwell amongst men, calling it from empty speculations to a practical strain. Thus we are taught in spiritual knowledge by the word of God. The Son, the eternal Word, when he came to dwell with men, and so brought life, and wisdom, and all blessings from the heavens down unto them, taught them, both by his doctrine and perfect example, how to walk ; and his Apostles do, conformably, aim at this in their holy writings, joining with the mysteries of faith, those rules of life which show men the straight way to happiness.

And as it is spoken of the largeness of Solomon's wisdom, that *he spake of all trees, from the cedar in Lebanon to the hyssop that grows out of the wall,* (1 Kings iv. 33,) so in this, we may see the perfection of the Holy Scriptures, that they give those directions that are needful to all ranks and sorts of men.   They speak not only of the duties of kings, how they ought to behave themselves on their thrones, and the duty of their subjects towards them in that dignity, and how ministers and others ought to carry themselves in the *house of God;* but they come into private houses, and give economic rules for them ; teaching parents, and children, and masters, yea, and servants, how to acquit themselves one to another.   Thus here, *Servants, be subject to your masters.*

As this is a just plea for all the people of God, that they have a right to the use of this Book, being so useful for all sorts, and that they ought not to be debarred from it ; so, it is a just plea against a great part of those that debar themselves the use of it, through sloth-fulness and earthly-mindedness, seeing it is so contempered, that there may be many things, yea, all the main things in it profitable for all, fitted to the use of the lowest estate and lowest capacities of men. Yea, it takes (as we see) particular notice of their condition ; stoops down to take the meanest servant by the hand, to lead him in the way to heaven ; and not only in that part of it which is the general way of Christians, but even in those steps of it that lie within the walk of their particular calling ; as here, teaching not only the duties of a Christian, but of a *Christian servant.*

Obs. 1. The Scriptures are a deep that few can wade far into, and none can wade through, (as those waters, Ezek. xlvii. 5,) but yet, all may come to the brook and refresh themselves with drinking of the streams of its living water, and go in a little way, according to their strength and stature.   Now this (I say) may be spoken to our shame, and I wish it might shame you to amendment, that so many of you either use not the Scriptures at all, or, in using, do not use them ; you turn over the leaves, and, it may be, run through the lines, and con-sider not what they advise you.   Masters, learn your part, and serv-ants too, hearken what they say to you, for they pass not you by, they vouchsafe to speak to you too, but you vouchsafe not to hear them, and observe their voice.   How can you think that the reading of this Book concerns you not, when you may hear it address such particular directions to you ?   Wisdom goes not only to the gates of palaces, but to the common gates of the cities, and to the public highways, and calls to the simplest that she may make them wise.   Besides that you dishonour God, you prejudice yourselves ; for does not that neglect of God and His word justly procure the disorder and disobedience of your servants towards you, as a fit punishment from His righteous hand, although they are unrighteous, and are procuring further judg-ment to themselves in so doing ?   And not only thus is your neglect

of the word a cause of your trouble by the justice of God, but it is so
in regard of the nature of the word, inasmuch as if you would respect
it, and make use of it in your houses, it would teach your servants to
respect and obey you, as here you see it speaks for you ; and therefore you wrong both it and yourselves, when you silence it in your
families.

Obs. 2. The Apostle having spoken of subjection to public authority,
adds this of subjection to private domestic authority. It is a thing of
much concernment, the right ordering of families ; for all other societies, civil and religious, are made up of these.   Villages, and cities,
and churches, and commonwealths, and kingdoms, are but a collec-
tion of families ; and therefore such as these are, for the most part,
such must the whole societies predominantly be.   One particular
house is but a very small part of a kingdom, yet, the wickedness and
lewdness of that house, be it but of the meanest in it, of servants one
or more, and though it seem but a small thing, yet goes in to make up
that heap of sin which provokes the wrath of God, and draws on public
calamity.

And this particularly, when it declines into disorder, proves a public
evil.   When servants grow generally corrupt, and disobedient, and un-
faithful, though they be the lowest part, yet the whole body of a commonwealth cannot but feel very much the evil of it ; as a man does
when his legs and feet grow diseased, and begin to fail him.

We have here, 1. Their duty. 2. The due extent of it. 3. The
right principle of it.

1st, Their duty, *be subject.*   Keep your order and station under
your masters, and that *with fear,* and inward reverence of mind and
respect to them ; for that is the very life of all obedience.   Then their
obedience hath in it diligent doing, and patient suffering : both these
are in that word, *be subject.*   Do faithfully to your utmost that which
is intrusted to you, and obey all their just commands, for action, indeed,
goes no further ; but suffer patiently even their unjust rigours and se-
verities.   And this being the harder part of the two, and yet, a part
that the servants of those times bore, many of them being more
hardly and slavishly used than any with us, (especially those that were
Christian servants under unchristian masters,) therefore the Apostle insists most on this.   And this is the extent of the obedience here required, that it be paid to all kinds of masters, *not to the good only, but
also to the evil;* not only to obey, but to suffer, and suffer patiently, and
not only deserved, but even wrongful and unjust punishment.

Now because this particular concerns Servants, let them reflect
upon their own carriage and examine it by this rule ; and truly the
greatest part of them will be found very unconformable to it, being
either closely fraudulent and deceitful, or grossly stubborn and disobedient, abusing the lenity and mildness of their masters, or murmuring at their just severity.   So far are they from the patient endurance
of the least undue word of reproof, much less of sharper punishment,
either truly, or, in their opinion, undeserved.   And truly, if any who
profess religion, dispense with this in themselves, they mistake the
matter very much ; for religion ties them the more, whether children
or servants, to be most submissive and obedient even to the worst

kind of parents and masters, *always in the Lord;* not obeying any unjust command, though they may and ought to suffer patiently (as it is here) their unjust reproofs or punishments.

But on the other side, this does not justify, nor at all excuse the unmerciful austerities and unbridled passion of masters ; it is still a perverseness and crookedness in them, as the word is here, σκολιοῖς, and must have its own name, and shall have its proper reward from the sovereign Master and Lord of all the world.

2ndly, There is here, also, the due extent of this duty, namely, *To the froward.* It is a more deformed thing, to have a distorted, crooked mind, or a froward spirit, than any crookedness of the body. How can he that hath servants under him expect their obedience, when he cannot command his own passion, but is a slave to it ? And unless much conscience of duty possess servants, (more than is commonly to be found with them,) it cannot but work a master into much disaffection and disesteem with them, when he is of a turbulent spirit, a *troubler of his own house,* imbittering his affairs and commands with rigidness and passion, and ready to take things by that side which may offend and trouble him, thinking his servant slights his call, when he may as well think he hears him not, and upon every slight occasion, real or imagined, flying out into reproachful speeches, or proud threats, contrary to the Apostle St. Paul's rule, which he sets over against the duty of servants : *Forbearing threatening, knowing that your Master also is in heaven, and that there is no respect of persons with Him.* Eph. vi. 9. Think, therefore, when you shall appear before the judgment-seat of God, that your carriage shall be examined and judged as well as theirs ; and think, that though we regard much those differences of masters and servants, yet they are nothing with God, they vanish away in His presence.

Consider *who made thee to differ.* Might He not, with a turn of His hand, have made your stations just contrary, have made thee the servant, and thy servant the master ? But we willingly forget those things that should compose our mind to humility and meekness, and blow them up with such fancies as please and feed our natural vanity, and make us somebody in our own account.

However, that Christian servant who falls into the hands of a froward master, will not be beaten out of his station and duty of obedience by all the hard and wrongful usage he meets with, but will take that as an opportunity of exercising the more obedience and patience, and will be the more cheerfully patient, because of his innocence, as the Apostle here exhorts.

Men do indeed look sometimes upon this as a just plea for impatience, that they suffer unjustly, which yet is very ill logic ; for, as the philosopher said, "Would any man that frets because he suffers unjustly, wish to deserve it, that he might be patient ?" Now, to hear them, they seem to speak so, when they exclaim, that the thing that vexeth them most, is, that they have not deserved any such thing as is inflicted on them. Truly, desert of punishment may make a man more silent upon it, but innocence, rightly considered, makes him more patient. Guiltiness stops a man's mouth, indeed, in suffering, but surely it doth not quiet his mind ; on the contrary, it is that which mainly disturbs and grieves him; it is the sting of suffering, as sin is said to be of death, 1 Cor. xv. 56. And therefore, when there is no guilt, the pain of sufferings cannot but be much abated; yea, the Apostle here declares, that to suffer undeserved, and withal patiently, is glorious to a man, and acceptable to God. It is commendable, indeed, to be truly patient even in deserved sufferings, but the deserving them tarnishes the lustre of that patience, and makes it look more like constraint; which is the Apostle's meaning, in preferring spotless suffering much before it. And this is indeed the true glory of it, that it pleaseth God; (so it is rendered in the close of the 20th verse, for the other word of *glory* in the beginning of it;) it is a pleasing thing in God's eyes, and therefore He will thank a man for it, as the word is, χάρις παρὰ Θεῷ. Though we owe all our patience under all kinds of afflictions as a duty to Him, and though this grace is His own gift, yet He hath obliged himself by His royal word, not only to accept of it, but to praise it, and reward it in His children. Though they lose their thanks at the world's hands, and be rather scoffed at and taunted in all their doings and sufferings, it is no matter; they can expect no other there; but their *reward is on high*, in the sure and faithful hand of their Lord.

How often do men work earnestly, and do and suffer much, for the uncertain wages of glory and thanks amongst men! And how many of them fall short of their reckoning, either dying before they came to that state where they think to find it, or not finding it where they looked for it, and so they live but to feel the pain of their disappointment! Or, if they do attain their end, such glory and thanks as men have to give them, what amounts it to? Is it any other than a handful of nothing, the breath of their mouths, and themselves much like it, a vapour dying out in the air? The most real thanks they give, their solidest rewards, are but such as a man cannot take home with him: or if they go so far with him, yet, at furthest, he must leave them at the door, when he is to enter his everlasting home. All the riches, and palaces, and monuments of honour that he had, and that are erected to him after death, as if he had then some interest in them, reach him not at all. Enjoy them who will, he does not, *he hath no portion of all that is done under the sun;* his own end is to him the end of the world.

But he that would have abiding glory and thanks, must turn his eye another way for them. All men desire glory, but they know neither what it is, nor how it is to be sought. He is upon the only right bargain of this kind, *whose praise* (according to St. Paul's word) *is not of men, but of God.* Rom. ii. 29. If men commend him not, he accounts it no loss, nor any gain if they do; for he is bound for a country where that coin goes not, and whither he cannot carry it, and therefore he gathers it not. That which he seeks in all, is, that he may be approved and accepted of God, whose thanks is no less, to the least of those He accepts, than a crown of unfading glory. Not a poor *servant* that fears His name, and is obedient and patient for His sake, but shall be so rewarded.

There be some kind of graces and good actions, which men (such as regard any grace) take special notice of, and commend highly,—such as are of a magnific and remarkable nature, as martyrdom, or doing or suffering for religion in some public way. There be again.

other obscure graces, which, if men despise them not, yet they esteem not much, as meekness, gentleness, and patience under private crosses, known to few or none.   And yet, these are of great account with God, and therefore should be so with us ; these are indeed of more universal use, whereas the other are but for high times, as we say, for rare occasions : these are every one's work, but few are called to the acting of the other.   And the least of these graces shall not lose its reward, in whose person soever, as St. Paul tells us, speaking of this same subject, *Knowing that whatsoever good thing any man doeth, the same shall he receive of the Lord, whether he be bond or free.*   Eph. vi. 8.

This is the bounty of that great Master we serve.   For what are we and all we can do, that there should be the name of reward attached to it ?   Yet he keeps all in reckoning ; not a poor lame prayer, not a tear nor a sigh, poured forth before Him shall be lost.   Not any cross, whether from His own hand immediately, or coming through men's hands, that is taken, what way soever it come, as out of His hand, and carried patiently, yea, and welcomed, and embraced for His sake, but He observes our so entertaining of it.   Not an injury that the meanest servant bears Christianly, but goes upon account with Him.   And He sets them down so, as that they bear much value through His estimate and way of reckoning of them, though in themselves they are all less than nothing ; as a worthless counter stands for hundreds or thousands, according to the place you set it in.   Happy they who have to deal with such a Lord, and who, be they servants or masters, are vowed servants to Him !   *When He comes, His reward shall be with Him.*   Rev. xxii. 12.

The 3rd thing is, the Principle of this obedience and patience.   *For conscience towards God.*   This imports, first, the knowledge of God, and of His will in some due measure, and then a conscientious respect unto Him and His will so known, taking it for their only rule in doing and suffering.

Observe, 1. This declares to us the freeness of the grace of God in regard to men's outward quality, that He doth often bestow the riches of His grace upon persons of mean condition.   It is supposed here, that this *conscience towards God,* this saving knowledge and fear of His name, is to be found in Servants : therefore, the Apostle takes them within the address of his letter amongst those who are *elect, according to the foreknowledge of God,* (ch. i. ver. 2,) and sharers of those dignities he mentions, (ch. ii. ver. 9,) *a chosen generation.*   The honour of a spiritual royalty may be concealed under the meanness of a servant ; and this grace may be conferred upon the servant, and denied to the master, as is here supposed.   It may fall out that a perverse, crooked-minded master may have a servant uprightly minded, being endowed with a tender conscience towards God.   And thus the Lord does to counteract the pride of man, and to set off the lustre of His own free grace.   He hath all to choose from, and yet chooses where men would least imagine.   See Matt. xi. 25 ; 1 Cor. i. 27.

Observe, 2. Grace finds a way to exert itself in every estate where it exists, and regulates the soul according to the particular duties of that estate.   Whether it find a man high or low, a master or a servant, it requires not a change of his station, but works a change on his heart, and teaches him how to live in it.   The same spirit that makes a Christian master pious, and gentle, and prudent in commanding, makes a Christian servant faithful, and obsequious, and diligent in obeying.   A skilful engraver makes you a statue indifferently of wood, or stone, or marble, as they are put into his hand ; so, Grace forms a man to a Christian way of walking in any estate.   There is a way for him in the meanest condition to glorify God, and to adorn the profession of religion ; no estate so low as to be shut out from that ; and a rightly-informed and rightly-affected conscience towards God, shows a man that way, and causes him to walk in it.   As the astrologers say that the same stars that made Cyrus to be chosen king amongst the armies of men when he came to be a man, made him to be chosen king amongst the shepherd's children when he was a child ; thus Grace will have its proper operation in every estate.

In this, men readily deceive themselves ; they can do any thing well in imagination, better than the real task that is in their hands.   They presume that they could do God good service in some place of command, who serve Him not, as becomes them, in that which is by far the easier, the place of obeying wherein he hath set them.   They think that if they had the ability and opportunities that some men have, they would do much more for religion, and for God, than they do ; and yet they do nothing, but spoil a far lower part than that, which is their own, and is given them to study and act aright in.   But our folly and self-ignorance abuse us : it is not our part to choose what we should be, but to be what we are to His glory who gives us to be such.   Be thy condition never so mean, yet, thy *conscience towards God*, if it be within thee, will find itself work in that.   If it be little that is intrusted to thee, in regard of thy outward condition, or any other way, *be thou faithful in that little*, as our Saviour speaks, and thy reward shall not be little : *He shall make thee ruler over much.*   Matt. xxv. 23.

Observe, 3.   As a corrupt mind debaseth the best and most excellent callings and actions, so the lowest are raised above themselves, and ennobled by a spiritual mind.   Magistrates or ministers, though their calling and employments be high, may have low intentions, and draw down their high calling to those low intentions ; they may seek themselves, and their own selfish ends, and neglect God.   And a sincere Christian may elevate his low calling by this conscience towards God, observing His will, and intending His glory in it.   An eagle may fly high, and yet have its eye down upon some carrion on the earth : even so, a man may be standing on the earth, and on some low part of it, and yet have his eye upon heaven, and be contemplating it.   That which men cannot at all see in one another, is the very thing that is most considerable in their actions, namely, the principle whence they flow, and the end to which they tend.   This is the form and life of actions,—that by which they are earthly or heavenly.   Whatsoever be the matter of them, the spiritual mind hath that alchemy indeed, of turning base metals into gold, earthly employments into heavenly.   The handy-work of an artisan or servant who regards God, and eyes Him even in that work, is much holier than the *prayer of a hypocrite ;* and a servant's enduring the private wrongs and harshness of a froward master, bearing it patiently *for conscience towards God*, is more acceptable to God, than the sufferings of such as may endure much for a public good cause, without a good and upright heart.

This habitude and posture of the heart towards God, the Apostle St. Paul presses much upon servants, Eph. vi. 8, as being very needful to allay the hard labour and harsh usage of many of them. This is the way to make all easy, to undergo it for God. There is no pill so bitter, but respect and love to God will sweeten it. And this is a very great refreshment and comfort to Christians in the mean estate of servants or other labouring men, that they may offer up their hardship and bodily labour as a sacrifice to God, and say, Lord, this is the station wherein Thou hast set me in this world, and I desire to serve Thee in it. What I do is for Thee, and what I suffer I desire to bear patiently and cheerfully for Thy sake, in submission and obedience to Thy will.

For conscience.] In this there is, 1. A reverential compliance with God's disposal, both in allotting to them that condition of life, and in particularly choosing their master for them ; though possibly not the mildest and pleasantest, yet the fittest for their good. There is much in firmly believing this, and in heartily submitting to it ; for we would, naturally, rather carve for ourselves, and shape our own estate to our mind, which is a most foolish, yea, an impious presumption : as if we were wiser than He who hath done it, and as if there were not as much, and, it may be, more possibility of true contentment in a mean, than in a far higher condition ! The master's mind is often more toiled than the servant's body. But if our condition be appointed us, at least we would have a voice in some qualifications and circumstances of it ; as in this, if a man must serve, he would wish willingly that God would allot him a meek, gentle master. And so, in other things, if we must be sick, we would be well accommodated, and not want helps ; but to have sickness, and want means and friends for our help, this we cannot think of without horror. But this submission to God is never right, till all that concerns us be given up into His hand, to do with it, and with every article and circumstance of it, as seems good in His eyes. 2. In this *conscience*, there is a religious and observant respect to the rule which God hath set men to walk by in that condition ; so that their obedience depends not upon any external inducement, failing when that fails, but flows from an inward impression of the law of God upon the heart. Thus, a servant's obedience and patience will not be pinned to the goodness and equity of his master, but when that fails, will subsist upon its own inward ground ; and so, generally, in all other estates. This is the thing that makes sure and constant walking ; makes a man *step even* in the ways of God. When a man's obedience springs from that unfailing, unchanging reason, the command of God, it is a natural motion, and therefore keeps on, and rather grows than abates ; but they who are moved by things outward, must often fail, because those things are not constant in their moving : as, for instance, when a people are much acted on by the spirit of their rulers, as the Jews when they had good kings. 3. In this *conscience*, there is a tender care of the glory of God, and the adornment of religion, which the Apostle premised before these particular duties, as a thing to be specially regarded in them. The honour of our Lord's name, is that which we should set up as the mark to aim all our actions at. But, alas! either we think not on it, or our hearts slip out, and start from their aim, *like bows of deceit,* as the word is, Psal. lxxviii. 57. 4. There is the comfortable persuasion of God's approbation and acceptance, (as it is expressed in the following verse, of which somewhat before,) and the hope of that reward He hath promised, as it is, Col. iii. 24 : *Knowing that of the Lord ye shall receive the inheritance, for ye serve the Lord Christ.* No less than *the inheritance!* So, then, such servants as these, are *sons and heirs of God, coheirs with Christ.* Thus he that is a servant, may be in a far more excellent state than his master. The servant may hope for and aim at a kingdom, while the master is embracing a dunghill. And such a one will think highly of God's free grace, and the looking ever to that inheritance makes him go cheerfully through all pains and troubles here, as *light* and *momentary,* and not worth the naming in comparison of *that glory that shall be revealed.* In the mean time, the best and most easy condition of the sons of God cannot satisfy them, nor stay their sighs and *groans, waiting* and longing for *that day of their full redemption.* Rom. viii. 16, 23.

Now this is the great rule, not only for servants, but for all the servants of God in what state soever, *to set the Lord always before them,* Psal. xvi. 8, and to study with St. Paul, *to have a conscience void of offence towards God and man,* Acts xxiv. 16 ; to eye, and to apply constantly to their actions and their inward thoughts, the command of God ; to walk by that rule abroad, and at home in their houses, and in the several ways of their calling ; (as an exact workman is ever and anon laying his rule to his work, and squaring it ;) and *for the conscience they have towards God,* to do and suffer His will cheerfully in every thing, being content that He choose their condition and their trials for them ; only desirous to be assured, that He hath chosen them for His own, and given them a right to the *glorious liberty of the sons of God,* Rom. viii. 21 ; still endeavouring to walk in that way which leads to it, overlooking *this moment,* and all things in it, accounting it a very indifferent matter what is their outward state here, provided they may be happy in eternity. Whether we be high or low here, bond or free, it imports little, seeing that all these differences will be so quickly at an end, and there shall not be so much as any track or footstep of them left. With particular men, it is so in their graves ; you may distinguish the greater from the less by their tombs, but by their dust you cannot : and with the whole world it shall be so in the end. All monuments and palaces, as well as cottages, shall be made fire, as our Apostle tells us. *The elements shall melt with fervent heat, and the earth, and all the works therein, shall be burnt up.* 2 Pet. iii. 10.

Ver. 21. For even hereunto were ye called : because Christ also suffered for us, leaving us an example, that ye should follow his steps :
22. Who did no sin, neither was guile found in his mouth :
23. Who, when he was reviled, reviled not again ; when he suffered, he threatened .not ; but committed himself to him that judgeth righteously.

THE rules that God hath set men to live by, are universally just, and there is a universal obligation upon all men to obey them; but as they are particularly addressed to His own people in His word, *they*, out of question, are particularly bound to yield obedience, and have many peculiar persuasives to it, not extending to others, which are therefore usually represented to them, and pressed upon them, in the Holy Scriptures. Thus the preface of the Law runs to Israel: Besides that *I am Jehovah*, and have supreme power to give men laws, it is added, *I am thy God*, especially thy deliverer from slavery and bondage, and so have a peculiar right to thy obedience. Deut. vii. 6. Thus, the Apostle here urgeth this point in hand, of inoffensiveness and patience, particularly in Christian servants, but so as it fits every Christian in his station, *For hereunto*, says he, *ye are called*. Whatsoever others do, though they think it too straight a rule, yet you are tied to it by your own calling and profession as you are Christians; and this is evidently the highest and clearest reason that can be, and of greatest power with a Christian, namely, the example of Jesus Christ himself: *For Christ also suffered for us*, &c.

So, it is all but one entire argument, *viz.*, that they ought thus to behave themselves, because it is the very thing they are called to, as their conformity to Jesus Christ, whose they profess to be, yea, with whom, as Christians, they profess themselves to be one.

Hereunto were ye called.] This, in the general, is a thing that ought to be ever before our eye, to consider the nature and end of our calling, and to endeavour in all things to act suitably to it; to think in every occurrence, What doth the calling of a Christian require of me in this? But the truth is, the most do not mind this. We profess ourselves to be Christians, and never think what kind of behaviour this obliges us to, and what manner of persons it becomes us to be *in all holy conversation*, but *walk disorderly*, out of our rank, *inordinately*. You that are profane, were you called by the Gospel to serve the world and your lusts? Were you called to swearing, and rioting, and voluptuousness? Hear you not the Apostle testifying the contrary, in express terms, that *God hath not called us to uncleanness, but unto holiness?* 1 Thess. iv. 7. You that are of proud, contentious spirits, do you act suitably to this holy calling? No; for *we are called to peace*, says the same Apostle. 1 Cor. vii. 15. But we study not this holy calling, and therefore we walk so incongruously, so unlike the Gospel: *we lie and do not the truth*, as St. John speaks, 1 John i. 6: our actions belie us.

The particular things that Christians are here said to be called to, are, *suffering*, as their lot, and *patience*, as their duty, even under the most unjust and undeserved sufferings.

And both these are as large as the sphere of this calling. Not only servants and others of a mean condition, who, lying low, are the more subject to rigours and injuries, but generally, all who are called to godliness, are likewise called to sufferings. 2 Tim. iii. 12. All that will follow Christ, must do it in his livery; they must take up their cross. This is a very harsh and unpleasing article of the Gospel to a carnal mind, but the Scriptures conceal it not. Men are not led blindfold into sufferings, and drawn into a hidden snare by the Gospel's invitations; they are told it very often, that they may not pretend a surprisal, nor have any just plea for starting back again. So our Saviour tells his disciples, why he was so express and plain with them in this, *These things have I told you that ye be not offended,* John xvi. 1 ; as if he had said, I have showed you the ruggedness of your way, that you may not stumble at it, taking it to be a smooth, plain one. But then, where this is spoken of, it is usually allayed with the mention of those comforts that accompany these sufferings, or of that glory which follows them. The doctrine of the Apostles, which was so verified in their own persons, was this, *That we must, through much tribulation, enter into the kingdom of God,* Acts xiv. 22. An unpleasant way indeed, if you look no farther ; but a *kingdom* at the end of it, and that *the kingdom of God,* will transfuse pleasure into the most painful step in it all. It seems a sad condition that falls to the share of godly men in this world, to be eminent in sorrows and troubles. *Many are the afflictions of the righteous,* Psal. xxxiv. 19 : but that which follows, weighs them abundantly down in consolation, that the Lord himself is engaged in their afflictions, both for their deliverance out of them in due time, and, in the mean time, for their support and preservation under them : *The Lord delivers them out of them all,* and till he does that, *He keepeth all their bones.* This was literally verified in the natural body of Christ, as St. John observes, John xix. 36, and it holds spiritually true in his mystical body. The Lord supports the spirits of believers in their troubles, with such solid consolations as are the pillars and strength of their souls, as the bones are of the body, which the Hebrew word for them imports. So, *He keepeth all his bones :* and the desperate condition of wicked men is opposed to this, ver. 21, to illustrate it, *Evil shall slay the wicked.*

Thus, John xvi. 33, they are forewarned in the close, what to expect at the world's hands, as they were divers times before in that same sermon ; but it is a sweet testament, take it altogether : *Ye shall have tribulation in the world, but peace in Me.* And seeing He hath jointly bequeathed these two to his followers, were it not great folly to renounce such a bargain, and to let go that peace for fear of this trouble ? The trouble is but *in the world,* but the *peace* is *in Him,* who weighs down thousands of worlds.

So, then, they do exceedingly mistake and misreckon, who would reconcile Christ and the world, who would have the Church of Christ, or, at least, themselves for their own shares, enjoy both kinds of peace together ; would willingly have peace in Christ, but are very loth to part with the world's peace. They would be Christians, but they are very ill satisfied when they hear of any thing but ease and prosperity in that estate, and willingly forget the tenor of the Gospel in this ; and so, when times of trouble and sufferings come, their minds are as new and uncouth to it, as if they had not been told of it beforehand. They like better St. Peter's carnal advice to Christ, to avoid suffering, Matt. xvi. 22, than his Apostolic doctrine to Christians, teaching them, that as Christ *suffered,* so they likewise *are called to suffering.* Men are ready to think as Peter did, that Christ should favour himself more in his own body, his Church, than to expose it to so much suffering ; and most would be of Rome's mind in this, at least in affection, that the badge of the Church should be pomp and prosperity, and not the cross : the true cross and afflictions are too heavy and painful.

But *God's thoughts are not as ours:* those whom He calls to a kingdom, He calls to sufferings as the way to it.   He will have the heirs of heaven know, that they are not at home on earth, and that *this is not their rest.*   He will not have them, with the abused world, fancy a happiness here, and, as St. Augustine says, *Beatam vitam quærere in regione mortis*—seek a happy life in the region of death.   The reproaches and wrongs that encounter them shall elevate their minds often to that land of peace and rest, *where righteousness dwells.* 2 Pet. iii. 13. The hard taskmaster shall make them weary of Egypt, which otherwise, possibly, they would comply too well with ; shall dispose them for deliverance, and make it welcome, which, it may be, they might but coldly desire, if they were better used.

He knows what He does, who secretly serves His own good purposes by men's evil ones, and, by the *ploughers that make long furrows* on the back of His Church, (Psal. cxxix. 3,) makes it a fruitful field to Himself.   Therefore, it is great folly and unadvisedness, to take up a prejudice against His way, to think it might be better as we would model it, and to complain of the order of things, whereas we should complain of disordered minds : but we had rather have all altered and changed for us, the very course of Providence, than seek the change of our own perverse hearts.   But the right temper of a Christian is, to run always cross to the corrupt stream of the world and human iniquity, and to be willingly carried along with the stream of Divine providence, and not at all to stir a hand, no, nor a thought, to row against that mighty current ; and not only is he carried with it upon necessity, because there is no steering against it, but cheerfully and voluntarily ; not because he must, but because he would.

And this is the other thing to which Christians are jointly called ; as to suffering, so to *calmness of mind* and *patience in suffering,* although their suffering be most unjust ; yea, this is truly a part of that duty they are called to, to maintain that integrity and inoffensiveness of life that may make their sufferings at men's hands always unjust. The entire duty here, is innocence and patience ; doing willingly no wrong to others, and yet cheerfully suffering wrong when done to themselves.   If either of the two be wanting, their suffering does not credit their profession, but dishonours it.   If they be patient under deserved suffering, their guiltiness darkens their patience ; and if their sufferings be undeserved, yea, and the cause of them honourable, yet impatience under them stains both their sufferings and their cause, and seems in part to justify the very injustice that is used against them ; but when innocence and patience meet together in suffering, their sufferings are in their perfect lustre.   These are they who honour religion, and shame the enemies of it.   It was the concurrence of these two that was the very triumph of the martyrs in times of persecution, that tormented their tormentors, and made them *more than conquerors,* even in sufferings.

Now that we are called both to suffering and to this manner of suffering, the Apostle puts out of question, by the supreme example of our Lord Jesus Christ ; for the sum of our calling is, *to follow Him.* Now in both these, in suffering, and in suffering innocently and patiently, the whole history of the Gospel testifies how complete a pattern He is. And the Apostle gives us here a summary, yet a very clear account of it.

The words have in them these two things : I. The perfection of this example. II. Our obligation to follow it.

I. The example he sets off to the full, 1. In regard of the greatness of our Saviour's sufferings. 2. In regard of His spotlessness and patience in suffering.

The first, we have in that word, *He suffered;* and afterwards, at ver. 24, we have His crucifixion and His stripes expressly specified.

Now this is reason enough, and carries it beyond all other reason, why Christians are called to a suffering life, seeing the Lord and Author of that calling suffered himself so much. *The Captain,* or Leader, *of our salvation,* as the Apostle speaks, was *consecrated by suffering,* Heb. ii. 10 : that was the way by which *He entered into the holy place,* where He is now *our everlasting High Priest, making intercession for us.* If He be our Leader to salvation, must not we follow Him in the way He leads, whatsoever it is ? If it be (as we see it is) by the way of sufferings, we must either follow on in that way, or fall short of salvation ; for there is no other leader, nor any other way than that which He opened ; so that there is not only a congruity in it, that His followers be conformed to Him in suffering, but a necessity, if they will follow Him on, till they attain to glory. And the consideration of both these, cannot but argue a Christian into a resolution for this *via regia,* this royal way of suffering that leads to glory, through which their King and Lord himself went to His glory. It could hardly be believed at first, that this was *His* way, and we can as hardly yet believe that it must be ours. *O fools, and slow of heart to believe! Ought not Christ to have suffered these things, and so to enter into his glory?* Luke xxiv. 25, 26.

Would you be at glory, and will you not follow your Leader in the only way to it ? Must there be another way cut out for you by yourself ? O absurd ! *Shall the servant be greater than his master?* John xiii. 6. Are not you fairly dealt with ? If you have a mind to Christ, you shall have full as much of the world's good-will as He had : *if it hate you,* He bids you remember, *how it hated Him.* John xv. 18.

But though there were a way to do otherwise, would you not, if the love of Christ possessed your hearts, rather choose to share with Him in His lot, and would you not find delight in the very trouble of it ? Is not this conformity to Jesus, the great ambition of all his true-hearted followers ? *We carry about in the body the dying of the Lord Jesus,* says the great Apostle, 2 Cor. iv. 10. Besides the unspeakable advantage to come, which goes linked with this, that *if we suffer with Him, we shall reign with him,* (2 Tim. ii. 12,) there is a glory, even in this present resemblance, that we are conformed to the image of the Son of God in sufferings. Why should we desire to leave Him ? Are you not one with Him ? Can you choose but have the same common friends and enemies ? Would you willingly, if it might be, could you find in your heart to be friends with that world which hated your Lord and Master ? Would you have nothing but kindness and ease, where He had nothing but enmity and trouble ? Or would you not rather, when you think aright of it, refuse and disdain to be so unlike

Him? As that good Duke said, when they would have crowned him King of Jerusalem, *No*, said he, *by no means, I will not wear a crown of gold where Jesus was crowned with thorns.*

2. His spotlessness and patience in suffering, are both of them set here before us; the one ver. 22, the other ver. 23.

Whosoever thou art who makest such a noise about the injustice of what thou sufferest, and thinkest to justify thy impatience by thine innocence, let me ask thee, Art thou more just and innocent than He who is here set before thee? Or, art thou able to come near Him in this point? *Who did no sin, neither was guile found in his mouth.* This is to signify perfect holiness, according to that declaration, James iii. 2, *If any man offend not in word, the same is a perfect man.* Man is a little world, a world of wickedness; and that little part of him, *the tongue*, is termed by St. James *a world of iniquity.* But all Christ's words, as well as His actions, and all His thoughts, flowed from a pure spring that had not any thing defiled in it; and therefore no temptation, either from men or Satan, could seize on Him. Other men may seem clear as long as they are unstirred, but move and trouble them, and the mud arises; but He was nothing but holiness, a pure fountain, all purity to the bottom; and therefore stir and trouble Him as they would, He was still alike clear. *The prince of this world cometh, and hath nothing in me.* John xiv. 39.

This is the main ground of our confidence in Him, that He is *a holy, harmless, undefiled High Priest :* and *such a one became us*, says the Apostle, who are so sinful. Heb. vii. 26. The more sinful we are, the more need that our High Priest should be sinless; and being so, we may build upon His perfection, as standing in our stead, yea, we are invested with Him and His righteousness.

Again, *there was no guile found in His mouth.* This serves to convince us concerning all the promises that He hath made, that they are nothing but truth. Hath he said, *Him that cometh to me I will in no wise cast out?* John vi. 37. Then you need not fear, how unworthy and vile soever you may be; do but come to Him, and you have His word that He will not shut the door against you. And as He hath promised access, so he hath further promised ease and soul's rest to those that come, Matt. xi. 30. Then be confident to find that in Him too, for there was never a false or guileful word found in His mouth.

But to consider it only in the present action, this speaks Him the most innocent sufferer that ever was, not only judicially just in His cause, but entirely just in His person, altogether righteous; and yet, condemned to death, and an opprobrious death of malefactors, and set betwixt two, as chief of the three! *I am*, says he, *the rose of Sharon, and the lily of the valley;* and the spouse saith of Him, *My well-beloved is white and ruddy,* Cant. ii. 1, 10 : thus, indeed, He was in His death, ruddy in his bloodshed, and white in his innocence, and withal in his meekness and patience; the other thing wherein he is here so exemplary.

Who, when he was reviled, reviled not again.] This spotless Lamb of God, was a Lamb both in guiltlessness and silence; and the Prophet Isaiah expresses the resemblance, in that *He was brought as a Lamb to the slaughter*, Isa. liii. 7. He suffered not only an unjust sentence of death, but withal unjust revilings, *the contradictions of sinners.* No one ever did so little deserve revilings ; no one ever could have said so much in his own just defence, and to the just reproach of his enemies ; and yet, in both, he preferred silence. No one could ever threaten so heavy things as He could against his enemies, and have made good all he threatened, and yet no such thing was heard from Him. The heavens and the earth, as it were, spoke their resentment of His death who made them ; but He was silent ; or what He spoke makes this still good, how far he was from revilings and threatenings. As spices pounded, or precious ointment poured out, give their smell most, thus, *His name was an ointment* then *poured forth,* together with His blood, (Cant. i. 3,) and filling heaven and earth with its sweet perfume, was a savour of rest and peace in both, appeasing the wrath of God, and so quieting the consciences of men. And even in this particular was it then most fragrant, in that all the torments of the cross, and all the revilings of the multitude, racked him as it were for some answer, yet could draw no other from Him than this, *Father, forgive them, for they know not what they do.*

But for those to whom this mercy belonged not, the Apostle tells us what He did ; instead of revilings and threatenings, *He committed all to Him who judgeth righteously.* And this is the true method of Christian patience, that which quiets the mind, and keeps it from the boiling, tumultuous thoughts of revenge, to turn the whole matter into God's hand, to resign it over to Him, to prosecute when and as He thinks good. Not as the most, who had rather, if they had power, do for themselves, and be their own avengers ; and because they have not power, do offer up such bitter curses and prayers for revenge unto God, as are most hateful to Him, and are far from this calm and holy way of committing matters to His judgment. The common way of referring things to God, is indeed impious and dishonourable to Him, being really no other than calling Him to be a servant and executioner to our passion. We ordinarily mistake His justice, and judge of it according to our own precipitant and distempered minds. If wicked men be not crossed in their designs, and their wickedness evidently crushed, just when we would have it, we are ready to give up the matter as desperate, or at least to abate of those confident and reverential thoughts of Divine justice which we owe Him. Howsoever things go, this ought to be fixed in our hearts, that *He who sitteth in heaven* judgeth righteously, and executes that His righteous judgment in the fittest season. We poor worms, whose whole life is but a *hand-breadth* in itself, and is *as nothing* unto God, think a few months or years a great matter ; but to Him who *inhabiteth eternity, a thousand years are but as one day,* as our Apostle teaches us, in his second Epistle, chap. iii. 8.

Our Saviour, in that time of his humiliation and suffering, committed himself and his cause (for that is best expressed, in that nothing is expressed but *He committed)* to *Him who judgeth righteously,* and the issue shall be, that *all his enemies shall become his footstool,* and He himself shall judge them. But that which is given us here to learn from his carriage toward them in his suffering, is, that quietness and moderation of mind, even under unjust sufferings, make us like Him : not to reply to reproach with reproach, as our custom is, to give one ill word for another, or two for one, to be sure not to be behind. Men take a pride in this, and think it ridiculous simplicity so to suffer, and this makes strifes and contention so much abound ; but it is a great mistake. You think it greatness of spirit to bear nothing, to put up with no wrong, whereas, indeed, it is great weakness, and baseness. It is true greatness of spirit to despise the most of those things which set you usually on fire one against another ; especially, being done after a Christian manner, it were a part of the spirit of Christ in you: and is there any spirit greater than that, think you ? Oh that there were less of the spirit of the Dragon, and more of the spirit of the Dove amongst us !

II. Our obligation to follow the example of Christ, besides being enforced by its own excellency, is intimated in these two things contained in the words : 1. The design of His behaviour for this use, to be as an example to us. 2. Our interest in Him, and those His sufferings, wherein He so carried himself.

1. That His behaviour was intended as an example, *Leaving us an example*, &c. He left His footsteps as a copy, (as the word in the original, ὑπογραμμον, imports,) to be followed by us : every step of His, is a letter of this copy ; and particularly in this point of suffering, He wrote us a pure and perfect copy of obedience, in clear and great letters, in His own blood.

His whole life is our rule: not, indeed, His miraculous works, His footsteps walking on the sea, and such like, they are not for our following ; but His obedience, holiness, meekness, and humility are our copy, which we should continually study. The shorter and more effectual way, they say, of teaching, is by example ; but above all, this matchless Example is the happiest way of teaching. *He that follows me*, says our Lord, *shall not walk in darkness.* John viii. 12.

He that aims high, shoots the higher for it, though he shoot not so high as he aims. This is what ennobles the spirit of a Christian, the propounding of this our high pattern, the example of Jesus Christ.

The imitation of men in worthless things, is low and servile ; the imitation of their virtues is commendable, but if we aim no higher, it is both imperfect and unsafe. The Apostle St. Paul will have no imitation, but with regard to this Supreme Pattern : *Be ye followers of me, as I am of Christ.* 1 Cor. xi. 1. One Christian may take the example of Christ as exhibited in many things in another, but still he must examine all by the original primitive copy, the footsteps of Christ himself, following nothing but as it is conformable to that, and looking chiefly on Him, both as the most perfect and most effectual example. See Heb. xii. 2. There is *a cloud of witnesses* and examples, but look above them all, to Him, who is as high above them, as the sun is above the clouds. As in the Covenant of Grace the way is better, a living way indeed, so, there is this advantage also, that we are not left to our own skill for following it, but taught by the Spirit. In the delivery of the Law, God showed His glory and greatness by the manner of giving it, but the Law was written only in dead tables. But Christ, the living law, teaches by obeying it, how to obey it ; and this, too, is the advantage of the Gospel, that the law is twice written over unto believers, first, in the example of Christ, and then, inwardly in their hearts by his Spirit. There is, together with that copy of all grace in Him, a spirit derived from Him, enabling believers to follow Him in their measure. They may not only see Him *as the only begotten Son of God, full of grace and truth*, as it is John i. 14, but, as there it follows, *they receive of his fulness grace for grace.* The love of Christ makes the soul delight to converse with him ; and converse and love together make it learn his behaviour : as men that live much together, especially if they do much affect one another, will insensibly contract one another's habits and customs.

The other thing obliging us is, 2ndly, Our interest in Him and His sufferings; *He suffered for us.* And to this the Apostle returns, ver. 24. Observe only from the tie of these two, that if we neglect His example set before us, we cannot enjoy any right assurance of His suffering for us ; but if we do seriously endeavour to follow Him, then, we may expect to obtain life through His death, and those steps of His wherein we walk, will bring us ere long to be *where He is.*

Ver. 24. Who his own self bare our sins in his own body on the tree, that we, being dead to sins, should live unto righteousness : by whose stripes ye were healed.

THAT which is deepest in the heart, is generally most in the mouth ; that which abounds within, runs over most by the tongue or pen. When men light upon the speaking of that subject which possesses their affection, they can hardly be taken off, or drawn from it again. Thus the Apostles in their writings, when they make mention any way of Christ suffering for us, love to dwell on it, as that which they take most delight to speak of ; such delicacy, such sweetness is in it to a spiritual taste, that they like to keep it in their mouth, and are never out of their theme when they insist on Jesus Christ, though they have but named Him by occasion of some other doctrine ; for He is the great subject of all they have to say.

Thus here, the Apostle had spoken of Christ in the foregoing words very fitly to his present subject, setting Him before Christian servants, and all suffering Christians, as their complete example, both in point of much suffering, and of perfect innocence and patience in suffering ; and he had expressed their obligation to study and follow that example ; yet, he cannot leave it so, but having said that all those His sufferings, wherein He was so exemplary, were for us, as a chief consideration for which we should study to be like Him, he returns to that again, and enlarges upon it in words partly the same, partly very near those of that Evangelist among the Prophets, Isaiah liii. 4.

And it suits very well with his main scope, to press this point, as giving both very much strength and sweetness to the exhortation ; for surely it is most reasonable, that we willingly conform to Him in suffering, who had never been an example of suffering, nor subject at all to sufferings, nor in any degree capable of them, but for us ; and it is most comfortable in *these light sufferings of this present moment*, to consider that He hath freed us from these sufferings of eternity, by suffering Himself in our stead in the fulness of time.

That Jesus Christ is, in doing and in suffering, our supreme and matchless example, and that He came to be so, is a truth ; but that He is nothing further, and came for no other end, is you see a high point of falsehood. For how should man be enabled to learn and follow that example of obedience, unless there were more than an example in Christ? and what would become of that great reckoning of disobedience that man stands guilty of? No, these are notions far too narrow. He came to *bear our sins in his own body on the tree*, and for this purpose, had a body fitted for him and given him to bear this burden, to do this as the will of his Father, to stand for us instead of all offerings and sacrifices; and *by that will*, says the Apostle, *we are sanctified, through the offering of the body of Jesus Christ, once for all*. Heb. x. 9.

This was His business, not only to rectify sinful man by His example, but to redeem him by His blood. *He was a Teacher come from God:* as a Prophet, He teaches us the way of life, and as the best and greatest of prophets, is perfectly like His doctrine; and His actions, (which in all teachers is the liveliest part of doctrine,) His carriage in life and death, is our great pattern and instruction. But what is said of his Forerunner, is more eminently true of Christ: He is *a Prophet, and more than a Prophet*,—a Priest satisfying justice for us, and a King conquering sin and death for us; an example indeed, but more than an example,—our *sacrifice*, and *our life*, our *all in all*. It is our duty to *walk as He walked*, to make Him the pattern of our steps; (1 John ii. 6;) but our comfort and salvation lie in this, that *He is the propitiation for our sins*, ver. 2. So, in the first chapter of that Epistle, ver. 7, *We are to walk in the light, as He is in the light;* but for all our walking, we have need of that which follows, that bears the great weight,—*The blood of Jesus Christ cleanseth us from all sin.* And so still, that glory which He possesseth in His own person, is the pledge of ours: He is there for *us, He lives to make.intercession for us*, says the Apostle, Heb. vii. 25; and, *I go to prepare a place for you*, says our Lord himself, John xiv. 2.

We have in the words these two great points, and in the same order as the words lie: I. The Nature and Quality of the sufferings of Jesus Christ; and, II. The End of them.

I. In this expression of the Nature and Quality of the sufferings of Christ, we are to consider, 1. The Commutation of the persons, *He himself—for us*. 2. The Work undertaken and performed, *He bare our sins in His own body on the tree.*

1. The act or sentence of the Law against the breach of it standing in force, and Divine justice expecting satisfaction, Death was the necessary and inseparable consequent of Sin. If you say, the supreme Majesty of God, being accountable to none, might have forgiven all without satisfaction, we are not to contest that, nor foolishly to offer to sound the bottomless depth of His absolute prerogative. Christ implies in his prayer, Matt. xxvi. 39, that it was *impossible* that he could escape *that cup;* but the impossibility is resolved into his Father's will, as the cause of it. But this we may clearly see, following the track of the Holy Scriptures, (our only safe way,) that this way wherein our salvation is contrived, is most excellent, and suitable to the greatness and goodness of God; so full of wonders of wisdom and love, that the Angels, as our Apostle tells us before, cannot forbear looking on it, and admiring it: for all their exact knowledge, yet

they still find it infinitely beyond their knowledge, still in astonish-
ment and admiration of what they see, and still in search, looking in
to see more ; those cherubim still having their eyes fixed on this
Mercy-Seat.

Justice might indeed have seized on rebellious man, and laid the pronounced punishment on him.   Mercy might have freely acquitted him,
and pardoned all.   But can we name any place where Mercy and Justice, as relating to condemned man, could have met and shined jointly
in full aspect, save only in Jesus Christ ?—in whom indeed, *Mercy and
Truth met, and Righteousness and Peace kissed each other*, Psal. lxxxv.
10 ; yea, in whose person the parties concerned, that were at so great
a distance, met so near, as nearer cannot be imagined.

And not only was this the sole way for the consistency of these two,
Justice and Mercy, but take each of them severally, and they could
not have been manifested in so full lustre in any other way.   God's
just hatred of sin did, out of doubt, appear more in punishing His
own only begotten Son for it, than if the whole race of mankind had
suffered for it eternally.   Again, it raises the notion of mercy to the
highest, that sin is not only forgiven us, but for this end God's own
co-eternal Son is given to us, and for us.   Consider what He is, and
what we are ; He the *Son of His love*, and we, enemies.   Therefore
it is emphatically expressed in the words, *God so loved the world*, John
iii. 16 : that Love amounts to this much, that is, was so great, as *to
give his Son;* but how great that Love is, cannot be uttered.   *In this,*
says the Apostle, Rom. v. 8, *God commendeth His love to us*, sets it off
to the highest, gives us the richest and strongest evidence of it.

The foundation of this plan, this appearing of Christ for us, and
undergoing and answering all in our stead, lies in the decree of God,
where it was plotted and contrived, in the whole way of it, from eternity ; and the Father and the Son being one, and their thoughts and
will one, They were perfectly agreed on it ; and those likewise for
whom it should hold, were agreed upon, and their names written down,
according to which they are said to be *given unto Christ to redeem.*
And just according to that model did all the work proceed, and was
accomplished in all points, perfectly answering to the pattern of it in
the mind of God.   As it was preconcluded there, that the Son should
undertake the business, this matchless piece of service for His Father,
and that by His interposing men should be reconciled and saved ; so
that He might be altogether a fit person for the work, it was resolved,
that as He was already fit for it by the almightiness of His Deity and
Godhead, and the acceptableness of His person to the Father, as the
Son of God, so he should be further fitted by wonderfully uniting
weakness to Almightiness, the frailty of man to the power of God.
Because suffering for man was a main point of the work, therefore,
as His being the Son of God made Him acceptable to God, so His
being the Son of man made Him suitable to man, in whose business
He had engaged himself, and suitable to the business itself to be performed.   And not only was there in Him, by his human nature, a conformity to man, (for that might have been accomplished by a new
created body,) but a consanguinity with man, by a body framed of the
same piece,—this Redeemer, a Kinsman, (as the Hebrew word *goel*

is,)—only purified for His use, as was needful, and framed after a peculiar manner, in the womb of a virgin, as it is expressed, Heb. x. 5, *Thou hast fitted a body for me,*—having no sin itself, because ordained to have so much of our sins : as it is here, *He bare our sins in His own body.*

And this looks back to the primitive transaction and purpose. *Lo! I come to do thy will,* says the Son. Psal. xl. 7. *Behold my servant whom I have chosen,* says the Father, (Isa. xliii. 10,) this master-piece of my works ; no one in heaven or earth is fit to serve me, but my own Son. And as He came into the world according to that decree and will, so He goes out of it again in that way. *The Son of man goeth as is determined,* Luke xxii. 22 : it was wickedly and maliciously done by men against Him, but it was *determined* (which is what he there speaks of) wisely and graciously by His Father, with His own consent. As in those two-faced pictures, look upon the crucifying of Christ one way, as complotted by a treacherous disciple and malicious priests and rulers, and nothing more deformed and hateful than the authors of it ; but view it again, as determined in God's counsel, for the restoring of lost mankind, and it is full of unspeakable beauty and sweetness,—infinite wisdom and love in every trait of it.

Thus also, as to the persons for whom Christ engaged to suffer, their coming unto Him looks back to that first donation of the Father, as flowing from that : *All that the Father giveth me shall come unto me.* John vi. 37.

Now this being God's great design, it is that which He would have men eye and consider more than all the rest of His works ; and yet it is least of all considered by the most ! The other Covenant, made with the first Adam, was but to make way, and, if we may so speak, to make work for this. For He knew that it would not hold ; therefore, as this New Covenant became needful by the breach of the other, so, the failing of that other sets off and commends the firmness of this. The former was made with a man in his best condition, and yet he kept it not : even then, he proved vanity, as it is, Psal. xxxix. 5, *Verily, every man, in his best estate, is altogether vanity.* So that the second, that it might be stronger, is made with a Man indeed, to supply the place of the former, but he is *God-Man,* to be surer than the former, and therefore it holds. And this is the difference, as the Apostle expresses it, that the first Adam, in that Covenant, was laid as a foundation, and, though we say not that the Church, in its true notion, was built on him, yet, the estate of the whole race of mankind, the materials which the Church is built of, lay on him for that time ; and it failed. But upon this rock, the second Adam, is the Church so firmly built, that *the gates of hell cannot prevail against her. The first man, Adam, was made a living soul ; the last Adam was made a quickening* (or life-giving) *spirit.* 1 Cor. xv. 45. The first had life, but he transferred it not, yea, he kept it not for himself, but drew in and transferred death ; but the Second, by death, conveys life to all that are reckoned his seed : *He bare their sins.*

2. As to the work itself. He bare them *on the tree.* In that outside of His suffering, the visible kind of death inflicted on Him, in that it was hanging on the tree of the cross, there was an analogy

with the end and main work ; and it was ordered by the Lord with regard unto that end, being a death declared *accursed by the Law*, as the Apostle St. Paul observes, Gal. iii. 13, and so declaring Him who was *God blessed for ever*, to have been *made a curse* (that is, accounted as accursed) for us, that we might be blessed in Him, *in whom*, according to the promise, *all the nations of the earth are blessed*.

But that wherein lay the strength and main stress of His sufferings, was this invisible weight which none could see who gazed on Him, but which He felt more than all the rest : *He bare our sins*. In this there are three things. 1. The weight of sin. 2. The transferring of it upon Christ. 3. His bearing of it.

[1.] He bare sin as a heavy burden ; so the word *bearing* imports in general, (ἀνήνεγκεν,) and those two words particularly used by the Prophet, Isa. liii. 4, to which these allude, (סבל נשא) imply the *bearing of some great mass* or *load*. And such sin is ; for it hath the wrath of an offended God hanging at it, indissolubly tied to it, of which, who can bear the least ? And therefore the least sin, being the procuring cause of it, will press a man down for ever, that he shall not be able to rise. *Who can stand before Thee when once Thou art angry?* says the Psalmist, Psal. lxxvi. 7. And the Prophet, Jer. iii. 12, *Return, backsliding Israel, and I will not cause my wrath to fall upon thee—to fall* as a great weight, or as a millstone, and crush the soul.

But, senseless, we go light under the burden of sin, and feel it not, we complain not of it, and are therefore truly said to be *dead in it;* otherwise it could not but press us, and press out complaints. *O! wretched man that I am! who shall deliver me?* A profane, secure sinner thinks it nothing to break the holy Law of God, to please his flesh, or the world ; he counts sin a light matter, *makes a mock* of it, as Solomon says, Prov. xiv. 9. But a stirring conscience is of another mind : *Mine iniquities are gone over my head; as a heavy burden, they are too heavy for me.* Psal. xxxviii. 4.

Sin is such a burden as makes the very frame of heaven and earth, which is not guilty of it, yea, the whole creation, to crack and groan, (it is the Apostle's doctrine, Rom. viii. 22,) and yet, the impenitent heart, whose guiltiness it is, continues unmoved, groaneth not ; for your accustomed groaning is no such matter.

Yea, to consider it in connexion with the present subject, where we may best read what it is, Sin was a heavy load to Jesus Christ. In Psal. xl. 12, the Psalmist, speaking in the person of Christ, complains heavily, *Innumerable evils have compassed me about; Mine iniquities* (not His, as done by Him, but yet His, by His undertaking to pay for them) *have taken hold of me, so that I am not able to look up ; they are more than the hairs of my head, therefore my heart faileth me.* And surely, that which pressed *Him* so sore who upholds heaven and earth, no other in heaven or on earth could have sustained and surmounted, but would have sunk and perished under it. Was it, think you, the pain of that common outside of his death, though very painful, that drew such a word from him, *My God, my God, why hast thou forsaken me?* Or was it the fear of that beforehand, that pressed a *sweat of blood* from him ? No, it was this burden of sin, the first of which was committed in the garden of Eden, that then began to be laid upon Him and fastened upon his shoulders in the garden of Gethsemane, ten thousand times heavier than the cross which he was caused to bear. That might be for a while turned over to another, but this could not. This was the cup he trembled at more than at that gall and vinegar to be afterwards offered to him by his crucifiers, or any part of his external sufferings : it was the bitter cup of wrath due to sin, which his Father put into his hand, and caused him to drink, the very same thing that is here called the *bearing our sins in his body.*

And consider, that the very smallest sins contributed to make up this load, and made it so much the heavier ; and therefore, though sins be comparatively smaller and greater, yet learn thence to account no sin in itself small, which offends the great God, and which lay heavy upon your great Redeemer in the day of his sufferings.

At His apprehension, besides the soldiers, that invisible crowd of the sins he was to suffer for, came about him, for it was these that laid strongest hold on him : he could easily have shaken off all the rest, as appears, Matt. xxvi. 33, but our sins laid the arrest on him, being accounted His, as it is in that forecited place, Psal. xl. 12, *Mine iniquities.* Now amongst these were even those sins we call small ; they were of the number that took him, and they were amongst those instruments of his bloodshed. If the greater were as the spear that pierced his side, the less were as the nails that pierced his hands and his feet, and the very least as the thorns that were set on his precious head. And the multitude of them made up what was wanting in their magnitude ; though they were small, they were many.

[2.] They were transferred upon Him by virtue of that covenant we spoke of. They became His debt, and He responsible for all they came to. Seeing you have accepted of this business according to My will, (may we conceive the Father saying to his Son,) you must go through with it ; you are engaged in it, but it is no other than what you understood perfectly before ; you knew what it would cost you, and yet, out of joint love with Me to those I named to be saved by you, you were as willing as I to the whole undertaking. Now therefore the time is come, that I must lay upon you the sins of all those persons, and you must bear them ; the sins of all those believers who lived before, and all who are to come after, to the end of the world. *The Lord laid on Him the iniquity of us all,* says the Prophet, (Isa. liii. 6,) took it off from us, and charged it on him, made it *to meet on Him,* or *to fall in together,* as the word in the original imports. The sins of all, in all ages before and after, who were to be saved, all their guiltiness met together on His back upon the Cross. Whosoever of all that number had least sin, yet had no small burden to cast on Him : and to give accession to the whole weight, *every man hath had his own way of wandering,* as the Prophet there expresseth it, and He paid for all ; all fell on Him. And as in testimony of his meekness and patience, so, in this respect likewise, was He so silent in His sufferings, that though His enemies dealt most unjustly with Him, yet He stood as convicted before the justice-seat of His Father, under the imputed guilt of all our sins, and so eyeing Him, and accounting His business to be chiefly with Him, He did patiently bear the due punishment of all our sins at His Father's hand, according to that of the Psalmist, *I was dumb, I opened not my mouth because Thou didst it.* Psal. xxxix. 9. Therefore the Prophet immediately subjoins the description of his silent carriage, to that which he had spoken of, the confluence of our iniquities upon Him : *As a sheep before her shearers is dumb, so He openeth not His mouth.* Isa. liii. 7.

And if our sins were thus accounted His, then, in the same way, and for that very reason, His sufferings and satisfaction must of necessity be accounted ours.   As He said for his disciples to the men who came to take him, *If it be me ye seek, then let these go free;* so He said for all believers, to his Father, His wrath then seizing on him, If on me Thou wilt lay hold, then let these go free.   And thus the agreement was : *He was made sin for us who knew no sin, that we might be made the righteousness of God in Him.* 2 Cor. v. *ult.*

So, then, there is a union betwixt believers and Jesus Christ, by which this interchange is made ; He being charged with their sins, and they clothed with His satisfaction and righteousness.   This union is founded, 1*st*, in God's decree of Election, running to this effect, that they should live in Christ, and so, choosing the Head and the whole mystical Body as one, and reckoning their debt as his, in His own purpose, that He might receive satisfaction, and they salvation, in their Head, Christ.   The execution of that purpose and union began in Christ's incarnation, it being for them, though the nature He assumed is theirs in common with other men.   It is said, Heb. ii. 16, *He took not on Him the nature of angels, but the seed of Abraham,* the company of believers : He became man for their sakes, because they are men. That He is of the same nature with unbelieving men who perish, is but by accident, as it were ; there is no good to them in that, but the great evil of deeper condemnation, if they hear of Him, and believe not ; but He was made man to be like, yea, to be one with the Elect, *and He is not ashamed to call them brethren,* as the Apostle there says, Heb. ii. 11. 2*ndly,* This union is also founded in the actual intention of the Son so made man ; He presenting himself to the Father in all He did and suffered, *as for them,* having them, and them only, in His eye and thoughts, in all.   *For their sakes do I sanctify myself.* John xvii. 1, 9. Again, 3*rdly,* This union is applied and performed in them, when they are converted and ingrafted into Jesus Christ by faith ; and this doth actually discharge them of their own sins, and entitle them to His righteousness, and so, justify them in the sight of God.   4*thly,* The consummation of this union, is in glory, which is the result and fruit of all the former.   As it began in heaven, it is completed there ; but betwixt these two in heaven, the intervention of those other two degrees of it on earth was necessary, being intended in the first, as tending to the attainment of the last.   These four steps of it are all distinctly expressed in our Lord's own prayer, John xvii. 1*st,* God's purpose that the Son should give *eternal life to those whom He hath given Him,* ver. 2. 2*ndly,* The Son's undertaking and accomplishing their redemption, in ver. 4 : *I have finished the work which Thou gavest me to do.* 3*rdly,* The application of this union, and its performance in them, by their *faith,* their *believing,* and *keeping His word,* ver. 6, 8, and in several of the subsequent verses. And then, lastly, the consummation of this union, ver. 24 : *I will that they whom Thou hast given me be with me where I am.* There meet the first donation, and the last.

Now to obtain this life for them, Christ died *in their stead.* He appeared as the High Priest, being perfectly and truly what the name was on their plate of gold, *Holiness to the Lord,* Exod. xxviii. 36, and so *bearing their iniquity,* as it is there added of Aaron, ver. 38. But because the high priest was not the Redeemer, but only prefigured him, he did not himself suffer for the people's sin, but turned it over upon the beasts which he sacrificed, signifying that translation of sin, by laying his hand upon the head of the beast. But Jesus Christ is both the great High Priest and the great sacrifice in one ; and this seems to be here implied in these words, *Himself bare our sins in His own body,* which the priest under the Law did not. So, Isa. liii. 10, and Heb. ix. 12, *He made His soul an offering for sin.* He offered up himself, his *whole self.* In the history of the Gospel, it is said, that *His soul was heavy,* and chiefly suffered ; but it is the bearing sin in *His body,* and offering it, that is oftenest mentioned as the visible part of the sacrifice, and as His way of offering it, not excluding the other. Thus (Rom. xii. 1) we are exhorted to give *our bodies,* in opposition to the bodies of beasts, and they are therefore called *a living sacrifice,* which they are not without the soul. So, Christ's bearing it *in His body,* imports the bearing of it in his soul too.

[3.] His *bearing* of our sins, hints that He was active and willing in his suffering for us ; it was not a constrained offering. *He laid down his life,* as He himself tells us, John x. 18 ; and this expression here, *He bare,* implies, He took willingly off, lifted from us that burden, to bear it Himself. It was counted an ill sign amongst the heathens, when the beasts went unwillingly to be sacrificed, and drew back, and a good omen when they went willingly. But never was sacrifice so willing as our Great Sacrifice ; and we may be assured He hath appeased his Father's wrath, and wrought atonement for us. Isaac was in this a type of Christ ; we hear of no reluctance ; he submitted quietly to be bound when he was to be offered up. There are two words used in Isaiah, ch. liii. ver. 4, the one signifying *bearing,* the other, *taking away.* This *bearing* includes, also, that *taking away of the sins of the world,* spoken of by St. John, ch. i. ver. 29, which answers to both ; and so He, the Great Antitype, answers to both the goats, the sin-offering and the .scape-goat, Lev. xvi. He did bear our sins on his cross, and from thence did bear them away to his grave, and there they are buried ; and they whose sins He did so bear, and take away, and bury, shall hear no more of them as theirs to bear. Is He not, then, worthy to be beheld, in that notion under which John, in the forementioned text, viewed Him, and designates Him ?—*Behold the Lamb of God, which beareth and taketh away the sins of the world!*

You, then, who are gazing on vanity, be persuaded to turn your eyes this way, and behold this lasting wonder, this Lord of Life dying ! But the most, alas ! want a due eye for this Object. It is the eye of faith alone, that looks aright on Him, and is daily discovering new worlds of excellency and delight in this crucified Saviour ; that can view Him daily, as hanging on the Cross, without the childish, gaudy help of a crucifix, and grow in the knowledge of that Love which passeth knowledge, and rejoice itself in frequent thinking and speaking of Him, instead of those idle and vain thoughts at the best, and empty discourses, wherein the most delight, and wear out the day. What is all knowledge but painted folly in comparison of this? Hadst thou Solomon's faculty to discourse of all plants, and hadst not the right knowledge of this *root of Jesse;* wert thou singular in the knowledge of the stars and of the course of the heavens, and couldst walk through the spheres with a *Jacob's staff,* but ignorant of this *star of Jacob;* if thou knewest the histories of all time, and the life and death of all the most famous princes, and could rehearse them all, but dost not spiritually know and apply to thyself the death of Jesus as thy life; thou art still a wretched fool, and all thy knowledge with thee shall quickly perish. On the other side, if thy capacity or breeding hath denied thee the knowledge of all these things wherein men glory so much, yet, do but learn *Christ crucified,* and what wouldst thou have more? That shall make thee happy for ever. *For this is life eternal, to know thee the only true God, and Jesus Christ whom thou hast sent.* John xvii. 3.

Here St. Paul takes up his rest, *I determined to know nothing but Jesus Christ and him crucified.* 1 Cor. ii. 2. As if he had said, Whatsoever I knew besides, I resolved to be as if I knew nothing besides this, the only knowledge wherein I will rejoice myself, and which I will labour to impart to others. I have tried and compared the rest, and find them all unworthy of their room beside this, and my whole soul too little for this. I have passed this judgment and sentence on all. I have adjudged myself to deny all other knowledge, and confined myself within this circle, and I am not straitened. No, there is room enough in it; it is larger than heaven and earth, *Christ, and Him crucified;* the most despised and ignominious part of knowledge, yet the sweetest and most comfortable part of all: the root whence all our hopes of life and all our spiritual joys do spring.

But the greatest part of mankind hear this subject as a story. Some are a little moved with the present sound of it, but they draw it not home into their hearts, to make it theirs, and to find salvation in it, but still cleave to sin, and love sin better than Him who suffered for it.

But you whose hearts the Lord hath deeply humbled under a sense of sin, come to this depth of consolation, and try it, that you may have experience of the sweetness and riches of it. Study this point tho roughly, and you will find it answer all, and quiet your consciences. Apply this *bearing of sin* by the Lord Jesus for you, for it is published and made known to you for this purpose. This is the genuine and true use of it, as of the *brazen serpent,* not that the people might emptily gaze on the fabric of it, but that those that looked on it might be cured. When all that can be said, is said against you, "It is true," may you say, "but it is all satisfied for; He on whom I rest, made it His, and did bear it for me." The person of Christ is of more worth than all men, yea, than all the creatures, and therefore, his life was a full ransom for the greatest offender.

And as for outward troubles and sufferings, which were the occasion of this doctrine in this place, they are all made exceeding light by the removal of this great pressure. Let the Lord lay on me what He will, seeing He hath taken off my sin, and laid that on His own Son in my stead. I may suffer many things, but He hath borne that for me, which alone was able to make me miserable.

And you that have this persuasion, how will your hearts be taken up with His love, *who has so loved you as to give himself for you;* who interposed Himself to bear off from you the stroke of everlasting death, and encountered all the wrath due to us, and went through with that great work, by reason of his unspeakable love ! Let Him never go forth from my heart, who for my sake refused to go down from the cross.

II. The End of these Sufferings. *That we being dead to sin, should live unto righteousness.*] The Lord doth nothing in vain ; He hath not made the least of his works to no purpose ; *in wisdom hath He made them all,* says the Psalmist. And this is true, not only in regard of their excellent frame and order, but of their end, which is a chief point of wisdom. So then, in order to the right knowledge of this great work put into the hands of Jesus Christ, it is of special concern to understand what is its end.

Now this is the thing which Divine wisdom and love aimed at in that great undertaking, and therefore it will be our truest wisdom, and the truest evidence of our reflex love, to intend the same thing, that in this, *the same mind may be in us, that was in Christ Jesus* in his suffering for us ; for this very end it is expressed, *That we being dead to sin, should live to righteousness.*

In this there are three things to be considered : 1st, What this death and life is ; 2ndly, The designing of it in the sufferings and death of Jesus Christ ; 3rdly, The effecting of it by them.

1*st,* What this death and life is. Whatsoever it is, surely it is no small change that bears the name of the great and last natural change that we are subject to, a *death,* and then another kind of life succeeding to it.

In this the greatest part of mankind are mistaken, that they take any slight alteration in themselves for true conversion. A world of people are deluded with superficial moral changes in their life, some rectifying of their outward actions and course of life, and somewhat too in the temper and habit of their mind. Far from reaching the bottom of nature's wickedness, and *laying the axe to the root of the tree,* it is such a work as men can make a shift with by themselves. But the renovation which the Spirit of God worketh, is like Himself : it is so deep and total a work, that it is justly called by the name of the most substantial works and productions : *a new birth,* and more than that, *a new creation,* and here, a *death* and a kind of *life* following it.

This *death to sin,* supposes a former *living in it,* and to it ; and while a man does so, he is said indeed to be *dead in sin,* and yet withal, this is true, that he lives in sin, as the Apostle, speaking of widows, joins the expressions, 1 Tim. v. 6, *She that liveth in pleasure, is dead while she liveth.* So Eph. ii. 1, *Dead in trespasses and sins,* and he adds, *wherein ye walked,* which imports a life, such a one as it is ; and more expressly, ver. 3, *We had our conversation in the lusts of our flesh.* Now, thus to live in sin, is termed being dead in it, because, in that condition, man is indeed dead in respect of that divine life of the soul, that happy being which it should have in union with God, for which it was made, and without which it had better not be at all. For that life, as it is different from its natural being, and a kind of life above it, so it is contrary to that corrupt being and life it hath in sin ; and therefore, to live in sin, is to be dead in it, being a deprivement of that divine being, that life of the soul in God, in comparison whereof not only the base life it hath in sin, but the very natural life it hath in the body, and which the body hath by it, is not worthy of the name of life. You see the body, when the thread of its union with the soul is cut, become not only straightway a motionless lump, but, within a little time, a putrefied, noisome carcass ; and thus the soul by sin cut off from God who is its life, as is the soul that of the body, hath not only no moving faculty in good, but becomes full of rottenness and vileness : as the word is, Psal. xiv. 2, *They are gone aside and become filthy.* The soul, by turning away from God, turns filthy ; yet, as a man thus spiritually dead, lives naturally, so, because he acts and spends that natural life in the ways of sin, he is said to *live in sin.* Yea, there is somewhat more in that expression than the mere passing of his life in that way ; for instead of that happy life his soul should have in God, he pleases himself in the miserable life of sin, that which is his death, as if it were the proper life of his soul : *living in it* imports that natural propension he hath to sin, and the continual delight he takes in it, as in his element, and living to it, as if that were the very end of his being. In that estate, neither his body nor his mind stirreth without sin. Setting aside his manifest breaches of the Law, those actions that are evidently and totally sinful, his natural actions, his eating and drinking, his religious actions, his praying, and hearing, and preaching, are sin at the bottom. And generally, his heart is no other than a forge of sin. *Every imagination,* every fiction of things framed there, *is only evil continually,* Gen. vi. 5 : every day, and all the day long, it is his very trade and life.

Now, in opposition to this life of sin, this living in it and to it, a Christian is said to *die to sin,* to be cut off or separated from it. In our miserable natural state, there is as close a union betwixt us and sin, as betwixt our souls and bodies : it lives in us, and we in it, and the longer we live in that condition, the more the union grows, and the harder it is to dissolve it ; and it is as old as the union of soul and body, begun with it, so that nothing but the death here spoken of can part them. And this death, in this relative sense, is mutual : in the work of conversion, sin dies, and the soul dies to sin, and these two are really one and the same thing. The Spirit of God kills both at one blow, sin in the soul, and the soul to sin : as the Apostle says of himself and the world, Gal. vi. 14, each is crucified to the other.

And there are in it chiefly these two things, which make the difference, [1.] The solidity, and [2.] The universality of this change here represented under the notion of Death.

Many things may lie in a man's way betwixt him and the acting of divers sins which possibly he affects most.   Some restraints, either outward or inward, may be upon him, the authority of others, the fear of shame or punishment, or the check of an enlightened conscience; and though, by reason of these, he commit not the sin he would, yet he *lives in it,* because he *loves* it, because he would commit it : as we say, the soul lives not so much where it animates, as where it loves. And generally, that metaphorical kind of life, by which man is said to live in any thing, hath its principal seat in the affection : that is the immediate link of the union in such a life ; and the untying and death consists chiefly in the disengagement of the heart, the breaking off the affection from it.   *Ye that love the Lord,* says the Psalmist, *hate evil,* Psal. xcvii. 10.   An unrenewed mind may have some temporary dis-likes even of its beloved sins in cold blood, but it returns to like them within a while.   A man may not only have times of cessation from his wonted way of sinning, but, by reason of the society wherein he is, and the withdrawing of occasions to sin, and divers other causes, his very desire after it may seem to himself to be abated, and yet he may be not dead to sin, but only asleep to it ; and therefore, when a temptation, backed with opportunity and other inducing circumstances, comes and jogs him, he awakes, and arises, and follows it.

A man may for a while distaste some meat which he loves, (possibly upon a surfeit,) but he quickly regains his liking of it.   Every quarrel with sin, every fit of dislike to it, is not that hatred which is implied in dying to sin.   Upon the lively representation of the deformity of his sin to his mind, certainly a natural man may fall out with it ; but this is but as the little jars of husband and wife, which are far from dissolving the marriage : it is not a fixed hatred, such as amongst the Jews inferred a divorce—*If thou hate her, put her away ;* that is to die to it ; as by a legal divorce the husband and wife are civilly dead one to another in regard of the tie and use of marriage.

Again ; some men's education, and custom, and moral principles, may free them from the grossest kind of sins, yea, a man's temper may be averse from them, but they are alive to their own kind of sins, such as possibly are not so deformed in the common account, covet-ousness, or pride, or hardness of heart, and either a hatred or a disdain of the ways of holiness, which are too strict for them, and exceed their size.   Besides, for the good of human society, and for the interest of his own Church and people, God restrains many natural men from the height of wickedness, and gives them moral virtues.   There be very many, and very common sins, which more refined natures, it may be, are scarcely tempted to ; but as in their diet, and apparel, and other things in their natural life, they have the same kind of being with other persons, though they are more neat and elegant, so, in this living to sin, they live the same life with other ungodly men, though with a little more delicacy.

They consider not that the devils are not in themselves subject to, nor capable of, many of those sins that are accounted grossest amongst men, and yet are greater rebels and enemies to God than men are.

But to be *dead to sin* goes deeper, and extends further than all this ; it involves a most inward alienation of heart from sin, and most universal, from all sin, an antipathy to the most beloved sin.   Not only doth the believer forbear sin, but he hates it—*I hate vain thoughts*, Psal. cxix. 113 ; and not only doth he hate some sins, but all—*I hate every false way*, ver. 128.   A stroke at the heart does it, which is the certainest and quickest death of any wound.   For in this dying to sin, the whole man of necessity dies to it ; the mind dies to the device and study of sin, that vein of invention becomes dead ; the hand dies to the acting of it ; the ear, to the delightful hearing of things profane and sinful ; the tongue, to the world's dialect of oaths, and rotten speaking, and calumny, and evil speaking, which is the commonest effect of the tongue's life in sin,—the very natural heat of sin exerts and vents itself most that way ; the eye becomes dead to that intemperate look that Solomon speaks of, when he cautions us against *eyeing the wine when it is red, and well-coloured in the cup*, Prov. xxiii. 31 : it is not taken with looking on the glittering skin of that *serpent* till it *bite* and *sting*, as there he adds.   It becomes also dead to that unchaste look which kindles fire in the heart, to which Job blindfolded and deadened his eyes, by an express compact and agreement with them : *I have made a covenant with mine eyes.*   Job xxxi. 1.

The eye of a godly man is not fixed on the false sparkling of the world's pomp, honour, and wealth ; it is dead to them, being quite dazzled with a greater beauty.   The grass looks fine in the morning, when it is set with those liquid pearls, the drops of dew that shine upon it ; but if you can look but a little while on the body of the sun, and then look down again, the eye is as it were dead ; it sees not that faint shining on the earth that it thought so gay before : and as the eye is blinded, and dies to it, so, within a few hours, that gaiety quite evanishes and dies itself.

Men think it strange that the Godly are not fond of their diet, that their appetite is not stirred with desire of their delights and dainties ; they know not that such as be Christians indeed, are dead to those things, and the best dishes that are set before a dead man, give him not a stomach.   The godly man's *throat is cut to those meats*, as Solomon advises in another subject, Prov. xxiii. 2.   But why may not you be a little more sociable to follow the fashion of the world, and take a share with your neighbours, may some say, without so precisely and narrowly examining every thing ?   It is true, says the Christian, that the time was when I advised as little with conscience as others, but sought myself, and pleaded myself, as they do, and looked no further ; but that was when *I was alive to those ways ;* but now, truly, *I am dead to them :* and can you look for activity and conversation from a dead man ?   The pleasures of sin wherein I lived, are still the same, but I am not the same.   Are you such a sneak and a fool, says the natural man, as to bear affronts, and swallow them, and say nothing ?   Can you suffer to be so abused by such and such a wrong ?   Indeed, says the Christian again, I could once have resented an injury, as you or another would, and had somewhat of what you call high-heartedness, when I was alive after your fashion ; but now, that humour is not only something cooled, but it is killed in me : it is cold dead, as ye say ; and a greater Spirit, I think, than my own, hath taught me another lesson, hath made me both deaf and dumb that way, and hath given me a new vent, and another language, and another Party to speak to on such occasions. *They that seek my hurt,* says David, *speak mischievous things, and imagine deceits all the day long.* What doth he in this case ? *But I, as a deaf man, heard not, and I was as a dumb man that openeth not his mouth.* And why ? *For in thee, O Lord, do I hope.* Psal. xxxviii. 12—15. And for this deadness that you despise, I have seen Him who died for me, *who, when he was reviled, reviled not again.*

This is the true character of a Christian ; he is *dead to sin.* But, alas ! where is this Christian to be found ? And yet, thus is every one who truly partakes of Christ ; he is dead to sin really. Hypocrites have an historical kind of death like this, as players in tragedies. Those players have loose bags of blood that receive the wound : so the hypocrite in some externals, and it may be, in that which is as near him as any outward thing, his purse, may suffer some bloodshed of that for Christ. But this death to sin is not a swooning fit, that one may recover out of again : the Apostle, Rom. vi. 4, adds, that the believer *is buried with Christ.*

But this is an unpleasant subject, to talk thus of death and burial. The very name of death, in the softest sense it can have, makes a sour, melancholy discourse. It is so indeed, if you take it alone, if there were not, for the life that is lost, a far better one immediately following ; but so it is here ; *living unto righteousness* succeeds *dying to sin.*

That which makes natural death so affrightful, the *king of terrors,* as Job calls it, ch. xviii. 14, is mainly this faint belief and assurance of the resurrection and glory to come ; and without some lively apprehension of this, all men's moral resolutions and discourses are too weak cordials against this fear. They may set a good face on it, and speak big, and so cover the fear they cannot cure ; but certainly, they are a little ridiculous who would persuade men to be content to die, by reasoning from the necessity and unavoidableness of it, which, taken alone, rather may beget a desperate discontent than a quiet compliance. The very weakness of that argument is, that it is too strong, *durum telum.* That of company is fantastic : it may please the imagination, but satisfies not the judgment. Nor are the miseries of life, though an argument somewhat more proper, a full persuasive to meet death without reluctance : the oldest, the most decrepit, and most diseased persons, yet naturally fall not out with life, but could have a mind to it still ; and the very truth is this, the worst cottage any one dwells in, he is loth to go out of till he knows of a better. And the reason why that which is so hideous to others, was so sweet to martyrs, (Heb. xi. 35,) and other godly men who have heartily embraced death, and welcomed it though in very terrible shapes, was, because they had firm assurance of immortality beyond it. The ugly Death's head, when the light of glory shines through the holes of it, is comely and lovely. To look upon Death as Eternity's birth-day, is that which makes it not only tolerable, but amiable. *Hic dies postremus, æterni natalis est,* is a word I admire more than any other that ever dropt from a heathen.

Thus here, the strongest inducement to this Death, is the true notion and contemplation of this Life unto which it transfers us. It is most necessary to represent this, for a natural man hath as great an aversion every whit from this figurative death, this *dying to sin*, as from natural death; and there is the more necessity of persuading him to this, because his consent is necessary to it. No man dies this death to sin unwillingly, although no man is naturally willing to it. Much of this death consists in a man's consenting thus to die; and this is not only a lawful, but a laudable, yea, a necessary self-murder. *Mortify, therefore, your members which are upon the earth*, says the Apostle, Col. iii. 5. Now no sinner would be content to *die to sin*, if that were all ; but if it be passing to a more excellent *life*, then he gaineth, and it were a folly not to seek this death. It was a strange power of Plato's discourse of the soul's immortality, that moved a young man, upon reading it, to throw himself into the sea, that he might leap through it to that immortality : but truly, were this life of God, this *life to righteousness*, and the excellency and delight of it, known, it would gain many minds to this death whereby we step into it.

But there is a necessity of a new being as the principle of new action and motion. The Apostle says, *While ye served sin, ye were free from righteousness*, Rom. vi. 20 ; so it is, while ye were alive to sin, ye were dead to righteousness. But there is a new breath of life from Heaven, breathed on the soul. Then lives the soul indeed, when it is one with God, and sees *light in his light*, Psal. xxxii. 9,—hath a spiritual knowledge of him, and therefore sovereignly loves him, and delights in his will. And this is indeed *to live unto righteousness*, which, in a comprehensive sense, takes in all the frame of a Christian life, and all the duties of it towards God and towards men.

By this new nature, the very natural motion of the soul so taken, is obedience to God ; and walking in the paths of righteousness, it can no more live in the habit and ways of sin, than a man can live under water. Sin is not the Christian's element; it is as much too gross for his renewed soul, as the water is for his body : he may fall into it, but he cannot breathe in it ; cannot take delight and continue to live in it. *But his delight is in the law of the Lord*, Psal. i. 2. That is the walk which his soul refreshes itself in ; he loves it entirely, and loves it most, where it most crosses the remainders of corruption that are within him. He bends the strength of his soul to please God ; aims wholly at that; it takes up his thoughts early and late. He hath no other purpose in his being and living, than only to honour his Lord. This is, *to live to righteousness*. He doth not make a by-work of it, a study for his spare hours : no, it is his main business, his all. *In his law doth he meditate day and night*. This life, like the natural one, is seated in the heart, and from thence diffuses itself to the whole man ; he *loves* righteousness, and *receiveth the truth* (as the Apostle speaks) *in the love of it*. A natural man may do many things which, as to their shell and outside, are righteous ; but he lives not to righteousness, because his heart is not possessed and ruled by the love of it. But this life makes the godly man delight to walk uprightly and to speak of righteousness ; his language and ways carry the resemblance of his heart. I know it is easiest to act that part of religion which is in the tongue, but the Christian, nevertheless, ought not to be spiritually dumb. Because some birds are taught to speak, men do not for that give it over, and leave off to speak. *The mouth of the righteous speaketh wisdom, and his tongue talketh of judgment.* And his feet strive to keep pace with his tongue, which gives evidence of its unfeignedness ; *None of his steps shall slide*, or, he shall not stagger in his steps. But that which is betwixt these, is the common spring of both : *The law of God is in his heart;* see Psal. xxxvii. 30, 31 ; and from thence, as Solomon says, *are the issues of his life*, Prov. iv. 3. That law in his heart, is the principle of *this living to righteousness.*

2. The second thing here, is, that it was the design of the sufferings and death of Christ, to produce in us this death and life : *He bare sin*, and died for it, that we might die to it.

Out of some conviction of the consequence of sin, many have a confused desire to be justified, to have sin pardoned, who look no further : they think not on the importance and necessity of Sanctification, the nature whereof is expressed by this *dying to sin*, and *living to righteousness.*

But here we see that Sanctification is necessary as inseparably connected with Justification, not only as its companion, but as its end, which, in some sort, raises it above the other. We see that it was the thing which God eyed and intended, in taking away the guiltiness of sin, that we might be renewed and sanctified. If we compare them in point of time, looking backward, holiness was always necessary unto happiness, but satisfying for sin, and the pardon of it, were made necessary by sin ; or, if we look forward, the estate we are appointed to, and for which we are delivered from wrath, is an estate of perfect holiness. When we reflect upon that great work of redemption, we see it aimed at there, *Redeemed to be holy*, Eph. v. 25, 26 ; Tit. ii. 14. And if we go yet higher, to the very spring, the decree of election, with regard to that it is said, Eph. i. 14, *Chosen before, that we should be holy.* And the end shall suit the design : *Nothing shall enter into the new Jerusalem that is defiled*, or unholy ; nothing but perfect purity is there ; not a spot of sinful pollution, not a *wrinkle* of the old man. For this end was that great work undertaken by the Son of God, that he might frame out of polluted mankind a new and holy generation to his Father, who might compass His throne in the life of glory, and give Him pure praises, and behold His face in that eternity. Now, for this end it was needful, according to the all-wise purpose of the Father, that the guiltiness of sin and sentence of death should be once removed ; and thus, the burden of that lay upon Christ's shoulders on the cross. That done, it is further necessary, that souls so delivered be likewise purified and renewed, for they are designed for perfection of holiness in the end, and it must begin here.

Yet it is not possible to persuade men of this, that Christ had this in his eye and purpose when he was lifted up upon the cross, and looked upon the whole company of those his Father had given him to save, that he would redeem them to be a number of holy persons. We would be redeemed ; who is there that would not ? But Christ would have his redeemed ones holy ; and they who are not true to this His end, but cross and oppose Him in it, may hear of Redemption long and often, but little to their comfort. Are you resolved still to abuse and delude yourselves ? Well, whether you will believe it or

not, this is once more told you : there is unspeakable comfort in the
death of Christ, but it belongs only to those who *are dead to sin, and
alive to righteousness.* This circle shuts out the impenitent world ;
there it closes, and cannot be broken through ; but all who are penitent, are by their effectual calling lifted into it, translated from that
accursed condition wherein they were. So then, if you will live in
your sins, you may ; but then, resolve withal to bear them yourselves,
for Christ, in his bearing of sin, meant the benefit of none, but such
as in due time are thus dead, and thus alive with Him.

3. But then, in the third place, Christ's sufferings and death effect
all this. [1.] As the exemplary cause, the lively contemplation of
Christ crucified, is the most powerful of all thoughts, to separate the
heart and sin. But, [2.] besides this example, working as a moral
cause, Christ is the effective natural cause of this death and life ; for
he is one with the believer, and there is a real influence of his death
and life into their souls. This mysterious union of Christ and the
believer, is that whereon both their justification and sanctification, the
whole frame of their salvation and happiness, depends. And in this
particular view the Apostle still insists on it, speaking of Christ and
believers as one in his death and resurrection, *crucified with him,
dead with him, buried with him, and risen with him.* Rom. vi. 4, &c.
Being arisen he applies his death to those he died for, and by it kills
the life of sin in them, and so is avenged on it for its being the cause of
his death : according to that expression of the Psalmist, *Raise me up,
that I may requite them.* Psal. xli. 10. Christ infuses, and then
actuates and stirs up that faith and love in them, by which they are
united to him ; and these work powerfully in producing this.

[3.] Faith looks so stedfastly on its suffering Saviour, that, as they
say, *Intellectus fit illud quod intelligit,* The mind becomes that which
it contemplates. It makes the soul like him, assimilates and *conforms
it to his death,* as the Apostle speaks, Phil. iii. 10. That which
Papists fabulously say of some of their saints, that they received the
impression of the wounds of Christ in their body, is true, in a spiritual
sense, of the soul of every one that is indeed a saint and a believer : it
takes the very print of his death, by beholding him, and *dies to sin ;*
and then takes that of his rising again, and *lives to righteousness.* As
it applies it to *justify,* so to *mortify,* drawing virtue from it. Thus
said one, " Christ aimed at this in all those sufferings which, with so
much love, he went through; and shall I disappoint him, and not serve
his end ? "

[4.] That other powerful grace of Love joins in this work with
Faith ; for love desires nothing more than likeness and conformity :
though it be a painful resemblance, so much the better and fitter to
testify love. Therefore it will have the soul die with Him who died
for it, and the very same kind of death : *I am crucified with Christ,*
says the great Apostle, Gal. ii. 20. The love of Christ in the soul
takes the very nails that fastened him to the cross, and crucifies the
soul to the world, and to sin. *Love is strong as death,* particularly in
this. The strongest and liveliest body, when death seizes it, must
yield, and that become motionless which was so vigorous before :
thus the soul that is most active and unwearied in sin, when this love

seizes it, is killed to sin; and as death separates a man from his dearest friends and society, this love breaks all its ties and friendship with sin. Generally, as Plato hath it, love takes away one's living in one's self, and transfers it into the party loved; but the divine love of Christ doth it in the truest and highest manner.

By whose stripes ye were healed.] The misery of fallen man, and the mercy of his deliverance, are both of them such a depth, that no one expression, yea, no variety of expressions added one to another, can fathom them. Here we have divers very significant ones. 1. The guiltiness of sin as an intolerable burden, pressing the soul and sinking it, and that transferred and laid on a stronger back: *He bare.* Then, 2. The same wretchedness, under the notion of a strange disease, by all other means incurable, *healed by His stripes.* And, 3. It is again represented by the forlorn condition of a sheep wandering, and our salvation to be found only in the love and wisdom of our great Shepherd. And all these are borrowed from that sweet and clear prophecy in the fifty-third chapter of Isaiah.

The polluted nature of man is no other than a bundle of desperate diseases: he is spiritually dead, as the Scriptures often teach. Now this contradicts not, nor at all lessens the matter; but only because this misery, justly called *death*, exists in a subject animated with a natural life, therefore, so considered, it may bear the name and sense of sickness, or wounds: and therefore it is gross misprision,—they are as much out in their argument as in their conclusion, who would extract out of these expressions, any evidence that there are remains of spiritual life, or good, in our corrupted nature. But they are not worthy the contest, though vain heads think to argue themselves into life, and are seeking that life, by logic, in miserable nature, which they should seek, by faith, in Jesus Christ, namely, in these *his stripes*, by which *we are healed.*

It were a large task to name our spiritual maladies; how much more, severally to unfold their natures! Such a multitude of corrupt, false principles in the mind, which, as gangrenes, do spread themselves through the soul, and defile the whole man; that total gross blindness and unbelief in spiritual things, and that stone of the heart, hardness and impenitency; lethargies of senselessness and security; and then, (for there be such complications of spiritual diseases in us, as in naturals are altogether impossible,) such burning fevers of inordinate affections and desires, of lust, and malice, and envy, such racking and tormenting cares of covetousness, and *feeding on earth and ashes,* (as the Prophet speaks in another case, Isa. xliv. 20,) according to the depraved appetite that accompanies some diseases; such tumours of pride and self-conceit, that break forth, as filthy botches, in men's words and carriage one with another! In a word, what a wonderful disorder must needs be in the natural soul, by the frequent interchanges and fight of contrary passions within it! And, besides all these, how many deadly wounds do we receive from without, by the temptations of Satan and the world! We entertain them, and by weapons with which they furnish us, we willingly wound ourselves; as the Apostle says of them *who will be rich,* they *fall into divers snares and noisome lusts, and pierce themselves through with many sorrows.* 1 Tim. vi. 9, 10.

Did we see it, no infirmary or hospital was ever so full of loathsome and miserable spectacles, as, in a spiritual sense, our wretched nature is in any one of us apart : how much more when multitudes of us are met together ! But our evils are hid from us, and we perish miserably in a dream of happiness ! This makes up and completes our wretchedness, that we feel it not with our other diseases ; and this makes it worse still. This was the Church's disease, Rev. iii. 17 : *Thou sayest, I am rich, and knowest not that thou art poor,* &c. We are usually full of complaints of trifling griefs which are of small moment, and think not on nor feel our dangerous maladies : as he who showed a physician his sore finger, but the physician told him, he had more need to think on the cure of a dangerous imposthume within him, which he perceived by looking at him, though himself did not feel it.

In dangerous maladies or wounds, there be these evils : a tendency to death, and with that, the apprehension of the terror and fear of it, and the present distemper of the body. So, there are in sin, 1. The guiltiness of sin binding over the soul to death, the most frightful, eternal death ; 2. The terror of conscience in the apprehension of that death, or the wrath that is the consequence and end of sin ; 3. The raging and prevailing power of sin, which is the ill habitude and distemper of the soul. But these *stripes*, and that blood which issued from them, are a sound cure. Applied unto the soul, they take away the guiltiness of sin, and death deserved, and free us from our engagement to those everlasting scourgings and lashes of the wrath of God ; and they are likewise the only cure of those present terrors and pangs of conscience, arising from the sense of that wrath and sentence of death upon the soul. Our iniquities which met on Him, laid open to the rod that back which in itself was free. Those hands which never wrought iniquity, and those feet which never declined from the way of righteousness, yet, for our works and wanderings, were pierced ; and that tongue dropped with vinegar and gall on the cross, which never spoke a guileful nor sinful word. The blood of those stripes is that balm issuing from that Tree of Life so pierced, which can alone give ease to the conscience, and heal the wounds of it : they deliver from the power of sin, working by their influence a loathing of sin, which was the cause of them ; they cleanse out the vicious humours of our corrupt nature, by opening that issue of repentance : *They shall look on Him, and mourn over Him whom they have pierced,* Zech. xii. 10.

Now, to the end it may thus cure, it must be applied : it is the only receipt, but, in order to heal, it must be received. The most sovereign medicines cure not in any other manner, and therefore, still their first letter is, R, *Recipe,* take such a thing.

This is amongst the wonders of that great work, that the sovereign Lord of all, who binds and looses at His pleasure the influences of heaven, and the power and workings of all the creatures, would himself in our flesh be thus bound, the only Son bound as a slave, and scourged as a malefactor ! And his willing obedience made this an acceptable and expiating sacrifice, amongst the rest of his sufferings : *He gave his back to the smiters.* Isa. l. 6.

Now, it cannot be, that any one who is thus healed, reflecting upon this cure, can again take any constant delight in sin. It is impossible so far to forget both the grief it bred themselves, and that which it cost their Lord, as to make a new agreement with it, to live in the pleasure of it.

His stripes.] Turn your thoughts, every one of you, to consider this ; you that are not healed, that you may be healed ; and you that are, apply it still to perfect the cure in that part wherein it is gradual and not complete ; and for the ease you have found, bless and love Him who endured so much uneasiness to that end. There is a sweet mixture of sorrow and joy in contemplating these Stripes ; sorrow, surely, by sympathy, that they were *His* stripes, and joy, that they were our healing. Christians are too little mindful and sensible of this, and, it may be, are somewhat guilty of that with which Ephraim is charged, Hos. xi. 3, *They knew not that I healed them.*

Ver. 25. For ye were as sheep going astray ; but are now returned unto the Shepherd and Bishop of your souls.

In these few words, we have a brief and yet clear representation of the wretchedness of our natural condition, and of our happiness in Christ. The resemblance is borrowed from the same place in the prophet Isaiah, chap. liii. ver. 6.

Not to press the comparison, or, as it is too usual with commentators, to strain it beyond the purpose, in reference to our lost estate, this is all, or the main circumstance wherein the resemblance with sheep holds,—our *wandering,* as forlorn and exposed to destruction, like a sheep that has strayed and wandered from the fold. So taken, it imports, indeed, the loss of a better condition, the loss of the safety and happiness of the soul, of that good which is proper to it, as the suitable good of the brute creature here named, is, safe and good pasture.

That we may know there is no one exempt in nature from the guiltiness and misery of this wandering, the Prophet is express as to the universality of it. *All we have gone astray.* And though the Apostle here applies it in particular to his brethren, yet, it falls not amiss to any others. *Ye were as sheep going astray.* Yea, the Prophet there, to the collective universal, adds a distributive, *Every man to his own way,* or, a man to his way. They agree in this, that they all wander, though they differ in their several ways. There is an inbred proneness to stray in them all, more than in sheep, which are creatures naturally wandering, for each man hath his own way.

And this is our folly, that we flatter ourselves by comparison, and every one is pleased with himself because he is free from some wanderings of others ; not considering that he is a wanderer too, though in another way ; he hath his way, as those he looks on have theirs. And as men agree in wandering, though they differ in their way, so those ways agree in this, that they lead unto misery, and shall end in that. Think you there is no way to hell, but the way of open profaneness ?   Yes, surely, many a way that seems smooth and *clean in a man's own eyes,* and yet will end in condemnation.   Truth is but one, Error endless and interminable.   As we say of natural life and death, so may we say in respect of spiritual, the way to life is one, but there are many out of it.   *Lethi mille aditus.*   Each one hath not opportunity nor ability for every sin, or every degree of sin, but each sins after his own mode and power.   Isa. xl. 20.

Thy tongue, it may be, wanders not in the common path-road of oaths and curses, yet it wanders in secret calumnies, in detraction and defaming of others, though so conveyed as it scarcely appears ; or, if thou speak them not, yet thou art pleased to hear them.   It wanders, in trifling away the precious hours of irrecoverable time, with vain, unprofitable babblings in thy converse ; or, if thou art much alone, or in company much silent, yet, is not thy foolish mind still hunting vanity, following this self-pleasing design or the other, and seldom, and very slightly, if at all, conversant with God and the things of heaven, which, although they alone have the truest and the highest pleasure in them, yet, to thy carnal mind are tasteless and unsavoury ? There is scarcely any thing so light and childish, that thou wilt not more willingly and liberally bestow thy retired thoughts on, than upon those excellent, incomparable delights.   Oh ! the foolish heart of man ! When it may seem deep and serious, how often is it at Domitian's exercise in his study, *catching flies !*

Men account little of the wandering of their hearts, and yet truly, that is most of all to be considered ; for *from thence are the issues of life,* Prov. iv. 23.   It is the heart that hath forgotten God, and is roving after vanity : this causes all the errors of men's words and actions.   A wandering heart makes wandering eyes, feet, and tongue : it is the leading wanderer that misleads all the rest.   And as we are here called *straying sheep,* so, within the heart itself of each of us, there is as it were a whole wandering flock, a multitude of fictions, (Gen. viii. 21,) ungodly devices.   The word that signifies the evil of the thought in Hebrew, here, רע from רעה is taken from that which signifies feeding of a flock, and it likewise signifies wandering ; and so these meet in our thoughts, they are a great flock and a wandering flock.   This is the natural freedom of our thoughts ; they are free to wander from God and heaven, and to carry us to perdition.   And we are guilty of many pollutions this way, which we never acted.   Men are less sensible of heart-wickedness, if it break not forth ; but the heart is far more active in sin than any of the senses, or the whole body.   The motion of spirits is far swifter than that of bodies.   The mind can make a greater progress in any of these wanderings in one hour, than the body is able to follow in many days.

When the body is tied to attendance in the exercises wherein we are employed, yet, know you not,—it is so much the worse if you do not know, and feel it, and bewail it,—know you not, I say, that the heart can take its liberty, and leave you nothing but a carcass ?   This the unrenewed heart doth continually.   *They come and sit before me as my people, but their heart is after their covetousness.*   Ezek. xxxiii. 31. It hath another way to go, another God to wait on.

But are now returned.]   Whatsoever are the several ways of our straying, all our wandering originates in the aversion of the heart from God, whence of necessity follows a continual unsettledness and disquiet. The mind, *as a wave of the sea, tossed to and fro with the wind*, tumbles from one sin and vanity to another, and finds no rest ; or, as a sick person tosses from one side to another, and from one part of his bed to another, and perhaps changes his bed, in hope of ease, but still it is farther off, thus is the soul in all its wanderings.   But shift and change as it will, no rest shall it find until it come to this *returning*.   Jer. ii. 36, *Why gaddest thou about so much to change thy way?   Thou shalt be ashamed of Egypt as thou wast of Assyria?*   Nothing but sorrow and shame, till you change all those ways for this one.   *Return, O Israel, says the Lord, if thou wilt return, return unto me.*   It is not changing one of your own ways for another, that will profit you ; but *in returning to me* is your salvation.

Seeing we find in our own experience, besides the woeful end of our wanderings, the present perplexity and disquiet of them, why are we not persuaded to this, to give up with them all ?· *Return unto thy rest, O my soul*, says David, Psal. cxvi. 7 : this were our wisdom.

But is not that God in whom we expect rest, incensed against us for our wandering ? and is he not, being offended, *a consuming fire?* True, but this is the way to find acceptance and peace, and satisfying comforts in returning : come first to this Shepherd of souls, Jesus Christ, and by him, come unto the Father.   *No man comes unto the Father*, says he, *but by me.*   This is *via regia*, the high and right way of returning unto God.   John x. 11, *I am the good Shepherd;* and ver. 9, *I am the door: by me if any man enter in, he shall be saved.* But if he miss this Door, he shall miss salvation too.   *Ye are returned*, says the Apostle, *unto the Shepherd and Bishop of your souls.*

There be three things necessary to restore us to our happiness, whence we have departed in ʋur wanderings : 1. To take away the guiltiness of those former wanderings.   2. To reduce us into the way again.   3. To keep and lead us in it.

Now all these are performable only by this great Shepherd.   1. He did satisfy for the offence of our wanderings, and so remove our guiltiness.   He himself, the Shepherd, became a sacrifice for his flock, a sheep, or spotless lamb.   So Isa. liii. 6, *We like sheep have gone astray;* and immediately after the mention of our straying, it is added, *The Lord laid*, or, *made meet on him, the iniquity of us all*, of all our strayings ; and ver. 7, *He is brought as a lamb to the slaughter.* He who is our Shepherd, the same is the Lamb for sacrifice.   So our Apostle, (ch. i.) *We are redeemed, not by silver and gold, but by the precious blood of Christ, as of a lamb without blemish and without spot.* So John x. 11, *He is the good Shepherd that lays down his life for his sheep.*   Men think not on this ; many of them who have some thoughts of returning and amendment, think ʟot that there is a satisfaction due for past wanderings ; and therefore they pass by Christ, and consider not the necessity of returning to him, and by him to the Father.

2. He brings them back into the way of life : *Ye are returned.* But think not it is by their own knowledge and skill, that they discover their error, and find out the right path, or that by their own

strength they return into it. No, if we would contest grammaticisms, the word here is passive : *ye are returned*, reduced, or caused to return. But this truth hangs not on so weak notions as are often used, either for or against it. In that prophecy, Ezek. xxxiv. 16, God says, *I will seek and bring again*, &c. And, Psal. xxiii. 3, David says, *he restoreth* or *returneth my soul*. And that this is the work of this Shepherd, the Lord Jesus God-man, is clearly and frequently taught in the Gospel. He came for this very end : it was his errand and business in the world, *to seek and to save that which was lost*. And thus it is represented in the parable, Luke xv. 4, 5 : he *goes after that which is lost until he find it*, and then, having found it, doth not only show it the way, and say to it, Return, and so leave it to come after, but *he lays it on his shoulder*, and brings it home ; and notwithstanding all his pains, instead of complaining against it for wandering, he rejoices in that he hath found and recovered it : *he lays it on his shoulder rejoicing*. And in this, there is as much of the resemblance as in any other thing. Lost man can no more return unsought, than a sheep that wandereth, which is observed of all creatures to have least of that skill. Men may have some confused thoughts of returning, but to know the way and to come, unless they be sought out, they are unable. This is David's suit, though acquainted with the fold, *I have gone astray like a lost sheep: Lord, seek thy servant*. Psal. cxix. *ult.* This did our great and good Shepherd, through those difficult ways he was to pass for finding us, wherein he not only hazarded, but really laid down his life ; and those shoulders which did bear the iniquity of our wanderings, by expiation, upon the same doth he bear and bring us back from it by effectual conversion.

3. He keeps and leads us on in that way into which he hath restored us. He leaves us not again to try our own skill, whether we can walk to heaven alone, being set into the path of it, but he still conducts us in it by his own hand, and that is the cause of our persisting in it, and attaining the blessed end of it. *He restoreth my soul*, says the Psalmist, Psal. xxiii. 2 ; and that is not all : he adds, *He leadeth me in the paths of righteousness for his name's sake*. Those paths are the *green pastures* meant, and the *still waters* that he speaks of. And thus we may judge whether we are of his flock. Are we *led in the paths of righteousness?* Do we delight ourselves in him, and in his ways ? Are they the proper refreshment of our souls ? Do we find *his words sweet unto our taste?* Are we taken with the *green pastures* in it, and the crystal streams of consolations that glide through it ? Can we discern *his voice*, and does it draw our hearts, so that we follow it ? John x. 27.

The Shepherd and Bishop.] It was the style of Kings, to be called Shepherds ; and is the dignity of the Ministers of the Gospel, to have both these names. But this great Shepherd and Bishop is peculiarly worthy of these names, as supreme ; he alone is the universal Shepherd and Bishop, and none but an antichrist, who makes himself as Christ, killing and destroying the flock, will assume this title which belongs only to the Lord, the great Owner of his flock. He himself is their great Shepherd and Bishop. All shepherds and bishops who are truly such, have their function and place from him ; they hold of him, and follow his rule and example, in their inspection of the flock. It were the happiness of kingdoms, if magistrates and kings would set him, his love, and meekness, and equity, before their eyes in their government. And all those who are properly his bishops, are under especial obligations to study this pattern, to warm their affections to the flock, and to excite a tender care of their salvation, by looking on this *Arch-bishop* and *Arch-shepherd*, (as our Apostle calls him,) and in their measure, to follow his footsteps, spending their life and strength in seeking the good of his sheep, considering that they are subordinately shepherds of souls, that is, in dispensing spiritual things ; so far the title is communicable.

The Lord Jesus is supremely and singularly such : they under him are shepherds of souls, because their diligence concerns the soul, which excludes not the body in spiritual respects, as it is capable of things spiritual and eternal, by its union with the soul. But Christ is sovereign Shepherd of souls above all, and singular, in that he not only teaches them the doctrine of salvation, but purchased salvation for them, and inasmuch as he reaches the soul powerfully, which ministers by their own power cannot do. He lays hold on it, and restores, and leads it, and causes it to walk in his ways. In this sense it agrees to him alone, as supreme, in the incommunicable sense.

And from his guidance, power, and love, flows all the comfort of his flock. When they consider their own folly and weakness, this alone gives them confidence, that his hand guides them ; and they believe in his strength, far surpassing that of the roaring lion, (John x. 28—30,) his wisdom, in knowing their particular state and their weakness, and his tender love, in pitying them, and applying himself to it. Other shepherds, even faithful ones, may mistake them, and not know the way of leading them in some particulars, and they may be sometimes wanting in that tender affection that they owe ; or, if they have that, yet they are not able to bear them up, and support them powerfully ; but this Shepherd is perfect in all these respects. Isa. xl. 11. The young and weak Christian, or the elder at weak times, when they are big and heavy with some inward exercise of mind, which shall bring forth advantage and peace to them afterwards, them he *leads gently*, and uses them with the tenderness that their weakness requires.

And, in the general, he provides for his flock, and heals them when they are any way hurt, and washes them and makes them fruitful ; so that they are as that flock, described Cant. iv. 2 ; they are comely, but their Shepherd much more so : *Formosi pecoris custos, formosior ipse*. They are given him in the Father's purpose and choice, and so, those that return, are, even while they wander, *sheep* in some other sense than the rest which perish. They are, in the secret love of Election, of Christ's sheepfold, though not as yet actually brought into it. But when his time comes, wheresoever they wander, and how far off soever, even those who have strayed most, yet he restores them, and rejoices heaven with their return, and leads them till he bring them to partake of the joy that is there. That is the end of the way wherein he guides them. John x. 27, 28, *They hear my voice, and follow me.*   And they shall never repent of having done so.   To follow him, is to follow life, for *He is the life.*   He is in that glory which we desire; and where would we be, if not where he is, who, at his departure from the world, said, *Where I am, there they shall be also?*   To this happy meeting and heavenly abode, may God, of his infinite mercy, bring us, through *Jesus Christ our Lord!* Amen.

FIRST PETER

CHAPTER 3

Ver. 1. Likewise, ye wives, be in subjection to your own husbands; that, if any obey not the word, they also may without the word be won by the conversation of the wives.

THE *tabernacle of the sun* (Psal. xix. 4) is set high in the heavens; but it is so, that it may have influence below upon the earth.   And the *word of God*, which is spoken of there immediately after, as being in many ways like it, holds resemblance in this particular: it is a sublime heavenly light, and yet descends, in its use, to the lives of men, in the variety of their stations, to warm and to enlighten, to regulate their affections and actions in whatsoever course of life they are called to.   By a perfect revolution or circuit, as there it is said of the sun, it visits all ranks and estates; *its going forth is from the end of heaven, and its circuit unto the ends of it, and there is nothing hid from the heat of it;* it disdains not to teach the very servants, in their low condition and employments, how to behave themselves, and sets before them no meaner example than that of Jesus Christ, which is the highest of all examples.   So here, the Apostle proceeds to give rules adapted to that relation which is the main one in families, that of *Husbands and Wives.*   As for the order, it is indifferent; yet, possibly, he begins here at the duties of wives, because his former rules were given to inferiors, to subjects and servants; and the duty he commends particularly here to them, is, *subjection; Likewise, ye wives, be in subjection,* &c.

After men have said all they can, and much, it may be, to little purpose, in running the parallel between these two estates of life, marriage and celibacy, the result will be found, I conceive, all things being truly estimated, very little odds, even in natural respects, in the things themselves, saving only as the particular condition of persons, and the hand of Divine Providence, turn the balance the one way or the other.   The writing of satires against either, or panegyrics on the one in prejudice of the other, is but a caprice of men's minds, according to their own humour; but in respect of religion, the Apostle, having scanned the subject to the full, leaves it indifferent, only requiring in those who are so engaged, hearts as disengaged as may be, *that they that marry be as if they married not,* &c.   1 Cor. vii. 29, 31.   Within a while, it will be all one; as he adds that grave reason, *For th fashion* [σχῆμα] *of this world passeth*—it is but a pageant, a show of an hour long, [παράγει,] *goes by,* and is no more seen.   Thus, the great pomps and solemnities of marriages of kings and princes, in former times, where are they?   Oh! how unseemly is it to have an immortal soul drowned in the esteem and affection of any thing that perishes, and to be cold and indifferent in seeking after a good that will last as long as itself! Aspire to that good which is the only match for the soul, that close union with God which cannot be dissolved, which he calls an everlasting marriage, Hos. ii. 19; that will make you happy, either with the other, or without it. All the happiness of the most excellent persons, and the very top of all affection and prosperity meeting in human marriages, are but a dark and weak representation of the solid joy which is in that mysterious Divine union of the spirit of man with the *Father of spirits*, from whom it issues. But this by the way.

The common spring of all mutual duties, on both sides, must be supposed to be *love;* that peculiar conjugal love which makes them one, will infuse such sweetness into the authority of the Husband and the obedience of the Wife, as will make their lives harmonious, like the sound of a well-tuned instrument; whereas without that, having such a universal conjuncture of interest in all their affairs, they cannot escape frequent contests and discords, which is a sound more unpleasant than the jarring of untuned strings to an exact ear. And this should be considered in the choice, that it be not, as it is too often, (which causeth so many domestic ills,) contracted only as a bargain of outward advantages, but as a union of hearts. And where this is not, and there is something wanting in this point of affection, there, if the parties, or either of them, have any saving knowledge of God, and access to him in prayer, they will be earnest suitors for his help in this, that his hand may set right what no other can; that he who is love itself, may infuse that mutual love into their hearts now, which they should have sought sooner. And certainly, they who sensibly want this, and yet seek it not of him, what wonder is it, though they find much bitterness and discontent? Yea, where they agree, if it be only in natural affection, their observance of the duties required, is not by far either so comfortable and pleasing, or so sure and lasting, as when it ariseth from a religious and Christian love in both, which will cover many failings, and take things by the best side.

Love is the prime duty in both, the basis of all; but because the particular character of it, as proper to the Wife, is conjugal obedience and subjection, therefore that is usually specified, as Eph. v. 12, *Wives, submit yourselves unto your own husbands, as unto the Lord;* so here. Now, if it be such obedience as ought to arise from a special kind of love, then the Wife would remember this, that it must not be constrained, uncheerful obedience; and the Husband would remember, that he ought not to require base and servile obedience; for both these are contrary to that love, whereof this obedience must carry the true tincture and relish, as flowing from it: there all will hold right, where love commands, and love obeys.

This subjection, as all other, is qualified thus, that it be *in the Lord.* His authority is primitive, and binds first, and all others have their patents and privileges from him; therefore he is supremely and absolutely to be observed in all. If the Husband would draw the Wife to an irreligious course of life, he is not to be followed in this, but in all things indifferent, this obedience must hold; which yet forbids not a modest advice and representation to the Husband, of that which is more convenient; but that done, a submissive yielding to the Husband's will is the suiting of this rule.   Yea, possibly, the Husband may not only imprudently, but unlawfully will that which, if not in its own nature a thing unlawful, the Wife by reason of his will may obey lawfully, yea, could not lawfully disobey.

Now, though this subjection was a fundamental law of pure nature, and came from that hand, which made all things in perfect order, yet sin, which hath imbittered all human things with a curse, hath disrelished this subjection, and made it taste somewhat of a punishment, (Gen. iii. 16,) and that as a suitable punishment of the woman's abuse of the power she had with the man, to the drawing of him to disobedience against God.

The bitterness in this subjection arises from the corruption of nature in both: in the Wife, a perverse desire rather to command, or at least a repining discontent at the obligation to obey: and this is increased by the disorder, and imprudence, and harshness of Husbands, in the use of their authority.

But in a Christian, the conscience of Divine appointment will carry it, and weigh down all difficulties; for the Wife considers her station, that she is set in it, [$\dot{v}\pi o\tau a\sigma\sigma o\mu\acute{e}\nu a\iota,$] it is the rank the Lord's hand hath placed her in, and therefore she will not break it: from respect and love to him, she can digest much frowardness in a husband, and make that her patient subjection a sacrifice to God: Lord, I offer this to thee, and for thy sake I humbly bear it.

The worth and love of a Husband may cause that respect, where this rule moves not; but the Christian Wife who hath love to God, though her husband be not so comely, nor so wise, nor any way so amiable, as many others, yet, because he is her *own husband*, and because of the Lord's command in the general, and his providence in the particular disposal of his own, therefore she loves and obeys.

That if any obey not the word.]   This supposes a particular case, and applies the rule to it, taking it for granted that a believing wife will cheerfully observe and respect a believing husband, but if he is an unbeliever, yet that unties not this engagement; yea, there is something in this case which presses it and binds it the more, a singular good which probably may follow upon obeying such.   By *that good conversation*, they may be gained, who believe not the word: not that they could be fully converted without the word, but having a prejudice against the word, that may be removed by the carriage of a believing wife, and they may be somewhat mollified, and prepared, and induced to hearken to religion, and take it into consideration.

This gives not Christians a warrant to draw on themselves this task, and make themselves this work, by choosing to be joined to an unbeliever, either a profane or merely an unconverted husband or wife; but teacheth them, being so matched, what should be their great desire, and their suitable carriage in order to the attainment of it.   And in the primitive Christian times, this fell out often: by the Gospel preached, the husband might be converted from gross infidelity, Judaism, or Paganism, and not the wife; or the wife, (which is the supposition here,) and not the husband; and then came in the use of this consideration.

And this is the freedom of Divine Grace, to pick and choose where it will, *one of a family, or two of a tribe*, as the Prophet hath it, Jer. iii. 14 ; and according to our Saviour's word, *two in one bed, the one taken and the other left*, Luke xvii. 34 ; some selected ones in a congregation, or, in a house, a child, possibly, or servant, or wife, while it leaves the rest. The Apostle seems to imply particularly, that there were many instances of this, wives being converts, and their husbands unbelieving. We can determine nothing as to their conjecture, who think that there will be more of that sex, here called the *weaker vessels*, than of the other, who shall be vessels of honour, which God seasons with grace here, and hereafter will fill with glory ; but this is clear, that many of them are converted, while many men, and divers of them very wise and learned men, having the same or far greater means and opportunities, do perish in unbelief. This, I say, evidences the liberty and the power of the Spirit of God, that *wind that bloweth where it listeth ;* and withal it suits with the word of the Apostle, that the Lord this way abases those things that men account so much of, *and hath chosen the weak things of the world to confound the mighty.* 1 Cor. i. 26. Nor doth the pliableness and tenderness of their affections (though Grace, once wrought, may make good use of that) make their conversion easier, but the harder rather, for through nature's corruption they would by that be led to yield more to evil than to good ; but the efficacy of Grace appears much in establishing their hearts in the love of God, and in making them, when once possessed with that, to be inflexible and invincible by the temptations of the world, and the strength and sleights of Satan.

That which is here said of *their conversation*, holds of the Husband in the like case, and of friends and kindred, and generally of all Christians, in reference to them with whom they converse ; that their spotless, holy carriage as Christians, and in their particular station, as Christian husbands, or wives, or friends, is a very likely and hopeful means of converting others who believe not. Men who are prejudiced, observe actions a great deal more than words. In those first times especially, the blameless character of Christians did much to the increasing of their number.

Strive, ye wives, and others, to adorn and commend the religion you profess to others, especially those nearest you, who are averse. Give no just cause of scandal and prejudice against religion. Beware not only of gross failings and ways of sin, but of such imprudences as may expose you and your profession. Study both a holy and a wise carriage, and pray much for it. *If any of you lack wisdom, let him ask of God, that giveth to all men liberally, and upbraideth not, and it shall be given him.* Jam. i. 5.

But if wives and other private Christians be thus obliged, how much more the ministers of the word ! Oh that we could remember our deep obligations to holiness of life ! It has been rightly said, *Either teach none, or let your life teach too. Cohelleth, anima concionatrix*, the *preaching soul*, must the preacher be, (Eccl. i. 1,) the word of life springing from inward affection, and then, *vita concionatrix*, the *preaching life*. The Sunday's sermon lasts but an hour or two, but holiness of life is a continued sermon all the week long.

They also without the word may be won.] The conversion of a soul is an inestimable gain ; it is a high trading and design to go about it. Oh the precious soul ! but how undervalued by most ! Will we believe Him who knew well the price of it, for he paid it, that the whole visible world is not worth one soul, the gaining of it all cannot countervail that loss ? Matt. xvi. 26. This, wives, and husbands, and parents, and friends, if themselves converted, would consider seriously, and apply themselves to pray much that their unconverted relations, in nature dead, may be enlivened, and that they may receive them from death ; and they would esteem nothing, rest in no natural content or gain without that, at least, without using incessant diligence in seeking it, and their utmost skill and pains. But above all, this is the peculiar task of ministers, as the Apostle often repeats it of himself, that *unto the Jews* he *became as a Jew*, that he might *gain the Jews*, &c. 1 Cor. ix. All gains on earth are base in comparison with this. *Me malè amando, me perdidi, et te solum quærendo et purè amando, me et te pariter inveni :* By loving self amiss, myself I lost ; by seeking Thee, and singly, sincerely loving Thee, at once myself and Thee I found.— (Thomas à Kempis.) A soul converted is *gained* to itself, *gained* to the pastor, or friend, or wife, or husband, who sought it, and *gained* to Jesus Christ ; added to his treasury, who thought not his own precious blood too dear to lay out for this gain.

Ver. 2. While they behold your chaste conversation coupled with fear.

As all graces are connected in their own nature, so it is altogether necessary that they be found in connexion for the end here propounded, the conversion of those who are strangers to religion, and possessed with false notions of it, and prejudices against it. It is not the regularity of some particular actions, nor the observance of some duties, that will serve ; but it is an even, uniform frame of life that the Apostle here teaches Christian wives, particularly in reference to this end, the gaining or conversion of unbelieving husbands. And this we have both in that word, *their conversation,* which signifies the whole course and tract of their lives, and in the particular specifying of the several duties proper to that relation and state of life. 1. Subjection. 2. Chastity. 3. Fear. 4. Modesty in outward ornaments. 5. The inward ornaments of meekness and quietness of spirit.

The combination of these things makes up such a wife, and the exercise of them throughout her life makes up such a conversation, as adorns and commends the religion she professes, and is a fit, and may be a successful, means of converting the husband who as yet professes it not.

Chaste conversation.] It is the proper character of a Christian, to study purity in all things, as the word (ἁγνὴν) in its extent signifies. Let the world turn that to a reproach, call them as you will, this is sure, that none have less fancy and presumption of *purity,* than those who have most desire of it. But the particular pureness here intended is, as it is rendered, that of *chastity,* as the word is often taken ; it being a grace that peculiarly deserves that name, as the sins contrary to it are usually and deservedly called *uncleanness.* It is the pure whiteness of the soul to be chaste, to abhor and disdain the swinish puddle of lust, than which there is nothing that doth more debase the excellent soul; nothing that more evidently draws it down below itself, and makes it truly brutish.   The three kinds of chastity—virginal, conjugal, and vidual, are all of them acceptable to God, and suitable to the profession of a Christian : therefore, in general only, whatsoever be our condition in life, let us in that way conform to it, and follow the Apostle's rule, *possessing* these our earthen *vessels*, our bodies, in *holiness* and *honour;* (by which is there expressed this same chastity ;) and this we shall do if we rightly remember our calling as Christians, in what sort of life soever ; as there he tells us, *God hath not called us to uncleanness, but unto holiness.* 1 Thess. iv. 7.

With fear.]   Either a reverential respect to their husbands, or, the fear of God; whence flows best both that and all other observance, whether of conjugal or any other Christian duties.   Be not presumptuous, as some, because you are chaste, but so contemper your conversation with a religious fear of God, that you dare not take liberty to offend him in any other thing, and, according to his institution, with a reverential fear of your husbands, shunning to offend them.   But, possibly, this fear doth particularly relate to the other duty with which it was joined, *Chaste conversation with fear;* fearing the least stain of chastity, or the very least appearance of any thing not suiting with it. It is a delicate, timorous grace, afraid of the least air, or shadow of any thing that hath but a resemblance of wronging it, in carriage, or speech, or apparel, as follows in the 3rd and 4th verses.

Ver. 3. Whose adorning let it not be that outward adorning of plaiting the hair, and of wearing of gold, or of putting on of apparel ;
4. But let it be the hidden man of the heart, in that which is not corruptible, even the ornament of a meek and quiet spirit, which is in the sight of God of great price.

THAT nothing may be wanting to the qualifying of a Christian wife, she is taught how to dress herself ; supposing a general desire, but especially in that sex, of ornament and comeliness : the sex which began first our engagement to the necessity of clothing, having still a peculiar propensity to be curious in that, to improve the necessity to an advantage.

The direction here given, corrects the misplacing of this diligence, and addresses it right : *Let it not be of the outward man, in plaiting,* &c.

Our perverse, crooked hearts turn all we use into disorder.   Those two necessities of our life, *food* and *raiment,* how few know the right measure and bounds of them !   Unless poverty be our carver and cut us short, who, almost, is there, that is not bent to something excessive ! Far more are beholden to the lowliness of their estate, than to the lowliness of their mind, for sobriety in these things ; and yet, some will not be so bounded neither, but will profusely lavish out upon trifles, to the sensible prejudice of their estate.

It is not my purpose, nor do I think it very needful, to debate many particulars of apparel and ornament of the body, their lawfulness or unlawfulness : only,

First, It is out of doubt, that though clothing was first drawn on by necessity, yet, all regard of comeliness and ornament in apparel, is not unlawful; nor doth the Apostle's expression here, rightly considered, fasten that upon the adorning he here speaks of. He doth no more universally condemn the use of gold for ornament, than he doth any other comely raiment, which here he means by that general word of *putting on of apparel;* for his [*not*] is comparative,—*not this adorning, but the ornament of a meek spirit,* that rather, and as being much more comely and precious; as that known expression, *I will have mercy and not sacrifice.*

Secondly, According to the different place and quality of persons, there may be a difference in this: thus, the robes of judges and princes are not only for personal ornament, but because there is in them, especially to vulgar eyes which seldom look deeper than the outside of things, there is, I say, in that apparel a representation of authority or majesty, which befits their place; and besides this, other persons who are not in public place, men or women, (who are here particularly directed,) yet may have in this some mark of their rank; and in persons otherwise little distant, some allowance may be made for the habits and breeding of some beyond others, or the quality of their society, and those with whom they converse.

Thirdly, It is not impossible that there may be in some an affected pride in the meanness of apparel, and in others, under either neat or rich attire, a very humble, unaffected mind; using it upon some of the aforementioned engagements, or such like, and yet, the heart not at all upon it. *Magnus qui fictilibus utitur tanquam argento, nec ille minor qui argento tanquam fictilibus,* says Seneca: Great is he who enjoys his earthenware as if it were plate, and not less great is the man to whom all his plate is no more than earthenware.

Fourthly, It is as sure as any of these, that real excess and vanity in apparel will creep in, and will always willingly convey itself under the cloak of some of these honest and lawful considerations. This is a prime piece of our heart's deceit, not only to hold out fair pretences to others, but to put the trick upon ourselves, to make ourselves believe we are right and single-minded in those things wherein we are directly serving our lusts, and feeding our own vanity.

Fifthly, To a sincere and humble Christian, very little either dispute or discourse concerning this will be needful. A tender conscience, and a heart purified from vanity and weaned from the world, will be sure to regulate this, and all other things of this nature, after the safest manner, and will be wary, 1. of lightness and fantastic garb in apparel, which is the very bush or sign hanging out, that tells a vain mind lodges within; and, 2. of excessive costliness, which both argues and feeds the pride of the heart, and defrauds, if not others of their dues, yet, the poor of thy charity, which, in God's sight, is a due debt too. Far more comfort shalt thou have on thy death-bed, to remember that such a time, instead of putting lace on my own clothes, I helped a naked back to clothing, I abated somewhat of my former superfluities, to supply the poor's necessities—far sweeter will this be, than to remember that I could needlessly cast away many pounds to serve my pride, rather than give a penny to relieve the poor.

As conscientious Christians will not exceed in the thing itself, so, in as far as they use lawful ornament and comeliness, they will do it without bestowing much either of diligence or delight on the business.

To have the mind taken and pleased with such things, is so foolish and childish a thing, that if most might not find it in themselves, they would wonder at it in many others, of years and common sense. *Non bis pueri, sed semper:* Not twice children, but always. And yet, truly, it is a disease that few escape. It is strange upon how poor things men and women will be vain, and think themselves somebody; not only upon some comeliness in their face or feature, which though poor, is yet a part of themselves, but of things merely without them; that they are well lodged, or well mounted, or well apparelled, either richly, or well in fashion. Light, empty minds are, like bladders, blown up with any thing. And they who perceive not this in themselves, are the most drowned in it; but such as have found it out, and abhor their own follies, are still hunting and following these in themselves, to beat them out of their hearts and to shame them from such fopperies. The soul fallen from God, hath lost its true worth and beauty; and therefore it basely descends to these mean things, to serve and dress the body, and take share with it of its unworthy borrowed ornaments, while it hath lost and forgotten God, and seeks not after him, knows not that he alone is the beauty and ornament of the soul, (Jer. ii. 32,) his Spirit and the graces of it, its rich attire, as is here particularly specified in one excellent grace, and it holds true in the rest.

The Apostle doth indeed expressly, on purpose, check and forbid vanity and excess in apparel, and excessive delight in lawful decorum, but his prime end is to recommend this other ornament of the soul, *the hidden man of the heart.*

It is the thing the best philosophy aimed at, as some of their wisest men do express it, to reduce men, as much as may be, from their body to their soul; but this is the thing that true religion alone doth effectually and thoroughly, calling them off from the pampering and feeding of a morsel for the worms, to the nourishing of that immortal being infused into it, and directing them to the proper nourishment of souls, the *Bread that came down from heaven.* John vi. 27.

So here, the Apostle pulls off from Christian women their vain outside ornaments: but is not this a wrong, to spoil all their dressing and fineness? No, he doth this, only to send them to a better wardrobe: there is much profit in the change.

All the gold and other riches of the temple, prefigured the excellent graces of Christians: of Christ, indeed, first, as having all fulness in himself, and as furnishing it to them; but secondarily, of Christians, as the living temples of God. So, Psalm xlv. 13, the Church is *all glorious,* but it is *within.* And the embroidery, the variety of graces, the lively colours of other graces, shine best on the dark ground of humility. Christ delights to give much ornament to his Church, commends what she hath, and adds more. *Thy neck is comely with chains: we will make thee borders of gold.* Cant. i. 10, 11.

The particular grace the Apostle recommends, is particularly suitable to his subject in hand, the conjugal duty of wives; nothing so much adorning their whole carriage as this *meekness* and *quietness of spirit.*

But it is, withal, the comeliness of every Christian in every estate. It is not a woman's garment or ornament, improper for men. There is somewhat (as I may say) of a particular cut or fashion of it for wives towards their husbands, and in their domestic affairs; but men, all men, ought to wear of the same stuff, yea, if I may so speak, of the same piece, for it is in all one and the same spirit, and fits the stoutest and greatest commanders. Moses was a great general, and yet not less great in this virtue, *the meekest man on earth.*

Nothing is more uncomely in a wife than an uncomposed, turbulent spirit, that is put out of frame with every trifle, and inventive of false causes of disquietness and fretting to itself. And so in a husband, and in all, an unquiet, passionate mind lays itself naked, and discovers its own deformity to all. The greatest part of things that vex us, do so not from their own nature or weight, but from the unsettledness of our minds. *Multa nos offendunt quæ non lædunt:* Many things offend us which do not hurt us. How comely is it to see a composed, firm mind and carriage, that is not lightly moved!

I urge not a stoical stupidity, but that in things which deserve sharp reproof, the mind keep in its own station and seat still, not shaken out of itself, as the most are; that the tongue utter not unseemly, rash words, nor the hand act any thing that discovers the mind hath lost its command for the time. But truly, the most know so ill how to use just anger upon just cause, that it is easier, and the safer extreme, not to be angry, but still calm and serene, as the upper region; not as the place of continual tempest and storms, as the most are. Let it pass for a kind of sheepishness to be meek; it is a likeness to Him who *was as a sheep before the shearers, not opening his mouth;* it is a portion of *His* spirit.

The Apostle commends his exchange of ornaments, by two things. 1. This is incorruptible, and therefore fits an incorruptible soul. Your varieties of jewels and rich apparel are perishing things; you shall one day see a heap made of all, and that all on a flame. And in reference to yourselves, they perish sooner. When death strips you of your nearest garment, your flesh, all the others, which were but loose upper garments above it, must off too: it gets, indeed, a covering to the grave, but the soul is left stark naked, if no other clothing be provided for it, for the body was but borrowed; then it is made bare of all. But spiritual ornaments, and this of humility, and meekness amongst them, remain and are incorruptible; they neither wear out, nor go out of fashion, but are still the better for the wearing, and shall last eternity, and shine there in full lustre.

And, 2. Because the opinion of others is much regarded in matter of apparel, and it is mostly in respect to this that we use ornament in it, he tells us of the account in which this is held: men think it poor and mean, nothing more exposed to contempt than the *spirit of meekness,* it is mere folly with men,—that is no matter; this overweighs all their disesteem, *It is with God of great price;* and things are indeed as he values them, and no otherwise. Though it be not the country fashion, yet it is the fashion at Court, yea, it is the King's own fashion, Matt. xi. 29, *Learn of me, for I am meek and lowly of heart.* Some who are court-bred, will send for the masters of fashions; though they

live not in the Court, and though the peasants think them strange
dresses, yet they regard not that, but use them as finest and best.
Care not what the world say ; you are not to stay long with them.
Desire to have both fashions and stuffs from *Court*, from heaven, this
spirit of meekness, and it shall be sent you. It is never right in any
thing with us, till we attain to this, to tread on the opinion of men, and
eye nothing but God's approbation.

Ver. 5. For after this manner in the old time the holy women also, who trusted in
God, adorned themselves, being in subjection unto their own husbands :
6. Even as Sara obeyed Abraham, calling him lord : whose daughters ye are, as
long as ye do well, and are not afraid with any amazement.

THE Apostle enforces his doctrine by example, the most compendious
way of teaching. Hence, the right way to use the Scriptures, is, to
regulate our manners by them ; as by their precepts, so by their examples. And for this end it is that a great part of the Bible is historical. There is not in the Saints a transmigration of souls, but there
is, so to speak, a oneness of soul, they being in all ages partakers of
the self-same Spirit. Hence, pious and obedient wives, are here called
the *daughters of Sarah.* Such women are here designated as, 1. Holy ;
2. Believing ; 3. Firm and resolute ; *not afraid with any amazement.*
Though by nature they are fearful, yet they are rendered of undaunted
spirits, by a holy, clean, and pure conscience. Believing wives who
fear God, are not terrified ; their minds are established in a due obedience to God, and also towards their husbands.

Ver. 7. Likewise, ye husbands, dwell with them according to knowledge, giving
honour unto the wife, as unto the weaker vessel, and as being heirs together of
the grace of life ; that your prayers be not hindered.

YOUR wives are subject to you, but you likewise are subject to this
word, by which all ought, in all stations, to be directed, and by which,
however, all shall one day be judged. And you are *alike* subject as
they [ὁμοίως] : parents as children, masters as servants, and kings as
their subjects ; all hold of a Superior, and it is high treason against
the majesty of God, for any, in any place of command, to dream of an
unbounded, absolute authority, in opposition to him.

A spirit of prudence, or *knowledge*, particularly suitable and relating
to this subject, is required as the light and rule by which the Husband's whole economy and carriage is to be guided. It is required
that he endeavour after that civil prudence for the ordering of his
affairs which tends to the good of his family : but chiefly a pious,
religious prudence, for regulating his mind and carriage as a Christian
husband ; that he study the rule of Scripture in this particular, which
many do not, neither advising with it what they should do, nor laying
it, by reflection, upon their past actions, examining by it what they
have done. Now this is the great fault in all practical things : most
know something of them, but inadvertency and inconsideration, our
not ordering our ways by that light, is the thing that spoils all.

Knowledge is required in the Wife, but more eminently in the *Husband,* as the head, the proper seat of knowledge. It is possible, that
the Wife may sometimes have the advantage of knowledge, either
natural wit and judgment, or a great measure of understanding of

spiritual things ; but this still holds, that the Husband is bound to
improve the measure both of natural and of spiritual gifts, that he hath,
or can attain to, and to apply them usefully to the ordering of his conjugal carriage, and that he understand himself obliged somewhat the
more, in the very notion of a husband, both to seek after and to use
that prudence which is peculiarly required for his due deportment.
And a Christian wife, who is more largely endowed, yet will show all
due respect to the measure of wisdom, though it be less, which is
bestowed upon her husband.

Dwell with them.] This, indeed, implies and supposes their abiding
with their wives, so far as their calling and lawful affairs permit ; but
I conceive, that what it expressly means, is, all the conversation and
duties of that estate ; that they so behave themselves in dwelling with
them, as becomes *men of knowledge*, wise and prudent husbands ;
which returns them usually the gain of the full reverence and respect
due to them, of which they rob and divest themselves, who are either of
a foolish or trifling carriage, or of too austere and rigid a conversation.

Giving honour unto the Wife.] This, I conceive, is not, as some
take it, convenient maintenance, though that is a requisite duty too,
and may be taken in under this word ; but it seems to be, chiefly, a
due conjugal esteem of them, and respect to them, the Husband not
vilifying and despising them, which will be apt to grieve and exasperate them ; not disclosing the weaknesses of the wife to others, nor
observing them too narrowly himself, but hiding them both from
others' and his own eyes by love ; not seeing them further than love
itself requires; that is, to the wise rectifying of them by mild advices
and admonitions that flow from love.   And to this the reasons, indeed,
suit well.   It seems at first a little incongruous, *Honour* because *weaker*,
but not when we consider the kind of honour ; not of reverence as
superior, for that is their part, but of esteem and respect, without
which, indeed, love cannot consist, for we cannot love that which we
do not in some good measure esteem.   And care should be taken that
they be not contemned and slighted, even because they are weaker ;
for of all injuries, contempt is one of the most smarting and sensible,
especially to weak persons, who feel most exactly the least touches of
this.   *Omne infirmum naturâ querelum ; Every weak being is naturally
peevish ;* whereas greater spirits are a little harder against opinion, and
more indifferent for it.   Some wives may, indeed, be of a stronger
mind and judgment than their husbands, yet these rules respect the
general condition of the sexes, and speak of the females as ordinarily
weaker.

Again, Love, which is ever to be supposed one article, and the main
one, (for nothing, indeed, can be right where that supposition proves
false,) love, I say, supposed, this reason is very enforcing, that the
weaker the vessels be, the more tenderly they should be used ; and the
more a prudent passing by of frailties is needful, there love will study
it, and bestow it the more.   Yea, this tie, you know, makes two one ;
and that which is a part of ourselves, the more it needs in that respect,
the *more comeliness we put upon it*, as the Apostle St. Paul tells us,
1 Cor. xii. 23.   And this further may be considered, that there is a
mutual need of this *honouring* which consists in not despising and in

covering of frailties, as is even implied in this, that the Woman is not called simply weak, but the *weaker*, and the Husband, who is generally, by nature's advantage, or should be, the stronger, yet is weak too ; for both are vessels of earth, and therefore frail ; both polluted with sin, and therefore subject to a multitude of sinful follies and frailties. But as the particular frailty of their nature pleads on behalf of women for that *honour*, so, the other reason added, is taken, not from their particular disadvantage, but from their common privilege and advantage of grace as Christians, that the Christian Husband and Wife are equally *co-heirs* of the same *grace of life.*

As being heirs together of the grace of life.] This is that which most strongly binds all these duties on the hearts of Husbands and Wives, and most strongly indeed binds their hearts together, and makes them one. If each be reconciled unto God in Christ, and so an heir of life, and one with God, then are they truly one in God with each other ; and that is the surest and sweetest union that can be. Natural love hath risen very high in some husbands and wives ; but the highest of it falls very far short of that which holds in God. Hearts concentring in him, are most and excellently one. That love which is cemented by youth and beauty, when these moulder and decay, as soon they do, fades too. That is somewhat purer, and so more lasting, which holds in a natural or moral harmony of minds ; yet, these likewise may alter and change by some great accident. But the most refined, most spiritual, and most indissoluble, is that which is knit with the highest and purest Spirit. And the ignorance or disregard of this, is the great cause of so much bitterness, or so little true sweetness, in the life of most married persons ; because God is left out, because they meet not as one in him.

Heirs together.] Loth will they be to despise one another, who are both bought with the precious blood of one Redeemer, and loth to grieve one another. Being in him brought into peace with God, they will entertain true peace betwixt themselves, and not suffer any thing to disturb it. They have hopes to meet, one day, where is nothing but perfect concord and peace ; they will therefore live as heirs of that life here, and make their present estate as like to heaven as they can, and so, a pledge and evidence of their title to that inheritance of peace which is there laid up for them. And they will not fail to put one another often in mind of those hopes and that inheritance, and mutually to advance and further each other towards it. Where this is not the case, it is to little purpose to speak of other rules. Where neither party aspires to this heirship, live they otherwise as they will, there is one common inheritance abiding them, one inheritance of everlasting flames ; and, as they do increase the sin and guiltiness of one another by their irreligious conversation, so that which some of them do wickedly here, upon no great cause, they shall have full cause for doing there ; cause to curse the time of their coming together, and that shall be a piece of their exercise for ever. But happy those persons, in any society of marriage or friendship, who converse together as those that shall live eternally together in glory. This indeed is the sum of all duties.

Life.] A sweet word, but sweetest of all in this sense ! That life above, is indeed alone worthy the name; and this we have here, in comparison, let it not be called life, but a continual dying, an incessant journey towards the grave. If you reckon years, it is but a short moment to him that attains the fullest old age; but reckon miseries and sorrows, it is long to him that dies young. Oh that this only blessed life were more known, and then it would be more desired!

Grace.] This is the tenor of this heirship, Free Grace: this *life* is a free gift. Rom. vi. *ult.* No life so spotless, either in marriage or virginity, as to lay claim to this life upon other terms. If we consider but a little, what it is, and what we are, this will be quickly out of question with us; and we shall be most gladly content to hold it thus by deed of gift, and shall admire and extol that Grace which bestows it.

That your prayers be not hindered.] He supposes in Christians the necessary and frequent use of this; takes it for granted, that the heirs of life cannot live without prayer. This is the proper breathing and language of these heirs, none of whom are dumb; they can all speak. These heirs, if they be alone, they pray alone; if heirs together, and living together, they pray together. Can the husband and wife have that love, wisdom, and meekness, which may make their life happy, and that blessing which may make their affairs successful, while they neglect God, the only giver of these and all good things? You think these needless motives, but you cannot think how it would sweeten your converse if it were used: it is prayer that sanctifies, seasons, and blesses all. And it is not enough that they pray when with the family, but even husband and wife together by themselves, and also, with their children; that they, especially the mother, as being most with them in their childhood, when they begin to be capable, may draw them apart, and offer them to God, often praying with them, and instructing them in their youth; for they are pliable while young, as glass is when hot, but after, will sooner break than bend.

But above all, Prayer is necessary as they are heirs of heaven, often sending up their desires thither. You that are not much in prayer, appear as if you look for no more than what you have here. If you had an inheritance and treasure above, would not your hearts delight to be there? Thus the heart of a Christian is in the constant frame of it, but after a special manner Prayer raises the soul above the world, and sets it in heaven; it is its near access unto God, and dealing with him, specially about those affairs which concern that inheritance. Now in this lies a great part of the comfort a Christian can have here; and the Apostle knew this, that he would gain any thing at their hands, which he pressed by this argument, that otherwise they would be *hindered in their prayers.* He knew that they who are acquainted with prayer, find such unspeakable sweetness in it, that they will rather do any thing than be prejudiced in that.

Now the breach of conjugal love, the jars and contentions of husband and wife, do, out of doubt, so leaven and imbitter their spirits, that they are exceeding unfit for prayer, which is the sweet harmony of the soul in God's ears: and when the soul is so far out of tune as those distempers make it, he cannot but perceive it, whose ear is the most exact of all, for he made and tuned the ear, and is the fountain of harmony. It cuts the sinews and strength of prayer, makes breaches and gaps, as wounds at which the spirits fly out, as the cutting of a vein, by which, as they speak, it bleeds to death. When the soul is calm and composed, it may behold the face of God shining on it. And those who pray together, should not only have hearts in tune within themselves in their own frame, but tuned together ; especially husband and wife, who are one, they should have hearts consorted and sweetly tuned to each other for prayer. So the word is, (ἐὰν συμφωνήσωσιν,) Matt. xviii. 19.

And it is true, in the general, that all unwary walking in Christians wrongs their communion with Heaven, and casts a damp upon their prayers, so as to clog the wings of it. These two mutually help one another, *prayer* and *holy conversation:* the more exactly we walk, the more fit are we for prayer ; and the more we pray, the more are we enabled to walk exactly ; and it is a happy life to find the correspondence of these two, *calling on the Lord*, and *departing from iniquity.* 1 Tim. ii. 19. Therefore, that you may pray much, live holily ; and, that you may live holily, be much in prayer. Surely such are the heirs of glory, and this is their way to it.

Ver. 8. Finally, be ye all of one mind, having compassion one of another, love as brethren, be pitiful, be courteous.

HERE the particular rules the Apostle gives to several relations, fall in again to the main current of his general exhortation, which concerns us all as Christians. The return of his discourse to this universality, is expressed in that *Finally*, and the universality of these duties, in *All.* It is neither possible nor convenient to descend to every particular ; but there is supposed in a Christian an ingenuous and prudent spirit, to adapt those general rules to his particular actions and conversation ; squaring by them beforehand, and examining by them after. And yet therein the most fail. Men hear these as general discourses, and let them pass so ; they apply them not, or, if they do, it is readily to some other person. But they are addressed to all, that each one may regulate himself by them ; and so these divine truths are like a well-drawn picture, which looks particularly upon every one amongst the great multitude that look upon it. And this one verse hath a cluster of five Christian graces or virtues. That which is in the middle, as the stalk or root of the rest, *Love*, and the others growing out of it, two on each side, *Unanimity* and *Sympathy* on the one, and *Pity* and *Courtesy* on the other. But we shall take them as they lie.

Of one mind.] This doth not only mean union in judgment, but it extends likewise to affection and action ; especially in so far as they relate to and depend upon the other. And so, I conceive, it comprehends, in its full latitude, a harmony and agreement of minds, and affections, and carriage in Christians, as making up one body, and a serious study of preserving and increasing that agreement in all things, but especially in spiritual things, in which their communion doth primely consist. And because in this, the consent of their judgments in matters of religion is a prime point, therefore we will consider that a little more particularly.

And, *First*, What it is not.

1. It is not a careless indifferency concerning those things. Not to be troubled about them at all, nor to make any judgment concerning them, this is not a loving agreement, arising from oneness of spirit, but a dead stupidity, arguing a total spiritlessness. As the agreement of a number of dead bodies together, which indeed do not strive and contest, that is, they move not at all, because they live not; so that concord in things of religion, which is a not considering them, nor acting of the mind about them, is the fruit and sign either of gross ignorance, or of irreligion. They who are wholly ignorant of spiritual things, are content you determine and impose upon them what you will; as in the dark, there is no difference nor choice of colours, they are all one. But, 2. which is worse, in some this peaceableness about religion arises from a universal unbelief and disaffection; and that sometimes comes of the much search and knowledge of debates and controversies in religion. Men having so many disputes about religion in their heads, and no life of religion in their hearts, fall into a conceit that all is but juggling, and that the easiest way is, to believe, nothing; and these agree with any, or rather with none. Sometimes it is from a profane, supercilious disdain of all these things; and many there be among these of Gallio's temper, who *care for none of these things*, and who account all questions in religion, as he did, but matter of words and names. And by this all religions may agree together. But that were not a natural union produced by the active heat of the spirit, but a confusion rather, arising from the want of it; not a knitting together, but a freezing together, as cold congregates all bodies, how heterogeneous soever, sticks, stones, and water; but heat makes first a separation of different things, and then unites those that are of the same nature.

And to one or other of these two is reducible much of the common quietness of people's minds about religion. All that implicit Romish agreement which they boast of, what is it, but a brutish ignorance of spiritual things, authorized and recommended for that very purpose? And amongst the learned of them, there are as many idle differences and disputes as amongst any. It is an easy way, indeed, to agree, if all will put out their eyes, and follow the blind guiding of their judge of controversies. This is that πάνσοφον φάρμακον, their great device for peace, to let the Pope determine all. If all will resolve to be cozened by him, he will agree them all. As if the consciences of men should only find peace by being led by the nose at one man's pleasure! A way the Apostle Paul clearly renounces: *Not for that we have dominion over your faith, but are helpers of your joy; for by faith ye stand.* 2 Cor. i. 24.

And though we have escaped this, yet much of our common union of minds, I fear, proceeds from no other than the afore-mentioned causes, want of knowledge, and want of affection to religion. You that boast you live conformably to the appointments of the Church, and that no one hears of your noise, we may thank the ignorance of your minds for that kind of quietness. But the unanimity here required, is another thing; and before I unfold it, I shall premise this—That although it be very difficult, and it may be impossible, to determine what things are alone fundamental in religion, under the notion of difference, intended by that word, yet it is undoubted, that there be some truths more absolutely necessary, and therefore accordingly more clearly revealed, than some others ; there are μέγαλα τοῦ νόμου, *great things of the Law*, and so of the Gospel. And though no part of Divine truth once fully cleared ought to be slighted, yet there are things that may be true, and still are but of less importance and of less evidence than others ; and this difference is wisely to be considered by Christians, for the interest of this agreement of minds here recommended. And concerning it we may safely conclude,

1. That Christians ought to have a clear and unanimous belief of the mysteries and principles of faith ; to agree in those without controversy. 2. They ought to be diligent in the research of truth in all things that concern faith and religion ; and withal to use all due means for the fullest consent and agreement in them all that possibly can be attained. 3. Perfect and universal consent in all, after all industry bestowed on it, for any thing we know, is not here attainable, neither betwixt all churches, nor all persons in one and the same church ; and therefore, though church-meetings and synods, as the fittest and most effectual way to this unity, should endeavour to bring the church to the fullest agreement that may be, yet they should beware lest the straining it too high in all things rather break it, and an over-diligence in appointing uniformities remove them further from it. Leaving a latitude and indifferency in things capable of it, is often a stronger preserver of peace and unity. But this by the way. We will rather give some few rules that may be of use to every particular Christian, toward this common Christian good of Unity of Mind.

1st, Beware of two extremes, which often cause divisions, *captivity to custom* on the one hand, and *affectation of novelty* on the other.

2ndly, Labour for a staid mind, that will not be tossed with every *wind of doctrine*, or appearance of reason, as some who, like vanes, are easily blown to any side with mistakes of the Scriptures, either arising in their own minds or suggested by others.

3rdly, In unclear and doubtful things be not pertinacious, as the weakest minds are readiest to be upon seeming reason, which, when tried, will possibly fall to nothing ; yet they are most assured, and cannot suffer a different thought in any from their own. There is naturally this *Popeness* in every man's mind, and most, I say, in the shallowest ; a kind of fancied *infallibility* in themselves, which makes them *contentious*, (contrary to the Apostle's rule, Phil. ii. 3, *Let nothing be done through strife or vain-glory*,) and as earnest upon differing in the smallest punctilio as in a high article of faith. Stronger spirits are usually more patient of contradiction, and less violent, especially in doubtful things ; and they who see furthest are least peremptory in their determinations. The Apostle, in his Second Epistle to Timothy, hath a word, *the spirit of a sound mind:* it is a good, sound constitution of mind, not to feel every blast, either of seeming reason to be taken with it, or of cross opinion to be offended at it.

4thly, Join that which is there, *the spirit of love*, in this particular : not at all abating affection for every light difference. And this the most are a little to blame in ; whereas the abundance of that should rather fill up the gap of these petty disagreements, that they do not appear, nor be at all sensibly to be found. No more disaffection ought to follow this, than the difference of our faces and complexions, or feature of body, which cannot be found in any two alike in all things.

And these things would be of easier persuasion, if we considered, 1. How supple and flexible a thing human reason is, and therefore not lightly to be trusted to, especially in Divine things; for *here, we know but in part.* 1 Cor. xiii. 9. 2. The small importance of some things that have bred much noise and dissension in the world, as the Apostle speaks of the tongue, *How little a spark, how great a fire will it kindle!* James iii. 5. And a great many of those debates which cost men so much pains and time, are as far from clear decision as when they began, and are possibly of so little moment, that if they were ended their profit would not quit the cost. 3. Consider the strength of Christian charity, which, if it dwelt much in our hearts, would preserve this union of mind amidst very many different thoughts, such as they may be, and would teach us that excellent lesson the Apostle gives to this purpose, Phil. iii. 15, *Let us therefore, as many as be perfect, be thus minded: and if in any thing ye be otherwise minded, God shall reveal even this unto you. Nevertheless, whereto we have already attained, let us walk by the same rule, let us mind the same thing.* Let us follow our Lord unanimously in what he hath clearly manifested to us, and given us with one consent to embrace; as the spheres, notwithstanding each one hath its particular motion, yet all are wheeled about together with the first.

And this leads us to consider the further extent of this word, to agree in heart and in conversation, walking by the rule of those un-doubted truths we have received. And in this I shall recommend these two things to you :—

1. In the defence of the Truth, as the Lord shall call us, let us be of one mind, and all as one man. Satan acts by that maxim, and all his followers have it, *Divide and conquer;* and therefore let us hold that counter-maxim, *Union invincible.*

2. In the practice of that Truth, agree as one. Let your conversa-tion be uniform, by being squared to that one rule, and in all spi-ritual exercises join as one; be *of one heart and mind.* Would not our public worship, think you, prove much more both comfortable and profitable, if our hearts met in it as one, so that we would say of our hearing the word, as he, Acts x. 33, *We are all here present before God, to hear all things that are commanded of God?*—if our prayers ascended up as one pillar of incense to the Throne of grace; if they besieged it, as an army, *stipato agmine Deum obsidentes,* as Tertullian speaks, all surrounding it together to obtain favour for ourselves and the Church? This is much with God, the *consent of hearts* petition-ing. *Fama est junctas fortius ire preces:* It is believed that united prayers ascend with greater efficacy. So says our Saviour, Matt. xviii. 20, *Where two or three are gathered*—not their bodies within the same walls only, for so they are but so many carcasses tumbled together, and the promise of his being amongst us is not made to that, *for he is the God of the living and not of the dead,* Matt. xxii. 32; it is the spirit of darkness that abides amongst the tombs and graves; but—*gathered in my name,* one in that one holy name, **writ-**

ten upon their hearts, and uniting them, and so thence expressed in their joint services and invocations. So he says there of them who *agree upon any thing they shall ask*, (συμφωνήσουσιν,) if all their hearts present and hold it up together, if they make one cry or song of it, that harmony of their hearts shall be sweet in the Lord's ears, and shall draw a gracious answer out of his hand : *if ye agree*, your joint petitions shall be as it were an arrest or decree that shall stand in heaven : *it shall be done for them of my Father which is in heaven.* But alas ! where is our agreement ? The greater number of hearts say nothing, and others speak with such wavering and such a jarring, harsh noise, being out of tune, earthly, too low set, that they spoil all, and disappoint the answers. Were the censer filled with those united prayers heavenwards, it would be filled with fire earthwards against the enemies of the Church.

And in your private society seek unanimously your own and each other's spiritual good ; not only agreeing in your affairs and civil converse, but having *one heart and mind* as Christians. To eat and drink together, if you do no more, is such society as beasts may have : to do these in the excess, to eat and drink intemperately together, is a society worse than that of beasts, and below them. To discourse together of civil business, is to converse as men ; but the peculiar converse of Christians in that notion, as born again to immortality, an unfading inheritance above, is to further one another towards that, to put one another in mind of heaven and heavenly things. And it is strange that men who profess to be Christians, when they meet, either fill one another's ears with lies and profane speeches, or with vanities and trifles, or, at the best, with the affairs of the earth, and not a word of those things that should most possess the heart, and where the mind should be most set, but are ready to reproach and taunt any such thing in others. What ! are you ashamed of Christ and religion ? Why do you profess it then ? Is there such a thing, think ye, as the *communing of saints ?* If not, why say you believe it ? It is a truth, think of it as you will. The public ministry will profit little any where, where a people, or some part of them, are not thus one, and do not live together as of one mind, and use diligently all due means of edifying one another in their holy faith. How much of the primitive Christians' praise and profit is involved in the word, *They were together* [ὁμοθυμαδὸν] *with one accord, with one mind :* and so they grew ; *the Lord added to the Church.* Acts ii. 1, 44, 47.

Consider, 1. How the wicked are one in their ungodly designs and practices. *The scales of Leviathan*, as Luther expresses it, are *linked together;* shall not the Lord's followers be one in him ? They unite to undermine the peace of the Church ; shall not the godly join their prayers to countermine them ?

2. There is in the hearts of all the saints one spirit ; how then can they be but one ? Since they have the same purpose and journey, and tend to the same home, why should they not walk together in that way ? When they shall arrive there, they shall be fully one, and of one mind, not a jar nor difference, all their harps perfectly in tune to that one new song.

Having compassion.] This testifies, that it is not a bare speculative agreement of opinions that is the badge of Christian unity ; for this may accidentally be, where there is no further union ; but that they are themselves one, and have one life, in that they feel how it is one with another. There is a living sympathy amongst them, as making up one body, animated with one spirit : for that is the reason why the members of the body have that mutual feeling, even the most remote and distant, and the most excellent with the meanest. This the Apostle urges at large, Rom. xii. 4, and 1 Cor. xii. 14—17.

And this lively sense is in every living member of the body of Christ towards the whole, and towards each other particular part. This makes a Christian rejoice in the welfare and good of another, as if it were his own, and feel their griefs and distresses, as if himself were really a sharer in them ; for the word comprehends all feeling together, feeling of joy as well as grief. Heb. xiii. 3 ; 1 Cor. xii. 26. And always, where there is most of grace and of the Spirit of Jesus Christ, there is most of this sympathy. The Apostle St. Paul, as he was eminent in all grace, had a large portion of this. 2 Cor. xi. 29. And if this ought to be in reference to their outward condition, much more in spiritual things there should be rejoicing at the increases and flourishing of grace in others. That base envy which dwells in the hearts of rotten hypocrites, who would have all engrossed to themselves, argues that they move not further than the compass of *self;* that the pure love of God, and the sincere love of their brethren flowing from it, are not in them. But when the heart can unfeignedly rejoice in the Lord's bounty to others, and the lustre of grace in others, far outshining their own, truly it is an evidence that what grace such a one hath, is upright and good, and that the law of love is engraven on his heart. And where that is, there will be likewise, on the other side, a compassionate, tender sense of the infirmities and frailties of their brethren ; whereas some account it a sign of much advancement and spiritual proficiency, to be able to sit in judgment upon the qualifications and actions of others, and to lavish out severe censures round about them : to sentence one weak and of poor abilities, and another proud and lofty, and a third covetous, *&c.;* and thus to go on in a censor-like, magisterial strain. But it were truly an evidence of more grace, not to get upon the bench to judge them, but to sit down rather and mourn for them, when they are manifestly and really faulty, and as for their ordinary infirmities, to consider and bear them. These are the characters we find in the Scriptures, of stronger Christians, Rom. xv. 1 ; Gal. vi. 1. This holy and humble sympathy argues indeed a strong Christian. *Nil tam spiritualem virum indicat, quam peccati alieni tractatio: Nothing truly shows a spiritual man so much, as the dealing with another man's sin.* Far will he be from the ordinary way of insulting and trampling upon the weak, or using rigour and bitterness, even against some gross falls of a Christian : but will rather vent his compassion in tears, than his passion in fiery railings ; will bewail the frailty of man, and our dangerous condition in this life, amidst so many snares and temptations, and such strong and subtle enemies.

2ndly, As this sympathy works towards particular Christians in their several conditions, so, by the same reason, it acts, and that more eminently, towards the Church, and the public affairs that concern its good. And this, we find, hath breathed forth from the hearts of the saints in former times, in so many pathetical complaints and prayers for Zion. Thus David in his saddest times, when he might seem most dispensable to forget other things, and be wholly taken up with lamenting his own fall, yet, even there, he leaves not out the Church, Psal. li. 17, *In thy good pleasure, do good to Zion.* And though his heart was broken all to pieces, yet the very pieces cry no less for the building of Jerusalem's wall, than for the binding up and healing of itself. And in that cxxiind Psalm, which seems to be the expression of his joy on being exalted to the throne and sitting peaceably on it, yet he still thus prays for *the peace of Jerusalem.* And the penman of the cxxxviiith Psalm, makes it an execrable oversight to forget Jerusalem, or to remember it coldly or secondarily: no less will serve him than to *prefer it to his chief joy.* Whatsoever else is *top* or *head of his joy,* (as the word is,) Jerusalem's welfare shall be its crown, shall be set above it. And the prophet, whoever it was, that wrote that ciind Psalm, and in it poured out that prayer from *an afflicted soul,* comforts himself in this, that Zion shall be favoured. *My days are like a shadow that declineth, and I am withered like grass;* but it matters not what becomes of me; let me languish and wither away, provided Zion flourish; though I feel nothing but pains and troubles, *yet, Thou wilt arise and show mercy to Zion:* I am content: that satisfies me.

But where is now this spirit of high sympathy with the Church? Surely, if there were any remains of it in us, it is now a fit time to exert it. If we be not altogether dead, surely we shall be stirred with the voice of those late strokes of God's hand, and be driven to more humble and earnest prayer by it. When will men change their poor, base grumblings about their private concerns, Oh! what shall I do? &c., into strong cries for the Church of God, and the public deliverance of all these kingdoms from the raging sword? But vile selfishness undoes us, the most looking no further. If themselves and theirs might be secured, how many would regard little what became of the rest! As one said, *When I am dead let the world be fired.* But the Christian mind is of a larger sphere, looks not only upon more than itself in present, but even to after times and ages, and can rejoice in the good to come, when itself shall not be here to partake of it: it is more dilated, and liker unto God, and to our Head, Jesus Christ. *The Lord,* says the Prophet, (Isa. lxiii. 9,) *in all his people's affliction, was afflicted himself.* And Jesus Christ accounts the sufferings of his body, the Church, his own: *Saul, Saul, why persecutest thou me?* Acts ix. 4. The heel was trod upon on earth, and the Head crieth from heaven, as sensible of it. And this in all our evils, especially our spiritual griefs, is a high point of comfort to us, that our Lord Jesus is not insensible of them. This imboldens us to complain ourselves, and to put in our petitions for help to the throne of Grace through his hand, knowing that when he presents them, he will speak his own sense of our condition, and move for us as it were for himself, as we have it sweetly expressed, Heb. iv. 15, 16. Now, as it is our comfort, so it is our pattern.

Love as brethren.] Hence springs this feeling we speak of: love is the cause of union, and union the cause of sympathy, and of that unanimity mentioned before. They who have the same spirit uniting and animating them, cannot but have the same mind and the same feelings. And this spirit is derived from that Head, Christ, in whom Christians *live, and move, and have their being,* their new and excellent being, and so, living in him, they love him, and are one in him: they are *brethren,* as here the word is; their fraternity holds in him. He is the Head of it, *the first-born among many brethren,* Rom. viii. 29. Men are brethren in two natural respects, their bodies are of the same earth, and their souls breathed from the same God; but this third fraternity, which is founded in Christ, is far more excellent and more firm than the other two; for being one in him, they have there taken in the other two, inasmuch as in him is our whole nature: he is the *man Christ Jesus.* But to the advantage, and it is an infinite one, of being one in him, we are united to the Divine nature in him, *who is God blessed for ever,* Rom. ix. 5; and this is the highest, certainly, and the strongest union that can be imagined. Now this is *a great mystery,* indeed, as the Apostle says, Eph. v. 32, speaking of this same point, the union of Christ and his Church, whence their union and communion one with another, who make up that body, the Church, is derived. In Christ every believer is *born of God,* is his son; and so, they are not only brethren, one with another, who are so born, but Christ himself owns them as his brethren; *Both he who sanctifies, and they who are sanctified, are all of one, for which cause he is not ashamed to call them brethren.* Heb. ii. 11.

Sin broke all to pieces, man from God, and men from one another. Christ's work in the world was *union.* To make up these breaches he came down, and began the union which was his work, in the wonderful union made in his person that was to work it, making God and man one. And as the nature of man was reconciled, so, by what he performed, the persons of men are united to God. Faith makes them one with Christ, and he makes them one with the Father, and hence results this oneness amongst themselves: concentring and meeting in Jesus Christ, and in the Father through him, they are made one together. And that this was his great work, we may read in his prayer, John xvii., where it is the burden and main strain, the great request he so reiterates, *That they may be one, as we are one,* ver. 11. A high comparison, such as man durst not name, but after him who so warrants us! And again, ver. 21, *That they all may be one, as thou, Father, art in me, and I in thee, that they also may be one in us.*

So that certainly, where this exists, it is the ground-work of another kind of friendship and love than the world is acquainted with, or is able to judge of, and hath more worth in one drachm of it, than all the quintessence of civil or natural affection can amount to. The friendships of the world, the best of them, are but tied with chains of glass; but this fraternal love of Christians is a golden chain, both more precious, and more strong and lasting: the others are worthless and brittle.

The Christian owes and pays the general charity and good-will to all; but peculiar and intimate friendship he cannot have, except with such as come within the compass of this fraternal love, which, after a special manner, flows from God, and returns to him, and abides in him, and shall remain unto eternity.

Where this love is and abounds, it will banish far away all those dissensions and bitternesses, and those frivolous mistakings which are so frequent among most persons. It will teach men wisely and gently to admonish one another, where it is needful; but further than that, it will pass by many offences and failings, it will *cover a multitude of sins,* and will very much sweeten society, making it truly profitable; therefore the Psalmist calls it both *good and pleasant, that brethren dwell together in unity :* it perfumes all, as the precious ointment upon the head of Aaron. Psal. cxxxiii. 2, 3.

But many who are called Christians, are not indeed of this brotherhood, and therefore, no wonder they know not what this love means, but are either of restless, unquiet spirits, *biting and devouring one another,* as the Apostle speaks, or at the best, only civilly smooth and peaceable in their carriage, rather scorners than partakers of this spiritual love and fraternity. These are strangers to Christ, not brought into acquaintance and union with him, and therefore void of the life of grace, and the fruits of it, whereof this is a chief one. Oh! how few amongst multitudes that throng in as we do here together, are indeed partakers of the *glorious liberty of the sons of God,* or ambitious of that high and happy estate!

As for you that know these things, and have a portion in them, who have your *communion with the Father, and his Son Jesus Christ,* (1 John i. 3,) I beseech you, adorn your holy profession, and testify yourselves the disciples and the brethren of Jesus Christ by this mutual love. Seek to understand better what it is, and to know it more practically. Consider that source of love, that *love which the Father hath bestowed upon us,* in this, *that we should be called the sons of God,* (1 John iii. 1,) and so be brethren, and thence draw more of this sweet stream of love. *God is love,* says the same Apostle; therefore, surely, where there is most of God, there is most of this Divine grace, this holy love. Look upon and study much that infinite love of God and his Son Jesus Christ towards us. *He gave his only begotten Son ;* the Son *gave himself :* he sweetened his bitter cup with his transcendent love, and this he hath recommended to us, that *Even as he loved us, so should we love one another.* John xv. 12. We know we cannot reach this highest pattern ; that is not meant ; but the more we look on it, the higher we shall reach in this love, and shall learn some measure of such love on earth, as is in heaven, and that which so begins here, shall there be perfected.

Be pitiful, be courteous.] The roots of plants are hidden under ground, so that themselves are not seen, but they appear in their branches, and flowers, and fruits, which argue there is a root and life in them ; thus the graces of the Spirit planted in the soul, though themselves invisible, yet discover their being and life in the tract of a Christian's life, his words, and actions, and the frame of his carriage. Thus Faith shows that *it lives,* as the Apostle St. James teacheth at large, Jam. ii. 14, &c. And thus Love is a grace of so active a nature, that it is still working, and yet never weary. *Your labour of love,* says the Apostle, Heb. vi. 10 : it labours, but delight makes the hardest labour sweet and easy. And so proper is action to it, that all action is null without it. 1 Cor. xiii. 1—3. Yea, it knits faith and action together ; it is the link that unites them. *Faith worketh,* but it is, as the Apostle teaches us, *by love.* Gal. v. 6. So then, where this root is, these fruits will spring from it and discover it, *Pity* and *Courtesy.*

These are of a larger extent in their full sphere, than the preceding graces : for, from a general love due to all, they act towards all, to men, or humanity, in the general ; and this not from a bare natural tenderness, which softer complexions may have, nor from a prudent moral consideration of their possible falling under the like or greater calamities, but out of obedience to God, who requires this mercifulness in all his children, and cannot own them for his, unless in this they resemble him. And it is indeed an evidence of a truly Christian mind, to have much of this pity to the miseries of all, being rightly principled, and acting after a pious and Christian manner towards the sick and poor, of what condition soever ; yea, pitying most the spiritual misery of ungodly men, their hardness of heart, and unbelief, and earnestly wishing their conversion ; not repining at the long-suffering of God, as if thou wouldst have the bridge cut because thou art over, as St. Augustine speaks, but longing rather to see that *long-suffering and goodness of God lead them to repentance,* Rom. ii. 4 ; being grieved to see men ruining themselves, and diligently working their own destruction, *going in any way of wickedness,* (as Solomon speaks of one particularly,) *as an ox to the slaughter, or a fool to the correction of the stocks,* Prov. vii. 22. Certainly, the ungodly man is an object of the highest pity.

But there is a special debt of this pity to those whom we love as brethren in our Lord Jesus : they are most closely linked to us by a peculiar fraternal love. Their sufferings and calamities will move the bowels that have Christian affection within them. Nor is it an empty, helpless pity, but carries with it the real communication of our help to our utmost power. [εὔσπλαγχνοι.] Not only bowels that are moved themselves with pity, but that move the hand to succour ; for by this word, the natural affection of parents, and of the more tender parent, the mother, is expressed, who do not idly behold and bemoan their children being sick or distressed, but provide all possible help ; their bowels are not only stirred, but dilated and enlarged towards them.

And if our feeling bowels and helping hand are due to all, and particularly to the godly, and we ought to pay this debt in outward distresses, how much more in their soul-afflictions !—the rather, because these are most heavy in themselves, and least understood, and therefore least regarded ; yea, sometimes rendered yet heavier by natural friends, possibly by their bitter scoffs and taunts, or by their slighting, or, at best, by their misapplying of proper helps and remedies, which, as unfit medicines, do rather exasperate the disease ; therefore they that do understand, and can be sensible of that kind of wound, ought so much the more to be tender and pitiful towards it, and to deal mercifully and gently with it. It may be, very weak things sometimes trouble a weak Christian ; but there is in the spirit of the godly, a humble condescension learned from Christ, who *broke not the bruised reed, nor quenched the smoking flax.*

The least difficulties and scruples in a tender conscience, should not be roughly encountered ; they are as a knot in a silken thread, and require a gentle and wary hand to loose them.

Now, this tenderness of bowels and inclination to pity all, especially Christians, and them especially in their peculiar pressures, is not a weakness, as some kind of spirits take it to be ; this, even naturally, is a generous pity in the greatest spirits. Christian pity is not womanish, yea, it is more than manly, it is Divine. There is of natural pity most in the best and most ingenuous natures, but where it is spiritual, it is a prime lineament of the image of God ; and the more absolute and disengaged it is, in regard of those towards whom it acts, the more it is like unto God ; looking upon misery as a sufficient incentive of pity and mercy, without the ingredient of any other consideration. It is merely a vulgar piece of goodness, to be helpful and bountiful to friends, or to such as are within appearance of requital ; it is a trading kind of commerce, that : but pity and bounty, which need no inducements but the meeting of a fit object to work on, where it can expect nothing, save only the privilege of doing good, (which in itself is so sweet,) is God-like indeed. He is rich in bounty without any necessity, yea, or possibility of return from us ; for we have neither any thing to confer upon Him, nor hath he need of receiving any thing, who is the Spring of goodness and of being.

And that we may the better understand Him in this, he is pleased to express this his merciful nature in our notion and language, by *bowels of mercy and pity,* Isa. liv. 7, 8, and the *stirring* and *sounding* of them, Hos. xi. 8 ; by *the pity of a father,* Psalm ciii. 13, and by that *of a mother,* Isa. xlix. 15 ; as if nothing could be tender and significant enough to express his compassions. Hence, our redemption, Isa. lxiii. 9 ; hence, all our hopes of happiness. The gracious Lord saw his poor creatures undone by sin, and no power in heaven or on earth able to rescue them, but his own alone ; therefore his pity was moved, and his hand answers his heart. *His own arm brought salvation;* he sent *the Deliverer out of Zion, to turn away iniquity from Jacob.* Rom. xi. 26. And in all exigences of his children, he is overcome with their complaints, and cannot hold out against their moanings. He may, as Joseph, seem strange for a while, but cannot act that strangeness long. His heart moves and sounds to theirs, gives the echo to their griefs and groans ; as they say of two strings that are perfect unisons, touch the one, the other also sounds. *Surely I have heard Ephraim bemoaning himself......* *Is Ephraim my dear son?* Jer. xxxi. 18. Oh ! the unspeakable privilege to have Him for our Father, who is *the Father of mercies and compassions,* and those not barren, fruitless pityings, for he is withal *the God of all consolations.* Do not think that he can shut out a bleeding soul that comes to him, or refuse to take, and to bind up, and heal a broken heart that offers itself to him, puts itself into his hand, and entreats his help. Doth he require pity of us, and doth he give it to us, and is it not infinitely more in himself? All that is in angels and men, is but an insensible drop to that Ocean.

Let us then consider, that we are obliged both to pity, especially towards our Christian brethren, and to use all means for their help within our reach : to have bowels stirred with the report of such bloodsheds and cruelties as come to our ears, and to bestir ourselves according to our places and power for them. But surely all are to move this one way for their help, to run to the *Throne of Grace.* If your bowels sound for your brethren, let them sound that way for them, to represent their estate to Him who is highest, both in pity and in power, for he expects to be remembranced by us : he put that office upon his people, to be his recorders for Zion, and they are traitors to it, who neglect the discharge of that trust.

Courteous.] The former relates to the afflictions of others, this to our whole carriage with them in any condition. And yet, there is a particular regard to be paid to it in communicating good, in supplying their wants, or comforting them that are distressed ; that it be not done, or rather, I may say, undone in doing, with such supercilious roughness, venting itself either in looks or words, or any way, as sours it, and destroys the very being of a benefit, and turns it rather into an injury. And generally, the whole conversation of men is made unpleasant by cynical harshness and disdain.

This Courteousness which the Apostle recommends, is contrary to that evil, not only in the surface and outward behaviour : no ; religion doth not prescribe, nor is satisfied with such courtesy as goes no deeper than words and gestures, which sometimes is most contrary to that singleness which religion owns. These are the upper garments of malice ; saluting him aloud in the morning, whom they are undermining all the day. Or sometimes, though more innocent, yet it may be troublesome, merely by the vain affectation and excess of it. Even this becomes not a wise man, much less a Christian. An over-study or acting of that, is a token of emptiness, and is below a solid mind. Though Christians know such things, and could outdo the studiers of it, yet they (as it indeed deserves) do despise it. Nor is it that graver and wiser way of external plausible deportment, that answers fully this word ; it is the outer half indeed, but the thing is [φιλοφροσύνη,] a radical sweetness in the temper of the mind, that spreads itself into a man's words and actions ; and this not merely natural, a gentle, kind disposition, (which is indeed a natural advantage that some have,) but this is spiritual, a new nature descended from heaven, and so, in its original and kind, far excelling the other ; it supplies it where it is not in nature, and doth not only increase it where it is, but elevates it above itself, renews it, and sets a more excellent stamp upon it. Religion is in this mistaken sometimes, in that men think it imprints an unkindly roughness and austerity upon the mind and carriage. It doth indeed bar and banish all vanity and lightness, and all compliance and easy partaking with sin. Religion strains, and quite breaks that point of false and injurious courtesy, to suffer thy brother's soul to run the hazard of perishing, and to share in his guiltiness, by not admonishing him after that seasonable, and prudent, and gentle manner (for that indeed should be studied) which becomes thee as a Christian, and that particular respective manner which becomes thy station. These things rightly qualifying it, it doth no wrong to good manners and the courtesy here enjoined, but is truly a part of it, by due admonitions and reproofs to seek to reclaim a sinner; for it were the worst unkindness not to do it. *Thou shalt not hate thy brother, thou shalt in any wise rebuke thy brother, and not suffer sin upon him.* Lev. xix. 17.

But that which is true lovingness of heart and carriage, religion doth not only in no way prejudice, but you see requires it in the rule, and where it is wrought in the heart, works and causes it there; fetches out that crookedness and harshness which are otherwise invincible in some humours: *Emollit mores, nec sinit esse feros; Makes the wolf dwell with the lamb.* This, Christians should study, and belie the prejudices which the world take up against the power of Godliness; they should study to be inwardly so minded, and of such outward behaviour, as becomes that Spirit of Grace which dwells in them, endeavouring to gain *those that are without,* by their kind, obliging conversation.

In some copies it is [ταπεινόφρονες] *Humble;* and indeed, as this is excellent in itself, and a chief characteristic of a Christian, it agrees well with all those mentioned, and carries along with it this inward and real, not acted, courteousness. Not to insist on it now, it gains at all hands with God and with men; receives much grace from God, and kills envy, and commands respect and good-will from men.

Those showers of grace that slide off from the lofty mountains, rest on the valleys, and make them fruitful. *He giveth grace to the lowly,* loves to bestow it where there is most room to receive it, and most return of ingenuous and entire praises upon the receipt, and such is the humble heart. And truly, as much humility gains much grace, so it grows by it.

It is one of the world's reproaches against those who go beyond their size in religion, that they are proud and self-conceited. Christians, beware there be nothing in you justifying this. Surely they who have most true grace, are least guilty of this. Common knowledge and gifts may *puff up,* but grace does not.

He whom the Lord loads most with his richest gifts, stoops lowest, as pressed down with the weight of them. *Ille est qui superbire nescit, cui Deus ostendit misericordiam suam:* The free love of God humbles that heart most to which it is most manifested.

And towards men, humility graces all grace and all gifts; it glorifies God, and teaches others so to do. It is *conservatrix virtutum,* the *preserver of graces.* Sometimes it seems to wrong them by hiding them; but indeed, it is their safety. Hezekiah, by a vain showing of his jewels and treasures, forfeited them all: *Prodendo perdidit.*

Ver. 9. Not rendering evil for evil, or railing for railing; but contrariwise blessing; knowing that ye are thereunto called, that ye should inherit a blessing.

OPPOSITION helps grace both to more strength and more lustre. When Christian charity is not encountered by the world's malignance, it hath an easier task; but assaulted and overcoming, it shines the brighter, and rises the higher; and thus it is when it *renders not evil for evil.*

To repay good with evil is, amongst men, the top of iniquity; yet this is our universal guiltiness towards God, he multiplying mercies, and we vying with multiplied sins: as the Lord complains of Israel, *As they were increased so they sinned.* The lowest step of mutual good amongst men, is, not to be bent to provoke others with injuries, and, being unoffended, to offend none. But this, not to repay offences, nor *render evil for evil,* is a Christian's rule; and yet, further, to return *good* for *evil,* and *blessing* for *cursing,* is not only counselled, (as some vainly distinguish,) but commanded, Matt. v. 44.

It is true, the most have no ambition for this degree of goodness; they aspire no further than to do or say no evil unprovoked, and think themselves sufficiently just and equitable, if they keep within that; but this is lame, is only half the rule. Thou thinkest injury obliges thee, or, if not so, yet excuses thee, to revenge, or at least, disobliges thee, unties thy engagement of wishing and doing good. But these are all gross practical errors. For,

1st, The second injury done by way of revenge, differs from the first that provoked it little or nothing, but only in point of time; and certainly, no one man's sin can procure privilege to another, to sin in that or the like kind. If another hath broken the bonds of his allegiance and obedience to God, and of charity to thee, yet thou art not the less tied by the same bonds still.

2ndly, By revenge of injuries thou usurpest upon God's prerogative, who is *The Avenger,* as the Apostle teaches, Rom. xii. 19. This doth not forbid either the Magistrate's sword for just punishment of offenders, or the Soldier's sword in a just war; but such revenges as, without authority, or a lawful call, the pride and perverseness of men do multiply one against another; in which is involved a presumptuous contempt of God and his supreme authority, or at least, the unbelief and neglect of it.

3rdly, It cannot be genuine, upright goodness that hath its dependence upon the goodness of others who are about us: as they say of the vain-glorious man, his virtue lieth in the beholder's eye. If thy meekness and charity be such as lieth in the good and mild carriage of others towards thee, in their hands and tongues, thou art not owner of it intrinsically. Such quiet and calm, if none provoke thee, is but an accidental, uncertain cessation of thy turbulent spirit unstirred; but move it, and it exerts itself according to its nature, sending up that mud which lay at the bottom: whereas true grace doth then most manifest what it is, when those things which are most contrary surround and assault it; it cannot correspond and hold game with injuries and railings; it hath no faculty for that, for *answering evil with evil.* A tongue inured to graciousness, and mild speeches, and blessings, and a heart stored so within, can vent no other, try it and stir it as you will. A Christian acts and speaks, not according to what others are towards him, but according to what he is through the grace and Spirit of God in him; as they say, *Quicquid recipitur, recipitur ad modum recipientis:* The same things are differently received, and work differently, according to the nature and way of that which receives them.   A little spark blows up one of a sulphureous temper, and *many coals,* greater injuries and reproaches, are quenched and lose their force, being thrown at another of a *cool spirit,* as the original expression is, Prov. xvii. 27.

They who have malice, and bitterness, and cursings within, though these sleep, it may be, yet, awake them with the like, and the provision comes forth *out of the abundance of the heart:* give them an ill word, and they have another, or two for one, in readiness for you.   So, where the soul is furnished with spiritual blessings, their blessings come forth, even in answer to reproaches and indignities.   *The mouth of the wise is a tree of life,* says Solomon (Prov. x. 11); it can bear no other fruit, but according to its kind, and the nature of the root. An honest, spiritual heart, pluck at it who will, they can pull no other fruit than such fruit.   Love and meekness lodge there, and therefore, whosoever knocks, these make the answer.

Let the world account it a despicable simplicity, seek you still more of that dove-like spirit, the spirit of meekness and blessing.   It is a poor glory to vie in railings, to contest in that faculty, or in any kind of vindictive returns of evil: the most abject creatures have abundance of that great spirit, as foolish, poor-spirited persons account it; but *it is the glory of man to pass by a transgression,* (Prov. xix. 11,) it is the noblest victory.   And as we mentioned, the Highest Example, God, is our pattern in love and compassions: we are well warranted to endeavour to be like him in this.   Men esteem much more highly some other virtues which make more show, and trample upon these, love, and compassion, and meekness.   But though these violets grow low, and are of a dark colour, yet, they are of a very sweet and diffusive smell, odoriferous graces; and the Lord propounds himself our example in them, Matt. v. 44—48.   To *love them that hate you, and bless them that curse you,* is to be truly *the children of your Father,* your Father *which is in heaven.*   It is a kind of perfection: ver. 48, *Be ye therefore perfect, even as your Father which is in heaven is perfect. He maketh his sun to rise on the evil and on the good.*   Be you like it: howsoever men behave themselves, keep you your course, and let your benign influence, as you can, do good to all.   And Jesus Christ sets in himself these things before us, *Learn of me,* not to heal the sick, or raise the dead, but *learn, for I am meek and lowly in heart,* Matt. xi. 29.   And if you be his followers, this is your way, as the Apostle here addeth, *Hereunto are you called;* and this is the end of it, agreeably to the way, *that you may inherit a blessing.*

[Εἰδότες ὅτι.] [*Knowing that.*]   Understanding aright the nature of your holy calling, and then, considering it wisely, and conforming to it.

Those who have nothing beyond an external calling and profession of Christianity, are wholly blind in this point, and do not think what this imports, *A Christian.*   Could they be drawn to this, it were much, it were indeed all, to know to what they are called, and to answer to it, to walk like it.   But as one calls a certain sort of lawyers, *indoctum doctorum genus,* we may call the most, *an unchristian kind of Christians.*

Yea, even those who are really partakers of this spiritual and effectual call, yet are often very defective in this; in viewing their rule and laying it to their life, their hearts, and words, and actions, and squaring by it ; in often asking themselves, Suits this my calling ? Is this like a Christian ? It is a main point in any civil station, for a man to have a carriage suitable and convenient to his station and condition, that his actions become him : *Capus artis est decere quod facias.* But how many incongruities and solecisms do we commit, forgetting ourselves, who we are, and what we are called to ; to what as our duty, and to what as our portion and inheritance. And these indeed agree together ; we are *called* to an *undefiled, a holy inheritance,* and therefore, *called* likewise to be *holy* in our way to it ; for that contains all. We are *called* to a better estate at home, and *called* to be fitted for it while we are here ; *called* to an *inheritance of light,* and therefore, *called* to *walk* as *children of light ;* and so here, *called* to *blessing* as our inheritance, and to *blessing* as our duty ; for this [εἰς τουτο, *thereunto*] relates to both, looks back to the one, and forward to the other, the way, and the end, both *blessing.*

The fulness of this inheritance is reserved till we come to that land where it lieth ; there it abideth us ; but the earnests of that fulness of blessing are bestowed on us here ; *spiritual blessings in heavenly places in Christ* (Eph. i. 3) ; they descend from those heavenly places upon the heart, that precious name of our Lord Jesus poured on our hearts. If we be indeed interested in him, (as we pretend,) and have peace with God through our Lord Jesus Christ, we are put in possession of that blessing of forgiveness of sin, and on terms of love and amity with the Father, being reconciled by the blood of his Son, and then blessed with the anointing of the Spirit, the graces infused from heaven. Now, all these do so cure the bitter, accursed distempers of the natural heart, and so perfume it, that it cannot well breathe any thing but sweetness and blessing towards others : being itself thus blessed of the Lord, it echoes blessing both to God and men, echoes to his blessing of it ; and its words and whole carriage are *as the smell of a field that the Lord hath blessed,* as old Isaac said of his son's garments, Gen. xxvii. 27. The Lord having spoken pardon to a soul, and instead of the curse due to sin, blessed it with a title to glory, it easily and readily speaks pardon, and not only pardon, but blessing also, even to those that outrage it most, and deserve worst of it ; reflecting still on that, Oh ! what deserved I at my Lord's hands ! When so many talents are forgiven me, shall I stick at forgiving a few pence !

And then, *called to inherit a blessing ;* every believer *an heir of blessing !* And not only are the spiritual blessings he hath received, but even his largeness of blessing others is a pledge to him, an evidence of that heirship ; as those who are prone to cursing, though provoked, yet may look upon that as a sad mark, that they are heirs of a curse. Psal. cix. 17, *As he loved cursing, so let it come unto him.* Shall not they who delight in cursing, have enough of it, when they shall hear that doleful word, *Go, ye cursed,* &c. ? And, on the other side, as for the sons of blessing, who spared it not to any, the blessing they are heirs to is blessedness itself, and they are to be entered into it by that joyful speech, *Come, ye blessed of my Father.*

Men can but bless one another in good wishes, and can bless the Lord only in praises and applauding his blessedness ; but the Lord's blessing is, really *making blessed;* an operative word, which brings the thing with it.

Inherit a blessing.] Not called to be exempted from troubles and injuries here, and to be extolled and favoured by the world, but, on the contrary, rather to suffer the utmost of their malice, and to be the mark of their arrows, of wrongs, and scoffs, and reproaches. But it matters not, this weighs down all, *you are called to inherit a blessing,* which all their cursings and hatred cannot deprive you of. For as this inheriting of blessing enforces the duty of blessing others upon a Christian, so it encourages him to go through the hardest contrary measure he receives from the world. If the world should bless you, and applaud you never so loudly, yet their blessings cannot be called an inheritance ; they fly away, and die out in the air, have no substance at all, much less that endurance that may make them an inheritance. *Qui thesaurum tuum alieno in ore constituis, ignoras quod arca ista non clauditur?* You who trust your treasure to another man's keeping, are you aware that you are leaving it in an open chest ? And more generally, is there any thing here that deserves to be called ? The surest inheritances are not more than for term of life to any one man : their abiding is for others who succeed, but he removes. *Si hæc sunt vestra, tollite ea vobiscum* (S. BERNARD): If these things are yours, take them away with you. And when a man is to remove from all he hath possessed and rejoiced in here, then, *fool* indeed, if nothing be provided for the longer (oh ! how much longer) abode he must make elsewhere ! Will he not then bewail his madness, that he was hunting a shadow all his lifetime ? And may be, he is turned out of all his quiet possessions and easy dwelling before that (and in these times we may the more readily think of this); but at the utmost at night, when he should be for most rest, when that sad night comes after this day of fairest prosperity, the unbelieving, unrepenting sinner lies down in sorrow, in a woeful bed. Then must he, whether he will or no, enter on the possession of this inheritance of everlasting burnings. He hath an inheritance indeed, but he had better want it, and himself too be turned to nothing. Do you believe there are treasures which neither thief breaks into, nor is there any inward moth to corrupt them, an inheritance which, though the whole world be turned upside down, is in no hazard of a touch of damage, *a kingdom,* that not only cannot fall, but *cannot be shaken?* Heb. xii. 28. *Oh! be wise, and consider your latter end,* and whatsoever you do, look after this blessed inheritance. Seek to have the right to it in Jesus Christ, and the evidences and seals of it from his Spirit ; and if it be so with you, your hearts will be upon it, and your lives will be conformed to it.

Ver. 10. For he that will love life, and see good days, let him refrain his tongue from
evil, and his lips that they speak no guile.

THE rich bounty of God diffuses itself throughout the world upon all ; yet there is a select number who have peculiar blessings of his *right hand,* which the rest of the world share not in ; and even as to common blessings, they are differenced by a peculiar title to them, and sweetness in them: their blessings are blessings indeed, and entirely so, outside and inside, and more so within than they appear without :

the Lord himself *is their portion,* and *they are his.* This is their blessedness, which in a low estate they can challenge, and so outvie all the
painted prosperity of the world. Some kind of blessings do abundantly
run over upon others ; but *the cup of blessings* belongs unto the godly
by a new right from heaven, graciously couferred upon them. Others
are sent away *with gifts,* (as some apply that passage, Gen. xxv. 5, 6,)
but the inheritance is Isaac's. They are called to be *the sons of God,*
and are like him, as his children, in goodness and blessings. The inheritance of blessing is theirs alone :—*Called,* says the Apostle, *to inherit a blessing.* And all the promises in the great charter of both
Testaments run in that appropriating style, entailed to them, as the only
heirs. Thus this fitly is translated from the one Testament to the other,
by the Apostle, for his present purpose—*He that will love,* &c. See
Psal. xxxiv. 13, 14.

Consider, 1. The qualification required. 2. The blessing annexed
and ascertained to it ; the scope being, to recommend a rule so exact,
and for that purpose, to propound a good so important and desirable,
as a sufficient attractive to study and conform to that rule.

The rule is all of it one straight line, running through the whole
tract of a godly man's life ; yet you see clearly that it is not cut asunder indeed, but only marked into four, whereof, the two latter parcels
are somewhat longer, more generally reaching a man's ways, the two
former particularly regulating the tongue.

In the ten words of the law which God delivered in so singular a
manner both by word and writ from his own mouth and hand, there be
two, which if not wholly, yet most especially and most expressly concern the tongue, as a very considerable, though a small part of man ;
and of these four words, here two are bestowed on it.

The Apostle St. James is large in this, teaching the great concernment of this point. *It is a little member,* (says he, chap. iii. 5,) *but
boasteth great things,* needs a strong bridle ; and the bridling of it makes
much for the ruling the whole course of a man's life, as the Apostle
there applies the resemblance ; yea, he gives the skill of this as the very
character of perfection. And if we consider it, it must indeed be of
very great consequence how we use the tongue, it being the main outlet
of the thoughts of the heart and the mean of society amongst men in all
affairs civil and spiritual ; by which men give birth to the conceptions
of their own minds, and seek to beget the like in the minds of others.
The bit that is here made for men's mouths hath these two halves that
make it up : 1. To refrain from open evil speaking. 2. From double
and guileful speaking.

From evil.] This is a large field, the evil of the tongue ; but I give
it too narrow a name : we have good warrant to give it a much larger
—a whole universe, *a world of iniquity,* Jam. iii. 6, a vast bulk of evils,
and great variety of them, as of countries on the earth, or creatures in
the world ; and multitudes of such are venomous and full of deadly
poison, and not a few, monsters, new productions of wickedness *semper
aliquid novi,* as they say of Africa.

There be in the daily discourses of the greatest part of men, many
things that belong to this *world of evil,* and yet pass unsuspected, so
that we do not think them to be within its compass ; not using due

diligence and exactness in our discoveries of the several parts of it, although it is all within ourselves, yea, within a small part of ourselves, our tongues.

It were too quick a fancy to think to travel over this world of iniquity, the whole circuit of it, in an hour, yea, or so much as to aim exactly at all the parts that can be taken of it in the smallest map: but some of the chief we would particularly take notice of in the several four parts of it; for it will without constraint hold resemblance in that division, with the other, the habitable world.

I. *Profane* speech, that which is grossly and manifestly wicked; and in that part lie, 1. Impious speeches, which directly reflect upon the glory and name of God; blasphemies, and oaths, and cursings, of which there is so great, so lamentable abundance amongst us, the whole land overspread and defiled with it, the common noise that meets a man in streets and houses, and almost in all places where he comes; and to these, join what are not uncommon amongst us neither, scoffs and mocking at religion, the power and strictness of it, not only by the grosser sort, but by pretenders to some kind of goodness; for they who have attained to a self-pleasing pitch of civility or formal religion, have usually that point of presumption with it, that they make their own size the model and rule to examine all by. What is below it, they condemn indeed as profane; but what is beyond it, they account needless and affected preciseness; and, therefore, are as ready as others to let fly invectives or bitter taunts against it, which are the keen and poisoned shafts of the tongue, and a persecution that shall be called to a strict account. 2. Impure or filthy speaking, which either pollutes or offends the hearers, and is the noisome breath of a rotten, polluted heart.

II. Consider next, as another grand part of the tongue, *Uncharitable* speeches, tending to the defaming and disgrace of others; and these are likewise of two sorts: 1. Open railing and reproaches; 2. Secret slander and detraction. The former is unjust and cruel, but it is somewhat the less dangerous, because open. It is a fight in plain field; but truly it is no piece of a Christian's warfare to encounter it in the same kind. The sons of peace are not for these tongue-combats; they are often, no doubt, set upon so, but they have another abler way of overcoming it than by the use of the same weapon; for they break and blunt the point of ill-reproaches by meekness, and triumph over cursings with more abundant blessing, as is enjoined in the former words, which are seconded with these out of Psalm xxxiv. 13, 14. But they that enter the lists in this kind, and are provided one for another with enraged minds, are usually not unprovided of weapons, but lay hold on any thing that comes next;—*Furor arma ministrat;* as your drunkards in their quarrels, in their cups and pots, if they have any other great reproach, they lay about them with that, as their sword; but if they want that, true or untrue, pertinent or impertinent, all is one, they cast out any revilings that come next to hand. But there is not only wickedness, but something of baseness in this kind of conflicts, that makes them more abound amongst the baser sort, and not so frequent with such as are but of a more civil breeding and quality than the vulgar.

But the other kind—detraction, is more universal amongst all sorts, as being a far easier way of mischief in this kind, and of better conveyance. Railings cry out the matter openly, but detraction works all by surprises and stratagem, and mines under ground, and therefore is much more pernicious. The former are as the *arrows that fly by day*, but this, *as the pestilence that walketh in darkness*, (as these two are mentioned together in Psalm xci. 5, 6,) it spreads and infects secretly and insensibly, is not felt but in the effects of it ; and it works either by calumnies altogether forged and untrue, of which malice is inventive, or by the advantage of real faults, of which it is very discerning, and these are stretched and aggravated to the utmost. It is not expressible how deep a wound a tongue sharpened to this work will give, with a very little word and little noise,—*as a razor*, as it is called in Psal. lii. 2, which with a small touch cuts very deep,—taking things by the worst handle, whereas charity will try about all ways for a good acceptation and sense of things, and takes all by the best. This pest is still killing some almost in all companies ; it *casteth down many wounded*, as it is said of the strange woman, Prov. vii. 26. And they convey it under fair prefacing of commendation ; so giving them poison in wine, both that it may pass the better, and penetrate the more. This is a great sin, one which the Lord ranks with the first, when he sets them in order against a man, Psal. l. 20, *Thou sittest and speakest against thy brother.*

III. *Vain, fruitless* speeches are an evil of the tongue, not only those they call *harmless lies,* which some poor people take a pleasure in, and trade much in, light buffooneries and foolish jesting, but the greatest part of those discourses which men account the *blameless* entertainments one of another, come within the compass of this evil ; frothy, unsavoury stuff, tending to no purpose nor good at all ; *effectless words,* ἄργον, as our Saviour speaks, Matt. xii. 36, of which we must *render an account in the day of judgment,* for that very reason. They are in this *world of evil,* in the tongue ; if no other way ill, yet ill they are, as the Arabian deserts and barren sands, because they are fruitless.

IV. *Doubleness and guile :* so great a part, that it is here particularly named a part, though the evil of it is less known and discerned ; and so there is in it, as I may say, much *terra incognita ;* yet it is of a very large compass, as large, we may confidently say, as all the other three together. What of men's speech is not manifestly evil in any of the other kinds, is the most of it naught this way : speech good to appearance, plausible and fair, but not upright ; not silver, but *silver dross,* as Solomon calls it ; burning lips, &c. Prov. xxvi. 23. Each almost, some way or other, speaking falsehood and deceit to his neighbour ; and daring to act thus falsely with God in his services, and our protestations of obedience to him ; religious speeches abused by some in hypocrisy, as holy vestments, for a mask or disguise ; doing nothing but *compassing him about with lies,* as he complains of Ephraim, Hos. xi. 12 ; deceiving indeed ourselves, while we think to deceive Him who cannot be deceived, and *will not be mocked,* Psal. xvii. 1 ; Gal. vi. 7. He saw through the disguise and hypocrisy of his own people, when they came to inquire at him, and yet still entertained their heart-idols, as he tells the prophet, Ezek. xiv. 3.

The sins of each of us, would we enter into a strict account of ourselves, would be found to arise to a great sum in this kind ; and they that do put themselves upon the work of self-trial, find, no doubt, abundant matter of deepest humbling, though they had no more, even in the sin of their lips, and are by it often astonished at the Lord's patience, considering his holiness ; as Isaiah cried out, ch. vi. 5 : having seen the Lord in a glorious vision, this in particular falls upon his thoughts concerning himself and the people — *polluted lips : Woe is me,* &c. And indeed it is a thing the godly mind cannot be satisfied with, to make mention of the Lord, till their lips be *touched with a coal from* the heavenly fire of *the altar ;* and they especially that are called to be the Lord's messengers, will say as St. Bernard, " Had " the prophet need of a coal to unpollute his lips, then do ministers " require *totum globum igneum,* a whole globe of fire." Go through the land, and see if the sins of this kind will not take up much of the bill against us, which the Lord seems now to have taken into his hands and to be reading, and about to take order with it, because we will not. Would we set ourselves to read it, he would let it fall. Is it not because of oaths that the *land mourns,* or I am sure hath now high cause to mourn ? Mockings at *the power of godliness* fly thick in most congregations and societies. And what is there to be found almost but mutual detractions and supplantings of the good name of another, *tongues taught to speak lies,* Jer. ix. 4, 5, and that frame, or sew and *weave together deceits,* as it is in Psal. l. 19 ? And even the godly, as they may be subject to other sins, so may they be under some degree of this ; and too many are very much subject, by reason of their unwatchfulness and not staying themselves in this point, though not to profane, yet to vain, and it may be to detractive speeches ; sometimes possibly not with malicious intention, but out of an inadvertence of this evil, readier to stick on the failings of men, and it may be of other Christians, than to consider, and commend, and to follow what is laudable in them ; and it may be in their best discourses, not endeavouring to have hearts purified, as becomes them, from all guile and self-ends. Oh ! it is a thing needs much diligent study, and is worth it all, to be thoroughly sincere and unfeigned in all, and particularly in these things. Our Saviour's innocence is expressed so, *In his mouth was found no guile.* (Chap. ii. of this Epistle, ver. 22.)

But to add something for remedy of these evils in some part discovered ; for to vanquish this world of evils is a great conquest.

1. It must be done at the heart ; otherwise it will be but a mountebank cure, a false imagined conquest. The weights and wheels are *there,* and the clock strikes according to their motion. Even he that speaks contrary to what is within him, guilefully contrary to his inward conviction and knowledge, yet speaks conformably to what is within him in the temper and frame of his heart, which is double, *a heart and a heart,* as the Psalmist hath it, Psal. xii. 2. A guileful heart makes guileful tongue and lips. It is the work-house, where is the forge of deceits and slanders, and other evil speakings ; and the tongue is only the outer shop where they are vended, and the lips the door of it ; so then such ware as is made within, such and no other can be set out. From evil thoughts, evil speakings ; from a profane heart, profane

words; and from a malicious heart, bitter or calumnious words; and from a deceitful heart, guileful words, well varnished, but lined with rottenness.   And so in the general, *from the abundance of the heart the mouth speaketh*, as our Saviour teaches, Matt. xii. 34.   That which the heart is full of, runs over by the tongue: if the heart be full of God, the tongue will delight to speak of him; much of heavenly things within, will sweetly breathe forth something of their smell by the mouth; and if nothing but earth is there, all that man's discourse will have an earthly smell; and if nothing but wind, vanity and folly, the speech will be airy, and vain, and purposeless.   *The mouth of the righteous speaketh wisdom:—the law of his God is in his heart*, Psal. xxxvii. 30, 31.   *Thy law*, says David, (Psal. xl. 8,) *is within my heart*, or, as the Hebrew phrase is, *in the midst of my bowels;* and that, as from the centre, sends forth the lines and rays of suitable words, and *I will not, cannot refrain*, as there it is added, verse 9, *I have preached righteousness: lo, I have not refrained my lips.*   So no more can the evil heart *refrain the tongue from evil*, as here is directed. *The tongue of the righteous*, says Solomon, *is as fine silver, but the heart of the wicked is little worth.*   Prov. x. 20.   It makes the antithesis *in the root;* his *heart* is little worth, and therefore his *tongue* has no silver in it; he may be *worth thousands*, (as we speak,) that is, indeed, in his chests or lands, and yet himself, his heart, and all the thoughts of it, not worth a penny.

If thou art inured to oaths or cursing, in any kind or fashion of it, taking the great *name of God* any ways *in vain*, do not favour thyself in it as a small offence: to excuse it by custom, is to wash thyself with ink; and to plead that thou art long practised in that sin, is to accuse thyself deeper.   If thou wouldst indeed be delivered from it, think not that a slight dislike of it (when reproved) will do; but seek for a due knowledge of the majesty of God, and thence a deep reverence of him in thy heart; and that will certainly cure that habituated evil of thy tongue; will quite alter that bias which the custom thou speakest of hath given it; will cast it in a new mould, and teach it a new language; will turn thy regardless abuse of that name, by vain oaths and asseverations, into a holy frequent use of it in prayers and praises. Thou wilt not then dare dishonour that blessed name, which saints and angels bless and adore; but wilt set in with them to bless it.

None that know the weight of that name will dally with it, and *lightly lift it up;* (as that word translated *taking in vain*, in the third commandment, signifies;) they that do continue to *lift it up in vain*, as it were, to sport themselves with it, will find the weight of it falling back upon them, and crushing them to pieces.

In like manner, a purified heart will unteach the tongue all filthy, impure speeches, and will give it a holy strain; and the spirit of charity and humility will banish that mischievous humour, which sets so deep in the most, of reproaching and disgracing others in any kind either openly or secretly.   For it is wicked self-love and pride of heart whence these do spring, searching and disclosing the failings of others, on which love will rather cast a mantle to hide them.

It is an argument of a candid, ingenuous mind, to delight in the good name and commendation of others; to pass by their defects, and take notice of their virtues ; and to speak and hear of those willingly, and not endure either to speak or hear of the other; for in this indeed you may be little less guilty than the evil speaker, in taking pleasure in it, though you speak it not. And this is a piece of men's natural perverseness, to drink in tales and calumnies ;* and he that doth this, will readily, from the delight he hath in hearing, slide insensibly into the humour of evil speaking. It is strange how most persons dispense with themselves in this point, and that in scarcely any societies shall we find a hatred of this ill, but rather some tokens of taking pleasure in it ; and until a Christian sets himself to an inward watchfulness over his heart, not suffering in it any thought that is uncharitable, or vain self-esteem, upon the sight of others' frailties, he will still be subject to somewhat of this, in the tongue or ear at least. So, then, as for the evil of guile in the tongue, a sincere heart, *truth in the inward parts*, powerfully redresses it ; therefore it is expressed, Psal. xv. 2, *That speaketh the truth from his heart;* thence it flows. Seek much after this, to speak nothing with God, nor men, but what is the sense of a single unfeigned heart. O sweet truth ! excellent but rare sincerity ! he that *loves that truth within,* alone can work it there ; seek it of him.

2ndly, Be choice in your society, *Sit not with vain persons,* Psal. xxvi. 4, whose tongues have nothing else to utter, but impurity, or malice, or folly. Men readily learn the dialect and tone of the people amongst whom they live. If you sit down in the chair of scorners, if you take a seat with them, you shall quickly take a share of their diet with them, and sitting amongst them, take your turn, in time, of speaking with them in their own language. But frequent the company of grave and godly persons, in whose hearts and lips, piety, and love, and wisdom are set, and it is the way to learn their language.

3rdly, Use a little of the bridle in the quantity of speech.† Incline a little rather to sparing than lavishing, for *in many words there wants not sin*. That flux of the tongue, that prattling and babbling disease, is very common ; and hence so many impertinences, yea, so many of those worse ills in their discourses, whispering about, and inquiring, and censuring this and that. A childish delight ! and yet most men carry it with them all along to speak of persons and things not concerning us.‡ And this draws men to speak many things which agree not with the rules of wisdom, and charity, and sincerity. *He that refraineth his lips is wise,* saith Solomon, Prov. x. 19 : a vessel without a cover, cannot escape uncleanness. Much might be avoided by a little refraining of this ; much of the infection and sin that are occasioned by the many babblings that are usual. And were it no worse, is it not a sufficient evil, that they waste away that time, precious time, which cannot be recovered, which the most just or most thankful man in the world cannot restore ? He that spares speech, *favours his tongue* indeed, as the Latin phrase is [*favere linguæ*]; not he that looses the reins and lets it run. He that refrains his lips, may ponder and pre-examine what he utters, whether it be profitable and reasonable or no ; and so the tongue of the just is as *fined silver,* Prov. x. 20 ; it

---

* Obtrectatio et livor primis auribus accipiuntur.
† Χωρὶς τὸ τ' εἰπεῖν πολλὰ καὶ τὰ καίρια.   ÆSCHYL.
‡ Οὐδὲν οὕτως ἡδὺ τοῖς ἀνθρώποις ὡς τῶ λαλεῖν τὰ ἀλλότρια.   2 ORAT. 1.

is refined in the wise forethought and pondering of the heart: according to the saying, *Bis ad limam priusquam semel ad linguam.* *Twice to the file ere once to the tongue.* Even to utter knowledge and wise things profusely, holds not of wisdom, and a little usually makes most noise ; as the Hebrew proverb is, *Stater in lagena bis bis clamat.* *A penny in an earthen pot keeps a great sound and tinkling.* Certainly it is the way to have much inward peace, to be wary in this point. Men think to have solace by much free unbounded discourse with others, and when they have done, they find it otherwise, and sometimes contrary. He is wise that hath learned to speak little with others, and much with himself and with God. How much might be gained for our souls, if we would make a right use of this silence ! So David, dumb to men, found his tongue to God, Psal. xxxviii. 13, 15. A spiritually-minded man is quickly weary of other discourse, but of that which he loves and wherewith his affection is possessed and taken up : *Grave æstimant quicquid illud non sonat quod intus amant.* And by experience, a Christian will find it, when the Lord is pleased to show him most favour in prayer or other spiritual exercise, how unsavoury it makes other discourses after it ; as they who have tasted something singularly sweet, think other things that are less sweet, altogether tasteless and unpleasant.

4*thly,* In the use of the tongue, when thou dost speak, divert it from evil and guile, by a habit of, and delight in, profitable and gracious discourse. Thus St. Paul makes the opposition, Eph. iv. 29. Let there be no *rotten communication,* (σαπρὸς λογὸς,) and yet he urges not total silence neither, but enjoins such speech *as may edify and administer grace to the hearers.* Now in this we should consider, to the end such discourses may be more fruitful, both what is the true end of them, and the right means suiting it. They are not only, nor principally, for the learning of some new things, or the canvassing of debated questions, but their chief good is the warming of the heart ; stirring up in it love to God, and remembrance of our present and after estate, our mortality and immortality ; and extolling the ways of holiness, and the promises and comforts of the Gospel, and the excellency of Jesus Christ ; and in these sometimes one particular, sometimes another, as our particular condition requires, or any occasion makes them pertinent. Therefore in these discourses, seek not so much either to vent thy knowledge, or to increase it, as to know more spiritually and effectually what thou dost know. And in this way those mean, despised truths, that every one thinks he is sufficiently seen in, will have a new sweetness and use in them, which thou didst not so well perceive before, (for these flowers cannot be sucked dry,) and in this humble, sincere way thou shalt *grow in grace and in knowledge* too.

There is no sweeter entertainment than for travellers to be remembering their country, their blessed home, and the happiness abiding them there, and to be refreshing and encouraging one another in the hopes of it ; strengthening their hearts against all the hard encounters and difficulties in the way ; often overlooking this moment, and helping each other to higher apprehensions of that vision of God which we expect.

And are not such discourses much more worthy the choosing, than the base trash we usually fill one another's ears withal? Were our tongues given us to exchange folly and sin? or were they not framed for the glorifying of God, and therefore are called *our glory?* Some take the expression for the soul; but they must be one in this work, and then, indeed, are both our tongues and our souls truly our glory, when they are busied in exalting his, and are tuned together to that. *That my glory may sing praise to thee and not be silent.* Psal. xxx. 12. Instead of calumnies, and lies, and vanities, the carrion which flies— base minds feed on, to delight in Divine things and extolling of God, is for a *man to eat Angels' food.* An excellent task for the tongue is that which David chooseth, Psal. xxxv. 28 : *And my tongue shall speak of thy righteousness, and of thy praise all the day long.* Were the day ten days long, no vacant room for any unholy, or offensive, or feigned speech! And they lose not, who love to speak praise to Him, for he loves to speak peace to them! and instead of the world's vain tongue-liberty, to have such intercourse and discourse, is no sad, melancholy life, as the world mistakes it.

Ver. 11. Let him eschew evil, and do good; let him seek peace, and ensue it.

THIS is a full and complete rule; but it is our miserable folly, to mistake so far, as to embrace evil under the notion of good; and not only contrary to the nature of the thing, but contrary to our own experience, still to be pursuing that which is still flying further off from us, catching at a vanishing shadow of delight, with nothing to fasten upon but real guiltiness and misery. Childish minds! we have been so often gulled, and yet never grow wiser, still bewitched and deluded with dreams : *a deceived heart* (a mocked or deluded heart) *hath turned him aside.* Isa. xliv. 20. When we think that we are surest, have that hand that holds fastest, our right hand, upon some good, and that now surely we are sped,—even then it proves *a lie in our right hand,* slips through as a handful of air and proves nothing, promises fair, but doth but mock us ; (as the same word is used by Jacob, Gen. xxxi. 7, expressing the unfaithfulness of his uncle, who changed his ways so often ;) yet still we foolishly and madly trust it ! When it makes so gross a lie, that we might easily, if we took it to the light, see through it, being a lie so often discovered, and of known falsehood, yet, some new dream or disguise makes it pass with us again, and we go round in that mill, having our eyes put out, like Samson, and still we are where we were, engaged in perpetual fruitless toil. Strange! that the base deceitful lusts of sin should still keep their credit with us! but *the beast hath a false prophet* at his side, Rev. xix. 20, to commend him and set him off with new inventions, and *causes us to err by his lies,* as it is said of the false prophets, Jer. xxiii. 32. But evil it is still ; not only void of all good, but the very deformity and debasement of the soul ; defacing in it the Divine image of its Maker, and impressing on it the vile image of Satan. And then, further, it is attended with shame and sorrow : even at the very best, *it is a sowing of the wind,*—there is no solid good in it,—and withal a *reaping of the whirlwind,* vexations and horrors. Hos. viii. 7. They that know it under a sense of this after-view, as attended with the wrath of an offended God, — ask them what they think of it ;

whether they would not, in those thoughts, choose any trouble or pain, though ever so great, rather than willingly to adventure on the ways of sin.

Obedience is that good, that beauty and comeliness of the soul, that conformity with the holy will of God, that hath peace and sweetness in it; the hardest exercise of it is truly delightful even at present, and hereafter it shall fully be so. Would we but learn to consider it thus, to know sin to be the greatest evil, and the holy will of God the highest good, it would be easy to persuade and prevail with men to comply with this advice, to *eschew* the one, and *do* the other.

These do not only reach the actions, but require an intrinsical aversion of the heart from sin, and a propension to holiness and the love of it.

Eschew.] The very motion and bias of the soul must be turned from sin, and carried towards God. And this is principally to be considered by us, and inquired after within us,—*an abhorrence of that which is evil*, as the Scripture speaks, Rom. xii. 9 : not a simple forbearing, but hating and loathing it, and this springing from the love of God. *Ye that love the Lord, hate evil*, says the Psalmist, xcvii. 10. You will do so, cannot choose but do so; and so may you know that love to him to be upright and true.

And where this love is, the avoidance of sin, and walking in holiness, or *doing good*, will be, 1. More constant, not wavering with the variation of outward circumstances, of occasion, or society, or secrecy, but going on in its natural course ; as the sun is as far from the earth, and goes as fast, under a cloud, as when it is in our sight, and goes cheerfully, because from a natural principle it *rejoiceth as a strong man to run*, Psal. xix. 5, such is the obedience of a renewed mind. And, 2. More universal, as proceeding from an abhorrence of all sin ; as natural antipathies are against the whole kind of any thing. 3. More exact, keeping afar off from the very appearances of sin, and from all the inducements and steps towards it. And this is the true way of *eschewing* it.

Not a little time of constrained forbearance during a night, or the day of participating of the communion, or a little time before and some few days after such services ; for thus, with the most, sin is not dispossessed and cast out, but retires inward and lurks in the heart. Being beset with those ordinances, it knows they last but awhile, and therefore it gets into its strength, and keeps close there, till they be out of sight and disappear again, and be a good way off, so that it thinks itself out of their danger, a good many days having passed, and then it comes forth and returns to exert itself with liberty, yea, it may be, with more vigour, as it were to regain the time it hath been forced to lose and lie idle in.

They again miss of the right manner of this eschewing, who think themselves, possibly, somebody in it, in that they do avoid the gross sins wherein the vulgar sort of sinners wallow, or do eschew such evils as they have little or no inclination of nature to. But where the heart stands against sin, as a breach of God's law and an offence against his majesty, as Joseph, *Shall I do this evil, and sin against God ?* Gen. xxxix. 9, there, it will carry a man against all kind of sin, the most refined and the most beloved sin, wherein the truth of this aversion is most tried and approved. As they who have a strong natural dislike of some kind of meat, dress it as you will, and mingle it with what they love best, yet will not willingly eat of it ; and if they be surprised and deceived some way to swallow some of it, yet they will discover it afterwards, and be restless till they have vomited it up again ; thus is it with the heart which hath that inward contrariety to sin wrought in it by a new nature,—it will consent to no reconcilement with it, nor with any kind of it; as in those deadly feuds which were against whole families and names without exception. The renewed soul will *have no fellowship with the unfruitful works of darkness*, as the Apostle speaks, Eph. v. 11. *For what agreement is there betwixt light and darkness ?* 2 Cor. vi. 14. And this hatred of sin works most against sin in a man's self; as in things we abhor, our reluctance rises most when they are nearest us. A godly man hates sin in others, as hateful wheresoever it is found ; but because it is nearest him in himself, he hates it most there. They who by their nature and breeding are somewhat delicate, like not to see any thing uncleanly any where, but least of all in their own house, and upon their own clothes or skin. This makes the godly man, indeed, flee not only the society of evil men, but from himself ; he goes out of his old self; and till this be done, a man does not indeed flee sin, but carries it still with him as an evil companion, or an evil guide rather, that misleads him still from the paths of life. And there is much, first in the true discovery, and then in the thorough disunion of the heart from that sin which is most of all a man's self, that from which he can with the greatest difficulty escape, *that besets him the most*, εὐπερίστατος, Heb. xii. 1, and lieth in his way on all hands, hath him at every turn : to disengage one's self and get free from that, to eschew that evil, is difficult indeed. And the task in this is the harder, if this evil be, as oftentimes it may be, not some gross sin, but one more subtle, less seen, and therefore not so easily avoided ; but for this an impartial search must be used : if it be amongst those things that seem most necessary, and that cannot be dispensed with, an idol hid amongst the stuff, yet thence must it be drawn forth and cast out.

The right eschewing of evil, involves a wary avoidance of all occasions and beginnings of it. *Flee from sin* (says the wise man) *as from a serpent*. Eccles. ii. 2. We are not to be tampering with it, and coming near it, and thinking to charm it ; " For (as one says) who will not laugh at the charmer that is bitten by a serpent ?" He that thinks he hath power and skill to handle it without danger, let him observe Solomon's advice concerning the strange woman : he says not only, *Go not into her house*, but, *Remove thy way far from her, and come not near the door of her house*. Prov. v. 8. So teaches he wisely for the avoiding of that other sin near to it, *Look not on the wine when it is red in the cup*, Prov. xxiii. 31. They that are bold and adventurous, are often wounded : thus, *He that removeth stones shall be hurt thereby*. Eccles. x. 9. If we know our own weakness and the strength of sin, we shall fear to expose ourselves to hazards, and be willing even to abridge ourselves of some things lawful when they prove dangerous; for he that will do always all he lawfully may, shall often do something that lawfully he may not.

Thus for the other, [*Do good,*] the main thing is, to be inwardly principled for it; to have a heart stamped with the love of God and his commandments; to do all for conscience of his will, and love to him, and desire of his glory. A good action, even the best kind of actions, in an evil hand, and from an evil, unsanctified heart, passes amongst evils. *Delight in the Lord* and in his ways. David's *Oh how love I thy law!* Psal. cxix. 17, tells that he esteems it above the richest and pleasantest things on earth, but how much he esteems and loves it he cannot express.

And upon this will follow (as observed in regard to eschewing evil) a constant track and course of obedience, moving directly contrary to the stream of wickedness about a man, and also against the bent of his own corrupt heart within him; a serious desire and endeavour to do all the good that is within our calling and reach, but especially that particular good of our calling, that which *is in our hand,* and is peculiarly required of us. For in this some deceive themselves; they look upon such a condition as they imagine were fit for them, or such as is in their eye when they look upon others, and they think if they were such persons, and had such a place, and such power and opportunities, they would do great matters, and in the mean time they neglect that good to which they are called, and which they have in some measure power and place to do. This is the roving, sickly humour of our minds, and speaks their weakness; as sick persons would still change their bed, or posture, or place of abode, thinking to be better. But a staid mind applies itself to the duties of *its own station,* and seeks to glorify him who set it there, reverencing his wisdom in disposing of it so. And there is certainty of a blessed approbation of this conduct. Be thy station never so low, it is not the high condition, but much fidelity, secures it: *Thou hast been faithful in little,* Luke xix. 17. We must care not only to answer occasions, when they call, but to catch at them, and seek them out; yea, to frame occasions of doing good, whether in the Lord's immediate service, delighting in that, private and public, or in doing good to men, in assisting one with our means, another with *our admonitions, another* with counsel or comfort as we can; labouring not only *to have something* of that good which is most contrary to our nature, but even *to be eminent in that,* setting Christian resolution, and both the example and strength of our Lord, against all oppositions, and difficulties, and discouragements: *Looking unto Jesus the author and finisher of our faith,* Heb. xii. 2.

We see, then, our Rule, and it is the rule of peace and happiness; what hinders but we apply our hearts to it? This is our work, and setting aside the advantage that follows, consider the thing in itself: 1. The opposition of sin and obedience, under the name of *evil* and *good;* 2. The composition of our rule in these expressions, *Eschew* and *Do.* Consider it thus—*evil* and *good,* and it will persuade us to *eschew* and *do.*

And if you are persuaded to it, then, 1. Desire light from above, to discover to you what is evil and offensive to God in any kind, and what pleaseth him, what is his will; (for that is the rule and reason of good in our actions, *that ye may prove what is the good, and holy, and acceptable will of God,* Rom. xii. 2 ;) and to discover in yourselves what is most adverse and repugnant to that will. 2. Seek a renewed mind to hate that evil, even such as is the closest and most connatural to you, and to love that good, even that which is most contrary. 3. Seek strength and skill, that by another Spirit than your own, you may *avoid evil and do good,* and resist the incursions and solicitings of evil, the artifices and violences of Satan, who is both a *serpent* and a *lion;* and seek for power against your own inward corruption, and the fallacies of your own heart. And thus you shall be able for *every good work,* and be kept, in such a measure as suits your present estate, *blameless in spirit, soul, and body, to the coming of Jesus Christ.* 1 Thess. v. 23.

"Oh!" but says the humble Christian, "I am often entangled and "plunged in soul-evils, and often frustrated in my thoughts against "these evils, and in my aims at the good, which is my task and duty."

And was not this Paul's condition ? May you not complain in his language ? And happy will you be, if you do so with some measure of his feeling ; happy in crying out of *wretchedness!* Was not this his malady, *When I would do good, evil is present with me?* Rom. vii. 21. But know at once, that though thy duty is this, *to eschew evil and do good,* yet thy salvation is more surely founded than on thine own good. That perfection which answers to justice and the Law, is not required of thee. Thou art to *walk, not after the flesh, but after the Spirit;* but in so walking, whether in a low or a high measure, still thy comfort lieth in this, that *there is no condemnation to them that are in Christ Jesus,* as the Apostle begins the next chapter (Rom. viii.) after his sad complaints. Again, consider his thoughts in the close of the viith chapter, on perceiving the work of God in himself, and distinguishing that from the corrupt motions of nature, and so finding at once matter of heavy complaint, and yet of cheerful exultation : *O wretched man that I am!* and yet with the same breath, *Thanks to God, through Christ Jesus our Lord.*

So then, mourn with him, and yet rejoice with him, and go on with courage as he did, still *fighting the good fight of faith.* When thou fallest in the mire, be ashamed and humbled, yet return and wash in *the fountain opened,* and return and beg new strength *to walk more surely.* Learn to trust thyself less, and God more, and up and be doing against thy enemies, how tall and mighty soever be the sons of Anak. *Be of good courage,* and the Lord shall be with thee, and *shall strengthen thy heart,* and establish thy goings.

Do not lie down to rest upon lazy conclusions, that it is well enough with thee, because thou art out of the common puddle of profaneness ; but look further, to *cleanse thyself from all filthiness of flesh and spirit, perfecting holiness in the fear of God.* 2 Cor. vii. 1. Do not think thy little is enough, or that thou hast reason to despair of attaining more, but press, *press hard toward the mark and prize of thy high calling.* Phil. iii. 14. Do not think all is lost, because thou art at present foiled. *Novit se sæpe vicisse post sanguinem,* says Seneca : The experienced soldier knows that he hath often won the day after a fall, or a wound received ; and be assured that, after the short combats of a moment, follows an eternity of triumph.

Let him seek peace and ensue it.] Omitting the many acceptations of the word *Peace*, here particularly external peace with men, I conceive, is meant ; and this is to be sought, and not only to be sought when it is willingly found, but we are to pursue and follow it when it seems to fly away ; but yet, so to pursue it, as never to step out of the way of holiness and righteousness after it, and to forsake this rule that goes before it, of *eschewing evil and doing good.* Yea, mainly in so doing is peace to be sought and pursued, and it is most readily to be found and overtaken in that way : for *the fruit of righteousness is peace.* James iii. 18.

1st, Consider that an unpeaceable, turbulent disposition is the badge of a wicked mind ; *as the raging sea, still casting up mire and dirt.* Isa. lvii. 20. But this love of peace, and in all good ways seeking and pursuing it, is the true character *of the children of God,* who is *the God of peace.* True, the ungodly (to prevent their own just challenge, as Ahab) call the friends of true religion, disturbers, and the *troublers of Israel,* 1 Kings xviii. 17 ; and this will still be their impudence : but, certainly, they *that love the welfare of Jerusalem, do seek, and pray for,* and work for *peace* all they can, as a chief blessing, and the fruitful womb of multitudes of blessings.

2ndly, Consider, then, that to be deprived of peace, is a heavy judgment, and calls for our prayers and tears to pursue it and entreat its return ; calls us to seek it from His hand who is the sovereign dispenser of peace and war, to seek to *be at peace with him, and thereby good, all good shall come unto us,* (Job xxii. 21,) and particularly this great good of outward peace in due time ; and the very judgment of war shall in the event be turned into a blessing. We may pursue it amongst men, and not overtake it ; we may use all good means, and fall short ; but pursue it up as far as the throne of grace, seek it by prayer, and that will overtake it, will be sure to find it in God's hand, *who stilleth the waves of the sea, and the tumults of the people. If he give quietness, who then can disturb ?* Psal. lxv. 7 ; Job xxxiv. 29.

He that will love life.] This is the attractive,—*Life. Long life and days of good,* is the thing men most desire ; for if they be evil days, then so much the worse that they be long, and the shortest of such seem too long ; and if short, being good, this cuts off the enjoyment of that good : but these two complete the good, and suit it to men's wishes,— length and prosperity of life.

It is here supposed that all would be happy, that all desire it, being carried to that by nature, to seek their own good : but he that *will love it,* that means here, that will wisely love it, that will take the way to it, and be true to his desire, *must refrain his tongue from evil, and his lips that they speak no guile ; he must eschew evil and do good, seek peace and ensue it.* You desire to see good days, and yet hinder them by sinful provocations ; you desire good clear days, and yet cloud them by your guiltiness.

Thus many desire good here, yea, and confusedly desire the good of the life to come, because they hear it is life, and long life, and that good is to be found in it, yea, nothing but good: but in this is our folly, we will not love it wisely. The face of our desire is towards it, but in our course we are rowing from it down into the dead sea. You would all have better times, peace and plenty, and freedom from the molestation and expense of our present condition : why will you not be persuaded to seek it in the true way of it ?

But how is this ? Do not the righteous often pass their days in distress and sorrow, so as to have *few and evil days*, as Jacob speaks, Gen. xlvii. 9 ? Yet is there a truth in this promise, annexing outward good things to godliness, *as having the promises of this life and that which is to come.* 1 Tim. iv. 8. And it is so accomplished to them, when the Lord sees it convenient and conducive to their highest good : but that he most aims at, and they themselves do most desire; and therefore, if the abatement of outward good, either as to the length or sweetness of this life, serve his main end and theirs better, they are agreed upon this gainful commutation of good for infinitely better.

The life of a godly man, though short in comparison of the utmost of nature's course, yet may be long in value, in respect of his activity and attainment to much spiritual good. He may be said to live much in a little time; whereas they that wear out their days in folly and sin, *diu vivunt sed parum, i. e.,* they live long, but little; or, as the same writer again speaks, *non diu vixit, diu fuit, i. e.,* he lived not long, but existed long. And the good of the godly man's days, though unseen good, surpasses all the world's mirth and prosperity, which makes a noise, but is hollow within, as the *crackling of thorns,* a great sound, but little heat, and quickly done. As St. Augustine says of Abraham, he had *dies bonos in Deo, licet malos in seculo,* good days in God, though evil days in his generation; a believer can make up an ill day with a good God, and enjoying him, he hath solid peace. But then that which is abiding, that length of days, and that dwelling in the house of God in that length of days, is what *eye hath not seen, nor ear heard,* &c. 1 Cor. ii. 9. They are, indeed, *good days,* or rather one everlasting day, which has *no need of the sun, nor of the moon,* but immediately flows from the first and increated Light, *the Father of lights;* his glory shines in it, *and the Lamb is the Light thereof.*

Ver. 12. For the eyes of the Lord are over the righteous, and his ears are open unto their prayers : but the face of the Lord is against them that do evil.

THE wisest knowledge of things is, to know them in their causes ; but there is no knowledge of causes so happy and useful, as clearly to know and firmly to believe the universal dependence of all things upon the First and Highest Cause, the Cause of causes, the Spring of being and goodness, the wise and just Ruler of the world.

This the Psalmist, Psalm xxxiv. 15, 16, as here with him the Apostle, give us the true reason of that truth they have averred in the former words, the connexion of holiness and happiness. If life, and peace, and all good be in God's hand to bestow when it pleaseth him, then surely the way to it is an obedient and regular walking in observance of his will ; and the way of sin is the way to ruin: *For the eyes of the Lord are upon the righteous,* &c., *and his face is against them that do evil.*

In the words there is a double opposition ; of persons, and of their portion.

1*st*, Of persons, The *righteous* and *evil-doers.* These two words are often used in the Scriptures, and particularly in the book of Psalms, to express the godly and the wicked ; and so this righteousness is not absolute perfection or sinlessness, nor is the opposed evil every act of sin or breach of God's law : but the righteous be they that are students of obedience and holiness, that desire to walk as in the sight of God, and to *walk with God*, as Enoch did ; that are glad when they can any way serve him, and grieved when they offend him ; that feel and bewail their unrighteousness, and are earnestly breathing and advancing forward ; have a sincere and unfeigned love to all the commandments of God, and diligently endeavour to observe them ; that vehemently hate what most pleases their corrupt nature, and love the command that crosses it most ; this is an imperfect kind of perfection. See Phil. iii. 12, 15.

On the other side, evil-doers are they that commit sin *with greediness;* that walk in it, make it their way ; that live in sin as their element, *taking pleasure in unrighteousness,* as the Apostle speaks, 2 Thess. ii. 12 ; their great faculty, their great delight lies in sin ; they are skilful and cheerful evil-doers. Not any one man in all kinds of sins ; that is impossible ; there is a concatenation of sin, and one disposes and induces to another ; but yet one ungodly man is commonly more versed in and delighted with some one kind of sin, another with some other. He forbears none because it is evil and hateful to God, but as he cannot travel over the whole globe of wickedness, and go the full circuit, he walks up and down in his accustomed way of sin. No one mechanic is good at all trades, nor is any man expert in all arts ; but he is an evil-doer that follows the particular trade of the sin he hath chosen, is active and diligent in that, and finds it sweet. In a word, this opposition lieth mainly in the bent of the affection, or in the way it is set. The godly man hates the evil he possibly by temptation hath been drawn to do, and loves the good he is frustrated of, and, having intended, hath not attained to do. The sinner who hath his denomination from sin as his course, hates the good which he is sometimes forced to do, and loves that sin which many times he does not, either wanting occasion and means, so that he cannot do it, or through the check of an enlightened conscience, possibly dares not do ; and though so bound up from the act, as a dog in a chain, yet the habit, the natural inclination and desire in him, is still the same, the strength of his affection is carried to sin. So in the weakest godly man, there is that predominant sincerity and desire of holy walking, according to which he is called a righteous person, the Lord is pleased to give him that name, and account him so, being upright in heart, though often failing. There is a righteousness of a higher strain, upon which his salvation hangs ; that is not in him, but upon him ; he is clothed with it : but this other kind, which consists of sincerity, and of true and hearty, though imperfect obedience, is the righteousness here meant, and opposed to evil-doing.

2*ndly*, Their opposite condition, or portion, is expressed in the highest notion of it, that wherein the very being of happiness and misery lieth, the favour and anger of God.   As their natures differ most by the habit of their affection towards God, as their main distinguishing character, so the difference of their estate consists in the point of his affection towards them, expressed here, in our language, by the divers aspects of his countenance ; because our love or hatred usually looks out, and shows itself that way.

Now for the other word expressing his favour to the righteous, by *the openness of his ear*,—the opposition in the other needed not be expressed ; for either the wicked pray not, or if they do, it is indeed no prayer, the Lord doth not account or receive it as such ; and if his face be set against them, certainly his ear is shut against them too, and so shut that it openeth not to their loudest prayer.   *Though they cry in mine ears with a loud voice, yet will I not hear them*, says the Lord, Ezek. viii. 18.

And before we pass to the particulars of their condition, as here we have them described, this we would consider a little, and apply it to our present business,—Who are the persons whom the Lord thus regards, and to whose prayer he opens his ear.

This we pretend to be seeking after, that the Lord would look favourably upon us, and hearken to our suits, for ourselves, and this land, and the whole Church of God within these kingdoms.   Indeed *the fervent prayer of a faithful man availeth much* [πολὺ ἰσχύει] ; it is of great strength, a mighty thing, that can bind and loose the influences of heaven (as there is instanced, James v. 16) ; and if the prayer of a righteous man, be it but of one righteous man, how much more the combined cries of many of them together !   And that we judge not the righteousness there and here mentioned to be a thing above human estate, Elias, says the Apostle, *was a man*, and *a man subject to like passions as we are*, and yet such a righteous person as the Lord had an eye and gave ear to in so great a matter.   But where are those righteous fasters and prayers in great congregations ?   How few, if any, are to be found, who are such but in the lowest sense and measure, real lovers and inquirers after holiness !   What are our meetings here, but assemblies of evil-doers, rebellious children, ignorant and profane persons, or dead, formal professors ; and so, the more of us, the worse, incensing the Lord the more ; and the multitude of prayers, though we could and would continue many days, all to no purpose from such as we.   *Though ye make many prayers, when ye multiply prayer, I will not hear ; and when ye spread forth your hands, I will hide mine eyes from you.*   Isa. i. 11.   Your hands are so filthy, that if you would follow me to lay hold of me with them, you drive me further off ; as one with foul hands following a person that is neat, to catch hold of him ; and *if you spread them out before me*, my eyes are pure, you will make me turn away ; I cannot endure to look upon them, *I will hide mine eyes from you.*   And fasting, added with prayer, will not do it, nor make it pass.   *When they fast, I will not hear their cry.*   Jer. xiv. 12.

It is the sin of his people that provokes him, instead of looking favourably upon them, to have *his eyes upon them for evil and not for good*, as he threatens, Amos ix. 4 ; and therefore, without putting away of that, prayer is lost breath, doth no good.

They that still retain their sins, and will not hearken to his voice, how can they expect but that justly threatened retaliation, Prov. i. 26, 28, and that the Lord, in holy scorn, in the day of their distress, should send them for help and comfort to those things which they have made their gods, and preferred before him in their trouble? *They will say, Arise and save us. But where are the gods that thou hast made thee? Let them arise, if they can save thee in the time of thy trouble.* Jer. ii. 28.

And not only do open and gross impieties thus disappoint our prayers, but the lodging of any sin in our affection. *If I regard iniquity in my heart,* says the Psalmist, (Psal. lxvi. 18,) *the Lord will not hear my voice.* The word is, *If I see iniquity;* if mine eye look pleasantly upon it, his will not look so upon me, nor shall I find his ear so ready and open. He says not, If I do sin, but, *If I regard it in my heart.* The heart's entertaining and embracing a sin, though it be a smaller sin, is more than the simple falling into sin. And as the ungodly do for this reason lose all their prayers, a godly man may suffer this way, in some degree, upon some degree of guiltiness. The heart being seduced, it may be, and entangled for a time by some sinful lust, Christians are sure to find a stop in their prayers, that they neither go nor come so quickly and so comfortably as before. Any sinful humour, as rheums do our voice, binds up the voice of prayer, makes it not so clear and shrill as it was wont; and the accusing guilt of it ascending, shuts up the Lord's ear, that he doth not so readily hear and answer as before. And thus that sweet correspondence is interrupted, which all the delights of the world cannot compensate. If, then, you would have easy and sweet accesses to God in prayer,

1. Seek a holy heart; entertain a constant care and study of holiness; admit no parley with sin; do not so much as hearken to it, if you would be readily heard.

2. Seek a broken heart; the Lord is ever at hand to that, as it is in Psal. xxxiv., whence the Apostle cites the words now under our consideration, *He is nigh to them that are of a contrite spirit,* ver. 18, &c.; it is an excellent way to prevail. The breaking of the heart multiplies petitioners; every piece of it hath a voice, and a very strong and very moving voice, that enters his ear, and stirs the bowels and compassions of the Lord towards it.

3. Seek a humble heart. That may present its suit always; the court is constantly there, even within it; the Great King loves to make his abode and residence in it. Isa. lvii. 15. This is the thing that the Lord so delights in and requires; he will not fail to accept of it; it is his choice. Mic. vi. 7, 8, *Wherewith shall I come before the Lord? &c. He hath showed thee, O man, what is good; and what doth the Lord require of thee, but to do justly, and love mercy?* There is this righteousness, and that as a great part making it up, *to walk humbly with thy God;* in the original, *humble to walk with thy God;* he cannot agree with a proud heart; he hates, resists it; and *two cannot walk together unless they be agreed,* as the prophet speaks, Amos iii. 3. The humble heart only is company for God, hath liberty to walk and converse with him. *He gives grace to the humble;* he bows his ear, if thou lift not up thy neck: proud beggars he turns away with

disdain, and the humblest suitors always speed best with him.   *The righteous*, not such in their own eyes, but in his, through his gracious dignation and acceptance.   And is there not reason to come humbly before Him,—base worms, to the most holy and most high God ?

The eyes of the Lord.]   We see, 1. That both are *in his sight*, the righteous and the wicked ; all of them, and all their ways.   His eye is on the one, and his face on the other, as the word is ; but so on these as to be against them.   It is therefore rendered as denoting his eye of knowledge and observance, marking them and their actions, which is equally upon both.   *There is no darkness nor shadow of death where the workers of iniquity may hide themselves.* Job xxxiv. 22.   Foolishly and wretchedly done, to do that, or think that, which we would hide from the Lord, and then to think that we can hide it !   The prophet speaks woe to such : *Woe to them that dig deep to hide their counsel from the Lord, and their works are in the dark, and they say, Who seeth us, and who knoweth us ?* Isa. xxix. 15.   And this is the grand principle of all wickedness, (not, it may be, expressly stated, but secretly lying in the soul,) an habitual forgetting of God and his eye, not considering that he beholds us.   *Ye that forget God*, says the Psalmist (l. 22); thence all impiety proceeds ; and, on the other side, *the remembrance* of his eye, is a radical point of piety and holiness, in which the cxxxixth Psalm is large and excellent.

But, 2. as the Lord doth thus equally see both, so as that his eye and countenance imports his mind concerning them and towards them, the manner of his beholding them is different, yea, contrary.   And from the other,—the beholding them in common—knowing their ways —arises this different beholding, which (as usually words of sense signify also the affection, *verba sensûs connotant affectus*) is the approving and disliking, the loving and hating them, and their ways : so he peculiarly *knows the righteous* and their *ways*, Psal. i. 6, and *knows not, never knew, the workers of iniquity ;* even those that by their profession would plead most acquaintance, and familiar converse, *eating and drinking in his presence*, and yet, *I know you not, whence you are.* Luke xiii. 26.   It is not a breaking off from former acquaintance ; no, he doth not that ; he disavows none that ever were truly acquainted with him.   So the other evangelist hath it, Matt. vii. 29 ; of those that thought to have been in no small account, *I never knew you, depart from me ;* and the convincing reason lies in that, *ye workers of iniquity :* none of his favourites and friends are such.

Thus here, his eye, his gracious eye for good, is on the righteous ; and his face, his angry looks, his just wrath, against evil-doers.

In the xith Psalm we have this expressed much after the same way.   First, what we spoke of God's knowing and beholding in common the righteous and wicked, and their ways, is represented by his *sitting on high*, where he may mark, and see clearly throughout all places and all hearts.   *His throne is in heaven, his eyes behold, his eyelids try the children of men*, ver. 4.   He sits in heaven, not as in a chair of rest, regardless of human things, but on *a throne* for governing and judging ; though with as little uneasiness and disturbance, as if there were nothing to be done that way.   *His eyes behold*, not in a fruitless contemplation or knowledge, but *His eyelids try*, which signifies an intent inspection, such as men usually make with a kind of motion of their eyelids. Then upon this is added the different portion of the righteous and wicked, in his beholding them and dealing with them: *The Lord trieth the righteous*, ver. 5, approves what is good in them, and by trial and affliction doth purge out what is evil; and in both these there is love; *but the wicked, and him that loveth violence, his soul hateth;* and therefore, as here, *his face is against them.* His soul and face are all one, but these things are expressed after our manner. He looks upon them with indignation; and thence come the storms in the next verse, *Snares rained down*, ver. 6; the wariest foot cannot avoid such snares, they come down upon them from above: *Fire and brimstone and burning tempest* (alluding to *Sodom's* judgment, as an emblem of the punishment of all the wicked); *this is the portion of their cup.* There is a cup for them; but his children drink not with them. *They* have another cup; *the Lord* himself *is the portion of their cup.* Psal. xvi. 5. As the xith Psalm closes, *The righteous Lord loveth righteousness: his countenance doth behold the upright:* that is another beholding than the former, a gracious, loving beholding; as here, *His eyes are upon the righteous.*

Now the persuasion of this truth is the main establishment of a godly mind, amidst all the present confusions that appear in things; and it is so here intended, as well as in the Psalm I have mentioned, and throughout the Scriptures.

To look upon the present flourishing and prosperity of evil-doers, and on the distresses and sorrows of the godly, is a dark, obscure matter in itself; but the way to be cleared and comforted, is, to look above them to the Lord. *They looked unto him and were lightened.* Psal. xxxiv. 5. That answers all doubts, to believe this undoubted providence and justice, the eye of God that sees all, yea, rules all these things. And in the midst of all the painted happiness of wicked men, this is enough to make them miserable. *The Lord's face is against them;* and they shall surely find it so. He hath wrath and judgment in store, and *will bring it forth to light*, will execute it in due time; he is preparing for them that cup spoken of, and they shall drink it. So, in the saddest condition of his Church and a believing soul, to know this, that the Lord's eye is even then upon them, and that he is upon thoughts of peace and love to them, is that which settles and composes the mind. Thus, in that Psalm before cited, it was such difficulties that did drive David's thoughts to that for satisfaction: *If the foundations be destroyed, what can the righteous do?* Psal. xi. 3. In the time of such great shakings and confusions, the righteous man can do nothing to it, but the righteous Lord can do enough; He can do all, *The righteous Lord that loveth righteousness.* While all seems to go upside down, *He is on his throne*, he is *trying and judging*, and will appear to be judge. This is the thing that faithful souls should learn to look to, and not lose view and firm belief of, and should desire the Lord himself to raise their minds to it, when they are ready to sink. Natural strength and resolution will not serve the turn; floods may come that will arise above that; something above a man's own spirit must support him: therefore say with David, Psal. lxi. 2, *When my spirit is overwhelmed, lead me to the rock that is higher than I.* They think sometimes it is so hard with them, that he regards not ; but he assures them to the contrary, *I have graven thee upon the palms of mine hands*, Isa. xlix. 16. I cannot look upon my own hands, but I must remember thee : *And thy walls are continually before me.* This is what the spouse seeks for, *Set me as a seal upon thine arm.* Cant. viii. 6.

Now a little more particularly to consider the expressions, and their scope here ; how is that made good which the former words teach, that they who walk in the ways of wickedness can expect no good, but are certainly miserable ? Thus : *the face of the Lord is against them.* Prosper they may in their affairs and estates, may have riches, and posterity, and friends, and the world caressing them and smiling on them on all hands ; but there is that one thing that damps all, *the face of the Lord is against them.* This they feel not indeed for the time ; it is an invisible ill, out of sight and out of mind with them ; but there is a time of the appearing of *this face of the Lord against them, the revelation of his righteous judgment,* as the Apostle speaks, Rom. ii. 5. Sometimes they have precursory days of it here ; there is, however, one great prefixed day, *a day of darkness* to them indeed, wherein they shall know what this is, that now sounds so light, *to have the face of the Lord against them.* A look of it is more terrible than all present miseries combined together ; what then shall the eternity of it be ? *to be punished* (as the Apostle speaks) *with everlasting destruction from the presence of the Lord, and the glory of his power!* 2 Thess. i. 9.

Are we not then impertinent, foolish creatures, who are so thoughtful how our poor business here succeed with us, and how we are accounted of in the world, and how the faces of men are towards us, and scarcely ever enter into a secret, serious inquiry how the countenance of God is to us, whether favourably shining on us, or still angrily *set against us,* as it is against all impenitent sinners ?

The face of the soul being towards God, turned away from the world and sin, argues for it, that his face is not against it, but that he hath graciously looked upon it, and by a look of love hath drawn it towards himself ; for we act not first in that. *Non amatur Deus nisi de Deo :* There is no love of God but what comes from God. It is he that prevents us, and by the beams of his love kindles love in our hearts. Now the soul that is thus set towards him, it may be, doth not constantly see here his face shining full and clear upon it, but often clouded ; nay, it may be, such a soul hath not yet at all seen it sensibly ; yet this it may conclude, " Seeing *my desires are towards him,* " and my chief desire is the sweet *light of his countenance,* though as " yet I find not his face shining on me, yet I am persuaded it is not " *set against me* to destroy me." Misbelief, when the soul is much under its influence and distempered by it, may suggest this sometimes too ; but yet still there is some spark of hope that it is otherwise, that the eye of the Lord's pity is even in that estate upon us, and will in time manifest itself to be so.

To the other question, What assurance have the godly for that *seeing of good,* these blessings you speak of ? This is the answer : *The eyes of the Lord are upon them, and his ears open to their prayer.* If you

think him wise enough to know what is good for them, and rich
enough to afford it, they are sure of one thing, he loves them ; they
have his good will ; his heart is towards them, and therefore his eye
and his ear.   Can they then want any good ?   If *many days* and outward good things be indeed good for them, they cannot miss of these.
He hath given them already much better things than these, and hath
yet far better in store for them ; and what way soever the world go
with them, this itself is happiness enough, that they are in his love,
whose loving-kindness is better than life. Psal. lxiii. 3.   Sweet days have
they that live in it.   What better days would courtiers wish, than to
be still in the eye and favour of the king, to be certain of his good
will towards them, and to know of access and of a gracious acceptance of all their suits ?   Now thus it is with all the servants of the
Great King, without prejudice one to another ; he is ready to receive
their requests, and able and willing to do them all good.   Happy
estate of a believer !   He must not account himself poor and destitute
in any condition, for he hath favour at court ; he hath the King's eye
and his ear ; *the eyes of the Lord are upon him, and his ears open to
his prayers.*

The eyes of the Lord are upon the righteous.]   This hath in it,
1. His love, the propension of his heart towards them.   The eye is
the servant of the affection ; it naturally turns that way most, where
the heart is.   Therefore thus the Lord is pleased to speak of his love
to his own.   He views still all the world, but he looks upon them
with a peculiar delight ; his eye is still on them, as it were, turned
towards them from all the rest of the world.   Though he doth not
always let them see these his looks, (for it is not said, they always are
in sight of it ; no, not here ;) yet still, his eye is indeed upon them,
attracted by the beauty of grace in them, his own work indeed, the
beauty that he himself hath put upon them.   And so as to the other,
his ear too ; he is willing to do for them what they ask ; he loves even
to hear them speak ; finds a sweetness in the voice of their prayers,
that makes his ear not only *open to their prayers,* but desirous of them
as sweet music.   Thus he speaks of both, Cant. ii. 14, *My dove, let me
see thy countenance, let me hear thy voice, for sweet is thy voice, and
thy countenance is comely.*

2. The phrase expresses his good providence and readiness to do
them good ; to supply their wants, and order their affairs for them ;
to answer their desires, and thus to let them find the fruits of that love
which so leads his eye and ear towards them.   *His eye is upon them;*
he is devising and thinking what to do for them ; it is the thing he
thinks on most.   His eyes are upon all, but they are busied, as he is
pleased to express it, *they run to and fro through the earth, to show
himself strong in behalf of them, whose heart is perfect towards him,* &c.
2 Chron. xvi. 9.   So Deut. xi. 12, *His eyes are all the year on the
land.*   No wonder, then, he answers their suits in what is good for
them, when it is still in his thoughts before.   *He prevents them with
the blessings of his goodness,* Psalm xxi. 3 : they cannot be so mindful
of themselves, as he is of them.

This is an unspeakable comfort, when a poor believer is in great
perplexity of any kind in his outward or spiritual condition.   " Well,

"I see no way; I am blind in this, but there are *eyes upon me,* that "see well what is best. The Lord is minding me, and bringing about "all to my advantage. *I am poor and needy, indeed, but the Lord* "*thinketh on me,* Psal. xl. 17." That turns the balance. Would not a man, though he had nothing, think himself happy, if some great prince was busily thinking how to advance and enrich him? Much more, if a number of kings were upon this thought, and devising together. Yet *these thoughts might perish,* as the Psalmist speaks, Psal. cxlvi. 4. How much more solid happiness is it to have Him, whose power is greatest, and whose thoughts fail not, eyeing thee, and devising thy good, and asking us, as it were, *What shall be done to the man whom the king will honour?*

And his ears are open unto their prayer.] What suits thou hast, thou mayest speak freely; he will not refuse thee any thing that is for thy good.

"O! but I am not *righteous,* and all this is for the righteous only." Yet thou wouldst be such a one. Wouldst thou indeed? then in part thou art: (as he who modestly and wisely changed the name of *wise men* into *philosophers,* lovers of wisdom:) art thou not righteous? yet, (φιλοδίκαιος) a *lover of righteousness* thou art; then thou art one of the righteous. If still thine own unrighteousness be in thine eye, it may and should be so, to humble thee; but if it should scare thee from coming unto God, and offering thy suits with this persuasion, that *his ear is open,* should it make thee think that his favourable eye is not toward thee, yet there is mercy; creep in under the robe of his Son. Thou art sure *he* is *Jesus Christ the righteous,* and that the Father's eye is on him with delight, and then it shall be so on thee, being in him. Put thy petitions into his hand, who is the great Master of Requests; thou canst not doubt that he hath access, and that he hath that ear open to him, which thou thinkest shut to thee.

The exercise of prayer being so important, and bearing so great a part in the life and comfort of a Christian, it deserves to be very seriously considered. We will therefore subjoin some few considerations concerning it.

Prayer may be considered in a threefold notion. 1. As a duty we owe to God. As it is from him we expect and receive all, it is a very reasonable homage and acknowledgment, thus to testify the dependence of our being and life on him, and the dependence of our souls upon him, for being, and life, and all good; that we be daily suitors before his throne, and go to him for all. 2. As it constitutes the dignity and the delight of a spiritual mind, to have so near access unto God, and such liberty to speak to him. 3. As a proper and sure means, by Divine appointment and promise, of obtaining at the hands of God those good things that are needful and convenient for us. And although some believers of lower knowledge do not (it may be) so distinctly know, and others not so particularly consider, all these in it, yet there is a latent notion of them all in the heart of every godly person, which stirs them and puts them on to the constant use of prayer, and to a love of it.

And as they are in these respects inclined and bent to the exercise of prayer, the Lord's ear is in like manner inclined to hear their prayer in these respects. 1. He takes it well at their hands, that they do offer it up as due worship to him, that they desire thus as they can to serve him. He accepts of those offerings graciously, passes by the imperfections in them, and hath regard to their sincere intention and desire. 2. It pleases him well that they delight in prayer, as converse with him; that they love to be much with him, and to speak to him often, and still aspire, by this way, to more acquaintance with him; that they are ambitious of this. 3. He willingly hears their prayers as the expressions of their necessities and desires; being both rich and bountiful, he loves to have blessings drawn out of his hands that way; as full breasts delight to be drawn. The Lord's treasure is always full, and therefore he is always communicative. In the first respect, prayer is acceptable to the Lord *as incense and sacrifice*, as David desires, Psal. cxli. 12 : the Lord receives it as Divine worship done to him. In the second respect, prayer is as the visits and sweet entertainment and discourse of friends together, and so is pleasing to the Lord, as the free opening of the mind, the *pouring out of the heart to him*, as it is called, Psal. lxii. 8 ; and David, in Psal. v. 1, calls it *his words* and *his meditation;* the word for that signifies *discourse* or *conference.* And, in the third sense, the Lord receives prayer as the suits of petitioners who are in favour with him, and whom he readily accords to. And this the word for *supplication* in the original, and the word here rendered *prayer*, and that rendered *cry*, in the Psalm, do mean ; and in that sense, the Lord's open ear and hearkening hath in it his readiness to answer, as one that doth hear, and to answer graciously and really, as hearing favourably.

I shall now add some directions : I. For prayer, that it may be accepted and answered. II. For observing the answers of it.

I. For prayer. 1. The qualification of the heart that offers it. 2. The way of offering it.

1. As to the qualification of the heart, it must be in some measure, 1*st*, A holy heart, according to that word here, *the righteous.* There must be *no regarding iniquity*, no entertaining of friendship with any sin, but a permanent love and desire of holiness. Thus, indeed, a man prays within himself, as in a sanctified place, whither the Lord's ear inclines, as of old to the Temple. He needs not run superstitiously to a church, &c. *Intra te ora, sed vide priùs an sis templum Dei:* Pray inwardly, but first see whether thou art thyself a temple of God. The sanctified man's body is the *temple of the Holy Ghost,* as the Apostle speaks, 1 Cor. vi. 19 ; and his soul is the priest in it that offers sacrifice : both holy to the Lord, consecrated to him. 2*ndly*, It must be a believing heart, for there is no praying without this. Faith is the very life of prayer, whence spring hope and comfort with it, to uphold the soul, and keep it steady under storms with the promises ; and as Aaron and Hur to Moses, keeping it from fainting, strengthening the hands when they would begin to fail. Such is the force of that word, Psal. x. 17 ; for the *preparing of the heart* which God gives as an assurance and pledge of his *inclining his ear to hear,* signifies the *establishing of the heart;* that, indeed, is a main point of its preparedness, and due disposition for prayer. Now this is done by faith, without which, the soul, as the Apostle St. James speaks, is a rolling

unquiet thing, *as a wave of the sea*, of itself unstable as the waters, and then *driven with the wind and tossed* to and fro with every temptation. See and feel thine own unworthiness as much as thou canst, for thou art never bidden to believe in thyself; no, but.that is countermanded as faith's great enemy. But what hath thy unworthiness to say against free promises of grace, which are the basis of thy faith? So then believe, that you may pray: this is David's advice, Psal. lxii. 8, *Trust in him at all times, ye people*, and then, *pour out your hearts before him.* Confide in him as a most faithful and powerful friend, and then you will open your hearts to him.

2. For the way of offering up prayer. It is a great art, a main point of the secret of religion, to be skilled in it, and of great concern for the comfort and success of it. Much is here to be considered, but for the present take these advices briefly. [1.] Offer not to speak to him without the heart in some measure seasoned and prepossessed with the sense of his greatness and holiness. And there is much in this; considering wisely to whom we speak, *the King, the Lord of glory*, and setting the soul before him, in his presence; and then reflecting on ourselves, and seeing what we are, how wretched, and base, and filthy, and unworthy of such access to so great a Majesty. The want of this *preparing of the heart* to speak in the Lord's ear, by the consideration of God and ourselves, is that which fills the excuse of prayer with much guiltiness; makes the heart careless, and slight, and irreverent, and so displeases the Lord, and disappoints ourselves of that comfort in prayer, and those answers of it, of which otherwise we should have more experience. We rush in before him with any thing, provided we can tumble out a few words; and do not weigh these things, and compose our hearts with serious thoughts and conceptions of God. The soul that studies and endeavours this most, hath much to do to attain to any right apprehensions of him; (for *how little know we of him!*) yet should we, at least, set ourselves before him as the purest and greatest Spirit; a being infinitely more excellent than our minds or any creature can conceive. This would fill the soul with awe and reverence, and ballast it, so as to make it go more even through the exercise; to consider *the Lord*, as that prophet saw him, *sitting on his throne, and all the host of heaven standing by him*, on his right hand and on his left, 1 Kings xxii. 19, and thyself a defiled sinner coming before him, *velut e palude suâ vilis ranuncula*, as a vile frog creeping out of some pool, as St. Bernard expresses it: how would this fill thee with holy fear! Oh! his greatness and our baseness, and oh! the distance! This is Solomon's advice: *Be not rash with thy mouth, and let not thy heart be hasty to utter any thing before God, for God is in heaven and thou upon earth, therefore let thy words be few.* Eccl. v. 2. This would keep us from our ordinary babblings, that heart-nonsense, which, though the words be sense, yet, through the inattention of the heart, are but as impertinent, confused dreams in the Lord's ear; as there it follows, ver. 3.

[2.] When thou addressest thyself to prayer, desire and depend upon the assistance and inspiration of the Holy Spirit of God; without which thou art not able truly to pray. It is a supernatural work, and therefore the principle of it must be supernatural. He that hath nothing of the Spirit of God, cannot pray at all : he may howl as a beast in his necessity or distress, or may speak words of prayer, as some birds learn the language of men ; but pray he cannot. And they that have that Spirit, ought to seek the movings and actual workings of it in them in prayer, as the particular *help of their infirmities*, teaching both what to ask, (a thing which of ourselves we know not,) and then enabling them to ask, breathing forth their desires in such sighs and groans, as are the breath not simply of their own, but of God's Spirit.

[3.] As these two precautions are to be taken before prayer, so, in the exercise of it, you should learn to keep a watchful eye over your own hearts throughout, for every step of the way, that they start not out. And in order to this, strive to keep up a continual remembrance of that presence of God, which, in the entry of the work, is to be set before the eye of the soul. And our endeavour ought to be to fix it upon that view, that it turn not aside nor downwards, but from beginning to end keep sight of him, who sees and marks whether we do so or no. They that are most inspective and watchful in this, will still be faulty in it ; but certainly the less watchful, the more faulty. And this we ought to do, to be aspiring daily to more stability of mind in prayer, and to be driving out somewhat of that roving and wandering, which is so universal an evil, and certainly so grievous, not to those who have it most, but who observe and discover it most and endeavour most against it. A strange thing ! that the mind, even the renewed mind, should be so ready, not only at other times, but in the exercise of prayer, wherein we peculiarly come so near to God, yet even then to slip out and leave him, and follow some poor vanity or other instead of him ! Surely the godly man, when he thinks on this, is exceedingly ashamed of himself, cannot tell what to think of it. *God is exceeding joy*, whom, in his right thoughts, he esteems so much above the world and all things in it, yet to use him thus !—when he is speaking to him, to break off from that, and hold discourse, or change a word with some base thought that steps in, and whispers to him ; or, at the best, not to be stedfastly minding the Lord to whom he speaks, and possessed with the regard of his presence, and of his business and errand with him.

This is no small piece of our misery here : these wanderings are evidence to us, that we are not at home. But though we should be humbled for this, and still be labouring against it, yet should we not be so discouraged, as to be driven from the work. Satan would desire no better than that ; it were to help him to his wish. And sometimes a Christian may be driven to think, " What ! shall I still do thus, " abusing my Lord's name, and the privilege he hath given me ? I " had better leave off." No, not so by any means. Strive against the miserable evil that is within thee, but cast not away thy happiness. Be doing still. It is a froward, childish humour, when any thing agrees not to our mind, to throw all away. Thou mayest come off, as Jacob, with *halting* from thy *wrestlings*, and yet obtain the *blessing* for which thou wrestlest.

[4.] Those graces which are the due qualities of the heart, disposing it for prayer in the exercise of it, should be excited and acted, as holiness, the love of it, the desire of increase and growth of it, so, the humbling and melting of the heart, and chiefly faith, which is mainly set on work in prayer, draw forth the sweetness and virtues of the promises, teaching us to desire earnestly their performance to the soul, and to believe that they shall be performed ; to have before our eyes His goodness and faithfulness who hath promised, and to rest upon that. And for success in prayer, exercising faith in it, it is altogether necessary to interpose the Mediator, and to look through him, and to speak and petition by him, who warns us of this, that there is no other way to speak : *No man cometh to the Father but by me.* John xiv. 6. As the Jews, when they prayed, looked toward the temple, where was the mercy-seat, and the peculiar presence of God, [*Schechinah,*] thus ought we in all our praying to look on Christ, who is our *propitiatory*, and *in whom the fulness of the Godhead dwells bodily.* Col. ii. 9. The forgetting of this, may be the cause of our many disappointments.

[5.] Fervency ; not to seek coldly : that presages refusal. There must be fire in the sacrifice, otherwise it ascends not. There is no sacrifice without incense, and no incense without fire. Our remiss, dead hearts are not likely to do much for the Church of God, nor for ourselves. Where are those strong cries that should pierce the heavens ? *His ear is open to their cry.* He hears the faintest, coldest prayer, but not with that delight and propenseness to grant it ; his ear is not on it, as the word there is, Psal. lv. 17 ; he takes no pleasure in hearing it ; but cries, heart-cries, oh ! these take his ear, and move his bowels ; for these are the voice, the cries of his own children. A strange word of encouragement to importunity is that, *Give him no rest,* Isa. lxii. 7, suffer him not to be in quiet till *he make Jerusalem a praise in the earth.* A few such suitors, in these times, were worth thousands such as we are. Our prayers stick in our breasts, scarcely come forth ; much less do they go up and ascend with that piercing force that would open up the way for deliverances to come down.

But in this there must be some difference between temporal and spiritual things. That prayer which is in the right strain, cannot be too fervent in any thing ; but the desire of the thing in temporals may be too earnest. A feverish, distempered heat diseases the soul ; therefore, in these things, a holy indifferency concerning the particular may, and should be, joined with the fervency of prayer. But in spiritual things, there is no danger in vehemency of desire. *Covet* these, *hunger and thirst* for them, be incessantly ardent in the suit ; yet even in these, in some particulars, (as with respect to the degree and measure of grace, and some peculiar furtherances,) they should be presented so with earnestness, as that withal it be with a reference and resignation of it to the wisdom and love of our Father.

II. For the other point, the answer of our prayers, which is implied in this *openness of the ear*, it is a thing very needful to be considered and attended to. If we think that prayer is indeed a thing that God takes notice of, and hath regard to in his dealings with his children, it is certainly a point of duty and wisdom in them, to observe how he takes notice of it, and bends his ear to it, and puts his hand to help, and so answers it. This both furnishes matter of praise, and stirs up the heart to render it. Therefore, in the Psalms, the *hearing of prayer* is so often observed and recorded, and made a part of the song of praise. And withal it endears both God and prayer unto the soul, as we have both together, Psal. cxvi. 1, *I love the Lord because he hath heard my voice and my supplications.* The transposition in the original is pathetical, *I love, because the Lord hath heard my voice.* I am in love, and particularly this causes it ; I have found so much kindness in the Lord, I cannot but love. *He hath heard my voice.* And then it wins his esteem and affection to prayer. Seeing I find this virtue in it, we shall never part again ; *I will call upon him as long as I live.* Seeing prayer draweth help and favours from heaven, I shall not be to seek for a way, in any want or strait that can befall me.

In this there is need of direction ; but too many rules may as much confuse a matter, as too few, and do many times perplex the mind and multiply doubts ; as many laws do multiply pleading. Briefly, then,

1. Slothful minds do often neglect the answers of God, even when they are most legible in the grant of the very thing itself that was desired. It may be through a total inadvertence in this kind, through never thinking on things as answers of our requests ; or possibly, a continual eager pursuit of more, turns away the mind from considering what it hath upon request obtained ; we are still so bent upon what further we would have, that we never think what is already done for us, which is one of the most ordinary causes of ingratitude.

2. But though it be not in the same thing that we desire that our prayers are answered, yet, when the Lord changes our petitions in his answers, it is always for the better. He regards (according to that known word of St. Augustine, *Si non ad voluntatem, ad utilitatem*) our *well* more than our *will.* We beg deliverance ; we are not unanswered, if he give patience and support. Be it under a spiritual trial or temptation, *My grace is sufficient for thee.* And where the Lord doth thus, it is certainly better for the time, than the other would be. Observe here, *His ears are open to the righteous,* but *his eyes are on them too.* They have not so his ear as to induce him blindly to give them what they ask, whether it be fit or no ; but *his eye is on them,* to see and consider their estate, and to know better than themselves what is best, and accordingly to answer. This is no prejudice, but a great privilege, and the happiness of his children, that they have a Father who knows what is fit for them, and *withholds no good* from them. And this commutation and exchange of our requests a Christian observing, may usually find out the particular answer of his prayers ; and if sometimes he doth not, then his best way is not to subtilize and amuse himself much in that, but rather to keep on in the exercise, knowing (as the Apostle speaks in another case) this for certain, *that their labour shall not be in vain in the Lord,* 1 Cor. xv. ult. ; and as the Prophet hath it, Isa. xlv. 19, *He hath not said unto the house of Jacob, Seek ye me in vain.*

3. Only this we should always remember, not to set bounds and limits to the Lord in point of time, not to set him a day, that thou wilt attend so long and no longer. How patiently will some men bestow long attendance on others, where they expect some very poor good or

courtesy at their hands! Yet we are very brisk and hasty with him who never delays us but for our good, to ripen those mercies for us which we, as foolish children, would pluck while they are green, and have neither that sweetness and goodness in them which they shall have in his time. All his works are done in their season. Were there nothing to check our impatiences, but his greatness, and the greatness of those things we ask for, and our own unworthiness, these consider-ations might curb them, and persuade us how reasonable it is that we should wait. He is a King well worth waiting on; and there is in the very waiting on him, an honour and a happiness far above us. And the things we seek are great, forgiveness of sins, evidence of sonship and heirship; heirship of a kingdom; and we condemned rebels, born heirs of the bottomless pit! And shall such as we be in such haste with such a Lord in so great requests! But further, the attendance which this reason enforces, is sweetened by the consideration of his wisdom and love, that he hath foreseen and chosen the very hour for each mercy fit for us, and will not delay it a moment. Never any yet repented their waiting, but found it fully recompensed with the oppor-tune answer, in such a time as they were then forced to confess was the only best. *I waited patiently,* says the Psalmist, *in waiting I waited,* but it was all well bestowed, *He inclined to me and heard my cry, brought me up,* &c., Psal. xl. 1. And then he afterwards falls into admiration of the Lord's method, his *wonderful workings and thoughts to us-ward.* "While I was waiting and saw nothing, thy *thoughts* "*were towards* and for me, and thou didst then *work* when thy good-"ness was most remarkable and *wonderful.*"

When thou art in great affliction, outward or inward, thou thinkest (it may be) he regards thee not. Yea, but he doth. Thou art his gold, he knows the time of refining thee, and of then taking thee out of the furnace; he is versed and skilful in that work. Thou sayest, "I have cried long for power against sin, and for some evidence of "pardon, and find no answer to either;" yet, leave him not. He never yet cast away any that sought him, and stayed by him, and resolved, whatsoever came of it, to lie at his footstool, and to wait, were it all their life-time, for a good word or a good look from him. And they choose well who make that their great desire and expectation; for one of his good words or looks will make them happy for ever; and as he is truth itself, they are sure not to miss of it. *Blessed are all they that wait for him.* And thou that sayest, thou canst not find pardon of sin, and power against it; yet consider, whence are those desires of both, which thou once didst not care for. Why dost thou hate that sin which thou didst love, and art troubled and burdened with the guilt of it, under which thou wentest so easily, and which thou didst not feel before? Are not these something of his own work? Yes, surely. And know he will not leave it unfinished, nor *forsake the work of his hands.* Psal. cxxxviii. 8. *His eye may be on thee* though thou seest him not, *and his ear open to thy cry,* though for the present he speaks not to thee as thou desirest. It is not said, that his children always see and hear him sensibly; but yet, when they do not, he is beholding them and hearing them graciously, and will show himself to them, and answer them seasonably.

David says, Psal. xxii. 2, *I cry in the day-time, and thou hearest not, and in the night season, and am not silent;* yet will he not entertain hard thoughts of God, nor conclude against him ; on the contrary, he acknowledges, *Thou art holy*, ver. 3, where, by *holiness*, is meant his faithfulness (I conceive) to his own ; as it follows, *Thou that inhabitest the praises of Israel*, to wit, for the favours he hath showed his people, as ver. 4, *Our fathers trusted in thee*.

Let the Lord's open ear persuade us to make much use of it. *Clavis diei et sera noctis:* The key of day and the lock of night. Be much in this sweet and fruitful exercise of prayer, together and apart, under the sense of these three considerations mentioned above ; the duty, the dignity, and the utility of prayer.

1. The *duty*. It is due to the Lord to be worshipped and acknowledged thus, as the fountain of good. How will men crouch and bow one to another upon small requests ; and shall He only be neglected by the most, from whom *all* have *life and breath and all things!* (as the Apostle speaks in his sermon, Acts xvii. 25). And then,

2. Consider the *dignity* of this, to be admitted into so near converse with the highest Majesty. Were there nothing to follow, no answer at all, Prayer pays itself in the excellency of its nature, and the sweetness that the soul finds in it. Poor wretched man, to be admitted into heaven while he is on earth, and there to come and speak his mind freely to the Lord of heaven and earth, as his Friend, as his Father ! to empty all his complaints into his bosom ; when wearied with the follies and miseries of the world, to refresh his soul in his God. Where there is any thing of his love, this is a privilege of the highest sweetness ; for they who love, find much delight in discoursing together, and count all hours short, and think the day runs too fast, that is so spent ; and they who are much in this exercise, the Lord doth impart *his secrets* much to them. See Psal. xxv. 14.

3. Consider again, it is the most profitable exercise ; no lost time, as profane hearts judge it, but only time gained. All blessings attend this work. It is the richest traffic in the world, for it trades with heaven, and brings home what is most precious there. And as holiness disposes to prayer, so prayer befriends holiness, increases it much. Nothing so refines and purifies the soul as frequent prayer. If the often conversing with wise men doth so teach and advance the soul in wisdom, how much more then will converse with God ! This makes the soul despise the things of the world, and in a manner makes it Divine ; winds up the soul from the earth, acquainting it with delights that are infinitely sweeter.

The natural heart is full-stuffed with prejudices against the way of holiness, which dissuade and detain it ; and therefore the Holy Scriptures most fitly dwell much on this point, asserting the true advantage of it to the soul, and removing those mistakes which it has in respect of that way.

Thus here, and to press it the more home, ver. 10, &c., the Apostle, having used the Psalmist's words, now follows it forth in his own, and extends what was said concerning the particular way of meekness and love, &c., in the general doctrine, to all the paths of *righteousness*.

The main conclusion is, that happiness is the certain consequent and fruit of holiness; all good, even outward good, so far as it holds good, and is not inconsistent with a higher good. If we did believe this more, we should feel it more, and so, upon feeling and experiment, believe it more strongly. All the heavy judgments we feel or fear, are they not the fruit of our own ways, of profaneness, and pride, and malice, and abounding ungodliness? All cry out of hard times, evil days; and yet, who is taking the right way to better them? Yea, who is not still helping to make them worse? Are we not ourselves the greatest enemies of our own peace? Who looks either rightly backward, reflecting on his former ways, or rightly forward, to direct better his way that is before him? Who either says, *What have I done?* (as Jer. viii. 6,) or, *What ought I to do?* (Acts xvi. 30.) And indeed, the one of these depends on the other. *Consilium futurum ex præterito venit* (SENECA): " Future determination springs from the past." *I considered my ways,* says David, turned them over and over, (as the word is,) *and then I turned my feet unto thy testimonies,* Psal. cxix. 59.

Are there any, for all the judgments fallen on us, or that threaten us, returning apace with regret and hatred of sin, hastening unto God, and *mourning and weeping as they go,* bedewing each step with their tears? Yea, where is that newness of life that the word has called for so long, and that now the word and the rod together are so loudly calling for? Who is more *refraining his tongue from evil, and his lips from guile;* changing oaths, and lies, and calumnies, into a new language, into prayers, and reverent speaking of God, and joining a suitable, consonant carriage? Who is *eschewing evil and doing good,* labouring to be fertile in holiness, *to bring forth much fruit to God?* This were the way *to see good days* indeed; this is the way to the longest life, the only long life and *length of days,* one eternal day: as St. Augustine comments on those words, *One day in thy courts is better than a thousand,* Psal. lxxxiv. 7. *Millia dierum desiderant homines, et multum volunt hic vivere; contemnant millia dierum, desiderent unum, qui non habet ortum et occasum, cui non cedit hesternus, quem non urget crastinus.* " Men desire thousands of days, and wish to live long here: rather let them despise thousands of days, and desire that one which hath neither dawn nor darkening, to which no yesterday gives place, which yields to no to-morrow."

The reason added is above all exception, it is supreme: *The eyes of the Lord,* &c. If He who made times and seasons, and commands and forms them as he will, if he can give *good days,* or make men happy, then the only sure way to it must be the way of his obedience; to be in the constant favour of the great King, and still in his gracious thoughts; to have his eye and his ear. If this will serve the turn, (and if this do it not, I pray you, what will?) then the righteous man is the only happy man, *For the eyes of the Lord are upon him,* &c. Surer happy days may be expected hence, than theirs who draw them from the aspect of the stars; the eyes of the Father of lights benignly beholding them, the *trine aspect* of the blessed Trinity. The love he carries to them, draws his eye still towards them; there is no forgetting of them, nor slipping of the fit season to do them good: his mind, I may say, runs on that. He sees how it is with them, and receives their suits gladly, rejoicing to put favours upon them. He is their assured friend, yea, he is their Father; what then can they want? Surely they cannot miss of any good that his love and power can help them to.

But his face is against them that do evil.] So our happiness and misery are in *his face*, his looks. Nothing so comfortable as his favourable face, nothing so terrible again as his face—*his anger*, as the Hebrew word is often taken, that signifies *his face*. And yet, how many sleep sound under this misery! But believe it, it is a dead and a deadly sleep; the Lord standing in terms of enmity with thee, and yet thy soul *at ease!* Pitiful, accursed ease! I regard not the differences of your outward estate; that is not a thing worth the speaking of. If thou be poor and base, and in the world's eye but a wretch, and withal under the hatred of God, as being an impenitent, hardened sinner, those other things are nothing; this is the top, yea, the total sum of thy misery. Or be thou beautiful, or rich, or noble, or witty, or all these together, or what thou wilt, yet, is *the face of the Lord against thee?* Think as thou wilt, thy estate (*splendida miseria*) is not to be envied, but lamented: I cannot say, much good do it thee, with all thy enjoyments, for it is certain they can do thee no good; and if thou dost not believe this now, the day is at hand wherein thou shalt be forced to believe it, finding it then irrevocably true. If you will, you may still follow *the things of the world, walk after the lusts of your own hearts,* neglect God, and please yourselves, but, as Solomon's word is of judgment, Eccl. ix. 9, *Remember that the face of the Lord is against thee,* and in that judgment he shall unvail it, and let thee see it against thee. Oh, the most terrible of all sights!

The godly often do not see the Lord's favourable looks, while he is eyeing them; and the wicked usually do not see nor perceive, neither will believe, that *his face is against them;* but, besides that the day of full discovery is coming, the Lord doth sometimes let both the one and the other know somewhat how he stands affected towards them. In peculiar deliverances and mercies he tells his own, that he forgets them not, but both sees and hears them when they think he does neither, after that loving and gracious manner which they desire, and which is here meant; and sometimes, he lets forth glances of his bright countenance, darts in a beam upon their souls that is more worth than many worlds. And on the other side, he is pleased sometimes to make it known that his face is against the wicked, either by remarkable outward judgments, which to them are the vent of his just enmity against them, or to some he speaks it more home in horrors and affrights of conscience, which to them are earnests and pledges of their full misery, that *inheritance of woe* reserved, as the joys and comforts of believers are, of their *inheritance of glory.*

Therefore, if you have any belief of these things, be persuaded, be entreated to forsake the way of ungodliness. Do not flatter yourselves and dream of escaping, when you hear of outward judgments on your neighbours and brethren, but tremble and be humbled. Remember our Saviour's words, *Think ye that those on whom the tower of Siloam fell, were greater sinners than others? I tell you, nay, but except you repent, you shall all likewise perish,* Luke xiii. 4, 5. This seeming harsh word, he who was wisdom and sweetness itself uttered, and even in it spoke like a Saviour : he speaks of perishing, that they might not perish, and presses repentance by the heavy doom of impenitence.

When you hear of this, there is none of you would willingly choose it, that the Lord's face should be against you, although upon very high offers made to you of other things.   You think, I know, that the very sound of it is somewhat fearful, and on the other side, have possibly some confused notion of his favour, as a thing desirable ; and yet do not bestir yourselves, to avoid the one and inquire after the other ; which is certainly by reason of your unbelief.   For if you think of the love of God, as his word speaks of it, and as you will say you do, whence is it, I pray you, that there is no trifle in this world that will not take more deeply with you, and which you follow not with more earnestness, than this great business of reconciliation with God, in order to your finding his face not against you, but graciously towards you, *his eyes upon you, and his ears open to your prayer.*

Your blessedness is not,—no, believe it, it is not where most of you seek it, in things below you.   How can that be ?   It must be a higher good to make you happy.   While you labour and sweat for it in any thing under the sun, your pains run all to waste ; you seek a happy life in the region of death.   Here, here it is alone, in the love and favour of God, in having his countenance and friendship, and free access and converse ; and this is no where to be found, but in the ways of holiness.

Ver. 13. And who is he that will harm you, if ye be followers of that which is good ?

THIS the Apostle adds, as a further reason of the safety and happiness of that way he points out, a reason drawn from its own nature.   There is something even intrinsical in a meek, and upright, and holy carriage, that is apt, in part, to free a man from many evils and mischiefs which the ungodly are exposed to, and do readily draw upon themselves.   Your spotless and harmless deportment will much bind up the hands even of your enemies, and sometimes, possibly, somewhat allay and cool the malice of their hearts, that they cannot so rage against you as otherwise they might.   It will be somewhat strange and monstrous to range against the innocent.   *Who is he that will harm you?*   Here are two things : I. The carriage.   II. The advantage of it.

I. Their carriage is expressed : *followers of that which is good.* The Greek word is, *imitators.*

There is an imitation of men that is impious and wicked, which consists in taking the copy of their sins.   Again, there is an imitation which, though not so grossly evil, yet is poor and servile, being in mean things, yea, sometimes descending to imitate the very imperfections of others, as fancying some comeliness in them ; as some of Basil's scholars, who imitated his slow speaking, which he had a little in the extreme, and could not help.   But this is always laudable, and worthy of the best minds, to be *imitators of that which is good,* wheresoever they find it ; for that stays not in any man's person, as the ultimate pattern, but rises to the highest grace, being man's nearest

likeness to God, his image and resemblance, (and so, following the example of the saints in holiness, we look higher than them, and consider
them as receivers, but God as the first owner and dispenser of grace,)
bearing his stamp and superscription, and belonging peculiarly to him,
in what hand soever it be found, as carrying the mark of no other owner
than him.

The word of God contains our copy in its perfection, and very
legible and clear ; and so, the imitation of good, in the complete rule
of it, is the regulating of our ways by the word.   But even there we
find, besides general rules, the particular tracks of life of divers eminent holy persons, and those on purpose set before us, that we may
know holiness not to be an idle, imaginary thing, but that men have
really been holy, though not altogether sinless, yet, holy and spiritual
in some good measure ; have shined as lights amidst a perverse generation, as greater stars in a dark night, and were yet *men*, as St. James
says of Elias, like us in nature (ὁμοιοπαθεις) and in the frailty of it ;
subject to like passions as we are. James v. 17.   Why may we not
then aspire to be holy as they were, and attain to it ?—although we
should fall short of the degree, yet not stopping at a small measure,
but running further, *pressing still forward toward the mark ;* following
them in the way they went, though at a distance ; not reaching them,
and yet walking, yea, running after them as fast as we can ; not
judging of holiness by our own sloth and natural averseness, taking
it for a singularity fit only for rare, extraordinary persons, such as
prophets and apostles were, or as the Church of Rome fancies those
to be, to whom it vouchsafes a room in the roll of saints.   Do you not
know that holiness is the only *via regia*, this *following of good* the path
wherein all the children of God must walk, one following after another,
each striving to equal, and, if they could, to outstrip even those they
look on as most advanced in it ?   This is, amongst many others, a mis-
conceit in the Romish Church, that they seem to make holiness a kind
of impropriate good, which the common sort can have little share in,
almost all piety being shut up within cloister-walls, as its only fit
dwelling : but it hath not liked their lodging, it seems ; it has flown
over the walls away from them, for there is little of it even there to be
found.   Their opinion, however, places it there, as having little to do
abroad in the world ; whereas, the truth is, that all Christians. have
this for their common task, though some are under more peculiar
obligations to study this one copy.   Look on the rule of holiness, and
be followers of it, and followers or imitators one of another, so far as
their carriage agrees with that primitive copy, as written after it.   *Be
ye followers of me,* μιμηται, says the Apostle, even to the meanest Christians amongst those he wrote to, but thus, *as I am of Christ.* 1 Cor.
xi. 1.

Is it thus with us ?   Are we zealous and emulous followers of that
which is good, exciting each other by our example to a holy and Christian conversation, *provoking one another* (so the Apostle's word is) *to
love and to good works?* Heb. x. 24.   Or, are not the most mutual
corrupters of each other, and of the places and societies where they
live ; some leading, and others following, in their ungodliness ; not
regarding the course of those who are most desirous to walk holily, or,

if at all, doing it with a corrupt and evil eye, not in order to study and follow what is good in them, their way of holiness, but to espy any the least wrong step, to take exact notice of any imperfection or malignant slander, and by this, either to reproach religion, or to hearten or harden themselves in their irreligion and ungodliness, seeking warrant for their own willing licentiousness in the unwilling failings of God's children? And, in their converse with such as themselves, they are following their profane way, and flattering and blessing one another in it. "What need we be so precise?" And, "If I should not do as others, they would laugh at me, I should pass for a fool." Well, thou wilt be a fool of the most wretched kind, rather than be accounted one by such as are fools, and know not at all wherein true wisdom consists.

Thus the most are carried with the stream of this wicked world, their own inward corruption easily agreeing and suiting with it; every man, as a drop, falling into a torrent, and easily made one, and running along with it into that dead sea where it empties itself.

But those whom the Lord hath a purpose to sever and save, he carries in a course contrary even to that violent stream. And these are the students of holiness, *the followers of good*, who bend their endeavours thus, and look on all sides diligently, on what may animate and advance them; on the example of the saints in former times, and on the good they espy in those who live together with them; and above all, studying that perfect rule in the Scriptures, and that highest and first Pattern there so often set before them, even the Author of that rule, the Lord himself, *to be holy as he is holy, to be bountiful and merciful as their heavenly Father*, and in all labouring to be, as the Apostle exhorts, *followers of God as dear children.* Eph. v. 1, 2. [Τέλος ἀνθρώπου ὁμοίωσις Θεῷ, says Pythagoras.] Children who are beloved of their father, and do love and reverence him, will be ambitious to be like him, and particularly aim at the following of any virtues or excellency in him. Now, thus it is most reasonable that it should be in the children of God, their Father being the highest and best of all excellency and perfection.

But this excellent pattern is drawn down nearer their view, in the Son Jesus Christ; where we have that Highest Example made low, and yet losing nothing of its perfection, so that we may study God in man, and read all our lesson, without any blot, even in our own nature. And this is truly the only way to be the best proficients in this following and imitating of all good. In him we may learn all, even those lessons which men most despise, God teaching them by acting them, and calling us to follow : *Learn of me, for I am meek and lowly in heart.* Matt. xi. 29. But this is too large a subject. Would you advance in all grace? Study Christ much, and you shall find not only the pattern in him, but strength and skill from him, to follow it.

II. The advantage ; *Who is he that will harm you?*

The very name of it says so much ; it is *a good*, worthy the following for itself. But there is this further to enforce it, that, besides higher benefit, it oftentimes cuts off the occasions of present evils and disturbances, which otherwise are incident to men. *Who is he that will harm you?* Men, evil men, will often be overcome by our blameless and harmless behaviour.

1. In the life of a godly man, taken together in the whole body and frame of it, there is a grave beauty or comeliness, which oftentimes forces some kind of reverence and respect to it, even in ungodly minds.

2. Though a natural man cannot love them spiritually, as graces of the Spirit of God, (for so only the partakers of them are lovers of them,) yet he may have, and usually hath, a natural liking and esteem of some kind of virtues which are in a Christian, and are not, in their right nature, to be found in any other, though a moralist may have somewhat like them ; *meekness,* and *patience,* and *charity,* and *fidelity,* &c.

3. These, and other such like graces, do make a Christian life so inoffensive and calm, that, except where the matter of their God or religion is made the crime, malice itself can scarcely tell where to fasten its teeth or lay hold ; it hath nothing to pull by, though it would, yea, oftentimes, for want of work or occasions, it will fall asleep for awhile. Whereas ungodliness and iniquity, sometimes by breaking out into notorious crimes, draws out the sword of civil justice, and where it rises not so high, yet it involves men in frequent contentions and quarrels. Prov. xxiii. 29. How often are the lusts, and pride, and covetousness of men, paid with dangers, and troubles, and vexation, which, besides what is abiding them hereafter, do even in this present life spring out of them ! These, the godly pass free of by their just, and mild, and humble carriage. *Whence so many jars and strifes* among the greatest part, but from their unchristian hearts and lives, *from their lusts that war in their members,* as St. James says, their self-love and unmortified passions? One will abate nothing of his will, nor the other of his. Thus, where pride and passion meet on both sides, it cannot be but a fire will be kindled ; when hard flints strike together, the sparks will fly about : but a soft, mild spirit is a great preserver of its own peace, kills the power of contest ; as woolpacks, or such like soft matter, most deaden the force of bullets. *A soft answer turns away wrath,* says Solomon, Prov. xv. 1, beats it off, *breaks the bone,* as he says, the very strength of it, as the bones are of the body.

And thus we find it, those who think themselves high-spirited, and will bear least, as they speak, are often, even by that, forced to bow most, or to burst under it ; while humility and meekness escape many a burden, and many a blow, always keeping peace within, and often without too.

Reflection 1. If this were duly considered, might it not do somewhat to induce your minds to love the way of religion, for that it would so much abate the turbulency and unquietness that abound in the lives of men, a great part whereof the most do procure by the earthliness and distemper of their own carnal minds, and the disorder in their ways that arises thence ?

Reflection 2. You whose hearts are set towards God, and your feet entered into his ways, I hope will find no reason for a change, but many reasons to commend and endear those ways to you every day more than the last, and, amongst the rest, even this, that in them you escape many even present mischiefs which you see the ways of the world are full of. And, if you will be careful to ply your rule and study your copy better, you shall find it more so. The more you *follow that which is good*, the more shall you avoid a number of outward evils, which are ordinarily drawn upon men by their own enormities and passions. Keep as close as you can to the genuine, even track of a Christian walk, and labour for a prudent and meek behaviour, adorning your holy profession, and this shall adorn you, and sometimes gain *those that are without*, yea, even your enemies shall be constrained to approve it.

It is well known how much the spotless lives and patient sufferings of the primitive Christians did sometimes work upon their beholders, yea, on their persecutors, and persuaded some who would not share with them in their religion, yet to speak and write on their behalf. Seeing, then, that reason and experience do jointly aver it, that the lives of men conversant together have generally a great influence one upon another, (for example is an animated or living rule, and is both the shortest and most powerful way of teaching,)—

[1.] Whosoever of you are in an exemplary or leading place in relation to others, be it many or few, be ye, first, *followers of God.* Set before you the rule of holiness, and withal, the best and highest examples of those who have walked according to it, and then you will be leading in it those who are under you, and they being bent to follow you, in so doing will *follow that which is good.* Lead and draw them on, by admonishing, and counselling, and exhorting ; but especially, by walking. Pastors, be [τύποι] *ensamples* to the flock, or *models*, as our Apostle hath it, 1 Pet. v. 3, that they may be stamped aright, taking the impression of your lives. Sound doctrine alone will not serve. Though the water you give your flocks be pure, yet, if you lay spotted rods before them, it will bring forth spotted lives in them. Either teach not at all, or teach by the rhetoric of your lives.* Elders, be such in grave and pious carriage, whatsoever be your years ; for young men may be so, and, possibly, gray hairs may have nothing under them but gaddishness and folly many years old, habituated and inveterate ungodliness. Parents and Masters, let your children and servants read in your lives the life and power of godliness, the Practice of Piety not lying in your windows or corners of your houses, and confined within the clasp of the book bearing that or any such like title, but shining in your lives.

[2.] You that are easily receptive of the impression of example, beware of the stamp of unholiness, and of a carnal, formal course of profession, whereof the examples are most abounding ; but, though they be fewer who bear the lively image of God impressed on their hearts and expressed in their actions, yet study these, and be followers of them, as they are of Christ. I know you will espy much irregular and unsanctified carriage in us who are set up for the ministry, and if you look round, you will find the world lying in wickedness ; yet if there be any who have any sparks of Divine light in them, converse with those, and follow them.

* Ἡ μὴ διδάσκειν, ἡ διδάσκειν τῷ τρόπῳ.

[3.] And, generally, this I say to all, (for none are so complete but they may espy some imitable and emulable good, even in meaner Christians,) acquaint yourselves with the word, the rule of holiness ; and then, with an eye to that, look on one another, and be zealous of progress in the ways of holiness. Choose to converse with such as may excite you and advance you, both by their advice and example. Let not a corrupt generation in which you live, be the worse by you, nor you the worse by it. As far as you necessarily engage in some conversation with those who are unholy, let them not pull you into the mire, but, if you can, help them out. And let not any custom of sin prevailing about you, by being familiarly seen, gain upon you, so as to think it fashionable and comely, yea, or so as not to think it deformed and hateful. Know, that you must row against the stream of wickedness in the world, unless you would be carried with it to the dead sea, or lake of perdition. Take that grave counsel given, Rom. xii. 2 : *Be not conformed to this world, but be ye transformed by the renewing of your mind;* that is, the daily advancement in renovation, purifying and refining every day.

Now, in this way you shall have sweet inward peace and joy, as well as some outward advantage, in that men, except they are monstrously cruel and malicious, will not so readily *harm you;* it will abate much of their rage. But, however, if you do not escape suffering by your holy carriage, yea, *if you suffer* even for it, yet in that *are you happy* (as the Apostle immediately adds) :—

Ver. 14. But and if ye suffer for righteousness' sake, happy are ye : and be not afraid of their terror, neither be troubled.

IN this verse are two things ; First, Even in the most blameless way of a Christian, his suffering is supposed. Secondly, His happiness, even in suffering, is asserted.

I. Suffering is supposed, notwithstanding righteousness, yea, *for righteousness;* and that, not as a rare, unusual accident, but as the frequent lot of Christians ; as Luther calls Persecution, *malus genius Evangelii, The evil genius of the Gospel.* And we, being forewarned of this, as not only the possible, but the frequent lot of the saints, ought not to hearken to the false prophecies of our own self-love, which divines what it would gladly have, and easily persuades us to believe it. Think not that any prudence will lead you by all opposi-tions and malice of an ungodly world. Many winter blasts will meet you in the most inoffensive way of religion, if you keep straight to it. Suffering and war with the world, is a part of the godly man's portion here, which seems hard, but take it altogether, it is sweet : none in their wits will refuse that legacy entire, *In the world ye shall have trouble, but in me ye shall have peace.* John xvi. *ult.*

Look about you, and see if there be any estate of man, or course of life, exempted from troubles. The greatest are usually subject to greatest vexations ; as the largest bodies have the largest shadows attending them. We need not tell nobles and rich men, that content-ment doth not dwell in great palaces and titles, nor in full coffers ; they feel it, that they are not free of much anguish and molestation, and that a proportionable train of cares, as constantly as of servants, follows great place and wealth. Riches and trouble, or noise, are signified by the same Hebrew word. Compare Job xxxvi. 19, with xxx. 24. And kings find that their crowns, which are set so richly with diamonds without, are lined with thorns within. And if we speak of men who are *servants to unrighteousness*, besides what is to come, are they not often forced to suffer, amongst the service of their lusts, the distempers that attend unhealthy intemperance, the poverty that dogs luxury at the heels, and the fit punishment of voluptuous persons in painful diseases, which either quickly cut the thread of life, or make their aged bones full of the sins of their youth? Job xx. 11. Take what way you will, there is no place or condition so fenced and guarded, but public calamities, or personal griefs, find a way to reach us.

Seeing, then, we must suffer, whatever course we take, this kind of suffering, *to suffer for righteousness*, is far the best. What Julius Cæsar said ill of doing ill, *Si violandum est jus, regnandi causa violandum*, we may well say of suffering ill; If it must be, it is best to be for a kingdom. And these are the terms on which Christians are called to suffer for righteousness: *If we will reign with Christ*, certain it is, *we must suffer with him;* and, *if we do suffer with him*, it is as certain, *we shall reign with him*. 2 Tim. ii. 12. And therefore such sufferers are *happy*.

But I shall prosecute this suffering for righteousness, only with relation to the Apostle's present reasoning. His conclusion he establishes, 1. From the favour and protection of God; 2. From the nature of the thing itself. Now we would consider the consistence of this supposition with those reasons.

1st, From the favour or protection of God. *The eyes of the Lord* being *on the righteous* for their good, and *his ear open to their prayer*, how is it that, notwithstanding all this favour and inspection, they are so much exposed to suffering, and even for the regard and affection they bear towards him, *suffering for righteousness?* These seem not to agree well; yet they do.

It is not said that his eye is so on them, as that he will never see them afflicted, nor have them suffer any thing; no, but this is their great privilege and comfort in suffering, that his gracious eye is then upon them, and sees their trouble, and his ear towards them, not so as to grant them an exemption, (for that they will not seek for,) but seasonable deliverance, and, in the mean while, strong support, as is evident in that xxxivth Psalm. If his eye be always on them, he sees them suffer often, for *their afflictions are many*, (ver. 19,) and if his ear be to them, he hears many sighs and cries pressed out by sufferings. And they are content; this is enough, yea, better than not to suffer; they suffer, and often directly for him, but he sees it all, takes perfect notice of it, therefore it is not lost. And they are forced to cry, but none of their cries escape his ear. He hears, and he manifests that he sees and hears, for *he delivers them;* and, till he does, he keeps them from being crushed under the weight of the suffering: *He keeps all his bones, not one of them is broken* (verse 20). He sees, yea, appoints and provides these conflicts for his choicest servants. He sets his champions to encounter the malice of Satan and the world, for his sake, to give proof of the truth and the strength of their love to him for whom they suffer, and to overcome even in suffering.

He is sure of his designed advantages out of the sufferings of his Church and of his saints for his name. He loses nothing, and they lose nothing ; but their enemies, when they rage most, and prevail most, are ever the greatest losers. His own glory grows, the graces of his people grow, yea, their very number grows, and that sometimes most by their greatest sufferings. This was evident in the first ages of the Christian Church. Where were the glory of so much invincible love and patience, if they had not been so put to it ?

2ndly, For the other argument, that the said *following of good* would preserve from *harm*, it speaks truly the nature of the thing, what it is apt to do, and what, in some measure, it often doth ; but considering the nature of the world, *its enmity against God* and religion, that strong poison in the serpent's seed, it is not strange that it often proves otherwise ; that, notwithstanding the righteous carriage of Christians, yea, even *because* of it, they suffer much. It is a resolved case, *All that will live godly, must suffer persecution*, 2 Tim. iii. 12. It meets a Christian in his entrance to the way of the kingdom, and goes along all the way. No sooner canst thou begin to seek the way to heaven, but the world will seek how to vex and molest thee, and make that way grievous ; if no other way, by scoffs and taunts, intended as bitter blasts to destroy the tender blossom or bud of religion, or, as Herod, to kill Christ newly born. You shall no sooner begin to inquire after God, but, twenty to one, they will begin to inquire whether thou art gone mad. But if thou knowest *who it is whom thou hast trusted*, and whom thou lovest, this is a small matter. What though it were deeper and sharper sufferings, yet still, *if you suffer for righteousness, happy are you.*

Which is the IInd thing that was proposed, and more particularly imports, 1. That a Christian under the heaviest load of sufferings for righteousness, is yet still *happy*, notwithstanding those sufferings. 2. That he is happier even by those sufferings. And,

1. All the sufferings and distresses of this world are not able to destroy the happiness of a Christian, nor to diminish it ; yea, they cannot at all touch it : it is out of their reach. If it were built on worldly enjoyments, then worldly privations and sufferings might shake it, yea, might undo it : when those rotten props fail, that which rests on them must fall. He that hath set his heart on his riches, a few hours can make him miserable. He that lives on popular applause, it is almost in any body's power to rob him of his happiness ; a little slight or disgrace undoes him. Or, whatsoever the soul fixes on of these moving, unfixed things, pluck them from it, and it must cry after them, *Ye have taken away my gods.* But the believer's happiness is safe, out of the reach of shot. He may be impoverished, and imprisoned, and tortured, and killed, but this one thing is out of hazard ; he cannot be miserable ; still, in the midst of all these, he subsists a happy man. If all friends be shut out, yet the visits of the Comforter may be frequent, bringing him glad tidings from heaven, and communing with him of the love of Christ and solacing him in that. It was a

great word for a heathen to say of his false accusers, *Kill me they may, but they cannot hurt me.* How much more confidently may the Christian say so! Banishment he fears not, for his country is above; nor death, for that sends him home into that country.

The believing soul having hold of Jesus Christ, can easily despise the best and the worst of the world, and defy all that is in it; can share with the Apostle in that defiance which he gives, *I am persuaded that neither death nor life shall separate me from the love of God, which is in Christ Jesus our Lord,* Rom. viii. *ult.* Yea, what though the frame of the world were a dissolving, and falling to pieces! This happiness holds, and is not stirred by it; for it is built upon that Rock of eternity, that stirs not, nor changes at all.

Our main work, truly, if you will believe it, is this; to provide this immovable happiness, which amidst all changes, and losses, and sufferings, may hold firm. You *may be free, choose it rather*—not to stand to the courtesy of any thing about you, nor of any man, whether enemy or friend, for the tenure of your happiness. Lay it higher and surer, and if you be wise, provide such a peace as will remain untouched in the hottest flame, such a light as will shine in the deepest dungeon, and such a life as is safe even in death itself, that life which is *hid with Christ in God,* Col. iii. 3.

But if in other sufferings, even the worst and saddest, the believer is still a happy man, then, more especially in those that are the best kind, sufferings for righteousness. Not only do they not detract from his happiness, but,

2. They concur and give accession to it; he is happy even so by suffering. As will appear from the following considerations.

[1.] It is the happiness of a Christian, until he attain perfection, to be advancing towards it: to be daily refining from sin, and growing richer and stronger in the graces that make up a Christian, a new creature; to attain a higher degree of patience, and meekness, and humility; to have the heart more weaned from the earth and fixed on heaven. Now, as other afflictions of the saints do help them in these, their sufferings for righteousness, the unrighteous and injurious dealings of the world with them have a particular fitness for this purpose. Those trials that come immediately from God's own hand, seem to bind to a patient and humble compliance, with more authority, and (I may say) necessity; there is no plea, no place for so much as a word, unless it be directly and expressly against the Lord's own dealing; but unjust suffering at the hands of men, requires that respect unto God, (without whose hand they cannot move,) that for his sake, and for reverence and love to him, a Christian can go through those with that mild evenness of spirit which overcomes even in suffering.

And there is nothing outward more fit to persuade a man to give up with the world and its friendship, than to feel much of its enmity and malice, and that directly venting itself against religion, making that the very quarrel, which is of all things dearest to a Christian, and in the highest esteem with him.

If the world should caress them, and smile on them, they might be ready to forget their home, or at least to abate in the frequent thoughts and fervent desires of it, and to turn into some familiarity with the world, and favourable thoughts of it, so as to let out somewhat of their hearts after it ; and thus, Grace would grow faint by the diversion and calling forth of the spirits : as in summer, in the hottest and fairest weather, it is with the body.

It is an observation confirmed by the experience of all ages, that when the Church flourished most in outward peace and wealth, it abated most of its spiritual lustre, which is its genuine and true beauty, *opibus major, virtutibus minor ;* and when it seemed most miserable by persecutions and sufferings, it was most happy in sincerity, and zeal, and vigour of grace. When the moon shines brightest towards the earth, it is dark heavenwards ; and, on the contrary, when it appears not, it is nearest the sun, and clear towards heaven.

[2.] Persecuted Christians are happy in acting and evidencing, by those sufferings for God, their love to him. Love delights in difficulties, and grows in them. The more a Christian suffers for Christ, the more he loves him, and accounts him the dearer ; and the more he loves him, still the more can he suffer for him.

[3.] They are happy, as in testifying love to Christ and glorifying him, so in their conformity with him, which is love's ambition. Love affects likeness and harmony at any rate. A believer would readily take it as an affront, that the world should be kind to him, that was so harsh and cruel to his beloved Lord and Master. Canst thou expect, or wouldst thou wish, smooth language from that world which reviled thy Jesus, which called him Beelzebub? Couldst thou own and accept friendship at its hands, which buffeted him, and shed his blood ? Or, art thou not, rather, most willing to share with him, and of St. Paul's mind, *an ambassador in chains ;* [Πρεσβένω ἐν ἀλύσει] *God forbid that I should glory in any thing save in the cross of Christ, whereby the world is crucified unto me, and I unto the world.* Gal. vi. 14.

[4.] Suffering Christians are happy in the rich supplies of spiritual comfort and joy, which in those times of suffering are usual ; so that as *their sufferings for Christ do abound, their consolations in him abound much more,* as the Apostle testifies, 2 Cor. i. 5. God is speaking most peace to the soul, when the world speaks most war and enmity against it ; and this compensates abundantly. When the Christian lays the greatest sufferings men can inflict in the one balance, and the least glances of God's countenance in the other, he says, it is worth all the enduring of those to enjoy this : he says with David, Psal. cix. 28, *Let them curse, but bless Thou :* let them frown, but smile Thou. And thus God usually doth ; he refreshes such as are prisoners for him, with visits which they would gladly buy again with the hardest restraints and debarring of nearest friends. The world cannot but misjudge the state of suffering Christians ; it sees, as St. Bernard speaks, their crosses, but not their anointings : *vident cruces nostras, unctiones non vident.* Was not Stephen, think you, in a happy posture even in his enemies' hands ? Was he afraid of the showers of stones coming about his ears, who saw the heavens opened, and Jesus standing on the Father's right hand, so little troubled with their stoning of him, that, as the text hath it, in the midst of them *he fell asleep ?* Acts vii. 60.

[5.] If those sufferings be so small, that they are weighed down even by present comforts, and so the Christian be happy in them in that regard, how much more doth the *weight of glory* that follows surpass these sufferings! They *are not worthy to come in comparison*, they are as nothing to that *glory that shall be revealed*, in the Apostle's arithmetic; Rom. viii. 18, [λογίζομαι] when I have cast up the sum of the sufferings of this present time, this instant *now*, [τὸ νῦν,] they amount to just nothing in respect of that glory. Now, these sufferings are happy, because they are the way to this happiness, and pledges of it, and, if any thing can do, they raise the very degree of it. However, it is an *exceeding excellent weight of glory*. The Hebrew word which signifies *glory*, signifies *weight*. Earthly glories are all *too light*, τὸ ἐλαφρὸν, except in the weight of the cares and sorrows that attend them; but that hath the weight of complete blessedness. Speak not of all the sufferings, nor of all the prosperities of this poor life, nor of any thing in it, as worthy of a thought, when *that glory* is named; yea, let not this life be called *life*, when we mention that other life, which our Lord, by his death, hath purchased for us.

Be not afraid of their terror.] No time, nor place in the world, is so favourable to religion, that it is not still needful to arm a Christian mind against the outward oppositions and discouragements he shall meet with in his way to heaven. This is the Apostle's scope here; and he doth it, 1*st*, by an Assertion, 2*ndly*, by an Exhortation: the Assertion, that, in *suffering for righteousness*, they *are happy;* the Exhortation, agreeably to the Assertion, that *they fear not.* Why should they fear any thing, who are assured of happiness, yea, who are the more happy by reason of those very things that seem most to be feared?

The words are in part borrowed from the Prophet Isaiah, who relates them as the Lord's words to him and other godly persons with him in that time, countermanding in them that carnal, distrustful fear, which drove a profane king and people to seek help rather any where than in God, who was their strength: *Fear not their fear, nor be afraid; but sanctify the Lord of hosts himself, and let him be your fear, and let him be your dread.* Isa. viii. 12, 13. This the Apostle extends as a universal rule for Christians in the midst of their greatest troubles and dangers.

The things opposed here, are, a perplexing, troubling *fear of sufferings*, as the soul's distemper, and a *sanctifying of God in the heart*, as the sovereign cure of it, and the true principle of a healthful, sound constitution of mind.

Natural fear, though not evil in itself, yet, in the natural man, is constantly irregular and disordered in the actings of it, still missing its due object, or measure, or both; either running in a wrong channel, or over-running the banks. As there are no pure elements to be found here in this lower part of the world, but only in the philosophers' books, (who define them as pure, but they find them so no where,) thus we may speak of our natural passions, as not sinful in their nature, yet in us who are naturally sinful, yea, full of sin, they cannot escape the mixture and alloy of it.

Sin hath put the soul into universal disorder, so that it neither loves nor hates what it ought, nor as it ought; hath neither right joy, nor sorrow, nor hope, nor fear. A very small matter stirs and troubles it; and as waters that are stirred, (so the word [ταραχθῆτε] signifies,) having dregs in the bottom, become muddy and impure, thus the soul, by carnal fear, is confused, and there is neither quiet nor clearness in it. A *troubled sea*, as it *cannot rest*, so, in its restlessness, it *casts up mire*, as the prophet speaks, Isa. lvii. 20. Thus it is with the unrenewed heart of man: the least blasts that arise, disturb it and make it restless, and its own impurity makes it cast up mire. Yea, it is never right with the natural man: either he is asleep in carnal confidence, or, being shaken out of that, he is hurried and tumbled to and fro with carnal fears: he is either in a lethargy, or in a fever, or trembling ague. When troubles are at a distance, he is ready to fold his hands, and take his ease, as long as it may be; and then, being surprised when they come rushing on him, his sluggish ease is paid with a surcharge of perplexing and affrighting fears. And is not this the condition of the most?

Now, because these evils are not fully cured in the Believer, but he is subject to carnal security, (as David, *I said in my prosperity, I shall never be moved,*) and he is filled with undue fears and doubts in the apprehensions or feeling of trouble, (as the Psalmist likewise complaining, confesses the dejection and disquietness of his soul, and again, that he had almost lost his standing, *My feet had well nigh slipped,*) therefore, it is very needful to caution them often with such words as these, *Fear not their fear, neither be ye troubled.* You may take it objectively, *their fear :* Be not afraid of the world's malice, or any thing it can effect. Or it may be taken subjectively, as the prophet means: Do not you fear after the manner of the world; be not distrustfully troubled with any affliction that can befall you. Surely it is pertinent in either sense, or in both together; *Fear not what they can do, nor fear as they do.*

If we look on the condition of men, ourselves and others, are not the minds of the greatest part continually tossed, and their lives worn out between vain hopes and fears,* providing incessantly new matter of disquiet to themselves?

Contemplative men have always taken notice of this grand malady in our nature, and have attempted in many ways the cure of it, have bestowed much pains in seeking out prescriptions and rules for the attainment of a settled tranquillity of spirit, free from the fears and troubles that perplex us; but they have proved but mountebanks, who give big words enough, and do little or nothing, *all physicians of no value*, or of nothing, good for nothing, as Job speaks. Job xiii. 4. Some things they have said well concerning the outward causes of the inward evil, and of the inefficacy of inferior outward things to help it; but they have not descended to the bottom and inward cause of this our wretched unquiet condition; much less have they ascended to the true and only remedy of it. In this, Divine light is needful, and here we have it in the following verse.

---

* Hæc inter dubii vivimus et morimur.

Ver. 15. But sanctify the Lord God in your hearts: and be ready always to give an answer to every man that asketh you a reason of the hope that is in you with meekness and fear.

IMPLYING the cause of all our fears and troubles to be this, our ignorance and disregard of God; and the due knowledge and acknowledgment of him, to be the only establishment and strength of the mind.

In the words we may consider these three things: 1. This Respect of God, as it is here expressed, *Sanctify the Lord God.* 2. The Seat of it, *In your hearts.* 3. The Fruit of it, the power that this sanctifying of God in the heart hath, to rid that heart of those fears and troubles to which it is here opposed as their proper remedy.

Sanctify the Lord God.] He is holy, most holy, the Fountain of holiness. It is he, he alone, who powerfully sanctifies us, and then, and not till then, we sanctify him. When he hath made us holy, we know and confess him to be holy, we worship and serve our holy God, we glorify him with our whole souls and all our affections. We sanctify him by acknowledging his greatness, and power, and goodness, and (which is here more particularly intended) we do this by a holy fear of him, and faith in him. These within us confess his greatness, and power, and goodness: as the Prophet is express, *Sanctify him, and let him be your fear and your dread,* Isa. viii. 13; and then he adds, If thus you sanctify him, you shall further sanctify him. *He shall be your sanctuary:* you shall account him so, in believing in him, and shall find him so, in his protecting you; you shall repose on him for safety. And these particularly cure the heart of undue fears.

In your hearts.] We are to be sanctified in our words and actions, but primarily in our hearts, as the root and principle of the rest. He *sanctifies* his own *throughout,* makes their language and their lives holy, but first, and most of all, their hearts. And as he chiefly sanctifies the heart, it chiefly sanctifies him; acknowledges and worships him often when the tongue and body do not, and possibly cannot well join with it: it fears, and loves, and trusts in him, which properly the outward man cannot do, though it does follow and is acted on by these affections, and so shares in them according to its capacity.

Beware of an external, superficial sanctifying of God, for he accepts it not; he will interpret that a profaning of him and his name. *Be not deceived, God is not mocked.* Gal. vi. 7. He looks through all visages and appearances, in upon the heart; sees how it entertains him, and stands affected to him; whether it be possessed with reverence and love, more than either thy tongue or carriage can express. And if it be not so, all thy seeming worship is but injury, and thy speaking of him is but babbling, be thy discourse never so excellent; yea, the more thou hast seemed to sanctify God, while thy heart hath not been chief in the business, thou shalt not, by such service, have the less, but the more fear and trouble in the day of trouble, when it comes upon thee. No estate is so far off from true consolation, and so full of horrors, as that of the rotten-hearted hypocrite: his rotten heart is sooner shaken to pieces than any other. If you would have heart-peace in God, you must have this heart-sanctifying of him. It is the heart that is vexed and troubled with fears, the disease is there;

and if the prescribed remedy reach not thither, it will do no good. But let your hearts sanctify him, and then he shall fortify and establish your hearts.

This sanctifying of God in the heart, composes the heart, and frees it from fears.

First, In general, the turning of the heart to consider and regard God, takes it off from those vain, empty, windy things, that are the usual causes and matter of its fears. It feeds on wind, and therefore the bowels are tormented within. The heart is subject to disturbance, because it lets out itself to such things, and lets in such things into itself, as are ever in motion, and full of instability and restlessness; and so, it cannot be at quiet, till God come in and cast out these, and keep the heart within, that it wander out no more to them.

Secondly, Fear and Faith in the Believer, more particularly work in this.

1. That Fear, as greatest, overtops and nullifies all lesser fears: the heart possessed with this fear, hath no room for the other. It resolves the heart, in point of duty, what it should and must do, that it must not offend God by any means, lays that down as indisputable, and so eases it of doubtings and debates in that kind—whether shall I comply with the world, and abate somewhat of the sincerity and exact way of religion to please men, or to escape persecution or reproaches: no, it is unquestionably best, and only necessary *to obey him rather than men*, to retain his favour, be it with displeasing the most respected and considerable persons we know; yea, rather to choose the universal and highest displeasure of all the world for ever, than his smallest discountenance for a moment. It counts that the only indispensable necessity, to cleave unto God, and obey him. If I pray, I shall be accused, might Daniel think, but yet, pray I must, come on it what will. So, if I worship God in my prayer, they will mock me, I shall pass for a fool; no matter for that, it must be done: I must call on God, and strive to walk with him. This sets the mind at ease, not to be halting betwixt two opinions, but resolved what to do. *We are not careful*, said they, *to answer thee, O king—our God can deliver us*, but if not, this we have put out of deliberation, *we will not worship the image*. Dan. iii. 16. As one said, *Non oportet vivere, sed oportet navigare*, so we may say, It is not necessary to have the favour of the world, nor to have riches, nor to live, but it is necessary to hold fast the truth, and to walk holily, to sanctify the name of our Lord, and honour him, whether in life or death.

2. Faith in God clears the mind, and dispels carnal fears. It is the most sure help: *What time I am afraid*, says David, *I will trust in thee*. Psalm lvi. 3. It resolves the mind concerning the event, and scatters the multitude of perplexing thoughts which arise about that: What shall become of this and that? What if such an enemy prevail? What if the place of our abode grow dangerous, and we be not provided, as others are, for a removal? No matter, says Faith, though all fail, I know of one thing that will not; I have a refuge which all the strength of nature and art cannot break in upon or demolish, *a high defence, my rock in whom I trust*. Psalm lxii. 5, 6. The firm belief

of, and resting on his power, and wisdom, and love, gives a clear, satisfying answer to all doubts and fears. It suffers us not to stand to jangle with each trifling, grumbling objection, but carries all before it, makes day in the soul, and so chases away those fears that vex us only in the dark, as affrightful fancies do. This is indeed *to sanctify God*, and to give him his own glory, to *rest on him*. And it is a fruitful homage which is thus done to him, returning us so much peace and victory over fears and troubles, in the persuasion that nothing *can separate from his love;* that only we feared, and so, the things that cannot reach that, can be easily despised.

Seek to have the Lord in your hearts, and sanctify him there. He shall make them strong, and carry them through all dangers. *Though I walk*, says David, *through the valley of the shadow of death, I will fear no ill, for thou art with me.* Psal. xxiii. So xxvii. 1. What is it that makes the Church so firm and stout : *Though the sea roar, and the mountains be cast into the midst of the sea, yet we will not fear?* It is this : *God is in the midst of her ; she shall not be moved.* Psal. xlvi. 2, 5. No wonder ; he is immovable, and therefore doth establish all where he resides. If the world be in the middle of the heart, it will be often shaken, for all there is continual motion and change ; but God in it, keeps it stable. Labour, therefore, to get God into your hearts, residing in the midst of them, and then, in the midst of all conditions, they shall not move.

Our condition is universally exposed to fears and troubles, and no man is so stupid but he studies and projects for some fence against them, some bulwark to break the incursion of evils, and so to bring his mind to some ease, ridding it of the fear of them. Thus the most vulgar spirits do in their way ; for even the brutes, from whom such do not much differ in their actings, and course of life too, are instructed by nature to provide themselves and their young ones with shelter, the birds their nests, and the beasts their holes and dens. Thus, men gape and pant after gain with a confused, ill-examined fancy of quiet and safety in it, if once they might reach such a day, as to say with the rich fool in the gospel, *Soul, take thine ease, thou hast much goods laid up for many years;* though warned by his short ease, and by many watch-words, yea, by daily experience, that days may come, yea, one day will, when fear and trouble shall rush in, and break over the highest tower of riches; that there is a day, called the *day of wrath*, wherein they *profit not at all.* Prov. xi. 4. Thus, men seek safety in the greatness, or multitude, or supposed faithfulness of friends; they seek by any means to be strongly underset this way, to have many, and powerful, and trust-worthy friends. But wiser men, perceiving the unsafety and vanity of these and all external things, have cast about for some higher course. They see a necessity of withdrawing a man from externals, which do nothing but mock and deceive those most who trust most to them ; but they cannot tell whither to direct him. The best of them bring him *into himself*, and think to quiet him so, but the truth is, he finds as little to support him there ; there is nothing truly strong enough within him, to hold out against the many sorrows and fears which still from without do assault him. So then, though it is well done, to call off a man from outward things, as moving sands, that he build not on them, yet this is not enough ; for his own spirit is as unsettled a piece as is in all the world, and must have some higher strength than its own, to fortify and fix it. This is the way that is here taught, *Fear not their fear, but sanctify the Lord your God in your hearts;* and if you can attain this latter, the former will follow of itself.

In the general, then, God taking the place formerly possessed by things full of motion and unquietness, makes firm and establishes the heart. More particularly,

On the one hand, the fear of God turns other fears out of doors ; there is no room for them where this great fear is ; and though greater than they all, yet, it disturbs not as they do, yea, it brings as great quiet as they brought trouble. It is an ease to have but one thing for the heart to deal withal, for many times the multitude of carnal fears is more troublesome than their weight, as flies that vex most by their number.

Again, this fear is not a terrible apprehension of God as an enemy, but a sweet, composed reverence of God as our King, yea, as our Father ; as very great, but no less good than great ; so highly esteeming his favour, as fearing most of all things to offend him in any kind ; especially if the soul should either have been formerly, on the one hand, under the lash of his apprehended displeasure, or, on the other side, have had some sensible tastes of his love, and have been entertained in his *banqueting house,* where *his banner over it was love.* Cant. ii. 4.

His children fear him for his goodness ; are afraid to lose sight of that, or to deprive themselves of any of its influences ; desire to live in his favour, and then, for other things they are not very thoughtful.

On the other hand, Faith carries the soul above all doubts, assures it that if sufferings, or sickness, or death come, nothing can separate it from him. This suffices ; yea, what though he may hide his face for a time, though that is the hardest of all, yet there is no separation. Faith sets the soul in God, and where is safety, if it be not there ? It rests on those persuasions it hath concerning him, and that interest it hath in him. Faith believes that he sits and rules the affairs of the world, with an all-seeing eye and an all-moving hand. The greatest affairs surcharge him not, and the very smallest escape him not. He orders the march of all armies, and the events of battles, and yet, thou and thy particular condition slip not out of his view. The very *hairs of thy head are numbered;* are not then all thy steps, and the hazards of them, known to him, and all thy desires before him ? Doth he not *number thy wanderings,* every weary step thou art driven to, and *put thy tears in his bottle?* Psal. lvii. 8. Thou mayest assure thyself, that however thy matters seem to go, all is contrived to subserve thy good, especially thy chief and highest good. There is a regular motion in them, though the wheels do seem to run cross. *All these things are against me,* said old Jacob, and yet, they were all for him.

In all estates, I know of no heart's ease, but to believe ; to sanctify and honour thy God, in resting on his word. If thou art but persuaded of his love, surely that will carry thee above all distrustful fears. If thou art not clear in that point, yet depend and resolve to stay by him, yea, to stay on him, till he show himself unto thee. Thou hast some fear of him; thou canst not deny it without gross injury to him and thyself; thou wouldst willingly walk in all well-pleasing unto him: well then, *who is among you that feareth the Lord, though he see no* present *light, yet, let him trust in the name of the Lord, and stay upon his God.* Isa. l. 10. Press this upon thy soul, for there is not such another charm for all its fears and disquiet; therefore, repeat it still with David, sing this still, till it be stilled, and chide thy distrustful heart into believing: *Why art thou cast down, O my soul? why art thou disquieted within me?   Hope in God, for I shall yet praise him.* Psalm xlii. 5. Though I am all out of tune for the present, never a right string in my soul, yet, he will put forth his hand, and redress all, and I *shall yet once again praise,* and therefore, even now, I will hope.

It is true, some may say, God is a safe shelter and refuge, but he is holy, and holy men may find admittance and protection, but can so vile a sinner as I look to be protected, and taken in under his safe-guard? Go try. *Knock* at his door, *and* (take it not on our word, but on his own) *it shall be opened to thee;* that once done, thou shalt have a happy life of it in the worst times. Faith hath this privilege, never to be ashamed; it takes sanctuary in God, and sits and sings *under the shadow of his wings,* as David speaks, Psalm lxiii. 7.

Whence the unsettledness of men's minds in trouble, or when it is near, but because they are far off from God? The heart is shaken as the leaves of the tree with the wind, there is no stability of spirit; God is not sanctified in it, and no wonder, for He is not known. Strange this ignorance of God, and of the precious promises of his word! The most, living and dying strangers to him! When trouble comes, they have not him *as a known refuge,* but have to begin to seek after him, and to inquire the way to him; they cannot go to him as acquainted, and engaged by his own covenant with them. Others have some empty knowledge, and can discourse of Scripture, and ser-mons, and spiritual comforts, while yet they have none of that fear and trust which quiet the soul: they have notions of God in their heads, but God is not sanctified in their hearts.

If you will be advised, this is the way to have a high and strong spirit indeed, and to be above troubles and fears: seek for a more lively and divine knowledge of God than most as yet have, and rest not till you bring him into your hearts, and then you shall rest indeed in him.

Sanctify him by fearing him. *Let him be your fear and your dread,* not only as to outward, gross offences; fear an oath, fear to profane the Lord's holy day, but fear also all irregular earthly desires; fear the distempered affecting of any thing, the entertaining of any thing in the secret of your hearts, that may give distaste to your Be-loved. Take heed, respect the Great Person you have in your com-pany, who lodges within you, the Holy Spirit. *Grieve him not;* it will turn to your own grief if you do, for all your comfort is in his hand, and flows from him. If you be but in heart dallying with sin, it will unfit you for suffering outward troubles, and make your spirit low and base in the day of trial; yea, it will fill you with inward trouble, and disturb that peace which, I am sure, you who know it esteem more than all the peace and flourishing of this world.   Outward troubles do not molest or stir inward peace, but an unholy, unsanctified affection doth.   All the winds without cause not an earthquake, but that within its own bowels doth.   Christians are much their own enemies in unwary walking ; hereby they deprive themselves of those comforts they might have in God, and so are often almost as perplexed and full of fears, upon small occasions, as worldlings are.

Sanctify him by believing.   Study the main question, your *reconcilement* with him ; labour to bring that to some point, and then, in all other occurrences, Faith will uphold you, by enabling you to rely on God as now yours.   For these three things make up the soul's peace : 1*st*, To have right apprehensions of God, looking on him in Christ, and according to that covenant that holds in him.   And, 2*ndly*, A particular apprehension, that is, laying hold on him in that covenant as gracious and merciful, as satisfied and appeased in Christ, smelling in his sacrifice (which was himself) a savour of rest, and setting himself before me, that I may rely on him in that notion.   3*rdly*, A persuasion, that by so relying on him, my soul is as one, yea, is one with him.   Yet, while this is wanting, as to a believer it may be, the other is our duty, to sanctify the Lord in believing the word of grace, and believing on him, reposing on his word.   And this, even severed from the other, doth deliver, in a good measure, from distracting fears and troubles, and sets the soul at safety.

Whence is it, that in times of persecution or trouble, men are troubled within, and racked with fears, but because, instead of depending upon God, their hearts are glued to such things as are in hazard by those troubles without, their estates, or their ease, or their lives ?   The soul destitute of God esteems so highly these things, that it cannot but exceedingly feel when they are in danger, and fear their loss most, gaping after some imagined good : Oh ! if I had but this, I were well ;—but then, such or such a thing may step in and break all my projects. And this troubles the poor spirit of the man who hath no higher designs than such as are so easily blasted, and still, as any thing in man lifts up his soul to *vanity*, it must needs fall down again into *vexation*. There is a word or two in the Hebrew for *idols*, that signify withal *troubles*,* and *terrors*.† And so it is certainly : all our idols prove so to us ; they fill us with nothing but anguish and troubles, with unprofitable cares and fears, that are good for nothing, but to be fit punishments of that folly out of which they arise.   The ardent love or self-willed desire of prosperity, or wealth, or credit in the world, carries with it, as inseparably tied to it, a bundle of fears and inward troubles. *They that will be rich*, says the Apostle, *fall into a snare, and many noisome and hurtful lusts*, and, as he adds in the next verse, *they pierce themselves through with many sorrows.* 1 Tim. vi. 9.   He who hath set his heart upon an estate, or a commodious dwelling and lands, or upon a healthful and long life, cannot but be in continued alarms, renewing his fears concerning them.   Especially in troublous times, the least rumour of any thing that threateneth to deprive him of those

* [*Tigirim,*] Isa. xlv. 16, from [*Tszus,*] arctavit, hostiliter egit.
† [*Miphletzeth,*] 1 Kings xv. 13, from [*Phalatz,*] contremiscere, et [*Emim,*] Job xv. 25, from [*Aim,*] formidabilis, terrificus.

advantages, strikes him to the heart, because his heart is in them. I am well seated, thinks he, and I am of a sound, strong constitution, and may have many a good day. Oh! but besides the arrows of pestilence that are flying round about, the sword of a cruel enemy is not far off. This will affright and trouble a heart void of God. But if thou wouldst readily answer and dispel all these, and such like fears, *sanctify the Lord God in thy heart.* The soul that eyes God, renounces these things, looks on them at a great distance, as things far from the heart, and which therefore cannot easily trouble it, but it looks on God as within the heart, *sanctifies him in it,* and rests on him.

The word of God cures the many foolish hopes and fears that we are naturally subject to, by representing to us hopes and fears of a far higher nature, which swallow up and drown the other, as inundations and land-floods do the little ditches in those meadows that they overflow. *Fear not,* says our Saviour, *him that can kill the body*—What then ? Fear must have some work—he adds, *But fear him who can kill both soul and body.* Thus, in the passage cited here, *Fear not their fear, but sanctify the Lord, and let him be your fear and your dread.* And so, as for the hopes of the world, care not though you lose them for God : there is a *hope in you* (as it follows here) that is far above them.

Be ready always to give an answer.] The real Christian is *all for Christ,* hath given up all right of himself to his Lord and Master, to be all his, to do and suffer for him, and, therefore, he surely will not fail in this which is least, to speak for him upon all occasions. If he sanctify him in his heart, the tongue will follow, *and be ready* [πρὸς ἀπολογίαν] *to give an answer,* a defence or apology. Of this, here are four things to be noted.

1*st,* The need of it, *Men will ask an account.*

2*ndly,* The matter or subject of it, *The hope in you.*

3*rdly,* The manner, *With meekness and fear.*

4*thly,* The faculty for it, *Be ready.*

1. The need of a defence or apology. Religion is always the thing in the world that hath the greatest calumnies and prejudices cast upon it : and this engages those who love it, to endeavour to clear and disburden it of them. This they do chiefly by the course of their lives. The saints, by their blameless actions and patient sufferings, do write most real and convincing *Apologies ;* yet sometimes it is expedient, yea, necessary, to add verbal defences, and to vindicate not so much themselves, as their Lord and his truth, as suffering in the reproaches cast upon them. Did they rest in their own persons, a regardless contempt of them were usually the fittest answer ; *Spreta vilescerent.* But where the holy profession of Christians is likely to receive either the main or the indirect blow, and a word of defence may do any thing to ward it off, there we ought not to spare to do it.

Christian prudence goes a great way in the regulating of this ; for holy things are not to be cast to dogs. Some are not capable of receiving rational answers, especially in Divine things ; they were not only lost upon them, but religion dishonoured by the contest. But we are to answer every one that *inquires a reason,* or an account ; which supposes something receptive of it. We ought to judge ourselves engaged to give it, be it an enemy, if he will hear; if it gain him not, it may in part convince and cool him; much more, should it be one who ingenuously inquires for satisfaction, and possibly inclines to receive the truth, but is prejudiced against it by false misrepresentations of it: for Satan and the profane world are very inventive of such shapes and colours as may make truth most odious, drawing monstrous miscon-sequences out of it, and belying the practices of Christians, making their assemblies horrible and vile by false imputations; and thus are they often necessitated to declare the true tenor, both of their belief and their lives, in confessions of faith, and remonstrances of their carriage and custom.

The very name of Christians, in the primitive times, was made hate-ful by the foulest aspersions of strange wickednesses committed in their meetings; and these passed credibly through with all who were not particularly acquainted with them. Thus it also was with the Wal-denses; and so, both were forced to publish Apologies. And, as here enjoined, every one is bound, seasonably to clear himself, and his bre-thren, and religion: *Be ye always ready.* It is not always to be done to every one, but being ready to do it, we must consider when, and to whom, and how far. But,

2. All that they are to give account of is comprised here under this, *The hope that is in you.* Faith is the root of all graces, of all obe-dience and holiness; and Hope is so near in nature to it, that the one is commonly named for the other: for the things that *Faith* appre-hends and lays hold on as present, in the truth of Divine promises, *Hope* looks out for as to come, in their certain performance. To be-lieve a promise to be true before it be performed, is no other than to believe that it shall be performed; and Hope expects that.

Many rich and excellent things do the saints receive, even in their mean, despised condition here; but their *hope* is rather mentioned as the subject they may speak and give account of with most advantage, both because all they receive, at present, is but as nothing, compared to what they hope for, and because, such as it is, it cannot be made known at all to a natural man, being so clouded with their afflictions and sorrows. These he sees, but their graces and comforts he cannot see; and, therefore, the very ground of higher hopes, of somewhat to come, though he knows not what it is, speaks more satisfaction. To hear of another life, and a happiness hoped for, any man will confess it says something, and deserves to be considered.

So, then, the whole sum of religion goes under this word, *the hope that is in you,* for two reasons: first, for that it doth indeed all resolve and terminate into things to come; and secondly, as it leads and carries on the soul towards them by all the graces in it, and all the exercise of them, and through all services and sufferings; aiming at this, as its main scope, to keep that life to come in the believer's eye, till he get it in his hand; to sustain the hope of it, and bring him to possess it. Therefore the Apostle calls Faith, *the substance of things hoped for,* that which makes them be before they be, gives a solidity and substance to them. The name of *hope,* in other things, scarcely suits with such a meaning, but sounds a kind of uncertainty, and is somewhat airy; for, of all other hopes but this, it is a very true word of Seneca's, *Spes*

est nomen boni incerti: Hope is the name of an uncertain good. But
the Gospel, being entertained by Faith, furnishes a Hope that hath
substance and reality in it; and all its truths do concentrate into this,
to give such a hope. There was in St. Paul's word, besides the fitness
for his stratagem at that time, a truth suitable to this, where he designates his whole cause for which he was called in question, by the name
of his *Hope of the resurrection.* Acts xxiii. 6.

And, indeed, this hope carries its own apology in it, both for itself
and for religion. What can more pertinently answer all exceptions
against the way of godliness than this, to represent what hopes the
saints have who walk in that way? If you ask, Whither tends all this
your preciseness and singularity? Why cannot you live as your neighbours and the rest of the world about you? Truly, the reason is this:
we have somewhat further to look to than our present condition, and
far more considerable than any thing here; we have a hope of blessedness after time, a hope to dwell in the presence of God, where our
Lord Christ is gone before us; and we know that *as many as have
this hope must purify themselves even as he is pure.* 1 John iii. 3.
The City we tend to is holy, and *no unclean thing shall enter into it.*
Rev. xxi. 17. The hopes we have cannot subsist in the way of the
ungodly world; they cannot breathe in that air, but are choked and
stifled with it; and therefore we must take another way, unless we
will forego our hopes, and ruin ourselves for company. But all that
bustle of godliness you make, is (say you) but ostentation and hypocrisy. That may be your judgment, but, if it were so, we had but
a poor bargain. Such persons *have their reward;* that which they
desire, *to be seen of men,* is given them, and they can look for no more;
but we should be loth to have it so with us. That which our eye is
upon, is to come; our hopes are the thing which upholds us. We
know that we shall appear before the Judge of hearts, where shows
and formalities will not pass, and we are persuaded, that *the hope of
the hypocrite shall perish:* (Job viii. 13:) no man shall be so much
disappointed and ashamed as he. But the *Hope* that we have, *maketh
not ashamed.* Rom. v. 5. And while we consider that, so far are we
from the regarding of men's eyes, that, were it not we are bound to
profess our hope, and avow religion, and to walk conformably to it,
even before men, we would be content to pass through altogether
unseen: and we desire to pass as if it were so, as regardless either of
the approbation, or of the reproaches and mistakes of men, as if there
were no such thing, for it is indeed nothing.

Yea, the hopes we have make all things sweet. Therefore do we go
through disgraces and sufferings with patience, yea, with joy, because
of that Hope of glory and joy laid up for us. A Christian can *take
joyfully the spoiling of his goods, knowing that he hath in heaven a
better and an enduring substance.* Heb. x. 34.

The Hope.] All the estate of a believer lieth in hope, and it is a
royal estate. As for outward things, the children of God have what
he thinks fit to serve them, but those are not their portion, and therefore he gives often more of the world to those who shall have no more
hereafter; but all their flourish and lustre is but a base advantage, as
a lackey's gaudy clothes, which usually make more show than his who

is heir of the estate. How often, under a mean outward condition, and very despicable every way, goes an heir of glory *born of God*, and so royal; born to a *crown that fadeth not*, an estate of hopes, but so rich and so certain hopes, that the least thought of them surpasses all the world's possessions! Men think of somewhat for the present, *a bird in hand*, as you say, the best of it: but the odds is in this, that when all present things shall be past and swept away, as if they had not been, then shall these Hopers be in eternal possession; *they* only shall have all for ever, who seemed to have little or nothing here.

Oh! how much happier, to be the meanest expectant of the glory to come, than the sole possessor of all this world! These expectants are often kept short in earthly things, and, had they the greatest abundance of them, yet they cannot rest in that. Even so, all the spiritual blessings that they do possess here, are nothing to *the hope that is in them*, but as an earnest-penny to their great inheritance, which, indeed, confirms their hope, and assures unto them that full estate; and therefore, be it never so small, they may look on it with joy, not so much regarding it simply in itself, as in relation to that which it seals and ascertains the soul of. Be it never so small, yet it is a pledge of the great glory and happiness which we desire to share in.

It is the grand comfort of a Christian, to look often beyond all that he can possess or attain here; and as to answer others, when he is put to it concerning his Hope, so to *answer himself* concerning all his present griefs and wants : I have a poor traveller's lot here, little friendship and many straits, but yet I may go cheerfully homewards, for thither I shall come, and there I have riches and honour enough, a palace and a crown abiding me. Here, nothing but *depth calling unto depth*, one calamity and trouble, as waves, following another : but I have a hope of that *rest that remaineth for the people of God.* I feel the infirmities of a mortal state, but my hopes of immortality content me under them. I find strong and cruel assaults of temptations breaking in upon me, but, for all that, I have the assured hope of a full victory, and then, of everlasting peace. *I find a law in my members* rebelling against *the law of my mind*, which is the worst of all evils, so much strength of corruption within me; yet, there is withal a hope within me of deliverance, and I look over all to that; *I lift up my head, because the day of my redemption draws nigh.* This I dare avow and proclaim to all, and am not ashamed *to answer* concerning this blessed Hope.

3. But for the Manner of this, it is to be done with *meekness and fear;* meekness towards men, and reverential fear towards God.

With meekness.] A Christian is not, therefore, to be blustering and flying out into invectives, because he hath the better of it, against a man that questions him touching this Hope; as some think themselves certainly authorized to rough speech, because they plead for truth, and are on its side. On the contrary, so much the rather study meekness, for the glory and advantage of the truth. It needs not the service of passion; yea, nothing so disserves it, as passion when set to serve it. The *Spirit of truth* is withal the *Spirit of meekness.* The Dove that rested on that great Champion of truth, who is The Truth itself, is from him derived to the lovers of truth, and they ought to seek the participation of it. Imprudence makes some kind of Christians lose much of their labour, in speaking for religion, and drive those further off, whom they would draw into it.

And fear.] Divine things are never to be spoken of in a light, perfunctory way, but with a reverent, grave temper of spirit; and, for this reason, some choice is to be made both of time and persons. The confidence that attends this hope, makes the believer not fear men, to whom he answers, but still he fears his God, for whom he answers, and whose interest is chief in those things he speaks of. The soul that hath the deepest sense of spiritual things, and the truest knowledge of God, is most afraid to miscarry in speaking of him, most tender and wary how to acquit itself when engaged to speak of and for God.

4. We have the faculty for this apology, *Be ready*. In this are implied knowledge, and affection, and courage. As for knowledge, it is not required of every Christian, to be able to prosecute subtilties, and encounter the sophistry of adversaries, especially in obscure points; but all are bound to know so much, as to be able to aver that hope that is in them, the main doctrine of grace and salvation, wherein the most of men are lamentably ignorant. Affection sets all on work; whatever faculty the mind hath, it will not suffer it to be useless, and it hardens it against hazards in defence of the truth.

But the only way so to know and love the truth, and to have courage to avow it, is, to have the Lord *sanctified in the heart.* Men may dispute stoutly against Popery and errors, and yet be strangers to God and this hope. But surely it is the liveliest defence, and that which alone returns comfort within, when it arises from the peculiar interest of the soul in God, and in those truths and that hope which are questioned: it is then like pleading for the nearest friend, and for a man's own rights and inheritance. This will animate and give edge to it, when you apologize, not for a hope you have heard or read of barely, but for a hope *within you;* not merely a hope in believers in general, but in *you*, by a particular sense of that hope within.

But, although you should find it not so strong in you, as to your particular interest, yet are you seeking after it, and desiring it mainly? Is it your chief design to attain unto it? Then forbear not, if you have occasion, to speak for it, and commend it to others, and to maintain the sweetness and certainty of it.

And, to the end you may be the more established in it, and so the stronger to answer for it, not only against men, but against that great adversary who seeks so much to infringe and overbear it, know the right foundation of it; build it never on yourselves, or any thing in yourselves. The work of grace may evidence to you the truth of your hope, but the ground it fastens on is Jesus Christ, in whom all our rights and evidences hold good; his death assuring us of freedom from condemnation, and his life and possession of glory being the foundation of our hope. Heb. vi. 19. If you would have it immovable, rest it there; lay all this hope on him, and, when assaulted, fetch all your answers for it from him, for it is *Christ in you*, that is your *hope of glory.* Col. i. 27.

Ver. 16. Having a good conscience; that, whereas they speak evil of you, as of evil-doers, they may be ashamed that falsely accuse your good conversation in Christ.

THE *prosperity of fools is their destruction,* says Solomon, Prov. i. 32. But none of God's children die of this disease—of too much ease. He knows well how to breed them, and fit them for a kingdom. He keeps them in exercise, but yet so as they are not surcharged. He not only directs them how to overcome, but enables and supports them in all their conflicts, and gives them victory. One main thing, tending to their support and victory, is what is here required in the saints, and is withal wrought and maintained in them by the Spirit of God, *Having a good conscience,* &c.

I. We have here Two Parties opposed in contest—the evil tongues of the ungodly, and the good conscience and conversation of the Christian: *they speak evil of you, and falsely accuse you,* but do you have *a good conscience.*

II. The Success of their Contest: the good conscience prevails, and the evil-speakers are ashamed.

I. The parties engaged: *They speak evil.*] This is a general evil in the corrupt nature of man, though in some it rises to a greater height than in others. Are not tables and chambers, and almost all societies and meetings, full of it? And even those who have some dislikings of it, are too easily carried away with the stream, and, for company's sake, take a share, if not by lending their word, yet lending their ear, and willingly hearing the detractions of others; unless it be of their friends, or such as they have interest in, they insensibly slide into some forced complacency, and easily receive the impression of calumnies and defamings. But the most are more active in this evil, can cast in their penny to make up the shot; have their taunt or criticism upon somebody in readiness, to make up the feast, such as most companies entertain one another withal, but it is a vile diet. Satan's name, as the Syriac calls him, is, *an Eater of calumnies.* This tongue-evil hath its root in the heart, in a perverse constitution there, in pride and self-love. An overweening esteem that men naturally have of themselves, mounts them into the Censor's chair, gives them a fancied authority of judging others, and self-love, a desire to be esteemed; and, for that end, they spare not to depress others, and load them with disgraces and injurious censures, seeking upon their ruins to raise themselves: as Sallust speaks, *Ex alieni nominis jacturâ gradum sibi faciunt ad gloriam.*

But this bent of the unrenewed heart and tongue to evil-speaking, works and vents in the world most against those who walk most contrary to the course of the world; against such, this furnace of the tongue, *kindled from hell,* as St. James tells us, is made seven times hotter than ordinary. As for sincere Christians, they say, A company of hypocrites, Who so godly? but yet they are false, and malicious, and proud, &c. No kind of carriage in them shall escape, but there shall be some device to wrest and misname it. If they be cheerful in society, that shall be accounted more liberty than suits with their profession; if of a graver or sad temper, that shall pass for sullen severity. Thus perversely were John the Baptist and Christ censured by the Jews. Matt. xi. 18, 19. If they be diligent and wary in their affairs, then, in the world's construction, they are as covetous and worldly as any; if careless and remiss in them, then, silly, witless creatures, good for nothing. Still something stands cross.

The enemies of religion have not any where so quick an eye, as in observing the ways of such *as seek after God: my remarkers,* David calls them, Psal. lvi. 6,—they who scan my ways, as the word implies,—will not let the least step pass unexamined. If nothing be found faulty, then their invention works, either forging complete falsehoods, or disguising something that lies open to mistake. Or, if they can catch hold on any real failing, there is no end of their triumph and insultations. 1. They aggravate and raise it to the highest. 2. While they will not admit to be themselves judged of by their constant walk, they scruple not to judge of the condition of a Christian by any one particular action wherein he doth, or seems at least to, miscarry. 3. They rest not there, but make one failing of one Christian the reproach of all: Take up your devotees, there is never a one of them better. 4. Nor rest they there, but make the personal failings of those who profess it, the disgrace of religion itself. Now, all these are very crooked rules, and such as use them are guilty of gross injustice. For,

1. There is a great difference between a thing taken favourably, and the same action misconstrued. And,

2. A great difference betwixt one particular act, and a man's estate or inward frame, which they either consider not, or willingly or maliciously neglect.

3. How large is the difference that there is betwixt one and another in the measure of grace, as well as of prudence, either in their natural disposition, or in grace, or possibly in both! Some who are honest in the matter of religion, yet, being very weak, may miscarry in such things as other Christians come seldom near the hazard of. And though some should wholly forsake the way of godliness, wherein they seemed to walk, yet why should that reflect upon such as are real and stedfast in it? *They went out from us,* says the Apostle, *but were not of us.* 1 John ii. 19. *Offences* of this kind *must* be, but the *woe* rests on him by *whom they come,* not on other Christians. And if it spread further than the party offending, the woe is to the profane world, that take offence at religion because of him: as our Saviour hath expressed it, *Woe to the world because of offences!* Matt. xviii. 7; they shall stumble and fall, and break their necks upon these stumbling-blocks or scandals. Thou who art profane, and seest the failing of a minister or Christian, and art hardened by it, this is a judgment to thee, that thou meetest with such a block in thy way. *Woe to the world!* It is a judgment on a place, when God permits religion, in the persons of some, to be scandalous.

4. Religion itself remains still the same: whatsoever be the failings and blots of one or more who profess it, it is itself pure and spotless. If it teach not holiness, and meekness, and humility, and all good, purely, then except against it. But if it be *a straight golden reed* by which the temple is measured, (Rev. xxi. 15,) then let it have its

own esteem, both of straightness and preciousness, whatsoever uneven-
ness be found in those who profess to receive it.

Suspect and search yourselves, even in general, for this evil of evil-
speaking. Consider that we are to give [λογον λογῶν] *an account of
words;* and if of idle [ἄργον ῥῆμα] workless words, how much more of
lying or biting words !—*De verbo mendaci aut mordaci,* as St. Bernard
has it. Learn more humility and self-censure. Blunt that fire-edge
upon your own hard and disordered hearts, that others may meet with
nothing but charity and lenity at your hands.

But particularly beware of this, in more or less, in earnest or in jest,
to reproach religion, or those who profess it. Know how particularly
the glorious name of GOD is interested in that ; and they who dare
be affronting him, what shall they say ? How shall they stand, when
he calls them to account ? If you have not attained to it, yet do not
bark against it, but the rather esteem highly of religion. Love it, and
the very appearance of it, wherever you find it. Give it respect and
your good word at least ; and, from an external approbation, oh !
that you would aspire to inward acquaintance with it, and then no
more were needful to be said in this ; it would commend itself to you
sufficiently. But, in the mean time, be ashamed, be afraid of that
professed enmity against God that is amongst you, a malignant, hateful spirit against those who desire to walk holily, whetting your tongues
against them.

Consider, what do you mean ? This religion which we all profess,
is it the way to heaven, or is it not ? Do you believe this word, or
not ? If you do not, what do you here ? If you do, then you must
believe too, that those who walk closest by this rule are surest in that
way ; those who dare not share in your oaths, and excessive cups, and
profane conversation. What can you say ? It is not possible to open
your mouth against them, without renouncing this word and faith :
therefore, either declare you are no Christians, and that Christ is not
yours, or, in his name, I enjoin you, that you dare no more speak an ill
word of Christianity, and the power of religion, and those who seek
after it. There are not many higher signs of a reprobate mind, than
to have a bitter, virulent spirit against the children of God. Seek that
tie of affection and fraternity, on which the beloved Apostle, St. John,
lays such stress, when he says, *Hereby we know that we are translated
from death to life, because we love the brethren.* 1 John iii. 14.

But because those hissings are the natural voice of the serpent's seed,
expect them, you that have a mind to follow Christ, and take this
guard against them that you are here directed to take : *Having a good
conscience.*

It is a fruitless, verbal debate, whether Conscience be a faculty or
habit, or not. As in other things, so in this, which most of all requires
more solid and useful consideration, the vain mind of man feedeth on
the wind, loves to be busy to no purpose, *magno conatu magnas nugas.*
How much better is it to have this supernatural goodness of conscience, than to dispute about the nature of it ; to find it duly teaching
and admonishing, reproving and comforting, rather than to define it
most exactly ! *Malo sentire compunctionem, quam scire ejus defi-
nitionem.*

When all is examined, Conscience will be found to be no other than the *mind of man under the notion of a particular reference to himself and his own actions.* And there is a twofold goodness of the Conscience, *purity* and *tranquillity;* and this latter flows from the former, so that the former is the thing we ought primarily to study, and the latter will follow of itself. For a time, indeed, the conscience that is in a good measure pure, may be unpeaceable, but still it is the apprehension and sense of present or former impurity, that makes it so; for, without the consideration of guiltiness, there is nothing that can trouble it: it cannot apprehend the wrath of God, but with relation unto sin.

The goodness of conscience here recommended, is, *the integrity and holiness of the whole inward man in a Christian.* So, the ingredients of it are, 1. A due light or knowledge of our rule: that, like the lamps in the Temple, must be still burning within, as filthiness is always the companion of darkness. Therefore, if you would have a good conscience, you must by all means have so much light, so much knowledge of the will of God, as may regulate you, and show your way, may teach you how to do, and speak, and think, as in his presence.

2. A constant regard and using of this light, applying it to all things; not sleeping, but working by it; still seeking a nearer conformity with the known will of our God; daily redressing and ordering the affections by it; not sparing to knock off whatsoever we find irregular within, that our hearts may be polished and brought to a right frame by that rule. And this is the daily inward work of the Christian, his great business, *to purify himself as the Lord is pure.* 1 John iii. 3.

And, 3. For the advancing of this work, there is needful a frequent search of our hearts and of our actions, not only to consider what we are to do, but what we have done. These reflex inquiries, as they are a main part of the Conscience's proper work, are a chief means of making and keeping the Conscience good; first, by acquainting the soul with its own state, with the motions and inclinations that are most natural to it; secondly, by stirring it up to work out, and purge away by repentance, the pollution it hath contracted by any outward act or inward motion of sin; and, thirdly, this search both excites and enables the Conscience to be more watchful; teaches how to avoid and prevent the like errors for the time to come. As natural wise men labour to gain thus much out of their former oversights in their affairs, to be the wiser and warier by them, and lay up that as bought wit, which they have paid dear for, and therefore are careful to make their best advantage of it; so God makes the consideration of their falls preservatives to his children from falling again, makes a medicine of this poison.

Thus, that the conscience may be good, it must be enlightened, and it must be watchful, both advising before, and after censuring, according to that light.

The greater part of mankind little regard this: they walk by guess, having perhaps ignorant consciences, and the blind, you say, swallow many a fly. Yea, how many consciences are without sense, *as seared with a hot iron,* 1 Tim. iv. 2; so stupified, that they feel nothing! Others rest satisfied with a civil righteousness, an imagined goodness of conscience, because they are free from gross crimes. Others, who know the rule of Christianity, yet study not a conscientious respect to it in all things : they cast some transient looks upon the rule and their own hearts, it may be, but sit not down to compare them, make it not their business, have time for any thing but that, *Non vacant bonæ menti.* They do not, with St. Paul, exercise themselves in this, *to have a conscience void of offence towards God and men.* Acts xxiv. 16. Those were his *Ascetics* [ἀσκῶ] ; he exhausted himself in striving against what might defile the conscience ; or, as the word signifies, *elaborately wrought and dressed* his conscience, [ἀσκήσασα χιτῶνα,] Hom. Think you, while other things cannot be done without diligence and intention, that this is a work to be done at random ? No, it is the most exact and curious of all works, to have the conscience right, and keep it so ; as watches, or other such neat pieces of workmanship, except they be daily wound up and skilfully handled, will quickly go wrong. Yea, besides daily inspection, conscience should, like those, at some times be taken to pieces, and more accurately cleansed, for the best kept will gather soil and dust. Sometimes a Christian should set himself to a more solemn examination of his own heart, beyond his daily search ; and all little enough to have so precious a good as this, '*a good conscience.* They who are most diligent and vigilant, find nothing to abate as superfluous, but still need of more. The heart is to be *kept with all diligence,* or above all keeping. Prov. iv. 23. Corruption within is ready to grow and gain upon it, if it be never so little neglected, and from without, to invade it and get in. We breathe in a corrupt, infected air, and have need daily to *antidote* the heart against it.

You that are studying to be excellent in this art of a good conscience, go on, seek daily progress in it. The study of conscience is a more sweet, profitable study than that of all science, wherein is much vexation, and, for the most part, little or no fruit. Read this book diligently, and correct your *errata* by that other book, the word of God. Labour to have it pure and right. Other books and works are [περιεργὰ] *curious,* and [παρεργὰ] *by-works,* they shall not appear ; but this is one of the books that shall be opened in that great day, *according to which we must be judged.* Rev. xx. 12.

On this follows a good conversation, as inseparably connected with a good conscience. Grace is of a lively, active nature, and doth act like itself. Holiness in the heart, will be holiness in the life too ; not some good actions, but a good conversation, a uniform, even tract of life, the whole revolution of it regular. The inequality of some Christians' ways doth breed much discredit to religion, and discomfort to themselves.

But observe here, 1. The order of these two. 2. The principle of both.

1. The order. First, the Conscience good, and then the Conversation. *Make the tree good and the fruit will be good,* says our Saviour. Matt. xii. 33. So, here, a good conscience is the root of a good conversation. Most men begin at the wrong end of this work. They would reform the outward man first : that will do no good, it will be but dead work.

Do not rest upon external reformations, they will not hold ; there is no abiding, nor any advantage, in such a work.   You think, when reproved, Oh! I will mend and set about the redress of some outward things.   But this is as good as to do nothing.   The *mind and conscience being defiled,* as the Apostle speaks, Tit. i. 15, doth defile all the rest: it is a mire in the spring; although the pipes are cleansed, they will grow quickly foul again.   If Christians in their progress in grace would eye this most, that the conscience be growing purer, the heart more spiritual, the affections more regular and heavenly, their outward carriage would be holier; whereas the outward work of performing duties, and being much exercised in religion, may, by the neglect of this, be labour in vain, and amend nothing soundly.   To set the outward actions right, though with an honest intention, and not so to regard and find out the inward disorder of the heart, whence that in the actions flows, is but to be still putting the index of a clock right with your finger, while it is foul or out of order within, which is a continual business, and does no good.   Oh! but a purified conscience, a soul renewed and refined in its temper and affections, will make things go right without, in all the duties and acts of our callings.

2. The principle of good in both, is Christ : *Your good conversation in Christ.*   The conversation is not good, unless in him ; so neither is the conscience.

[1.] *In him,* as to our persons : we must be in him, and then, the conscience and conversation will be good in him.   The conscience that is morally good, having some kind of virtuous habits, yet being out of Christ, is nothing but pollution in the sight of God.   It must be washed in his blood, ere it can be clean ; all our pains will not cleanse it, floods of tears will not do it ; it is blood, and that blood alone, that hath the virtue of *purging the conscience from dead works.* Heb. ix. 14.

[2.] *In him,* as the perfect pattern of holiness ; the heart and life must be conformed to him, and so made truly good.

[3.] *In him,* as the Source of Grace, whence it is first derived, and always fed, and maintained, and made active : a Spirit goes forth from him that cleanseth our spirits, and so, makes our conversation clean and holy.

If thou wouldst have thy conscience and heart purified and pacified, and have thy life certified, go to Christ for all, make use of him ; as of his blood to wash off thy guiltiness, so of his Spirit to purify and sanctify thee.   If thou wouldst have thy heart reserved for God, pure as his temple ; if thou wouldst have thy lusts cast out which pollute thee, and findest no power to do it ; go to him, desire him to scourge out that filthy rabble, that abuse his house and make it a den of thieves.   Seek this, as the only way to have thy soul and thy ways righted, to *be in Christ,* and then, *walk in him.*   Let thy conversation be in Christ.   Study him, and follow him : look on his way, on his graces, his obedience, and humility, and meekness, till, by looking on them, they make the very idea of thee new, as the painter doth of a face he would draw to the life.   So behold his glory, that thou mayest be *transformed from glory to glory.*   But, as it is there added, this must be *by the Spirit of the Lord.*   2 Cor. iii. 18.   Do not, therefore, look on him simply, as an example without thee, but as life within thee.

Having *received him,* walk not only like him, but *in him,* as the Apostle St. Paul speaks, Col. ii. 6.   And as the word is here, *have your conversation,* not only according to Christ, but *in Christ.   Draw from his fulness grace for grace.*   John i. 16.

II. The other thing in the words, is, the advantage of this good conscience and conversation.   1. There is even an external success attends it, in respect of the malicious, ungodly world : *They shall be ashamed that falsely accuse you.*   Thus often it is even most evident to men ; the victory of innocency, silent innocency, most strongly confuting all calumny, making the ungodly, false accusers hide their heads.   Thus, without stirring, the integrity of a Christian conquers ; as a rock, unremoved, breaks the waters that are dashing against it. And this is not only a lawful, but a laudable way of revenge, shaming calumny out of it, and punishing evil speakers by well doing ; showing really how false their accusers were.   This is the most powerful apology and refutation ; as the sophister who would prove there was no motion, was best answered by the philosopher's rising up and walking.   And without this good conscience and conversation, we cut ourselves short of other apologies for religion, whatsoever we say for it.   One unchristian action will disgrace it more than we can repair by the largest and best framed speeches on its behalf.

Let those, therefore, who have given their names to Christ honour him, and their holy profession, most this way.   Speak for him as occasion requires ;—why should we not, provided it be *with meekness and fear,* as our Apostle hath taught ?—but let this be the main defence of religion : live suitably to it, and commend it so.   Thus all should do who are called Christians ; they should adorn that holy profession with holy conversation.   But the most are nothing better than spots and blots, some wallowing in the mire, and provoking one another to all uncleanness.   Oh ! the unchristian life of Christians ! an evil to be much lamented, more than all the troubles we sustain ! But these, indeed, do thus deny Christ, and declare that they are not his.   So many as have any reality of Christ in you, be so much the more holy, the more wicked the rest are.   Strive to make it up, and to honour that name which they disgrace.   And if they will reproach you, because ye walk not with them, and cast the mire of false reproaches on you, take no notice, but go on your way ; it will dry, and easily rub off.   Be not troubled with misjudgings ; shame them out of it by your blameless and holy carriage, for that will do most to put lies out of countenance.   However, if they continue impudent, the day is at hand, wherein all the enemies of Christ shall be *all clothed over* and covered *with shame,* and they who have kept a good conscience, and walked in Christ, *shall lift up their faces with joy.*

2ndly, There is an intrinsical good in this goodness of conscience, that sweetens all sufferings : as it follows,—

Ver. 17. For it is better, if the will of God be so, that ye suffer for well doing, than for evil doing.

THERE is a necessity of suffering in any way wherein ye can walk ; if ye choose the way of wickedness, you shall not, by doing so, escape suffering ; and that supposed, this is by far the better, to suffer *in well doing*, and *for* it, than to suffer either *for doing evil*, or simply to suffer *in that way*, (as the words run,) κακοποιοῦντας πάσχειν, *to suffer doing evil.*

The way of the ungodly is not exempt from suffering, even at present. Setting aside the judgment and wrath to come, they often suffer from the hands of men, whether justly or unjustly, and often from the immediate hand of God, who is always just, both in this and the other, causing the sinner *to eat of the fruit of his own ways.* Prov. i. 30. When profane, ungodly men offer violences and wrongs one to another, in this God is just against both, in that wherein they themselves are both unjust: they are both rebellious against him, and so, though they intend not to take up his quarrel, he means it Himself, and sets them to lash one another. The wicked profess their combined enmity against the children of God, yet they are not always at peace amongst themselves: they often revile and defame each other, and so it is kept up on both sides. Whereas the godly cannot hold them game in that, being like their Lord, *who, when he was reviled, reviled not again.* Besides, although the ungodly flourish at some times, yet they have their days of suffering, are subject to the common miseries of the life of man, and the common calamities of evil times; the sword and the pestilence, and such like public judgments. Now, in what kind soever it be that they suffer, they are at a great disadvantage, compared with the godly, in their sufferings.

Here impure consciences may lie sleeping, while men are at ease themselves; but when any great trouble comes and shakes them, then, suddenly, the conscience begins to awake and bustle, and proves more grievous to them, than all that comes on them from without. When they remember their despising of the ways of God, their neglecting of him and holy things, whence they are convinced how comfort might be reaped in these days of distress, this cuts and galls them most, looking back at their licentious, profane ways; each of them strikes to the heart. As the Apostle calls sin, *the sting of death*, so is it of all sufferings, and the sting that strikes deepest into the very soul: no stripes are like those that are secretly given by an accusing conscience. *Surdo verbere cedit.* JUV.

A sad condition it is, to have from thence the greatest anguish, whence the greatest comfort should be expected; to have thickest darkness, whence they should look for the clearest light. Men who have evil consciences, love not to be with them, are not much with themselves: as St. Augustine compares them to such as have shrewd wives, they love not to be much at home. But yet, outward distress sets a man inward, as foul weather drives him home, and there, where he should find comfort, he is met with such accusations as are *like a continual dropping*, as Solomon speaks of a contentious woman, Prov. xix. 3. It is a most wretched state, to live under sufferings or afflictions of any kind, and be a stranger to God; for a man to have God and his conscience against him, that should be his solace in times of distress; being knocked off from the comforts of the world, whereon he rested, and having no provision of spiritual comfort within, nor expectation from above.

But the children of God, in their sufferings, especially in such as are encountered for God, can retire within themselves, and rejoice in the testimony of a good conscience, yea, in the possession of Christ dwelling within them.   All the trouble that befalls them, is but as the rattling of hail upon the tiles of the house, to a man who is sitting within a warm room at a rich banquet; and such is a good conscience, a feast, yea, *a continual feast.*   The Believer looks on his Christ, and in him reads his deliverance from condemnation, and that is a strong comfort, a cordial that keeps him from fainting in the greatest distresses.   When the conscience gives this testimony, that sin is forgiven, it raises the soul above outward sufferings.   Tell the Christian of loss of goods, or liberty, or friends, or life, he answers all with this: Christ is mine, and my sin is pardoned; that is enough for me.   What would I not have suffered, to have been delivered from the wrath of God, if any suffering of mine in this world could have done that?   Now that is done to my hand, all other sufferings are light; they are *light* and *but for a moment.*   One thought of eternity drowns the whole time of the world's duration, which is but as one instant, or twinkling of an eye, betwixt eternity before, and eternity after; how much less is any short life, (and a small part of that is spent in sufferings,) yea, what is it, though it were all sufferings without interruption, which yet it is not!   When I look forward to the crown, all vanishes, and I think it *less than nothing.*   Now, these things the good conscience speaks to the Christian in his sufferings; therefore, certainly, his choice is best, who provides it for his companion against evil and troublous times. If moral integrity went so far, (as truly it did in some men who had much of it,) that they scorned all hard encounters, and esteemed this a sufficient bulwark, a strength impregnable, *Hic murus aheneus esto, nil conscire sibi,* how much more the Christian's good conscience, which alone is truly such!

As the Christian may thus look inward, and rejoice in tribulation, so there is another look, *upward,* that is here likewise mentioned, that allays very much all the sufferings of the saints : *If the will of God be so.*

The Christian mind hath still one eye to this, looking above the hand of men, and all inferior causes, in suffering, whether for the name of God, or otherwise; he looks on the sovereign will of God, and sweetly complies with that in all.   Neither is there any thing that doth more powerfully compose and quiet the mind than this; it makes it invincibly firm and content, when it hath attained this self-resignation to the *will of God,* so as to agree to that in every thing.   This is the very thing wherein tranquillity of spirit lies: it is no riddle, nor hard to be understood, yet few attain it.   And, I pray you, what is gained by our reluctances and repinings, but pain to ourselves?   God *doth what he will,* whether we consent or not.   Our disagreeing doth not prevent his purposes, but our own peace: if we will not be led, we are drawn.   We must suffer, if he will; but if we will what he wills, even in suffering, that makes it sweet and easy; when our mind goes along with his, and we willingly move with that stream of providence, which will carry us with it, even though we row against it; in which case we still have nothing but toil and weariness for our pains.

But this hard argument of Necessity is needless to the child of God, who, persuaded of the wisdom and love of his Father, knows that to

be truly best for him that his hand bestows. Sufferings are unpleasant to the flesh, and it will grumble ; but the voice of the Spirit of
God, in his children, is that of that good king, (Isa. xxxix. 8,) *Good
is the word of the Lord.* Let him do with me as seemeth good in his
eyes. My foolish heart would think these things I suffer might be
abated, but my wise and heavenly Father thinks otherwise. He hath
his design of honour to himself, and good to me in these, which I
would be loth to cross if I might. I might do God more service by
those temporal advantages, but doth not he know best what is fit?
Cannot he advance his grace more by the want of these things I
desire, than I could do myself by having them ? Cannot he make me
a gainer by sickness and poverty, and disgraces, and loss of friends and
children, by making up all in himself, and teaching me more of his
all-sufficiency ? Yea, even concerning the affairs of my soul, I am to
give up all to his good pleasure. Though I desire the light of his
countenance above all things in this world, yet, if he see fit to hide it
sometimes, if that be his will, let me not murmur. There is nothing
lost by this obedient temper ; yea, what way soever he deals with us,
there is much more advantage in it. No soul shall enjoy so much in
all estates, as that which hath divested and renounced itself, and hath
no will but God's.

Ver. 18. For Christ also hath once suffered for sins, the just for the unjust, (that he
might bring us to God,) being put to death in the flesh, but quickened by the Spirit.

THE whole life of a Christian, is a steady aiming at conformity with
Christ ; so that in any thing, whether doing or suffering, there can be
no argument so apposite and persuasive as his example, and no exercise of obedience, either active or passive, so difficult, but the view
and contemplation of that example will powerfully sweeten it. The
Apostle doth not decline the frequent use of it. Here we have it thus:
For Christ also suffered.

Though the doctrine of Christian suffering is the occasion of his
speaking of Christ's suffering, yet he insists on it beyond the simple
necessity of that argument, for its own excellency and for further usefulness. So we shall consider the double capacity. I. As an encouragement and engagement for Christians to suffer. II. As the great
point of their faith, whereon all their hopes and happiness depend,
being the means of their restoration to God.

I. The due consideration of Christ's sufferings doth much temper
all the sufferings of Christians, especially such as are directly for
Christ.

It is some known ease to the mind, in any distress, to look upon
examples of the like, or greater distress, in present or former times.
Ferre quam sortem patiuntur omnes. It diverts the eye from continual
poring on our own suffering ; and, when we return to view it again, it
lessens it, abates of the imagined bulk and greatness of it. Thus public, thus spiritual troubles are lightened ; and particularly the sufferings and temptations of the godly, by the consideration of this as their
common lot, their highway, not new in the person of any : *No temptation has befallen you, but what is common to men.* 1 Cor. x. 13. If
we trace the lives of the most eminent saints, shall we not find every

notable step that is recorded, marked with a new cross, one trouble following on another, *velut undâ pellitur unda,* as the waves do, in an incessant succession ? Is not this manifest in the life of Abraham, and of Jacob, and the rest of God's worthies, in the Scriptures ? And doth not this make it an unreasonable, absurd thought, to dream of an exemption ? Would any one have a new untrodden way cut out for him, free of thorns, and strewed with flowers all along ? Does he expect to meet with no contradictions, nor hard measure from the world, or imagine that there may be such a dexterity necessary, as to keep its good will, and the friendship of God too ? This will not be ; and it is a universal conclusion, *All that will live godly in Christ Jesus, must suffer persecution.* 2 Tim. iii. 12. This is the path to the kingdom, that which all the sons of God, the heirs of it, have gone in, even Christ ; according to that well-known word, One son without sin, but not one without suffering : *Christ also suffered.*

The example and company of the saints in suffering is very considerable, but that of Christ is more so than any other, yea, than all the rest together. Therefore the Apostle, having represented the former at large, ends in this, as the top of all, Heb. xii. 1, 2. *There is a race set before us,* it is to be run, and *run with patience,* and *without fainting :* now, he tells us of a *cloud of witnesses,* a cloud made up of instances of believers suffering before us, and the heat of the day wherein we run is somewhat cooled even by that cloud compassing us ; but the main strength of our comfort here, lies in *looking to Jesus,* in the eyeing of his sufferings and their issue. The considering and contemplating of him will be the strongest cordial, will keep you from *wearying* and *fainting* in the way, as it is verse 3.

The singular power of this instance, lies in many particulars considerable in it. To specify some chief things briefly in the steps of the present words : Consider, 1. The Greatness of the Example.

[1.] The greatness of the person, *Christ,* which is marked out to us by the manner of expression, [καὶ Χριστὸς,] *Christ also ;* besides and beyond all others, *even Christ himself.*

There can be no higher example. Not only are the sons of adoption sufferers, but the *begotten,* the *only begotten Son,* the Eternal Heir of glory, in whom all the rest have their title, their sonship and heirship, derived from, and dependent on his ; not only all the saints, but the King of saints. Who now shall repine at suffering ? Shall the wretched sons of men refuse to suffer, after the suffering of the spotless, glorious Son of God ? As St. Bernard speaks of pride, *Ubi se humiliavit Majestas, vermiculus infletur et intumescat*—After Majesty, Highest Majesty, to teach us humility, hath so humbled himself, how wicked and impudent a thing will it be for a worm to swell, to be high conceited ! Since thus our Lord hath taught us by suffering in his own person, and hath dignified sufferings so, we should certainly rather be ambitious than afraid of them.

[2.] The greatness and the continuance of his sufferings. That which the Apostle speaks here, of *his once suffering,* hath its truth ; taking in all, *he suffered once;* his whole life was one continued line of suffering, from the manger to the cross. All that lay betwixt was suitable ; his estate and entertainment throughout his whole life, agreed well with so mean a beginning, and so reproachful an end, of it. Forced upon a flight, while he could not go, and living till he appeared in public, in a very mean, despised condition, as the carpenter's son ; and, afterwards, his best works paid with envy and revilings, called a *wine-bibber*, and *a caster out of devils by the prince of devils;* his life often laid in wait and sought for. Art thou mean in thy birth and life, despised, misjudged, and reviled, on all hands ? Look how it was with Him, who had more right than thou hast to better entertainment in the world. Thou wilt not deny it was his own ; *it was made by him, and he was in it, and it knew him not.* Are thy friends harsh to thee ? *He came unto his own, and his own received him not.* Hast thou a mean cottage, or art thou drawn from it and hast no dwelling, and art thou every way poor and ill-accommodated ? He was as poor as thou canst be, *and had not where to lay his head,* worse provided than the *birds* and *foxes!* But then, consider to what a height his sufferings rose in the end, that most remarkable part of them here meant by his *once suffering for sins.* If thou shouldst be cut off by a violent death, or in the prime of thy years, mayst thou not look upon him as going before thee in both these ? And in so ignominious a way ! Scourged, buffeted, and spit on, he endured all, *he gave his back to the smiters,* and then, as the same prophet hath it, *he was numbered amongst the transgressors.* Isa. liii. *ult.* When they had used him with all that shame, they hanged him betwixt two thieves, and they that passed by *wagged their heads,* and darted taunts at him, as at a mark fixed to the cross : *they scoffed and said, He saved others, himself he cannot save. He endured the cross, and despised the shame,* says the Apostle, Heb. xii. 2.

Thus we see the outside of his sufferings. But the Christian is subject to grievous temptations and sad desertions, which are heavier by far than the sufferings which indeed the Apostle speaks of here. Yet, even in these, this same argument of his holds. For our Saviour is not unacquainted with, nor ignorant of, either of those, though still *without sin.* If any of *that* had been in any of his sufferings, it had not furthered, but undone all our comfort in him. But *tempted* he was ; he suffered that way too, and the temptations were terrible, as you know. And was there not some strong conflict when he fell down and prayed in the garden, and *sweat drops of blood?* Was there not an awful eclipse, when he cried out on the cross, *My God, my God, why hast thou forsaken me ?* So that, even in these, we may apply this comfort, and stay ourselves or our souls on him, and go to him as a compassionate High Priest. Heb. iv. 15. *For Christ also suffered.*

2. Consider the Fitness of the Example. As the same is every way great, yea, *greatest,* so it is fit, the *fittest* to take with a Christian, to set before him, as being so near a pattern, wherein he hath so much interest. As the argument is strong in itself, so, to the new man, the Christian man, it is particularly strongest ; it binds him most, as it is not far-fetched, but *exemplum domesticum,* a home pattern ; as when you persuade men to virtue, by the example of those that they have a near relation to. They are *his servants,* and shall they, or would they, think to *be greater than their Master,* to be exempt from his lot in the world ? They are *his soldiers,* and will they refuse to follow him, and

to endure with him? *Suffer hardship*, says the Apostle to Timothy, *as a good soldier of Jesus Christ.* 2 Tim. ii. 3. Will not a word from him put a vigour in them to go after him, whether upon any march or service, when he calls them friends, *Commilitones*, as they tell us was Julius Cæsar's word, which wrought so much on his trained bands? Yea, *he is not ashamed to call them brethren*, (Heb. ii. 11,) and will they be ashamed to share with him, and to be known by their suitable estate to be his brethren?

3. Consider the Efficacy of the Example. There is, from these sufferings of Christ, such a result of safety and comfort to a Christian, as makes them a most effectual encouragement to suffering, which is this: if he *suffered once*, and that was *for sin*, now that heavy, intolerable suffering for sin is once taken out of the Believer's way, it makes all other sufferings light, exceeding light, as nothing in his account. *He suffered once for sin*, so that to them who lay hold on him this holds sure, that sin is never to be suffered for in the way of strict justice again, as not by him, so not by them who are in him; for *he suffered for sins once*, and it was for *their* sins, every poor believer's. So, now the soul, finding itself rid of that fear, goes cheerfully through all other hazards and sufferings.

Whereas the soul, perplexed about that question, finds no relief in all other enjoyments; all propositions of lower comforts are unsavoury and troublesome to it. Tell it of peace and prosperity; say, however the world go, you shall have ease and pleasure, and you shall be honoured and esteemed by all; though you could make a man sure of these, yet if his conscience be working and stirred about the matter of his sin, and the wrath of God which is tied close to sin, he will wonder at your impertinency, in that you speak so far from the purpose. Say what you will of these, he still asks, What do you mean by this? Those things answer not to me. Do you think I can find comfort in them, so long as my sin is unpardoned, and there is a sentence of eternal death standing above my head? I feel even an impress of somewhat of that hot indignation, some flashes of it flying and lighting upon the face of my soul, and how can I take pleasure in these things you speak of? And though I should be senseless and feel nothing of this all my life, yet, how soon shall I have done with it, and the delights that reach no further! And then to have *everlasting burnings*, an eternity of wrath to enter to! How can I be satisfied with that estate?—All you offer a man in this posture, is as if you should set dainty fare, and bring music with it, before a man lying almost pressed to death under great weights, and should bid him eat and be merry, but lift not off his pressure: you do but mock the man and add to his misery. On the contrary, he that hath got but a view of his Christ, and reads his own pardon in Christ's sufferings, can rejoice in this, in the midst of all other sufferings, and look on death without apprehension, yea, with gladness, for the *sting is out*. Christ hath made all pleasant to him by this one thing, that *he suffered once for sins*. Christ hath perfumed the cross and the grave, and made all sweet. The pardoned man finds himself light, skips and leaps, and, *through Christ strengthening him*, he can encounter any trouble. If you think to shut up his spirit within outward sufferings, he is now, as Samson in his strength, able to carry away on his back the gates with which you would enclose him. Yea, he can submit patiently to the Lord's hand in any correction : Thou hast forgiven my sin, therefore deal with me as thou wilt ; all is well.

Refl. 1. Let us learn to consider more deeply, and to esteem more highly, Christ and his suffering, to silence our grumbling at our petty, light crosses ; for so they are, in comparison of his. Will not the great odds of his perfect innocency, and of the nature and measure of his sufferings ; will not the sense of the redemption of our souls from death by his death ; will none of these, nor all of them, argue us into more thankfulness and love to him, and patience in our trials ? Why will we then be called Christians ? It is impossible to be fretful and malcontent with the Lord's dealing with us in any kind, till first we have forgotten how he dealt with his dearest Son for our sakes. As St. Bernard speaks, *Enimvero non sentient sua, qui illius vulnera intuentur :* They truly feel not their own wounds, who contemplate his. But these things are not weighed by the most. We hear and speak of them, but our hearts receive not the impressions of them ; therefore we repine against our Lord and Father, and drown a hundred great blessings in any little trouble that befalls us.

Refl. 2. Seek surer interest in Christ and his suffering, than the most either have attained, or are aspiring to ; otherwise all that he suffered here will afford thee no ease or comfort in any kind of suffering. No, though thou suffer for a good cause, even for his cause, still this will be an extraneous, foreign thing to thee, and to tell thee of his sufferings, will work no otherwise with thee than some other common story. And as in the day of peace thou regardest it no more, so, in the day of thy trouble, thou shalt receive no more comfort from it. Other things which you esteemed, shall have no comfort to speak to you : *though you pursue them with words,* (as Solomon says of the poor man's friends, Prov. xix. 7,) *yet they shall be wanting to you.* And then you will surely find how happy it were to have this to turn you to, that the Lord Jesus suffered for sins, and for your sins, and therefore hath made it a light and comfortable business to you, to undergo momentary passing sufferings.

Days of trial will come ; do you not see they are on us already ? Be persuaded, therefore, to turn your eyes and desires more towards Christ. This is the thing we would still press : the support and happiness of your souls lie on it. But you will not believe it. Oh that you knew the comforts and sweetness of Christ ! Oh that one would speak, who knew more of them ! Were you once but entered into this knowledge of him, and the virtue of his sufferings, you would account all your days but lost wherein you have not known him ; and in all times, your hearts would find no refreshment like to the remembrance of his love.

Having somewhat considered these Sufferings, as the Apostle's argument for his present purpose, we come now,

II. To take a nearer view of the particulars by which he illustrates them, as the main point of our faith and comfort. Of them, here are two things to be remarked, their Cause and their Kind.

First, Their Cause ; both their meritorious cause and their final cause ; first, what in us procured these sufferings unto Christ, and secondly, what those his sufferings procured unto us. Our guiltiness brought suffering upon him ; and his suffering brings us unto God.

1st, For the meritorious cause, what in us brought sufferings on Christ. The evil of sin hath the evil of punishment inseparably connected with it. We are under a natural obligation of obedience unto God, and he justly urges it; so that where the *command* of his law is broken, the *curse* of it presently followeth. And though it was simply in the power of the supreme Lawgiver to have dispensed with the infliction, yet, having in his wisdom purposed to be known a just God in that way, following forth the tenor of his law, of necessity there must be a suffering for sin.

Thus, the angels who keep not their station, falling from it, fell into a dungeon, where they are, *under chains of darkness, reserved to the judgment of the great day.* Jude 6. Man also fell under the sentence of death, but in this is the difference betwixt man and them : they were not one of them, as the parent or common root of the rest, but each one fell or stood for himself alone, so a part of them only perished ; but Man fell altogether, so that not one of all the race could escape condemnation, unless some other way of satisfaction be found out. And here it is : *Christ suffered for sins, the just for the unjust. Father*, says he, *I have glorified thee on earth.* John xvii. 3. In this plot, indeed, do all the Divine attributes shine in their full lustre ; infinite mercy, and immense justice, and power, and wisdom. Looking on Christ as ordained for that purpose, *I have found a ransom*, says the Father, one fit to redeem man, a kinsman, one of that very same stock, the Son of man ; one able to redeem man by satisfying me, and fulfilling all I lay upon him ; *My Son, my only begotten Son, in whom my soul delights.* And he is willing, undertakes all, says, *Lo, I come*, Psal. xl. 7 : We are agreed upon the way of this redemption ; yea, upon the persons to be redeemed. It is not a roving, blind bargain, a price paid for we know not whom. Hear his own words : *Thou hast given the Son* (says the Son to the Father) *power over all flesh, that he should give eternal life to as many as Thou hast given him ;* and *all mine are thine, and thine are mine, and I am glorified in them.* John xvii. 2, 10.

For the sins of these he suffered, standing in their room ; and what he did and suffered according to the law of that covenant, was done and suffered by them. All the sins of all the elect were made up into a huge bundle, and bound upon his shoulders. So the prophet speaks in their name : *Surely He hath borne our griefs, and carried our sorrows :* and, *The Lord laid [or made to meet] on Him the iniquity of us all.* Isa. liii. 5. He had spoken of many ways of sin, and said, *We have turned every one to his own way ;* here he binds up all in the word *iniquity*, as all one sin, as if it were that one transgression of the first Adam, that brought on the curse of his seed, borne by the Second Adam, to take it away from all that are his seed, who are in him as their Root.

He is the great High Priest appearing before God with the names of the elect upon his shoulders, and in his heart bearing them and all their burdens, and offering for them, not any other sacrifice than *himself;* charging all their sin on himself, as the priest did the sins of the people on the head of the sacrifice. *He, by the Eternal Spirit,* says the Apostle, *offered up himself without spot unto God, spotless and sinless,* Heb. ix. 14; and so he alone is fit to take away our sin, being a satisfactory oblation for it. He suffered: in him was our ransom, and thus it was paid. In the man, Christ, was the Deity, and so his blood was, as the Apostle calls it, *the blood of God,* Acts xx. 28; and he being pierced, it came forth, and was told down as the rich price of our redemption. *Not silver, nor gold, nor corruptible things,* as our Apostle hath it before, *but the precious blood of Christ, as of a lamb without blemish.*

Obs. 1. Shall any man offer to bear the name of a Christian, who pleases himself in the way of sin, and can delight and sport himself with it, when he considers this, that Christ suffered for sin? Do not think it, you who still account sin sweet, which he found so bitter, and account that light, which was so heavy to him, and made his *soul heavy to the death.* You are yet far off from him. If you were in him, and one with him, there would be some harmony of your hearts with his, and some sympathy with those sufferings, as endured by your Lord, your Head, and for you. They who, with a right view, see him as pierced by their sins, that sight pierces them, and makes them mourn, brings forth tears, beholding the gushing forth of his blood. This makes the real Christian an avowed enemy to sin. Shall I ever be friends with that, says he, which killed my Lord? No, but I will ever kill it, and do it by applying his death. The true penitent is sworn to be the death of sin: he may be surprised by it, but there is no possibility of reconcilement betwixt them.

Thou that livest kindly and familiarly with sin, and either openly declarest thyself for it, or hast a secret love for it, where canst thou reap any comfort? Not from these sufferings. To thee, continuing in that posture, it is all one as if Christ had not suffered for sins; yea, it is worse than if no such thing had been, that there is salvation, and terms of mercy offered unto thee, and yet thou perishest; that there is *balm in Gilead,* and yet thou art not healed. And if thou hast not comfort from Jesus crucified, I know not whence thou canst have any that will hold out. Look about thee, tell me what thou seest, either in thy possession or in thy hopes, that thou esteemest most, and layest thy confidence on. Or, to deal more liberally with thee, see what estate thou wouldst choose, hadst thou thy wish; stretch thy fancy to devise an earthly happiness. These times are full of unquietness; but give thee a time of the calmest peace, not an air of trouble stirring; put thee where thou wilt, far off from fear of sword and pestilence, and encompass thee with children, friends, and possessions, and honours, and comfort, and health to enjoy all these; yet one thing thou must admit in the midst of them all: within a while thou must die, and having no real portion in Christ, but only a deluding dream of it, thou sinkest through that death into another death far more terrible. Of all thou enjoyest, nothing goes along with thee but unpardoned sin, and that delivers thee up to endless sorrow. *Oh that you were wise,* and *would consider your latter end!* Do not still gaze about you upon trifles, but yet be entreated to take notice of your Saviour, and receive him, that he may be yours. Fasten your belief and your love on him. Give all your heart to him, who stuck not to give himself an offering for your sins.

Obs. 2. To you who have fled unto him for refuge, if sensible of the Church's distress, be upheld with this thought, that He who suffered for it, will not suffer it to be undone. All the rage of enemies, yea, *the gates of hell shall not prevail against it.* He may, for a time, suffer the Church to be brought low for the sins of his people, and other wise reasons, but he will not utterly forsake it. Though there is much chaff, yet he hath a precious number in these kingdoms, for whom he shed his blood : many God hath called, and many he has yet to call ; he will not lose any of his flock which he bought so dear, (Acts xx. 28,) and for their sake he will, at one time or another, repair our breaches, and establish his throne in these kingdoms. For yourselves, what can affright you while this is in your eye ? Let others tremble at the apprehension of sword or pestilence ; but surely, you have for them and all other hazards, a most satisfying answer in this : My Christ hath suffered for sin ; I am not to fear that ; and *that* set aside, I know the worst is but death—I am wrong ; truly, that is the best : to be *dissolved, and be with Christ, is* [πολλῷ μᾶλλον κρεῖσσον] *much more better.* Phil. i. 23. *So being justified by faith,* believers *have peace with God,* and *rejoice in hope of the glory of God, glorying even in tribulations.* Rom. v. 1—3.

This were a happy estate indeed. But what shall they think who have no assurance, they who doubt that Christ is theirs, and that he suffered for their sins ? I know no way but to believe on him, and then you shall know that he is yours. From this arises the grand mistake of many : they would first know that Christ is theirs, and then would believe ; which cannot be, because he becomes ours by believing. It is that which gives title and propriety to him. He is set before sinners as a Saviour who hath suffered for sin, that they may look to him and be saved ; that they may lay over their souls on him, and then they may be assured he suffered for them.

Say, then, what is it that scares thee from Christ ? This, thou seest, is a poor groundless exception, for he is set before thee as a Saviour to believe on, that so he may be thy Saviour. Why wilt thou not come unto him ? Why refusest thou to believe ? Art thou a sinner ? Art thou unjust ? Then, he is fit for thy case : he suffered for sins, *the Just for the unjust.* Oh ! but so many and so great sins ! Yea, is that it ? It is true indeed, and good reason thou hast to think so ; but, 1*st,* Consider whether they be excepted in the proclamation of Christ, the pardon that comes in his name: if not, if he make no exception, why wilt thou ? 2*ndly,* Consider if thou wilt call them greater than this sacrifice, *He suffered.* Take due notice of the greatness and worth, first, of his person, and then, of his sufferings, and thou wilt not dare to say thy sin goes above the value of his suffering, or that thou art too unjust for him to justify thee. Be as unrighteous as thou canst be, art thou convinced of it ? then, know that Jesus the just is more righteous than thy unrighteousness. And, after all is said that any sinner hath to say, they are yet, without exception, *blessed who trust in him.* Psal. ii. *ult.*

2ndly, We have the *final cause* of his sufferings, *That he might bring us to God.*] It is the chief point of wisdom, to proportion means to their end: therefore, the all-wise God, in putting his only Son to so hard a task, had a high end in this, and this was it, *That he might bring us unto God.* In this we have three things: *1st*, The nature of this good, nearness unto God. *2ndly*, Our deprivement of it, by our own sin. *3rdly*, Our restoration to it, by Christ's sufferings.

[1.] The nature of this good. God hath suited every creature he hath made, with a convenient good to which it tends, and, in the obtainment of which it rests and is satisfied. Natural bodies have all their own natural place, whither, if not hindered, they move incessantly till they be in it; and they declare, by resting there, that they are (as I may say) where they would be. Sensitive creatures are carried to seek a sensitive good, as agreeable to their rank in being, and, attaining that, aim no further. Now, in this is the excellency of man, that he is made capable of a communion with his Maker, and, because capable of it, is unsatisfied without it: the soul, being cut out (so to speak) to that largeness, cannot be filled with less. Though he is fallen from his right to that good, and from all right desire of it, yet, not from a capacity of it, no, nor from a necessity of it, for the answering and filling of his capacity.

Though the heart once gone from God, turns continually further away from him, and moves not towards him, till it be renewed, yet even in that wandering, it retains that natural relation to God, as its centre, that it hath no true rest elsewhere, nor can by any means find it. It is made for him, and is therefore still restless till it meet with him.

It is true, the natural man takes much pains to quiet his heart by other things, and digests many vexations with hopes of contentment in the end and accomplishment of some design he hath; but still the heart misgives. Many times he attains not the thing he seeks; but if he do, yet he never attains the satisfaction he seeks and expects in it, but only learns from that to desire something further, and still hunts on after a fancy, drives his own shadow before him, and never overtakes it; and if he did, yet it is but a shadow. And so in running from God, besides the sad end, he carries an interwoven punishment with his sin, the natural disquiet and vexation of his spirit, fluttering to and fro, and *finding no rest for the sole of his foot;* the *waters* of inconstancy and vanity *covering the whole face of the earth.*

We study to debase our souls, and to make them content with less than they are made for; yea, we strive to make them carnal, that they may be pleased with sensible things. And in this, men attain a brutish content for a time, forgetting their higher good. But certainly, we cannot think it sufficient, and that no more were to be desired beyond ease and plenty, and pleasures of sense, for then, a beast in good case and a good pasture, might contest with us in point of happiness, and carry it away; for that sensitive good he enjoys without sin, and without the vexation that is mixed with us in all.

These things are too gross and heavy. The soul, the immortal soul, descended from heaven, must either be more happy or remain miserrable. The highest, the increated Spirit, is the proper good, *the Father of spirits*, that pure and full good which raises the soul above itself;

whereas all other things draw it down below itself. So, then, it is never well with the soul, but when it is near unto God, yea, in its union with him, married to him : mismatching itself elsewhere, it hath never any thing but shame and sorrow. *All that forsake thee shall be ashamed,* says the prophet, Jer. xvii. 13 ; and the Psalmist, *They that are afar off from thee shall perish,* Psal. lxxiii. 27. And this is indeed our natural miserable condition, and it is often expressed this way, by estrangedness and distance from God. See Eph. ii., where the Gentiles are spoken of as *far off* by their profession and nation, but both Jews and Gentiles are far off by their natural foundation, and both are brought near by the blood of the new covenant.

[2.] And this is the second thing here implied, that we are *far off by reason of sin;* otherwise there were no need of Christ, especially in this way of suffering for sin, *to bring us unto God.* At the first, sin, as the breach of God's command, broke off man, and separated him from God, and ever since the soul remains naturally remote from God. 1. It lies under a sentence of exile, pronounced by the justice of God ; condemned to banishment from God, who is the light and life of the soul, as the soul itself is of the body. 2. It is under a flat impossibility of returning by itself; and that in two respects : first, because of the guiltiness of sin standing betwixt, as an unpassable mountain or wall of separation ; secondly, because of the dominion of sin keeping the soul captive, yea, still drawing it farther off from God, increasing the distance and the enmity every day. Nor is there either in heaven or under heaven, any way to remove this enmity, and make up this distance, and restore man to the possession of God, but this one, by Christ, and by him suffering for sins.

[3.] Our restoration to nearness to God is by Christ's sufferings. He endured the sentence pronounced against man, yea, even in this particular notion of it, as a sentence of exile from God : one main ingredient in his suffering, was that sensible desertion by his heavenly Father, of which he cried out, *My God, my God, why hast thou forsaken me !* And, by suffering the sentence pronounced, he took away the guiltiness of sin, he himself being *spotless and undefiled.* *For such an High Priest became us,* Heb. vii. 26 : the more defiled we were, the more did we stand in need of an undefiled Priest and Sacrifice ; and he was both. Therefore the Apostle here very fitly mentions this qualification of our Saviour, as necessary for restoring us unto God, *the Just for the unjust.* So taking on himself, and taking away, the guilt of sin, setting his strong shoulder to remove that mountain, he made way or access for man unto God.

This the Apostle hath excellently expressed, Eph. ii. 16, *He hath reconciled us by his cross, having slain the enmity :* he killed the quarrel betwixt God and us, killed it by his death ; brings the parties together, and hath laid a sure foundation of agreement in his own sufferings ; appeases his Father's wrath by them, and by the same, appeases the sinner's conscience. All that God hath to say in point of justice, is answered there ; all that the poor humbled sinner hath to say, is answered too. He hath offered up such an atonement as satisfies the Father, so that he is content that sinners should come in and be reconciled. And then, Christ gives notice of this to the soul, to remove all jealousies. It is full of fear: though it would, it dares not approach unto God, apprehending him to be *a consuming fire.* They who have done the offence, are usually the hardest to reconcile, because they are still in doubt of their pardon. But Christ assures the soul of a full and hearty forgiveness, quenching the flaming wrath of God by his blood. No, says Christ, upon my warrant come in; you will now find my Father otherwise than you imagine: he hath declared himself satisfied at my hands, and is willing to receive you, to be heartily and thoroughly friends; never to hear a word more of the quarrel that was betwixt you; to grant a full oblivion. And if the soul bear back still through distrust, he takes it by the hand, and draws it forward, leads it unto his Father; (as the word προσαγάγη imports;) presents it to him, and leaves not the matter till it be made a full and sure agreement.

But for this purpose, that the soul may be both able and willing to come unto God, the sufferings of Christ take away that other impediment. As they satisfy the sentence, and thereby remove the guiltiness of sin, so he hath by them purchased a deliverance from the tyrannous *power* of sin, which detains the soul from God, after all the way has been made for its return. And he hath a power of applying his sufferings to the soul's deliverance, in that kind too. He opens the prison doors to them who are led captive; and because the great chain is upon the heart willingly enthralled in sin, he, by his sovereign power, takes off that, frees the heart from the love of sin, and shows what a base, slavish condition it is in, by representing, in his effectual way, the goodness of God, his readiness to entertain a returning sinner, and the sweetness and happiness of communion with him. Thus he powerfully persuades the heart to shake off all, and, without further delay, to return unto God so as to be received into favour and friendship, and to walk in the way of friendship, with God, to give up itself to his obedience, to disdain the vile service of sin, and live suitably to the dignity of fellowship and union with God.

And there is nothing but the power of Christ alone, that is able to effect this, to persuade a sinner to return, to bring home a heart unto God. Common mercies of God, though they have a leading faculty to repentance, (Rom. ii. 4,) yet the rebellious heart will not be led by them. The judgments of God, public or personal, though they ought to drive us to God, yet the heart, unchanged, runs the further from God. Do we not see it by ourselves and other sinners about us? They look not at all towards him who smites, much less do they return; or if any more serious thoughts of returning arise upon the surprise of an affliction, how soon vanish they, either the stroke abating, or the heart, by time, growing hard and senseless under it! Indeed, when it is renewed and brought in by Christ, then all other things have a sanctified influence, according to their quality, to stir up a Christian to seek after fuller communion, closer walk, and nearer access to God. But leave Christ out, I say, and all other means work not this way: neither the works nor the word of God sounding daily in his ear, *Return, return.* Let the noise of the rod speak it too, and both join together to make the cry the louder, *yet the wicked will do wickedly,* Dan. xii. 10; will not hearken to the voice of God, will not *see the hand of God lifted up*, Isa. xxvi. 11 ; will not be persuaded to go in and seek peace and reconcilement with God, though declaring himself provoked to punish, and to behave himself as an enemy against his own people. How many are there, who, in their own particular, have been very sharply lashed with divers scourges on their bodies, or their families, and yet are never a whit the nearer God for it all, their hearts are proud, and earthly, and vain, as ever ! and let him lay on ever so much, they will still be the same. Only a Divine virtue, going forth from Christ *lifted up, draws men* unto him ; and, being come unto him, he brings them unto the Father.

Reflection 1. You who are still strangers to God, who declare your-selves to be so, by living as strangers far off from him, do not still continue to abuse yourselves so grossly. Can you think any consola-tion yours that arises from the sufferings of Christ, while it is so evident they have not gained their end upon you, have not brought you to God ? Truly, most of you seem to think, that our Lord Jesus suffered rather to the end we might neglect God, and disobey him securely, than to re-store us to him. Hath he purchased you a liberty to sin ? Or is it not deliverance from sin, which alone is true liberty, the thing he aimed at, and agreed for, and laid down his life for ?

2. Why let we his blood still run in vain as to us ? He hath *by it opened up our way to God,* and yet we refuse to make use of it ! Oh how few come in ! Those who are brought unto God, and received into friendship with him, entertain that friendship, they delight in his company, love to be much with him : is it so with us ? By being so near, they become like unto him, know his will better every day, and grow more conformable to it. But, alas ! in the most, there is nothing of this.

3. But even they who are brought unto God, may be faulty in this, in part, not applying so sweet a privilege. They can comply and be too friendly with the vain world, can pass many days without a lively communion with God, not aspiring to the increase of that, as the thing our Lord hath purchased for us, and that wherein all our happiness and welfare lie, here and hereafter. Your hearts are cleaving to folly ; you are not delighting yourselves in the Lord, not refreshed with this nearness to him, and union with him ; your thoughts are not often on it, nor is it your study to walk conformably to it : certainly it ought to be thus, and you should be persuaded to endeavour that it may be thus with you.

4. Remember this for your comfort, that as you are brought unto God by Jesus Christ, so you are kept in that union by him. It is a firmer knot than the first was ; there is no power of hell can dissolve it. He suffered once to bring us once unto God, never to depart again. As he suffered once for all, so we are brought once for all. We may be sensibly nearer at one time than at another, but yet we can never be separate or cut off, being once knit by Christ, as the bond of our union. *Neither principalities, nor powers,* (&c.,) *shall be able to separate us from the love of God,* because it holds *in Christ Jesus our Lord.* Rom. viii. 37, 38.

Secondly, as to the Kind of our Lord's Sufferings ; *Being put to death in the flesh, but quickened by the Spirit.*] The true life of a

Christian, is, to eye Christ in every step of his life, both as his rule, and as his strength; looking to him as his pattern, both in doing and suffering, and drawing power from him for going through both: for the look of Faith doth that, fetches life from Jesus to enable it for all, being without him able for nothing. Therefore the Apostle doth still set this before his brethren; and having mentioned Christ's sufferings in general, the condition and end of it, he here specifies the particular kind of it, that which was the utmost point, *put to death in the flesh*, and then adds this issue out of it, *quickened by the Spirit*.

This is at once the strongest engagement, and the strongest encouragement. Was he, our Head, crowned with thorns, and shall the Body look for garlands? Are we redeemed from hell and condemnation by him, and can any such refuse any service he calls them to? They who are *washed in the Lamb's blood, will follow him whithersoever he goes;* (Rev. xiv. 4;) and, following him through, they shall find their journey's end overpay all the troubles and sufferings of the way. *These are they,* said the Elder who appeared in vision to John, *who came out of great tribulation:* tribulation and great tribulation, yet, they came out of it, and gloriously too, arrayed in *long white robes!* The scarlet Strumpet (as follows in that book) dyed her garments red in the blood of the saints; but this is their happiness, that *their garments are washed white in the blood of the Lamb.* Rev. vii. 14.

Once take away sin, and all suffering is light. Now, that is done by this, *His once suffering for sin:* those who are in him shall hear no more of that as condemning them, binding over to suffer that wrath which is due to sin. Now, this puts an invincible strength into the soul for enduring all other things, how hard soever.

Put to death.] This is the utmost point, and that which men are most startled at, *to die:* and a violent death, *put to death;* and yet, he hath led in this way, who *is the Captain of our salvation. In the flesh.* Under this second phrase, his human nature, and his Divine nature and power, are distinguished. *Put to death in the flesh,* is a very fit expression, not only (as is usual) taking the flesh for the whole manhood, but because death is most properly spoken of that very person, or his flesh. The whole man suffers death, a dissolution, or taking to pieces, and the soul suffers a separation, or dislodging; but death, or the privation of life and sense, belongs particularly to the flesh or body. But the *Spirit,* here opposed to the *flesh* or body, is certainly of a higher nature and power than is the human soul, which cannot of itself return to re-inhabit and quicken the body.

Put to death.] His death was both voluntary and violent. That same power which restored his life could have kept it exempted from death; but the design was for death. He therefore took our flesh, to put it off thus, and to offer it up as a sacrifice, which, to be acceptable, must of necessity be free and voluntary; and, in that sense, he is said to have died even by that same Spirit, which here, in opposition to death, is said to quicken him. See Heb. ix. 14, *Through the Eternal Spirit, he offered himself without spot unto God.* They accounted it an ill-boding sign when the sacrifices came constrained to the altar, and drew back, and, on the contrary, were gladdened with the hopes of success, when they came cheerfully forward; but never sacrifice came so willingly all the way, and from the first step knew whither he was going. Yet, because no other sacrifice would serve, he was most content to become one; *Sacrifices and burnt offerings Thou didst not desire: then said I, Lo, I come.* Psal. xl. 6, 7. He was not only a willing sacrifice, as Isaac, bound peaceably, and laid on the altar, but his own sacrificer. The beasts, if they came willingly, yet offered not themselves; but he *offered up himself;* and thus, not only by a willingness far above all those *sacrifices of bullocks and goats,* but *by the eternal Spirit,* he offered up himself. Therefore he says, in this regard, *I lay down my life for my sheep;* it is not pulled from me, but I lay it down. And so it is often expressed by [ἀπέθανε] *he died;* and yet, this suits with it, [θανατωθεὶς,] *put to death.* Yea, it was also expedient to be thus, that his death should be violent, and so, the more penal, to carry the more clear expression of a punishment, and such a violent death as had both ignominy and a curse tied to it, and this inflicted in a judicial way; (though, as from the hands of men, most unjustly;) that he should stand, and be judged, and condemned to death as a guilty person, carrying in that person the persons of so many who should otherwise have fallen under condemnation, as indeed guilty. *He was numbered with transgressors,* (as the prophet hath it,) *bearing the sins of many.* Isa. liii. *ult.*

Thus, then, there was, in his death, external violence joined with internal willingness. But what is there to be found but complications of wonders in our Lord Jesus? Oh! high, inconceivable mystery of godliness! *God manifested in the flesh!* Nothing in this world so strange and sweet as that conjuncture, *God-Man, humanitas Dei!* What a strong foundation of friendship and union betwixt the person of man and God, that their natures met in so close embraces in one Person! And, then, look on, and see so poor and despised an outward condition through his life, yet, having hid under it the majesty of God, *all the brightness of the Father's glory!* And this is the top of all, that he was *put to death in the flesh;* the Lord of life dying, the Lord of glory clothed with shame! But it quickly appeared what kind of person it was that died, by this, *he was put to death,* indeed, *in the flesh, but quickened by the Spirit.*

Quickened.] He was indeed too great a morsel for the Grave to digest. For all its vast craving mouth and devouring appetite, crying, *Sheol, Give, give,* yet was it forced to give him up again, as the fish to give up the prophet Jonah, who, in that, was the figure of Christ. The chains of that prison are strong, but he was too strong a prisoner to be held by them; as our Apostle hath it in his sermon, (Acts ii. 24,) that it was *not possible that he should be kept by them.* They thought all was sure when they had rolled to the stone, and sealed it; that then the Grave had indeed shut her mouth upon Him; it appeared a done business to them, and looked as if it were very complete in his enemies' eyes, and very desperate to his friends, his poor disciples and followers. Were they not near the point of giving over, when they said, *This is the third day,* &c., and, *We thought this had been he that should have delivered Israel?* Luke xxiv. 21. And yet, he was then with them, who was indeed the *deliverer* and *salvation of Israel.* That rolling of the stone to the grave, was as if they had rolled it towards the east in the night, to stop the rising of the sun the next morning; much further above all their watches and their power was this *Sun of Righteousness* in his rising again. That body which was entombed was united to the spring of life, the Divine Spirit of the Godhead that quickened it.

Reflection 1. Thus the Church, which is likewise his body, when it seems undone, when it is brought to the lowest posture and state, yet, by virtue of that mystical union with Jesus Christ, (as his natural body, by personal union with his Deity,) shall be preserved from destruction, and shall be delivered and raised in due time. Yea, as he was nearest his exaltation in the lowest step of his humiliation, so is it with his Church: when things are brought to the most hopeless appearance, then shall light arise out of darkness. *Cum duplicantur lateres venit Moses.*

Therefore, as we ought to seek a more humble sense of Sion's distress, so we should also be solicitous not to let go this hope, that her mighty Lord will, in the end, be glorious in her deliverance, and that all her sufferings and low estate shall be as a dark ground to set off the lustre of her restoration, when the Lord shall visit her with salvation; as in the rising of Jesus Christ, his almighty power and Deity were more manifested than if he had not died. And therefore we may say confidently, with the Psalmist to his Lord, Psal. lxxi. 20, *Thou who hast showed me great and sore troubles, shalt quicken me again, and shalt bring me up from the depths of the earth: Thou shalt increase my greatness, and comfort me on every side.* Yea, the Church comes more beautiful out of the deepest distress: let it be overwhelmed with waves, yet it sinks not, but rises up as only washed. And in this confidence we ought to rejoice, even in the midst of our sorrows; and, though we live not to see them, yet, even in beholding afar off, to be gladdened with the great things the Lord will do for his Church in the latter times. He will certainly *make bare his holy arm in the eyes of the nations*, and *all the ends of the earth shall see the salvation of our God*. Isa. lii. 10. His King whom he *hath set on his holy hill*, shall grow in his conquests and glory, and all that rise against him *shall he break with a rod of iron*. Psal. ii. He was humbled once, but his glory shall be for ever. *As many were astonished at him, his visage being marred more than any man*, they shall be as much astonished at his beauty and glory: *So shall he sprinkle many nations; the kings shall shut their mouths at him*. Isa. lii. 14, 15. According as here we find that remarkable evidence of his Divine power in rising from the dead: *Put to death in the flesh, but quickened by the Spirit.*

Ref. 2. Thus may a believing soul at the lowest, when, to its own sense, it is given over unto death, and swallowed up of it, as it were *in the belly of hell*, yet look up to this Divine power. He whose soul was not left there, will not leave thine there. Yea, when thou art most sunk in thy sad apprehensions, and far off to thy thinking, then is he nearest to raise and comfort thee; as sometimes it grows darkest immediately before day. Rest on his power and goodness, which never failed any who did so. *It is He* (as David says) *who lifts up the soul from the gates of death.* Psal. ix. 13.

Ref. 3. Would any of you be cured of that common disease, the fear of death? Look this way, and you shall find more than you seek; you shall be taught, not only not to fear, but to love it. Consider, 1. His death: *He died.* By that, thou who receivest him as thy life, mayest be sure of this, that thou art, by that his death, freed from the second death. *Descendit huc vita nostra, et tulit mortem nostram, et occidit eam de abundantiâ vitæ suæ:* He who is our life, says Augustine, descended hither, and bore our death, killing it by the abounding of his life. And that is the great point. Let that have the name which was given to the other, *the most terrible of all terrible things;* and, as the second death is removed, this death which thou art to pass through, is, I may say, beautified and sweetened; the ugly visage of it becomes amiable, when ye look on it in Christ, and in his death: that puts such a pleasing comeliness upon it, that whereas others fly from it with affright, the Believer cannot choose but embrace it. He longs to lie down in that bed of rest, since his Lord lay in it, and hath warmed that cold bed, and purified it with his fragrant body. 2. But especially be looking forward to his return thence, *quickened by the Spirit;* this being to those who are in him the certain pledge, yea, the effectual cause, of that blessed resurrection which is in their hopes. There is that union betwixt them, that they shall rise by the communication and virtue of his rising; not simply by his power, for so the wicked to their grief shall be raised, but they by his life, as theirs. Therefore it is so often reiterated, John vi., where he speaks of himself as the *living* and *life-giving Bread* to Believers, *I will raise them up at the last day.* This comfort we have even for the house of clay we lay down; and as for our more considerable part, our immortal souls, this his death and rising hath provided for them, at their dislodging, an entrance into that glory where he is. Now, if these things were lively apprehended and laid on, Christ made ours, and the first resurrection manifest in us, were we quickened by His Spirit to newness of life, certainly there would not be a more welcome and refreshing thought, nor a sweeter discourse to us, than that of death. And no matter for the kind of it. Were it a violent death, so was his. Were it what we account most judgment-like amongst diseases, the plague; was not his death very painful? And was it not an accursed death? And by that curse endured by him in his, is not the curse taken away to the Believer? Oh how welcome will that day be, that day of deliverance! To be out of this woeful prison, I regard not at what door I go out, being at once freed from so many deaths, and let in to enjoy him who is my life.

Ver. 19. By which also he went and preached unto the spirits in prison;
20. Which sometime were disobedient, when once the longsuffering of God waited in the days of Noah, while the ark was a preparing, wherein few, that is, eight souls were saved by water.
21. The like figure whereunto even baptism doth also now save us (not the putting away of the filth of the flesh, but the answer of a good conscience toward God,) by the resurrection of Jesus Christ.

THERE is nothing that so much concerns a Christian to know, as the excellency of Jesus Christ, his person and works; so that it is always pertinent to insist much on that subject. The Apostle, having spoken of this Spirit or Divine nature, and the power of it, as raising him from the dead, takes occasion to speak of another work of that Spirit, to wit, the emission and publishing of his Divine doctrine ; and that, not as a new thing following his death and rising, but as the same in substance with that which was, by the same Spirit, promulgated long before, even to the first inhabitants of the world.   *Quickened by the Spirit,* that is, in our days, says the Apostle ; but then, long before that, by the same Spirit, *He went and preached to the spirits in prison.*

This place is somewhat obscure in itself, but, as it usually happens, made more so by the various fancies and contests of interpreters, aiming or pretending to clear it.   These I like never to make a noise of.   They who dream of the *descent of Christ's soul into hell,* think this place sounds somewhat that way ; but, being examined, it proves no way suitable, nor can, by the strongest wresting, be drawn to fit their purpose.   For, 1. That it was to preach, he went thither, they are not willing to avow ; though the end they assign is as groundless and imaginary as this is.   2. They would have his business to be with the spirits of the faithful deceased before his coming ; but here we see it is with the disobedient.   And, 3. His Spirit here is the same with the sense of the foregoing words, which mean not his soul, but his eternal Deity.   4. Nor is it *the spirits that were in prison,* as they read it, but *the spirits in prison,* which, by the opposition of their former condition, *sometime,* or *formerly disobedient,* doth clearly speak their present condition, as the just consequence and fruit of their disobedience.

Other misinterpretations I mention not, taking it as agreeable to the whole strain of the Apostle's words,* that Jesus Christ did, before his appearing in the flesh, speak by his Spirit in his servants to those of the foregoing ages, yea, the most ancient of them, declaring to them the way of life, though rejected by the unbelief of the most part. This is interjected in the mentioning of Christ's sufferings and exaltation after them.   And, after all, the Apostle returns to that again, and to the exhortation which he strengthens by it : but so as that this discourse taken in, is pertinently adapted to the present subject. The Apostle's aim in it we may conceive to be this, (his main scope being to encourage his brethren in the faith of Christ, and the way of holiness, against all opposition and hardship,) so to instruct his brethren in Christ's perpetual influence into his Church in all ages, even before his incarnation, as that they might, at the same time, see

---

* Thus I then thought, but do now apprehend another sense, as probable, if not more, even that so much rejected by most interpreters: the mission of the Spirit, and preaching of the Gospel by it, after his resurrection, preaching to sinners, and converting them, according to the prophecy which he first fulfilled in person, and, after, more amply in his Apostles.   That prophecy I mean, Isa. lx. 1.   The Spirit came upon him, and it was sent from him on his Apostles, to preach to *spirits in prison ; to preach liberty to those captives,* captive spirits, and therefore called *spirits in prison,* to illustrate the thing the more, by opposition to that Spirit of Christ, *the Spirit of liberty,* setting them free.   And this is to show the greater efficacy of Christ's preaching, than of Noah's ; though he was a signal preacher of righteousness, yet only himself and his family, eight persons, were saved by him ; but multitudes of all nations by the Spirit and preaching of Christ in the Gospel ; and that by the seal of baptism, the resurrection of Christ being represented in the return from the water, and our dying with him, by immersion ; and that figure of Baptism is like their Ark.

the great unbelief of the world, yea, their opposing of Divine truth, and the small number of those who receive it, and so not be discouraged by the fewness of their number, and the hatred of the world, finding that salvation in Jesus Christ, dead and risen again, which the rest miss of by their own wilful refusal. And this very point he insists on clearly in the following chapter, ver. 3, 4. And the very ways of ungodliness there specified, which believers renounce, were those that the world was guilty of in those days, and in which they were surprised by the Flood : *They ate and drank till the Flood came upon them.*

In the words of these three verses, we have three things : First, An assertion concerning the preaching of Christ, and the persons he preached to. Secondly, The designation and description of the time or age wherein that was, and the particular way of God's dealing with them. Thirdly, The adapting or applying of the example to Christians.— First, the Assertion concerning the preaching of Christ, and the persons he preached to, in these words, which I take together, *By the which Spirit he went and preached to the spirits in prison, which sometime were disobedient.*

In these words we have A Preacher and his Hearers. With regard to the Preacher, we shall find here, 1st, His ability. 2ndly, His activity in the use of it.

1st, His ability is altogether singular and matchless, the very spring of all abilities, the Spirit of Wisdom himself, being the co-eternal Son of God. That Spirit he preached by, was the same as that by which he raised himself from the dead ; and without this Spirit there is no preaching. Now he was, as our Apostle calls him, *a preacher of righteousness*, but it was by the power of this Spirit ; for in him did this Spirit preach. The Son is the wisdom of the Father. His name is The Word ; not only for that by him *all things were created*, as John hath it, John i. 4, the Son being that power by which, as by the word of his mouth, all things were made ; but he is *The Word*, likewise, *as revealing the Father*, declaring to us the counsel and will of God : therefore he is, by the same Evangelist, in the same place, called that *Light which illuminates the world*, John i. 9, without which, Man, called the lesser world, the intellectual world, were as the greater world without the sun. And all who bring aright the doctrine of saving wisdom, derive it necessarily from him ; all preachers draw from this sovereign Preacher, as the fountain of Divine light. As all the planets receive their light from the sun, and by that diffusing itself amongst them, it is not diminished in the sun, but only communicated to them, remaining still full and entire in it as its source ; thus doth the Spirit flow from Christ, in a particular degree, unto those he sends forth in his name, and it is in them that he preaches by the power and light of his eternal Spirit.

Hither, then, must all those come who would be rightly supplied and enabled for that work. It is impossible to speak duly of him in any measure, but by his Spirit ; there must be particular access, and a receiving of instructions from him, and a transfusion of his Spirit into ours. Oh! were it thus with us, how sweet were it to speak of him ! To be much in prayer, much in dependence on him, and drawing from him, would do much more in this, than reading and studying, seeking after arts, and tongues, and common knowledge. These, indeed, are not to be despised nor neglected. *Utilis lectio, utilis eruditio, sed magis unctio necessaria, quippe quæ sola docet de omnibus*, says Bernard : *Reading is good, and learning good, but above all, anointing is necessary, that anointing that teacheth all things.* And you who are for your own interest, be earnest with this Lord, this Fountain of Spirit, to let forth more of it upon his messengers in these times. You would receive back the fruit of it, were ye busy this way ; you would find more life and refreshing sweetness in the word of life, how weak and worthless soever they were who brought it ; it should descend as sweet showers upon the valleys, and make them fruitful.

2nd, We have the activity of Christ as a preacher. By this Spirit, it is said here, *He preached.* Not only did he so in the days of his abode on earth, but in all times, both before and after. He never left his Church altogether destitute of saving light, which he dispensed himself, and conveyed by the hands of his servants ; therefore it is said, *He preached*, that this may be no excuse for times after he is ascended into heaven, no, nor for times before he descended to the earth in human flesh. Though he preached not then, nor does now in his flesh, yet *by his Spirit* he then preached, and still doth ; so that according to what was chief in him, he was still present with his Church, and preaching in it, and is so to the end of the world, this his infinite Spirit being every where. Yet, it is said here, by which *he went and preached*, signifying the remarkable clearness of his administration that way. As when he appears eminently in any work of his own, or in taking notice of our works, God is said to come down ; (as in reference to those cities of Babel and Sodom, *Let us go down*, and, *I will go down and see*, Gen. xi. 5, 7 ; xviii. 21 ; so, Exod. iii. 8, *I am come down to deliver Israel ;*) thus here, so clearly did he admonish them by Noah, coming, as it were, himself, on purpose to declare his mind to them. And this word, I conceive, is the rather used to show what equality there is in this. He came, indeed, visibly, and dwelt amongst men, when he became flesh ; yet, before that he visited them by his Spirit ; he went by that, and preached. And so, in after-times, himself being ascended, and not having come visibly in his flesh to all, but to the Jews only, yet, in the preaching of the Apostles to the Gentiles, as the great Apostle says of him in that expression, Eph. ii. 17, *He came and preached to you which were afar off.* And this he continues to do in the ministry of his word ; and therefore, says he, *He that despiseth you, despiseth me.* Luke x. 16.

Were this considered, it could not but procure far more respect to the word, and more acceptance of it. Would you think that, in his word, Christ speaks by his eternal Spirit, yea, that he comes and preaches, addresses himself particularly to you in it : could you slight him thus, and turn him off with daily refusals, or delays at least ? Think, it is too long you have so unworthily used so great a Lord, who brings unto you so great salvation ; who came once in so wonderful a way to work that salvation for us in his flesh, and is still coming to offer it unto us by his Spirit ; who does himself preach to us, telling us what he undertook on our behalf, and how he hath performed all, and that now nothing rests but that we receive him, and believe on him, and all is ours.   But alas ! from the most the return is, what we have here, *disobedience*.

Which sometime were disobedient.] There are two things in these hearers, by which they are characterized ; their present condition in the time the Apostle was speaking of them, *spirits in prison*, and their former disposition, when the Spirit of Christ was preaching to them, *sometime disobedient*.   This latter went first in time, and was the cause of the other ; therefore, of it first.

1. *Sometime disobedient.*] If you look to their visible subordinate preacher, you find he was a holy man, and an able and diligent preacher of righteousness, both in his doctrine, and in the track of his life, which is the most powerful preaching ; on both which accounts it seems strange that he prevailed so little.   But it appears much more so, if we look higher, even to this height at which the Apostle points, that almighty *Spirit of Christ* who preached to them.   And yet, they were disobedient !   The word is [ἀπειθήσασι], *they were not persuaded;* it signifies both unbelief and disobedience, and that very fitly, unbelief being in itself the grand disobedience : it is the mind's not yielding to Divine truth, and so the spring of all disobedience in affection and action.   And this *root of bitterness*, this unbelief, is deeply fastened in our natural hearts ; and without a change in them, a taking them to pieces, they cannot be good.   It is as a tree firmly rooted, which cannot be plucked up without loosening the ground round about it. And this accursed root brings forth fruit unto death, because the word is not believed, neither the threats of the Law, nor the promises of the Gospel ; therefore men cleave unto their sins, and speak peace unto themselves while they are under the curse.

It may seem very strange that the Gospel is so fruitless amongst us ; yea, that neither word nor rod, both preaching aloud to us the doctrine of humiliation and repentance, persuades any man to return, or so much as to turn inward, and question himself, to say, What have I done ?   But thus it will be, till the Spirit be poured from on high, to open and soften hearts.   This is to be desired, as much wanting in the ministry of the word ; but were it there, that would not serve, unless it were by a concurrent work within the heart meeting the word, and making the impressions of it there : for here we find the Spirit went and preached ; and yet, the spirits of the hearers still remained unbelieving and disobedient.   It is therefore a combined work of this Spirit in the preacher and the hearers, that makes it successful, otherwise it is but shouting in a dead man's ear ; there must be *something within*, as one said in a like case.

2. *To the spirits in prison.*]   That is now their posture ; and because he speaks of them as in that posture, he calls them spirits ; for it is their spirits that are in that prison.   He likewise calls them spirits to whom the Spirit of Christ preached, because it is indeed that which the preaching of the word aims at ; it hath to do with the spirits of men.   It is not content to be at their ear with a sound, but works on their minds and spirits some way, either to believe and receive, or to

be hardened and sealed up to judgment by it, which is for rebels. If disobedience follow on the preaching of that word, *the prison* follows on that disobedience ; and that word, by which they would not be bound to obedience, binds them over to that prison, whence they shall never escape, nor be released for ever.

Take notice of it, and know that you are warned, you who will not receive salvation, offering, pressing itself upon you. You are every day in that way of disobedience, hastening to this perpetual imprisonment.

Consider, you now sit and hear this word ; so did those who are here spoken of : they had their time on earth, and much patience was used towards them. And though you are not to be swept away by a flood of waters, yet you are daily carried on by the flood of time and mortality. Psal. xc. 5. And how soon you shall be on the other side, and sent into eternity, you know not. I beseech you, be yet wise ; hearken to the offers yet made you ; for in his name I yet once again make a tender of Jesus Christ, and salvation in him, to all that will let go their sins, to lay hold on him. Oh ! do not destroy yourselves. You are in prison ; he proclaims unto you liberty. Christ is still following us himself with treaties. *Clamans dictis, factis, morte, vitâ, descensu, ascensu, clamans ut redeamus ad eum* (Augustine): Crying aloud by his words, by his deeds, by his death, by his life, by his coming down from heaven, by his ascension into it, crying to us to return to him. Christ proclaims your liberty, and will you not accept of it ? Think, though you are pleased with your present thraldom and prison, it reserves you (if you come not forth) to this other prison, that shall not please you : these chains of spiritual darkness in which you are, unless you be freed, will deliver you up to the *chains of everlasting darkness,* wherein these hopeless prisoners are *kept to the judgment of the great day.* But if you will receive Jesus Christ, presently upon that, life, and liberty, and blessedness are made yours. *If the Son make you free, you shall be free indeed.* John viii. 35.

When once the long-suffering of God waited in the days of Noah.] There are two main continuing wonders in the world, the bounty of God, and the disloyalty of man ; and the succession of times is nothing but new editions of these two. One grand example is here set before us, an œcumenical example, as large as the whole world ; on the part of God, much patience, and yet, on man's part, invincible disobedience. Here are two things in the instance. 1*st,* The Lord's general dealing with the world of the ungodly at that time. 2*ndly,* His peculiar way with his own chosen, Noah and his family : he waited patiently for all the rest, but he effectually saved them.

Observe, first, The *time* designated thus, *In the days of Noah.* There were many great and powerful persons in those days, who overtopped Noah (no doubt) in outward respects ; as, in their stature, the proud giants. And they begot children, *mighty men of old, men of renown,* as the text hath it, Gen. vi. 3 ; and yet, as themselves perished in the flood, so their names are drowned. They had their big thoughts, certainly, that their houses and *their names* should *continue,* as the Psalmist speaks, (Psal. xlix. 11,) and yet they are sunk in perpetual oblivion ; while Noah's name, who walked in humble obedience, you see in these most precious records of God's own book, still looks fresh, and smells sweet, and hath this honour, that the very age of the world is marked with this name, to be known by it: *In the days of Noah*. That which profane ambitious persons do idolatrously seek after they are often remarkably disappointed of. They would have their names memorable and famous, yet they rot; they are either buried with them, or remembered with disgrace, rotting above ground, as carcasses uninterred, and so are the more noisome; it being as little credit to them to be mentioned, as for Pilate that his name is in the Confession of Faith. But the name and remembrance of the righteous is still sweet and delightful; as the name of Abraham the Father of the faithful, and those of Isaac and Jacob: their names are embalmed indeed, so that they cannot rot, embalmed with God's own name, [*Eternal*] THAT name being wrapped about theirs, *the God of Abraham, Isaac, and Jacob*.

Thus is Noah here mentioned as preferred of God; and so, in the Second Epistle, as *a preacher of righteousness*, and Heb. xi., among those worthies whose honour is, that *they believed*. This is only a name, a small thing, not to be mentioned in comparison of their other privileges, and especially of that venerable life and glory which they are heirs too; and indeed it is a thing they regard very little; yet, this we see, that even this advantage follows them, and flies from the vain and ungodly who haunt and pursue it.

The Lord's dealing with the wicked in those times, before he swept them away by the deluge, is represented in these two particulars: 1. Long-suffering, and withal, 2. Clear warning.

1. Long-suffering—long forbearing to be angry, as the Hebrew word is in the proclamation of the Divine name, Exod. xxxiv. 6, which supposes a great provocation, and the continuance of it, and yet, patience continuing. And in this appears the goodness of God: considering how hateful sin is to him, and how powerful he is to punish it, how easy were it, if it pleased him, in one moment to cut off all the ungodly, high and low, throughout the whole world! Yet he bears, and forbears to punish! Oh, what a world of sin is every day committed in nations, in cities, and villages, yea, in families, which he doth not strike with present judgments, and not only forbears to punish, but multiplies his common mercies on them, *sun and rain and fruitful seasons*. Acts xiv. 17.

Yea, there is so much of this, that it falls under a gross misconstruction; yet, he bears that too. *Because sentence against an evil work is not speedily executed, therefore the heart of the sons of men is fully set in them to do evil*. Eccles. viii. 11. Because there is not so much as *a word* of it for the time, (so the word is) this swells and fills the heart of man, and makes it *big to do evil*. And not only is the Lord's long-suffering mistaken by the ungodly, but even by his own, who should understand him better, and know the true sense of his ways, yet sometimes they are misled in this point: beholding his forbearance of punishing the workers of iniquity, instead of magnifying his patience, they fall very near into questioning his justice and providence. See Psal. xiii., Jer. xii., Job xx., &c. Our narrow, hasty spirits, left to their own measures, take not in those larger views that would satisfy us in respect to the ways of God, and forget the immense largeness of his wise designs, his deep reach from one age to another, yea, from eternity to eternity. We consider not, 1. How easily he can right himself, in point of justice, when he will ; that none can make escape from him, how loose soever their guard seem, and how great liberty soever appears in their present condition. *Nemo decoquit huic creditori.* 2. That as he can most easily, so he will most seasonably, be known in executing judgment ; and that his justice shall shine the brighter, by all that patience he hath used, by the sun of prosperity. 3. We think not how little that time is to him, which seems long to us, to whom *a thousand years are as one day.* It seemed a long time of the Church's distress and their enemies' triumph, in those seventy years of the Babylonish captivity ; and yet, in God's language, it is spoken of as *a moment, a small moment,* Isa. liv. 7. However, in the issue, the Lord always clears himself. He is indeed long-suffering and patient, but the impenitent abusers of his patience pay interest for all the time of that forbearance, in the weight of judgment when it comes upon them. But thus, we see, the Lord deals. Thus he dealt with the world in the beginning, *when all flesh had corrupted their way ; yet,* saith he, *their days shall be one hundred and twenty years.* Gen. vi. 3.

Let us learn to curb and cool our brisk humours towards even stubborn sinners. Be grieved at their sin, for that is your duty ; but think it not strange, nor fret at it, that they continue to abuse the long-suffering of God, and yet, that he continues ever abused by suffering them. Zeal is good, but as it springs from love, if it be right, so it is requited by love, and carries the impressions of it : of love to God, and so, a complacency in his way, liking it because it is his ; and of love to men, so as to be pleased with that waiting for them, in the possibility, at least, of their being reclaimed ; knowing that, however, if they return not, yet the Lord will not lose his own at their hands. *Wilt thou,* said those two fiery disciples, *that we call for fire, as Elias?* Oh ! but the spirit of the dove rested on Him who told them, *They knew not what spirit they were of.* Luke ix. 55. *q. d.* You speak of Elias, and you think you are of his spirit in this motion, but you mistake yourselves ; this comes from another spirit than you imagine. Instead of looking for such sudden justice without you, look inward, and see whence that is : examine and correct that within you.

When you are tempted to take ill that goodness and patience of God to sinners, consider, 1. Can this be right, to differ from his mind in any thing ? Is it not our only wisdom, and ever safe rule, to think as he thinks, and will as he wills ? And I pray you, does he not hate sin more than you do ? Is not his interest in punishing it deeper than yours ? And if you be zealous for his interest, as you pretend, then be so with him, and in his way ; for starting from that, surely you are wrong. Consider, 2. Did he not wait for thee ? What had become of thee, if long-suffering had subserved his purpose of further mercy, of free pardon to thee ? And why wilt thou not always allow that to which thou art so much obliged ? Wouldst thou have the bridge cut, because thou art so over ? Surely thou wilt not own so gross a thought. Therefore, esteem thy God still the more, as thou seest the

more of his long-suffering to sinners ; and learn for him, and with him,
to bear and wait.

2. But this was not a dumb forbearance, such as may serve for a
surprise, but continual teaching and warning were joined with it, as
remarked before.   We see, they wanted not preaching of the choicest
kind.   He, the *Son of God*, by his Eternal *Spirit, went and preached
to them;* it was his truth in Noah's mouth.   And with that, we have
a continued real sermon, expressed in this verse, *While the ark was
preparing:* that spoke God's mind, and every knock (as the usual observation is) of the hammers and tools used in building, preached to
them, threatening aloud designed judgment, and exhorting to prevent
it.   And therefore that word is added, ἐξεδέχετο, that the long-suffering of God *waited*, or expected : expected a believing of his word,
and a returning from their wickedness.   But we see no such thing
followed ; they took their own course still, and therefore the Lord took
his.   They had polluted the earth with their wickedness ; now the
Lord would have the cleansing by repentance; that being denied, it
must be another way, by a flood.   And because they and their sins
remained one, they would not part with them, therefore was one work
made of both ; they and their sins, as inseparable, must be cleansed
away together.

Thus impenitency under much long-suffering, makes judgment full
and complete.   I appeal to you, hath not the Lord used much forbearance towards us ?   Hath he not patiently spared us, and clearly warned
us, and waited long for the fruit of all ?   Hath any thing been wanting ?   Have not temporal mercies been multiplied on us ?   Have not
the spiritual riches of the Gospel been opened up to us ?

And each of you, for yourselves, consider how it is with you after
so much long-suffering of God, which none of you can deny he hath
used towards you, and so many gracious invitations, with that patience.   Have they gained your hearts, or do you still remain servants
to sin, still strangers to him, and formal worshippers ?   I beseech
you, think on it, what will be the issue of that course.   Is it a light
matter to you, *to die in your sins*, and to have *the wrath of God abiding on you?* to have refused Christ so often, and that after you have
been so often requested to receive salvation ?   After the Lord hath followed you with entreaties, hath called to you so often, *Why will ye
die?* yet, wilfully to perish, and withal to have all these entreaties
come in and accuse you, and make your burden heavier ?   Would you
willingly die in this estate ?   If not, then think that yet he is waiting,
if at length you will return.   This one day more of his waiting you
have, and of his speaking to you ; and some who were here with you
the last day, are taken away since.   *Oh that we were wise, and would
consider our latter end!*   Though there were neither sword nor pestilence near you, you must die, and, for any thing you know, quickly.
Why wear you out the day of grace and those precious seasons still,
as uncertain of Christ, yea, as undiligent after him, as you were long
ago ?   As you love your souls, be more serious in their business.   This
was the undoing of the sinners we are speaking of ; they were all for
present things.   *They ate and drank, they married*, in a continued
course, without ceasing, and without minding their after-estate.   Luke

xvii. 27.   They were drowned in these things, and that drowned them in a flood. Noah did also eat and drink, but his main work was, during that time, the preparing of the ark. The necessities of this life the children of God are tied to, and forced to bestow some time and pains on them; but the thing that takes up their hearts, that which the bent of their souls is set on, is their interest in Jesus Christ: and all your wise designs are but a pleasing madness, till this be chief with you. Others have had as much of God's patience, and as fair opportunity, as you, whose souls and Christ had never met, and now know that they never shall. They had their time of worldly projects and enjoyment, as you now have, and followed them, as if they had been immortally to abide with them; but they are passed away as a shadow, and we are posting after them, and within awhile shall lie down in the dust.   Oh! how happy they whose hearts are not here, trading with vanity and gathering vexation, but whose thoughts are on that blessed life above trouble!   Certainly, they who pass for fools in the world, are the only *children of wisdom*, they who have renounced their lusts and their own wills, have yielded up themselves to Jesus, taking him for their King, and have their minds resting on him as their salvation.

While the ark was a preparing.] Observe, the delay of the Lord's determined judgment on the ungodly was indeed long-suffering towards them, but here was more in it to Noah and his family; the providing for their preservation, and, till that was completed for them, the rest were spared.   Thus, the very forbearance which the ungodly do enjoy, is usually involved with the interest of the godly; something of that usually goes into it; and so it is in a great part for their sakes, that the rest are both spared and furnished with common mercies.   The saints are usually the scorn and contempt of others, yet are they, by that love the Lord carries towards them, the very arches and pillars of states, and kingdoms, and families, where they are, yea, of the world, *(Semen sanctum statumen terræ,)* the frame whereof is continued mainly in regard to them. Isa. vi. 13.   But they who are ungrateful to the great Maker and Upholder of it, and regardless of him, what wonder if they take no notice of the advantage they receive by the concernment of his children in the world?   Observe here,

I. The Work. II. The end of it. I. In the Work, the preparing of the ark, observe, 1st, God's appointment; 2ndly, Noah's obedience.

1st, It was God's appointment. His power was not tied to this, yet his wisdom chose it. He who steered the course of this ark safely all that time, could have preserved those he designed it for without it; but thus it pleases the Lord, usually, to mix his most wonderful deliverances with some selected means; exercising, in that way, our obedience in their use, yet so as that the singular power of his hand in them, whereon faith rests, doth clearly appear, doing by them what, in a more natural way, they could not possibly effect.

2ndly, For the obedience of Noah, if we should insist on the difficulties, both in this work and in the way of their preservation by it, it would look the clearer, and be found very remarkable.   Considering the length of the work, the great pains in providing materials, especially considering the opposition that probably he met with in it from the profane about him, the mightier of them, or, at least, the hatred and continual scoffs of all sorts, it required principles of an invincible resolution to go through with it. What (would they say) means this old dotard to do? Whither this monstrous voyage? And inasmuch as it spoke, as no doubt he told them, their ruin and his safety, this would incense them so much the more. You look far before you, and what! shall we all perish, and you alone escape? But through all, the sovereign command and gracious promise of his God carried him, regarding their scoffs and threats as little in making the Ark, as he did afterwards the noise of the waters about it, when he was sitting safe within it. This his obedience, having indeed so boisterous winds to encounter, had need of a well-fastened root, that it might stand and hold out against them all, and so it had. The Apostle St. Paul tells us what the root of it was: *By faith, being warned of God, he prepared an ark.* Heb. xi. 7. And there is no living and lasting obedience but what springs from that root. He believed what the Lord spake of his determined judgment on the ungodly world, and from the belief of that arose that holy fear which is expressly mentioned, Heb. xi. 7, as exciting him to this work; and he believed the word of promise, which the Lord spake concerning his preservation by the Ark: and the belief of these two carried him strongly on to the work, and through it, against all counter-blasts and opposition; overcame both his own doubtings and the mockings of the wicked, while he still looked to Him who was the master and contriver of the work.

Till we attain such a fixed view of our God, and such firm persuasion of his truth, and power, and goodness, it will never be right with us; there will be nothing but wavering and unsettledness in our spirits and in our ways. Every little discouragement from within or from without, that meets us, will be likely to turn us over. We shall not walk in an even course, but still be reeling and staggering, till Faith be set wholly upon its own basis, the proper foundation of it: not set betwixt two upon one strong prop, and another that is rotten, partly on God, and partly on creature helps and encouragements, or our own strength. Our only safe and happy way is, in humble obedience, in his own strength to follow his appointments, without standing and questioning the matter, and to resign the conduct of all to his wisdom and love; to put the rudder of our life into his hand, to steer the course of it as seemeth him good, resting quietly on his word of promise for our safety. Lord, whither thou wilt, and which way thou wilt, be thou my guide, and it sufficeth.

This absolute following of God, and trusting him with all, is marked as the true character of faith in Abraham; his going after God away from his country, *not knowing,* nor asking, *whither he went,* secure in his guide. And so, in that other greater point of offering his son, he silenced all disputes about it, by that mighty conclusion of faith, *accounting that he was able to raise him from the dead.* Heb. xi. 8, 19. Thus it is said, ver. 7, *By faith, Noah prepared the ark.* He did not argue and question, How shall this be done, and if it were, how shall I get all the kinds of beasts gathered together to put into it, and how shall it be ended, when we are shut in? No, but he believed firmly that it should be finished by him, and he be saved by it ; and he was not disappointed.

II. The End of this work was the *saving of* Noah and his family from the general Deluge, wherein all the rest perished.

Here it will be fit to consider the point of the preservation of the godly in ordinary and common calamities, briefly in these positions.

1. It is certain that the children of God, as they are not exempted from the common, universal calamities and evils of this life, which befall the rest of men, so not from any particular kind of them. As it is *appointed* for them, with all others, *once to die*, so we find them not privileged from any kind of disease, or other way of death ; not from falling by sword, or by pestilence, or in the frenzy of a fever, or any kind of sudden death : yea, when these, or such like, are on a land by way of public judgment, the godly are not altogether exempted from them, but may fall in them with others ; as we find Moses dying in the wilderness with those he brought out of Egypt. Now though it was for a particular failing in the wilderness, yet it evinces, that there is in this no infringement upon their privileges, nothing contrary to the love of God towards them, and his covenant with them.

2. The promises made to the godly of preservation, from common judgments, have their truth, and are made good in many of them who are so preserved, though they do not hold absolutely and universally. For they are ever to be understood in subordination to their highest good ; but when they are preserved, they ought to take it as a gracious accomplishment even of these promises to them, which the wicked, many of whom do likewise escape, have no right to, but are preserved for after judgment.

3. It is certain, that the curse and sting is taken out of all those evils incident to the godly with others, in life and death, which makes the main difference, though to the eye of the world invisible. And it may be observed, that in those common judgments of sword, or pestilence, or other epidemic diseases, a great part of those who are cut off are of the wickedest, though the Lord may send of those arrows to some few of his own, to call them home.

The full and clear distinction of the godly and the wicked, being reserved for their after-estate in eternity, it needs not seem strange, that in many things it appears not here. One thing, above all others most grievous to the child of God, may take away the wonder of other things they suffer in common, that is, the remainders of sin in them while they are in the flesh : though there is a spirit in them above it, and contrary to it, which makes the difference, yet, sometimes the too much likeness, especially in the prevailings of corruption, doth confuse the matter, not only to others' eyes, but to their own.

4. Though the great distinction and severing be reserved to that great and solemn day which shall clear all, yet the Lord is pleased, in part, more remarkably at some times to distinguish his own from the ungodly, in the execution of temporal judgments, and to give these as preludes of that final and full judgment. And this instance of Noah was one of the most eminent in that kind, being the most general judgment that ever befell the world, or that shall befall it till the last, and so, the liveliest figure of it ; this was by water, as the second

shall be by fire. It was most congruous that it should resemble it in this, as the chief point ; the saving of righteous Noah and his family from it, prefiguring the eternal salvation of believers, as our Apostle teacheth.

Wherein few, that is, eight persons, were saved by water.] This great point of the fewness of those who are saved in the other greater salvation, as in this, I shall not now prosecute : only,

1. If so few, then, the inquiry into ourselves, whether we be of these few, should be more diligent, and followed more home, than it is as yet with the most of us. We are wary in our trifles, and only in this easily deceived, yea, our own deceivers in this great point. Is not this folly far beyond what you usually say of some, *Penny wise and pound foolish;* to be wise for a moment, and fools for eternity ?

2. You who are indeed seeking the way of life, be not discouraged by your fewness. It hath always been so. You see here, how few of the whole world were saved. And is it not better to be of the few in the Ark, than of the multitude in the waters ? Let them fret, as ordinarily they do, to see so few more diligent for heaven ; as no doubt they did in the case of Noah. And this is what galls them, that any should have higher names and surer hopes this way : What ! are none but such as you going to heaven ? Think you all of us damned ? What can we say, but that there is a flood of wrath awaiting many, and certainly, all that are out of the Ark shall perish in it.

3. This is that main truth that I would leave with you : look on Jesus Christ as the Ark, of whom this was a figure, and believe it, out of Him there is nothing but certain destruction, a deluge of wrath, all the world over, on those who are out of Christ. Oh ! it is our life, our only safety, to be in him. But these things are not believed. Men think they believe them, and do not. Were it believed, that we are under the sentence of eternal death in our natural state, and that there is no escape but by removing out of ourselves unto Christ, oh, what thronging would there be to him ! Whereas, now, he invites, and calls, and how few are persuaded to come to him ! Noah believed the Lord's word of judgment against the world, believed his promise made to him, and prepared an ark. Is it not a high sign of unbelief, that, there being an ark of everlasting salvation ready prepared to our hand, we will not so much as come to it ? Will you be persuaded certainly, that the Ark-door stands open ? His offers are free ; do but come and try if he will turn you away. No, he will not : *Him that comes to me, I will in no wise cast out.* John vi. 37. And as there is such acceptance and sure preservation in him, there is as sure perishing without him, trust on what you will. Be you of a giant's stature, (as many of them were,) to help you to climb up (as they would surely do when the Flood came on) to the highest mountains and tallest trees, yet, it shall overtake you. Make your best of your worldly advantages, or good parts, or civil righteousness, all shall prove poor shifts from the flood of wrath, which rises above all these, and drowns them. Only the Ark of our salvation is safe. Think how gladly they would have been within the Ark, when they found death without it ; and now it was too late ! How would many who now despise Christ, wish to honour him one day ! Men, so long as they

thought to be safe on the earth, would never betake them to the Ark, would think it a prison ; and could men find salvation any where else, they would never come to Christ for it : this is, because they know him not. But yet, be it necessity, let that drive thee in ; and then being in him, thou shalt find reason to love him for himself, besides the salvation thou hast in him.

You who have fled into him for refuge, wrong him not so far as to question your safety. What though the floods of thy former guiltiness rise high, thine Ark shall still be above them ; and the higher they rise, the higher he shall rise, shall have the more glory in freely justifying and saving thee. Though thou find the remaining power of sin still within thee, yet it shall not sink thine Ark. There was in this Ark, sin, yet they were saved from the Flood. If thou dost believe, that puts thee in Christ, and he will bring thee safe through without splitting or sinking.

As thou art bound to account thyself safe in him, so to admire that love which set thee there. Noah was a holy man : but whence were both his holiness and his preservation while the world perished, but because *he found favour* or *free grace*, as the word is, in the eyes of the Lord ? And no doubt, he did much contemplate this, being secure within, when the cries of the rest drowning were about him. Thus think thou : Seeing so few are saved in this blessed Ark wherein I am, in comparison of the multitudes that perish in the deluge, whence is this ? why was I chosen, and so many about me left, why, but because it pleased him ? But all is strait here. We have neither hearts nor time for ample thoughts of this love, till we be beyond time ; then shall we admire and praise without ceasing, and without wearying.

As the Example the Apostle here makes use of, is great and remarkable, so, *Thirdly*, it is fit and suitable for the instruction of Christians, to whom he proceeds to adapt and apply it, in the particular resemblance of it to the rule of Christianity. *The like figure whereunto, even Baptism, doth also now save us.*

In these words we have, I. The End of Baptism. II. The proper virtue or efficacy of it for that End. And, III. A resemblance in both these to Noah's preservation in the Flood.

I. The End of Baptism, *to save us.* This is the great common end of all the ordinances of God ; that one high mark they all aim at. And the great and common mistake in regard to them, is, that they are not so understood and used. We come and sit awhile, and, if we can keep awake, give the word the hearing ; but how few of us receive it as *the ingrafted word that is able to save our souls !* Were it thus taken, what sweetness would be found in it, which most who hear and read it are strangers to ! How precious would those lines be, if we looked on them thus, and saw them meeting and concentring in salvation as their end ! Thus, likewise, were the sacraments considered indeed as seals of this inheritance, annexed to the great charter of it, seals of salvation, this would powerfully beget a fit appetite for the Lord's Supper, when we are invited to it, and would beget a due esteem of Baptism ; would teach you more frequent and fruitful thoughts of your own Baptism, and more pious considerations of it when you require it for your children.   A natural eye looks upon bread, and wine, and water, and sees the outward difference of their use there, that they are set apart and differenced (as is evident by external circumstances) from their common use ; but the main of the difference, wherein their excellency lies, it sees not, as the eye of faith above that espies salvation under them.   And oh, what a different thing are they to it, from what they are to a formal user of them ! We should aspire to know the hidden rich things of God, that are wrapped up in his ordinances.   We stick in the shell and surface of them, and seek no further ; that makes them unbeautiful and unsavoury to us, and that use of them turns into an empty custom.   Let us be more earnest with Him who hath appointed them, and made this their end, *to save us*, that he would clear up the eye of our souls, to see them thus under this relation, and to see how they are suited to this their end, and tend to it.   And let us seriously seek salvation in them, from his own hand, and we shall find it.

Doth save us.]   So that this salvation of Noah and his family from the Deluge, and all outward deliverances and salvations, are but dark shadows of this.   Let them not be spoken of, these reprisals and prolongings of this present life, in comparison of the deliverance of the soul from death, the second death ; the stretching of a moment, compared to the concernment of eternity.   How would any of you welcome a full and sure protection from common dangers, if such were to be had, that you should be ascertained of safety from sword and pestilence ; that whatever others suffered about you, you and your family should be free !   And those who have escaped a near danger of this kind are apt to rest there, as if no more were to be feared ; whereas this common favour may be shown to those who are afar off from God.   And what though you be not only thus far safe, but I say, if you were secured for the future, (which none of you absolutely are,) yet, when you are put out of danger of sword and plague, still death remains, and sin and wrath may be remaining with it.   And shall it not be all one, to die under these in a time of public peace and welfare, as if it were now ?   Yea, it may be something more unhappy, by reason of the increase of the heap of sin and wrath, guiltiness being augmented by life prolonged ; and more grievous to be pulled away from the world in the midst of peaceable enjoyment, and to have everlasting darkness succeed to that short sun-shine of thy day of ease ; happiness of a short date, and misery for ever !   What availed it wicked Ham to outlive the Flood, to inherit a curse after it ; to be kept undrowned in the waters, to see himself and his posterity blasted with his father's curse ?   Think seriously, what will be the end of all thy temporary safety and preservation, if thou share not in this salvation, and find not thyself sealed and marked for it ?   What will it avail, to flatter thyself with a dream of happiness, and *walk in the light* of a few *sparks* that will soon die out, and *then lie down in sorrow?* Isa. l. 11. A sad bed that, which the most have to go to, after they have wearied themselves all the day, all their life, in a chase of vanity !

II. The next thing is, the power and virtue of this means for its end.   That Baptism hath a power, is clear, in that it is so expressly said, *it doth save us:* what kind of power is equally clear from the way it is here expressed; not by a natural force of the element; though adapted and sacramentally used, it only can wash away the filth of the body; its physical efficacy or power reaches no further: but it is in the hand of the Spirit of God, as other sacraments are, and as the word itself is, to purify the conscience, and convey grace and salvation to the soul, by the reference it hath to, and union with, that which it represents. It saves *by the answer of a good conscience unto God*, and it affords that, *by the resurrection of Jesus from the dead.*

Thus, then, we have a true account of the power of this, and so of other sacraments, and a discovery of the error of two extremes: (1.) Of those who ascribe too much to them, as if they wrought by a natural, inherent virtue, and carried grace in them inseparably. (2.) Of those who ascribe too little to them, making them only signs and badges of our profession. Signs they are, but more than signs merely representing; they are means exhibiting, and seals confirming, grace to the faithful. But the working of faith, and the conveying of Christ into the soul to be received by faith, is not a thing put into them to do of themselves, but still in the Supreme Hand that appointed them: and he indeed both causes the souls of his own to receive these his seals with faith, and makes them effectual to confirm that faith which receives them so. They are then, in a word, neither empty signs to them who believe, nor effectual causes of grace to them who believe not.

The mistake, on both sides, arises from the want of duly considering the relative nature of these seals, and that kind of union that is betwixt them and the grace they represent, which is real, though not natural or physical, as they speak, so that, though they do not save all who partake of them, yet they do really and effectually save believers, (for whose salvation they are means,) as the other external ordinances of God do. Though they have not that power which is peculiar to the Author of them, yet a power they have, such as befits their nature, and by reason of which they are truly said to sanctify and justify, and so to save, as the Apostle here avers of Baptism.

Now, that which is intended for our help, our carnal minds are ready to turn into a hinderance and disadvantage. The Lord representing invisible things to the eye, and confirming his promises even by visible seals, we are apt, from the grossness of our unspiritual hearts, instead of stepping up by that which is earthly, to the Divine spiritual things represented, to stay in the outward element, and go no further. Therefore, the Apostle, to lead us into the inside of this seal of Baptism, is very clear in designating the effect and fruit of it: *Not* (says he) the *putting away the filth of the flesh;* (and water, if you look no further, can do no more;) there is an invisible impurity upon our nature, chiefly on our invisible part, our soul: this washing means the taking away of that, and where it reaches its true effect, it doth so purify the conscience, and makes it good, truly so, in the sight of God, who is the judge of it.

Consider, 1. It is a pitiful thing to see the ignorance of the most, professing Christianity, and partaking of the outward seals of it, yet not knowing what they mean; not apprehending the spiritual dignity and virtue of them. Blind in the *mysteries of the kingdom*, they are not so much as sensible of that blindness. And being ignorant of the nature of these holy things, they cannot have a due esteem of them, which arises out of the view of their inward worth and efficacy. A confused fancy they have of some good in them, and this rising to the other extreme, to a superstitious confidence in the simple performance and participation of them, as if that carried some inseparable virtue with it, which none could miss of, who are sprinkled with the waters of Baptism, and share in the elements of bread and wine in the Lord's Supper.

And what is the utmost plea of the most for their title to heaven, but that in these relative and external things they are Christians; that they are baptized, hear the word, and are admitted to the Lord's table?—Not considering how many have gone through all these, who yet, daily, are going on in the ways of death, never coming near Jesus Christ, *who is the way, and the truth, and the life,* whom the word, and the seals of it, hold forth to Believers. And they are washed in his blood, and quickened with his life, and made like him, and co-heirs of glory with him.

2. Even those who have some clearer notion of the nature and fruit of the seals of grace, yet are in a practical error, in that they look not with due diligence into themselves, inquiring after the efficiency of them in their hearts; do not study the life of Christ, to know more what it is, and then, to search into themselves for the truth and the growth of that life within them. Is it not an unbecoming thing, for a Christian (when he is about to appear before the Lord at his table, and so looks something more narrowly within) to find as little faith, as little Divine affection, a heart as unmortified to the world, as cold towards Christ, as before his last address to the same table, after the intervening, possibly, of many months; in which time, had he been careful often to reflect inwards on his heart, and to look back upon that new sealing in his last participation, he might probably have been more conformable? And, truly, as there is much guiltiness cleaves to us in this, so, generally, much more in reference to this other sacrament that is here the Apostle's subject, *Baptism,* which being but once administered, and that in infancy, is very seldom and slightly considered by many, even real Christians. And so we are at a loss in that profit and comfort, that increase of both holiness and faith, which the frequent recollecting of it, after a spiritual manner, would no doubt advance us to. And not only do we neglect to put ourselves upon the thoughts of it in private, but, in the frequent opportunities of such thoughts in public, we let it pass unregarded, are idle, inconsiderate, and so, truly guilty beholders. And the more frequently we have these opportunities, the less are we touched with them; they become common, and work not, and the slighting of them grows as common with us as the thing. Yea, when the engagement is more special and personal, when parents are to present their infants to this ordinance, (and then might, and certainly ought to have a more particular and fixed eye upon it, and themselves as being sealed with it, to ask within after the fruit and power of it, and to stir up themselves anew to the actings of faith, and to ambition after newness of life, and, with earnest prayer for their children, to be suitors for themselves, for further evidence of their interest in Christ;) yet possibly, many are not much

engaged in these things even at such times, but are more busied to prepare their house for entertaining their friends, than to prepare their
hearts for offering up their infant unto God to be sealed, and withal to
make a new offer of their own hearts to him, to have renewed on them
the inward seal of the covenant of grace, the outward seal whereof they
did receive, as it is now to be conferred upon their infant.

Did we often look upon the face of our souls, the beholding of the
many spots with which we have defiled them after our washing might
work us to shame and grief, and would drive us by renewed application
to wash often in that blood which that water figures, which alone can
fetch out the stain of sin ; and then, it would put us upon renewed
purposes of purity, to walk more carefully, to avoid the pollutions of
the world we walk in, and to purge out the pollutions of the hearts
that we carry about with us, which defile us more than all the world
besides. It would work a holy disdain of sin, often to contemplate
ourselves as washed in so precious a laver. Shall I, would the Christian say, considering that I am now cleansed in the precious blood of
my Lord Jesus, run again into that puddle out of which he so graciously took me, and made me clean ? Let the swine wallow in it : he
hath made me of his sheepfold. He hath made me of that excellent
order for which all are consecrated by that washing, who partake of it :
*He hath washed us in his blood, and made us kings and priests unto
God the Father.* Am I of these, and shall I debase myself to the vile
pleasures of sin ? No, I will think myself too good to serve any sinful
lusts : seeing that he hath looked on me, and taken me up, and washed
and dignified me, and that I am wholly his, all my study and business
shall be to honour and magnify him.

The answer of a good conscience, &c.] The taking away of spiritual
filthiness, as the true and saving effect of baptism, the Apostle here expresses by that which is the further result and effect of it, *The answer
of a good conscience unto God;* for it is the washing away of that
filthiness which both makes the conscience good, and, in making it such,
fits it to make answer unto God. A good conscience, in its full sense,
is a pure conscience and a peaceable conscience ; and it cannot, indeed,
be peaceably good, unless it be purely good. And although, on the
other side, it may want the present enjoyment of peace, being purified,
yet, certainly, in a purified conscience, there is a title and a right to
peace ; it is radically there, even when it appears not ; and, in due
time, it shall appear, shall spring forth, bud, and flourish.

The purified and good condition of the whole soul may well, as here
it doth, go under the name of the good conscience, it being so prime a
faculty of it, and as the glass of the whole soul, wherein the estate of it
is represented. Therefore, Heb. ix., the efficacy of the blood of Christ
is expressed thus, that it *purifieth our consciences from dead works;*
which expression is the same thing in effect with that here, *the answer
of a good conscience unto God.*

The answer, [ἐπερώτημα,] the asking or questioning of conscience,
which comprises likewise its answer ; for the word intends the whole
correspondence of the conscience with God, and with itself as towards
God, or in the sight of God. And indeed, God's questioning it, is by
itself ; it is his deputy in the soul. He makes it pose itself for him.

and before him, concerning its own condition, and so, the answer it gives itself in that posture, he as it were sitting and hearing it in his presence, is an answer made unto him.   This questioning and answering (if such a thing were at this time, as it was certainly soon after) yet means not the questions and answers used in the baptism of persons who, being of years, professed their faith in answering the questions moved ; it possibly alludes unto that ; but it further, by way of resemblance, expresses the inward questioning and answering which is transacted within, betwixt the soul and itself, and the soul and God, and so is allusively called ἐπερώτημα, a questioning and answering, but it is distinctively specified, εἰς Θεὸν : whereas the other was towards men, this is unto God.

A good conscience is a waking, speaking conscience, and the conscience that questions itself most, is of all sorts the best ; that which is dumb, therefore, or asleep, and is not active and frequent in self-inquiries, is not a good conscience.   The word is judicial, ἐπερώτημα, alluding to the *interrogation* used in law for the trial and executing of processes.   And this is the great business of conscience, to sit, and examine, and judge within ; to *hold courts* in the soul.   And it is of continual necessity that it be so : there can be no *vacation* of this judicature, without great damage to the estate of the soul : yea, not a day ought to pass without a session of conscience within ; for daily disorders arise in the soul, which, if they pass on, will grow and gather more, and so breed more difficulty in their trial and redress.   Yet men do easily turn from this work as hard and unpleasant, and make many a long vacation in the year, and protract it from one day to another. In the morning they must go about their business, and at night they are weary and sleepy, and all the day long one affair steps in after another ; and in case of that failing, some trifling company or other ; and so their days pass on, while the soul is overgrown with impurities and disorders.

You know what confusions, and disorders, and evils will abound amongst a rude people, where there is no kind of court or judicature held.   Thus is it with that unruly rabble, the lusts and passions of our souls, when there is no discipline or judgment within, or where there is but a neglect and intermission of it for a short time.   And the most part of souls are in the posture of ruin : their vile affections, as a headstrong, tumultuous multitude, that wlll not suffer a deputed judge to sit amongst them, cry down their conscience, and make a continual noise, that the voice of it may not be heard, and so, force it to desist and leave them to their own ways.

But you who take this course, know, you are providing the severest judgment for yourselves by this disturbing of judgment, as when a people rise against an inferior judge, the prince or supreme magistrate who sent him, hearing of it, doth not fail to vindicate his honour and justice in their exemplary punishment.

Will you not answer unto conscience, but, when it begins to speak, turn to business or company, that you may not hear it ?   Know, that it and you must answer unto God ; and when he shall make inquiry, it must report, and report as the truth is, knowing that there is no hiding the matter from him ; Lord, there are, to my knowledge, a world of enormities within the circuit I had to judge, and I would have judged them, but was forcibly withstood and interrupted ; and was not strong enough to resist the tumultuous power that rose against me ; now the matter comes into thine own hand to judge it thyself. What shall the soul say in that day, when conscience shall make such an answer unto God, and it shall come under the severity of his justice for all ? Whereas, if it had given way to the conscience to find out, and judge, and rectify matters, so that it could have answered concerning its procedure that way, God would accept this as the answer of a good conscience, and what conscience had done, he would not do over again : It hath judged ; then, I acquit. *For if we would judge ourselves,* (says the Apostle,) *we should not be judged.* 1 Cor. xi. 31.

The questioning or inquiry of conscience, and so, its report or answer unto God, extends to all the affairs of the soul, all the affections and motions of it, and all the actions and carriage of the whole man. The open wickedness of the most, testifies against them, that though sprinkled with water in Baptism, yet they are strangers to the power and gracious efficacy of it. Not being *baptized with the Holy Ghost and with fire,* they have still their dross and filth remaining in them, and nothing else appearing in their ways ; so that their consciences cannot so much as make a good answer for them unto men, much less unto God. What shall it answer for them, being judged, but that they are swearers, and cursers, and drunkards, or unclean ? or that they are slanderers, delighting to pass their hours in descanting on the actions and ways of others, and looking through the miscoloured glass of their own malice and pride ; that they are neglecters of God and holy things, lovers of themselves and their own pleasures, more than lovers of God ? And have such as these impudence enough to call themselves Christians, and to pretend themselves to be such as are washed in the blood of Christ ? Yes, they do this. But be ashamed and confounded in yourselves, you that remain in this condition. Yea, although thou art blameless in men's eyes, and possibly in thy own eyes too, yet thou mayest be *filthy* still in the sight of God. There is such *a generation,* a multitude of them, *that are pure in their own eyes, and yet are not washed from their filthiness;* (Prov. xxx. 12 ;) moral evil persons who are most satisfied with their own estate, or such as have further *a form of godliness,* but their lusts are not mortified by *the power of it,* secret pride, and earthliness of mind, and vain-glory, and carnal wisdom, being still entertained with pleasure within.

These are foul pollutions, filthy and hateful in the sight of God ; so that where it is thus, that such guests are in peaceable possession of the heart, there the blood and Spirit of Christ are not yet come ; neither can there be this answer of a good conscience unto God.

This *answer of a good conscience unto God,* as likewise its questioning, to enable itself for that answer, is touching two great points, which are of chief concern to the soul, its *justification,* and its *sanctification;* for Baptism is the seal of both, and purifies the conscience in both respects. *That* water is the figure both of the blood and the water, the justifying blood of Christ, and the pure water of the sanctifying Spirit of Christ : he takes away the condemning guiltiness of sin, by the one, and the polluting filthiness, by the other.

Now, the Conscience of a real Believer inquiring within, upon right discovery will make this answer unto God : Lord, I have found that there is no standing before thee, for the soul in itself is overwhelmed with a world of guiltiness : but I find a blood sprinkled upon it, that hath, I am sure, virtue enough to purge it all away, and to present it pure unto thee; and I know that wheresoever thou findest that blood sprinkled, thine anger is quenched and appeased immediately upon the sight of it. Thine hand cannot smite where that blood is before thine eye.—And this the Lord does agree to, and authorizes the Conscience, upon this account, to return back an answer of safety and peace to the soul.

So for the other point : Lord, I find a living work of holiness on this soul : though there is yet corruption there, yet it is as a continual grief and vexation, it is an implacable hatred, there is no peace betwixt them, but continual enmity and hostility ; and if I cannot say much of the high degrees of grace, and faith in Christ, and love to him, and heavenliness of mind, yet, I may say, there is a beginning of these : at least, this I most confidently affirm, that there are real and earnest desires of the soul after these things. It would know and conform to thy will, and be delivered from itself and its own will ; and though it were to the highest displeasure of all the world, it would gladly walk in all well-pleasing unto thee. Now, he who sees the truth of these things, knowing it to be thus, owns it as his own work, and engages himself to advance it, and bring it to perfection. This is a taste of that intercourse which the purified conscience hath with God, as the saving fruit of Baptism.

And all this it doth, not of itself, but by virtue of *the resurrection of Jesus Christ*, which refers both to the remote effect, *salvation*, and to the nearer effect, as a means and pledge of that, *the purifying of the conscience*.

By this his death, and the effusion of his blood in his sufferings, are not excluded, but are included in it, his resurrection being the evidence of that whole work of expiation, both completed and accepted: full payment being made by our Surety, and so, he set free, his freedom is the cause and the assurance of ours. Therefore the Apostle St. Paul expresses it so, that *he died for our sins, and rose for our righteousness;* and our Apostle shows us the worth of our *living hope* in this same resurrection, chap. i. ver. 3. *Blessed be the God and Father of our Lord Jesus Christ, who according to his abundant mercy, hath begotten us again unto a lively hope, by the resurrection of Jesus Christ from the dead.*

Now, that Baptism doth apply and seal to the Believer his interest in the death and resurrection of Christ, the Apostle St. Paul teaches to the full, Rom. vi. 4 : *We are buried with him*, says he, *by baptism into his death, that like as Christ was raised up from the dead by the glory of the Father, even so we should also walk in newness of life.* The dipping into the waters representing our dying with Christ ; and the return thence, our rising with him.

The last thing is, the resemblance of Baptism, in these things, to the saving of Noah in the Flood. And it holds in that we spoke of last ; for he seemed to have rather entered into a grave, as dead, than into a safeguard of life, in going into the Ark; yet, being buried there, he rose again, as it were, in his coming forth to begin a new world. The waters of the Flood drowned the ungodly, as a heap of filthiness washed them away, them and their sin together as one, being inseparable; and upon the same waters, the Ark floating, preserved Noah. Thus, the waters of Baptism are intended as a deluge to drown sin and to save the Believer, who by faith is separated both from the world and from his sin; so, it sinks, and he is saved.

And there is, further, another thing specified by the Apostle, wherein, though it be a little hard, yet he chiefly intends the parallel; the *fewness* of those that are saved by both. For though many are sprinkled with the elemental water of Baptism, yet few, so as to attain by it the *answer of a good conscience towards God*, and to live by participation of the resurrection and life of Christ.

Thou that seest the world perishing in a deluge of wrath, and art now most thoughtful for this, how thou shalt escape it, fly into Christ as thy safety, and rest secure there. Thou shalt find life in his death, and that life further ascertained to thee in his rising again. So full and clear a title to life hast thou in these two, that thou canst challenge all adversaries upon this very ground, as unconquerable whilst thou standest on it, and mayest speak thy challenge in the Apostle's style, *It is God that justifieth, who shall condemn?* But how know you that he justifies? *It is Christ that died, yea rather, that is risen, who sitteth at the right hand of God, who also maketh intercession for us.* Rom. viii. 33, 34. It alludes to that place, Isa. l. 8, where Christ speaks of himself, but in the name of all who adhere to him; *He is near that justifies me: who is he that will contend with me?* So that what Christ speaks there, the Apostle, with good reason, imparts to each believer as in him. If no more is to be laid to Christ's charge, he being now acquitted, as is clear by his rising again; then, neither to thine, who art clothed with him, and one with him.

This is the grand answer of a good conscience; and, in point of justifying them before God, there can be no answer but this. What have any to say to thee? Thy debt is paid by him who undertook it; and he is free. Answer all accusations with this, *Christ is risen.*

And then, for the mortifying of sin, and strengthening of thy graces, look daily on that death and resurrection. Study them, set thine eye upon them, till thy heart take on the impression of them by much spiritual and affectionate looking on them. *Beholding the glory of thy Lord* Christ, then, be *transformed into it.* 2 Cor. iii. 18. It is not only a moral pattern or copy, but an effectual cause of thy sanctification, having real influence into thy soul. Dead with him, and again alive with him! Oh happiness and dignity unspeakable, to have this life known and cleared to your souls! If it were, how would it make you live above the world, and all the vain hopes and fears of this wretched life, and the fear of death itself! Yea, it would make that visage of death most lóvely, which to the world is most affrightful.

It is the Apostle's maxim, that the *carnal mind is enmity against God;* and as it is universally true of every carnal mind, so of all the motions and thoughts of it. Even where it seems to agree with God, yet it is still contrary; if it acknowledge and conform to his ordinance, yet, even in so doing, it is on directly opposite terms to him, particularly in this, that what he esteems most in them, the carnal mind makes least account of. He chiefly eyes and values the inside ; the natural man dwells and rests in the shell and surface of them. God, according to his spiritual nature, looks most on the more spiritual part of his worship and worshippers ; the carnal mind is in this just like itself, altogether for the sensible, external part, and unable to look beyond it. Therefore the Apostle here, having taken occasion to speak of Baptism in terms that contain a parallel and resemblance between it and the Flood, is express in correcting this mistake. It is not, says he, *the putting away of the filth of the flesh, but the answer of a good conscience.*

Were it possible to persuade you, I would recommend one thing to you : learn to look on the ordinances of God suitably to their nature, spiritually, and inquire after the spiritual effect and working of them upon your consciences. We would willingly have all religion reduced to externals ; this is our natural choice ; and we would pay all in this coin, as cheaper and easier by far, and would compound for the spiritual part, rather to add and give more external performance and ceremony. Hence, the natural complacency in Popery, which is all for this service of the flesh and body-services ; and to those prescribed by God, will deal so liberally with him in that kind, as to add more, and frame new devices and rites, what you will in this kind, sprinklings, and washings, and anointings, and incense. But whither tends all this ? Is it not a gross mistaking of God, to think him thus pleased ? Or is it not a direct affront, knowing that he is not pleased with these, but desires another thing, to thrust that upon him which he cares not for, and refuse him what he calls for ?—that single, humble heart-worship and walking with him, that purity of spirit and conscience which only he prizes ; no outward service being acceptable, but for these, as they tend to this end and do attain it. Give me, saith he, nothing, if you give not this. Oh ! saith the carnal mind, any thing but this thou shalt have ; as many washings and offerings as thou wilt, *thousands of rams, and ten thousand rivers of oil; yea,* rather than fail, *let the fruit of my body go for the sin of my soul.* Mic. vi. 6. Thus we : will the outward use of the word and sacraments do it ? then, all shall be well. Baptized we are ; and shall I hear much and communicate often, if I can reach it ? Shall I be exact in point of family worship ? Shall I pray in secret ? All this I do, or at least I now promise. Ay, but when all that is done, there is yet one thing may be wanting, and if it be so, all that amounts to nothing. Is thy conscience purified and made good by all these ; or art thou seeking and aiming at this, by the use of all means ? Then certainly thou shalt find life in them. But does thy heart still remain uncleansed from the old ways, not purified from the pollutions of the world ? Do thy beloved sins still lodge with thee, and keep possession of thy heart ? Then art thou still a stranger to Christ, and an enemy to God. The word and seals of life are dead to thee, and thou art still dead in the use of them all. Know you not that many have made shipwreck upon the very rock of salvation ? that many who were baptized as well as you, and as constant attendants on all the worship and ordinances of God as you, yet have remained without Christ, and died in their sins, and are now past recovery ?   Oh that you would be warned !   There are still multitudes running headlong that same course, tending to destruction, through the midst of all the means of salvation ; the saddest way of all to it, through word and sacraments, and all heavenly ordinances, to be walking hell-wards !   Christians, and yet no Christians ; baptized, and yet unbaptized !   As the Prophet takes in the profane multitude of God's own people with the nations, Jer. ix. 26, *Egypt, and Judah, and Edom; all these nations are uncircumcised :* and the worst came last ; *and all the house of Israel are uncircumcised in the heart :* thus, thus, the most of us are unbaptized in the heart.   And as this is the way of personal destruction, so it is that, as the Prophet there declares, which brings upon the Church so many public judgments ; and as the Apostle tells the Corinthians, (1 Ep. xi. 30,) that for the abuse of the Lord's table, *many were sick, and many slept.*   Certainly, our abuse of the holy things of God, and want of their proper spiritual fruits, are amongst the prime sins of this land, for which so many slain have fallen in the fields by the sword, and in the streets by pestilence ; and more are likely yet to fall, if we thus continue to provoke the Lord to his face.   For, it is the most avowed, direct affront, to profane his holy things ; and this we do while we answer not their proper end, and are not inwardly sanctified by them. We have no other word, nor other sacraments, to recommend to you, than those which you have used so long to no purpose ; only we would call you from the dead forms, to seek the living power of them, that you perish not.

You think the *renouncing of Baptism* a horrible word, and that we would speak so only of witches ; yet it is a common guiltiness that cleaves to all who renounce not the filthy lusts and the self-will of their own hearts.   For Baptism carries in it a renouncing of these ; and so the cleaving unto these, is a renouncing of it.   Oh ! we all were sealed or God in Baptism ; but who lives as if it was so ?   How few have the impression of it on the conscience, and the expression of it in the walk and fruit of their life !   We do not, as clean-washed persons, abhor and fly all pollutions, *all fellowship with the unfruitful works of darkness.*

We have been a long time hearers of the Gospel, whereof Baptism is the seal, and most of us often at the Lord's table.   What hath all this done upon us ?   Ask within : are your hearts changed ?   Is there a new creation there ?   Where is that spiritual-mindedness ?   Are your hearts dead to the world and sin, and alive to God, *your consciences purged from dead works ?*

What mean you ?   Is not this the end of all the ordinances, to make all clean, and to renew and make good the conscience, to bring the soul and your Lord into a happy amity, and a good correspondence, that it may not only be on speaking terms, but often speak and converse with him ?—may have liberty both to demand and answer, as the original word implies ? that it may speak the language of faith and humble obedience unto God, and that he may speak the language of peace to it, and both, the language of the Lord each to the other ?

That conscience alone is good, which is much busied in this work, in demanding and answering ; which speaks much with itself, and much with God.   This is both the sign that it is good, and the means to make it better.   That soul will doubtless be very wary in its walk, which takes daily account of itself, and renders up that account unto God.   It will not live by guess, but naturally examine each step before-hand, because it is resolved to examine all after; will consider well what it should do, because it means to ask over again what it hath done, and not only to answer itself, but to make a faithful report of all unto God ; to lay all before him, continually upon trial made ; to tell him what is in any measure well done, as his own work, and bless him for that ; and tell him, too, all the slips and miscarriages of the day, as our own ; complaining of ourselves in his presence, and still entreating free pardon, and more wisdom to walk more holily and exactly, and gaining, even by our failings, more humility and more watchfulness.

If you would have your consciences answer well, they must inquire and question much beforehand.   Whether is this I purpose and go about, agreeable to my Lord's will ?   Will it please him ?   Ask that more, and regard that more, than this, which the most follow : Will it please or profit myself ?   Fits that my own humour ?   And examine not only the bulk and substance of thy ways and actions, but the man-ner of them, how thy heart is set.   So think it not enough to go to church, or to pray, but *take heed how ye hear;* consider how pure He is, and how piercing his eye, whom thou servest.

Then, again, afterwards ; think it not enough, I was praying, or hearing, or reading, it was a good work, what need I question it fur-ther ?   No, but be still reflecting and asking how it was done : How have I heard, how have I prayed ?   Was my heart humbled by the discoveries of sin, from the word ?   Was it refreshed with the promises of grace ?   Did it lie level under the word, to receive the stamp of it ?   Was it in prayer set and kept in a holy bent towards God ?   Did it breathe forth real and earnest desires into his ear ; or was it remiss, and roving, and dead in the service ?   So in my society with others, in such and such company, what was spent of my time, and how did I employ it ?   Did I seek to honour my Lord, and to edify my brethren, by my carriage and speeches ; or did the time run out in trifling, vain discourse ?   When alone, what is the carriage and walk of my heart ?   Where it hath most liberty to move in its own pace, is it delighted in converse with God ?   Are the thoughts of heavenly things frequent and sweet to it ; or does it run after the earth and the delights of it, spinning out itself in impertinent, vain contrivances ?

The neglect of such inquiries, is that which entertains and increases the impurity of the soul, so that men are afraid to look into themselves, and to look up to God.   But oh ! what a foolish course is this, to shift off what cannot be avoided !   In the end, answer must be made to that All-seeing Judge with whom we have to do, and to whom we owe our accounts.

And, truly, it should be seriously considered, what makes this good conscience, which makes an acceptable answer unto God.   That ap-pears by the opposition, *not the putting away the filth of the flesh;* then, it *is* the putting away of *soul-filthiness;* so it is the renewing and purifying of the conscience, that makes it good, pure, and peaceable. In the purifying, it may be troubled, which is but the stirring in cleansing of it, and makes more quiet in the end, as physic, or the lancing of a sore; and after it is in some measure cleansed, it may have fits of trouble, which yet still add further purity and further peace. So there is no hazard in that work; but all the misery is, a dead security of the conscience while remaining filthy, and yet unstirred; or, after some stirring or pricking, as a wound not thoroughly cured, skinned over, which will but breed more vexation in the end; it will fester and grow more difficult to be cured, and if it be cured, it must be by deeper cutting and more pain, than if at first it had endured a thorough search.

O my brethren! take heed of sleeping unto death in carnal ease. Resolve to take no rest till you be in the element and place of soul-rest, where solid rest indeed is. Rest not till you be with Christ. Though all the world should offer their best, turn them by with disdain; if they will not be turned by, throw them down, and go over them, and trample upon them. Say, you have no rest to give me, nor will I take any at your hands, nor from any creature. There is no rest for me till I be under His shadow, who endured so much trouble to purchase my rest, and whom having found, I may sit down quiet and satisfied; and when the men of the world make boast of the highest content, I will outvie them all with this one word, *My Beloved is mine, and I am his.*

The answer of a good conscience toward God.] The conscience of man is never rightly at peace in itself, till it be rightly persuaded of peace with God, which, while it remains filthy, it cannot be; for he is holy, and iniquity cannot dwell with *him*. What *communion betwixt light and darkness?* 2 Cor. vi. 14. So then the conscience must be cleansed, ere it can look upon God with assurance and peace. This cleansing is sacramentally performed by Baptism; effectually, by the Spirit of Christ and the blood of Christ; and he lives to impart both: therefore here is mentioned his resurrection from the dead, as that, by virtue whereof we are assured of this purifying and peace. Then can the conscience, in some measure with confidence, answer, Lord, though polluted by former sins, and by sin still dwelling in me, yet thou seest that my desires are to be daily more like my Saviour; I would have more love and zeal for thee, more hatred of sin. It can answer with St. Peter, when he was posed, *Lovest thou me?* Lord, I appeal to thine own eye, who seest my heart: *Lord, thou knowest that I love thee;* at least I desire to love thee, and to desire thee; and that is love. Willingly would I do thee more suitable service, and honour thy name more; and I do sincerely desire more grace for this, that thou mayest have more glory; and I entreat the light of thy countenance for this end, that, by seeing it, my heart may be more weaned from the world, and knit unto thyself. Thus it answers touching its inward frame and the work of holiness by the Spirit of holiness dwelling in it. But, to answer Justice, touching the point of guilt, it flies *to the Blood of sprinkling,* fetches all its answer thence, turns over the matter upon it, and that Blood answers for it; for it doth speak, and *speak better things than the blood of Abel,* Heb. xii.

24 ; speaks full payment of all that can be exacted from the sinner ; and that is a sufficient answer.

The conscience is then, in this point, at first made speechless, driven to a nonplus in itself, hath from itself no answer to make ; but then it turns about to Christ, and finds what to say : Lord, there is indeed in me nothing but guiltiness ; I have deserved death ; but I have fled into the City of refuge which thou hast appointed ; there I resolve to abide, to live and die there. If Justice pursue me, it shall find me there : I take sanctuary in Jesus. The arrest laid upon me, will light upon him, and he hath wherewithal to answer it. He can straightway declare he hath paid all, and can make it good. He hath the acquaintance to show ; yea, his own liberty is a real sign of it. He was in prison, and is let free, which tells that all is satisfied. Therefore the answer here rises out of the *resurrection of Jesus Christ.*

And in this very thing lies our peace, and our way, and all our happiness. Oh! it is worth your time and pains, to try your interest in this ; it is the only thing worthy your highest diligence. But the most are out of their wits, running like a number of distracted persons, and still in a deal of business, but to what end they know not. You are unwilling to be deceived in those things which, at their best and surest, do but deceive you when all is done ; but are content to be deceived in that which is your great concernment. You are your own deceivers in it ; gladly gulled with shadows of faith and repentance, false touches of sorrow, and false flashes of joy, and are not careful to have your souls really unbottomed from themselves, and built upon Christ ; to have him your treasure, your righteousness, your all, and to have him your answer unto God your Father. But if you will yet be advised, let go all, to lay hold on him : lay your souls on him, and leave him not. He is *a tried foundation-stone,* and *he that trusts on him, shall not be confounded.*

Ver. 22. Who is gone into heaven, and is on the right hand of God ; angels and authorities and powers being made subject unto him.

THIS is added on purpose to show us further, what he is, how high and glorious a Saviour we have !

We have here four points or steps of the exaltation of Christ :—
1. Resurrection from the dead. 2. Ascension into heaven. 3. Sitting at the right hand of God. 4. In that posture, his royal authority over the angels. The particulars are clear in themselves. Of the sitting at the right hand of God, you are not ignorant that it is a borrowed expression, drawn from earth to heaven, to bring down some notion of heaven to us ; to signify to us in our language, suitably to our customs, the supreme dignity of Jesus Christ, God and Man, the Mediator of the new covenant, his matchless nearness unto his Father, and the sovereignty given him over heaven and earth. And that of the subjection of angels, is but a more particular specifying of that his dignity and power, as enthroned at the Father's right hand, they being the most elevated and glorious creatures : so that his authority over all the world is implied in that subjection of the highest and noblest part of it. His victory and triumph over the angels of darkness, is an evidence of his invincible power and greatness, and matter

of comfort to his saints ; but this here intends his supremacy over the glorious elect angels.

That there is amongst them priority, we find ; that there is a comely order in their differences, cannot be doubted ; but to marshal their degrees and stations above, is a point, not only of vain, fruitless curiosity, but of presumptuous intrusion. Whether these are names of their different particular dignities, or only different names of their general excellency and power, as I think it cannot be certainly well determined, so it imports us not to determine : only, this we know, and are particularly taught from this place, that whatsoever is their common dignity, both in names and differences, they are all subject to our glorious Head, Christ.

What confirmation they have in their estate by him, (though piously asserted by divines,) is not so infallibly clear from the alleged scriptures, which may bear another sense. But this is certain, that he is their King, and they acknowledge him to be so, and do incessantly admire and adore him. They rejoice in his glory, and in the glory and happiness of mankind through him. They yield him most cheerful obedience, and serve him readily in the good of his Church, and of each particular believer, as he deputes and employs them.

This is the thing here intended, having in it these two : his Dignity above them, and his Authority over them.

1. Such is his Dignity, that even that nature which he stooped below them to take on, he hath carried up and raised above them ; the very earth, the flesh of man, being exalted in his person above all those heavenly spirits, who are of so excellent and pure a being in their nature, and from the beginning of the world have been clothed with so transcendent glory. A parcel of clay is made so bright, and set so high, as to outshine those bright flaming spirits, those Stars of the morning, that flesh being united to the Fountain of Light, the blessed Deity in the person of the Son.

In coming to fetch and put on this garment, he made himself *lower than the angels ;* but carrying it with him, at his return to his eternal throne, and sitting down with it there, it is raised high above them ; as the Apostle teaches excellently and amply : *To which of them said he, Sit on my right hand ?* Heb. i. 2.

This they look upon with perpetual wonder, but not with envy or repining. No, amongst all their eyes, no such eye is to be found. Yea, they rejoice in the infinite wisdom of God in this design, and his infinite love to poor lost mankind. It is wonderful, indeed, to see him filling the room of their fallen brethren with new guests from earth, yea, with such as are born heirs of hell ; but that not only sinful men should thus be raised to a participation of glory with them who are spotless, sinless spirits, but their flesh, in their Redeemer, should be dignified with a glory so far beyond them,—this is that mystery the angels are intent on looking and prying into, and cannot, nor ever shall, see the bottom of it, for it hath none.

2. Jesus Christ is not only exalted above the angels in absolute dignity, but in relative authority over them. He is made Captain over those heavenly bands ; they are all under his command, for all services wherein it pleases him to employ them ; and the great

employment he hath, is the attending on his Church, and on particular elect ones. *Are they not all ministering spirits, sent forth to minister to them that shall be heirs of salvation?* Heb. i. *ult.* They are the servants of Christ, and in him, and at his appointment, the servants of every believer ; and are many ways serviceable and useful for their good, which truly we do not duly consider. There is no danger of overvaluing them, and inclining to worship them upon this consideration ; yea, if we take it right, it will rather take us off from that. The angel judged his argument strong enough to St. John against that, that he was but *his fellow servant.* Rev. xix. 10. But this is more, that they are servants to us, although not therefore inferior, it being an honorary service. Yet certainly they are inferior to our Head, and so, to his mystical body, taken in that notion, as a part of him.

Reflection 1. The height of this our Saviour's glory will appear the more, if we reflect on the descent from which he ascended to it. Oh ! how low did we bring down so high a Majesty, into the pit wherein we had fallen, by climbing to be higher than he had set us ! It was high indeed, as we were fallen so low, and yet he, against whom our sin was committed, came down to help us up again, and to take hold of us,—*took us on ;* so the word is, [ἐπιλαμβάνεται,] Heb. ii. 16. *He took not hold of the angels,*—let them go, hath left them to die for ever,—*but he took hold of the seed of Abraham,* and took on him indeed their flesh, dwelling amongst us, and in a mean part. He *emptied himself,* ἐκένωσε, (Phil. ii. 7,) and became of no repute. And further, after he descended to the earth, and into our flesh, in it he became *obedient to death* upon the cross, and descended into the grave. And by these steps, he was walking towards that glory wherein he now is : *he abased himself, wherefore,* says the Apostle, *God hath highly exalted him.* Phil. ii. 8. So he says of himself, *Ought not Christ first to suffer these things, and so enter into his glory?* Luke xxiv. 26. Now this, indeed, it is pertinent to consider. The Apostle is here upon the point of Christ's sufferings ; that is his theme, and therefore he is so particular in the ascending of Christ to his glory. Who, of those that would come thither, will refuse to follow him in the way wherein he led, he [ἀρχηγὸς] *the Leader of our faith?* Heb. xii. 2. And who, of those who follow him, will not love and delight to follow him through any way, the lowest and darkest ? It is excellent and safe, and then, it ends you see where.

Refl. 2. Think not strange of the Lord's method with his Church, in bringing her to so low and desperate a posture many times. Can she be in a condition more seemingly desperate than was her Head—not only in ignominious sufferings, but dead and laid in the grave, and the stone rolled to it and sealed, and all made sure ? And yet he arose and ascended, and now sits in glory, and shall sit *till all his enemies become his footstool.* Do not fear for him, that they shall overtop, yea, or be able to reach him who is exalted higher than the heavens ; neither be afraid for his Church, which is his body, and, if her Head be safe and alive, cannot but partake of safety and life with him. Though she were, to sight, dead and laid in the grave, yet shall she arise thence, and be more glorious than before (Isa. xxvi. 19) ; and still, the deeper her distress, shall rise the higher in the day of deliverance.

Thus, in his dealing with a soul, observe the Lord's method. Think it not strange that he brings a soul low, very low, which he means to comfort and exalt very high in grace and glory: that he leads it by hell-gates to heaven; that it be at that point, *My God, my God, why hast thou forsaken me?* Was not the Head put to use that word, and so to speak it, as the head speaks for the body, seasoning it for his members, and sweetening that bitter cup by his own drinking of it? Oh! what a hard condition may a soul be brought unto, and put to think, *Can He love me, and intend mercy for me, who leaves me to this!* And yet, in all, the Lord is preparing it thus for comfort and blessedness.

Refl. 3. Turn your thoughts more frequently to this excellent subject, the glorious high estate of our *great High Priest.* The angels admire this mystery, and we slight it! They rejoice in it, and we, whom it certainly more nearly concerns, are not moved with it; we do not draw that comfort and instruction from it, which it would plentifully afford, if it were sought after. It would comfort us against all troubles and fears to reflect, is He not on high, who hath undertaken for us? Doth any thing befall us, but it is past first in heaven? And shall any thing pass there to our prejudice or damage? He sits there, and is upon the counsel of all, who hath loved us, and given himself for us; yea, who, as he descended thence for us, did likewise ascend thither again for us. He hath made our inheritance which he purchased, there sure to us, taking possession for us, and in our name, since he is there, not only as the Son of God, but as our Surety, and as our Head. And so, the Believer may think himself even already possessed of this right, inasmuch as his Christ is there. The saints are glorified already in their Head. *Ubi Caput meum regnat ibi me regnare credo: Where he reigns, there I believe myself to reign,* says Augustine. And consider, in all thy straits and troubles, outward or inward, they are not hid from him. He knows them, and feels them, thy compassionate High Priest hath a gracious sense of thy frailties and griefs, fears and temptations, and will not suffer thee to be surcharged. He is still presenting thy estate to the Father, and using that interest and power which he hath in his affection, for thy good. And what wouldst thou more? Art thou one whose heart desires to rest upon him, and cleave to him? Thou art knit so to him, that his resurrection and glory secure thee thine. His life and thine are not two, but one life, as that of the head and members; and if he could not be overcome of death, thou canst not neither. Oh! that sweet word, *Because I live, ye shall live also.* John xiv. 19.

Let thy thoughts and carriage be moulded in this contemplation rightly, ever to look on thy exalted Head. Consider his glory; see not only thy nature raised in him above the angels, but thy person interested by faith in that his glory; and then, think thyself too good to serve any base lust. Look down on sin and the world with a holy disdain, being united to Him who is so exalted and so glorious. And let not thy mind creep here; engage not thy heart to any thing that time and this earth can afford. Oh! why are we so little where there is such a spring of delightful and high thoughts for us? *If ye be risen with Christ, seek those things which are above, where he sits.* Col.

iii. 1. What mean you? Are ye such as will let go your interest in this once crucified, and now glorified, Jesus? If not, why are ye not more conformable to it? Why does it not possess your hearts more? Ought it not to be thus? Should not our hearts be where our treasure, where our blessed Head is? Oh! how unreasonable, how unfriendly is it, how much may we be ashamed to have room in our hearts for earnest thoughts, or desires, or delights, about any thing besides him!

Were this deeply wrought upon the hearts of ,those that have a right in it, would there be found in them any attachment to the poor things that are passing away? Would death be a terrible word? Yea, would it not be one of the sweetest, most rejoicing thoughts to solace and ease the heart under all pressures, to look forward to that day of liberty? This infectious disease* may keep possession of all the winter, and grow hot with the year again. Do not flatter yourselves, and think it is past; you have yet remembering strokes to keep it in your eye. But, however, shall we abide always here? Or is there any reason, when things are duly weighed, why we should desire it? Well, if you would be united beforehand, and so feel your separation from this world less, this is the only way : Look up to Him who draws up all hearts that do indeed behold him. Then, I say, thy heart shall be removed beforehand; and the rest is easy and sweet. When that is done, all is gained. And consider, how he desires the completion of our union with him. Shall it be his request and earnest desire, and shall it not be ours too, *that where he is, there we may be also?* John xvii. 24. Let us expect it with patient submission, yet striving by desires and suits, and looking out for our release from this body of sin and death.

FIRST PETER

CHAPTER 4

Ver. 1. Forasmuch then as Christ hath suffered for us in the flesh, arm yourselves likewise with the same mind; for he that hath suffered in the flesh hath ceased from sin.

THE main of a Christian's duty lies in these two things, patience in suffering, and avoidance of sin, ἀνέχου καὶ ἀπέχου, and they have a natural influence upon each other. Although affliction simply doth not, yet affliction sweetly and humbly carried, doth purify and disengage the heart from sin, wean it from the world and the common ways of it. And again, holy and exact walking keeps the soul in a sound, healthful temper, and so enables it to patient suffering, to bear things more easily ; as a strong body endures fatigue, heat, cold, and hardship, with ease, a small part whereof would surcharge a sickly constitution. The consciousness of sin, and careless unholy courses, do wonderfully weaken a soul, and distemper it, so that it is not able to endure much ; every little thing disturbs it. Therefore, the Apostle

---

* This probably refers to the Pestilence in 1665. See the lecture on chap. iv. 6.
"Though the Pestilence doth not affright you so," &c.

hath reason, both to insist so much on these two points in this Epistle, and likewise to interweave the one so often with the other, pressing jointly throughout, the cheerful bearing of all kinds of afflictions, and the careful forbearing of all kinds of sin; and out of the one discourse he slides into the other ; as here.

And as the things agree in their nature, so, in their great pattern and principle, Jesus Christ: and the Apostle still draws both from thence ; that of patience, ch. iii. 18, that of holiness, here : *Forasmuch, then, as Christ hath suffered for us*, &c.

The chief study of a Christian, and the very thing that makes him to be a Christian, is, conformity with Christ. *Summa religionis imitari quem colis: This is the sum of religion*, (said that wise heathen, Pythagoras,) *to be like him whom thou worshippest*. But this example being in itself too sublime, is brought down to our view in Christ ; the brightness of God is veiled, and veiled in our own flesh, that we may be able to look on it. The inaccessible light of the Deity is so attempered in the humanity of Christ, that we may read our lesson by it in him, and may direct our walk by it. And that truly is our only way ; there is nothing but wandering and perishing in all other ways, nothing but darkness and misery out of him ; but *he that follows me*, says he, *shall not walk in darkness*, John viii. 12. And therefore is he set before us in the Gospel, in so clear and lively colours, that we may make this our whole endeavour, to be like him.

Consider here, 1. The high engagement to this conformity. 2. The nature of it. 3. The actual improvement of it.

1. The engagement lies in this, that he suffered for us. Of this we have treated before. Only, in reference to this, had he come down, as some have mis-imagined it, only to set us this perfect way of obedience, and give us an example of it in our own nature, this had been very much: that the Son of God should descend to teach wretched man, and the great King descend into man, and dwell in a tabernacle of clay, to set up a school in it, for such ignorant, accursed creatures, and should, in his own person, act the hardest lessons, both in doing and suffering, to lead us in both. But the matter goes yet higher than this. Oh ! how much higher hath he suffered, not simply as our rule, but as our surety, and in our stead ! *He suffered for us in the flesh*. We are the more obliged to make his suffering our example, because it was to us more than an example ; it was our ransom.

This makes the conformity reasonable in a double respect. [1.] It is *due*, that we follow him, who led thus as the *Captain of our salvation ;* that we follow him in suffering, and in doing, seeing both were so for us. It is strange how some armies have addicted themselves to their head, so as to be at his call night and day, in summer and winter, to refuse no travail or endurance of hardship for him, and all only to please him, and serve his inclination and ambition ; as Cæsar's trained bands, especially the veterans, it is a wonder what they endured in counter-marches, and in traversing from one country to another. But besides that our Lord and Leader is so great and excellent, and so well deserves following for his own worth, this lays upon us an obligation beyond all conceiving, that he first suffered for us, that he endured such hatred of men, and such wrath of God the Father, and went through death, so vile a death, to procure our life. What can be too bitter to endure, or too sweet to forsake, to follow Him ? Were this duly considered, should we cleave to our lusts, or to our ease ? Should we not be willing to go through fire and water, yea, through death itself, yea, were it possible, through many deaths, to follow him ?

[2.] Consider, as this conformity is *due*, so it is made *easy* by that his suffering for us. Our burden which pressed us to hell being taken off, is not all that is left, to suffer or to do, as nothing ? Our chains which bound us over to eternal death being knocked off, shall we not walk, shall we not run, in his ways ? Oh ! think what that burden and yoke was which he hath eased us of, how heavy, how unsufferable it was, and then we shall think, what he so truly says, that all he lays on is sweet ; *his yoke easy, and his burden light.* Oh ! the happy change, to be rescued from the vilest slavery, and called to conformity and fellowship with the Son of God !

2. The nature of this conformity, (to show the nearness of it,) is expressed in the very same terms as in the pattern : it is not a remote resemblance, but the same thing, even *suffering in the flesh.* But that we may understand rightly what suffering is here meant, it is plainly this, *ceasing from sin.* So that *suffering in the flesh*, here, is not simply the enduring of afflictions, which is a part of the Christian's conformity to his Head, Christ, (Rom. viii. 29,) but implies a more inward and spiritual suffering. It is the suffering and the dying of our corruption, the taking away of the life of sin by the death of Christ: the death of his sinless flesh works in the believer the death of sinful flesh, that is, the corruption of his nature, which is so usually in Scripture called *flesh.* Sin makes man base, drowns him in flesh and the lusts of it, makes the very soul become gross and earthly, turns it, as it were, to flesh. So, the Apostle calls the very mind that is unrenewed, *a carnal mind.* Rom. viii. 7.

And what doth the mind of a natural man hunt after and run out into, from one day and year to another ? Is it not on the things of this base world, and *(corporis negotium)* the concernment of his flesh ? What would he have, but be accommodated to eat, and drink, and dress, and live at ease ? *He minds earthly things*, savours and relishes them, and cares for them. Examine the most of your pains and time, and your strongest desires, and most serious thoughts, whether they go not this way, to raise yourselves and yours in your worldly condition. Yea, the highest projects of the greatest natural spirits, are but earth still, in respect of things truly spiritual. All their state designs go not beyond this poor life that perishes in the flesh, and is daily perishing, even while we are busiest in upholding it and providing for it. Present things and this lodge of clay, this flesh and its interest, take up most of our time and pains: the most ? yea, all, till that change be wrought which the Apostle speaks of, till Christ be put on : Rom. xiii. 14. *Put ye on the Lord Jesus Christ*, and then, the other will easily follow, which follows in the words, *Make no provision for the flesh, to fulfil the lusts thereof.* Once in Christ, and then your necessary general care for this natural life will be regulated and moderated by the Spirit.

And as for all unlawful and enormous desires of the flesh, you shall be rid of providing for these. Instead of all provision for the life of the flesh in that sense, there is another guest, and another life, for you now to wait on and furnish for. In them who are in Christ, that flesh is dead; they are freed from its drudgery. *He that hath suffered in the flesh, hath rested from sin.*

Ceased from sin.] He is at rest from it, a godly death, as they who *die in the Lord* rest from their labours. Rev. xiv. 13. He that hath suffered in the flesh and is dead to it, dies indeed in the Lord, rests from the base turmoil of sin; it is no longer his master. As our sin was the cause of Christ's death, his death is the death of sin in us; and that, not simply as he bore a moral pattern of it, but as the real work- ing cause of it, it hath an effectual influence on the soul, kills it to sin. *I am crucified with Christ,* says St. Paul. Gal. ii. 20. Faith so looks on the death of Christ, that it takes the impression of it, sets it on the heart, kills it unto sin. Christ and the Believer do not only become one in law, so that his death stands for theirs, but one in nature, so that his death for sin causes theirs to it. They are *baptized into his death.* Rom. vi. 3.

This suffering in the flesh being unto death, and such a death, *(cruci- fying,)* hath indeed pain in it; but what then? It must be so like his, and the Believer be like him, in willingly enduring it. All the pain of his suffering in the flesh, his love to us digested and went through with; so, all the pain to our nature in severing and pulling us from our beloved sins, and in our dying to them, if his love be planted in our hearts, that will sweeten it, and make us delight in it. Love desires nothing more than likeness, and shares willingly in all with the party loved; and above all love, this Divine love is purest and highest, and works most strongly that way; takes pleasure in that pain, and is a voluntary death, as Plato calls love. It is *strong as death,* says Solo- mon. Cant. viii. 6. As death makes the strongest body fall to the ground, so doth the love of Christ make the most active and lively sinner dead to his sin; and as death severs a man from his dearest and most familiar friends, thus doth the love of Christ, and his death flow- ing from it, sever the heart from its most beloved sins.

I beseech you, seek to have your hearts set against sin, to hate it, to wound it, and be dying daily to it. Be not satisfied, unless ye feel an abatement of it, and a life within you. Disdain that base service, and being bought at so high a rate, think yourselves too good to be slaves to any base lust. You are called to a more excellent and more honourable service. And of this suffering in the flesh, we may safely say, what the Apostle speaks of the sufferings with and for Christ, (Rom. viii. 17,) that the partakers of these sufferings are co-heirs of glory with Christ: *If we suffer thus with him, we shall also be glorified with him;* if we die with him, we shall live with him for ever.

3. We have the actual improvement of this Conformity: *Arm your- selves with the same mind,* or *thoughts* of this mortification. Death, taken naturally, in its proper sense, being an entire privation of life, admits not of degrees; but this figurative death, this mortification of the flesh in a Christian, is gradual. In so far as he is renewed, and is animated and acted on by the Spirit of Christ, he is thoroughly

mortified; (for this death, and that new life joined with it, and here added, *ver.* 2, go together and grow together ;) but because he is not totally renewed, and there is in him the remains of that corruption still, which is here called flesh, therefore it is his great task, to be gaining further upon it, and overcoming and mortifying it every day. And to this tend the frequent exhortations of this nature: *Mortify your members that are on the earth.* So Rom. vi. *Likewise reckon yourselves dead to sin,* and, *Let it not reign in your mortal bodies.* Thus here, *Arm yourselves with the same mind,* or with this very thought. Consider and apply that suffering of Christ in the flesh, to the end that you, with him suffering in the flesh, may cease from sin. Think that it ought to be thus, and seek that it may be thus, with you.

Arm yourselves.] There is still fighting, and sin will be molesting you ; though wounded to death, yet will it struggle for life, and seek to wound its enemy ; it will assault the graces that are in you. Do not think, if it be once struck, and you have given it a stab near to the heart, by the *sword of the Spirit,* that therefore it will stir no more. No, so long as you live in the flesh, in these bowels there will be re-mainders of the life of this flesh, your natural corruption ; therefore ye must be armed against it. Sin will not give you rest, so long as there is a drop of blood in its veins, one spark of life in it : and that will be so long as you have life here. This old man is stout, and will fight himself to death ; and at the weakest it will rouse up itself, and exert its dying spirits, as men will do sometimes more eagerly than when they were not so weak, nor so near death.

This the children of God often find to their grief, that corruptions which they thought had been cold dead, stir and rise up again, and set upon them. A passion or lust, that after some great stroke lay a long while as dead, stirred not, and therefore they thought to have heard no more of it, though it shall never recover fully again, to be lively as before, yet will revive in such a measure as to molest, and possibly to foil them yet again. Therefore is it continually necessary that they live in arms, and put them not off to their dying day ; till they put off the body, and be altogether free of the flesh. You may take the Lord's promise for victory in the end ; that shall not fail ; but do not promise yourself ease in the way, for that will not hold. If at some times you be undermost, give not all for lost : he hath often won the day, who hath been foiled and wounded in the fight. But likewise take not all for won, so as to have no more conflict, when sometimes you have the better, as in particular battles. Be not desperate when you lose, nor secure when you gain them : when it is worse with you, do not throw away your arms, nor lay them away when you are at best.

Now, the way to be armed is this, *the same mind:* How would my Lord, Christ, carry himself in this case ? And what was *his* business in all places and companies ? Was it not to do the will, and advance the glory, of his Father ? If I be injured and reviled, consider how would he do in this ? Would he repay one injury with another, one reproach with another reproach ? *No, being reviled, he reviled not again.* Well, through his strength, this shall be my way too. Thus ought it to be with the Christian, framing all his ways, and words, and very thoughts, upon that model, *the mind of Christ*, and studying in all things to walk even as he walked; studying it much, as the reason and rule of mortification, and drawing from it, as the real cause and spring of mortification.

The pious contemplation of his death will most powerfully kill the love of sin in the soul, and kindle an ardent hatred of it. The Believer, looking on his Jesus as crucified for him and *wounded for his transgression*, and taking in deep thoughts of his spotless innocency, which deserved no such thing, and of his matchless love, which yet endured it all for him, will then naturally think, Shall I be a friend to that which was his deadly enemy ? Shall sin be sweet to me, which was so bitter to him, and that for my sake ? Shall I ever lend it a good look, or entertain a favourable thought of that which shed my Lord's blood ? Shall I live in that for which he died, and died to kill it in me ? Oh ! let it not be.

To the end it may not be, let such really apply *that* death, to work this on the soul ; (for this is always to be added, and is the main thing indeed ;) by holding and fastening that death close to the soul, effectually to kill the effects of sin in it ; to stifle and crush them dead, by pressing that death on the heart ; looking on it, not only as a most complete model, but as having a most effectual virtue for this effect ; and desiring him, entreating our Lord himself, who communicates himself and the virtue of his death to the Believer, that he would powerfully cause it to flow in upon us, and let us feel the virtue of it.

It is, then, the only thriving and growing life, to be much in the lively contemplation and application of Jesus Christ ; to be continually studying him, and conversing with him, and drawing from him, *receiving of his fulness, grace for grace.* John i. 16. Wouldst thou have much power against sin, and much increase of holiness, let thine eye be much on Christ ; set thine heart on him ; let it dwell in him, and be still with him. When sin is likely to prevail in any kind, go to him, tell him of the insurrection of his enemies, and thy inability to resist, and desire him to suppress them, and to help thee against them, that they may gain nothing by their stirring, but some new wound. If thy heart begin to be taken with, and move towards, sin, lay it before him ; the beams of his love shall eat out that fire of those sinful lusts. Wouldst thou have thy pride, and passions, and love of the world, and self-love, killed, go sue for the virtue of his death, and that shall do it. Seek his Spirit, the Spirit of meekness, and humility, and Divine love. Look on him, and he shall draw thy heart heavenwards, and unite it to himself, and make it like himself. And is not that the thing thou desirest ?

Ver. 2. That he no longer should live the rest of his time in the flesh to the lusts of men, but to the will of God.

3. For the time past of our life may suffice us to have wrought the will of the Gentiles, when we walked in lasciviousness, lusts, excess of wine, revellings, banquetings, and abominable idolatries.

THE chains of sin are so strong, and so fastened on our nature, that there is in us no power to break them off, till a mightier and stronger

Spirit than our own come into us.   The Spirit of Christ dropped into
the soul, makes it able to *break through a troop, and leap over a wall,*
as David speaks of himself, when furnished with the strength of his
God. Psal. xviii. 29.   Men's resolutions fall to nothing ; and as a
prisoner who attempts to escape, and does not, is bound faster, thus
usually it is with men in their self-purposes of forsaking sin : they leave
out Christ in the work, and so remain in their captivity, yea, it grows
upon them.   And while we press them to free themselves, and show
not Christ to them, we put them upon an impossibility.   But a look to
him makes it feasible and easy.   Faith in him, and that love to him
which faith begets, break through and surmount all difficulties.   It is
the powerful love of Christ, that kills the love of sin, and kindles the
love of holiness in the soul ; makes it a willing sharer in his death,
and so a happy partaker of his life.   For that always follows, and
must of necessity, as here is added : *He that hath suffered in the flesh,
hath ceased from sin,*—is crucified and dead to it ; but he loses nothing ; yea, it is his great gain, to lose that deadly life of the flesh for
a new spiritual life, a life indeed *living unto God ;* that is the end why
he so dies, that he may thus live— *That he no longer should live to the
lusts of men,* and yet live far better, *live to the will of God.*   He that is
one with Christ by believing, is one with him throughout, in death and
in life.   As Christ rose from the dead, so he that is dead to sin with
him, through the power of his death, rises to that new life with him,
through the power of his resurrection.   And these two constitute our
sanctification, which whosoever do partake of Christ, and are found
in him, do certainly draw from him.   Thus are they joined, Rom. vi.
11 : *Likewise reckon you yourselves dead indeed to sin, but alive to God,*
and both *through Christ Jesus our Lord.*
     All they who do really come to Jesus Christ, as they come to him
as their Saviour, to be clothed with him, and made righteous by him,
so they come likewise to him as their Sanctifier, to be made new and
holy by him, to die and live with him, to *follow the Lamb wheresoever
he goes,* through the hardest sufferings, and death itself.   And this
spiritual suffering and dying with him, is the universal way of all his
followers ; they are all martyrs thus in the crucifying of sinful flesh,
and so dying for him, and with him.   And they may well go cheerfully through.   Though it bear the unpleasant name of *death,* yet, as
the other death is, (which makes it so little terrible, yea, often to appear
so very desirable to them,) so is this, the way to a far more excellent
and happy life ; so that they may pass through it gladly, both for the
company and the end of it.   It is with Christ they go into his death, as
unto life in his life.   Though a believer might be free from these terms,
he would not.   No, surely.   Could he be content with that easy-life
of sin, instead of the Divine life of Christ ?   No, he will do thus, and
not accept of deliverance, that he may obtain (as the Apostle speaks of
the martyrs) *a better resurrection.* Heb. xi. 35.   Think on it again,
you to whom your sins are dear still, and this life sweet ; you are yet
far from Christ and his life.
     The Apostle, with the intent to press this more home, expresses
more at large the nature of the opposite estates and lives that he speaks
of, and so, 1. Sets before his Christian brethren the dignity of that

new life; and then, 2. By a particular reflection upon the former life, he presses the change. The former life he calls a living *to the lusts of men;* this new spiritual life, a living *to the will of God.*

The lusts of men.] Such as are common to the corrupt nature of man; such as every man may find in himself, and perceive in others. The Apostle, in the third verse more particularly, for further clearness, specifies those kinds of men that were most notorious in these lusts, and those kinds of lusts that were most notorious in men. Writing to the dispersed Jews, he calls sinful lusts *the will of the Gentiles,* as having least control of contrary light in them; (and yet, the Jews walked in the same, though they had the Law as a light and rule for avoiding of them;) and implies, that these lusts were unbeseeming even their former condition as Jews, but much more unsuitable to them, as now Christians. Some of the grossest of these lusts he names, meaning all the rest, all the ways of sin, and so representing their vileness in the more lively manner. Not, as some take it, when they hear of such heinous sins, as if it were to lessen the evil of sins of a more civil nature by the comparison, or as if freedom from these were a blameless condition, and a change of it needless; no, the Holy Ghost means it just contrary, that we may judge of all sin, and of our sinful nature, by our estimate of those sins that are most discernible and abominable. All sin, though not equal in degree, yet is of one nature, and originally springs from one root, arising from the same unholy nature of man, and contrary to the same holy nature and will of God.

So then, 1. Those who walk in these highways of impiety, and yet will have the name of *Christians,* they are the shame of Christians, and the professed enemies of Jesus Christ, and of all others the most hateful to him: they seem to have taken on his name, for no other end than to shame and disgrace it. But he will vindicate himself, and the blot shall rest upon these impudent persons, who dare hold up their faces in the Church of God as parts of it, and are indeed nothing but the dishonour of it, spots and blots; who dare profess to worship God as his people, and remain unclean, riotous, and profane persons. How suits thy sitting here before the Lord, and thy sitting with vile ungodly company on the ale-bench? How agrees the word, sounds it well, There goes a drunken Christian, an unclean, a basely covetous, or earthly-minded Christian. And the naming of the latter is not besides the text, but agreeable to the very words of it; for the Apostle warrants us to take it under the name of *idolatry,* and in that name he reckons it to be mortified by a Christian: Col. iii. 5. *Mortify therefore your members which are upon the earth, fornication, uncleanness, inordinate affection, evil concupiscence, and covetousness, which is* IDOLATRY.

2. But yet, men who are someway exempted from the blot of these foul impieties, may still remain slaves to sin, alive to it, and dead to God, living to the lusts of men, and not to the will of God, pleasing others and themselves, and displeasing him. And the smoothest, best bred, and most moralized natural man, is in this base thraldom; and he is the more miserable, in that he dreams of liberty in the midst of his chains, thinks himself clean by looking on those that wallow in gross profaneness; takes measure of himself by the most crooked lives

of ungodly men about him, and so thinks himself very straight ; but
lays not the straight rule of the will of God to his ways and heart,
which if he did, he would then discover much crookedness in his ways,
and much more in his heart, that now he sees not, but takes it to be
square and even.

Therefore I advise and desire you to look more narrowly to yourselves in this, and see whether you be not still living to your own lusts
and wills instead of to God, seeking, in all your ways, to advance and
please yourselves, and not him. Is not the bent of your hearts set
that way ? Do not your whole desires and endeavours run in that
channel, how you and yours may be somebody, and how you may have
wherewithal to serve the flesh, and to be accounted of and respected
amongst men ! And if we trace it home, all a man's honouring and
pleasing of others tends to, and ends in, pleasing of himself : it resolves into that. And is it not so meant by him ? He pleases men,
either that he may gain by them, or be respected by them, or that something that is still pleasing to himself may be the return of it. So, self
is the grand idol, for which all other heart-idolatries are committed ;
and, indeed, in the unrenewed heart there is no scarcity of them. Oh !
what multitudes, what heaps, if the wall were digged through, and the
light of God going before us, and leading us in to see them ! The
natural motion and way of the natural heart, is no other than still seeking out new inventions, a forge of new gods, still either forming them
to itself, or worshipping those it hath already framed ; committing
spiritual fornication from God, with the creature, and multiplying lovers
every where, as it is tempted ; as the Lord complains of his people,
upon every high hill, and under every green tree. Jer. ii. 20 ; iii. 6.

You will not believe so much ill of yourselves, will not be convinced
of this unpleasant but necessary truth ; and this is a part of our self-
pleasing, that we please ourselves in this, that we will not see it, either
in our callings and ordinary ways, or in our religious exercises. For
even in these, we naturally aim at nothing but ourselves ; either our
reputation, or, at best, our own safety and peace ; either to stop the
cry of conscience for the present, or to escape the wrath that is to
come ; but not in a spiritual regard of the will of God, and out of pure
love to himself for himself ; yet, thus it should be, and that love, the
divine fire in all our sacrifices. The carnal mind is in the dark, and
sees not its vileness in living to itself, will not confess it to be so. But
when God comes into the soul, he lets it see itself, and all its idols and
idolatries, and forces it to abhor and loathe itself for all its abominations : and having discovered its filthiness to itself, then he purges and
cleanses it for himself, *from all its filthiness, and from all its idols,*
(Ezek. xxxvi. 25,) according to his promise, and comes in and takes
possession of it for himself, enthrones himself in the heart. And it is
never right nor happy till that be done.

But to the will of God.] We readily take any little slight change
for true conversion, but we may see here that we mistake it : it doth
not barely knock off some obvious apparent enormities, but casts all in
a new mould, alters the whole frame of the heart and life, kills a man,
and makes him alive again. And this new life is contrary to the old ;
for the change is made with that intent, *that he live no longer to the*

lusts of men, but to the will of God.   He is now, indeed, *a new creature,* having a new judgment and new thoughts of things, and so, accordingly, new desires and affections, and answerably to these, new actions.   *Old things are passed away and dead, and all things are become
new.*   2 Cor. v. 17.

Political men have observed, that in states, if alterations must be,
it is better to alter many things than a few.   And physicians have the
same remark for one's habit and custom for bodily health, upon the
same ground ; because things do so relate one to another, that except
they be adapted and suited together in the change, it avails not ; yea,
it sometimes proves the worse in the whole, though a few things in
particular seem to be bettered.   Thus, half-reformations in a Christian
turn to his prejudice : it is only best to be reformed throughout, and
to give up with all idols ; not to live one half to himself and the world,
and, as it were, another half to God, for that is but falsely so, and, in
reality, it cannot be.   The only way is, to make a heap of all, to have
all sacrificed together, and to live to no lust, but altogether and only to
God.   Thus it must be : there is no monster in the new creation, no
half new creature, *either all, or not at all, ὅλος ἢ μὴ ὅλως.*   We have
to deal with the Maker and the Searcher of the heart in this turn, and
he will have nothing unless he have the heart, and none of that neither,
unless he have it all.   If thou pass over into his kingdom, and become
his subject, thou must have him for thy only Sovereign.   *Omnisque
potestas impatiens consortis:* Royalty can admit of no rivalry, and least
of all, the highest and best of all.   If Christ be thy King, then his laws
and sceptre must rule all in thee ; thou must now acknowledge no
foreign power ; that will be treason.

And if he be thy Husband, thou must renounce all others.   Wilt thou
provoke him to jealousy ?   Yea, beware how thou givest a thought or
a look of thy affection any other way, for he will spy it, and will not
endure it.   The title of a husband is as strict and tender, as the other
of a king.

It is only best to be thus : it is thy great advantage and happiness,
to be thus entirely freed from so many tyrannous base lords, and to be
now subject to only one, and he so great, and withal so gracious and
sweet a King, *the Prince of Peace.*   Thou wast hurried before, and
racked with the very multitude of them.   Thy lusts, so many cruel task-
masters over thee, they gave thee no rest, and the work they set thee
to was base and slavish, more than the burdens, and pots, and toiling
in the clay of Egypt ; thou wast held to work in the earth, to pain, and
to soil and foul thyself with their drudgery.

Now thou hast but One to serve, and that is a great ease ; and it is
no slavery, but true honour, to serve so excellent a Lord, and in so
high services ; for he puts thee upon nothing but what is neat, and
what is honourable.   Thou art as *a vessel of honour* in his house, for
his best employments.   Now, thou art not in pain how to please this
person and the other, nor needest thou vex thyself to gain men, to
study their approbation and honour, nor to keep to thine own lusts
and observe their will.   Thou hast none but thy God to please in all ;
and if he be pleased, thou mayest disregard who be displeased.   His
will is not fickle and changing as men's are, and as thine own is.   He

hath told thee what he likes and desires, and he alters not ; so that
now thou knowest whom thou hast to do withal, and what to do,
whom to please, and what will please him, and this cannot but much
settle thy mind, and put thee at ease.   Thou mayest say heartily, as
rejoicing in the change of so many for one, and of such for such a
One, as the Church says, Isa. xxvi. 13, *O Lord our God, other lords
beside thee have had dominion over me, but now, by thee only will I
make mention of thy name;* now, none but thyself, not so much as
the *name* of them any more, away with them : through thy grace,
thou only shalt be my God.   It cannot endure that any thing be named
with thee.

Now, 1. That it may be thus, that we may wholly live *to the will of
God,* we must *know* his will, what it is.   Persons grossly ignorant of
God and of his will, cannot live to him.   We cannot *have fellowship
with him, and walk in darkness;* for HE *is light.* 1 John i. 6, 7.
This takes off a great many amongst us, who have not so much as a
common notion of the will of God.   But besides, that knowledge which
is a part, and (I may say) the first part, of the renewed image of God,
is not a natural knowledge of spiritual things, merely attained by human
teaching or industry, but it is a beam of God's own, issuing from himself, both enlightening and enlivening the whole soul : it gains the
affection and stirs to action, and so, indeed, it acts, and increases by
acting ; for the more we walk according to what we know of the will
of God, the more we shall be advanced to know more.   This is the
real *proving what is his good, and holy, and acceptable will.* Rom.
xii. 2.   So says Christ, *If any one will do the will of my Father, he
shall know of the doctrine.* John vii. 17.   Our lying off from the lively
use of known truth, keeps us low in the knowledge of God and communion with him.

2. So then, upon that knowledge of God's will, where it is spiritual
and from himself, follows the suiting of the heart with it, the affections
taking the stamp of it, and agreeing with it, *receiving the truth in the
love of it,* so that the heart may be transformed into it ; and now it is
not driven to obedience violently, but sweetly moving to it, by love
within the heart, framed to the love of God, and so of his will.

3. As Divine knowledge begets this affection, so this affection will
bring forth action, real obedience.   For these three are inseparably
linked, and each dependent on, and the product of, the others.   The
affection is not blind, but flowing from knowledge ; nor the actual obedience constrained, but flowing from affection ; and the affection is not
idle, seeing it brings forth obedience ; nor is the knowledge dead, seeing
it begets affection.

Thus the renewed, the living Christian, is all for God, a sacrifice
entirely offered up to God, and *a living sacrifice,* which lives to God.
He takes no more notice of his own carnal will ; hath renounced that
to embrace the holy will of God ; and therefore, though there is a contrary law and will in him, yet he does not acknowledge it, but only
the law of Christ, as now established in him ; that law of love, by
which he is sweetly and willingly led.   Real obedience consults not
now with flesh and blood, what will please them, but only inquires
what will please his God, and knowing his mind, thus resolves to

demur no more, nor to ask consent of any other ; that he will do, and it is reason enough to him : My Lord wills it, therefore, in his strength I will do it ; for now I live to his will, it is my life to study and obey it.

Now, we know what is the true character of the redeemed of Christ, that they are freed from the service of themselves and of the world, yea, dead to it, and have no life but for God, as altogether his.

Let it, then, be our study and ambition to attain this, and to grow in it ; to be daily further freed from all other ways and desires, and more wholly addicted to the will of our God ; displeased when we find any thing else stir or move within us but that, making that the spring of our motion in every work.

1. Because we know that his sovereign will is (and is most justly) the glory of his name, therefore we are not to rest till this be set up in our view, as our end in all things, and we are to account all our plausible doings as hateful, (as indeed they are,) which are not aimed at this end ; yea, endeavouring to have it as frequently and as expressly before us as we can, still keeping our eye on the mark ; throwing away, yea, undoing our own interest, not seeking ourselves in any thing, but him in all.

2. As living to his will is in all things to be our end, so, in all the way to that end, it is to be the rule of every step. For we cannot attain his end but in his way ; nor can we attain it without a resignation of the way to his prescription, taking all our directions from him, how we shall honour him in all. The soul that lives to him, hath enough to make any thing not only warrantable but amiable in seeking his will ; and he not only does it, but delights to do it. This is to live to him, to find it our life ; as we speak of a work wherein men do most, and with most delight employ themselves. That such a lust be crucified, is it thy will, Lord ? Then, no more advising, no more delay. How dear soever that was when I lived to it, it is now as hateful, seeing I live to thee who hatest it. Wilt thou have me forget an injury, though a great one, and love the person that hath wronged me ? While I lived to myself and my passions, this had been hard. But now, how sweet is it ! seeing I live to thee, and am glad to be put upon things most opposite to my corrupt heart ; glad to trample upon my own will, to follow thine. And this I daily aspire to and aim at, to have no will of my own, but that thine be in me, that I may live to thee, as one with thee, and thou my rule and delight ; yea, not to use the very natural comforts of my life, but for thee ; to eat, and drink, and sleep for thee ; and not to please myself, but to be enabled to serve and please thee ; to make one offering of myself and all my actions to thee, my Lord.

Oh ! it is the only sweet life, to be living thus, and daily learning to live more fully thus ! It is heaven this, a little scantling of it here, and a pledge of whole heaven. This is, indeed, the life of Christ, not only like his, but one with his ; it is his spirit, his life derived into the soul, and, therefore, both the most excellent, and, certainly, the most permanent life, for *he dieth no more*, and therefore this his life cannot be extinguished. Hence is the perseverance of the saints ; because they have one life with Christ, and so are alive unto God, once for all, for ever.

It is true, the former custom of sin would plead with grace old possession ; and this the Apostle implies here, that because *formerly we lived* to our lusts, they will urge that ; but he teaches us to beat it directly back on them, and turn the edge of it as a most strong reason against them : True, you had so long time of us, the more is our sorrow and shame, and the more reason that it be no longer so.

The rest of his time in the flesh, (that is, in this body,) is not to be spent as the foregoing, *in living to the flesh*, that is, the corrupt lusts of it, and the common ways of the world ; but, as often as the Christian looks back on that, he is to find it as a spur in his side, to be the more earnest, and more wholly busied in living much to God, having lived so long contrary to him, in living to the flesh. *The past may suffice.* There is a rhetorical figure *(a lyptote)* in that expression, meaning much more than the words express : It is *enough*—oh ! *too much*, to have lived so long so miserable a life.

Now, says the Christian, O corrupt lusts and deluding world, look for no more : I have served you too long. The rest, whatsoever it is, must be to the Lord, to live to him by whom I live ; and ashamed and grieved I am I was so long in beginning ; so much past, it may be the most of my short race past, before I took notice of God, or looked towards him. Oh ! how have I lost, and worse than lost, all my by-past days ! Now, had I the advantage and abilities of many men, and were I to live many ages, all should be to live to my God, and honour him. And what strength I have, and what time I shall have, through his grace, shall be wholly his. And when any Christian hath thus resolved, his intended life being so imperfect, and the time so short, the poorness of the offer would break his heart, were there not an eternity before him, wherein he shall live to his God, and in him, without blemish and without end.

Spiritual things being once discerned by a spiritual light, the whole soul is carried after them ; and the ways of holiness are never truly sweet, till they be thoroughly embraced, and till there be a full renunciation of all that is contrary to them. All his former ways of wandering from God, are very hateful to a Christian who is indeed returned and brought home ; and those are most of all hateful, wherein he hath most wandered and most delighted. A sight of Christ gains the heart, makes it break from all entanglements, both of its own lusts, and of the profane world about it. And these are the two things the Apostle here aims at. Exhorting Christians to the study of newness of life, and showing the necessity of it, that they cannot be Christians without it, he opposes their new estate and engagement, to the old customs of their former condition, and to the continuing custom and conceit of the ungodly world, that against both they may maintain that rank and dignity to which now they are called, and, in a holy disdain of both, walk as the redeemed of the Lord. Their own former custom he speaks to in these verses, and to the custom and opinion of the world, in those which follow. Both of these will set strong upon a man, especially while he is yet weak, and newly entered into that new estate.

Now, as to the first, his old acquaintance, his wonted lusts, will not fail to bestir themselves to accost him in their most obliging, familiar way, and represent their long-continued friendship. But the Christian, following the principles of his new being, will not entertain any long discourse with them, but cut them short, tell them that the change he hath made he avows, and finds it so happy, that these former delights may put off hopes of regaining him. No, they dress themselves in their best array, and put on all their ornaments, and say, as that known word of the courtesan, *I am the same I was;* the Christian will answer as he did, *I am not the same I was.* And not only thus will he turn off the plea of former acquaintance that sin makes, but turn it back upon it, as in his present thoughts, making much against it. The longer I was so deluded, the more reason now that I be wiser ; the more time so mispent, the more pressing necessity of redeeming it. Oh ! I have too long lived in that vile slavery. All was but husks I fed on. *I was laying out my money for that which was no bread, and my labour for that which satisfied not.* Isa. lv. 2. Now, I am on the pursuit of a good that I am sure will satisfy, will fill the largest desires of my soul ; and shall I be sparing and slack, or shall any thing call me off from it ? Let it not be. I who took so much pains, early and late, to serve and sacrifice to so base a god, shall I not now live more to my new Lord, the living God, and sacrifice my time and strength, and my whole self, to him ?

And this is still the regret of the sensible Christian, that he cannot attain that unwearied diligence and that strong bent of affection, in seeking communion with God, and living to him, which once he had for the service of sin : he wonders that it should be thus with him, not to equal that which it were so reasonable that he should so far exceed.

It is, beyond expression, a thing to be lamented, that so small a number of men regard God, the author of their being, that so few live to him in whom they live, returning that being and life they have, and all their enjoyments, as is due, to him from whom they all flow. And then, how pitiful is it, that the small number who are thus minded, mind it so remissly and coldly, and are so far outstripped by the *children of this world,* who follow painted follies and lies with more eagerness and industry than the *children of wisdom* do that certain and solid blessedness which they seek after ! *Plus illi ad vanitatem, quam nos ad veritatem :* They are more intent upon vanity, than we upon verity. Strange ! that men should do so much violence one to another, and to themselves in body and mind, for trifles and chaff ; and that there is so little to be found of that allowed and com-manded *violence,* for *a kingdom,* and *such a kingdom, that cannot be moved* (Heb. xii. 28) ; a word too high for all the monarchies under the sun.

And should not our diligence and violence in this so worthy a design, be so much the greater, the. later we begin to pursue it ? They tell it of Cæsar, that when he passed into Spain, meeting there with Alexander's statue, it occasioned him to weep, considering that he was up so much more early, having performed so many conquests in those years, wherein he thought he himself had done nothing, and was yet but beginning. Truly, it will be a sad thought to a really renewed mind, to look back on the flower of youth and strength as lost in vanity ; if not in gross profaneness, yet, in self-serving and self-pleasing, and in ignorance and neglect of God. And perceiving their few years so far spent ere they set out, they will account days precious, and make the more haste, and desire, with holy David, *enlarged hearts to run the way of God's commandments.* Psal. cxix. 32. They will study to live much in a little time ; and, having lived all the past time to no purpose, will be sensible they have none now to spare upon the lusts and ways of the flesh, and vain societies and visits. Yea, they will be redeeming all they can, even from their necessary affairs, for that which is more necessary than all other necessities, *the one thing needful,* to learn the will of our God, and live to it; this is our business, our *high calling,* the main and most excellent of all our employments.

Not that we are to cast off our particular callings, or omit due diligence in them; for that will prove a snare, and involve a person in things more opposite to godliness. But certainly, this *living to God* requires, 1. A fit measuring of thy own ability for affairs, and, as far as thou canst choose, fitting thy load to thy shoulders, not surcharging thyself with it. An excessive burden of businesses, either by the greatness or the multitude of them, will not fail to entangle thee and depress thy mind, and will hold it so down, that thou shalt not find it possible to walk upright and look upwards, with that freedom and frequency that becomes heirs of heaven.

2. The measure of thy affairs being adapted, look to thy affection in them, that it be regulated too. Thy heart may be engaged in thy little business as much, if thou watch it not, as in many and great affairs. A man may drown in a little brook or pool, as well as in a great river, if he be down and plunge himself into it, and put his head under water. Some care thou must have, that thou mayest not care. Those things that are thorns indeed, thou must make a hedge of them, to keep out those temptations that accompany sloth, and extreme want that waits on it; but let them be the hedge: suffer them not to grow within the garden. *If riches increase, set not thy heart on them,* nor set them in thy heart. That place is due to Another, is made to be the garden of thy beloved Lord, made for the best plants and flowers, and there they ought to grow, the love of God, and faith, and meekness, and the other fragrant graces of the Spirit. And know, that this is no common nor easy matter, to keep the heart disengaged in the midst of affairs, that still it be reserved for him whose right it is.

3. Not only labour to keep thy mind spiritual in itself, but by it put a spiritual stamp even upon thy temporal employments ; and so thou shalt live to God, not only without prejudice of thy calling, but even in it, and shalt converse with him in thy shop, or in the field, or in thy journey, doing all in obedience to him, and offering all, and thyself withal, as a sacrifice to him ; thou still with him, and he still with thee, in all. This is to live to the will of God indeed, to follow his direction, and intend his glory in all. Thus the wife, in the very oversight of her house, and the husband in his affairs abroad, may be living to God, raising their low employments to a high quality this way : Lord, even this mean work I do for thee, complying with thy will, who hast put me in this station, and given me this task. *Thy will be done.* Lord, I offer up even this work to thee. Accept of me, and of my desire to

obey thee in all.   And as in their work, so, in their refreshments and
rest, Christians do all for him.   *Whether ye eat or drink*, says the
Apostle, (1 Cor. x. 31,) *or whatsoever ye do, do all to the glory of God;*
doing all for this reason, because it is his will, and for this end, that he
may have glory; bending the use of all our strength and all his mercies
that way; setting this mark on all our designs and ways, This for the
glory of my God, and, This further for his glory, and so from one thing
to another throughout our whole life.   This is the art of keeping the
heart spiritual in all affairs, yea, of spiritualizing the affairs themselves
in their use, that in themselves are earthly.   This is the *elixir* that
turns lower metal into gold, the mean actions of this life, in a Christian's hands, into obedience and holy offerings unto God.

And were we acquainted with the way of intermixing holy thoughts,
ejaculatory eyeings of God, in our ordinary ways, it would keep the
heart in a sweet temper all the day long, and have an excellent influence into all our ordinary actions and holy performances, at those
times when we apply ourselves solemnly to them.   Our hearts would
be near them, not so far off to seek and call in, as usually they are
through the neglect of this.   This were to *walk with God* indeed; to
go all the day long as in our Father's hand; whereas, without this, our
praying morning and evening looks but as a formal visit, not delighting in that constant converse which yet is our happiness and honour,
and makes all estates sweet.   This would refresh us in the hardest
labour; as they that carry the spices from Arabia are refreshed with
the smell of them in their journey, and some observe, that it keeps
their strength, and frees them from fainting.

If you will then live to God indeed, be not satisfied without the
constant regard of him; and whosoever hath attained most of it, study
it yet more, *to set the Lord always before you*, as David professeth, and
then shall you have that comfort that he adds, He shall be still *at your
right hand, that you shall not be moved*.   Psal. xvi. 8.

And you that are yet to begin this, think what his patience is, that
after you have slighted so many calls, you may yet begin to seek him,
and live to him.   And then, consider, if you still despise all this
goodness, how soon it may be otherwise; you may be past the reach
of this call, and may not begin, but be cut off for ever from the hopes
of it.   Oh, how sad an estate! and the more so, by the remembrance
of these slighted offers and invitations!   Will you then yet return?
You that would share in Christ, let go those lusts to which you have
hitherto lived, and embrace him, and in him there is spirit and life
for you.   He shall enable you to live this heavenly life to the will
of God, *his God and your God, and his Father and your Father*.   John
xx. 17.   Oh! delay no longer this happy change.   How soon may that
puff of breath that is in thy nostrils, who hearest this, be extinguished!
And art thou willing to die in thy sins, rather than that they should
die before thee?   Thinkest thou it a pain to live to the will of God?
Surely it will be more pain to lie under his eternal wrath.   Oh! thou
knowest not how sweet they find it who have tried it.   Or thinkest
thou, I will afterwards?   Who can make thee sure either of that afterwards, or of that will?   If but afterwards, why not now presently,
without further debate?   Hast thou not served sin long enough?

May not the time passed in that service suffice? yea, is it not too much? Wouldst thou only live unto God as little time as may be, and think the dregs of thy life good enough for him? What ingratitude and gross folly is this! Yea, though thou wert sure of coming unto him and being accepted, yet, if thou knewest him in any measure, thou wouldst not think it a privilege to defer it, but willingly choose to be free from the world and thy lusts, to be immediately his, and wouldst, with David, *make haste, and not delay to keep his righteous judgments.* All the time thou livest without him, what a filthy, wretched life is it, if that can be called life that is without him! To live to sin, is to live still in a dungeon; but to live to the will of God, is to walk in liberty and light, to walk by light unto light, by the beginnings of it to the fulness of it, which is in his presence.

Ver. 4. Wherein they think it strange that ye run not with them to the same excess of riot, speaking evil of you:
5. Who shall give account to him that is ready to judge the quick and the dead.

GRACE, until it reach its home and end in glory, is still in conflict; there is a restless party within and without, yea, the whole world against it. It is a stranger here, and is accounted and used as such. *They think it strange that you run not with them, and they speak evil of you:* these wondering thoughts they vent in reproaching words.

In these two verses we have these three things: 1. The Christian's opposite course to that of the world. 2. The world's opposite thoughts and speeches of this course. 3. The supreme and final judgment of both.

1. The opposite course, in that *They run to excesses of riot—You run not with them.* They run to excesses (ἀσωτίας) *of riot* or *luxury.* Though all natural men are not, in the grossest kind, guilty of this, yet they are all of them in some way truly riotous or luxurious, lavishing away themselves, and their days, upon the poor perishing delights of sin, each according to his own palate and humour. As all persons that are riotous, in the common sense of it, gluttons or drunkards, do not love the same kind of meats or drink, but have several relishes or appetites, yet they agree in the nature of the sin; so the notion enlarged after that same manner, to the different custom of corrupt nature, takes in all the ways of sin: some are glutting in and continually drunk with pleasures and carnal enjoyments; others, with the cares of this life, which our Saviour reckons with surfeiting and drunkenness, as being a kind of it, and surcharging the heart as they do: as there he expresses it, Luke xxi. 34, *Take heed to yourselves, lest at any time your hearts be overcharged with surfeiting and drunkenness, and cares of this life.* Whatsoever it is that draws away the heart from God, that, how plausible soever, doth debauch and destroy us: we spend and undo ourselves upon it, as the word signifies, ἀσωτία, a making havoc of all. And the other word, ἀνάχυσις, signifies profusion, and dissolute lavishing, a pouring out of the affections upon vanity; they are scattered and defiled as water spilt upon the ground, that cannot be cleansed nor gathered up again. And, indeed, it passes all our skill and strength, to recover and recollect our hearts for God; he only can do it for himself. He who made it, can gather it, and

cleanse it, and make it anew, and unite it to himself. Oh! what a scattered, broken, unstable thing is the carnal heart, till it be changed, falling in love with every gay folly it meets withal, and running out to rest profusely upon things like its vain self, which suit and agree with it, and serve its lusts! It can dream and muse upon these long enough, upon any thing that feeds the earthliness or pride of it; it can be prodigal of hours, and let out floods of thoughts, where a little is too much, but is bounded and straitened where all are too little; hath not one fixed thought in a whole day to spare for God.

And truly, this *running out* of the heart is a continual drunkenness and madness: it is not capable of reason, and will not be stopped in its current by any persuasion; it is *mad upon its idols*, as the Prophet speaks, Jer. l. 38. You may as well speak to a river in its course, and bid it stay, as speak to an impenitent sinner in the course of his iniquity; and all the other means you can use, is but as the putting of your finger to a rapid stream, to stay it. But there is a Hand that can both stop and turn the most impetuous torrent of the heart, be it even *the heart of a king*, which will least endure any other controlment. Prov. xxi. 1.

Now, as the ungodly world naturally moves to this profusion with a strong and swift motion, *runs* to it, so, it *runs together* to it, and that makes the current both the stronger and the swifter; as a number of brooks falling into one main channel, make a mighty stream. And every man naturally is, in his birth, and in the course of his life, just as a brook, that of itself is carried to that stream of sin which is in the world, and then falling into it, is carried rapidly along with it. And if every sinner, taken apart, be so incontrovertible by all created power, how much more hard a task is a public reformation, the turning of a land from its course of wickedness! All that is set to dam up their way, doth at the best but stay them a little, and they swell, and rise, and run over with more noise and violence than if they had not been stopped. Thus we find outward restraints prove, and thus the very public judgments of God on us. They may have made a little interruption, but, upon the abatement of them, the course of sin, in all kinds, seems to be now more fierce, as it were, to regain the time lost in that constrained forbearance. So that we see the need of much prayer to entreat his powerful hand, that can turn the course of Jordan, that he would work, not a temporary, but an abiding change of the course of this land, and cause many souls to look upon Jesus Christ and flow into him, as the word is in Psal. xxxiv. 5.

This is their course, but *you run not with them*. The godly are a small and weak company, and yet run counter to the grand torrent of the world, just against them. And there is a Spirit within them, whence that their contrary motion flows; a Spirit strong enough to maintain it in them, against all the crowd and combined course of the ungodly. *Greater is he that is in you, than he that is in the world.* 1 John iv. 4. As Lot in Sodom, his righteous soul was not carried with them, but was *vexed with their ungodly doings*. There is, to a Believer, the example of Christ, to set against the example of the world, and the Spirit of Christ, against the spirit of the world; and these are by far the more excellent and the stronger. Faith looking to him, and drawing virtue from him, makes the soul surmount all discouragements and oppositions. So, Heb. xii. 2, *Looking to Jesus;* and that not only as an example worthy to oppose to all the world's examples; the saints were so, yet he more than they all; but further, He is *the Author and Finisher of our Faith;* and so we eye him, as having *endured the cross, and despised the shame,* and as having *sat down at the right hand of the throne of God,* not only that, in doing so, we may follow him in that way, unto that end, as our Pattern, but as our Head, from whom we borrow our strength so to follow *the Author and Finisher of our Faith.* And so, 1 John v. 4, *This is our victory, whereby we overcome the world, even our faith.*

The Spirit of God shows the Believer clearly both the baseness of the ways of sin, and the wretched measure of their end. That Divine light discovers the fading and false blush of the pleasures of sin, that there is nothing under them but true deformity and rottenness, which the deluded, gross world does not see, but takes the first appearance of it for true and solid beauty, and so is enamoured with a painted strumpet. And as he sees the vileness of that love of sin, he sees the final unhappiness of it, that *her ways lead to the chambers of death.* Methinks a Believer is as one standing upon a high tower, who sees the way wherein the world runs, in a valley, as an unavoidable precipice, a steep edge hanging over the bottomless pit, where all that are not reclaimed, fall over before they be aware; this they, in their low way, perceive not, and therefore walk and run on in the smooth pleasures and ease of it towards their perdition; but he that sees the end, will not *run with them.*

And as he hath, by that light of the Spirit, this clear reason for thinking on and taking another course, so, by that Spirit, he hath a very natural bent to a contrary motion, so that he cannot be one with them. That Spirit moves him upwards whence it came, and makes that, in so far as he is renewed, his natural motion. Though he hath a clog of flesh that cleaves to him, and so breeds him some difficulty, yet, in the strength of that new nature, he overcomes it, and goes on till he attain his end, where all the difficulty in the way presently is over-rewarded and forgotten. This makes amends for every weary step, that every one of those who walk in that way, shall *appear in Zion before God.* Psal. lxxxiv. 6.

2. We have their opposite thoughts and speeches of each other. *They think it strange, speaking evil of you.* The Christian and the carnal man are most wonderful to each other. The one wonders to see the other walk so strictly, and deny himself to those carnal liberties which the most take, and take for so necessary, that they think they could not live without them. And the Christian thinks it strange that men should be so bewitched, and still remain children in the vanity of their turmoil, wearying and humouring themselves from morning to night, running after stories and fancies, ever busy doing nothing; wonders that the delights of earth and sin can so long entertain and please men, and persuade them to give Jesus Christ so many refusals, to turn from their life and happiness, and choose to be miserable, yea, and take much pains to make themselves miserable. He knows the depravedness and blindness of nature in this; knows it by himself, that once he was so, and therefore wonders

not so much at them as they do at him; yet, the unreasonableness
and frenzy of that course now appears to him in so strong a light,
that he cannot but wonder at these woeful mistakes. But the ungodly
wonder far more at him, not knowing the inward cause of his different
choice and way. The Believer, as we said, is upon the hill; he is
going up, and looking back on them in the valley, sees their way
tending to, and ending in death, and calls them to retire from it as
loud as he can; he tells them the danger, but either they hear not,
nor understand his language, or will not believe him: finding present
ease and delight in their way, they will not consider and suspect the
end of it, but they judge him the fool who will not share with them,
and take that way where such multitudes go, and with such ease, and
some of them with their train, and horses, and coaches, and all their
pomp, while he, and a few straggling poor creatures like him, are
climbing up a craggy steep hill, and will by no means come off from
that way, and partake of theirs; not knowing, or not believing, that at
the top of that hill he climbs, is that happy, glorious city *the new Jerusalem*, whereof he is a citizen, and whither he is tending; not believing
that he knows the end both of their way and of his own, and therefore
would reclaim them if he could, but will by no means *return unto them:*
as the Lord commanded the Prophet, *Let them return unto thee, but return not thou unto them.* Jer. xv. 19.

The world thinks it strange that a Christian can spend so much time
in secret prayer, not knowing, nor being able to conceive of the sweetness of the communion with God which he attains in that way. Yea,
while he feels it not, how sweet it is, beyond the world's enjoyments, to
be but seeking after it, and waiting for it! Oh, the delight that there
is in the bitterest exercise of repentance, in the very tears, much more
in the succeeding harvest of joy! *Incontinentes veræ voluptatis ignari*,
says Aristotle: The intemperate are strangers to true pleasure. It is
strange unto a carnal man, to see the child of God disdain the pleasures of sin; he knows not the higher and purer delights and pleasures
that the Christian is called to, and of which he hath, it may be, some
part at present, but, however, the fulness of them in assured hope.

The strangeness of the world's way to the Christian, and of his to it,
though that is somewhat unnatural, yet affects them very differently.
He looks on the deluded sinner with pity, they on him with hate.
Their part, which is here expressed, of wondering, breaks out in re-
viling: *they speak evil of you;* and what is their voice? What mean
these precise fools? will they readily say. What course is this they
take, contrary to all the world? Will they make a new religion, and
condemn all their honest, civil neighbours that are not like them? Ay,
forsooth, do all go to hell, think you, except you, and those that follow
your way? We are for no more than good fellowship and liberty;
and as for so much reading and praying, those are but brain-sick,
melancholy conceits: a man may go to heaven like his neighbour,
without all this ado. Thus they let fly at their pleasure. But this
troubles not the composed Christian's mind at all: while curs snarl
and bark about him, the sober traveller goes on his way, and regards
them not. He that is acquainted with the way of holiness, can more
than endure the counter-blasts and airs of scoffs and revilings; he

accounts them his glory and his riches. So Moses *esteemed the reproach of Christ greater riches than the treasures in Egypt.* Heb. xi. 26. And besides many other things to animate, we have this which is here expressed,—

3rdly, The supreme and final judgment. Oh, how full is it! *They shall give account to Him that is ready to judge the quick and the dead* —hath this *in readiness,* τῷ ἑτοίμως ἔχοντι, hath the day set ; and it shall surely come, though you think it far off.

Though the wicked themselves forget their scoffs against the godly, and though the Christian slights them, and lets them pass, they pass not so ; they are all registered, and the great Court-day shall call them to account for all these riots and excesses, and withal, for all their reproaches of the godly, who would not run with them in these ways. Tremble, then, ye despisers and mockers of holiness, though you come not near it. What will you do when those you reviled shall appear glorious in your sight, and their King, the King of saints here,·much more glorious, and his glory their joy, and all terror to you ? Oh ! then, all faces that could look out disdainfully upon religion and the professors of it, shall *gather blackness,* and be bathed with shame, and the despised saints of God shall shout so much the more for joy.

You that would rejoice, then, in the appearing of that holy Lord and Judge of the world, let your way be now in holiness. Avoid and hate the common ways of the wicked world ; they live in their foolish opinion, and that shall quickly end, but the sentence of that day shall stand for ever.

Ver. 6. For for this cause was the Gospel preached also to them that are dead, that they might be judged according to men in the flesh, but live according to God in the spirit.

It is a thing of prime concernment for a Christian, to be rightly informed, and frequently put in mind, what is the true estate and nature of a Christian ; for this, the multitude of those that bear that name, either know not, or commonly forget, and so are carried away with the vain fancies and mistakes of the world. The Apostle hath characterized Christianity very clearly to us in this place, by that which is the very nature of it, *conformity with Christ,* and that which is necessarily consequent upon that, *disconformity with the world.* And as the nature and natural properties of things hold universally, those who in all ages are effectually called by the Gospel, are thus moulded and framed by it. Thus it was, says the Apostle, with your brethren who are now at rest, as many as received the Gospel ; and for this end was it preached to them, *that they might be judged according to men in the flesh, but live according to God in the Spirit.*

We have here, 1. The Preaching of the Gospel as the suitable means to a certain end. 2. The express nature of that end.

1. *For for this cause was the Gospel preached.* There is a particular end, and that very important, for which the preaching of the Gospel is intended ; this end many consider not, hearing it as if it were to no end, or not propounding a fixed, determined end in the hearing. This, therefore, is to be considered by those who preach this Gospel, that they aim aright in it at this end, and at no other,—no self-end. The legal priests were not to be squint-eyed, (Lev. xxi. 20,) nor must evangeli-

cal ministers be thus squinting to base gain, or vain applause. They should also make it their study, to find in themselves this work, this *living to God;* otherwise, they cannot skilfully or faithfully apply their gifts to work this effect on their hearers : and therefore acquaintance with God is most necessary.

How sounds it, to many of us at least, but as a well-contrived story, whose use is to amuse us, and possibly delight us a little, and there is an end,—and indeed no end, for this turns the most serious and most glorious of all messages into an empty sound. If we awake and give it a hearing, it is much : but for any thing further, how few deeply beforehand consider : I have a dead heart ; therefore will I go unto the word of life, that it may be quickened. It is frozen ; I will go and lay it before the warm beams of that Sun which shines in the Gospel. My corruptions are mighty and strong, and grace, if there be any in my heart, is exceeding weak ; but there is in the Gospel a power to weaken and kill sin, and to strengthen grace, and this being the intent of my wise God in appointing it, it shall be my desire and purpose in resorting to it, to find it to me according to his gracious design ; to have faith in my Christ, the fountain of my life, more strengthened, and made more active in drawing from him ; to have my heart more refined and spiritualized, and to have the sluice of repentance opened, and my affections to Divine things enlarged, more hatred of sin, and more love of God and communion with him.

Ask yourselves concerning former times ; and, to take yourselves even now, inquire within, Why came I hither this day ? What had I in mine eye and desires this morning ere I came forth, and in my way as I was coming ? Did I seriously propound an end, or not ; and what was my end ? Nor doth the mere custom of mentioning this in prayer, satisfy the question ; for this, as other such things usually do in our hand, may turn to a lifeless form, and have no heat of spiritual affection, none of David's panting and breathing after God in his ordinances ; such desires as will not be stilled without a measure of attainment, as the child's desire of the breast, as our Apostle resembles it, chap. ii. ver. 1.

And then again, being returned home, reflect on your hearts : Much hath been heard, but is there any thing done by it ? Have I gained my point ? It was not simply to pass a little time that I went, or to pass it with delight in hearing, *rejoicing in that light,* as they did in St. John Baptist's *for a season,* [πρὸς ὥραν,] as long as the hour lasts. It was not to have my ear pleased, but my heart changed ; not to learn some new notions, and carry them cold in my head, but to be quickened and purified, and *renewed in the spirit of my mind.* Is this done ? Think I now with greater esteem of Christ, and the life of faith, and the happiness of a Christian ? And are such thoughts solid and abiding with me ? What sin have I left behind ? What grace of the Spirit have I brought home ? Or what new degree, or, at least, new desire of it, a living desire, that will follow its point ? Oh ! this were good repetition.

It is a strange folly in multitudes of us, to set ourselves no mark, to propound no end in the hearing of the Gospel. The merchant sails not merely that he may sail, but for traffic, and traffics that he may be rich. The husbandman ploughs not merely to keep himself busy with no further end, but ploughs that he may sow, and sows that he may reap with advantage. And shall we do the most excellent and fruitful work fruitlessly, hear only to hear, and look no further ? This is indeed a great vanity, and a great misery, to lose that labour, and gain nothing by it, which duly used, would be of all others most advantageous and gainful: and yet all meetings are full of this !

Now, when you come, it is not simply to hear a discourse, and relish or dislike it in hearing, but a matter of life and death, of eternal death and eternal life; and the spiritual life, begotten and nourished by the word, is the beginning of that eternal life. It follows,

To them that are dead.] By which, I conceive, he intends such as had heard and believed the Gospel, when it came to them, and now were dead. And this, I think, he doth to strengthen those brethren to whom he writes ; he commends the Gospel, to the intent that they might not think the condition and end of it hard ; as our Saviour mollifies the matter of outward sufferings thus : *So persecuted they the Prophets that were before you,* Matt. v. 12 ; and the Apostle afterwards, in this chapter, uses the same reason in that same subject. So here, that they might not judge the point of mortification he presses, so grievous, as naturally men will do, he tells them, it is the constant end of the Gospel, and that they who have been saved by it, went that same way he points out to them. They that are dead before you, died in this way that I press on you, before they died ; and the Gospel was preached to them for that very end.

Men pass away, and others succeed, but the Gospel is still the same, hath the same tenor and substance, and the same ends. So Solomon speaks of the heavens and earth, that they remain the same, while *one generation passes, and another cometh.* Eccl. i. 4. The Gospel surpasses both in its stability, as our Saviour testifies : *They shall pass away, but not one jot of this word.* Matt. v. 18. And indeed they wear and wax old, as the Apostle teaches us ; but the Gospel is, from one age to another, of most unalterable integrity, hath still the same vigour and powerful influence as at the first.

They who formerly received the Gospel, received it upon these terms ; therefore think it not hard. And they *are* now *dead;* all the difficulty of that work of dying to sin, is now over with them. If they had not died *to* their sins by the Gospel, they had died *in* them, after a while, and so died eternally. It is therefore a wise prevention, to have sin judged and put to death in us before we die. If we will not part with sin, if we die in it, and with it, we and our sin perish together ; but if it die first before us, then we live for ever.

And what thinkest thou of thy carnal will and all the delights of sin ? What is the longest term of its life ? Uncertain it is, but most certainly very short; thou and these pleasures must be severed and parted within a little time ; however, thou must die, and then they die, and you never meet again. Now, were it not the wisest course to part a little sooner with them, and let them die before thee, that thou mayest inherit eternal life, and eternal delights in it, *pleasures for evermore?* It is the only wise bargain ; let us therefore delay it no longer.

This is our season of enjoying the sweetness of the Gospel. Others heard it before us in the places which now we fill; and now they are removed, and we must remove shortly, and leave our places to others, to speak and hear in. It is high time we were considering what we do here, to what end we speak and hear; high time to lay hold on that salvation which is held forth unto us, and, that we may lay hold on it, to let go our hold of sin and those perishing things that we hold so firm, and cleave so fast to. Do they that are dead, who heard and obeyed the Gospel, now repent of their repentance and mortifying of the flesh? Or rather, do they not think ten thousand times more pains, were it for many ages, all too little for a moment of that which now they enjoy, and shall enjoy to eternity? And they that are dead, who heard the Gospel and slighted it, if such a thing might be, what would they give for one of those opportunities which now we daily have, and daily lose, and have no fruit or esteem of them! You have lately seen, at least many of you, and you that shifted the sight, have heard of numbers, cut off in a little time, whole families swept away by the late stroke of God's hand,* many of which did think no other but that they might have still been with you here in this place and exercise, at this time, and many years after this. And yet, who hath laid to heart the lengthening out of this day, and considered it more as an opportunity of securing that higher and happier life, than as a little protracting of this wretched life, which is hastening to an end? Oh! therefore be entreated *to-day, while it is called To-day, not to harden your hearts.* Though the pestilence doth not now affright you so, yet, that standing mortality, and the decay of these earthen lodges, tells us that shortly we shall cease to preach and hear this Gospel. Did we consider, it would excite us to a more earnest search after our evidences of that eternal life that is set before us in the Gospel; and we should seek them in the characters of that spiritual life which is the beginning of eternal life within us, and is wrought by the Gospel in all the heirs of salvation.

Think therefore wisely of these two things, of what is the proper end of the Gospel, and of the approaching end of thy days; and let thy certainty of this latter, drive thee to seek more certainty of the former, that thou mayest partake of it; and then, this again will make the thoughts of the other sweet to thee. That visage of death, that is so terrible to unchanged sinners, shall be amiable to thine eye. Having found a life in the Gospel as happy and lasting as this is miserable and vanishing, and seeing the perfection of that life on the other side of death, thou wilt long for the passage.

Be more serious in this matter of daily hearing the Gospel. Consider why it is sent to thee, and what it brings, and think—It is too long I have slighted its message, and many who have done so are cut off, and shall hear it no more; I have it once more inviting me, and to me this may be the last invitation. And in these thoughts, ere you come, bow your knee to the Father of spirits, that this one thing may be granted you, that your souls may find at length the lively and mighty power of his Spirit upon yours, in the hearing of this Gospel, that *you may be judged according to men in the flesh, but live according to God in the Spirit.*

* A. D. 1665.

2. Thus is the particular nature of that end expressed. And not to perplex you with various senses, the Apostle intends, I conceive, no other than the dying to the world and sin, and living unto God, which is his main subject and scope in the foregoing discourse. That death was before called a *suffering in the flesh*, which is in effect the same; and therefore, though the words may be drawn another way, yet it is strange that interpreters have been so far wide of this their genuine and agreeable sense, and that they have been by almost all of them taken in some other import.

To be judged in the flesh, in the present sense, is to die to sin, or that sin die in us: and [1.] It is thus expressed suitably to the nature of it; it is to the flesh a violent death, and it is according to a sentence judicially pronounced against it. That guilty and miserable life of sin, is in the Gospel adjudged to death : there that arrest and sentence is clear and full. See Rom. vi. 6, &c.; viii. 13. That sin must die in order that the soul may live : it must be crucified in us, and we to it, that we may partake of the life of Christ, and of happiness in him. And this is called *to be judged in the flesh*, to have this sentence executed. [2.] The thing is the rather spoken of here under the term of being judged, in counterbalance of that judgment mentioned immediately before, ver. 5, the Last Judgment of quick and dead, wherein they who would not be thus judged, but mocked and despised those that were, shall fall under a far more terrible judgment, and the sentence of a heavy death indeed, even everlasting death; though they think they shall escape and enjoy liberty in living in sin. And that, *To be judged according to men*, is, I conceive, added, to signify the connaturalness of the life of sin to a man's now corrupt nature ; that men do judge it a death indeed, to be severed and pulled from their sins, and that a cruel death ; and the sentence of it in the Gospel is a heavy sentence, *a hard saying* to a carnal heart, that he must give up all his sinful delights, must die indeed in self-denial, must be separated from himself, which is to die, if he will be joined with Christ, and live in him. Thus men judge that they are adjudged to a painful death by the sentence of the Gospel. Although it is that they may truly and happily live, yet they understand it not so. They see the death, the parting with sin and all its pleasures ; but the life they see not, nor can any know it till they partake of it : it is known to him in whom it exists ; it is *hid with Christ in God*. Col. iii. 3. And therefore the opposition here is very fitly thus represented, that the death is *according to men in the flesh*, but the life is *according to God in the Spirit.*

As the Christian is adjudged to this *death in the flesh* by the Gospel, so he is looked on and accounted, by carnal men, as dead, for that he enjoys not with them what they esteem their life, and think they could not live without. One that cannot carouse and swear with profane men, is a silly dead creature, good for nothing ; and he that can bear wrongs, and love him that injured him, is a poor spiritless fool, hath no mettle or life in him, in the world's account. Thus is he *judged according to men in the flesh*,—he is as a dead man,—*but lives according to God in the Spirit;* dead to men, and alive to God, as ver. 2.

Now, if this life be in thee, it will act. All life is in motion, and is called *an act*, but most active of all is this most excellent, and, as I may call it, most lively life. It will be moving towards God, often seeking to him, making still towards him as its principle and fountain, exerting itself in holy and affectionate thoughts of him ; sometimes on one of his sweet attributes, sometimes on another, as the bee amongst the flowers. And as it will thus act within, so it will be outwardly laying hold on all occasions, yea, seeking out ways and opportunities to be serviceable to thy Lord ; employing all for him, commending and extolling his goodness, doing and suffering cheerfully for him, laying out the strength of desires, and parts, and means, in thy station, to gain him glory. If thou be alone, then not esteeming thyself alone, but with him, seeking to know more of him, and to be made more like him. If in company, then casting about how to bring his name into esteem, and to draw others to a love of religion and holiness by speeches, as it may be fit, and most by the true behaviour of thy carriage ;—tender over the souls of others, to do them good to thy utmost ; thinking, each day, an hour lost when thou art not busy for the honour and advantage of him to whom thou now livest ;—thinking in the morning, Now what may I do this day for my God ? How may I most please and glorify him, and use my strength, and wit, and my whole self, as not mine, but his ? And then, in the evening, reflecting, O Lord, have I seconded these thoughts in reality ? What glory hast thou had by me this day ? Whither went my thoughts and endeavours ? What busied them most ? Have I been much with God ? Have I adorned the Gospel in my converse with others ?—And if thou findest any thing done this way, this life will engage thee to bless and acknowledge him, the spring and worker of it. If thou hast stepped aside, were it but to *an appearance of evil*, or if any fit season of good hath escaped thee unprofitably, it will lead thee to check thyself, and to be grieved for thy sloth and coldness, and to see if more love would not beget more diligence.

Try it by sympathy and antipathy, which follow the nature of things : as we see in some plants and creatures that cannot grow, cannot agree together, and others that do favour and benefit mutually. If thy soul hath an aversion and reluctancy against whatever is contrary to holiness, it is an evidence of this new nature and life ; thy heart rises against wicked ways and speeches, oaths and cursings, and rotten communication ; yea, thou canst not endure unworthy discourses, wherein most spend their time ; thou findest no relish in the unsavoury societies of such as know not God, canst not *sit with vain persons*, but findest a delight in those who have the image of God upon them, such as partake of that Divine life, and carry the evidences of it in their carriage. David did not disdain the fellowship of the saints, and that it was no disparagement to him, is implied in the name he gives them, Psal. xvi. 2, *the excellent ones*, the magnific or noble, *adiri :* that word is taken from one that signifies a robe or noble garment, *adereth, toga magnifica ;* so he thought them nobles and kings as well as he ; they had *robes royal*, and therefore were fit companions of kings. A spiritual eye looks upon spiritual dignity, and esteems and loves them who are *born of God*, how low soever be their natural birth and breeding. The sons of God have of his Spirit in them, and are born to the same inheritance, where all shall have enough, and they are tending homewards by the conduct of the same Spirit that is in them ; so that there must be amongst them a real complacency and delight in one another.

And then, consider the temper of thy heart towards spiritual things, the word and ordinances of God, whether thou dost esteem highly of them, and delight in them ; whether there be compliance of the heart with Divine truths, something in thee, that suits and sides with them against thy corruptions ; whether in thy affliction thou seekest not to the puddles of earthly comforts, but hast thy recourse to the sweet crystal streams of the Divine promises, and findest refreshment in them. It may be, at some times, in a spiritual distemper, holy exercises and ordinances will not have that present sensible sweetness to a Christian, that he desires ; and some will for a long time lie under dryness and deadness this way ; yet there is here an evidence of this spiritual life, that thou stayest by the Lord, and reliest on him, and wilt not leave these holy means, how sapless soever to thy sense for the present. Thou findest for a long time little sweetness in prayer, yet thou prayest still, and, when thou canst say nothing, yet offerest at it, and lookest towards Christ thy life. Thou dost not turn away from these things to seek consolation elsewhere, but as thou knowest that life is in Christ, thou wilt stay till he refresh thee with new and lively influence. It is not any where but in him ; as St. Peter said, *Lord, whither should we go ? Thou hast the words of eternal life.* John vi. 68.

Consider with thyself, whether thou hast any knowledge of the growth or deficiencies of this spiritual life ; for it is here but begun, and breathes in an air contrary to it, and lodges in a house that often smokes and darkens it. Canst thou go on in formal performances, from one year to another, and make no advancement in the inward exercises of grace, and restest thou content with that ? It is no good sign. But art thou either gaining victories over sin, and further strength of faith and love, and other graces, or, at least, art thou earnestly seeking these, and bewailing thy wants and disappointments of this kind ? Then thou livest. At the worst, wouldst thou rather grow this way, be farther off from sin, and nearer to God, than grow in thy estate, or credit, or honours ? Esteemest thou more highly of grace than of the whole world ? There is life at the root ; although though findest not that flourishing thou desirest ; yet, the desire of it is life in thee. And, if growing this way, art thou content, whatsoever is thy outward estate ? Canst thou solace thyself in the love and goodness of thy God, though the world frown on thee ? Art thou unable to take comfort in the smiles of the world, when his face is hid ? This tells thee thou livest, and that he is thy life.

Although many Christians have not so much sensible joy, yet they account spiritual joy and the light of God's countenance the only true joy, and all other without it, madness ; and they cry, and sigh, and wait for it. Meanwhile, not only duty and the hopes of attaining a better state in religion, but even love to God, makes them to do so, to serve, and please, and glorify him to their utmost. And this is not a dead resting without God, but it is a stable compliance with his will in the highest point ; waiting for him, and living by faith, which is most acceptable to him. In a word, whether in sensible comfort or without it, still, this is the fixed thought of a believing soul, *It is good for me to draw nigh to God*, Psal. lxxiii. 28 ;—only good; and it will not live in a willing estrangedness from him, what way soever he be pleased to deal with it.

Now, for the entertaining and strengthening of this life, which is the great business and care of all that have it,—

1st, Beware of omitting and interrupting those spiritual means, which do provide it and nourish it. Little neglects of that kind will draw on greater, and great neglects will make great abatements of vigour and liveliness. Take heed of using holy things coldly and lazily, without affection : that will make them fruitless, and our life will not be advantaged by them, unless they be used in a lively way. Be active in all good within thy reach : as this is a sign of the spiritual life, so it is a helper and friend to it. A slothful, unstirring life, will make a sickly, unhealthy life. Motion purifies and sharpens the spirits, and makes men robust and vigorous.

2ndly, Beware of admitting a correspondence with any sin ; yea, do not so much as discourse familiarly with it, or look kindly toward it ; for that will undoubtedly cast a damp upon thy spirit, and diminish thy graces at least, and will obstruct thy communion with God. Thou knowest (thou who hast any knowledge of this life) that thou canst not go to him with that sweet freedom thou wert wont, after thou hast been but tampering or parleying with any of thy old loves. Oh ! do not make so foolish a bargain, as to prejudice the least of thy spiritual comforts, for the greatest and longest continued enjoyments of sin, which are base and but for a season.

But wouldst thou grow upwards in this life ? 3dly, Have much recourse to Jesus Christ thy Head, the spring from whom flow the animal spirits that quicken thy soul. Wouldst thou know more of God ? He it is who *reveals·the Father*, and reveals him as *his Father*, and, in him, *thy Father ;* and that is the sweet notion of God. Wouldst thou overcome thy lusts further ? Our victory is in him. Apply his conquest : *We are more than conquerors, through him that loved us.* Rom. viii. 37. Wouldst thou be more replenished with graces and spiritual affections ? His fulness is, for that use, open to us ; there is life, and more life, in him, and for us. This was his business here. He came, *that we might have life, and might have it more abundantly.* John x. 10.

Ver. 7. But the end of all things is at hand : be ye therefore sober, and watch unto prayer.

THE heart of a real Christian is really taken off from the world, and set heavenwards ; yet there is still in this flesh so much of the flesh hanging to it, as will readily poise all downwards, unless it be often wound up and put in remembrance of those things that will raise it still to further spirituality. This the Apostle doth in this Epistle, and particularly in these words, in which three things are to be considered.

I. A threefold duty recommended. II. The mutual relation that binds these duties to one another. III. The reason here used to bind them upon a Christian.

I. A threefold duty recommended, Sobriety, Watchfulness, and Prayer; and of the three, the last is evidently the chief, and is here so meant, and others being recommended, as suitable and subservient to it; therefore I shall speak first of Prayer.

And truly, to speak and to hear of this duty often, were our hearts truly and entirely acquainted with it, would have still new sweetness and usefulness in it. Oh, how great were the advantage of that lively knowledge of it, beyond the exactest skill in defining it, and in discoursing on the heads of doctrine concerning it !

Prayer is not a smooth expression, or a well-contrived form of words; not the product of a ready memory, or of a rich invention exerting itself in the performance. These may draw a neat picture of it, but still, the life is wanting. The motion of the heart God-wards, holy and divine affection, makes prayer real, and lively, and acceptable to the living God, to whom it is presented ; the pouring out of thy heart to him who made it, and therefore hears it, and understands what it speaks, and how it is moved and affected in calling on him. It is not the gilded paper and good writing of a petition, that prevails with a king, but the moving sense of it. And to that King who discerns the heart, heart-sense is the sense of all, and that which only he regards ; he listens to hear what that speaks, and takes all as nothing where that is silent. All other excellence in prayer is but the outside and fashion of it; this is the life of it.

Though prayer, precisely taken, is only petition, yet, in its fuller and usual sense, it comprehends the venting of our humble sense of vileness and sin, in sincere confession, and the extolling and praising of the holy name of our God, his excellency and goodness, with thankful acknowledgment of received mercies. Of these sweet ingredient perfumes is the incense of Prayer composed, and by the Divine fire of love it ascends unto God, the heart and all with it; and when the hearts of the saints unite in joint prayer, the pillar of sweet smoke goes up the greater and the fuller. Thus says that song of the spouse : *Going up from the wilderness, as pillars of smoke perfumed with myrrh and frankincense, and all the powders of the merchant.* Cant. iii. 6. The word there, (*Timeroth*, from *Temer*, a palm-tree,) signifies *straight pillars*, like the tallest, straightest kind of trees. And, indeed, the sincerity and unfeignedness of prayer makes it go up as a straight pillar, no crookedness in it, tending straight towards heaven, and bowing to no side by the way. Oh ! the single and fixed viewing of God, as it, in other ways, is the thing which makes all holy and sweet, so particularly does it in this Divine work of prayer.

It is true we have to deal with a God who of himself needs not this our pains, either to inform or to excite him : he fully knows our thoughts before we express them, and our wants before we feel them or think of them. Nor doth this affection and gracious bent to do his children good, wax remiss, or admit of the least abatement and forgetfulness of them.

But, instead of necessity on the part of God, which cannot be imagined, we shall find that equity, and that singular dignity and utility of it, on our part, which cannot be denied.

1. *Equity.* That thus the creature signify his homage to, and dependence on, his Creator, for his being and well-being ; that he take all the good he enjoys, or expects, from that Sovereign Good, declaring himself unworthy, waiting for all upon the terms of free goodness, and acknowledging all to flow from that spring.

2. *Dignity.* Man was made for communion with God his Maker ; it is the excellency of his nature to be capable of this end, the happiness of it to be raised to enjoy it. Now, in nothing more in this life, is this communion actually and highly enjoyed, than in the exercise of prayer ; in that he may freely impart his affairs, and estate, and wants, to God, as the most faithful and powerful Friend, the richest and most loving Father ; may use the liberty of a child, telling his Father what he stands in need of and desires, and communing with him with humble confidence, being admitted so frequently into the presence of so great a King.

3. The *Utility* of it. [1.] Prayer eases the soul in times of distress, when it is oppressed with griefs and fears, by giving them vent, and that in so advantageous a way, emptying them into the bosom of God. The very vent, were it but into the air, gives ease ; or speak your grief to a statue rather than smother it ; much more ease does it give to pour it forth into the lap of a confidential and sympathizing friend, even though unable to help us ; yet still more, of one who can help ; and, of all friends, our God is, beyond all comparison, the surest, and most affectionate, and most powerful. So Isa. lxiii. 9, both compassion and effectual salvation are expressed : *In all their affliction he was afflicted, and the angel of his presence saved them ; in his love and in his pity he redeemed them ; and he bare them, and carried them all the days of old.* And so, resting on his love, power, and gracious promises, the soul quiets itself in God upon this assurance, that it is not in vain to seek him, and that he *despiseth not the sighing of the poor.* Psal. xii. 5.

[2.] The soul is more spiritually affected with its own condition, by laying it open before the Lord ; becomes more deeply sensible of sin, and ashamed in his sight, in confessing it before him ; more dilated and enlarged to receive the mercies sued for, as the *opening wide of the mouth* of the soul, that it *may be filled;* more disposed to observe the Lord in answering, and to bless him, and trust on him, upon the renewed experiences of his regard to its distresses and desires.

[3.] All the graces of the Spirit are, in prayer, stirred and exercised, and, by exercise, strengthened and increased ; Faith, in applying the Divine promises, which are the very ground that the soul goes upon to God, Hope looking out to their performance, and Love particularly expressing itself in that sweet converse, and delighting in it, as love doth in the company of the person beloved, thinking all hours too short in speaking with him. Oh, how the soul is refreshed with freedom of speech with its beloved Lord ! And as it delights in that, so it is continually advanced and grows by each meeting and conference, beholding the excellency of God, and relishing the pure and sublime pleasures that are to be found in near communion with him. Looking upon the **Father** in the face of Christ, and using him as a Mediator in prayer, as still it must, it is drawn to further admiration of that bottomless love, which found out that way of agreement, that *new and living way* of our access, when all was shut up, and we must otherwise have been shut out for ever. And then, the affectionate expressions of that reflex love, seeking to find that vent in prayer, do kindle higher, and being as it were fanned and blown up, rise to a greater, and higher, and purer flame, and so tend upwards the more strongly. David, as he doth profess his love to God in prayer, in his Psalms, so no doubt it grew in the expressing : *I will love thee, O Lord my strength,* Psal. xviii. 1. And in Psal. cxvi. 1, he doth raise an incentive of love out of this very consideration of the correspondence of prayer—*I love the Lord because he hath heard;* and he resolves thereafter upon persistance in that course,—*therefore will I call upon him as long as I live.* And as the graces of the Spirit are advanced in prayer by their actings, so for this further reason, because prayer sets the soul particularly near unto God in Jesus Christ. It is then in his presence, and being much with God in this way, it is powerfully assimilated to him by converse with him ; as we readily contract their habits with whom we have much intercourse, especially if they be such as we singularly love and respect. Thus the soul is moulded further to the likeness of God, is stamped with clearer characters of him, by being much with him, becomes more like God, more holy and spiritual, and, like Moses, brings back a bright shining from the mount.

[4.] And not only thus, by a natural influence, doth prayer work this advantage, but even by a federal efficacy, suing for, and upon suit obtaining, supplies of grace as the chief good, and besides, all other needful mercies. It is a real means of receiving. *Whatsoever you shall ask, that will I do,* says our Saviour. John xiv. 13. God having established this intercourse, has engaged his truth and goodness in it, that if they call on him, they shall be heard and answered. If they prepare the heart to call, he will incline his ear to hear. Our Saviour hath assured us, that we may build upon his goodness, upon the affection of a father in him ; *He will give good things to them that ask,* says one Evangelist, (Matt. vii. 11,) *give the Holy Spirit to them that ask him,* says another, (Luke xi. 13,) as being *the good* indeed, the highest of gifts and the sum of all good things, and that for which his children are most earnest supplicants. Prayer for grace doth, as it were, set the mouth of the soul to the spring, draws from Jesus Christ, and is replenished out of his fulness, thirsting after it, and drawing from it that way.

And for this reason it is that our Saviour, and from him, and according to his example, the Apostles, recommend prayer much. *Watch and pray,* says our Saviour, Matt. xxvi. 41 ; and St. Paul, *Pray continually,* 1 Thess. v. 17. And our Apostle here particularly specifies this, as the grand means of attaining that conformity with Christ which he expresses : this is the highway to it, *Be sober and watch unto prayer.* He that is much in prayer, shall grow rich in grace. He shall thrive and increase most, who is busiest in this, which is our very traffic with heaven, and fetches the most precious commodities thence. He who sends oftenest out these ships of *desire*, who makes the most voyages to that land of spices and pearls, shall be sure to improve his stock most, and have most of heaven upon earth.

But the true art of this trading is very rare. Every trade hath something wherein the skill of it lies ; but this is deep and supernatural, is not reached by human industry. Industry is to be used in it, but we must know the faculty of it comes from above, that spirit of prayer without which learning, and wit, and religious breeding, can do nothing. Therefore, this is to be our prayer often, our great suit, for the spirit of prayer, that we may speak the language of the sons of God by the Spirit of God, which alone teaches the heart to pronounce aright those things that the tongue of many hypocrites can articulate well to man's ear. Only the children, in that right strain that takes him, call God their *Father*, and cry unto him as their Father ; and therefore, many a poor unlettered Christian far outstrips your school-rabbies in this faculty, because it is not effectually taught in those lower academies. They must be in God's own school, children of his house, who speak this language. Men may give spiritual rules and directions in this, and such as may be useful, drawn from the word that furnishes us with all needful precepts ; but you have still to bring these into the seat of this faculty of prayer, the heart, and stamp them upon it, and so to teach it to pray, without which there is no prayer. This is the prerogative royal of him who framed the heart of man within him.

But for advancing in this, and growing more skilful in it, Prayer is, with continual dependence on the Spirit, to be much used. Praying much, thou shalt be blest with much faculty for it. So then, askest thou, What shall I do, that I may learn to pray ? There be things here to be considered, which are expressed as serving this end ; but for the present take this, and chiefly this, By praying, thou shalt learn to pray.—Thou shalt both obtain more of the Spirit, and find more of the cheerful working of it in prayer, when thou puttest it often to that work for which it is received, and wherein it takes delight. And, as both advantaging all other graces and promoting the grace of prayer itself, this frequency and abounding in prayer is here very clearly intended, in that the Apostle makes it as the main of the work we have to do, and would have us keep our hearts in a constant aptness for it : *Be sober and watch*—to what end ?—*unto prayer*.

Be sober.] They that have no better, must make the best they can of carnal delights. It is no wonder they take as large a share of them as they can bear, and sometimes more. But the Christian is called to a more excellent state and higher pleasures ; so that he may behold men glutting themselves with these base things, and be as little moved to share with them, as men are taken with the pleasure a swine hath in wallowing in the mire.

It becomes the heirs of heaven to be far above the love of the earth, and in the necessary use of any earthly things, still to keep within the due measure of their use, and to keep their hearts wholly disengaged from an excessive affection to them. This is the Sobriety to which we are here exhorted.

It is true, that in the most common sense of the word, it is very commendable, and it is fit to be so considered by a Christian, that he flee gross intemperance, as a thing most contrary to his condition and holy calling, and wholly inconsistent with the spiritual temper of a renewed mind, with those exercises to which it is called, and with its progress in its way homewards. It is a most unseemly sight, to behold one simply by outward profession a Christian, overtaken with surfeiting and drunkenness, much more, given to the vile custom of it. All sensual delights, even the filthy lust of uncleanness, go under the common name of insobriety, intemperance, ἀκολασία: and they all degrade and destroy the noble soul, being unworthy of a man, much more of a Christian; and the contempt of them preserves the soul and elevates it.

But the Sobriety here recommended, though it takes in that too, yet reaches farther than temperance in meat and drink. It is the spiritual temperance of a Christian mind in all earthly things, as our Saviour joins these together, Luke xxi. 34, *surfeiting, and drunkenness, and cares of this life:* and under the *cares* are comprehended all the excessive desires and delights of this life, which cannot be followed and attended without distempered carefulness.

Many who are sober men and of temperate diet, yet are spiritually intemperate, drunk with pride, or covetousness, or passions; drunk with self-love and love of their pleasures and ease, with love of the world and the things of it, which cannot consist with the love of God, as St. John tells us, 1 John ii. 15; drunk with the inordinate, unlawful love even of their lawful calling and the lawful gain they pursue by it. Their hearts are still going after it, and so, reeling to and fro, never fixed on God and heavenly things, but either hurried up and down with incessant business, or, if sometimes at ease, it is as the ease of a drunken man, not composed to better and wiser thoughts, but falling into a dead sleep, contrary to the watching here joined with sobriety.

Watch.] There is a Christian rule to be observed in the very moderating of bodily sleep, and that particularly for the interest of prayer; but watching, as well as sobriety, here, implies chiefly the spiritual circumspectness and vigilancy of the mind, in a wary, waking posture, that it be not surprised by the assaults or sleights of Satan, by the world, nor by its nearest and most deceiving enemy, the corruption that dwells within, which, being so near, doth most readily watch unperceived advantages, and easily circumvent us. Heb. xii. 1. The soul of a Christian being surrounded with enemies, both of so great power and wrath, and so watchful to undo it, should it not be watchful for its own safety, and live in a military vigilancy continually, keeping constant watch and sentinel, and suffering nothing to pass that may carry the least suspicion of danger? Should he not be distrustful and jealous of all the motions of his own heart, and the smilings of the world? And in relation to these, it will be a wise course to take that word as a good caveat, Νῆφε καὶ μέμνησε ἀπιστεῖν. *Be watchful, and remember to mistrust.* Under the garment of some harmless pleasure, or some lawful liberties, may be conveyed into thy soul some thief or traitor, that will either betray thee to the enemy, or at least pilfer and steal of the most precious things thou hast. Do we not by experience find, how easily our foolish hearts are seduced and deceived, and therefore apt to deceive themselves? And by things that seem to have no evil in them, they are yet drawn from the height of affection to their

Supreme Good, and from communion with God, and study to please him ; which should not be intermitted, for then it will abate, whereas it ought still to be growing.

Now, II. The *mutual relation* of these duties is clear : they are each of them assistant and helpful to the other, and are in their nature inseparably linked together, as they are here in the words of the Apostle ; *Sobriety*, the friend of *watchfulness*, and *prayer*, of both. Intemperance doth of necessity draw on sleep : excessive eating and drinking, by sending up too many, and so, gross vapours, surcharge the brain ; and when the body is thus deadened, how unfit is it for any active employment. Thus the mind, by a surcharge of delights, or desires, or cares of earth, is made so heavy and dull, that it cannot awake ; hath not the spiritual activity and clearness that spiritual exercises, particularly prayer, do require. Yea, as bodily insobriety, full feeding and drinking, not only for the time indisposes to action, but, by the custom of it, brings the body to so gross and heavy a temper, that the very natural spirits cannot stir to and fro in it with freedom, but are clogged, and stick as the wheels of a coach in a deep miry way ; thus is it with the soul glutted with earthly things : the affections bemired with them, make it sluggish and inactive in spiritual things, and render the motions of the spirit heavy ; and, obstructed thus, the soul grows carnally secure and sleepy, and prayer comes heavily off. But when the affections are soberly exercised, and even in lawful things have not full liberty, with the reins laid on their necks, to follow the world and carnal projects and delights ; when the unavoidable affairs of this life are done with a spiritual mind, a heart kept free and disengaged ; then is the soul more nimble for spiritual things, for Divine meditation and prayer : it can watch and continue in these things, and spend itself in that excellent way with more alacrity.

Again, as this Sobriety, and the watchful temper attending it, enable for prayer, so prayer preserves these. Prayer winds up the soul from the earth, raises it above those things which intemperance feeds on, acquaints it with the transcending sweetness of Divine comforts, the love and loveliness of Jesus Christ ; and these most powerfully wean the soul from the low, creeping pleasures that the world gapes after and swallows with such greediness. He that is admitted to nearest intimacy with the king, and is called daily to his presence, not only in the view and company of others, but likewise in secret, will he be so mad as to sit down and drink with the kitchen-boys, or the common guards, so far below what he may enjoy ? Surely not.

Prayer, being our near communion with the great God, certainly sublimates the soul, and makes it look down upon the base ways of the world with disdain, and despise the truly besotting pleasures of it. Yea, the Lord doth sometimes fill those souls that converse much with him, with such beatific delights, such inebriating sweetness, as I may call it, that it is, in a happy manner, drunk with these ; and the more there is of this, the more is the soul above base intemperance in the use of the delights of the world. Whereas common drunkenness makes a man less than a man, this makes him more than a man : that sinks him below himself, makes him a beast ; this raises him above himself, and makes him an angel.

Would you, as surely you ought, have much faculty for prayer, and be frequent in it, and experience much of the pure sweetness of it? Then, deny yourselves more the muddy pleasures and sweetness of the world. If you would pray much, and with much advantage, then *be sober, and watch unto prayer.* Suffer not your hearts to long so after ease, and wealth, and esteem in the world: these will make your hearts, if they mix with them, become like them, and take their quality; will make them gross and earthly, and unable to mount up; will clog the wings of prayer, and you shall find the loss, when your soul is heavy and drowsy, and falls off from delighting in God and communion with him. Will such things as those you follow be able to countervail your damage? Can they speak you peace, and uphold you in a day of darkness and distress? Or may it not be such now, as will make them all a burden and vexation to you? But, on the other hand, the more you abate and let go of these, and come empty and hungry to God in prayer, the more room shall you have for his consolations; and therefore, the more plentifully will he pour in of them, and enrich your soul with them the more, the less you take in of the other.

Again, would you have yourselves raised to, and continued and advanced in, a spiritual, heavenly temper, free from the surfeits of earth, and awake and active for heaven? Be incessant in prayer.

But thou wilt say, I find nothing but heavy indisposedness in it, nothing but roving and vanity of heart, and so, though I have used it some time, it is still unprofitable and uncomfortable to me.—Although it be so, yet, hold on, give it not over. Or need I say this to thee? Though it were referred to thyself, wouldst thou forsake it and leave off? Then, what wouldst thou do next? For if there be no comfort in it, far less is there any for thee in any other way. If temptation should so far prevail with thee as to lead thee to try intermission, either thou wouldst be forced to return to it presently, or certainly wouldst fall into a more grievous condition, and, after horrors and lashings, must at length come back to it again, or perish for ever. Therefore, however it go, continue praying. Strive to believe that love thou canst not see; for where sight is abridged, there it is proper for faith to work. If thou canst do no more, lie before thy Lord, and look to him, and say, Lord, here I am, thou mayest quicken and revive me if thou wilt, and I trust thou wilt; but if I must do it, I will die at thy feet. My life is in thy hand, and thou art goodness and mercy; while I have breath I will cry, or, if I cannot cry, yet I will wait on, and look to thee.

One thing forget not, that the ready way to rise out of this sad, yet safe state, is, to be much in viewing the Mediator, and interposing him betwixt the Father's view and thy soul. Some who do orthodoxly believe this to be right, yet, (as often befalls us in other things of this kind,) do not so consider and use it in their necessity, as becomes them, and therefore fall short of comfort. He hath declared it, *No man cometh to the Father but by me.* How vile soever thou art, put thyself under his robe, and into his hand, and he will lead thee unto the Father, and present thee acceptable and blameless; and the Father shall receive thee, and declare himself well pleased with thee in his well-beloved Son, who hath covered thee with his righteousness, and brought thee so clothed, and set thee before him.

III. The third thing we have to consider, is, the reason which binds on us these duties : *The end of all things is at hand.*

We need often to be reminded of this, for even believers too readily forget it ; and it is very suitable to the Apostle's foregoing discourse of judgment, and to his present exhortation to sobriety and watchfulness unto prayer. Even the general end of all is *at hand;* though, since the Apostle wrote this, many ages are past. For, [1.] The Apostles usually speak of the whole time after the coming of Jesus Christ in the flesh, as *the last time,* for that two double chiliads of years passed before it, the one before, the other under the Law ; and in this third, it is conceived, shall be the end of all things. And the Apostles seem, by divers expressions, to have apprehended it in their days to be not far off. So St. Paul, 1 Thess. iv. 17 : *We which are alive, and remain, shall be caught up together with them in the clouds,*—speaking as if it were not impossible that it might come in their time ; which put him upon some explication of that correction of their mistakes, in his next Epistle to them, wherein, notwithstanding, he seems not to assert any great tract of time to intervene, but only that in that time great things were first to come. [2.] However, this might always have been said : in respect of succeeding eternity, the whole duration of the world is not considerable ; and to the Eternal Lord who made it, and hath appointed its period, *a thousand years are but as one day.* We think a thousand years a great matter, in respect of our short life, and more so through our shortsightedness, who look not through this to eternal life ; but what is the utmost length of time, were it millions of years, to a thought of eternity ? We find much room in this earth, but to the vast heavens it is but as a point. Thus, that which is but small to us, a field or little enclosure, a fly, had it skill, would divide into provinces in proportion to itself. [3.] To each man, the *end of all things* is, even after our measure, *at hand;* for when he dies, the world ends for him. Now this consideration fits the subject, and presses it strongly. Seeing all things shall be quickly at an end, even the frame of heaven and earth, why should we, knowing this, and having higher hopes, lay out so much of our desires and endeavours upon those things, that are posting to ruin ? It is no hard notion, to be sober and watchful to prayer, to be trading that way, and seeking higher things, and to be very moderate in these, which are of so short a date. As in themselves and their utmost term, they are of short duration, so more evidently to each of us in particular, who are so *soon cut off, and flee away.* Why should our hearts cleave to those things from which we shall so quickly part, and from which, if we will not freely part and let them go, we shall be pulled away, and pulled with the more pain, the closer we cleave, and the faster we are glued to them ?

This the Apostle St. Paul casts in seasonably, (though many think it not seasonable at such times,) when he is discoursing of a great point of our life, marriage, to work Christian minds to a holy freedom both ways, whether they use it or not ; not to view it, nor any thing here, with the world's spectacles, which make it look so big and so fixed, but to see it in the stream of time as passing by, and as no such great matter. 1 Cor. vii. 31. *The fashion of this world passeth away,* παράγει, as a pageant or show in a street, going through and quickly out of sight. What became of all the marriage solemnities of kings and princes of former ages, which they were so taken up with in their time? When we read of them described in history, they are as a night-dream, or a day-fancy, which passes through the mind and vanishes.

Oh! foolish man, that hunteth such poor things, and will not be called off till death benight him, and he finds his great work not done, yea, not begun, nor even seriously thought of. Your buildings, your trading, your lands, your matches, and friendships, and projects, when they take with you, and your hearts are after them, say, But for how long are all these? *Their end is at hand; therefore be sober, and watch unto prayer.* Learn to divide better; more hours for prayer, and fewer for them; your whole heart for it, and none of it for them. Seeing they will fail you so quickly, prevent them; become free: lean not on them till they break, and you fall into the pit.

It is reported of one, that, hearing the fifth chapter of Genesis read, so long lives, and yet, the burden still, *they died*—Seth lived nine hundred and twelve years, *and he died;* Enos lived nine hundred and five years, *and he died;* Methuselah nine hundred and sixty-nine years, *and he died;*—he took so deeply the thought of death and eternity, that it changed his whole frame, and turned him from a voluptuous, to a most strict and pious course of life. How small a word will do much, when God sets it into the heart! But surely, this one thing would make the soul more calm and sober in the pursuit of present things, if their term were truly computed and considered. How soon shall youth, and health, and carnal delights, be at an end! How soon shall state-craft and king-craft, and all the great projects of the highest wits and spirits, be lain in the dust! This casts a damp upon all those fine things. But to a soul acquainted with God, and in affection removed hence already, no thought so sweet as this. It helps much to carry it cheerfully through wrestlings and difficulties, through better and worse; they see land near, and shall quickly be at home: that is the way. *The end of all things is at hand;* an end of a few poor delights and the many vexations of this wretched life; an end of temptations and sins, the worst of all evils; yea, an end of the imperfect fashion of our best things here, an end of prayer itself, to which succeeds that new song of endless praises.

Ver. 8. And above all things have fervent charity among yourselves: for charity shall cover the multitude of sins.

THE graces of the Spirit are an entire frame, making up the new creature, and none of them can be wanting; therefore the doctrine and exhortation of the Apostles speak of them usually, not only as inseparable, but as one. But there is, amongst them all, none more comprehensive than this of *Love*, insomuch that St. Paul calls it *the fulfilling of the Law*, Rom. xiii. 10. Love to God is the sum of all relative to him, and so likewise is it towards our brethren. Love to God is that which makes us live to him, and be wholly his; that which most powerfully weans us from this world, and causeth us delight in communion with him in holy meditation and prayer. Now the Apostle adding here the duty of Christians to one another, gives this as the prime, yea, the sum of all; *Above all, have fervent love.*

Concerning this, consider, I. The Nature of it. II. The eminent Degree of it. And, III. The excellent Fruit of it.

I. The Nature of this Love. 1. It is a union, therefore called a *bond* or *chain*, that links things together. 2. It is not a mere external union, that holds in customs, or words, or outward carriage, but a union of hearts. 3. It is here not a natural, but a spiritual, supernatural union : it is the mutual love of Christians *as brethren.* There is a common benevolence and good will due to all ; but a more particular uniting affection amongst Christians, which makes them interchangeably one.

The Devil being an apostate spirit, revolted and separated from God, doth naturally project and work division. This was his first exploit, and it is still his grand design and business in the world. He first divided man from God ; put them at an enmity by the first sin of our first parents ; and the next we read of in their first child, was enmity against his brother. So, Satan is called by our Saviour, justly, *a liar and a murderer from the beginning,* John viii. 44 : he murdered man by lying, and made him a murderer.

And as the Devil's work is division, Christ's work is union. He came to *dissolve the works of the Devil,* ἵνα λύσῃ, by a contrary work, 1 John iii. 8. He came to make all friends ; to re-collect and re-unite all men to God, and man to man. And both those unions hold in him by virtue of that marvellous union of natures in his person, and that mysterious union of the persons of believers with him as their Head. So the word, ἀνακεφαλαιώσασθαι, signifies, Eph. i. 10, *To unite all in one head.*

This was his great project in all ; this he died and suffered for, and this he prayed for, John xvii. ; and this is strong above all ties, natural or civil, Union in Christ. This they have who are indeed Christians ; this they would pretend to have, if they understood it, who profess themselves Christians. If natural friendship be capable of that expression, *one spirit in two bodies,* Christian union hath it much more really and properly ; for there is, indeed, one spirit more extensive in all the faithful, yea, so one a spirit, that it makes them up into *one body* more extensive. They are not so much as divers bodies, only divers *members of one body.*

Now, this love of our brethren is not another from the love of God ; it is but the streaming forth of it, or the reflection of it. Jesus Christ sending his Spirit into the heart, unites it to God, in himself by love, which is indeed all, that *loving of God* supremely and entirely, with *all the mind and soul, all the* combined *strength of the heart!* And then, that same love, first wholly carried to him, is not divided or impaired by the love of our brethren, but is dilated, as derived from the other. God allows, yea, commands, yea, causes, that it stream forth, and act itself toward them, remaining still in him, as in its source and centre ; beginning at him, and returning to him, as the beams that diffuse themselves from the sun, and the light and heat, yet are not divided or cut off from it, but remain in it, and, by emanation, issue from it. In loving our brethren in God, and for him, not only because he commands us to love them, and so the law of love to him ties us to it, as his will ; but because that love of God doth naturally extend itself thus, and act thus ; in loving our brethren after a spiritual, Christian manner, we do, even in that, love our God.

Loving of God makes us one with God, and so gives us an impression of his Divine bounty in his Spirit.   And his love, the proper work of his Spirit, dwelling in the heart, enlarges and dilates it, as self-love contracts and straitens it : so that as self-love is the perfect opposite to the love of God, it is likewise so to brotherly love ; it shuts out and undoes both ; and where the love of God is rekindled and enters the heart, it destroys and burns up self-love, and so carries the affection up to himself, and in him forth to our brethren.

This is that bitter root of all enmity in man against God, and, amongst men, against one another, *Self*, man's heart turned from God towards himself ; and the very work of renewing grace is, to annul and destroy self, to replace God in his right, that the heart, and all its affections and motions, may be at his disposal ; so that, instead of self-will and self-love, which ruled before, now, the will of God, and the love of God, command all.

And where it is thus, there this φιλαδελφία, this love of our brethren, will be sincere.   Whence is it that wars, and contests, and mutual disgracings and despisings, do so much abound, but that men love themselves, and nothing but themselves, or in relation to themselves, as it pleases, or is advantageous to them ?   That is the standard and rule. All is carried by interest, so thence are strifes, and defamings, and bitterness against one another.   But the Spirit of Christ coming in, undoes all selfishness. And now, what is according to God, what he wills and loves, that is law, and a powerful law, so written on the heart, this law of love, that it obeys, not unpleasantly, but with delight, and knows no constraint but the sweet constraint of love.   To forgive a wrong, to love even thine enemy for him, is not only feasible now, but delectable, although a little while ago thou thoughtest it was quite impossible.

That Spirit of Christ, which is all sweetness and love, so calms and composes the heart, that peace with God, and that unspeakably blessed correspondence of love with him, do so fill the soul with lovingness and sweetness, that it can breathe nothing else.   It hates nothing but sin, it pities the sinner, and carries towards the worst that love of good will, desiring their return and salvation.   But as for those in whom appears the image of their Father, their heart cleaves to them as brethren indeed.   No natural advantages of birth, of beauty, or of wit, draw a Christian's love so much, as the resemblance of Christ ; wherever that is found, it is comely and lovely to a soul that loves him.

Much communion with God sweetens and calms the mind, cures the distempers of passion and pride, which are the avowed enemies of Love. Particularly, Prayer and Love suit well.

(1.) Prayer disposes to this Love. *He that loveth not, knoweth not God*, saith the beloved Apostle, *for God is love*. 1 John iv. 3.   He that is most conversant with love in the Spring of it, where it is purest and fullest, cannot but have the fullest measure of it, flowing in from thence into his heart, and flowing forth from thence unto his brethren.   If they who use the society of mild and good men, are insensibly assimilated to them, grow like them, and contract somewhat of their temper ; much more doth familiar walking with God powerfully transform the soul into his likeness, making it merciful, and loving, and ready to forgive, as he is.

(2.) This Love disposes to Prayer. To pray together, hearts must be consorted and tuned together ; otherwise how can they sound the same suits harmoniously ? How unpleasant, in the exquisite ear of God, who made the ear, are the jarring, disunited hearts that often seem to join in the same prayer, and yet are not set together in love ! And when thou prayest alone, while thy heart is imbittered and disaffected to thy brother, although upon an offence done to thee, it is as a mis-tuned instrument ; the strings are not accorded, are not in tune amongst themselves, and so the sound is harsh and offensive. Try it well thyself, and thou wilt perceive it ; how much more he to whom thou prayest ! When thou art stirred and in passion against thy brother, or not, on the contrary, lovingly affected towards him, what broken, disordered, unfastened stuff are thy requests ? Therefore the Lord will have this done first, the heart tuned : *Go thy way*, says he, *leave thy gift, and be reconciled to thy brother ; then come and offer thy gift.* Matt. v. 23.

Why is this which is so much recommended by Christ, so little regarded by Christians? It is given by him as the characteristic and badge of his followers ; yet, of those who pretend to be so, how few wear it ! Oh ! a little real Christianity were more worth than all that empty profession and discourse, that we think so much of. Hearts receiving the mould and stamp of this rule, these were living copies of the Gospel. *Ye are our epistle*, says the Apostle, 2 Cor. iii. 2. We come together, and hear, and speak, sometimes of one grace, and sometimes of another, while yet the most never seek to have their hearts enriched with the possession of any one of them. We search not to the bottom the perverseness of our nature, and the guiltiness that is upon us in these things ; or we shift off the conviction, and find a way to forget it when the hour is done.

That accursed root, self-love, which makes man an enemy to God, and men enemies and devourers one of another, who sets to the discovery and the displanting of it ? Who bends the force of holy endeavours and prayer, supplicating the hand of God for the plucking of it up ? Some natures are quieter and make less noise, but till the heart be possessed with the love of God, it shall never truly love either men in the way due to all, or the children of God in their peculiar relation.

Among yourselves, &c.] That is here the point : the peculiar love of the saints as thy brethren, glorying and rejoicing in the same Father, the sons of God, *begotten again* to that *lively hope* of glory. Now these, as they owe a bountiful disposition to all, are mutually to love one another as brethren.

Thou that hatest and reproachest the godly, and the more they study to walk as the children of their holy Father, hatest them the more, and art glad to find a spot on them to point at, or wilt dash mire on them where thou findest none, know that thou art in this the enemy of God ; know that the indignity done to them, Jesus Christ will take as done to himself. Truly, *we know that we have passed from death unto life, because we love the brethren : he that loveth not his brother, abideth in death.* 1 John iii. 4. So then, renounce this word, or else believe that thou art yet far from the life of Christ, who so hatest it in others. Oh !

but they are but a number of hypocrites, wilt thou say. If they be so, this declares so much the more thy extreme hatred of holiness, that thou canst not endure so much as the picture of it ; canst not see any thing like it, but thou must let fly at it. And this argues thy deep hatred of God. Holiness in a Christian is the image of God, and the hypocrite in the resemblance of it, is the image of a Christian ; so that thou hatest the very image of the image of God. For, deceive not thyself, it is not the latent evil in hypocrisy, but the apparent good in it that thou hatest. The profane man thinks himself a great zealot against hypocrisy ; he is still exclaiming against it ; but it is only this he is angry at, that all should not be ungodly, the wicked enemies of religion, as he is, either dissolute, or merely decent. And the decent man is frequently the bitterest enemy of all strictness beyond his own size, as condemning him, and therefore he cries it down, as all of it false and counterfeit wares.

Let me entreat you, if you would not be found *fighters against God*, let no revilings be heard amongst you, against any who are, or seem to be, followers of holiness. If you will not reverence it yourselves, yet reverence it in others ; at least, do not reproach it. It should be your ambition, else, why are you willing to be called Christians ? But if you will not *pursue holiness*, yet persecute it not. If you will not *have fervent love to the saints*, yet burn not with infernal heat of fervent hatred against them ; for truly, that is one of the most likely pledges of those flames, and of society with damned spirits, as love to the children of God is of that inheritance and society with them in glory.

You that are brethren, and united by that purest and strongest tie, as you are one in your Head, in your life derived from him, in your hopes of glory with him, seek to be more one in heart, in fervent love one to another in him. Consider the combinations and concurrences of the wicked against him and his *little flock*, and let this provoke you to more united affection. Shall the scales of Leviathan (as one alludes) stick so close together, and shall not the members of Christ be more one and undivided ? You that can feel it, stir up yourselves to bewail the present divisions, and the fears of more. Sue earnestly for that *one Spirit*, to act and work more powerfully in the hearts of his people.

II. Consider the eminent Degree of this Love. 1. Its eminency amongst the graces, *Above all*. 2. The high measure of it required, *Fervent love*, [ἐκτενῆ,] a high bent, or strain of it ; that which acts strongly, and carries far.

1. It is eminent, that which indeed among Christians preserves all, and knits all together, and therefore called, Col. iii. 14, *the bond of perfection:* all is bound up by it. How can they pray together, how advance the name of their God, or keep in and stir up all grace in one another, unless they be united in love ? How can they have access to God, or fellowship with him *who is love*, as St. John speaks, if, instead of this sweet temper, there be rancour and bitterness among them ? So then, uncharitableness and divisions amongst Christians, do not only hinder their civil good, but their spiritual much more ; and that not only *lucro cessante*, (as they speak,) interrupting the ways of mutual profiting, but *damno emergente*, it doth really damage them, and brings them to losses ; preys upon their graces, as hot withering winds on

herbs and plants. Where the heart entertains either bitter malice, or but uncharitable prejudices, there will be a certain decay of spirituality in the whole soul.

2. Again, for the *degree* of this love required, it is not a cold indifferency, a negative love, as I may call it, or a not willing of evil, nor is it a lukewarm wishing of good, but fervent and active love; for, if fervent, it will be active, a fire that will not be smothered, but will find a way to extend itself.

III. The Fruits of this Love follow. 1. *Covering of evil*, in this verse. 2. *Doing of good*, ver. 9, &c.

Charity shall cover the multitude of sins.] This expression is taken from Solomon, Prov. x. 12; and as covering sins is represented as a main act of love, so love is commended by it, this being a most useful and laudable act of it, that it *covers sins*, and *a multitude of sins.* Solomon saith, (and the opposition clears the sense,) *Hatred stirreth up strife*, aggravates and makes the worst of all, *but love covereth all sins*: it delights not in the undue disclosing of brethren's failings, doth not eye them rigidly, nor expose them willingly to the eyes of others.

Now this recommends Charity, in regard of its continual usefulness and necessity this way, considering human frailty, and that *in many things*, as St. James speaks, *we all offend*, James iii. 2; so that this is still needful on all hands. What do they think who are still picking at every appearing infirmity of their brethren? Know they not that the frailties that cleave to the saints of God while they are here, do stand in need of, and call for, this mutual office of love, to cover and pass them by? Who is there that stands not in need of this? If none, why are there any who deny it to others? There can be no society nor entertaining of Christian converse without it, without giving (as we speak) allowance; reckoning to meet with defects and weaknesses on all hands, and covering the failings of one another, seeing it is mutually needful.

Again, as the necessity of this commends it and the love whence it flows, so there is that laudable ingenuousness in it, that should draw us to the liking of it. It is the bent of the basest and most worthless spirits, to be busy in the search and discovery of others' failings, passing by all that is commendable and imitable, as base flies readily sitting on any little sore they can find, rather than upon the sound parts. But the more excellent mind of a real Christian loves not unnecessarily to touch, no, nor to look upon them, but rather turns away. Such never uncover their brother's sores, but to cure them; and no more than is necessary for that end: they would willingly have them hid, that neither they nor others might see them.

This bars not the judicial trial of scandalous offences, nor the giving information of them, and bringing them under due censure. The forbearing of this is not charity, but both iniquity and cruelty; and this cleaves too much to many of us. They that cannot pass over the least touch of a wrong done to themselves, can digest twenty high injuries done to God by profane persons about them, and resent it not. Such may be assured, that they are as yet destitute of love to God, and of Christian love to their brethren, which springs from it.

The uncovering of sin, necessary to the curing of it, is not only no breach of charity, but is indeed a main point of it, and the neglect of it the highest kind of cruelty. But further than that goes, certainly, this rule teaches the veiling of our brethren's infirmities from the eyes of others, and even from our own, that we look not on them with rigour; no, nor without compassion.

1. Love is skilful in finding out the fairest construction of things doubtful; and this is a great point. Take me the best action that can be named, pride and malice shall find a way to disgrace it, and put a hard visage upon it. Again, what is not undeniably evil, Love will turn it in· all the ways of viewing it, till it find the best and most favourable.

2. Where the thing is so plainly a sin, that this way of covering it can have no place, yet then will Love consider what may lessen it most; whether a surprise, or strength of temptation, or ignorance, (as our Saviour, *Father, forgive them, for they know not what they do,*) or natural complexion, or at least, will still take in human frailty, to turn all the bitterness of passion into sweet compassion.

3. All private reproofs, and where conscience requires public accusation and censure, even these will be sweetened in that compassion that flows from Love. If it be such a sore as must not lie covered up, lest it prove deadly, so that it must be uncovered, to be lanced and cut, that it may be cured, still this is to be done as loving the soul of the brother. Where the rule of conscience urges it not, then thou must bury it, and be so far from delighting to divulge such things, that, as far as, without partaking in it, thou mayest, thou must veil it from all eyes, and try the way of private admonition; and if the party appear to be humble and willing to be reclaimed, then forget it, cast it quite out of thy thoughts, that, as much as may be, thou mayest learn to forget it more. But this, I say, is to be done with the tenderest bowels of piety, feeling the cuts thou art forced to give in that necessary incision, and using mildness and patience. Thus the Apostle instructs his Timothy, *Reprove, rebuke, exhort,* but do it with *long-suffering, with all long-suffering.* 2 Tim. iv. 2. And even *them that oppose, instruct,* says he, *with meekness, if God peradventure will give them repentance to the acknowledging of the truth.* 2 Tim. ii. 25.

5. If thou be interested in the offence, even by unfeigned free forgiveness, so far as thy concern goes, let it be as if it had not been. And though thou meet with many of these, Charity will gain and grow by such occasions, and the more it hath covered, the more it can cover : *cover a multitude,* says our Apostle, *covers all sins,* says Solomon. Yea, though thou be often put to it by the same party, what made thee forgive once, well improved, will stretch our Saviour's rule to *seventy times seven times in one day.* Matt. xviii. 21.

And truly, in this men mistake grossly, who think it is greatness of spirit to resent wrongs, and baseness to forgive them : on the contrary, it is the only excellent spirit scarcely to feel a wrong, or, feeling, straightly to forgive it. It is the Greatest and Best of spirits that enables to this, the Spirit of God, that dove-like Spirit which rested on our Lord Jesus, and which from him is derived to all that are in him. I pray you, think, is it not a token of a tender, sickly body, to be altered with every touch from every blast it meets with ? And thus is it a sign of a poor, weak, sickly spirit, to endure nothing, to be distempered at the least air of an injury, yea, with the very fancy of it, where there is really none.

Inf. 1. Learn, then, to beware of those evils that are contrary to this charity. Do not dispute with yourselves in rigid remarks and censures, when the matter will bear any better sense.

2ndly, Do not delight in tearing a wound wider, and stretching a real failing to the utmost.

3rdly, In handling of it, study gentleness, pity, and meekness. These will advance the cure, whereas the flying out into passion against thy fallen brother, will prove nothing but as the putting of thy nail into the sore, that will readily rankle it and make it worse. Even sin may be sinfully reproved ; and how thinkest thou that sin shall redress sin, and restore the sinner ?

There is a great deal of spiritual art and skill in dealing with another's sin : it requires much spirituality of mind, and much, prudence, and much love, a mind clear from passion ; for that blinds the eye, and makes the hand rough, so that a man neither rightly sees, nor rightly handles the sore he goes about to cure ; and many are lost through the ignorance and neglect of that due temper which is to be brought to this work. Men think otherwise, that their rigours are much spirituality ; but they mistake it. *Brethren, if a man be overtaken in a fault, ye which are spiritual, restore such an one in the spirit of meekness, considering thyself, lest thou also be tempted.* Gal. vi. 1.

4thly. For thyself, as an offence touches thee, learn to delight as much in that Divine way of forgiveness, as carnal minds do in that base, inhuman way of revenge. It is not, as they judge, a glory to bluster and swagger for every thing, but the *glory of a man to pass by a transgression.* Prov. xix. 11. This makes him God-like. And consider thou often that Love which covers all thine, that Blood which was shed to wash off thy guilt. Needs any more be said to gain all in this that can be required of thee ?

Now, the other fruit of love, *doing good,* is first expressed in one particular, ver. 9, and then dilated to a general rule, at ver. 20.

Ver. 9. Use hospitality one to another without grudging.

HOSPITALITY, or kindness to strangers, is mentioned here as an important fruit of love, it being, in those times and places, in much use in travel, and particularly needful often among Christians one to another then, by reason of hot and general persecutions. But under this name, I conceive all other supply of the wants of our brethren in outward things to be here comprehended.

Now, for this, the way and measure, indeed, must receive its proportion from the estate and ability of persons. But certainly, the great straitening of hands in these things, is more from the straitness of hearts, than of means. A large heart, with a little estate, will do much with cheerfulness and little noise, while hearts glued to the poor riches they possess, or rather are possessed by, can scarcely part with any thing, till they be pulled from all.

Now, for the supplying of our brethren's necessities, one good help is, the retrenching of our own superfluities. Turn the stream into that channel where it will refresh thy brethren and enrich thyself, and let it not run into the dead sea. Thy vain, excessive entertainments, the gaudy variety of dresses, these thou dost not challenge, thinking it is of thine own; but know, (as it follows, ver. 10,) thou art but *steward* of it, and this is not faithfully laying out; thou canst not answer for it. Yea, it is robbery; thou robbest thy poor brethren who want necessaries, whilst thou lavishest thus on unnecessaries. Such a feast, such a suit of apparel, is direct robbery in the Lord's eye; and the poor may cry, That is mine that you cast away so vainly, by which both I and you might be profited. *Withhold not good from them to whom it is due, when it is in the power of thine hand to do it.* Prov. iii. 27, 28.

Without grudging.] Some look to the actions, but few to the intention and posture of mind in them; and yet that is the main: it is all indeed, even with men, so far as they can perceive it, much more with thy Lord, who always perceives it to the full. He delights in the good he does his creatures, and would have them be so affected to one another; especially he would have his children bear this trait of his likeness. See then, when thou givest alms, or entertainest a stranger, that there be nothing either of under-grumbling, or crooked self-seeking in it. Let the *left hand* have no hand in it, nor so much as *know* of it, as our Saviour directs, Matt. vi. 3. Let it not be to please men, or to please thyself, or simply out of a natural pity, or from the consideration of thy own possible incidency into the like case, which many think very well, if they be so moved; but here is a higher principle moving thee, love to God, and to thy brother in and for him. This will make it cheerful and pleasant to thyself, and well-pleasing to him for whom thou dost it. We lose much in actions, in themselves good, both of piety and charity, through disregard of our hearts in them; and nothing will prevail with us, to be more intent this way, to look more on our hearts, but this, to look more on Him who looks on them, and judges, and accepts all according to them.

Though all the sins of former ages gather and fall into the latter times, this is pointed out as the grand evil, *Uncharitableness.* The Apostle St. Paul tells us, 2 Tim. iii. 2, that *in the last days, men shall be covetous, slanderers, lovers of pleasure more than lovers of God*—but how? From whence all this confluence of evils? The spring of all is put first, and that is the direct opposite of Christian love: *men shall be* [φιλαυτοι] *lovers of themselves.* This is what kills the love of God, and the love of our brethren, and kindles that infernal fire of love to please themselves: riches make men voluptuous and covetous, &c. Truly, whatsoever become of men's curious computations of times, this wretched selfishness and decay of love may save us the labour of much *chronological* debate in this, and lead us, from this certain character of them, to conclude these to be the *latter times*, in a very strict sense. All other sins are come down along, and run combined now with this; but truly, uncharitableness is the main one. As old age is a rendezvous or meeting-place of maladies, but is especially subject to cold diseases, thus is it in the old age of the world: many sins abound, but especially coldness of love, as our Saviour foretells it, that in *the last days the love of many shall wax cold.* Matt. xxiv. 12.

As the disease of the youth of the world, was, the *abounding of lust,* (Gen. vi.,) so that of its age is, *decay of love.* And as that heat called for a total deluge of waters, so this coldness calls for fire, the kindling of a universal fire, that shall make an end of it and the world together. *Aqua propter ardorem libidinis, ignis propter teporem chari- tatis:* Water because of the heat of lust, fire because of the coldness of charity.

But they alone are the happy men, and have the advantage of all the world, in whom the world is burnt up beforehand, by another fire, that Divine fire of the love of God, kindled in their hearts, by which they ascend up to him, and are reflected from him upon their brethren, with a benign heat and influence for their good. Oh! be unsatisfied with yourselves, and restless till you find it thus, till you find your hearts possessed of this excellent grace of love, that you may have it, and use it, and it may grow by using and acting. I could, methinks, heartily study on this, and weary you with the reiterated pressing of this one thing, if there were hopes, in so wearying you, to weary you out of those evils that are contrary to it, and in pressing this grace, to make any real impression of it upon your hearts. Besides all the further good that follows it, there is in this love itself so much peace and sweetness, as abundantly pays itself, and all the labour of it; whereas pride and malice do fill the heart with continual vexations and disquiet, and eat out the very bowels wherein they breed. Aspire to this, to be wholly bent, not only to procure or desire hurt to none, but to wish and seek the good of all : and as for those that are in Christ, surely, that will unite thy heart to them, and stir thee up, according to thy opportunities and power, to do them good, as parts of Christ, and of the same body with thyself.

Ver. 10. As every man hath received the gift, even so minister the same one to another, as good stewards of the manifold grace of God.

THIS is the rule concerning the gifts and graces bestowed on men. And we have here, 1. Their difference in their kind and measure. 2. Their concordance in their source and use.

1. Their difference in their kind and measure is expressed in the first clause, *As every one hath received;* then, again, in the last clause, [ποικίλη χάρις] *various* or *manifold grace;* where χάρις, *grace,* is all one with the former, χάρισμα, *gift,* and is taken at large for all kind of endowments and furniture by which men are enabled for mutual good. One man hath riches, another, authority and command, another, wit, or eloquence, or learning ; and some, though eminent in some one, yet have a fuller conjuncture of divers of these. We find not more difference in visages and statures of body, than in qualifications and abilities of mind, which are the visage and stature of it, yea, the odds is far greater betwixt man and man in this, than it can be in the other.

2. Now, this difference accords well with the accordance here expressed in their common spring and common use. For the variety of these many gifts suits well with the singular riches and wisdom of their one Giver, and with the common advantage and benefit of the many receivers. And in the usefulness of that variety to the receivers

shine forth the bounty and wisdom of the Giver, in so ordering all that diversity to one excellent end.　So this ποικίλη χάρις, *manifold grace,* here, commends that πολυποίκιλος σοφία, *manifold wisdom,* that the Apostle speaks of, Eph. iii. 10.

There is such an admirable beauty in this variety, such a symmetry and contemperature of different, yea, of contrary qualities, as speaks his riches, that so divers gifts are from the same Spirit; a kind of *embroidering,** of many colours happily mixed, as the word ποικιλλειν signifies: as it is in the frame of the natural body of man, that lesser world, and in the composition of the greater world, thus it is in the Church of God, the mystical body of Jesus Christ, exceeding both in excellency and beauty.

And as there is such art in this contrivance, and such comeliness in the resulting frame, so it is no less useful.　And this chiefly commends the thing itself, and the supreme wisdom ordering it, that, as in the body each part hath not only its place for proportion and order, but its several use; and as in the world each part is beneficial to another, so here, every man's gift relates, and is fitted to some use for the good of others.

Infer. 1. The first thing which meets us here, it is very useful to know, that all is *received,* and received of *gift,* of most *free gift:* so the words do carry.　Now this should most reasonably check all murmuring in those who receive least, and all insulting in those that receive most.　Whatever it is, do not repine; but praise, how little soever it is, for it is a free gift.　Again, how much soever it is, *be not high-minded, but fear;* boast not thyself, but humbly bless thy Lord. *For if thou didst receive it, why dost thou boast, as if thou hadst not received it?* 1 Cor. iv. 7.

Inf. 2. Every man hath received some gift, no man all gifts; and this, rightly considered, would keep all in a more even temper.　As, in nature, nothing is altogether useless, so nothing is self-sufficient.　This should keep the meanest from repining and discontent: he that hath the lowest rank in most respects, yet something he hath received, that is not only a good to himself, but, rightly improved, may be so to others likewise.　And this will curb the loftiness of the most highly privileged, and teach them, not only to see some deficiencies in themselves, and some gifts in far meaner persons, which they want, but, besides the simple discovery of this, it will put them upon the use of what is in lower persons; not only to stoop to the acknowledgment, but even, withal, to the participation and benefit of it; not to trample upon all that is below them, but to take up and use things useful, though lying at their feet.　Some flowers and herbs, that grow very low, are of a very fragrant smell and healthful use.

Thou that carriest it so high, losest much by it.　Many poor Christians whom thou despisest to make use of, may have that in them which might be very useful for thee; but thou overlookest it, and treadest on it.　St. Paul acknowledgeth he was *comforted by the coming of Titus,* though far inferior to him.　Sometimes, a very mean, unlettered Christian may speak more profitably and comfortably, even to

---

* The Psalmist's word applied to the body. Psal. cxxxix. 12.

a knowing, learned man, than multitudes of his own best thoughts can do, especially in a time of weakness and darkness.

Inf. 3. As all is received and with that difference, so the third thing is, that all is received *to minister to each other*, and mutual benefit is the true use of all, suiting the mind of Him who dispenses all, and the way of his dispensation. Thou art not proprietary lord of any thing thou hast, but οἰκόνομος, *a steward;* and therefore oughtest gladly to be a good steward, that is, both faithful and prudent in thy intrusted gifts, using all thou hast to the good of the Household, and so to the advantage of thy Lord and Master. Hast thou abilities of estate, or body, or mind? Let all be thus employed. Thinkest thou that thy wealth, or power, or wit, is thine, to do with as thou wilt, to engross to thyself, either to retain useless, or to use; to hoard and wrap up, or to lavish out, according as thy humour leads thee? No, all is given as to a steward, wisely and faithfully to lay up and lay out. Not only thy outward and common gifts of mind, but even saving grace, which seems most intrusted and appropriated for thy private good, yet is not wholly for that: even thy graces are for the good of thy brethren.

Oh that we would consider this in all, and look back and mourn on the fruitlessness of all that hath been in our hand all our life hitherto! If it has not been wholly fruitless, yet how far short of that fruit we might have brought forth! Any little thing done by us looks big in our eye; we view it through a magnifying glass; but who may not complain that their means, and health, and opportunities of several kinds, of doing for God and for our brethren, have lain dead upon their hands, in a great part? As Christians are defective in other duties of love, so most in that most important duty, of advancing the spiritual good of each other. Even they who have grace, do not duly use it to mutual edification. I desire none to leap over the bounds of their calling, or the rules of Christian prudence in their converse; yea, this were much to be blamed; but I fear lest unwary hands, throwing on water to quench that evil, have let some of it fall aside upon those sparks that should rather have been stirred and blown up.

Neither should the disproportion of gifts and graces hinder Christians to *minister one to another:* it should neither move the weaker to envy the stronger, nor the stronger to despise the weaker; but each, in his place, is to be serviceable to the others, as the Apostle excellently presses, by that most fit resemblance of the parts of the body. *As the foot says not, Why am I not the eye or the head? the head cannot say of the foot, I have no need of thee.* 1 Cor. xii. 15, 21. There is no envy, no despising in the natural body. Oh, the pity there should be so much in the mystical! Were we more spiritual, less of this would be found. In the mean time, oh that we were more agreeable to that happy estate we look for, in our present aspect and carriage one towards another! Though all the graces of the Spirit exist, in some measure, where there is one, yet not all in a like measure. One Christian is more eminent in meekness, another in humility, a third in zeal, &c. Now, by their spiritual converse one with another, each may be a gainer; and in many ways may a private

Christian promote the good of others with whom he lives, by seasonable admonitions, and advice, and reproof, sweetened with meekness,
but most by holy example, which is the most lively and most effectual
speech.

Thou that hast greater gifts hast more intrusted in thy hand, and
therefore the greater thy obligation to fidelity and diligence. Men in
great place and public services, ought to stir themselves up by this
thought, to singular watchfulness and zeal. And in private converse
one with another, we ought to be doing and receiving spiritual good.
Are we not strangers here ? Is it not strange that we so often meet
and part, without a word of our home, or the way to it, or our advance
towards it ? Christians should be trading one with another in spiritual
things ; and he, surely, who faithfully uses most, receives most. This
is comprehended under that word : *To him that hath* (*i. e.* possesses
actively and usefully) *shall be given ; and from him that hath not* (*i. e.*
uses not) *shall be taken away even that which he hath.* Matt. xxv. 29.
Merchants can feel in their trading a dead time, and complain seriously
of it ; but Christians, in theirs, either can suffer it and not see it, or see
it and not complain, or, possibly, complain and yet not be deeply sensible of it.

Certainly, it cannot be sufficiently regretted, that we are so fruitless
in the Lord's work in this kind, that when we are alone we study it
not more, nor seek it more by prayer, to know the true use of all we
receive, and that we do not in society endeavour it accordingly ; but
we trifle out our time, and instead of the commerce of grace to our
mutual enriching, we trade in vanity, and are, as it were, children
exchanging shells and toys together.

This surely will lie heavy upon the conscience.when we reflect on it,
and shall come near the utter brink of time, looking forwards on eternity, and then looking back to our days, so vainly wasted, and worn
out to so little purpose. Oh ! let us awake, awake ourselves and one
another, to more fruitfulness and faithfulness, whatsoever be our received measure, less or more.

Be not discouraged : to have little in the account shall be no prejudice. The approbation runs not, *Thou hast much,* but, on the contrary, *Thou hast been faithful in little.* Great faithfulness in the use
of small gifts hath great acceptance, and a great and sure reward.
Great receipts engage to greater returns, and therefore require the
greater diligence ; and that not only for the increase of grace within, but
for the assistance of it in others. Retired contemplation may be more
pleasing, but due activity for God and his Church is more profitable.
Rachel was fair, but she was barren ; Leah blear-eyed, but fruitful.

Ver. 11. If any man speak, let him speak as the oracles of God ; if any man minis-
    ter, let him do it as of the ability which God giveth : that God in all things may
    be glorified through Jesus Christ, to whom be praise and dominion for ever and
    ever. Amen.

EVERY part of the Body of Christ, as it partakes of life with the rest,
so it imparts service to the rest. But there be some more eminent,
and, as I may say, *organic* parts of this Body, and these are more
eminently useful to the whole. Therefore the Apostle, having enlarged

into a general precept, adds a word in special reference to these special parts, the Preachers of the word, and (which here I conceive is meant by deacons or ministers) the other assistant officers of the Church of God.

These are co-ordained by Jesus Christ, as Lord of his own House, to be serviceable to him in it. He fits and sanctifies for this great work, all who are called unto it by himself. And they are directed for the acquitting of their great work, I. By a clear rule of the due manner. II. By the main end of its appointment.

I. Particular rules for the preaching of the word may be many, but this is a most comprehensive one which the Apostle gives : *If any man speak, let him speak as the oracles of God.* It is clear from the rule, what speaking is regulated, and for brevity it is once expressed. If any man speak the oracles of God, let him speak them like themselves, *as the oracles of God.*

It is a chief thing in all serious actions, to take the nature of them aright : for this mainly regulates them, and directs in their performance. And this especially should be regarded in those things that are of highest worth and greatest weight, in spiritual employments, wherein it is most dangerous, and yet with us most ordinary, to mistake and miscarry. Were prayer considered as presence and speech with the great God, the King of glory, oh, how would this mould the mind ! What watchful, holy, and humble deportment would it teach ! So that, truly, all directions for prayer might be summed up, after this same model, in this one, If any man pray, let him speak *as speaking with God;* just as here for preaching, If any man speak in that way, let him do it as *speaking from God,* that is, *as the oracles of God.* Under this, all the due qualifications of this holy work are comprised. I shall name but these three, which are primary, and others may be easily reduced to these : 1. *Faithfully.*   2. *Holily.*   3. *Wisely.*

1. In the first, *Fidelity,* it is supposed that a man should have a competent insight and knowledge in these Divine oracles, that first he learn before he teach ; which many of us do not, though we pass through the schools and classes, and through the books too, wherein these things are taught, and bring with us some provision, such as may be had there. He that would faithfully teach of God, must be *taught of God,* be θεοδιδακτὸς, *God-learned;* and this will help to all the rest : will help him to be faithful in delivering the message as he receives it, not detracting, or adding, or altering ; and as in setting forth that in general truths, so in the particular setting them home, declaring to his people their sins, and God's judgments following sin, especially in his own people.

2. A minister must speak *holily,* with that high esteem and reverence of the Great Majesty whose message he carries, that becomes the divinity of the message itself, those deep mysteries that no created spirits are able to fathom. Oh ! this would make us tremble in the dispensing of these oracles, considering our impurities and weaknesses, and unspeakable disproportion to so high a task. He had reason who said, " I am seized with amazement and horror as often as I begin to speak of God." And with this humble reverence is to be joined, ardent love to our Lord, to his truth, to his glory, and to

his people's souls. These holy affections stand opposite to our blind boldness in rushing on this sublime exercise as a common work, and our dead coldness in speaking of things which our hearts are not warmed with; and so no wonder what we say seldom reaches further than the ear, or, at furthest, than the understanding and memory of our hearers. There is a correspondence; it is the heart speaks to the heart, and the understanding and memory the same, and the tongue speaks but to the ear. Further, this holy temper shuts out all private passion in delivering Divine truths. It is a high profaning of his name and holy things, to make them speak our private pleas and quarrels; yea, to reprove sin after this manner is a heinous sin. To fly out into invectives, which, though not expressed so, yet are aimed as blows of self-revenge for injuries done to us, or fancied by us, this is to wind and draw the holy word of God to serve our unholy distempers, and to make it speak, not his meaning, but our own. Surely, this is not to speak *as the oracles of God*, but basely to abuse the word, as impostors in religion of old did their images, speaking behind them, and through them, what might make for their advantage. It is true, that the word is to be particularly applied to reprove most the particular sins which most abound amongst a people; but this is to be done, not in anger, but in love.

3. The word is to be spoken *wisely*. By this I mean, in the way of delivering it, that it be done gravely and decently; that light expressions, and affected flourishes, and unseemly gestures, be avoided; and that there be a sweet contemperature of authority and mildness. But *who is sufficient for these things?*

Now, you that hear should certainly meet and agree in this too. If any hear, let him hear *as the oracles of God;* not as a well-tuned sound, to help you to sleep an hour; not as a human speech or oration, to displease or please you for an hour, according to the suiting of its strain and your palate; not as a school lesson, to add somewhat to your stock of knowledge, to tell you somewhat you knew not before, or as a feast of new notions. Thus the most relish a preacher, while they try his gift, and it is new with them, but a little time disgusts them. But hear *as the oracles of God.* The discovery of sin and death lying on us, and the discovery of a Saviour, that takes these off; the sweet word of reconciliation, God wooing man; the Great King entreating for peace with a company of rebels,—not that they are too strong for him, oh! no, but, on the contrary, he could utterly destroy them in one moment: these are the things brought you in this word. Therefore come to it with suitable reverence, with ardent desires, and hearts open to receive it *with meekness, as the ingrafted word that is able to save your souls.* James i. 21. It were well worth one day's pains of speaking and hearing, that we could learn somewhat, at least, how to speak and hear henceforward; to speak, and to hear, *as the oracles of God.*

In the other rule, of *ministering as of the ability that God giveth,* we may observe: 1. Ability, and that received from God; for other ability there is none for any good work, and least of all, for the peculiar ministration of his spiritual affairs in his house. 2. The using of this ability received from him for them.

And this, truly, is a chief thing for ministers, and for individual Christians, still to depend on the influence and strength of God; to do all his works in that strength. The humblest Christian, how weak soever, is the strongest. There is a natural wretched independency in us, that we would be the authors of our own works, and do all without him, without whom indeed we can do nothing. Let us learn to go more out of ourselves, and we shall find more strength for our duties, and against our temptations. Faith's great work is, to renounce self-power, and to bring in the power of God to be ours. Happy they that are weakest in themselves, sensibly so. That word of the Apostle is theirs; they know what it means, though a riddle to the world: *When I am weak, then am I strong.* 2 Cor. xii. 10. Now,

II. The *End* of all this appointment is, *that in all God may be glorified through Jesus Christ.* All meet in this, if they move in their straight line: here concentre, not only these two sorts specified in this verse, but all sorts of persons that use aright any gift of God, as they are generally comprehended in the former verse. For this end relates to all, as it is expressed universally, *That in all,* in all persons and all things; the word bears both, and the thing itself extends to both.

Here we have, like that of the heavens, a circular motion of all sanctified good: it comes forth from God, through Christ, unto Christians, and moving in them to the mutual good of each other, returns through Christ unto God again, and takes them along with it, in whom it was, and had its motion.

All persons and all things shall pay this tribute, even they that most wickedly seek to withhold it; but this is the happiness of the saints, that they move willingly thus, are sweetly drawn, not forced or driven. They are gained to seek and desire this, to set in with God in the intention of the same end; to have the same purpose with him, his glory in all, and to prosecute his end by his direction, by the means and ways he appoints them.

This is his due, as God; and the declining from this, the squinting from this view to self-ends, especially in God's own peculiar work, is high treason. Yet, the base heart of man leads naturally this way, to intend himself in all, to raise his own esteem or advantage in some way. And in this the heart is so subtle, that it will deceive the most discerning, if they be not constant in suspecting and watching it. This is the great task, to overcome in this point; to have self under our feet, and God only in our eye and purpose in all.

It is most reasonable, his due as God the author of all, not only of all supervenient good, but even of being itself, seeing all is from him, that all be for him: *For of him, and through him, and to him are all things: to whom be glory for ever. Amen.* Rom. xi. *ult.*

As it is most just, so it is also most sweet, to aim in all at this, *that God be glorified:* it is the alone worthy and happy design, which fills the heart with heavenliness, and with a heavenly calmness; sets it above the clouds and storms of those passions which disquiet low, self-seeking minds. He is a miserable, unsettled wretch, who cleaves to himself and forgets God; is perplexed about his credit, and gain, and base ends, which are often broken, and which, when he attains, yet they and he must shortly perish together. When his estate, or designs, or any comforts fail, how can he look to him at whom he looked so little before? May not the Lord say, *Go to the gods whom thou hast served, and let them deliver and comfort thee;* seek comfort from thyself, as thou didst all for thyself? What an appalment will this be! But he that hath resigned himself, and is all for God, may say, confidently, that *the Lord is his portion.* This is the Christian's aim, to have nothing in himself, nor in any thing, but on this tenure: all for the glory of my God,—my estate, family, abilities, my whole self, all I have and am. And as the love of God grows in the heart, this purpose grows: the higher the flame rises, the purer it is. The eye is daily more upon it; it is oftener in the mind in all actions than before. In common things, the very works of our callings, our very refreshments, to eat, and drink, and sleep, are all for this end, and with a particular aim at it as much as may be; even the thought of it often renewed throughout the day, and at times, generally applied to all our ways and employments. It is this elixir that turns thy ordinary works into gold, into sacrifices, by the touch of it.

Through Jesus Christ.] The Christian in covenant with God, receives all this way, and returns all this way. And Christ possesses, and hath equal right with the Father to this glory, as he is equally the spring of it with him, as God. But it is conveyed through him as Mediator, who obtains all the grace we receive; and all the glory we return, and all our praise, as our spiritual sacrifice, is put into his hand as our High Priest, to offer up for us, that they may be accepted.

Now the holy ardour of the Apostle's affections, taken with the mention of this glory of God, carries him to a *doxology,* as we term it, a rendering of glory, in the middle of his discourse. Thus often we find in St. Paul likewise. Poor and short-lived is the glory and grandeur of men; like themselves, it is a shadow, and nothing; but this is solid and lasting, it is supreme, and abideth *for ever.* And the Apostles, full of divine affections, and admiring nothing but God, do delight in this, and cannot refrain from this at any time in their discourse: it is always sweet and seasonable, and they find it so. And thus are spiritual minds: a word of this nature falls on them as a spark on some matter that readily takes fire; they are straight inflamed with it. But alas! to us how much is it otherwise! The mention of the praise and glory of our God, is, to our hearts, as a spark falling either into a puddle of water, and foul water too, or at least, as upon green timber, that much fire will not kindle; there is so much moisture of our humours and corruptions, that all dies out with us, and we remain cold and dead.

But were not this a high and blessed condition, to be in all estates in some willing readiness to bear a part in this song, to acknowledge the greatness and goodness of our God, and to wish him glory in all? What are the angels doing? This is their business, and that without end. And seeing we hope to partake with them, we should even here, though in a lower key, and not so tunably neither, yet, as we may, begin it; and upon all occasions, our hearts should be often following in this sweet note, or offering at it, *To him be glory and dominion for ever.*

Ver. 12. Beloved, think it not strange concerning the fiery trial which is to try you, as though some strange thing happened unto you:
13. But rejoice, inasmuch as ye are partakers of Christ's sufferings; that, when his glory shall be revealed, ye may be glad also with exceeding joy.

THIS fighting life, surely, when we consider it aright, we need not be dissuaded from loving it, but have rather need to be strengthened with patience to go through, and to fight on with courage and assurance of victory; still combating in a higher strength than our own, against sin within and troubles without.   This is the great scope of this Epistle, and the Apostle often interchanges his advices and comforts in reference to these two.   *Against sin* he instructs us in the beginning of this chapter, urging us to be armed, *armed with the same mind* that was in Christ, and here again, *against suffering*, and both in a like way.   In the mortifying of sin, we suffer with him, as there he teaches, verse 1 of this chapter: and in the encountering of affliction, we suffer with him, as here we have it: and so, the same mind in the same sufferings will bring us to the same issue.   *Beloved, think it not strange concerning the fiery trial which is to try you, &c.   But rejoice, inasmuch as ye are partakers of Christ's sufferings; that, when his glory shall be revealed, ye likewise may be glad with exceeding joy.*

The words, to the end of the chapter, contain grounds of encouragement and consolation for the children of God in sufferings, especially in suffering for God.

These two verses have these two things: I. The close conjunction of sufferings with the estate of a Christian. II. The due composure of a Christian towards suffering.

I. It is no new, and therefore no strange thing, that sufferings, hot sufferings, fiery ones, be the companions of religion.   Besides the common miseries of human life, there is an accession of troubles and hatreds for that holiness of life to which the children of God are called.

It was the lot of the Church from her wicked neighbours, and in the Church, the lot of the most holy and peculiar servants of God, from the profane multitude.   *Woe is me, my mother,* says Jeremiah, *that thou hast borne me a man of strife, and a man of contention to the whole earth!* Jer. xv. 10.   And of all the Prophets, says not our Saviour, handling this same argument in his sermon, *So persecuted they the Prophets that were before you?* Matt. v. 12.   And afterwards, he tells them what they might look for: *Behold,* says he, *I send you forth as sheep in the midst of wolves.* Matt. x. 16.   And, in general, there is no following of Christ, but with his badge and burden.   Something is to be left, we ourselves are to be left—*Whosoever will be my disciple, let him deny himself;* and somewhat to take—*Take up his cross and follow me.* Matt. xvi. 24.   And doth not the Apostle give his scholars this universal lesson, as an infallible truth, *All that will live godly in Jesus Christ, shall suffer persecution?* Look, in the close of that roll of believers conquering in suffering, what a cluster of sufferings and torture you have. Heb. xi. 36, &c. Thus in the primitive times, the trial, and fiery trial, even literally so, continued long.   Those wicked emperors hated the very innocency of Christians; and the people, though they knew their blameless carriage, yet, when any evil came, would pick this quarrel, and still cry, *Christianos ad leones.*

Now this, if we look to inferior causes, is *not strange*, the malignant, ungodly world hating holiness, *hating the light*, yea, the very shadow of it. And the more the children of God walk like their Father and their home, the more unlike must they, of necessity, become to the world about them, and therefore become the very mark of all their enmities and malice.

And thus, indeed, the godly, though the *sons of peace*, are the improper causes, the occasion of much noise and disturbance in the world ; as their Lord, the Prince of Peace, avows it openly of himself in that sense, *I came not to send peace, but a sword, to set a man at variance with his father, and the daughter against the mother*, &c. Matt. x. 34. If a son in a family begin to inquire after God, and withdraw from their profane or dead way, oh, what a clamour rises presently ! " Oh, my son, or daughter, or wife, is become a plain fool," &c. And then is all done that may be, to quell and vex them, and make their life grievous to them.

The exact holy walking of a Christian really condemns the world about him ; shows the disorder and foulness of their profane ways. The life of religion, set by the side of dead formality, discovers it to be a carcass, a lifeless appearance ; and, for this, neither grossly wicked, nor decent, formal persons, can well digest it. There is in the life of a Christian a convincing light, that shows the deformity of the works of darkness, and a piercing heat, that scorches the ungodly, and stirs and troubles their consciences. This they cannot endure, and hence rises in them a contrary fire of wicked hatred, and hence the trials, the fiery trials of the godly. If they could get those precise persons removed out of their way, they think they might then have more room, and live at more liberty: as it is, Rev. xi. 10, a *carousing* [χαροῦσιν]. What a dance there was about the two dead bodies of the Two Witnesses ! *The people and nations rejoiced and made merry, and sent gifts one to another, because these two Prophets tormented them that dwelt on the earth.* And from the same hearth, I mean the same wickedness of heart in the world, are the fires of persecution kindled against the saints in the world, and the bonfires of joy when they are rid of them.

And as this is an infernal fire of enmity against God, so it is blown by that spirit whose element it is. Satan stirs up and blows the coal, and raises the hatred of the ungodly against Christians.

But while he, and they in whom he powerfully works, are thus working for their vile ends in the persecution of the saints, HE who sovereignly orders all, is working in the same his wise and gracious ends, and attains them, and makes the malice of his enemies serve his ends and undo their own. It is true, that by the heat of persecution many are scared from embracing religion : such as love themselves and their present ease, and others that seemed to have embraced it, are driven to let it go and fall from it ; but yet, when all is well computed, religion is still upon the gaining hand. Those who reject it, or revolt from it, are such as have no true knowledge of it, or share in it, nor in that happiness in which it ends. But they that are indeed united to Jesus Christ, do cleave the closer to him, and seek to have their hearts more fastened to him, because of the trials that they are, or may probably be put to. And in their victorious patience appears the invincible power of religion where it hath once gained the heart, that it cannot be beaten or burnt out : itself is a fire more mighty than all the fires kindled against it. The love of Christ conquers and triumphs in the hardest sufferings of life, and in death itself.

And this hath been the means of kindling it in other hearts, which were strangers to it, when they beheld the victorious patience of the saints, who conquered dying, as their Head did ; who wearied their tor⁻ mentors, and triumphed over their cruelty by a constancy far above it.

Thus, these fiery trials make the lustre of faith most appear, as gold shines brightest in the furnace; and if any dross be mixed with it, it is refined and purified from it by these trials, and so it remains, by means of the fire, purer than before. And both these are in the resemblance here intended ; that the fire of sufferings is for the advantage of believers, both as trying the excellency of faith, giving evidence of it, what it is, and also purifying it from earth and drossy mixtures, and making it more excellently what it is, raising it to a higher pitch of refinedness and worth. In these fires, as faith is tried, so the word on which faith relies is tried, and is found *all gold*, most precious, no refuse in it. The truth and sweetness of the promises are much confirmed in the Christian's heart, upon his experiment of them in his sufferings. His God is found to be as good as his word, being with him when he goes through the fire, (Isa. xliii. 2,) preserving him, so that he loses nothing except dross, which is a gainful loss, leaves only of his corruption behind him.

Oh ! how much worth is it, and how doth it endear the heart to God, to have found him sensibly present in the times of trouble, refreshing the soul with dews of spiritual comfort, in the midst of the flames of fiery trial.

One special advantage of these fires is, the purifying of a Christian's heart from the love of the world and of present things. It is true, the world at best is base and despicable, in respect to the high estate and hopes of a believer ; yet still there is somewhat within him, that would bend him downwards, and draw him to too much complacency in outward things, if they were much to his mind. Too kind usage might sometimes make him forget himself and think himself at home, at least so much as not to entertain those longings after home, and that ardent progress homewards, that become him. It is good for us, certainly, to find hardship, and enmities, and contempts here, and to find them frequent, that we may not think them *strange*, but ourselves *strangers*, and may think it were strange for us to be otherwise entertained. This keeps the affections more clear and disengaged, sets them upward. Thus the Lord makes the world displeasing to his own, that they may turn in to him, and seek all their consolations in himself. Oh, unspeakable advantage !

II. The composure of a Christian, in reference to sufferings, is prescribed in these two following, *resolving and rejoicing:* 1. Resolving to endure them, reckoning upon them, *Think it not strange,* μὴ ξενίζεσθε ; 2. Rejoicing in them, χαίρετε, *Be glad, inasmuch,* &c.

Be not strangers in it.] Which yet naturally we would be. We are willing to hear of peace and ease, and would gladly believe what we extremely desire. It is a thing of prime concern, to take at first a right notion of Christianity. This many do not, and so either fall off quickly, or walk on slowly and heavily; they do not reckon right the charges, take not into the account the duties of doing and suffering, but think to perform some duties, if they may with ease, and have no other foresight; they do not consider that self-denial, that fighting against a man's self, and fighting vehemently with the world, those trials, fiery trials, which a Christian must encounter with. As they observe of other points, so Popery is in this very compliant with nature, which is a very bad sign in religion. We would be content it were true that the true Church of Christ had rather prosperity and pomp for her badge than the cross; much ease and riches, and few or no crosses, except they were painted and gilded crosses, such as that Church hath chosen, instead of real ones.

Most men would give religion a fair countenance, if it gave them fair weather; and they that do indeed acknowledge Christ to be the Son of God, as St. Peter did, yet are naturally as unwilling as he was to hear the hard news of suffering; and if their advice might have place, would readily be of his mind, *Be it far from thee, Lord.* Matt. xvi. 22, 23. His good confession was not, but this kind advice was *from flesh and blood,* and from an evil spirit, as the sharp answer tells, *Get thee behind me, Satan, thou art an offence unto me.*

You know what kind of Messiah the Jews generally dreamed of, and therefore took offence at the meanness and sufferings of Christ, expecting an earthly king, and an outwardly flourishing state. And the disciples themselves, after they had been long with him, were still in that same dream, when they were contesting about imaginary places. Yea, they were scarcely well out of it, even after his suffering and death: all the noise and trouble of that had not well awaked them. *We trusted it had been he which should have restored Israel.* Luke xxiv. 21.

And, after all that we have read and heard of ancient times, and of Jesus Christ himself, his sufferings in the flesh, and of his Apostles and his saints, from one age to another, yet still we have our inclinations to this practice of driving troubles far off from our thoughts, till they come upon our backs, fancying nothing but rest and ease, till we be shaken rudely out of it.

How have we of late flattered ourselves, many of us one year after another, upon slight appearances, Oh, now it will be peace! And, behold, still trouble hath increased, and these thoughts have proved the lying visions of our own hearts, while *the Lord hath not spoken of it.* Ezek. xiii. 7. And thus, of late, have we thought it at hand, and taken ways of our own to hasten it, which, I fear, will prove fool's haste, as you say.

You that know the Lord, seek him earnestly for the averting of further troubles and combustions, which, if you look aright, you will find threatening us as much as ever. And withal, seek hearts prepared and fixed for days of trial, *fiery trial.* Yea, though we did obtain some breathing of our outward peace, yet shall not the followers of Christ want their trials from the hatred of the ungodly world. *If it persecuted me,* says he, *it will also persecute you.* John xv. 20.

Acquaint, therefore, your thoughts and hearts with sufferings, that when they come, thou and they not being strangers, may agree and comply the better. Do not afflict yourselves with vain fears beforehand of troubles to come, and so make uncertain evils a certain vexation by advance ; but thus forethink the hardest trial you are likely to be put to for the name and cause of Christ, and labour for a holy stability of mind, for encountering it if it should come upon you. Things certainly fall the lighter on us, when they fall first upon our thoughts. In this way, indeed, of an imagined suffering, the conquest beforehand may be but imaginary, and thou mayest fail in the trial. Therefore, be still humble and dependent on the strength of Christ, and seek to be previously furnished with much distrust of thyself, and much trust in him, with much denial of thyself, and much love to him ; and this preparing and training of the heart may prove useful, and make it more dexterous, when brought to a real conflict. In all, both beforehand and in the time of the trial, make thy Lord Jesus all thy strength. That is our only way in all to be conquerors, *to be more than conquerors, through him that loved us.* Rom. viii. 37.

Think it not strange, for it is not. Suit your thoughts to the experience and verdict of all times, and to the warnings that the Spirit of God hath given us in the Scriptures, and our Saviour himself from his own mouth, and in the example which he showed in his own person. But the point goes higher.

Rejoice.] Though we think not the sufferings *strange,* yet, may we not well think that rule somewhat strange, to *rejoice* in them ? No, it will be found as reasonable as the other, being duly considered. And it rests upon the same ground, which will bear both. *Inasmuch as you are partakers of the sufferings of Christ.*

If the children of God consider their trials, not in their natural bitterness, but in the sweet love from whence they spring, and the sweet fruits that spring from them, that we are our Lord's gold, and that he tries us in the furnace to purify us, (as in the former verse,) this may beget not only patience, but gladness even in the sufferings. But add we this, and truly it completes the reason of this way of rejoicing in our saddest sufferings, that in them we are *partakers of the sufferings of Christ.*

So then, 1. Consider this twofold connected participation, of the sufferings of Christ and of the after-glory. 2. The present joy, even in sufferings, springing from that participation.

I need not tell you, that this communion in sufferings, is not in point of expiation, or satisfaction to Divine justice, which was the peculiar end of the sufferings of Christ *personal,* but not of the common sufferings of Christ *mystical. He bare our sins in his own body on the tree,* and in bearing them, took them away : we bear his sufferings, as his body united to him by his Spirit. Those sufferings, which were his personal burden, we partake the sweet fruits of ; they are accounted ours, and we are acquitted by them ; but the endurance of them was his high and incommunicable task, in which none at all were with him. Our communion in these as fully completed by himself in his natural body, is the ground of our comfort and joy in those sufferings that are completed in his mystical body, the Church.

This is indeed our joy, that we have so light a burden, so sweet an exchange; the weight of sin quite taken off our backs, and all bound on his cross only, and our crosses, the badges of our conformity to him, laid indeed on our shoulders, but the great weight of them likewise held up by his hand, that they overpress us not. These fires of our trial may be corrective, and purgative of the remaining power of sin, and they are so intended; but Jesus Christ alone, in the sufferings of his own cross, was the burnt-offering, *the propitiation for our sins.*

Now, although he hath perfectly satisfied for us, and saved us by his sufferings, yet this conformity to him in the way of suffering is most reasonable. Although our holiness doth not stand in point of law, nor come in at all in the matter of justifying us, yet we are called and appointed to holiness in Christ, as assimilating us to him, our glorious Head; and we do really receive it from him, that we may be like him. So these our sufferings bear a very congruous likeness to him, though in no way as an accession to his in expiation, yet as a part of his image; and therefore the Apostle says, even in this respect, that we are *predestinated to be conformed to the image of his Son.* Rom. viii. 29. Is it fit that we should not follow where our Captain led, and went first, but that he should lead through rugged, thorny ways, and we pass about to get away through flowery meadows? As his natural body shared with his head in his sufferings, so ought his body mystical to share with him, as its Head,—the buffetings and spittings on his face, the thorny crowns on his head, a pierced side, nailed hands and feet: if we be parts of him, can we think that a body finding nothing but ease, and bathing in delights, can agree to a Head so tormented? I remember what that pious Duke said at Jerusalem, when they offered to crown him king there, *Nolo auream, ubi Christus spineam:* No crown of gold, where Christ Jesus was crowned with thorns.

This is the way we must follow, or else resolve to leave him; the way of the Cross is the royal way to the Crown. He said it, and reminded them of it again, that they might take the deep impression of it: *Remember what I said unto you, the servant is not greater than the Lord. If they have persecuted me, they will also persecute you; if they have kept my saying, they will keep yours also.* John xv. 20. And particularly in point of reproaches: *If they have called the master Beelzebub, how much more shall they call them of his household?* Matt. x. 24. A bitter scoff, an evil name, reproaches for Christ, why do these fret thee? They were a part of thy Lord's entertainment while he was here. Thou art, even in this, a *partaker of his sufferings*, and in this way is he bringing thee forward to the partaking of his glory. That is the other thing.

When his glory shall be revealed.] Now that he is hidden, little of his glory is seen. It was hidden while he was on earth, and now it is hidden in heaven, where he is. And as for his body here, his Church, it hath no pompous dress, nor outward splendour; and the particular parts of it, the saints, are poor despised creatures, the very refuse of men in outward respects and common esteem. So he himself is not seen, and his followers, the more they are seen and looked on by the world's eye, the more meanness appears. True, as in the days of his humiliation some rays were breaking forth through the veil of his flesh and the cloud of his low, despicable condition, thus it is sometimes with his followers : a glance of his image strikes the very eye of the world, and forces some acknowledgment and a kind of reverence in the ungodly ; but, commonly, Christ and his followers are covered with all the disgraces and ignominies the world can put on them.   But there is a day wherein he will appear, and it is at hand ; and then *he shall be glorious,* even *in his* despised *saints,* and *admired in them that believe,* 2 Thess. i. 10 : how much more in the matchless brightness of his own glorious person !

In the mean time, he is hidden, and they are hidden in him : *Our life is hid with Christ in God.*   Col. iii. 3.   The world sees nothing of his glory and beauty, and even his own see not much ; they have but a little glimmering of him, and of their own happiness in him ; know little of their own high condition, and what they are born to.   But in that bright day, he shall shine forth in his royal dignity, and *every eye shall see him,* and be overcome with his splendour.   Terrible shall it be to those that formerly despised him and his saints, but to them it shall be the gladdest day that ever arose upon them, a day that shall never set or be benighted ; the day they so much longed and looked out for, the full accomplishment of all their hopes and desires.   Oh, how dark were all our days without the hope of this day !

Then, says the Apostle, *ye shall rejoice* with exceeding *joy;* and to the end you may not fall short of that joy in the participation of glory, fall not back from a cheerful progress in the communion of those sufferings that are so closely linked with it, and will so surely lead unto it, and end in it.   For in this the Apostle's expressions, this glory and joy is set before them, as the great matter of their desires and hopes, and the certain end of their present sufferings.

Now, upon these grounds, the admonition will appear reasonable, and not too great a demand, *to rejoice* even *in sufferings.*

It is true, that passage in the Epistle to the Hebrews, ch. xii. 11, opposes present affliction to joy.   But, 1st, If you mark, it is but in the appearance, or outward visage, *It seemeth not to be matter of joy, but of grief.*   To look upon, it hath not a smiling countenance ; yet joy may be under it.   And, 2. Though to the flesh it is what it seems, grief, and not joy, yet there may be under it spiritual joy ; yea, the affliction itself may help and advance that joy.   3. Through the natural sense of it, there will be some alloy or mixture of grief, so that the joy cannot be pure and complete, but yet there may be joy even in it.   This the Apostle here clearly grants : *Rejoice* now *in* suffering that you may *rejoice exceedingly after* it, ἀγαλλιώμενοι, *leaping for joy.*   Doubtless, this joy, at present, is but a little parcel, a drop of that sea of joy.   Now it is joy, but more is reserved.   Then, *they shall leap for joy.*   Yet even at present, rejoice in *trial,* yea, in *fiery trial.*   This may be done.   The children of God are not called to so sad a life as the world imagines : besides what is laid up for them in heaven, they have, even here, their rejoicings and songs in their distresses, as those prisoners had their psalms even at midnight, after their stripes, and in their chains, before they knew of a sudden deliverance, (Acts xvi. 25.)   True, there may be a darkness within, clouding all the matter of their joy, but even that darkness is the seed-time of after-joy : light is sown in that darkness, and shall spring up : and not only shall they have a rich crop at full harvest, but even some first-fruits of it here, in pledge of the harvest.

And this they ought to expect, and to seek after with minds humble and submissive as to the measure and time of it, that they may be partakers of spiritual joy, and may by it be enabled to go patiently, yea, cheerfully, through the tribulations and temptations that lie in their way homeward. And for this end they ought to endeavour after a more clear discerning of their interest in Christ, that they may know they partake of him, and so that, in suffering, they are partakers of his sufferings and shall be partakers of his glory.

Many afflictions will not cloud and obstruct this, so much as one sin ; therefore, if ye would walk cheerfully, be most careful to walk holily. All the winds about the earth make not an earthquake, but only that within.

Now this Joy is grounded on this communion [1.] in sufferings, then, [2.] in glory.

[1.] Even in sufferings themselves. It is a sweet, a joyful thing to be a sharer with Christ in any thing. All enjoyments wherein he is not are bitter to a soul that loves him, and all sufferings with him are sweet. The worst things of Christ are more truly delightful than the best things of the world ; his afflictions are sweeter than their pleasures, his *reproach* more glorious than their honours, and more rich than their treasures, as Moses accounted them. Heb. xi. 26. Love delights in likeness and communion, not only in things otherwise pleasant, but in the hardest and harshest things, which have not any thing in them desirable, but only that likeness. So that this thought is very sweet to a heart possessed with this love : What does the world by its hatred, and persecutions, and revilings for the sake of Christ, but make me more like him, give me a greater share with him, in that which he did so willingly undergo for me ? *When he was sought for to be made a king*, as St. Bernard remarks, *he escaped ; but when he was sought to be brought to the cross, he freely yielded himself.* And shall I shrink and creep back from what he calls me to suffer for his sake ! Yea, even all my other troubles and sufferings, I will desire to have stamped thus, with this conformity to the sufferings of Christ, in the humble, obedient, cheerful endurance of them, and the giving up my will to my Father's.

The following of Christ makes any way pleasant. His faithful followers refuse no march after him, be it through deserts, and mountains, and storms, and hazards, that will affright self-pleasing, easy spirits. Hearts kindled and actuated with the Spirit of Christ, will *follow him wheresoever he goeth.*

As he speaks it for warning to his Disciples, *If they persecuted me, they will persecute you,* so he speaks it for comfort to them, and sufficient comfort it is, *If they hate you, they hated me before you.* John xv. 18, 20.

[2.] Then add the other : see whither it tends. *He shall be revealed in his glory,* and ye shall even overflow with joy in the partaking of that glory. Therefore, rejoice now in the midst of all your sufferings.

Stand upon the advanced ground of the promises and the covenant of Grace, and by faith look beyond this moment, and all that is in it, to that day wherein *everlasting joy shall be upon your heads,* a crown of it, and *sorrow and mourning shall flee away.* Isa. li. 11. Believe in this day, and the victory is won. Oh ! that blessed hope, well fixed and exercised, would give other manner of spirits. What zeal for God would it not inspire ! What invincible courage against all encounters ! How soon will this pageant of the world vanish, that men are gazing on, these pictures and fancies of pleasures and honours, falsely so called, and give place to the real glory of the sons of God, when this blessed Son, who is God, shall be seen appearing in full majesty, and all his brethren in glory with him, all clothed in their robes ! And if you ask, Who are they ? Why, *these are they who came out of great tribulation, and have washed their robes in the blood of the Lamb.* Rev. vii. 14.

Ver. 14. If ye be reproached for the name of Christ, happy are ye ; for the Spirit of glory and of God resteth upon you : on their part he is evil spoken of, but on your part he is glorified.

15. But let none of you suffer as a murderer, or as a thief, or as an evil-doer, or as a busy-body in other men's matters.

16. Yet if any man suffer as a Christian, let him not be ashamed ; but let him glorify God on this behalf.

THE WORD is the Christian's magazine, both of instructions and of encouragements, whether for *doing* or for *suffering;* and this Epistle is rich in both. Here, what the Apostle had said concerning suffering in general, he specifies in the particular case of suffering *reproaches.* But this seems not to come up to the height of that expression which he hath used before : he spoke of *fiery trial,* but this of *reproach* seems rather fit to be called an *airy trial,* the blast of vanishing words. Yet, upon trial, it will be found to be (as here it is accounted) a very sharp, a *fiery trial.*

First, then, of this particular kind of suffering ; and *Secondly,* of the comfort and advice furnished against it.

If ye be reproached.] If we consider both the nature of the thing and the strain of the Scriptures, we shall find that reproaches are amongst the sharpest sort of sufferings, and are indeed *fiery trials. The tongue is a fire,* says St. James, and reproaches are the flashes of that fire ; they are a subtle kind of flame, like that lightning which, as naturalists say, crusheth the bones, and yet breaks not the flesh ; they wound not the body, as do tortures and whips, but through a whole skin, they reach the spirit of a man, and cut it. So Psalm xlii. 10 : *As with a sword in my bones, mine enemies reproach me.* The fire of reproaches preys upon and dries up the *precious ointment of a good name,* to use Solomon's comparison, Eccl. vii. 4. A good name is in itself good, a prime outward good ; and take us according to our natural temper and apprehensions, (according to which we feel things,) most men are, and some excessively, too tender and delicate in it. Although, truly, I take it rather to be a weakness than true greatness of spirit, as many fancy it, to depend much on the opinion of others, and to feel it deeply, yet, I say, considering that it is commonly thus with men, and that there are the remains of this, as of other frailties in the children of God, it cannot well be but reproaches will ordinarily much afflict men, and to some kind of spirits, possibly, be more grievous than great bodily pain or suffering.

And inasmuch as they are thus grievous, the Scripture accounts them so, and very usually reckons them amongst sufferings : it is apt to name them more than any other kind of suffering, and that with good reason, not only for their piercing nature, (as we have said,) but withal for their frequency and multitude ; and some things we suffer do, as flies, more trouble by their number than by their weight.

Now, there is no one kind of suffering, of such constancy, and commonness, and abundance, as reproaches are. When other persecutions cease, yet these continue ; when all other fires of martyrdom are put out, these burn still. In all times and places, the malignant World is ready to revile religion ; not only avowed enemies of it, but the greatest part even of those that make a vulgar profession of it : they that outwardly receive the *form* of religion, are yet, many of them, inwardly haters of the *power* of it, and Christians who are such merely in name, will scorn and reproach those that are Christians indeed.

And this is done with such ease by every one, that these arrows fly thick : every one that hath a tongue can shoot them, even base *abjects* (Psal. xxxv. 15); and *the drunkards make songs*, as Jeremiah complains. The meanest sort can reach this point of persecution, and be active in it against the children of God. They who cannot or dare not offer them any other injury, will not fear, nor spare, to let fly a taunt or bitter word. So that whereas other sufferings are rarer, these meet them daily :—*While they say daily unto me, Where is thy God?* Psal. xlii. 10.

We see, then, how justly reproaches are often mentioned amongst and beyond other trials, and accounted persecution. See Matt. v. 10, 11 : *Blessed are ye when men shall revile you, and persecute you, and shall say all manner of evil against you falsely, for my sake.* In the history of the casting out of Hagar and her son, Gen. xxi. 9, all we find laid to Ishmael's charge is, *Sarah saw him mocking.* And as *he that was born after the flesh* did then, in this manner, *persecute him that was born after the Spirit,* (Gal. iv. 29,) even so it is now. And thus are reproaches mentioned amongst the sufferings of Christ in the Gospel, and not as the least : the railings and mockings that were darted at him, and fixed to the Cross, are mentioned more than the very nails that fixed him. And so, Heb. xii. 2, *The shame* of the Cross : though he was above it, and despised it, yet that *shame* added much to the burden of it. So, ver. 3 : *Consider him who endured the contradiction of sinners.*

Now the other thing is, that this is the lot of Christians, as it was of Christ. And why should they look for more kindness and better usage, and think to find acclamations and applauses from the World, which so vilified their Lord ? Oh, no ! The vain heart must be weaned from these, to follow Christ. If we will indeed follow him, it must be tamed to share with him in this point of suffering, not only mistakes and misconstructions, but bitter scoffings and reproaches. Why should not our minds ply and fold to this upon that very reason which he so reasonably presses again and again on his disciples ? *The servant is not greater than his master.*   And, in reference to this very thing, he adds : *If they have called the Master Beelzebub, how much more will they speak so of his servants !* Matt. x. 24, 25.

Infer. 1.   Seeing it is thus, I shall first press upon the followers of Christ, the Apostle's rule here, to keep their suffering spotless, that it may not be comfortless.   Resolve to endure it, but resolve, likewise, that it shall be on your part innocent suffering.   *Suffer not as evil-doers.* Besides that the ways of wickedness are most unsuitable to your holy calling, look to the enmity about you, and gain even out of that evil, this great good of more circumspect and holy walking.   Recollect who you are and where you are, your own weakness and the world's wickedness.   This our Saviour represents, and upon it gives that suitable rule : *Behold, I send you forth as sheep in the midst of wolves ; be ye therefore wise as serpents, and harmless as doves.—Prudens simplicitas.* Know you not what exact eyes of others are upon you ?   Will you not thence learn exactly to eye yourselves and all your ways, and seek of God, with David, *to be led in righteousness, because of your enemies, your observers?* Psal. xxvii. 11.

This is the rule here : ver. 16.   *Suffer as Christians,* holily and blamelessly, that the Enemy may not know where to fasten his hold. As the wrestlers anointed their bodies, that the hands of their antagonists might not fasten upon them, thus, truly, they that walk and suffer as Christians anointed with the Spirit of Christ, their enemies cannot well fasten their hold upon them.

To you, therefore, who love the Lord Jesus, I recommend this especially, to be careful that all your reproaches may be indeed for Christ, and not for any thing in you unlike to Christ ; that there be nothing save the matter of your rod,   Keep the quarrel as clean and unmixed as you can, and this will advantage you much, both within and without, in the peace and firmness of your minds, and in the refutation of your enemies.   This will make you *as a brazen wall,* as the Lord speaks to the Prophet : *they shall fight against you, but shall not prevail.* Jer. xv. 20.

Keep far off from all impure, unholy ways.   *Suffer not as evil-doers,* no, nor as *busy-bodies.*   Be much at home, setting things at rights within your own breast, where there is so much work, and such daily need of diligence, and then you will find no leisure for unnecessary, idle pryings into the ways and affairs of others ; and further than your calling and the rules of Christian charity engage you, you will not interpose in any matters without you, nor be found proud and censorious, as the World is ready to call you.

Shun the appearances of evil ; walk warily and prudently in all things. Be not *heady, nor self-willed,* no, not in the best thing.   Walk not upon the utter brink and hedge of your liberty, for then you shall be in danger of overpassing it.   Things that are lawful may be inexpedient, and, in case there is fear of scandal, ought either to be wholly forborne, or used with much prudence and circumspection.   Oh, study in all things to adorn the Gospel, and under a sense of your own unskilfulness and folly, beg wisdom from above, that *Anointing that will teach you all things,* much of that *holy Spirit that will lead you in the way of all truth;* and then, in that way, whatsoever may befall you, *suffer it,* and however you may be vilified and reproached, *happy are ye, for the Spirit of glory and of God resteth upon you.*

Infer. 2. But if to be thus reproached is to be happy, then, certainly, their reproachers are not less unhappy. If on those resteth the *Spirit of glory and of God,* what spirit is in these, but the spirit of Satan, and of shame and vileness? Who is the basest, most contemptible kind of person in the world? Truly, I think, an avowed contemner and mocker of holiness. Shall any such be found amongst us?

I charge you all in this name of Christ, that you do not entertain godless prejudices against the people of God. Let not your ears be open to, nor your hearts close with, the calumnies and lies that may be flying abroad of them and their practices; much less open your mouths against them, or let any disgraceful word be heard from you. And when you meet with undeniable real frailties, know the *law of love,* and to practise it. Think, This is blameworthy, yet let me not turn it to the reproach of those persons, who, notwithstanding, may be sincere, much less to the reproach of other persons professing religion, and then cast it upon religion itself.

My brethren, beware of sharing with the ungodly in this tongue persecution of Christians. There is a day at hand, wherein the Lord will make inquiry after these things. If we shall be made accountable for *idle words,* (as we are warned, Matt. xii. 36,) how much more for bitter, malicious words uttered against any, especially against the saints of God, whom, however the World may reckon, he esteems his precious ones, his treasure! You that now can look on them with a scornful eye, which way shall you look when they shall be beautiful and glorious, and all the ungodly clothed with shame? Oh, do not reproach them, but rather come in and share with them in the way of holiness, and in all the sufferings and reproaches that follow it; for if you partake of their disgraces, you shall share in glory with them, in the day of their Lord's appearing.

The words contain two things, the *evil* of these reproaches supposed, and the *good* expressed. The *evil* supposed, that they are trials, and hot trials, has been treated of already. Now as to the good expressed.

Happy are ye.] Ye are happy even at present, in the very midst of them; they do not trouble your happy estate, yea, they advance it. Thus solid, indeed, is the happiness of the saints, that in the lowest condition it remains the same; in disgraces, in caves, in prisons and chains, cast them where you will, still they are happy. A diamond in the mire, sullied and trampled on, yet still retains its own worth. But this is more, that the very things that seem to make them miserable, do not only not do that, but, on the contrary, do make them the more happy: they are gainers by their losses, and attain more liberty by their thraldoms, and more honour by their disgraces, and more peace by their troubles. The World and all their enemies are exceedingly befooled in striving against them: not only can they not undo them, but by all their enmity and practices, they do them pleasure, and raise them higher. With what weapons shall they fight? How shall a Christian's enemies set upon him? Where shall they hit him, seeing that all the wrongs they do him, do indeed enrich and ennoble him, and that the more he is depressed, he flourishes the more.   Certainly, the blessedness of a Christian is matchless and invincible.

But how holds this, that a Christian is *happy in reproaches and by them*?   It is not through their nature and virtue, for they are evil ; (so Matt. v. 11 ;) but first, by reason of the cause ; secondly, by reason of the accompanying and consequent comfort.

[1.] By reason of the *cause* of these reproaches.   This we have negatively at verse 15.   *Not as an evil-doer ;*—that stains thy holy profession, damps thy comfort, and clouds thy happiness, disprofits thee, and dishonours thy Lord.   But the cause is stated positively, ver. 14, 16—*for the name of Christ.*   And what is there so rough which that will not make pleasant, to suffer with Christ and for Christ, who suffered so much and so willingly for thee ?   Hath he not gone through all before thee, and made all easy and lovely ?   Hath he not sweetened poverty, and persecution, and hatred, and disgraces, and death itself, perfumed the grave, and turned it from a pit of horror into a sweet resting bed ?   And thus love of Christ judgeth : it thinks all lovely which is endured for him, is glad to meet with difficulties, and is ambitious of suffering for him.   Scorn or contempt is a thing of hard digestion, but much inward heat of love digests it easily.   Reproaches are bitter, but the reproaches of Christ are sweet.   Take their true value, Heb. xi. 26 : *The reproaches of Christ are greater riches than the treasures of Egypt :* his very worst things, better than the best of the world.   A touch of Christ turns all into gold : his reproaches are *riches*, as it is expressed there, and *honour*, as here.   *Happy !* Not only afterwards shall ye be happy, but *happy are ye* at present ; and that, not only in apprehension of that after happiness, as sure, and as already present to Faith realizing it, but even [2.] in that they now possess the presence and comforts of the Spirit.

For the Spirit of glory.]   This accompanies disgraces for him ; *his* Spirit, *the Spirit of glory and of God.*   With your sufferings goes the name of Christ, and the Spirit of Christ : take them thus, when reproaches are cast upon you for his name, and you are enabled to bear them by his Spirit.   And surely his Spirit is most fit to support you under them, yea, to raise you above them.   They are ignominious and inglorious, he is the Spirit of glory ; they are human reproaches, he, the Divine Spirit, *the Spirit of glory and of God,* that is, the glorious Spirit of God.

And this is the advantage : the less the Christian finds esteem and acceptance in the world, the more he turns his eye inward, to see what is there ; and there he finds the world's contempt counterpoised by a weight of excellency and glory, even in this present condition, as the pledge of the glory before him.   The reproaches be fiery ; but the *Spirit of glory resteth upon you,* doth not give you a passing visit, but stays within you, and is indeed yours.   And in this the Christian can take comfort, and let the foul weather blow over, let all the scoffs and contempts abroad pass as they come, having a glorious Spirit within, such a guest honouring him with his presence, abode, and sweet fellowship, being, indeed, one with him.   So that rich miser at Athens could say,—when they scorned him in the streets, he went home to his bags, and hugging himself there at the sight, let them say what they would :—

> ——— Populus me sibilat; at mihi plaudo
> Ipse domi, simul ac nummos contemplor in arca.

How much more reasonably may the Christian say, Let them revile and bark, I have riches and honour enough that they see not. And this is what makes the world, as they are a malicious party, so to be an incompetent judge of the Christian's estate. They see the rugged, unpleasant outside only : the right inside their eye cannot reach. We were miserable indeed, were our comforts such as they could see.

And while this is the constant estate of a Christian, it is usually most manifested to him in the time of his greatest sufferings. Then (as we said) he naturally turns inward and sees it most, and accordingly finds it most. God making this happy supplement and compensation, that when his people have least of the world they have most of himself ; when they are most covered with the world's disfavour, his favour shines brightest to them. As Moses, when he was in the cloud, had nearest access and speech with God ; so when the Christian is most clouded with distresses and disgraces, then doth the Lord often show himself most clearly to him.

If you be indeed Christians, you will not be so much thinking, at any time, how you may be free from all sufferings and despisings, but rather, how you may go strongly and cheerfully through them. Lo, here is the way : seek a real and firm interest in Christ, and a participation of Christ's Spirit, and then a look to him will make all easy and delightful. Thou wilt be ashamed within thyself to start back, or yield one foot, at the encounter of a taunt or reproach for him. Thou wilt think, For whom is it ? Is it not for Him who for my sake hid not his face from shame and spitting ? And further, He died : now, how should I meet death for him, who shrink at the blast of a scornful word ?

If you would know whether this his Spirit is and resteth in you, it cannot be better known than, 1st, By that very love, ardent love to him, and high esteem of him, and, from thence, a willingness, yea, a gladness to suffer any thing for him. 2nd, This *Spirit of glory* sets the heart on glory. True glory makes heavenly things excellent in our thoughts, and sets the world, the better and the worse, the honour and the dishonour of it, at a low rate.

The spirit of the world is a base, ignoble spirit, even the highest pitch of it. Theirs are but poor designs who are projecting for kingdoms, compared to those of the Christian, which ascend above all things under the sun, and above the sun itself, and therefore he is not shaken with the threats of the world, nor taken with its offers. Excellent is the answer which St. Basil gives, in the person of those martyrs, to that emperor who made them (as he thought) great proffers to draw them off : " Why," say they, " dost thou bid us so low as pieces of the world ? We have learned to despise it all." This is not stupidity, nor an affected stoutness of spirit, but a humble sublimity, which the natural spirit of a man cannot reach unto.

But wilt thou say still, This stops me, I do not find this Spirit in me: if I did, then I think I could be willing to suffer any thing.

To this, for the present, I say not more than this: **Dost** thou desire
that Christ may be glorified, and couldst thou be content it were by thy
suffering in any kind thou mayest be called to undergo for him? Art
thou willing to give up thy own interest to study and follow Christ's,
and to sacrifice thine own credit and name to advance his? Art thou
unwilling to do any thing that may dishonour him, but not unwilling to
suffer any thing that may honour him? Or wouldst thou be thus?
Then, be not disputing, but up and walk on in his strength.

Now, if any say, But his name is dishonoured by these reproaches
—True, says the Apostle, *on their part it is so, but not on yours.* They
that reproach you, do their best to make it reflect on Christ and his
cause, but thus it is only *on their part.* You are sufferers for his name,
and so you *glorify* it: your faith and patience, and your victory by
these, do declare the power of Divine grace, and the efficacy of the
Gospel. These have made torturers ashamed, and induced some beholders to share with those who were tortured. Thus, though the
profane world intends, as far as it can reach, to fix dishonour upon the
profession of Christ, yet it sticks not, but on the contrary, he is glorified
by your constancy.

And as the ignominy fastens not, but the glory from the endurance
does, so Christians are obliged, and certainly are ready, according to
the apostle's zeal, ver. 16, *to glorify God on this behalf*, that, as he
is glorified in them, so they may glorify and bless him who hath dignified them so; that whereas we might have been left to a sad sinking
task, to have suffered for various guilts, our God hath changed the
tenor and nature of our sufferings, and makes them to be *for the name
of Christ.*

Thus, a spiritual mind doth not swell on a conceit of constancy and
courage, which is the readiest way of self-undoing, but acknowledges
all to be *gift*, even suffering: *To you it is given not only to believe but
to suffer*, and so *to bless him* on that behalf. Phil. i. 29. Oh! this love
grows in suffering. See Acts v. 41, *They went away rejoicing that
they were counted worthy to suffer shame for his name.*

Consider, it is but a short while, and the wicked and their scoffs
shall vanish; *they shall not be.* This shame will presently be over,
this disgrace is of short date, but the glory, and the *Spirit of glory*,
are eternal. What though thou shouldst be poor, and defamed, and
despised, and be the common mark of scorn and all injuries, yet the
end of them all is at hand. This is now thy part, but the scene shall
be changed. Kings here, real ones, are in the deepest reality but
stage kings; but when thou comest to alter the person thou now
bearest, here is the odds: thou wast a fool in appearance, and for a
moment, but thou shalt be truly a king for ever.

Ver. 17. For the time is come that judgment must begin at the house of God: and if
it first begin at us, what shall the end be of them that obey not the Gospel of God?

THERE is not only perfect equity, but withal a comely proportion and
beauty in all the ways of God, had we eyes opened to discern them,
particularly in this point of the sufferings and afflictions of the Church.
The Apostle here sets it before his brethren, *For the time is come*, &c.
In which words, there is, 1*st*, A parallel of the Lord's dealing with

his own and with the wicked.   2*nd*, A persuasion to due compliance and confidence, on the part of his own, upon that consideration.

The parallel is in the *order* and the *measure* of punishing; and it is so that, for the *order*, it begins at the house of God, and ends upon the ungodly.   And that carries in it this great difference in the *measure*, that it passes from the one on whom it begins, and rests on the other on whom it ends, and on whom the full weight of it lies for ever.   It is so expressed: *What shall the end be*, &c., which imports, not only that judgment shall overtake them in the end, but that it shall be their end; they shall end in it, and it shall be endless upon them.

The time is.] Indeed, the whole time of this present life is so, is the time of suffering and purifying for the Church, compassed with enemies who will afflict her, and subject to those impurities which need affliction.   The children of God are in their under-age here: all their time they are children, and have their frailties and childish follies; and therefore, though they are not always under the stroke of the rod, for that they were not able to endure, yet they are under the discipline and use of the rod all their time.   And whereas the wicked escape till their day of full payment, the children of God are in this life chastised with frequent afflictions.   And so, *the time* [ὁ καιρὸς] may here be taken according as the Apostle St. Paul uses the same word, Rom. viii. 18, παθήματα τοῦ νῦν καιροῦ, *the sufferings of this present time*.

But withal, it is true, and appears to be here implied, that there are peculiar set times, which the Lord chooses for the correcting of his Church.   He hath the days prefixed and written in his *Ephemerides*, hath his days of correcting, wherein he goes round from one church to another.   We thought it would never come to us, but we have now found the smart of it.

And here the Apostle may probably mean the times of those hot persecutions that were then begun, and continued, though with some intervals, for two or three ages.   Thus, in the sixth chapter of the Apocalypse, after the *white horse*, immediately follow at his heels, *the red*, and *the black*, and *the pale horse*.   And as it was upon the first publishing of the Gospel, so usually, upon the restoring of it, or upon remarkable reformations of the Church and revivings of religion, follow sharp and searching trials.   As the lower cause of this is the rage and malice of Satan, and of the ungodly world acted and stirred by him, against the purity and prevalency of religion, so it is from a higher Hand for better ends.   The Lord will discover the multitudes of hypocrites and empty professors, who will at such a time readily abound, when religion is upon an advancing way, and the stream of it runs strong.   Now, by the counter-current of troubles, such fall back and are carried away.   And the truth of grace, in the hearts of believers, receives advantage from these hazards and sufferings; they are put to fasten their hold the better on Christ, to seek more experience of the real and sweet consolations of the Gospel, which may uphold them against the counter-blasts of suffering.   Thus is religion made a more real and solid thing in the hearts of true believers: they are entered to that way of receiving Christ and his cross together, that they may see their bargain, and not think it a surprise.

Judgment.] Though all her sufferings are not such, yet, commonly, there is that unsuitable and unwary walking among Christians, that even their sufferings for the cause of God, though unjust from men, are from God just punishments of their miscarriages towards him, in their former ways; their self-pleasing and earthliness, having too high a relish for the delights of this world, forgetting their inheritance and home, and conforming themselves to the world, walking too much like it.

Must begin.] The Church of God is punished, while the wicked are free and flourish in the world, possibly all their days; or, if judgment reach them here, yet it is later; it *begins at the house of God.* [1.] This holds in those who profess his name, and are of the visible Church, compared with them who are without the pale of it, and are its avowed enemies. [2.] In those who profess a desire of a more religious and holy course of life within the Church, compared with the profane multitude. [3.] In those who are indeed more spiritual and holy, and come nearer unto God, compared with others who fall short of that measure. In all these respects it holds, that the Lord doth more readily exercise them with afflictions, and correct their wanderings, than any others.

And this truly is most reasonable; and the reason lies in the very name given to the Church, *the house of God.* For,

1. There is *equity* in such a proceeding. The sins of the Church have their peculiar aggravations, which fall not upon others. That which is simply a sin in strangers to God, is, in his people, the breach of a known and received law, and a law daily unfolded and set before them: yea, it is against their oath of allegiance; it is perfidy and breach of covenant, committed both against the clearest light, and the strictest bonds, and the highest mercies. And still the more particular the profession of his name and the testimonies of his love, these make sin the more sinful, and the punishment of it the more reasonable. The sins of the Church are all twice dipped, *Dibapha, have a double dye.* Isa. i. 18. They are breaches of the Law, and they are, besides, ungrateful and disloyal breaches of promise.

2. As there is unquestionable *equity,* so there is an evident *congruity* in this. God is ruler of all the world, but particularly of his Church, here called *his house,* wherein he hath a special residence and presence; and therefore it is most suitable that there he be specially observed and obeyed, and if disobeyed, that he take notice of it and punish it; that he suffer not himself to be dishonoured to his face by those of his own house. And therefore, whosoever escapes, his own shall not. *You only have I known, of all the families of the earth: therefore will I punish you for all your iniquities.* Amos iii. 2. It is fit that He who righteously judges and rules all nations, should make his justice most evident and exemplary in his own house, where it may best be remarked, and where it will best appear how impartial he is in punishing sin. So a king, (as the Psalmist, Psal. ci. 2,) that he may rule the land well, makes his *own house* exemplary. It is, you know, one special qualification of a bishop and pastor, to be *one that ruleth well his own house, having his children in subjection; for if a man know not how to rule his own house, how shall he take care*

of the Church of God? 1 Tim. iii. 4.   Now this, therefore, more eminently appears in the Supreme Lord of the Church ; he rules it as his
own house, and therefore when he finds disobedience there, he will first
punish that.   So he clears himself, and the wicked world being afterwards punished, their mouths are stopped with the preceding punishment of the Church.   Will he not spare his own ?   Yea, they shall be
first scourged.   *What then shall be the end of them that obey not the
Gospel ?*

And indeed, the purity of his nature, if it be every where contrary
to all sinful impurity, cannot but most appear in his peculiar dwelling-
house ; that he will especially have neat and clean.   If he hate sin all
the world over, where it is nearest to him he hates it most, and testifies
his hatred of it most : he will not endure it in his presence.   As cleanly,
neat persons cannot well look upon any thing that is nasty, much less
will they suffer it to come near them, or touch them, or to continue in
their presence in the house where they dwell : so the Lord, *who is of
purer eyes than to behold iniquity,* will not abide it within his own doors ;
and the nearer any come to him, the less can he endure any unholiness
or sinful pollution in them.   *He will be sanctified in all that come nigh
him,* Lev. x. 3 ; so especially in his ministers.   Oh, how pure ought they
to be, and how provoking and hateful to him are their impurities !
Therefore, in that commission to the destroyers, Ezek. ix. 6, to which
the Apostle here may have some reference, *Go,* says he, *slay the old
and the young, and begin at my sanctuary.*   They were the persons who
had polluted his worship, and there the first stroke lighted.   And in a
spiritual sense, because all his people are his own elect priesthood, and
should be *holiness to the Lord ;* when they are not really so, and do not
sanctify him in their walking, he sanctifies himself, and declares his
holiness in his judgments on them.

3. There is mercy in this dispensation too ; even under the habit of
judgment, Love walks secretly and works.   So loving and so wise a
Father will not undo his children by sparing the rod, but *because he
loves, rebukes and chastens.*   See Heb. xii. 6 ; Prov. iii. 11 ; Apoc.
iii. 19.   His Church is his house ; therefore that he may delight in it,
and take pleasure to dwell in it, and make it happy with his presence,
he will have it often washed and made clean, and the filth and rubbish
scoured and purged out of it ; this argues his gracious purpose of
abiding in it.

And as he doth it that he may delight in his people, so he doth it
that they may delight in him, and in him alone.   He imbitters the
breast of the World, to wean them ; makes the World hate them, that
they may the more easily hate it ; suffers them not to settle upon it,
and fall into a complacency with it, but makes it unpleasant to them by
many and sharp afflictions, that they may with the more willingness
come off and be untied from it, and that they may remember home the
more, and seek their comforts above ; that finding so little below, they
may turn unto him, and delight themselves in communion with him.
That the sweet incense of their prayers may ascend the more thick, he
kindles those fires of trials to them.   For though it should not be so,
yet so it is, that in times of ease they would easily grow remiss and
formal in that duty.

He is gracious and wise, knows what he does with them, and *the thoughts he thinks towards them.* Jer. xxix. 11. All is for their advantage, for the purifying of their iniquities. Isa. xxvii. 9. He purges out their impatience, and earthliness, and self-will, and carnal security ; and thus refines them for vessels of honour. We see in a jeweller's shop, that as there are pearls and diamonds, and other precious stones, so there are files, cutting instruments, and many sharp tools, for their polishing ; and while they are in the work-house, they are continual neighbours to them, and often come under them. The Church is God's jewellery, his work-house, where his jewels are a polishing for his palace and house ; and those he espe-cially esteems and means to make most resplendent, he hath oftenest his tools upon.

Thus observe it, as it is in the Church compared to other societies, so is it in a congregation or family ; if there be one more diligently seeking after God than the rest, he shall be liable to meet with more trials, and be oftener under afflictions than any of the company, either under contempt and scorn, or poverty and sickness, or some one pres-sure or other, outward or inward. And those inward trials are the nearest and sharpest which the World sees least, and yet the soul feels most. And yet all these, both outward and inward, have love, un-speakable love in them all, being designed to purge and polish them, and, by the increasing of grace, to fit them for glory.

Inf. 1. Let us not be so foolish as to promise ourselves impunity on account of our relation to God as his Church in covenant with him. If once we thought so, surely our experience hath undeceived us. And let not what we have suffered harden us, as if the worst were past. We may rather fear it is but a pledge and beginning of sharper judgment. Why do we not consider our unhumbled and unpurified condition, and tremble before the Lord ? Would we save him a labour, he would take it well. Let us purify our souls, that he may not be put to further purifying by new judgments. Were we busy reading our present condition, we should see very legible foresigns of further judgments ; as for instance : [1.] The Lord taking away his eminent and worthy servants, who are as the very pillars of the public peace and welfare, and taking away counsel, and courage, and union from the rest ; forsaking us in our meetings, and leaving us in the dark to grope and rush one upon another. [2.] The dissensions and jarrings in the State and Church, are likely, from imagination, to bring it to a reality. These unnatural burnings threaten new fires of public judgments to be kindled amongst us. [3.] That general despising of the Gospel and abounding of profaneness through-out the land, not yet purged, but as our great sin remaining in us, calls for more fire and more boiling. [4.] The general coldness and deadness of spirit ; the want of zeal for God, and of the communion of saints, that mutual stirring up of one another to holiness ; and, which is the source of all, the restraining of prayer, a frozen benumb-edness in that so necessary work, that preventer of judgments, that binder of the hands of God from punishments, and opener of them for the pouring forth of mercies.—Oh ! this is a sad condition in itself, though it portended no further judgment, the Lord hiding himself, and the spirit of zeal and prayer withdrawn, and scarcely any lamenting it, or so much as perceiving it! Where are our days either of solemn prayer or praises, as if there were cause for neither! And yet, there is a clear cause for both. Truly, my brethren, we have need, if ever we had, to bestir ourselves. Are not these kingdoms, at this present, brought to the extreme point of their highest hazard? And yet, who lays it to heart?

Inf. 2. Learn to put a right construction on all God's dealings with his Church, and with thy soul. With regard to his Church, there may be a time wherein thou shalt see it not only tossed, but, to thy thinking, covered and swallowed up with tears : but wait a little, it shall arrive safe. This is a common stumbling-stone, but walk by the light of the word, and the eye of Faith looking on it, and thou shalt pass by and not stumble at it. The Church mourns, and Babylon sings—*sits as a queen;* but for how long ? She shall *come down and sit in the dust;* and Sion shall be glorious, *and put on her beautiful garments,* while Babylon shall not look for another revolution to raise her again ; no, she shall never rise. *And a mighty angel took up a stone like a great mill-stone, and cast it into the sea, saying, Thus, with violence, shall that great city Babylon be thrown down, and shall be found no more at all.* Rev. xviii. 21.

Be not hasty : take God's work together, and do not judge of it by parcels. It is indeed all wisdom and righteousness ; but we shall best discern the beauty of it, when we look on it in the frame, when it shall be fully completed and finished, and our eyes enlightened to take a fuller and clearer view of it than we can have here. Oh, what wonder, what endless wondering will it then command !

We read of Joseph hated, and sold, and imprisoned, and all most unjustly, yet because, within a leaf or two, we find him freed and exalted, and his brethren coming as supplicants to him, we are satisfied. But when we look on things which are for the present cloudy and dark, our short-sighted, hasty spirits cannot learn to wait a little, till we see the other side, and what end the Lord makes. We see *judgment beginning at the house of God,* and this perplexes us while we consider not the rest, *What shall be the end of them that obey not the Gospel?* God begins the judgment on his Church for a little time, that it may end and rest upon his enemies for ever. And indeed, he leaves the wicked last in the punishment, that he may make use of them for the punishment of his Church. They are *his rod,* Isa. x. 5 ; but when he hath done that work with them, they are *broken and burnt,* and that when they are at the height of their insolence and boasting, not knowing what hand moves them, and smites his people with them for a while, *till the day of their consuming come,* ver. 16, 24, 25. Let the vile enemy that hath shed our blood and insulted over us, rejoice in their present impunity, and in men's procuring of it, and pleading for it ; * there is another Hand whence we may look for justice. And though it may be, that the judgment begun at us, is not

---

* I am ready to believe this refers to the escape of many who had deserved the severest punishments, for their part in the grand Irish rebellion, but were screened by the favour of some great men in the reign of King Charles II.—[Dr. Doddridge.]

yet ended, and that we may yet further, and that justly, find them our scourge, yet, certainly, we may and ought to look beyond that, unto the end of the Lord's work, which shall be the ruin of his enemies, and the peace of his people, and the glory of his name.

Of them that obey not the Gospel.] The end of all the ungodly is terrible, but especially the end of such as heard the Gospel, and have not received and obeyed it.

The word ἀπειθούντων hath in it both unbelief and disobedience; and these are inseparable. Unbelief is the grand point of disobedience in itself, and the spring of all other disobedience; and the pity is, that men will not believe it to be thus.

They think it an easy and a common thing to believe. Who doth not believe? Oh, but rather, who does? *Who hath believed our report?* Were our own misery and the happiness that is in Christ believed, were the riches of Christ and the love of Christ believed, would not this persuade men to forsake their sins and the world, in order to embrace him?

But men run away with an extraordinary fancy of believing, and do not deeply consider what news the Gospel brings, and how much it concerns them. Sometimes, it may be, they have a sudden thought of it, and they think, I will think on it better at some other time. But when comes that time? One business steps in after another, and shuffles it out. Men are not at leisure to be saved.

Observe the phrase, *The Gospel of God.* It is his embassy of peace to men, the riches of his mercy and free love opened and set forth, not simply to be looked upon, but laid hold on; the glorious holy God declaring his design of agreement with man, in his own Son, his blood streaming forth in it to wash away uncleanness. And yet this Gospel is not obeyed! Surely, the conditions of it must be very hard, and the commands intolerably grievous, that are not hearkened to. Why, judge you if they be. The great command is, to receive that salvation; and the other is this, to love that Saviour; and there is no more. Perfect obedience is not now the thing; and the obedience which is required, that love makes sweet and easy to us, and acceptable to him. This is proclaimed to all who hear the Gospel, but the greatest part refuse it: they love themselves, and their lusts, and this present world, and will not change, and so they perish!

They perish—What is that? What is their end? I will answer that but as the Apostle doth, and that is even by asking the question over again, *What shall be their end?*

There is no speaking of it; a curtain is drawn: silent wonder expresses it best, telling that it cannot be expressed. How then shall it be endured? It is true, that there be resemblances used in Scripture, giving us some glance of it. We hear of a *burning lake, a fire that is not quenched, and a worm that dies not.* Isa. lxvi. 24; Mark ix. 44; Rev. xxi. 8. But these are but shadows to the real misery of them that obey not the Gospel. Oh, to be filled with the wrath of God, the ever-living God, for ever! What words or thoughts can reach it? Oh, eternity, eternity! Oh that we did believe it!

This same parallel of the Lord's dealing with the righteous and the wicked, is continued in the following verse, in other terms, for the clearer expression, and deeper impression of it.

Ver. 18. ꞌAnd if the righteous scarcely be saved, where shall the ungodly and the sinner appear?

It is true, then, that they are *scarcely saved;* even they who endeavour to walk uprightly in the ways of God, that is, *the righteous,* they are *scarcely saved.* This imports not any uncertainty or hazard in the thing itself as to the end, in respect of the purpose and performance of God, but only, the great difficulties and hard encounters in the way ; that they go through so many temptations and tribulations, so many *fightings without and fears within.* The Christian is so simple and weak, and his enemies are so crafty and powerful, the oppositions of the wicked world, their hatreds, and scorns, and molestations, the sleights and violence of Satan, and, worst of all, the strength of his own corruptions ; and by reason of abounding corruption, there is such frequent, almost continual, need of purifying by afflictions and trials, that he has need to be still under physic, and is of necessity at some times drained and brought so low, that there is scarcely strength or life remaining in him.

And, truly, all outward difficulties would be but matter of ease, would be as nothing, were it not for the encumbrance of lusts and corruptions within. Were a man to meet disgraces and sufferings for Christ, how easily would he go through them, yea, and rejoice in them, were he rid of the fretting impatience, the pride, and self-love, of his own carnal heart ! These clog and trouble him worst, and he cannot shake them off, nor prevail against them without much pains, many prayers and tears ; and many times, after much wrestling, he scarcely finds that he hath gained any ground : yea, sometimes he is foiled and cast down by them.

And so, in all other duties, such a fighting and continual combat, with a revolting, backsliding heart, the flesh still pulling and dragging downwards ! When he would mount up he finds himself as a bird with a stone tied to its foot ; he hath wings that flutter to be upwards, but is pressed down by the weight fastened to him. What struggling with wanderings and deadness in hearing, and reading, and prayer ! And what is most grievous is, that, by their unwary walking, and the prevailing of some corruption, they grieve the Spirit of God, and provoke him to hide his face, and withdraw his comforts. How much pain to attain any thing, any particular grace of humility, or meekness, or self-denial ; and if any thing be attained, how hard to keep and maintain it against the contrary party ! How often are they driven back to their old point. If they do but cease from striving a little, they are carried back by the stream. And what returns of doubtings and misbelief, after they thought they were got somewhat above them, insomuch that sometimes they are at the point of giving over, and thinking it will never be for them. And yet, through all these they are brought safe home. There is another strength than theirs which bears them up, and brings them through. But these things, and many more of this nature, argue the difficulty of their course, and that it is not so easy a thing to come to heaven as most imagine it.

Inference. Thou that findest so little stop and conflict in it, who goest thy round of external duties, and all is well, art no more troubled; thou hast need to inquire, after a long time spent in this way, Am I right? Have I not yet to begin? Surely, this looks not like the way to heaven, as it is described in the Scripture: it is too smooth and easy to be right.

And if the way of the righteous be so hard, then how hard shall be the end of the ungodly sinner that walks in sin with delight! It were strange if they should be at such pains, and with great difficulty attain their end, and he should come in amongst them in the end; they were fools indeed. True, if it were so. But what if it be not so? Then the wicked man is the fool, and shall find that he is, when he shall not be able to *stand in judgment.* Where shall he appear, when to the end he might not appear, he would be glad to be smothered under the weight of the hills and mountains, if they could shelter him from appearing?

And what is the aim of all this which we have spoken, or can speak, on this subject, but that ye may be moved to take into deeper thoughts the concernment of your immortal souls? Oh that you would be persuaded! Oh that you would betake yourselves to Jesus Christ, and seek salvation in him! Seek to be covered with his righteousness, and to be led by his Spirit in the ways of righteousness. That will seal to you the happy certainty of the End, and overcome for you all the difficulties of the Way. What is the Gospel of Christ preached for? What was the blood of Christ shed for? Was it not, that by receiving him we might escape condemnation? Nay, this drew him from heaven: *He came that we might have life, and that we might have it more abundantly.* John x. 10.

Ver. 19. Wherefore let them that suffer according to the will of God commit the keeping of their souls to him in well-doing, as unto a faithful Creator.

NOTHING doth so establish the mind amidst the rollings and turbulency of present things, as both a look above them, and a look beyond them; above them to the steady and good Hand by which they are ruled, and beyond them to the sweet and beautiful end to which, by that Hand, they shall be brought. This the Apostle lays here as the foundation of that patience and peace in troubles, wherewith he would have his brethren furnished. And thus he closes this chapter in these words: *Wherefore let them that suffer according to the will of God commit the keeping of their souls to him in well-doing, as unto a faithful Creator.*

The words contain the true principle of Christian patience and tranquillity of mind in the sufferings of this life, expressing both wherein it consists, and what are the grounds of it.

I. It lies in this, *committing the soul unto God.* The word ἐν ἀγαθοποιΐα, which is added, is a true qualification of this, that it be *in well doing,* according to the preceding doctrine, which the Apostle gives clearly and largely, *ver.* 15, 16. If men would have inward peace amidst outward trouble, they must walk by the rule of peace,

and keep strictly to it.   If you would commit your soul to the keeping of God, know that he is a holy God, and an unholy soul that
walks in any way of wickedness, whether known or secret, is no fit
commodity to put into his pure hand to keep.   Therefore, as you
would have this confidence to give your holy God the keeping of your
soul, and that he may accept of it, and take it off your hand, beware
of wilful pollutions and unholy ways.   Walk so as you may not discredit your Protector, and move him to be ashamed of you, and dis-
claim you.   Shall it be said that you live under his shelter, and yet
walk inordinately ?   As this cannot well be, you cannot well believe it
to be.   Loose ways will loosen your hold of him, and confidence in
him.   You will be driven to question your interest, and to think,
Surely I do but delude myself: can I be under his safeguard, and
yet follow the course of the world, and my corrupt heart ?   Certainly,
let who will be so, HE will not be a guardian and patron of wickedness.   No, *He is not a God that hath pleasure in wickedness, nor shall
evil dwell with him.*   Psal. v. 4.   If thou give thy soul to him to keep,
upon the terms of liberty to sin, he will turn it out of his doors, and
remit it back to thee to look to as thou wilt thyself.   Yea, in the ways
of sin, thou dost indeed steal it back, and carriest it out from him ;
thou puttest thyself out of the compass of his defence, goest without
the trenches, and art, at thine own hazard, exposed to armies of mischiefs and miseries.

Inference.   This, then, is primarily to be looked to : you that would
have safety in God in evil times, beware of evil ways ; for in these it
cannot be.   If you will be safe in him, you must stay with him, and
in all your ways keep within him *as your fortress.*   Now, in the ways
of sin you run out from him.

Hence it is we have so little established confidence in God in times
of trial.   We take ways of our own, and will be gadding, and so we
are surprised and taken, as they that are often venturing out into the
enemy's reach, and cannot stay within the walls.   It is no idle repetition, Psal. xci. 1 : *He that dwelleth in the secret places of the Most
High, shall abide under the shadow of the Almighty.*   He that wanders not, but stays there, shall find himself there hidden from danger.
They that rove out from God in their ways, are disquieted and tossed
with fears ; this is the *fruit of their own ways ;* but the soul that is
indeed given to him to keep, keeps near him.

Study pure and holy walking, if you would have your confidence
firm, and have boldness and joy in God.   You will find that a little
sin will shake your trust, and disturb your peace, more than the
greatest sufferings : yea, in those sufferings, your assurance and joy
in God will grow and abound most if sin be kept out.   That is the
trouble-feast that disquiets the conscience, which, while it continues
good, is a *continual feast.*   So much sin as gets in, so much peace will
go out.   Afflictions cannot break in upon it to break it, but sin doth.
All the winds which blow about the earth from all points, stir it not ;
only that within the bowels of it makes the earthquake.

I do not mean that for infirmities a Christian ought to be discouraged.   But take heed of walking in any way of sin, for that will
unsettle thy confidence.   Innocency and holy walking make the soul

of a sound constitution, which the counter-blasts of affliction wear not out, nor alter. Sin makes it so sickly and crazy, that it can endure nothing. Therefore, study to keep your consciences pure, and they shall be peaceable, yea, in the worst of times commonly most peaceable and best furnished with spiritual confidence and comfort.

Commit the keeping of their souls.] The Lord is an entire protector. He keeps the bodies, yea, all that belongs to the Believer, and, as much as is good for him, makes all safe, *keeps all his bones, not one of them is broken*, Psal. xxxiv. 18; yea, says our Saviour, *The very hairs of your head are numbered.* Matt. x. 30. But that which, as in the Believer's account, and in God's account, so, certainly in itself is most precious, is principally committed and received into his keeping, *their souls.* They would most gladly be secured in that here, and that shall be safe in the midst of all hazards. Their chief concern is, that, whatsoever be lost, this may not : this is the jewel, and therefore the prime care is of this. If the soul be safe, all is well ; it is riches enough. *What shall it profit a man, though he gain the whole world*, says our Saviour, *and lose his own soul?* Mark viii. 36. And so, what shall it disprofit a man, though he lose the whole world, if he gain his soul ? Nothing at all.

When times of trial come, oh, what a bustle to hide this and that ; to flee, and carry away and make safe that which is but trash and rubbish to the precious soul ; but how few thoughts of that ! Were we in our wits, that would be all at all times, not only in trouble, but in days of peace. Oh, how shall I make sure about my soul ? Let all go as it may, can I but be secured and persuaded in that point, I desire no more.

Now, the way is this, *commit them to God:* this many say, but few do. Give them into his hand, *lay them up* there, (so the word is,) and they are safe, and may be quiet and composed.

In patience possess your souls, says our Saviour, Luke xxiv. 19. Impatient, fretting souls are out of themselves ; their owners do not possess them. Now, the way to possess them ourselves in patience, is, thus to commit them to him in confidence ; for then only we possess them, when he keeps them. They are easily disquieted and shaken in pieces while they are in our own hands, but in his hand, they are above the reach of dangers and fears.

Inference. Learn from hence, what is the proper act of Faith : it rolls the soul over on God, ventures it in his hand, and rests satisfied concerning it, being there. And there is no way but this, to be quiet within, to be impregnable and immovable in all assaults, and fixed in all changes, believing in his free love. Therefore, be persuaded to resolve on that ;—not doubting and disputing, Whether shall I believe or not ? Shall I think he will suffer me to lay my soul upon him to keep, so unworthy, so guilty a soul ? Were it not presumption ?—Oh, what sayest thou ? Why dost thou thus dishonour him, and disquiet thyself ? If thou hast a purpose to walk in any way of wickedness, indeed thou art not for him ; yea, thou comest not near him to give him thy soul. But wouldst thou have it delivered from sin, rather than from trouble, yea, rather than from hell ? Is that the chief safety thou seekest, to be kept from iniquity, from thine own iniquity, thy beloved sins? Dost thou desire to dwell in him, and walk with him? Then, whatsoever be thy guiltiness and unworthiness, come forward, and give him thy soul to keep. If he should seem to refuse it, press it on him. If he stretch not forth his hand, lay it down at his foot, and leave it there, and resolve not to take it back. Say, Lord, thou hast made us these souls, thou callest for them again to be committed to thee; here is one. It is unworthy, but what soul is not so? It is most unworthy, but therein will the riches of thy grace appear most in receiving it. And thus leave it with him, and know, he will make thee a good account of it. Now, should you lose goods, or credit, or friends, or life itself, it imports not; the main concern is sure, if so be thy soul is out of hazard. *I suffer these things for the Gospel,* says the Apostle: *nevertheless, I am not ashamed*—Why?—*for I know whom I have trusted, and am persuaded that he is able to keep that which I have committed to him against that day.* 2 Tim. i. 12.

II. The *Ground* of this Confidence, is in these two things, the *ability* and the *fidelity* of him in whom we trust. There is much in a persuasion of the power of God. Though few think they question that, there is in us secret, undiscovered unbelief, even in that point. Therefore the Lord so often makes mention of it in the Prophets. See Isa. l. 3, &c. And, in this point, the Apostle Paul is particularly express: *I am persuaded that he is able to keep,* &c. So this Apostle: *Kept by the power of God through faith unto salvation, ready to be revealed in the last time.* Chap. i. ver. 5. This is very needful to be considered, in regard of the many and great oppositions, and dangers, and powerful enemies, that seek after our souls; *He is able to keep them, for he is stronger than all, and none can pluck them out of his hand,* says our Saviour. John x. 29. This the Apostle here implies in that word, *Creator:* if he was able to give them being, surely he is able to keep them from perishing. This relation of a Creator, implies likewise a benign propension and good-will to the works of his hands; if he gave them us at first, when once they were not, forming them out of nothing, will he not give us them again, being put into his hand for safety?

And as he is powerful, he is no less faithful, *a faithful Creator,* Truth itself. Those who believe on him, he never deceives or disappoints. Well might St. Paul say, *I know whom I have trusted.* Oh, the advantage of Faith! It engages the truth and the power of God: his royal word and honour lies upon it, to preserve the soul that Faith gives him in keeping. If he remain able and faithful to perform his word, that soul shall not perish.

There be in the words other two grounds of quietness of spirit in sufferings. [1.] It is according to the will of God. The believing soul, subjected and levelled to that will, complying with his good pleasure in all, cannot have a more powerful persuasive than this, that all is ordered by his will. This settled in the heart would settle it much, and make it even in all things; not only to know, but wisely and deeply to consider, that it is thus, that all is measured in heaven, every drachm of thy troubles weighed by that skilful Hand, which doth all things by weight, number, and measure.

And then, consider him as thy God and Father, who hath taken special charge of thee, and of thy soul : thou hast given it to him, and he hath received it. And, upon this consideration, study to follow his will in all, to have no will but his. This is thy duty, and thy wisdom. Nothing is gained by spurning and struggling, but to hurt and vex thyself ; but by complying, all is gained—sweet peace. It is the very secret, the mystery of solid peace within, to resign all to his will, to be disposed of at his pleasure, without the least contrary thought. And thus, like two-faced pictures, those sufferings and troubles, and whatsoever else, while beheld on the one side as painful to the flesh, hath an unpleasant visage, yet, go about a little, and look upon it as thy Father's will, and then it is smiling, beautiful, and lovely. This I would recommend to you, not only for temporals, as easier there, but in spiritual things, your comforts and sensible enlargements, to love all that he does. It is the sum of Christianity, to have thy will crucified, and the will of thy Lord thy only desire. Whether joy or sorrow, sickness or health, life or death, in all, in all, *Thy will be done.*

The other ground of quietness is contained in the first word, which looks back on the foregoing discourse, *Wherefore*—what ? Seeing that your reproachings and sufferings are not endless, yea, that they are short, they shall end, quickly end, and end in glory, be not troubled about them, overlook them. The eye of faith will do it. A moment gone, and what are they ? This is the great cause of our disquietness in present troubles and griefs ; we forget their end. We are affected by our condition in this present life, as if it were all, and it is nothing. Oh, how quickly shall all the enjoyments, and all the sufferings of this life pass away, and be as if they had not been !

FIRST PETER

CHAPTER 5

Ver. 1. The elders which are among you I exhort, who am also an elder, and a witness of the sufferings of Christ, and also a partaker of the glory that shall be revealed.

THE Church of Christ being one body, is interested in the condition and carriage of each particular Christian, as a part of it, but more especially in respect to those who are more eminent and organic parts of it. Therefore, the Apostle, after many excellent directions given to all his Christian brethren to whom he writes, doth most reasonably and fitly add this express exhortation to those who had the oversight and charge of the rest : *The Elders which are among you,* &c.

The words contain a particular definition of the persons exhorted and the persons exhorting.

I. The persons exhorted : *The Elders among you. Elders* here, as in other places, is a name, not of age, but of office ; yet the office is named by that age which is, or ought to be, most suitably qualified for it, importing, that men, though not aged, yet, if called to that office, should be noted for such wisdom and gravity of mind and carriage, as may give that authority, and command that respect, which is requisite for persons in their calling : not *novices,* as St. Paul speaks : not as a light bladder, being easily blown up, as young unstable minds are ;

but such as young Timothy was in humility and diligence, as the Apostle testifies of him, Phil. ii. 20, and as he further exhorts him to be, 1 Tim. iv. 12 : *Let no man despise thy youth, but be an example of believers in word, in conversation, in charity, in faith, in purity.*

The name of *Elders* indifferently signifies either age or their calling : and the name of *ruling elders* sometimes denotes civil rulers, sometimes pastors of the Church ; as, amongst the Jews, both offices often met in the same person. Here, it appears that pastors are meant, as the exhortation, of *feeding the flock*, evidences ; which though it sometimes signifies *ruling*, and here may comprise it, yet is chiefly by doctrine. And then the title given to Christ, in the encouragement which is added, confirms this interpretation : *The Chief Shepherd.*

A due frame of spirit and carriage in the Elders, particularly the Apostles of the Church, is a thing of prime concern for the good of it. It is one of the heaviest threatenings, when the Lord declares, that he will give a rebellious people such teachers and prophets as they deserved, and indeed desired : *If there be a man to prophesy of wine and strong drink, such a one shall be a prophet,* says he to that people. Mic. ii. 11. And, on the other side, amongst the sweetest promises of mercy, this is not the least, to be furnished with plenty of faithful teachers. Though profane men make no reckoning of it, yet, were it in the hardest times, they who know the Lord will account of it as he doth, a sweet allay of all sufferings and hardship : *Though the Lord give you the bread of adversity and the water of affliction, yet shall not thy teachers be removed into a corner, but thine eyes shall see thy teachers.* Isa. xxx. 20. Oh ! how rich a promise is that, Jer. iii. 15, *I will give you pastors according to my own heart.*

This promise is to be pressed and sued for by earnest prayer. Were people much in this duty, pastors would find the benefit of it, and so the people themselves would receive back their prayers, with much gain, into their own bosom : they would have the returned benefit of it, as the vapours that go up from below, fall down upon the earth again in sweet showers, and make it fruitful. Thus, went there many prayers up for pastors, their doctrine would *drop as rain, and distil as dew,* (Deut. xxx. 2,) and the sweet influence of it would make fruitful the valleys, humble hearts receiving it. And, at this time, it is very needful that the Lord be much importuned for the continuance and increase of his favour in this his Church. As they who have power should be more careful of those due means which, in schools of learning, or otherwise, are needful for qualifying men for this service ; so, all in general, both people and pastors, and such as are offering themselves to that service, should chiefly beg from the Higher Academy, that teaching, abundance of that Spirit promised to those employed in that work, that might make them *able ministers of the New Testament.*

Oh ! it is an inestimable blessing, to have the saving light of the Gospel shining clear in the faithful and powerful ministry of it. They thought so, who said of their worthy teacher, They had rather for them, that the sun should not shine, than that he should not teach. *Satius solem non lucere, quam Chrysostomum non docere.*

2. The person exhorting : *I, a co-presbyter,* or *fellow-elder* with you. The duty of mutual exhortation lies on Christians at large, though it

be little known amongst the greatest part; but truly, Pastors should be, as in other duties, so particularly in this, eminent and exemplary in their intercourses and converse, saying often one to another, Oh! let us remember to what we are called; to how high and heavy a charge; to what holiness and diligence; how great is the hazard of our miscarriage, and how great the reward of our fidelity. They should be often whetting and sharpening one another by these weighty and holy considerations.

And a witness of the sufferings of Christ. He did indeed give witness to Christ, by suffering for him the hatred and persecutions of the world in the publishing of the Gospel, and so was a witness and martyr before the time that he was put to death: and this I exclude not. But that which is more particularly here intended, is, his certain knowledge of the sufferings of Christ, in his own person, as an eyewitness of them, and upon that knowledge, a publisher of them. Luke xxiv. 48. And thus these two suit with the two motives urged, to bear home the exhortation: the one couched in that expression, *the flock of God*, (ver. 2,) his purchase with those his sufferings whereof I was an eye-witness; the other motive, in the words, *a crown of glory*, &c., ver. 4. As if he had said, I may speak the more confidently of that, for I am one of those who have a real interest in it, and a firm belief of it, *a partaker of the glory that shall be revealed.* And these, indeed, are the things which give weight to a man's words, make them powerful and pressing.

A witness of the sufferings of Christ. The Apostles had a singular advantage in this, who were αὐτόπται, *eye-witnesses;* and St. Paul, who wanted that, had it supplied by a vision of Christ, in his conversion. A spiritual view of Christ crucified, is generally, I will not say, absolutely, necessary to make a minister of Christ, but certainly very requisite for the due witnessing of him, and the displaying of the excellency and virtue of his sufferings, and for so preaching the Gospel that there shall need no other crucifix;* after so clear and lively a way, as that it may in some measure suit the Apostle's word, Gal. iii. 1, *Before whose eyes Jesus Christ hath been evidently set forth crucified among you.*

Men commonly read, and hear, and may possibly preach, of the sufferings of Christ as a common story, and in that way it may a little move a man, and wring tears from his eyes. But faith hath another kind of sight of them, and so works another kind of affections; and without that, the very eye-sight of them had availed the Apostles nothing; for how many saw him suffer as they did, who reviled, or at least despised him! But by the eye of faith to see the only begotten Son of God, as *stricken and smitten of God, bearing our sorrows,* and *wounded for our transgressions,* Jesus Christ, *the righteous,* reckoned amongst the unrighteous and malefactors; to see him stripped naked, and scourged, and buffeted, and nailed, and dying; and all for us; this is the thing that will bind upon us most strongly all the

---

* Alluding to the custom of many Popish preachers, to carry a little crucifix into the pulpit with them.—[Dr. Doddridge.]

duties of Christianity and of our particular callings, and best enable us, according to our callings, to bind them upon others. But our slender view of these things occasions a light sense of them, and that, cold incitements to answerable duty. Certainly, deep impressions would cause lively expressions.

Would we willingly stir up our own hearts and one another to holy diligence in our station, study more thoroughly Christ as suffering and dying: that is the very life of the Gospel and of our souls; it is all we have to learn, and all we have to teach and press on you. *I determined to know nothing among you, save Jesus Christ and him crucified,* to make Christ's Cross the sum of all my learning.

A partaker of the glory to be revealed.] As he was a witness of those sufferings, so a partaker of the glory purchased by those sufferings; and therefore, as one insighted and interested in what he speaks, the Apostle might fitly speak of that peculiar duty to which those sufferings and that glory do peculiarly persuade. This is the only way of speaking of those things, not as a discourser or contemplative student, but as *a partaker* of them. There is another force in a pastor's exhortation either to his people or his brethren, who brings his message written upon his own heart; who speaks of the guilt of sin, and the sufferings of Christ for it, as particularly feeling his own guilt, and looking on those sufferings as taking it away; speaks of free grace, as one who either hath drunken of the refreshing streams of it, or at least is earnestly thirsting after it; speaks of the love of Christ, from a heart kindled with it, and of the glory to come, as one who looks to be a sharer in it, and longs earnestly for it, as one who hath all his joy and content laid up in the hopes of it.

And thus with respect to Christians conversing with each other in their mutual exhortings and comfortings, all is cold and dead that flows not from some inward persuasion and experimental knowledge of Divine things. But that gives an edge and a sweetness to Christian conference:—to be speaking of Jesus Christ, not only as a King and as a Redeemer, but as *their* King, and *their* Redeemer, in David's style, *My King and my God,* and of his sufferings as theirs, applied by faith, and acquitting them in St. Paul's style, *Who loved me and gave himself for me;* to be speaking of the glory to come as *their* inheritance, that of which they are *partakers,* their home; as strangers meeting together abroad, in some foreign country, delight to speak of their own land, their parentage and friends, and the rich patrimony there abiding them. *Peregrinis in terris nulla est jucundior recordatio quam suæ civitatis:* Nothing is more delightful, says Augustine, to travellers in distant countries, than the remembrance of their native land. And this ought to be the entertainment of Christians when they meet. Away with trifling, vain discourses; cause all to give place to these refreshing remembrances of our home. Were our hearts much on that rich inheritance above, it would be impossible to refrain our tongues, and to pass on so silent concerning it; to find matter of empty pratings, and be pleased with them, and to have no relish of this. Whither go your hearts? They are out of their way, and abase themselves, that turn so much downwards, and are not more above the sun, eyeing still that blessed land where our purchased inheritance lies.

Oh, seek after more clear knowledge of this glory, and of your interest in it, that your hearts may rejoice in the remembrance of it ; that it be not to you as the description of a pleasant land, such as men read of in history, and have no portion in : they like it well, and are pleased with it while they read, be it but some imagined country or commonwealth finely fancied. But know this country of yours to be real, and no device ; and seek to know yourselves to be partakers of it.

This confidence depends not upon a singular revelation, but on the power of faith, and the light of the Spirit of God, which clears to his children the things that he hath freely given them ; though some of them at times, some, it may be, all, or most of their time, do want it, God so disposing it, that they scarcely clearly see their right, till they be in possession ; see not their heaven and home, till they arrive at it, or are hard upon it. Yet, truly, this we may and ought to seek after in humility and submission, that we may have the *pledge and earnest of our inheritance;* not so much for the comfort within us, (though that is allowed,) as that it may wean our hearts from things below, may raise us to higher and closer communion with God, and enable us more for his service, and excite us more to his praises, even here. What were a Christian without the hope of this glory ? As one said, *Tolle religionem, et nullus eris: Take away religion, and you take away the man.* And, having this hope, what are all things here to him ? How poor and despicable the better and worse of this life, and this life itself ! How glad is he that it will quickly end ! And what were the length of it to him, but a long continuance of his banishment, a long detainment from his home, and how sweet is the message that is sent for him to come home !

The glory to be revealed! It is hidden for the present, wholly unknown to the children of this world, and even but little known to the children of God, who are heirs of it. Yea, they who know themselves *partakers of it,* yet know not much what it is ; only this, that it is above all they know or can imagine. They may see things which make a great show here ; they may hear of more than they see ; they may think or imagine more than either they hear or see, or can distinctly conceive of ; but still they must think of this glory as beyond it all. If I see pompous shows, or read or hear of them, yet this I say of them, These are not as my inheritance: oh! it is far beyond them. Yea, does my mind imagine things far beyond them, golden mountains and marble palaces, yet those fall short of my inheritance, for it is such *as eye hath not seen, nor ear heard, nor hath it entered into the heart of man to conceive.* Oh the brightness of that glory when it shall be revealed ! How shall they be astonished, who shall see it, and not partake of it ! How shall they be filled with everlasting joy, who are heirs of it ! Were the heart much upon the thoughts of that glory, what thing is there in this perishing world, which could either lift it up or cast it down ?

Ver. 2. Feed the flock of God which is among you, taking the oversight thereof, not by constraint, but willingly; not for filthy lucre, but of a ready mind;
3. Neither as being lords over God's heritage, but being ensamples to the flock.
4. And when the chief Shepherd shall appear, ye shall receive a crown of glory that fadeth not away.

In these words we have, I. The Duty enjoined : *Feed the flock of God which is among you, taking the oversight of it.* II. The due Qualifications for this duty : *Not by constraint, not for filthy lucre, not as lording it over God's heritage, but willingly, of a ready mind,* and as *being ensamples to the flock.* III. The high Advantage to be expected : *An unfading crown of glory, when the Chief Shepherd shall appear.*

I. The Duty enjoined. Every step of the way of our salvation hath on it the print of infinite majesty, wisdom, and goodness, and this amongst the rest ; that men, sinful, weak men, are made subservient in that great work of bringing Christ and souls to meet ; that by the *foolishness of preaching,* (or what appears so to carnal wisdom,) the chosen of God are called, and come unto Jesus, and are made *wise unto salvation ;* and that the life which is conveyed to them by the *word of life* in the hands of poor men, is by the same means preserved and advanced. This is the standing work of the ministry, and this the thing here bound upon them that are employed in it, *to feed the flock of God that is among them.* Jesus Christ descended to purchase a Church, and descended to provide and furnish it, to send down his Spirit : *He ascended and gave gifts,* particularly *for the work of the ministry ;* and the great use of them is this, *Feed the flock of God.*

Not to say any more of this usual resemblance of a flock, as importing the weakness and tenderness of the Church, the continual need she stands in of inspection, and guidance, and defence, and the tender care of the Chief Shepherd for these things ; the phrase enforces the present duty of subordinate pastors, their care and diligence in feeding that flock. The due rule of discipline not excluded, the main part of this duty is by doctrine, the leading them into the wholesome and *green pastures* of saving truths revealed in the Gospel, accommodating the way of teaching to their condition and capacity ; and with this they should be, as much as possible, particularly acquainted, and suit diligently and prudently their doctrine to it. They are to *feed the sheep,* those more advanced ; *to feed the lambs,* the younger and weaker ; to have special care of the infirm ; to learn of their Master, the great Shepherd, to *bind up that which is broken,* and *strengthen that which is sick,* (Ezek. xxxiv. 16,)—those that are broken in spirit, that are exercised with temptations ; and *gently to lead those that are with young,* (Isa. xl. 11,)—those in whom the inward work of grace is as in the conception, and they heavy and weak with the weight of it, and the many difficulties and doubtings which are frequent companions and symptoms of that work. Oh, what dexterity and skilfulness, what diligence, and, above all, what affection and bowels of compassion, are needful for this task ! *Who is sufficient for these things?* 2 Cor. ii. 16. Who would not faint and give over in it, were not our Lord *the Chief Shepherd ;* were not all our sufficiency laid up in his rich fulness, and all our insufficiency covered in his gracious acceptance ?

Inf. 1. This is the thing we have to eye and study, to set him before us, and to apply ourselves in his strength to this work :—not to seek to *please*, but to *feed;* not to delight the ears, but to feed *the souls* of his people; to see that the food be according to his appointment; not empty or subtile notions, not light, affected expressions, but wholesome truths, solid food, spiritual things spiritually conceived, and uttered with holy understanding and affection.

And we are to consider this, wherein lies a very pressing motive; it is *the flock of God:* not our own, to use as we please, but committed to our custody by him, who loves highly and prizes his flock, and will require an account of us concerning it; his bought, his purchased flock, and at so dear a rate, as the Apostle St. Paul uses this same consideration, in the same argument, Acts xx. 28: *The flock of God that he hath bought with his own blood.* How reasonable is it that we bestow our strength and life on that flock for which our Lord laid down his life; that we be most ready to draw out our spirits for them for whom he let out his blood! *Had I,* says that holy man, Bernard, *some of that blood poured forth on the cross, how carefully would I carry it! And ought I not to be as careful of those souls that it was shed for?* (Advent, Serm. 3.) Oh, that price which was paid for souls, which He, who was no foolish merchant, but wisdom itself, gave for them! Were that price more in our eyes, and more in yours, nothing would so much take either you or us, as the matter of our souls. In this would our desires and endeavours meet, we to use, and you to improve, the means of saving your precious souls.

Inf. 2. This mainly concerns us indeed, who have charge of many, especially finding the right cure of one soul within us so hard: but you are concerned in it, each for one. At least remember, this is the end of the ministry, that you may be brought unto Christ; that you may be led to the sweet pastures and pleasant streams of the Gospel; that you may be spiritually fed, and may grow in that heavenly life, which is here begun in all those in whom it shall hereafter be perfected.

And as we ought in preaching, so ought you in hearing, to propound this end to yourselves, that you may be spiritually refreshed, and walk in the strength of that Divine nourishment. Is this your purpose when you come hither? Inquire of your own hearts, and see what you seek, and what you find, in the public ordinances of God's house. Certainly, the most do not so much as think on the due design of them; they aim at no end, and therefore can attain none; they seek nothing, but sit out their hour, asleep or awake, as it may happen. Or, possibly, some seek to be delighted for the time, as the Lord tells the Prophet, to hear, *as it were, a pleasant song,* Ezek. xxxiii. 32, if the gifts and strain of the speaker be any thing pleasing. Or, it may be, they seek to gain some new notions, to add somewhat to their stock of knowledge, either that they may be enabled for discourse, or, simply, that they may know. Some, it may be, go a little further; they like to be stirred and moved for the time, and to have some touch of good affection kindled in them: but this lasts but *for a while,* till their other thoughts and affairs get in, and smother and quench it; they are not careful to blow it up and improve it. How many, when they have been a little affected with the word, go out and fall into other discourses and thoughts: they either take in their affairs secretly, as it were under their cloak, and their hearts keep up a conference with them, or, if they forbear this, yet, as soon as they go out, they plunge themselves over head and ears in the world, and lose all which might have any way advantaged their spiritual condition. It may be, one will say, It was a good sermon. Is that to the purpose? But what think you it hath for your praise or dispraise? Instead of saying, Oh, how well was that spoken! you should say, Oh, how hard is repentance! how sweet a thing is faith! how excellent the love of Jesus Christ! That were your best and most real commendation of the sermon, with true benefit to yourselves.

If some of you be careful of repeating, yet, rest not on that : if you be able to speak of it afterwards upon occasion, there is somewhat requisite beside and beyond this, to evidence that you are indeed fed by the word, as the flock of God. As when sheep, you know, or other creatures, are nourished by their pasture, the food they have eaten appears, not in the same fashion upon them, not in grass, but in growth of flesh and fleece ; thus the word would truly appear to feed you, not by the bare discoursing of the word over again, but by the temper of your spirits and actions, if in them you really grow more spiritual, if humility, self-denial, charity, and holiness, are increased in you by it ; otherwise, whatsoever literal knowledge you attain, it avails you nothing. Though you heard many sermons every day, and attained further light by them, and carried a plausible profession of religion, yet, unless by the Gospel you be transformed into the likeness of Christ, and grace be indeed growing in you, you are but, as one says of the cypress trees, fair and tall, but fruitless.*

Are you not grieved and afraid, or may not many of you be so, who have lived many years under a fruitful ministry, and yet are as earthly and selfish, as unacquainted with God and his ways, as at the first? Consider this, that as the neglect of souls will lie heavy on unholy or negligent ministers, so, a great many souls are ruining themselves under some measure of fit means, and the slighting of those means will make their condition far heavier than that of many others. Remember our Saviour's word : *Woe to thee, Chorazin! Woe unto thee, Bethsaida! It shall be more tolerable for Tyre and Sidon in the day of judgment than for you.* Matt. xi. 21.

II. The discharge of this high task we have here duly qualified : the Apostle expresses the upright way of it, both negatively and positively.

There be three evils the Apostle would remove from this work, *constrainedness, covetousness,* and *ambition,* as opposed to *willingness, a ready mind,* and an exemplary temper and behaviour.

1. We are cautioned against *constrainedness,* μὴ ἀναγκαστῶς ; against being driven to the work by necessity, indigence, and want of other means of subsistence, as it is with too many ; making a trade of it to live by, and setting to it as to any other calling for that end ; yea, making it the refuge and forlorn resource of their insufficiency for other callings. And as men are not to undertake the work, driven to it by that hard weapon of necessity, so, being engaged in it, they are not to discharge the duties of it merely upon necessity, because of fines binding to it,

* Καλοὶ καὶ ὑψηλοὶ καὶ κάρπον οὐκ ἔχουσι.

or for fear of censure : this is a violent, forced motion, and cannot but be both very unpleasant and unprofitable, as to the proper end and profiting of this work. And as the principle of the motion in this service should not be a compelling necessity of any kind, but true *willingness of heart*, so this willingness should not arise from any thing but pure affection to the work.

2. Not *for filthy gain*, but purely from the inward bent of the mind. As it should not be a compulsive or violent motion by necessity from without, so it should not be an artificial motion by weights hung on within—avarice and love of gain. The former were a wheel, driven or drawn, going by force ; the latter, little better, as a clock made to go by art, by weights hung to it. But there should be a natural motion, like that of the heavens in their course. A willing obedience to the Spirit of God within, moving a man in every part of this holy work, that is προθυμῶς, his mind carried to it as the thing he delights in, and in which he loves to be exercised. So, Timothy *careth, γνησίως*, not artificially, but naturally. Phil. ii. 20. There may be in a faithful pastor very great reluctance in engaging and adhering to the work, upon a sense of the excellency of it and his own unfitness, and the deep apprehension of those high interests, the glory of God, and the salvation of souls ; and yet, he may enter into it, and continue in it, with this *readiness of mind* too ; that is, with most single and earnest desires of doing all he can for God, and *the flock of God ;* only grieved that there is in him so little suitableness of heart, so little holiness and acquaintance with God for enabling him to it. But might he find that, he were satisfied ; and, in expectation of that, he goes on, and waits, and is doing according to his little skill and strength, and cannot leave it. He is *constrained* indeed, but all the constraint is that of *love to Jesus*, and, for his sake, to the souls he hath bought ; (2 Cor. v. 14;) and all the *gain* sought, is, to *gain* souls to Christ ; which is far different from the constraint and the gain here prohibited ; yea, this is indeed that very willingness and readiness of mind which is opposed to that other constraint. That is without ; this is within : that other gain, is base, filthy gain, αἰσχροκέρδος ; this noble and divine.

Inf. 1. Far be it from us, that necessity and constraint should be the thing that moves us in so holy a work. The Lord whom we serve, sees into the heart, and if he find not that primarily moving, accounts all our diligence nothing. And let not base earth within be the cause of our willingness, but a mind touched with heaven. It is true, the temptations of earth with us, in the matter of gain, are not great ; but yet, the heart may cleave to them, as much as if they were much greater, and if it do cleave to them, they shall ruin us ; as well a poor stipend and glebe, if the affection be upon them, as a great deanery or bishopric. If a man fall into it, he may drown in a small brook, being under water, as well as in the great ocean. Oh, the little time that remains ! Let us join our desires and endeavours in this work, bend our united strength to serve him, that we may have joy in that day of reckoning.

And, indeed, there is nothing moves us aright, nor shall we ever find comfort in this service, unless it be from a cheerful inward *readiness of mind*, and that from the *love of Christ*. Thus said he to his Apostle,

Lovest thou me? Then feed my sheep and feed my lambs. John xxi. 16.
Love to Christ begets love to his people's souls, which are so precious
to him, and a care of feeding them. He devolves the working of love
towards him, upon his flock, for their good, puts them in his room, to
receive the benefit of our services, which cannot reach him considered
in himself: he can receive no other profit from it. Love, much love,
gives much unwearied care and much skill in this charge. How sweet
is it to him that loves, to bestow himself, *to spend and be spent,* upon
his service whom he loves! Jacob, in the same kind of service, endured all that was imposed on him, and found it light by reason of love,
the cold of the nights, and heat of the days: seven years he served for
his Rachel, *and they seemed to him but a few days, because he loved her.*
Gen. xxix. 20.

Love is the great endowment of a shepherd of Christ's flock. He
says not to Peter, Art thou wise, or learned, or eloquent? but, *Lovest
thou me? Then feed my sheep.*

3. The third evil is ambition, and that is either in the affecting of
undue authority, or the overstrained and tyrannical exercise of due
authority, or to seek those dignities that suit not with this charge, which
is not *dominium,* but *ministerium.* This temper, therefore, is forbidden, Luke xxii. 25, 26 : *The kings of the Gentiles exercise lordship over
them, but ye shall not be so.* There is a ministerial authority to be used
in discipline, and more sharpness with some than with others ; but
still, lowliness and moderation must be predominant, and not domi-
neering with rigour ; rather being examples to the flock in all holiness,
and especially in humility and meekness, wherein our Lord Jesus particularly propounds his own example : *Learn of me, for I am meek and
lowly of heart.*

But being ensamples.] Such a pattern as they may stamp and print
their spirits and carriage by, and be *followers of you, as you are of
Christ.* And without this, there is little or no fruitful teaching. Well
says Nazianzen, *Either teach not, or teach by living.* So the Apostle
exhorteth Timothy to be an *example in word,* but withal *in conversation.*
1 Tim. iv. 12. That is τύπος, the best printed copy.

But this pares off, will some think, all encouragements of learning ;
leaves no advantage, no respect, or authority. Oh, no : it removes
poor worthless encouragements out of the way, to make place for one
great one that is sufficient, which all the others together are not.

III. The high Advantage : *And when the Chief Shepherd shall appear, ye shall receive a crown of glory which fadeth not away.* Thou
shalt lose nothing by all that restraint from base gain, and vain glory,
and worldly power. No matter, let them all go for *a crown :* that weighs
them all down ; that shall abide for ever. Oh, how far more excellent! *A crown of glory,* pure, unmixed glory, without any ingrediency
of pride or sinful vanity, or any danger of it. And a crown *that fadeth
not,* ἀμαράντινον, of such a flower as withers not : not a temporary garland of fading flowers, such as all here are. *Woe to the crown of pride!*
says the Prophet, Isa. xxviii. 1. Though it be made of flowers growing in a fat valley, yet, their glorious beauty is a fading flower ; but
this will remain fresh and in perfect lustre to all eternity. May they
not well trample on base gain and vain applause, who have this crown

to look to? They that will be content with those, let them be; but *they have their reward,* and it is done and gone, when faithful followers are to receive theirs. Joys of royal pomp, marriages and feasts, how soon do they vanish as a dream! That of Ahasuerus lasted about half a year, but then it ended! And how many since that are gone and forgotten! But this day begins a triumph and a feast, that shall never either end or weary, affording still fresh, ever new delights. All things here, the choicest pleasures, cloy, but satisfy not: those above shall always satisfy, and never cloy, *when the Chief Shepherd shall appear.* And that shall shortly be: this moment will shortly be out.

What is to be refused in the way to this crown? All labour is sweet for it. And what is there here to be desired to detain our hearts that we should not most willingly let go, to rest from our labours, and receive our crown? Was ever any king sad to think that the day of his coronation drew nigh? And then, there will be no envy, nor jealousies: all will be kings, each with his crown, each rejoicing in the glory of the others, and all in His, who that day shall be *All in All.*

Ver. 5. Likewise, ye younger, submit yourselves unto the elder. Yea, all of you be subject one to another, and be clothed with humility: for God resisteth the proud, and giveth grace to the humble.

SIN hath disordered all; so that nothing is to be found but distemper and crookedness in the condition and ways of men towards God, and towards one another, till a new Spirit come in and rectify all. And very much of that redress lies in this particular grace of *humility,* here recommended by the Apostle.

That grace regulates the carriage, 1. Of the *younger* towards the *elder.* 2. Of all men *one to another.* 3. Of all towards God.

1st, The *Younger are to be subject to the Elder.* Which I take so to refer to difference of years, that it hath some aspect likewise to the relation of those that are under the discipline and government of the *elders,* πρεσβύτεροι, who, though not always such in years, ought, however, to suit that name in exemplary gravity and wisdom. It is no seigniory, but a ministry; yet, there is a sacred authority in it, when rightly carried, which both duly challenges, and effectually commands that respect and obedience which is fit for the right order and government of *the House of God.*

The Spirit of Christ in his ministers, is the thing that makes them truly *Elders,* and truly *worthy of double honour;* and without that, men may hunt after respect and credit by other parts, and the more they follow it, the faster it flies from them; or, if they catch any thing of it, they only grasp a shadow.

Infer. Learn, you my brethren, that obedience which is due to the discipline of God's House. This is all we plead for in this point. And know, if you refuse it, and despise the ordinance of God, he will resent the indignity as done to himself. And oh, that all who have that charge of his House upon them, would mind his interest wholly, and not rise in conceit of their power, but wholly employ and improve it for their Lord and Master, and look on no respect paid to themselves as for its own sake desirable, but only so far as is needful for the profitable discharge and advancement of his work in their hands! What are human differences and regards? How empty a vapour! And what-soever it is, nothing is lost by single and entire love of our Lord's glory, and total aiming at that. *Them that honour him, he will honour; and those that despise him, shall be despised.* 1 Sam. ii. 30.

But though this [*likewise*] implies, I conceive, somewhat relative to the former subject, yet, certainly, its full scope is more extensive, and directs us, touching the difference of years, to yield the *subjection*, that is, the respect and reverence which is due from younger to elder persons.

The presumption and unbridledness of youth require the pressing and binding on of this rule. And it is of undeniable equity, even writ-ten in nature, as due to aged persons. But, doubtless, those reap this due fruit in that season the most, who have ripened it most by the in-fluence of their grave and holy carriage. *The hoary head* is indeed *a crown,*—but when?—*when found in the way of righteousness.* Prov. xvi. 31. There it shines, and hath a kind of royalty over youth; other-wise, a graceless old age is a most despicable and lamentable sight. What gains an unholy old man or woman, by their scores of years, but the more scores of guiltiness and misery? And their white hairs speak nothing but ripeness for wrath. Oh! to be as *a tree planted in the house of the Lord, bringing forth fruit in old age.* Psal. xcii. 12, 13. Much experience in the ways of God, and much disdain of the world, and much desire of the love of God, a heavenly temper of mind and frame of life; this is the advantage of many years. But to have seen and felt the more misery, and *heaped up* the more sin, the greater bun-dle of it, *against the day of wrath,* a woeful *treasure* of it, threescore, or threescore and ten years a gathering, and with so much increase every day; no vacation, no dead years, no, not a day wherein it was not growing; how deplorable a case!

A sad reflection, to look back and think, What have I done for God? and to find nothing but such a world of sin committed against him! How much better he who gets home betimes in his youth, if once de-livered from sin and death, at one with God, and some way serviceable to him, or desiring to be so, and who hath a quick voyage, having lived much in a little time!

2. *All of you be subject one to another.* This yet further dilates the duty, makes it universally mutual; *one subject to another.* This directly turns about the vain contest of men, that arises from the natural mis-chief of self-love. Every one would carry it, and be best and highest. The very company of Christ, and his exemplary lowliness, and the meanness of himself and those his followers, all these did not bar out this frothy, foolish question, *Who shall be greatest?* And so far it was disputed, that it occasioned heat about it, *a strife amongst them.* Luke xxii. 24. Now, this rule is just opposite: each is to strive to be lowest, *subject one to another.*

This doth not annul either civil or church government, nor those dif-ferences that are grounded upon the law of nature, or of civil society; for we see immediately before, that such differences are allowed, and the particular duties of them recommended; but it only requires that all due respect, according to their station, be given by each Christian to another. And though there cannot be such a subjection of masters or parents to their servants and children, as is due to them from these, yet, a lowly, meek carrying of their authority, a tender respect of their youth, the receiving of an admonition from them duly qualified, is that which suits with the rule; and, in general, not delighting in the trampling on or abusing of any, but rather seeking the credit and good esteem of all as our own; taking notice of that good in them, wherein they are beyond us; (for all have some advantage, and none hath all;) and, in a word, (and it is the precept of St. Paul, like this of our Apostle here,) *In honour preferring one another,* Rom. xii. 10: *q. d.* Let this be all the strife, who shall put most respect each on another, according to the capacity and station of every one: *in giving honour, go each one before another.*

Now, that such carriage may be sincere, no empty compliment, or court holy water, (as they speak,) but a part of the solid holiness of a Christian, the Apostle requires the true principle of such deportment, the grace of *humility,* that a Christian *put on that;* not the appearance of it, to act in as a stage-garment, but the truth of it, as their constant habit. *Be ye clothed with humility.* It must appear in your outward carriage; so the resemblance of clothing imports. But let it appear as really it is; so the very name of it imports. It is not ταπεινοφανία, but ταπεινοφροσύνη; not *a show of humility,* but heart-lowliness, *humility of mind.*

As it is the bent of humility to hide other graces, so far as piety to God and our brethren will permit, so, it would willingly hide itself; it loves not to appear but as necessity urges. Appear it must, and it doth somewhat more appear than many other graces do, though it seeks not to appear. It is seen as a modest man or woman's apparel, which they wear not for the end that it may be seen; they do not gaudily flaunt and delight in dressing: though there is a decency as well as necessity, which they do and may have respect to, yet it is in so neat and unaffected a way, that they are a good example even in that point. Thus, humility in carriage and words, is as the decorum of this clothing, but the main is the real usefulness of it.

And therefore, a truly humble man desires not much to appear humble. Yea, were it not for disedifying his brethren, he would rather disguise and hide, not only other things by humility, but even humility itself, and would be content, upon the mistake of some words or gestures, to pass for proud and vain, being humble within, rather than to be big in his own eyes, under a semblance of outward lowliness. Yea, were it not that charity and piety do both forbid it, he would not care to do some things on purpose that might seem arrogant, to carry humility unseen, that doth so naturally delight in covering all graces, and is sorry that it cannot do so without being seen itself, as that garment that covers the rest must of necessity be seen itself. But seeing it must be so, it is with the least show that may be, as a dark veil cast about rich attire, hides their show, and makes very little itself.

This, therefore, is mainly to be studied, that the seat of humility be *the heart.* Although it will be seen in the carriage, yet as little as it can; as few words as may be concerning itself; and those it doth speak, must be the real thoughts of the mind, and not an affected voice of it differing from the inward sense: otherwise, humble speech and carriage only put on without, and not fastened in the inside, is the most refined and subtle, and indeed the most dangerous kind of pride. And this I would recommend as a safe way: Ever let thy thoughts concerning thyself be below what thou utterest; and what thou seest needful or fitting to say to thine own abasement, be not only content (which most are not) to be taken at thy word, and believed to be such by them that hear thee, but be desirous of it, and let that be the end of thy speech, to persuade them, and gain it of them, that they really take thee for as worthless and mean as thou dost express thyself.

Infer. But how little are we acquainted with the real frame of Christianity, the most living without a rule, not laying it to their words and ways at all, nor yielding so much as seeming obedience to the Gospel; while others take up a kind of profession, and think all consists in some religious performances, and do not study the inward reserve of their heart-evils, nor labour to have that temple purged; for the heart should be a temple, and it stands in much need of a sweeping out of the filthiness, and putting out of idols. Some there be, who are much busied about the matter of their assurance, still upon that point, which it is lawful, indeed, and laudable to inquire after, yet not so as to neglect other things more needful. It were certainly better for many, when they find no issue that way, to turn somewhat of their diligence to the study of Christian graces and duties in their station, and to task themselves for a time, were it to the more special seeking, first, of some one grace, and then, of another, as meekness, and patience, and this particularly of humility. To be truly heart-humble—many men despise it in others; but some that will commend it in the general, or in some of those in whom they behold it, yet seek not to *put it on* themselves. They love to be more gay, and to seem to be somebody, and not to abase themselves. It is the way, say they, to be undone. This clothing is too poor a stuff, and too sad a colour for them. Oh, my brethren, you know not the excellency of it. Ye look out at a distance and judge according to your light, vain minds. But will you see it by the light of the word, and then you shall perceive much hidden richness and comeliness in it. And do not only approve it, and call it comely on others, but put it on, and so it is most comely. And as it is with respect to all graces, so, particularly, as to this clothing of humility, though it make least show, yet, come near, and you will see it both rich and comely; and though it hides other graces, yet, when they do appear under it, as sometimes they will, a little glance of them so, makes them much more esteemed. Rebecca's beauty and her jewels were covered with a veil, but when they did appear, the veil set them off, and commended them, though at a distance it hid them.

Again: As in all graces, so particularly in this grace, take heed of a disguise or counterfeit of it. Oh for sincerity in all things, and particularly in this! To be low in thine own eyes, and willing to be so in the eyes of others, this is the very upright nature of heart-humility. 1st, Not to be deluded with a false conceit of advantages thou hast not. 2ndly, Not to be swelled with a vain conceit of those thou really hast. 3rdly, Not affecting to be esteemed by others, either upon their imagining thee to have some good that is not in thee, or discerning that which is. Is not the day at hand, when men will be taken off the false heights they stand on, and set on their own feet; when all the esteem of others shall vanish and pass away like smoke, and thou shalt be just what God finds and accounts thee, and neither more nor less? Oh! the remembrance of that day when a true estimate will be made of all, this would make men hang less upon the unstable conceits and opinions of one another, knowing our judgment and day shall shortly end. Be it little or much that thou hast, the lower and closer thou carriest it under this cloak, the safer shall it and thou be, the more shall it increase, and thou shalt be the liker Him in whom *all fulness dwells.* In this he hath most expressly set himself before us as our pattern; and one says well, " Surely, man might now be constrained to be proud, for whom God himself became humble."

Now, to work the heart to a humble posture, 1. Look *into thyself* in earnest: and, truly, whosoever thou be that hast the highest conceit of thyself, and the highest causes for it, a real sight of thyself will lay thy crest. Men look on any good, or any fancy of it, in themselves, with both eyes, and skip over, as unpleasant, their real defects and deformities. Every man is naturally his own flatterer; otherwise, flatteries, and false cryings up from others, would make little impression; but hence their success, they meet with the same conceit within. But let any man see his ignorance, and lay what he knows not over against what he knows; the disorders in his heart and affections, over against any right motion in them; his secret follies and sins, against his outwardly blameless carriage;—this man shall not readily love and embrace himself; yea, it shall be impossible for him not to abase and abhor himself.

2. Look on the good in others, and the evil in thyself: make that the parallel, and then thou wilt walk humbly. Most men do just the contrary, and that foolish and unjust comparison puffs them up.

3. Thou art not required to be ignorant of that good which really is so indeed; but beware of imagining *that* to be good which is not; yea, rather let something that is truly good pass thy view, and see it within, rather than beyond its true size. And then, whatsoever it be, see it not as thine own, but as God's, his free gift; and so, the more thou hast, looking on it in that view, thou wilt certainly be the more humble, as having the more obligations: the weight of them will press thee down, and lay thee still lower, as you see it in Abraham,— the clear visions and promises he had made him fall down flat to the ground. Gen. xv. 12.

4. Pray much for the spirit of humility, the Spirit of Christ, for that is it; otherwise, all thy vileness will not humble thee. When men hear of this or of other graces, and how reasonable they are, they think presently to have them, and do not consider the natural enmity and rebellion of their own hearts, and the necessity of receiving them from heaven. And therefore, in the use of all other means, be most dependent on that influence, and most in the use of that means which opens the heart most to that influence, and draws it down upon the heart, and that is Prayer.

Of all the evils of our corrupt nature, there is none more connatural and universal than pride, the grand wickedness, self-exalting in our own and others' opinion. Though I will not contest what was the first step in that complicated first sin, yet certainly this of pride was one, and a main ingredient in it,—that which the unbelief conceived going before, and the disobedience following after, were both servants to ; and ever since, it sticks still deep in our nature. St. Augustine says truly, *That which first overcame man, is the last thing he overcomes.* Some sins, comparatively, may die before us, but this hath life in it, sensibly, as long as we. It is as the heart of all, the first living, and the last dying ; and it hath this advantage, that, whereas other sins are fomented by one another, this feeds even on virtues and graces, as a moth that breeds in them, and consumes them, even in the finest of them, if it be not carefully looked to. This hydra, as one head of it is cut off, another rises up. It will secretly cleave to the best actions, and prey upon them. And therefore is there so much need that we continually watch, and fight, and pray against it, and be restless in the pursuit of real and deep humiliation, daily seeking to advance further in it ; to be nothing, and to desire to be nothing ; not only to bear, but to love our own abasement, and the things that procure and help it, to take pleasure in them, so far as may be without sin : yea, even in respect of our sinful failings, when they are discovered, to love the bringing low of ourselves by them, while we hate and grieve for the sin of them.

And, above all, it is requisite to watch ourselves in our best things, that self get not in, or, if it break in, or steal in at any time, that it be presently found out and cast out again ; to have that established within us, to do all for God, to intend him and his glory in all, and to be willing to advance his glory, were it by our own disgrace: not to make raising or pleasing thyself the rule of exercising thy parts and graces, when thou art called to use and bring them forth, but the good of thy brethren, and in that, the glory of thy Lord. Now, this is indeed to be severed from self and united to him, to have self-love turned into the love of God. And this is his own work ; it is above all other hands : therefore, the main combat against pride, and the conquest of it, and the gaining of humility, is certainly by prayer. God bestows himself upon them who are most abundant in prayer ; and they to whom he shows himself most are certainly the most humble.

Now, to stir us up to diligence in the exercise of this grace, take briefly a consideration or two.

1. Look on that above pointed at, the high example of lowliness set before us : Jesus Christ requiring our particular care to take this lesson from him. And is it not most reasonable ? He the most fair, the most excellent and complete of all men, and yet the most humble ! He more than a man, who yet willingly became, in some sort, less than a man, as it is expressed, Psal. xxii. 6, *a worm and no man.* And when Majesty itself *emptied itself,* and descended so low, shall a worm swell and be high-conceited ?

Then, consider, it was for *us* he humbled himself, to expiate our pride ; and therefore it is evidently the more just that we follow a pattern which is both so great in itself, and doth so nearly concern us. O humility, the virtue of Christ, (that which he so peculiarly espoused,) how dost thou confound the vanity of our pride !

2. Consider the safety of Grace under this clothing ; it is that which keeps it unexposed to a thousand hazards. Humility doth Grace no prejudice in covering it, but indeed shelters it from violence and wrong : therefore they do justly call it *conservatrix virtutum*, the preserver of graces ; and one says well, " That he who carries other graces without humility, carries a precious powder in the wind without a cover."

3. Consider the increase of grace by it, as here expressed ; the perfect enmity of God against pride, and his bounty towards humility. *He resisteth the proud, and giveth grace to the humble.*

God resisteth the proud, [ἀντιτάσσεται,] singles it out for his grand enemy, and sets himself in battle array against it : so the word is. It breaks the ranks of men in which he hath set them, when they are not subject, ὑποτασσόμενοι, as the word is before ; yea, Pride not only breaks rank, but rises up in rebellion against God, and doth what it can to dethrone him and usurp his place : therefore he orders his forces against it. And to be sure, if God be able to make his party good, Pride shall not escape ruin. He will break it, and bring it low : for he is set upon that purpose, and will not be diverted.

But he giveth grace,—pours it out plentifully upon humble hearts. His sweet dews and showers of grace slide off the mountains of pride, and fall on the low valleys of humble hearts, and make them pleasant and fertile. The swelling heart, puffed up with a fancy of fulness, hath no room for grace. It is lifted up, is not hallowed and fitted to receive and contain the graces that descend from above. And again, as the humble heart is most capacious, and, as being emptied and hollowed, can hold most, so it is the most thankful, acknowledges all as received, while the proud cries out that all is his own. The return of glory that is due from Grace, comes most freely and plentifully from a humble heart : God delights to enrich it with grace, and it delights to return him glory. The more he bestows on it, the more it desires to honour him with all ; and the more it doth so, the more readily he bestows still more upon it ; and this is the sweet intercourse betwixt God and the humble soul. This is the noble ambition of humility, in respect whereof all the aspirings of pride are low and base. When all is reckoned, the lowliest mind is truly the highest ; and these two agree so well, that the more lowly it is, it is thus the higher ; and the higher thus, it is still the more lowly.

Oh, my brethren, want of this is a great cause of all our wants. Why should our God bestow on us what we would bestow on our idol, self ? Or, if not to idolize thyself, yet to idolize the thing, the gift that Grace bestowed, to fetch thy believing and comforts from that, which is to put it in his place who gave, and *to make Baal of it,* as some would render Hosea ii. 8.* Now he will not furnish thee thus to his own prejudice therein. Seek, therefore, to have thy heart on a high design, seeking grace still, not to rest in any gift, nor to grow vain and regardless of him upon it. If we had but this fixed with us—What gift or grace I seek, what comfort I seek, it shall be no sooner mine, but it

---

* The words *Gnasu Lebagnol*, which we render *which they prepared for* Baal, may, as the margin notes, be translated *wherewith they made* Baal.—(Dr. Doddridge.)

shall be all thine again, and myself with it ; I desire nothing from thee, but that it may come back to thee, and draw me with it unto thee ; this is all my end, and all my desire :—the request thus presented would not come back so often unanswered.

This is the only way to grow quickly rich : come still poor to Him who hath enough ever to enrich thee, and desire of his riches, not for thyself, but for him.   Mind entirely his glory in all thou hast and seekest to have.   What thou hast, use so, and what thou wantest, vow that thou wilt use it so : let it be his in thy purpose, even before it be thine in possession, as Hannah did in her suit for a son ; 1 Sam. i. 11 ; and thou shalt obtain it as she did.   And then, as she was, be thou faithful in the performance : *Him whom I received* (says she) *by petition, I have returned to the Lord.*

It is undoubtedly the secret pride and selfishness of our hearts, that obstruct much of the bounty of God's hand in the measure of our graces, and the sweet embraces of his love, which we should otherwise find.   The more that we let go of ourselves, still the more should we receive of himself.   Oh, foolish we, who refuse so blessed an exchange !

To this humility, as in these words it is taken in the notion of our inward thoughts touching ourselves, and our carriage in relation to others, the Apostle joins the other humility, in relation to God ; being indeed the different actings of one and the same grace, and inseparably connected each with the other.

Ver. 6. Humble yourselves therefore under the mighty hand of God, that he may exalt you in due time.

THIS is pressed by a reason both of equity and necessity, in that word, *The mighty hand of God.*   He is Sovereign Lord of all, and all things do obeisance to him ; therefore, it is *just*, that you his people, professing loyalty and obedience to him, be most submissive and humble in your subjection to him in all things.   Again, mark *the necessity, his mighty hand :* there is no striving, it is a vain thing to flinch and struggle, for he doth what he will.   And his hand is so mighty, that the greatest power of the creature is nothing to it.   Yea, it is all indeed derived from him, and therefore cannot do any whit against him.   If thou wilt not yield, thou must yield : if thou wilt not be led, thou shalt be pulled and drawn.   Therefore, submission is your only course.

A third reason by which this duty is pressed, is that of utility, or the certain advantage of it.   As there is nothing to be gained, yea, rather, as you are certainly ruined by reluctance, so this humble submission is the only way to gain your point.   What would you have under any affliction, but be delivered and raised up ?   Thus alone can you attain that : *Humble yourselves, and he shall raise you up in due time.*

This is the end why he humbles you : he lays weights upon you, that you may be depressed.   Now, when this end is gained, that you are willingly so, then the weights are taken off, and you are lifted up by his gracious hand.   Otherwise, it is not enough, that he hath humbled you by his hand, unless you *humble yourselves* under his hand. Many have had great and many pressures, one affliction after another, and been humbled, and yet not made humble, as they commonly express the difference: humbled by force in regard of their outward condition, but not humbled in their inward temper; and therefore, as soon as the weight is off, like heaps of wool, they rise up again, and grow as big as they were.

If we would consider this in our particular trials, and aim at this deportment, it were our wisdom. Are they not mad, who, under any stroke, quarrel or struggle against God? What gain your children thus at your hands, but more blows? Nor is this only an unseemly and unhappy way, openly to resist and strive, but even secretly to fret and grumble; for he hears the least whispering of the heart, and looks most how that behaves itself under his hand. Oh, humble acceptance of his chastisement, is our duty and our peace; that which gains most on the heart of our Father, and makes the rod fall soonest out of his hand.

And not only should we learn this in our outward things, but in our spiritual condition, as the thing the Lord is much pleased with in his children. There is a stubbornness and fretting of heart concerning our souls, that arises from pride and the untamedness of our nature; and yet some take a pleasure in it, touching the matter of comfort and assurance, if it be withheld. Or, (which they take more liberty in,) if it be sanctification and victory over sin they seek, and yet find little or no success, but the Lord holding them under in these, they then vex themselves, and wax more discontented, and nothing pleases them: as peevish children, upon the refusal of somewhat they would have, take displeasure, and make no account of the daily provision made for them, and all the other benefits they have by the care and love of their parents. This is a folly very unbeseeming the children that are the *children of wisdom*, and should walk as such; and till they learn more humble respect for their Father's will, they are still the farther off from their purpose. Were they once brought to submit the matter, and give him heartily his will, he would readily give them theirs, as far as it were for their good: as you say to your children, of any thing they are too stiff and earnest in, and make a noise for, "Cry not for it, and you shall have it."

And this is the thing we observe not, that the Lord often, by his delays, is aiming at this; and were this done, we cannot think how graciously he would deal with us. His gracious design is, to make much room for grace by much humbling; especially in some spirits which need much trying, or when he means much to enable for some singular service. And thus, the time is not lost, as we are apt to imagine, but it furthers our end, while we think the contrary. It is necessary time and pains that are given to the unballasting of a ship, the casting out of the earth and sand, when it is to be laden with spices. We must be emptied more, if we would have more of that fulness and riches which we are longing for.

So long as we fume and chafe against his way, though it be in our best supplications, we are not in a posture for a favourable answer. Would we wring things out of his hand by fretfulness? That is not the way: no; but present humble, submissive suits: Lord, this is my desire, but thou art wise and gracious ; I refer the matter to thy will for the thing, and for the measure, and for the time, and all. Were we moulded to this composure, then were mercy near. When he hath gained this, broken our will and tamed our stoutness, then he relents and pities. See Jer. xxx. 17, 18. *Because they called thee an outcast, &c., thus saith the Lord, Behold, I will bring again the captivity of Jacob's tents, &c.*

This I would recommend in any estate, the humble folding under the Lord's hand, kissing the rod, and falling low before him ; and this is the way to be raised. But there may be some one who thinks he hath tried this awhile, and is still at the same point, hath gained nothing, and he may therefore be ready to fall back to his old repinings ; let such a one know that his humbling and compliance were not upright ; it was a fit of false, constrained submission, and therefore lasts not ; it was but a tempting of God, instead of submitting to him. " Oh, will he have a submission ? I will try it, but with this reserve, that if after such a time I gain not what I seek, I shall think it is lost, and that I have reason to return to my discontent." Though the man says not thus, yet this meaning is secretly under it. But wouldst thou have it right, it must be without condition, without reserve ; no time, nor any thing, prescribed : and then he will make his word good, *He will raise thee up*, and that

In due time. Not thy fancied time, but his own wisely appointed time. Thou thinkest, Now I am sinking ; if he help not now, it will be too late. Yet he sees it otherwise : he can let thee sink still lower, and yet bring thee up again. He doth but stay till the most fit time. Thou canst not see it now, but thou shalt see it, that his chosen time is absolutely best. *God waiteth to be gracious.* Isa. xxx. 18. Doth he wait, and wilt not thou ? Oh, the firm belief of his wisdom, power, and goodness, what difficulty will it not surmount ? So then, be humble under his hand. Submit not only thy goods, thy health, thy life, but thy soul. Seek and wait for thy pardon as a condemned rebel, with thy rope about thy neck. Lay thyself low before him, stoop at his feet, and crave leave to look up, and speak, and say—Lord, I am justly under the sentence of death : if I fall under it, thou art righteous, and I do here acknowledge it ; but there is deliverance in Christ, thither I would have recourse : yet, if I be beaten back, and kept out, and faith withheld from me, and I perish, as it were, in view of salvation ; if I see the rock, and yet cannot come at it, but drown ; what have I to say ? In this, likewise, thou art righteous. Only, if it seem good unto thee to save the vilest, most wretched of sinners, and to show great mercy in pardoning so great debts, the higher will be the glory of that mercy. However, here I am resolved to wait, till either thou graciously receive me, or absolutely reject me. If thou do this, I have not a word to say against it ; but because thou art gracious, I hope, I hope thou wilt yet have mercy on me.—I dare say that the promise in the text belongs to such a soul, and *it shall be raised up in due time.*

And what though most or all of our life should pass without much sensible taste even of spiritual comforts, a poor all it is ! Let us not over-esteem this *moment*, and so think too much of our better or worse condition in it, either in temporals, or even in spirituals, so far as regards such things as are more arbitrary and accessory to the name of our spiritual life. Provided we can humbly wait for free grace, and depend on the word of promise, we are safe. If the Lord will clearly shine on us, and refresh us, this is much to be desired and prized ; but if he so think fit, what if we should be all our days held at a distance, and under a cloud of wrath? It is but *a moment in his anger.* Psal. xxx. 5. Then follows a life-time in his favour, an endless life-time. It is *but weeping* (as it there follows) *for a night, and joy comes in the morning,* that clearer morning of Eternity, to which no evening succeeds.

Ver. 7. Casting all your care upon him ; for he careth for you.

AMONGST other spiritual secrets, this is one, and a prime one, the combination of lowliness and boldness, *humble confidence:* this is the true temper of a child of God towards his great and good Father ; nor can any have it, but they who are indeed his children, and have within them that *spirit of adoption* which he *sends into their hearts.* Gal. iv. 6.

And these two the Apostle here joins together : *Humble yourselves under the hand of God,* and yet, *Cast your care on him :* upon that same Hand under which you ought to humble yourselves, must you withal cast over your care, all your care ; *for he careth for you.*

Consider, I. The Nature of this Confidence, *Casting all your care on him.* II. The Ground or warrant of it, *For he careth for you.*

I. For the Nature of it. Every man hath some desires and purposes that are predominant with him, besides those that relate to the daily exigencies of life with which he is compassed ; and in both, according to their importance or his estimate of them, and the difficulties occurring in them, he is naturally carried to be proportionally thoughtful and careful in them. Now, the excess and distemper of this care, is one of the great diseases and miseries of man's life. Moral men, perceiving and feeling it, have been tampering at the cure, and prescribing after their fashion, but with little success. Some present abatement and allay of the paroxysm or extremity, their rules may reach ; but they never go near the bottom, the cause of the evil, and therefore cannot work a thorough, sound cure of it. Something they have spoken, somewhat fitly, of the surpassing of nature's rule and size in the pursuit of superfluous, needless things ; but, for the unavoidable care of things needful, they know no redress, but refer men entirely to their own industry and diligence. They can tell how little will serve him who seeks no more than what will serve, but how to be provided with that little, or to be assured of it, and freed from troubling care, they cannot tell.

Now, truly it were a great point, to be well instructed in the former ; and it is necessary for the due practice of the rule here given, touching necessary cares, first, to cut off cares unnecessary, to retrench all extravagant, superfluous desires. For, certainly, a great part of the troublous cares of men, relate merely to such things as have no other necessity in them, than what our disordered desires create, nor truly any real good in them, but what our fancy puts upon them. Some

are indeed forced to labour hard for their daily bread ; but, undoubtedly, a great deal of the sweat and toil of the greatest part of men is
about unnecessaries : *ad supervacua sudatur.*   Such an estate, so
much by the year, such a place, so much honour, and esteem, and rank
in the world,—these are the things that make some slaves to the
humours of others, whom they court, and place their dependence on,
for these ends ; and those, possibly, to whom they are so enthralled,
are themselves at as little liberty, but captivated to the humours of
some others, either above them, or who being below them, may give
accession and furtherance to their ends of enrichment, advancement,
or popularity.   Men who are set on these things, forge necessities to
themselves, and make vain things as necessary as food and raiment,
resolving that they will have them, or fall in the chase, being wilfully
and unavoidably bent on them.   *They that will be rich,* says the
Apostle, (1 Tim. vi. 9,) who are resolved on it upon any terms, meet
with terms hard enough,—*they fall into temptation, and a snare, and
into many foolish and hurtful lusts, which drown men in destruction
and perdition.   Drown* them ; there is no recovering, but still they are
plunged deeper and deeper.   *Foolish lusts ;* unreasonable, childish desires ; after one bargain, such another, and after one sin, another to
make even, and somewhat then to keep that whole, and so on without
end.   If their hearts are set upon purchase and land, still some house
or neighbour-field, some *Naboth's vineyard,* is in their eyes, and all the
rest is nothing without that, which discovers the madness of this humour, this dropsy-thirst.

And this is the first thing, indeed, to be looked to, that our desires
and cares be brought to a due compass.   And what would we have ?
Think we that contentment lies in so much, and no less ?   When that
is attained, it shall appear as far off as before.   When children are at
the foot of a high hill, they think it reaches the heavens, and yet, if
they were there, they would find themselves as far off as before, or at
least not sensibly nearer.   Men think, Oh, had I this, I were well ; and
when it is reached, it is but an advanced standing from which to look
higher, and spy out for some other thing.

We are indeed children in this, to think the good of our estate lies
in the greatness, and not in the fitness of it for us.   He were a fool
that would have his clothes so, and think the bigger and longer they
were, they would please him the better.   And certainly, as in apparel,
so in place and estate, and all outward things, their good lies not in
their greatness, but in their fitness for us.   Our Saviour tells us expressly, that *man's life consisteth not in the abundance of the things he
possesseth.*   Luke xii. 13.   Think you that great and rich persons live
more content ?   Believe it not.   If they will deal freely, they can tell
you the contrary ; that there is nothing but a show in them, and that
great estates and places have great grief and cares attending them, as
shadows are proportioned to their bodies.   And if they have no real
crosses, luxury frames troubles to itself ; like a variety of dishes corrupting the stomach, and causing variety of diseases.   And instead
of need, they have fantastic, vain discontents that will trouble men as
much as greater, be it but this hawk flies not well, or that dog runs not
well, to men whose hearts are in those games.

So then, I say, this is first to be regulated: all childish, vain, need-less cares are to be discharged, and, as being unfit to cast on thy God, are to be quite cast out of thy heart. Entertain no care at all but such as thou mayest put into God's hands, and make his on thy behalf; such as he will take off thy hand, and undertake for thee.

All needful, lawful care, and that only, will he receive. So then, rid thyself quite of all that thou canst not take this course with, and then, without scruple, take confidently this course with all the rest. Seek a well-regulated, sober spirit. In the things of this life, *be con-tent with food and raiment;* not delicates, but *food;* not ornament, but *raiment,* τροφὴν οὐ τρυφὴν, σκεπάσματα οὐ κοσμήματα; and conclude, that what thy Father carves to thee is best for thee, the fittest measure, for he knows it, and loves thee wisely. This course our Saviour would have thee take, Matt. vi. 31; first, to cut off superfluous care, then, to turn over on thy God the care of what is necessary. He will look to that, thou hast him engaged; and he can and will give thee beyond that, if he sees it fit.

Only, this is required of thee, to refer the matter to his discretion entirely. Now, in thy thus well-regulated affairs and desires, there is a diligent care and study of thy duty; this he lays on thee. There is a care of support in the work, and of the success of it; this thou oughtest to lay on him. And so, indeed, all the care is turned off from thee upon him, even that of duty, which from him lies on us. We offer our service, but for skill and strength to discharge it, that care we lay on him, and he allows us to do so; and then, for the event and success, with that we trust him entirely. And this is the way to walk contentedly and cheerfully homewards, leaning and resting all the way on him, who is both our *guide* and our *strength*, who hath us and all our good in his gracious hand. Much zeal for him, and desire of his glory, minding our duty in relation to that, is the thing he requires, and while we are bending our whole care to that, he undertakes the care of us and our condition: as that king said to his favourite, when persuading him to fidelity and diligence in his state-trust, "Do my affairs, and I will do yours." Such a word directly hath St. Chrysostom: Σὺ μερίμνησον τὰ τοῦ Θεοῦ, καὶ αὐτὸς μεριμνῆσει τὸ σόν: If thou have a concern for the things that are God's, he will also be careful with thee and thine.

The care of duty thus carried, is sweet and light, doth not cut and divide the mind; it is united and gathered in God, and rests there, and walks in his hand all the way. He bears the weight of all our works, and *works them in us*, and for us; and therein lies our peace, that *he ordains for us*. Isa. xxvi. 12. If thou wouldst shake off the yoke of obedience, thou art likewise to be shaken off thyself; but if, in humble diligence in the ways of God, thou walk on in his strength, there is nothing that concerns thee and thy work, but he will take the charge and care of, thyself and all thine interests. Art thou troubled with fears, enemies, and snares? Untrouble thyself of that, for he is with thee. He hath promised to *lead thee in a straight and safe path*, Psal. xxvii. 11; and to rebuke all thine enemies, to *subdue thine iniquities for thee*, Micah vii. 19; and to *fight against those that fight against thee*, Psal. xxxv. 1. *No weapon formed against thee shall prosper*, Isa. liv. 17 ; *yea, when thou passest through the water, and through the fire*, he *will be with thee*, Isa. xliii. 2. Doth thine own weakness discourage thee ? Hath he not engaged for that too ? So, lay over that care upon him. Hath he not spoken of *strengthening the weak hands and feeble knees*, and said, *that the lame shall leap as an hart?* Isa. xxxv. 3, 6. And though there is nothing in thyself but unrighteousness and weakness, yet there is in him, for thee, *righteousness and strength*, Isa. xlv. 24,—*righteousness*, to express the abundance of righteousness. When thou art ready to faint, a look to him will revive thee; a believing look draws in of his strength to thy soul, and renews it. Isa. xl. 29. And know, the more tender and weak thou art, the more tender he is over thee, and the more strong will he be in thee. *He feeds his flock like a shepherd*, and the weakest he is the most careful of : *they are carried in his arms and his bosom*, Isa. xl. 11, and it is easy for the feeblest to go so.

And as for the issue and success of thy way, let not that trouble thee at all : that is the care he would have thee wholly disburden thyself of, and lay entirely upon him. Do not vex thyself with thinking, how will this and that be, what if this and the other fall out. That is his part wholly, and if thou meddle with it, thou at once displeasest him, and disquietest thyself. This sin carries the punishment of it close tied to it. If thou wilt be struggling with that which belongs not to thee, and poising at that burden that is not thine, what wonder, yea, I may say, what pity if thou fall under it ? Art thou not well served ? Is it not just, that if thou wilt do for thyself, and bear for thyself, what thy Lord calls for to bear for thee, thou shouldst feel the weight of it to thy cost ?

But what is the way of this devolving of my burden ? There is a faculty in it that all persons have not : though they would do thus with it, they cannot ; it lies on them, and they are not able to cast it on God. The way is, doubtless, by praying and believing : these are the hands by which the soul can turn over to God what itself cannot bear : all cares, the whole bundle, is most dexterously transferred thus. *Be careful in nothing.* Phil. iv. 6. A great word ! Oh, but how shall it be ? Why thus, says he, *In all things make your requests known unto God*, and in a confident, cheerful way, *supplication* mixed with *thanksgiving;* so shall it be the more lively and active to carry forth and carry up thy cares, and discharge thee of them, and lay them on God. Whatsoever it is that presses thee, go tell thy Father ; put over the matter into his hand, and so thou shalt be freed from μερίμνα, that dividing, perplexing care, that the world is full of.

No more, but when thou art either to do or suffer any thing, when thou art about any purpose or business, go tell God of it, and acquaint him with it ; yea, burden him with it, and thou hast done for matter of caring : no more care, but quiet, sweet diligence in thy duty, and dependence on him for the carriage of thy matters. And in this prayer, Faith acts : it is a believing requesting. *Ask in faith, not doubting.* Jam. i. 6. So thou rollest over all on him ; that is the very proper working of faith, the carrying the soul, and all its desires, out of itself unto God, as expressed Psal. xxxvi. 5: *Roll over on God,—* make one bundle of all; roll thy cares, and thyself with them, as one burden, all on thy God.

Now Faith, to do this, stays itself on the promise. It cannot move but on firm ground, and the promises are its ground; and for this end is this added, *He careth for thee.*

This must be established in the heart. 1. The firm belief of the Divine Providence, that all things are managed and ruled by it, and that in the highest power and wisdom; that there is no breaking of his purposes, nor resisting of his power. *The counsel of the Lord standeth for ever, and the thoughts of his heart to all generations.* Psal. xxxiii. 11. 2. The belief of his gracious Providence to his own people, that he orders all for their true advantage, and makes all different lines and ways concentre in their highest good; all to meet in that, how opposite soever in appearance. See Rom. viii. 28. 3. A particular confidence of his good-will towards thee, and undertaking for thee. Now, if this be the question, the promise resolves thee: trust him, and he takes on the trust, and there is no other condition; cast on him thy care, and he takes it on, he cares for thee. His royal word is engaged not to give thee the slip, if thou do really lay it upon him. *Cast thy burden upon the Lord,* Psal. lv. 22;—hand it over, heave it upon him,—*and he shall sustain thee;* shall bear both, if thou trust him with both, both thee and thy burden: *He shall never suffer the righteous to be moved.*

Inf. 1. The children of God have the only sweet life. The world thinks not so, rather looks on them as poor, discontented, lowering creatures; but it sees not what an uncaring, truly secure life they are called to. While others are turmoiling and wrestling, each with his projects and burdens for himself, and are at length crushed and sinking under them, (for that is the end of all that do for themselves,) the child of God goes free from the pressure of all that concerns him, it being laid over on his God. If he use his advantage, he is not racked with musings, Oh! what will become of this and that; but goes on in the strength of his God as he may, offers up poor, but sincere endeavours to God, and is sure of one thing, that all shall be well. He lays his affairs and himself on God, and so hath no pressing care; no care but the care of love, how to please, how to honour his Lord. And in this, too, he depends on him, both for skill and strength; and touching the success of things, he leaves that as none of his to be burdened with, casts it on God, and since he careth for it, they need not both care, his care alone is sufficient. Hence springs peace, inconceivable peace. *Be careful for nothing, but in every thing, by prayer and supplication, with thanksgiving, let your requests be made known unto God. And the peace of God, which passeth all understanding, shall keep your hearts and minds, through Jesus Christ.* Phil. iv. 6, 7.

Inf. 2. But truly, the godly are much wanting to themselves, by not improving this their privilege. They too often forget this their sweet way, and fret themselves to no purpose; they wrestle with their burdens themselves, and do not entirely and freely *roll them over on God.* They are surcharged with them, and he calls for them, and yet they will not give them him. They think to spare him, but indeed, in this, they disobey, and dishonour, and so grieve him; and they find the grief return on themselves, and yet cannot learn to be wise.

Why deal we thus with our God and with our souls, grieving both at once? Let it never be, that for any outward thing thou perplex thyself, and ravel thy thoughts, as in thickets, with the cares of this life. Oh, how unsuitable are these to a child of God, for whom a life so far more excellent is provided! Hath he prepared a kingdom for thee, and will he not bestow thy charges in the way to it? Think it not: *He knoweth you have need of these things.* Matt. vi. 32. Seek not vain things, nor great things: for these, it is likely, are not fit for thee; but seek what is needful and convenient in his judgment, and refer thyself to that.

Then, as for thy spiritual estate, lay over upon God the care of that too. Be not so much in thorny questionings, doubting and disputing at every step, Oh, is this accepted, and that accepted? and, So much deadness! &c.; but apply thyself more simply to thy duty. Lamely as it may be, halt on, and believe that he is gracious and pities thee, and lay the care of bringing thee through upon him. Lie not complaining and arguing, but *up and be doing, and the Lord shall be with thee.* 1 Chron. xxii. 16. I am persuaded that many a soul that hath some truth of grace, falls much behind in the progress, by this accustomed way of endless questionings. Men can scarcely be brought to examine and suspect their own condition, being carnally secure, and satisfied that all is well; but then, when once they awaken and set to this, they are ready to entangle themselves in it, and neglect their way, by poring on their condition. They will not set cheerfully to any thing, because they want assurances and height of joy; and this course they take is the way to want it still. Walking humbly and sincerely, and offering at thy duty, and waiting on the Lord, is certainly the better way, and nearer that very purpose of thine; for *he meeteth him that rejoiceth and worketh righteousness, those that remember him in his ways.* Isa. lxiv. 5. One thing the Christian should endeavour to obtain, firm belief for the Church: all the care of that must be cast on God, that he *will beautify Zion,* and perform all his word to her. And then think, Do I trust him for the whole Church, and the great affairs concerning it, and shall I doubt him for myself, or any thing that concerns me? Do I confide in him for the steering and guidance of the whole ship, and shall I be peevishly doubting and distrusting about my pack in it?

Again, when, in addition to the present and the past, thou callest in after evils by advance, and art still revolving the dangers before, and thy weakness. It is good, indeed, to entertain by these holy fear and self-distrust; but by that, be driven in to trust on him who undertakes for thee, on him in whom thy strength lies, and be as sure and confident in him, as thou art, and justly art, distrustful of thyself.

Further, learn to prescribe nothing. Study entire resignation, for that is thy great duty and thy peace; that gives up all into the hand of thy Lord, and can it be in a better hand? First, refer the carving of outward things to him, heartily and fully. Then, stay not there, but go higher. If we have renounced the comforts of this world for God, let us add this, renounce even spiritual comforts for him too.

Put all in his will: If I be in light, blessed be thou; and if in darkness, even then, blessed be thou too.   As he saith of earthly treasures, *Gold is mine, and silver is mine,*—(and this may satisfy a Christian in those two, to desire no more of them than his Father sees fit to give, knowing that he, having all the mines and treasures of the world at his command, would not pinch and hold short his children, if it were good for them to have more;) even thus it is in respect to the other, the true riches: Is not the Spirit mine, may God say, and all comforts mine? I have them to bestow, and enough of them.   And ought not this to allay thy afflicting care, and to quiet thy repinings, and establish thy heart, in referring it to his disposal, as touching thy comforts and supplies? The whole golden mines of all spiritual comfort and good are his, and the Spirit itself.   Then, will he not furnish what is fit for thee, if thou humbly attend on him, and lay the care of providing for thee upon his wisdom and love? This were the sure way to honour him with what we have, and to obtain much of what we have not; for certainly he deals best with those that do most absolutely refer all to him.

Ver. 8. Be sober, be vigilant; because your adversary the devil, as a roaring lion, walketh about, seeking whom he may devour :
9. Whom resist stedfast in the faith, knowing that the same afflictions are accomplished in your brethren that are in the world.

THE children of God, if they rightly take their Father's mind, are always disburdened of perplexing carefulness, but never exempted from diligent watchfulness.   Thus we find here, they are allowed, yea, enjoined, to cast all their care upon their wise and loving Father, and are secured by his care.   He takes it well that they lay all over on him, yea, he takes it not well when they forbear him, and burden themselves.   He hath provided a sweet quiet life for them, could they improve and use it; a calm and firm condition in all the storms and troubles that are about them; however things go, to find content, and *be careful for nothing.*

Now, upon this, a carnal heart would imagine straight, according to its sense and inclination,—as it desires to have it, so would it dream that it is,—that then, a man devolving his care on God, may give up all watch and ward, and needs not apply himself to any kind of duty. But this is the ignorant and perverse mistake, the reasonless reasoning of the flesh.   You see these are here joined, not only as agreeable, but indeed inseparable : *Cast all your care on him, for he careth for you,* and withal, *Be sober, be vigilant.*

And this is the Scripture logic. *It is he that worketh in you to will and to do.* Phil. ii. 13.—Then, would you possibly think, I need not work at all, or, if I do, it may be very easily and securely.   No :— *therefore,* says the Apostle, because he worketh in you to will and to do, *work out your salvation,* yea, and do it *with fear and trembling;* work you in humble obedience to his command, and in dependence on him who *worketh all in you.*

Thus, here.   *Cast your care on Him,* not that you may be the more free to take your own pleasure and slothful ease, but, on the contrary, that you may be the more active and apt to watch: being freed from the burden of vexing carefulness, which would press and encumber you,

you are the more nimble, as one eased of a load, to walk, and work, and watch as becomes a Christian. And for this very purpose is that burden taken off from you, that you may be more able and disposed for every duty that is laid upon you.

Observe these two as connected, and thence gather, *First*, There is no right believing without diligence and watchfulness joined with it. That slothful reliance of most souls on blind thoughts of mercy will undo them: their faith is *a dead faith*, and a deadly faith; they are perishing and will not consider it. Such persons do not duly cast their care on God for their souls, for indeed they have no such care. *Secondly*, There is no right diligence without believing.

There is, as in other affairs, so, even in spiritual things, an anxious, perplexing care, which is a distemper and disturbance to the soul: it seems to have a heat of zeal and affection in it, but is, indeed, not the natural right heat that is healthful, and enables for action, but a diseased, feverish heat, that puts all out of frame, and unfits for duty. It seems to stir and further, but indeed it hinders, and does not hasten us, but so as to make us stumble: as if there was one behind a man, driving and thrusting him forward, and not suffering him to set and order his steps in his course, this were the ready way, instead of advancing him, to weary him, and possibly give him a fall.

Such is the distrustful care that many have in their spiritual course: they raise a hundred questions about the way of their performances, and their acceptance, and their estate, and the issue of their endeavours. Indeed, we should endeavour to do all by our rule, and to walk exactly, and examine our ways; especially in holy things, to seek some insight and faculty in their performance, suiting their nature and end, and His greatness and purity whom we worship. This should be minded diligently, and yet calmly and composedly; for diffident doubtings do retard and disorder all. But quiet stayedness of heart on God, dependence on him, on his strength for performance, and his free love in Christ for acceptance, this makes the work go kindly and sweetly on, makes it pleasing to God, and refreshing to thy soul.

Inf. Certainly, thou art a vexation to thyself, and displeasest thy Lord, when thou art questioning whether thou shalt go on or not, from finding in thy service so much deadness and hardness; thinking, therefore, that it were as good to do nothing, that thou dost but dishonour him in all. Now, thou considerest not, that in these very thoughts thou dost more wrong and dishonour him than in thy worst services; for thou callest in question his lenity and goodness, takest him, for a rigorous exacter, yea, representest him to thyself as a hard master, who is the most gentle and gracious of all masters. Do not use him so. Indeed, thou oughtest to *take heed to thy foot*, to see how thy heart is affected in his worship. Keep and watch it as thou canst, but in doing so, or in endeavouring to do, however thou find it, do not think he will use rigours with thee; but the more thou observest thine own miscarriages towards him, the less severely will he observe them. To think otherwise, to fret and repine that thy heart is not to his mind, nor indeed to thine own, to go on in a discontented impatience, this is certainly not the commanded watchfulness, but that forbidden carefulness.

Be sober.] This we have formerly spoken of, the Apostle having formerly exhorted to it once and again in this Epistle. It were easy to entertain men's minds with new discourse, if our task were rather to please than to profit; for there be many things which, with little labour, might be brought forth as new and strange to ordinary hearers. But there be a few things which chiefly concern us to know and practise, and these are to be more frequently represented and pressed. This Apostle, and other inspired writers, drew from too full a spring to be ebb of matter; but they rather chose profitable iterations, than unprofitable variety; and so ought we.

This Sobriety is not only temperance in meat and drink, but in all things that concern the flesh. Even that of diet is, though not all, yet a very considerable part of it; and this not only hath implied in it, that one exceed not in the quantity or quality, but even requires a regulating of ourselves in the manner of using our repast; that as we are not to make careful and studious provision, or to take up our thoughts how to please our palate, so, even in the use of sober, mean diet, we endeavour the mortifying of our flesh, not to eat and drink merely to please ourselves, or to satisfy our natural desire, but for God; even to propound this in our sitting down to it, in obedience to him; to use these helps of life, and the life itself, to be spent in his obedience, and in endeavouring to advance his glory.

It is a most shameful idol, a dunghill god indeed, to serve the belly, and to delight in feastings, or in our ordinary repast, laying the reins loose on our appetite, to take its own career. And yet, in this, men most commonly offend, even persons that are not notably intemperate, neither gluttonous nor drunken, and yet, I say, have not that holy, retained, bridled way of using their repast, with an eye upon a higher end.

But this Sobriety, in its ample sense, binds not only that sense of lust, but all the rest in the use of their several delights, yea, and in the whole man, all the affections of the soul, in relation to this world, and the things of it: we are to be in it as weaned from it, and raised above it in the bent of our minds; *to use it as if we used it not.* 1 Cor. vii. 31.

This we speak and hear of, but do not apply ourselves really to this rule. Each hath some trifle or earthly vanity, one or more, but especially some choice one, that he cannot be taken off from; as children readily have some toy that they set more by than the rest. We have childish hearts cleaving to vanity; one hankering after some preferment, another after some estate, lands, or houses, or money. And we are drunk in the pursuit of these, so that when our hearts should be fixed on Divine exercises, they cannot stand, but reel to and fro, or stumble down and fall asleep, roving after those thoughts of that which we affect, staggering ever and anon, or else, so plunged in them all the time, that we are as asleep in them.

Therefore, these two are here, and ordinarily, joined, *Be sober and watchful.* Glutting ourselves either with the delights, or with the desires and cares of earth, makes us sleepy: the fumes that arise from them surcharge us, and cast us into a deep sleep,—a secure unminding of God and of ourselves, the interest of our immortal souls.

The pleasures of sense are too gross for the Divine soul. Divine, I call it, for so by original it is; but we abase it, and make it flesh by those gross earthly things, and make it unfit to rise heavenwards. As insobriety, intemperance in diet, prejudices the very natural spirits, making them dull, clogs their passage, and makes them move as a coach in a miry way, thus doth all inordinate use and love of inferior things: it makes the soul of a low, heavy constitution, so that it cannot move freely in any thing that is spiritual. Yea, where there is some truth of grace, yet it is obstructed and dulled by taking in too much of the world, and feeding on it; which is no more proper for the finest part of the man, for the soul, than the coarse ploughman's diet is for delicate, tender bodies of higher breeding; yea, the disproportion is far greater.

If, then, you would have free spirits for spiritual things, keep them at a spare diet in all things temporal. Let not out your hearts to any thing here below. Learn to delight in God, and seek to taste of his transcendent sweetness : that will perfectly disrelish all lower delights. So your sobriety in abstaining from them shall be still further recompensed with more enjoyment of God, and you shall not lose pleasure by denying yourself the pleasures of earth, but shall change them for those that are unspeakably better and purer in their stead. He shall communicate himself unto you, the *light of whose countenance* feeds and satisfies the glorified spirits that are about his throne.

Be vigilant.] This watchfulness, joined with sobriety, extends to all the estates and ways of a Christian, being surrounded with hazards and snares. *He that despiseth his way shall die,* says Solomon. Prov. xix. 16. The most do thus walk at random : they give attendance on public worship, and have some customary way of private prayer, but do not further regard how they walk, what is their carriage all the day long, what they speak, how they are in company, and how alone, which way their hearts go early and late, what it is that steals away most of their affection from God.

Oh, my beloved, did we know our continual danger, it would shake us out of this miserable dead security that possesses us. We think not on it, but there are snares laid for us all the way, in every path we walk in, and every step of it; in our meat and drink ; in our calling and labour ; in our house at home; in our journeying abroad ; yea, even in God's house, and in our spiritual exercises, both there and in private. Knew we, or at least, considered we this, we should choose our steps more exactly, and look to our ways, to our words, to our thoughts, which truly, whatsoever noise we make, we really do not. *Ponder the path of thy feet,* says Solomon ; and before that, *Let thine eyes look right on, and let thine eyelids look straight before thee.* And further, *Put away a froward mouth, and perverse lips put far from thee.* But, first of all, as the main reason and spring of all, *Keep thy heart with all diligence,* or *above all keeping, for out of it are the issues of life.* Prov. iv. 23—26.

Because your adversary the devil.] An alarm to watchfulness is here given, from the watchfulness of our grand Adversary. There be other two usually ranked with him, as the leading enemies of our souls, the World and our own flesh ; but here, he is expressly named, who commands in chief, and orders and manages the war, using the service of the other two against us, as prime officers, under which most of the forces of particular temptations are ranked. Some others there be which he immediately commands and leads on himself, a regiment of his own, some spiritual temptations.

And we have need to be put in mind of the hostility and practices of Satan against us ; for if the most were put to it, they would be forced to confess that they very seldom think on their spiritual danger from this hand. As we keep loose guard against the allurements of the world, and of our own corruption, so we watch not against the devices of Satan, but go on by guess, and suspect nothing, and so are easily a prey to all.

The least enemy being despised and neglected, as men observe, proves often too great. The smallest appearances of evil, the least things that may prejudice our spiritual good, while we make no reckoning of them, may do us great mischief. Our not considering them makes them become considerable, especially being under the command of a vigilant and skilful leader, who knows how to improve advantages. Therefore, in things which we many times account petty, and not worthy our notice as having any evil in them, we should learn to suspect the address of this adversary, who usually hides himself, and couches under some covert, till he may appear irresistible, and seize on us ; and then, indeed, he *roars*.

And this seeking the destruction of souls is, you see, marked as all his work. The prey he hunts is souls, that they may be as miserable as himself. Therefore he is justly called *our adversary*, the enemy of holiness and of our souls ; first tempting to sin, and then accusing for sin, as his name here imports ; appearing against us upon the advantages he hath gained. He studies our nature, and fits his temptations to it ; knows the prevalency of lust, or earthliness, or that great and most general evil of pride, so like himself, and that is his throne in the heart. Sometimes *he boweth down*, as it is said of the lion, Psal. x. 9 ; he waits his opportunity craftily, and then assaults fiercely. And the children of God find sometimes so much violence in his temptations, that they surprise them ; such horrid thoughts cast in as poisoned arrows, or *fiery darts*, as the Apostle speaks, Eph. vi. 16. And this, his enmity, though it is against man in general, yet is most enraged against the children of God. He goes about and spies where they are weakest, and amongst them, directs his attacks most against those who are most advanced in holiness, and nearest unto God. They were once under his power, and now being escaped from him, he pursues them as Pharaoh did the Israelites, with all his forces, raging and roaring after them, as a prey that was once in his den, and under his paw, and now is rescued.

The resemblance hath in it, his strength, his diligence, and his cruelty. His strength, *a lion* ; his diligence, *going about and seeking* ; his cruelty, *roaring*, and *seeking to devour*.

Inf. Is it not most reasonable hence to press watchfulness ; to keep continual watch, to see what comes in, and what goes out ; to try what is under every offer of the world, every motion of our own natural hearts, whether there be not some treachery, some secret intelligence or not ?   Especially after a time of some .special seasons of grace, and some special new supplies of grace, received in such seasons, (as after the holy sacrament,) then will he set on most eagerly, when he knows of the richest booty. The pirates that let the ships pass as they go by empty, watch them well when they return richly laden : so doth this great pirate. Did he not assault our Saviour straight after his baptism ? ὁ πειράζων.   Matt. iv. 3.

And, that we may *watch*, it concerns us *to be sober*. The instruction is military : a drunken soldier is not fit to be on the watch. This, most of us are, with our several fancies and vanities, and so exposed to this adversary. And when we have gained some advantage in a conflict, or when the enemy seems to retire and be gone, yet, even then, are we to be watchful, yea, then especially. How many, presuming on false safeties that way, and sitting down to carouse, or lying down to sleep, have been re-assaulted and cut off! *Invadunt urbem somno vinoque sepultam.* Oh, beware when you think yourselves most safe ! That very thought makes you least safe. Keep always your spirits free from surcharges, and lavish profusion upon the world ; keep from applying your hearts to any thing in it, sitting down to it.   Oh ! no. Be like Gideon's army, fit to follow God, and to be victorious in him, not lying down to drink, but taking of it only as for necessity, in passing. Take our Saviour's own word, *Take heed lest at any time your hearts be surcharged with surfeitings and drunkenness and the cares of this life.* Luke xxi. 34. These will *overcharge* you and make you drunk, and cast you asleep.

Oh, mind your work and your warfare always, more than your ease and pleasure ! Seek it not here ; your rest is not here. Oh, poor short rest, if it were ! But follow the Lord Jesus through conflicts and sufferings. A little while, and you shall have certain victory, and after it everlasting triumph, rest, and pleasure, and a feast that shall not end, where there is no danger either of surfeiting or of wearying, but pure and perpetual delight. In this persuasion, you should be abstinent and watchful, and *endure hardship, as good soldiers of Jesus Christ,* as the Apostle speaks, 2 Tim. ii. 4, *not entangling yourselves with the affairs of this life,* and thus be ready for encounters. Stand watching, and if you be assaulted, *resist.*

Whom resist, stedfast in the faith.] To watchfulness courage should be joined. He that watches and yields, seems rather to watch to receive than to resist the enemy.

And this resistance should be continued even against multiplied assaults : for thou hast to deal with an enemy that will not easily give over, but will try several ways, and will redouble his onsets ;* sometimes very thick, to weary thee out, sometimes after a little forbearance interposed, to catch thee unawares, when he is not expected. But in all, faint not, but be stedfast in thy resistance.

This is easily said, say you, but how may it be ? How shall I be able so to do ? Thus :

Stedfast in the faith.] The most of men are under the power of one of these two evils, security or distrust ; and out of the one, we

---

* Οὐ δίδωσιν ἀνάπαυσιν, οὐδὲ νικῶν, οὐδὲ νικώμενος. Plutarch. in Vita Marcel.

readily fall into the other. Therefore the Apostle frames his exhortations, and the arguments in support of it, in opposition to both these; first, against security in the former verse, *Be sober and watch,* and presses that by the proper argument of great and continuing danger; here against distrust, *Whom resist, stedfast in the faith;* and he adds an encouraging consideration of the common condition of the children of God in the world : *Knowing that the same afflictions are accomplished in your brethren.*

Stedfast, or solid, *by faith.*] This is absolutely necessary for resistance. A man cannot fight upon a quagmire; there is no standing out without a standing, some firm ground to tread upon ; and this Faith alone furnishes. It lifts the soul up to the firm advanced ground of the promises, and fastens it there ; and there it is sure, even *as Mount Zion, that cannot be removed.* He says not, stedfast by your own resolutions and purposes, but *stedfast by faith.* The power of God, by faith becomes ours ; for that is contained and engaged in the word of promise. Faith lays hold there, and there finds Almighty strength. *And this is our victory,* says the Apostle St. John, *whereby we overcome the world, even our Faith.* 1 John v. 4. So faith is our victory, whereby we overcome *the prince of this world. Whom resist, stedfast in the faith.* And, universally, all difficulties, and all enemies, are overcome by *faith.* Faith sets the stronger *Lion of the tribe of Judah,* against this *roaring lion* of the bottomless pit ; that delivering Lion, against this devouring lion.

When the soul is surrounded with enemies on all hands, so that there is no way of escape, Faith flies above them, and carries up the soul to take refuge in Christ, and is there safe. That is the power of Faith; it sets a soul in Christ, and there it looks down upon all temptations as at the bottom of the rock, breaking themselves into foam. When the floods of temptation rise and gather, so great and so many, that the soul is even ready to be swallowed up, then, by faith, it says, Lord Jesus, thou art my strength, I look to thee for deliverance ; now appear for my help ! And thus it overcomes. The guilt of sin is answered by his blood, the power of sin is conquered by his Spirit ; and afflictions that arise are nothing to these: his love and gracious presence make them sweet and easy.

We mistake, if we think to do any thing, or to be any thing, without him ; and we mistake again, if we think any thing too hard to be done or suffered with him. *Without me you can do nothing,* says he, John xv. 5 ; and *I am able to do all things,* says the Apostle, or *can all things,* πάντα ἰσχύω, (so the word is,) *through Christ that strengthens me.* Phil. iv. 13. All things ! Oh, that is a big word, yet it is a true word ; and thus made good—through Christ empowering me ; that frees it both from falsehood and vanity. A humble confidence, for it is not in himself, but in Christ; and this boasting is good. *My soul shall make her boast in God,* says David, Psal. xxxiv. 2. Oh, they alone have warrant to boast and to triumph, even before the victory, who do it in this style ! Such may give a challenge to all the world, to all adverse powers of Earth and Hell, as the Apostle doth in his own and every believer's name, Rom. viii. 35, 38 : *Who shall separate us from the love of Christ?* &c. See the victory recorded in this same way, Apoc. xii. 11 : *And they overcame him*—but how?—*by the blood of the Lamb, and by the word of their testimony.* That Blood, and the word of their testimony, believing that word concerning that Blood, these are the strength and victory of a Christian.

Inf. Although, then, thou seest thyself the most witless and weak, and findest thyself nothing but a prey to the powers of darkness, yet know that, by believing, the wisdom and strength of Christ are thine. Thou art, and oughtest to find thyself, all weakness ; but he is all strength, Almightiness itself. Learn to apply his victory, and so it is thine. Be strong—how?—*in him, and the power of his might.* But thou wilt say, I am often foiled, yea, I cannot find that I prevail at all against mine enemies, but they still against me. Yet rely on him : he can turn the chase in an instant. Still cleave to him. When the whole powers of thy soul are, as it were, scattered and routed, rally them by believing. Draw thou but unto the standard of Jesus Christ, and the day shall be thine ; for victory follows that standard, and cannot be severed from it. Yea, though thou find the smart of divers strokes, yet, think that often a wounded soldier hath won the day. Believe, and it shall be so with thee.

And remember that thy defeats, through the wisdom and love of thy God, may be ordered to advance the victory ; to put courage and holy anger into thee against thine enemies ; to humble thee, and drive thee from thine own imagined strength, to make use of his real strength. And be not hasty ; think not at the very first to conquer. Many a hard conflict must thou resolve upon, and often shalt thou be brought very low, almost to a desperate point, to thy sense, past recovery ; then it is his time to step in, even in the midst of their prevailing. *Let God but arise, and his enemies shall be scattered.* Psal. lxviii. 1. Thus the Church hath found it in her greatest extremities, and thus likewise the believing soul.

Knowing that the same afflictions are accomplished in your brethren that are in the world.] There is one thing that much troubles the patience, and weakens the faith, of some Christians ; they are ready to think there is no one, yea, that there never was any one beloved of God, in such a condition as theirs. Thus sometimes they swell even their outward trials in imagination, but oftener their inward ones, which are most heavy and pressing to themselves, and the parallel of them in others least discernible by them. Therefore the Apostle St. Paul breaks this conceit, 1 Cor. x. 13, *No temptation hath taken you, but such as is common to men.* And here is the same truth, *The same afflictions are accomplished in your brethren.*

But we had rather hear of ease, and cannot, after all that is said, bring our hearts to comply with this, that temptations and troubles are the saints' portion here, and that this is the royal way to the kingdom. Our King led in it, and all his followers go the same way ; and besides the happy end of it, is it not sweet, even for this, simply, because he went in it ? Yet, this is the truth, and, taken altogether, is a most conformable truth : the whole brotherhood, *all our brethren,* go in it, and our Eldest Brother went first.

Ver. 10. But the God of all grace, who hath called us unto his eternal glory by Christ Jesus, after that ye have suffered a while, make you perfect, stablish, strengthen, settle you.

HIS divine doctrine and exhortations the Apostle closes with prayer, as we follow this rule in public after the word preached. So St. Paul frequently did, and so Christ himself, John xvii., after that sermon in the preceding chapters. It were well if both ministers and people would follow the same way more in private, each for themselves, and each for the other. The want of this is mainly the thing that makes our preaching and hearing so barren and fruitless. The ministers of the Gospel should indeed be as the angels of God, going betwixt him and his people; not only bringing down useful instructions from God to them, but putting up earnest supplications to God for them. In the tenth chapter of St. Luke, the disciples are sent forth and appointed to preach; and in the eleventh, we have them desiring to be taught to pray; *Lord, teach us to pray.* And without this, there can be little answer or success in the other; little springing up of this seed, though ministers sow it plentifully in preaching, unless they secretly water it with their prayers and their tears.

And people, truly, should keep some correspondence in this duty, and that, if other obligation will not persuade, even for their own advantage; for it returns unto them with abundant interest. If much of the Spirit be poured forth on ministers, are they not the more able to unfold the spiritual mysteries of the Gospel, and to build up their people in the knowledge of them? Oh that both of us were more abundant in this rich and sweet exercise!

But the God of all grace, who hath called us to eternal glory by Christ Jesus.] This prayer suits the Apostle St. Paul's word, in his direction to the Philippians (ch. iv. 6); it is *supplication with thanksgiving*, prayer with praise. In the prayer or petition, consider, 1st, the matter, and 2ndly, the style.

The matter, or thing requested, is expressed in divers brief words, *Make you perfect, stablish, strengthen, settle you;* which, though they be much of the same sense, yet are not superfluously multiplied, for they carry both the great importance of the thing, and the earnest desire in asking it. And though it be a little light and unsolid, to frame a different sense to each of them, (nor are any of the ways that such interpreters have taken in it, very satisfactory to any discerning judgment,) yet I conceive they are not altogether without some profitable difference. The first [*Perfect*] implies, more clearly than the rest, their advancement in victory over their remaining corruptions and infirmities, and their progress towards perfection. *Stablish,* hath more express reference to both the inward lightness and inconstancy that are natural to us, and the counter-blasts of persecutions and temptations, outward oppositions; and it imports the curing of the one, and support against the other. *Strengthen,* has respect to the growth of their graces, especially the gaining of further measures of those graces wherein they are weakest and lowest. And *settle,* though it seems the same, and in substance is the same with the other word, *stablish,* yet it adds somewhat to it very worthy of consideration; for it signifies, to found or fix upon a sure foundation, and so, indeed, may have an aspect to him who is the foundation and strength of believers, on whom they build by faith, even *Jesus Christ,* in whom we have all, both victory over sin, and increase of grace, and establishment of spirit, and power to persevere against all difficulties and assaults. He is that *corner foundation-stone laid in Zion, that they that build upon him may not be ashamed,* Isa. xxviii. 16 ; that *Rock* that upholds the house founded on it, in the midst of all winds and storms. Matt. vii. *ult.*

Observe, 1st, These expressions have in them that which is primarily to be sought after by every Christian, *perseverance* and *progress* in grace. These two are here interwoven ; for there be two words importing the one, and two the other, and they are interchangeably placed. This is often urged on Christians as their duty, and accordingly ought they to apply themselves to it, and use their highest diligence in it ; not to take the beginning of Christianity for the end of it, to think it enough if they are entered into the way of it, and to sit down upon the entry ; but to walk on, to *go from strength to strength,* and even through the greatest difficulties and discouragements, to pass forward with unmoved stability and fixedness of mind. They ought to be aiming at perfection. It is true, we shall still fall exceedingly short of it ; but the more we study it, the nearer shall we come to it ; the higher we aim, the higher shall we shoot, though we shoot not so high as we aim.

It is an excellent life, and it is the proper life of a Christian, to be daily outstripping himself, to be spiritually wiser, holier, more heavenly-minded to-day than yesterday, and to-morrow (if it be added to his life) than to-day ; *Suavissima vita est in dies sentire se fieri meliorem :* every day loving the world less, and Christ more, than on the former, and gaining every day some further victory over his secret corruptions ; having his passions more subdued and mortified, his desires in all temporal things more cool and indifferent, and in spiritual things, more ardent ; that miserable lightness of spirit cured, and his heart rendered more solid and fixed upon God, aspiring to more near communion with him, and labouring that particular graces may be made more lively and strong, by often exercising and stirring them up ; faith more confirmed and stayed, love more inflamed, composed meekness producing more deep humility. Oh, this were a worthy ambition indeed ! You would have your estates growing, and your credit growing ; how much rather should you seek to have your graces growing, and not be content with any thing you have attained to !

Obs. 2nd, But all our endeavours and diligence in this will be vain, unless we look for our perfecting and establishing from that *right hand,* without which we can do nothing. Thither the Apostle moves his desires for his brethren, and so teaches them the same address for themselves : *The God of all grace make you perfect.*

This prayer is grounded (as all prayer of faith must be) on the promise and covenant of God. He *is our rock, and his work is perfect.* Deut. xxxii. 4. He doth not begin a building, and then leave it off : none of his designs break in the middle, or fall short of their end. *He will perfect that good work which he hath begun, to the day of Jesus Christ.* Phil. i. 6. And how often is he called the *strength of those that trust in him, their buckler, and his way perfect.* Psal. xviii. 30.

Hence is the stability of grace, the perseverance of the saints ; it is founded upon His unchangeableness. Not that they are unchangeable, though truly sanctified, if they and their graces were left to their own management : no, it is he who not only gives that rich portion to those he adopts to be his children, but keeps it for them, and them in the possession of it. He *maintains the lot of our inheritance.* Psal. xvi. 5. And to build that persuasion of perseverance upon his truth and power engaged in it, is no presumption ; yea, it is high dishonour to him to question it.

But when Nature is set to judge of Grace, it must speak according to itself, and therefore very unsuitably to that which it speaks of. Natural wits apprehend not the spiritual tenor of the Covenant of Grace, but model it to their own principles, and quite disguise it : they think of nothing but their resolves and moral purposes ; or if they take up with some confused notion of grace, they imagine it put into their own hands, to keep or to lose it, and will not stoop to a continual dependence on the strength of Another, rather choosing that game of hazard, though it is certain loss and undoing, to do for themselves.

But the humble Believer is otherwise taught ; he *hath not so learned Christ.* He sees himself beset with enemies without, and buckled to a treacherous heart within, that will betray him to them ; and he dares no more trust himself to himself, than to his most professed enemies. Thus it ought to be, and the more the heart is brought to this humble petitioning for that ability, and strengthening, and perfecting, from God, the more shall it find both stability, and peace from the assurance of that stability.

And certainly, the more the Christian is acquainted with himself, the more will he go out of himself for his perfecting and establishing. He finds that when he thinks to go forward, he is driven backward, and that sin gets hold of him, oftentimes when he thought to have smitten it. He finds that such is the miserable inconstancy of his heart in spiritual things, the vanishing of his purposes and breaking off of his thoughts, that they usually die ere they be brought forth : so that when he hath thought, I will pray more reverently, and set myself to behold God when I speak to him, and watch more over my heart, that it fly not out and leave me,—possibly the first time he sets to it, thinking to be master of his intention, he finds himself more scattered, and disordered, and dead, than at any time before. When he hath conceived thoughts of humility and self-abasement, and thinks, Now I am down, and laid low within myself, to rise and look big no more,—some vain fancy creeps in anon, and encourages him, and raises him up to his old estate ; so that in this plight, had he not higher strength to look at, he would sit down and give over all, as utterly hopeless of ever attaining to his journey's end.

But when he considers whose work that is within him, even these small beginnings of desires, he is encouraged by the greatness of the work, not to despise and despair of the small appearance of it in its beginning, *not to despise the day of small things,* Zech. iv. 10 ; and knowing that it is *not by any power, nor by might, but by his Spirit,* that it shall be accomplished, he lays hold on that word, *Though thy beginning be small, yet thy latter end shall greatly increase.* Job viii. 7.

The Believer *looks to Jesus,* [ἀφορῶντες,] Heb. xii. 2,—*looks off* from all oppositions and difficulties, *looks* above them *to Jesus, the author and finisher of our faith; author,* and therefore *finisher.* Thus, that royal dignity is interested in the maintenance and completion of what he hath wrought. Notwithstanding all thy imperfections, and the strength of sin, he can and will subdue it. Notwithstanding thy condition is so light and loose, that it were easy for any wind of temptation to blow thee away, yet he shall hold thee in his right hand, and there thou shalt be firm as the earth, that is so settled by his hand, that though it hangs on nothing, yet nothing can remove it. Though thou art weak, he is strong ; and it is *he that strengthens thee, and renews thy strength,* Isa. xl. 28 : when it seems to be gone and quite spent, he makes it fresh, and greater than ever before. The word here rendered *renew,* signifies *change :* they shall have, for their own, his strength. A weak believer, and his strong Saviour, will be too hard for all that can rise against them. It is here fit, as in statues, *hominem cum basi metiri,* to measure the man with the basis on which he stands ; and there is no taking the right measure of a Christian but in that way.

Thou art now, indeed, exposed to great storms and tempests, but he builds thee on himself, makes thee, by believing, to found on him ; and so, though the winds blow and the rain fall, yet thou standest, being built on him, thy Rock. And this, indeed, is our safety, the more we cleave to our Rock and fasten on him. This is the only thing that *establishes* us, and *perfects,* and *strengthens* us ; therefore, well is that word added, θεμελιῶσαι, *found* you, or *settle* you, on your foundation. This is the firmness of the Church against the gates of hell ; he is a strong Foundation for its establishment, and a living Foundation, having influence into the Building, for perfecting it ; for it is a living House, and the foundation is a root sending life into the stones, so that *they grow up,* as this Apostle speaks, ch. ii. 4.

It is the inactivity of faith on Jesus, that keeps us so imperfect, and wrestling still with our corruptions, without any advancement. We wrestle in our own strength too often, and so are justly, yea, necessarily, foiled ; it cannot be otherwise till we make him our strength. This we are still forgetting, and had need to be put in mind of, and ought frequently to remind ourselves. We would be at doing for ourselves, and insensibly fall into this folly, even after much smarting for it, if we be not watchful against it. There is this wretched natural independency in us, that is so hard to beat out. All our projectings are but castles in the air, imaginary buildings without a foundation, till once laid on Christ. But never shall we find heart-peace, sweet peace, and progress in holiness, till we be driven from it, to make him all our strength ; till we be brought to do nothing, to attempt nothing, to hope or expect nothing, but in him ; and then shall we indeed find his fulness and all-sufficiency, and *be more than conquerors through him who hath loved us.*

But the God of all grace.] By reason of our many wants and great weakness, we had need to have a very full hand and a very strong hand to go to for our supplies and for support. And such we have indeed: our Father is the *God of all grace,* a spring that cannot be drawn dry, no, nor so much as any whit diminished.

The God of all Grace: the God of imputed grace, of infused and increased grace, of furnished and assisting grace. The work of salvation is all Grace from beginning to end. Free Grace in the plot of it, laid in the counsel of God, and performed by his own hand all of it; his Son sent in the flesh, and his Spirit sent into the hearts of his chosen, to apply Christ. All grace is in him, the living spring of it, and flows from him; all the various actings, and all the several degrees of grace. He is the God of pardoning grace, who *blotteth out the transgressions of* his own children, *for his own name's sake,* (Isa. xliii. 25,) who takes up all quarrels, and makes one act of oblivion serve for all reckonings betwixt him and them. And, as he is the God of pardoning grace, so withal, the God of sanctifying grace, who refines and purifies all those he means to make up into vessels of glory, and hath in his hand all the fit means and ways of doing this; purifies them by afflictions and outward trials, by the reproaches and hatreds of the world. The profane world little know how serviceable they are to the graces and comforts of a Christian, when they dishonour and persecute him; yea, little doth a Christian himself sometimes think how great his advantage is by those things, till he finds it, and wonders at his Father's wisdom and love. But most powerfully are the children of God sanctified by the Spirit within them, without which, indeed, no other thing could be of any advantage to them in this. That Divine fire kindled within them, is daily refining and sublimating them, that Spirit of Christ conquering sin, and by the mighty flame of his love, consuming the earth and dross that is in them; making their affections more spiritual and disengaged from all creature-delights. And thus, as they receive the beginnings of grace freely, so all the advances and increases of it; life from their Lord still flowing and causing them to grow, abating the power of sin, strengthening a fainting faith, quickening a languishing love, teaching the soul the ways of wounding strong corruptions, and fortifying its weak graces; yea, in wonderful ways advancing the good of his children by things not only harsh to them, as afflictions and temptations, but by that which is directly opposite in its nature, sin itself; raising them by their falls, and strengthening them by their very troubles; working them to humility and vigilance, and sending them to Christ for strength, by the experience of their weaknesses and failings.

And as he is the God of pardoning grace, and of sanctifying grace in the beginning and growth of it, so also the God of supporting grace, of that supervenient influence without which the graces placed within us would lie dead, and fail us in the time of greatest need. This is the immediate assisting power that bears up the soul under the hardest services, and backs it in the sharpest conflicts, communicating fresh auxiliary strength, when we, with all the grace we have dwelling within us, are surcharged. Then he steps in, and opposes his strength to a prevailing and confident enemy, that is at the point of insulting and triumph. When temptations have made a breach, and enter with full force and violence, he lets in so' much present help on a sudden, as makes them give back, and beats them out. *When the enemy comes in as a flood, the Spirit of the Lord lifts up a standard against him.* Isa. lix. 11. And no siege can be so close as to keep out this aid, for it comes from above.

And by this, a Christian learns that his strength is in God; whereas, if his received grace were always party enough, and able to make itself good against all incursions, though we know we have received it, yet being within us, we should possibly sometimes forget the receipt of it, and look on it more as ours than as his; more as being within us, than as flowing from him. But when all the forces we have, the standing garrison, are by far overmatched, and yet we find the assailants beaten back, then we must acknowledge him who sends such seasonable relief, to be, as the Psalmist speaks, *a very present help in trouble.* Psal. xlvi. 1.

All St. Paul's constant strength of grace inherent in him, could not fence him so well, as to ward off the piercing point of that sharp temptation, whatsoever it was, which he records, 2 Cor. xii. 7. The redoubled buffetings that he felt, came so thick upon him, that he was driven to his knees by it, to cry for help to be sent down, without which he found he could not hold out; and he had an answer assuring him of help, a secret support that should maintain them: *My grace is sufficient for thee: q. d.,* though thine own be not, that is, the grace which I have already given thee, yet *mine* is, that is, the grace which is in me, and which I will put forth for thy assistance.

And this is our great advantage and comfort, that we have a Protector who is Almighty, and who is always at hand, who can and will hear us whensoever we are beset and straitened. That captain had reason, who, on being required to keep Milan for the king of France, went up to the highest turret, and cried out three times, "King of France," and then refused the service, because the king heard him not, and nobody answered for him; meaning to imply the great distance, and so the difficulty of sending aid, when need should require. But we may be confident of our supplies in the most sudden surprisals. Our King can, and will hear us when we call, and will send relief in due season. We may be in apparent hazards, but we shall not be wholly vanquished: it is but crying to him in our greatest straits, and help appears. Possibly we see the host of enemies first, and that so great that there is no likelihood of escaping, but then, praying, we espy the fiery chariots and horsemen, and may say, *There are more with us than with them.* 2 Kings vi. 16.

The Apostle St. Paul calls our God, *the God of all consolation,* Rom. xv. 5, as here he is styled *the God of all grace.* And this is our rejoicing, that in his hand is all good, our sanctification and consolation, assistance and assurance, *grace and glory.* And this style suits most fitly with the present petition, that for our *perfecting, and stablishing, and strengthening in grace,* we have recourse to *the God of all Grace*, whose former gifts do not discourage us from seeking more, but indeed both encourage us, and engage him for the perfecting of it. It is his will, that we have constant recourse to him for all we want. He is so rich, and withal so liberal, that he delights in our seeking and drawing much from him; and it is by believing and praying, that we do draw from him. Were these plied, we should soon grow richer. But remember, all this grace that we would receive from the God of all Grace, must be from *God in Christ.* There it flows for us, and thither we are directed. *It was the Father's good pleasure, that in him should all fulness dwell,* Col. i. 19, and that *for us,* that we might know whither to go, and where to apply for it.

Now, for the further opening up of his riches, expressed in this title, *the God of all Grace,* there is added one great act of grace, which doth indeed include all the rest, for we have in it the beginning and the end of the work linked together; the first effect of grace upon us, in *effectual calling,* and the last accomplishment of it, in *eternal glory. Who hath called us to his eternal glory.*

This *calling,* I conceive, doth not simply mean the design of the Gospel in its general publication, wherein the outward call lies, that it holds forth, and sets before us, eternal glory as the result of Grace; but refers to the real bringing of a Christian to Christ, and uniting him with Christ, and so giving him a real and firm title to glory,— such a call, as powerfully works grace in the soul, and secures glory to the soul; gives it a right to that inheritance, and fits it for it; and sometimes gives it even the evident and sweet assurance of it. This assurance, indeed, all the heirs of glory have not ordinarily within them, and scarcely any have at all times equally clear. Some travel on in a covert, cloudy day, and get home by it, having so much light as to know their way, and yet do not at all clearly see the bright and full sunshine of assurance; others have it breaking forth at times, and anon under a cloud; and some have it more constantly. But as all meet in the end, so all agree in this in the beginning, that is, in the reality of the thing; they are made unalterably sure heirs of it, in their effectual calling.

And by this the Apostle advances his petition for their support, and establishment, and advancement in the way of grace. The way of our calling to so high and happy an estate, did we apply our thoughts more to it, would work on us, and persuade us to a more suitable temper of mind, and course of life; would give us more noble and sublime thoughts, and ways above the world; and the stronger were our persuasion of it, the more strongly should we be thus persuaded by it. And as it would thus prevail with us, so might we use it to prevail with God for all needful grace.

All you who hear the Gospel, are, in the general, called to this glory. It is told you where and how you may lay hold on it. You are told, that if you will let go your sins and embrace Jesus Christ, this glory shall be yours. It is his purchase, and the right of it lies in him, and not elsewhere; and the way to obtain a right to him is to receive him for a Saviour, and at the same time for Lord and King; to become his subjects, and so to be made kings. This is our message to you, but you will not receive it. You give it a hearing, it may be, but do not indeed hearken to the motion ; and this, of necessity, must proceed from unbelief. Were you indeed persuaded, that in coming unto Christ, you were immediately not only set free from a sentence of death, which is still standing over your head while you are out of him, but withal entitled to a crown, made heirs of a kingdom, an eternal kingdom,—I say, if this were believed, were it possible to slight him as the most do, and turn back the bargain, and bestow their money elsewhere upon trifles of no value, children's commodities, rattles, and painted toys ? Such are your greatest projects, even for earthly kingdoms, in respect of Christ, and this glory provided in him. How wonderful is it, that where this happiness is daily proclaimed, and you are not only informed of it, but entreated to receive it, not only is it offered you, but pressed and urged upon you, and you say you believe the matter ; yet still, the false glory and other vanities of this world amuse and entangle you, so that you close not with this rich offer of *eternal glory.*

But where any do close with it, it is indeed by a call that goes deeper than the ear, a word spoken home to within, a touch of the Spirit of God upon the heart, which hath a magnetic virtue to draw it, so that it cannot choose but follow, and yet chooses it most freely and sweetly ; doth most gladly open to let in Jesus Christ and his sweet government upon his own terms, takes him and all the reproaches and troubles that can come with him. And well it may, seeing, beyond a little passing trouble, abiding, eternal glory.

The state to which a Christian is called, is not a poor and sad estate, as the World judges ; it is no less than *eternal glory.* The World think it strange to see the believer abridge himself in the delights of sin, their common pursuits and eager graspings after gains, or honours, or pleasures of sense ; but they know not the infinite gain that he hath made, in that he hath exchanged this dross for downweight of pure gold. The World see what the Christian leaves, but they see not what he comes to, what his new purchase is, in another place ; they see what he suffers, but not what he expects, and shall attain as the end of those sufferings, which shall shortly end. But he, knowing well upon what conditions all these things run, may well say, *Non magna relinquo, magna sequor*—How small is what I forsake, how great that which I follow after !

It is Glory, Eternal Glory, *His eternal Glory*, true, real Glory. All here that is so named, is no more than a name, a shadow of glory ; it cannot endure the balance, but is found too light, as was said of a great monarch, Dan. v. ; and even many principalities and provinces, put into the scale one after another, still add no weight : yea, possibly, as a late political writer wittily observes of a certain monarch, " The more kingdoms you cast in, the scale is still the lighter." Men are naturally desirous of glory, and gape after it ; but they are naturally ignorant of the true nature and place of it : they seek it where it is not, and, as Solomon says of riches, *set their hearts on that which is not*, Prov. xxiii. 5—hath no subsistence or reality. But the glory above, is true, real glory, and bears weight, and so bears aright the name of glory, the term for which in the Hebrew [*Kebud*] signifies *weight;* and the Apostle's expression seems to allude to that sense: speaking of this same glory to come, he calls it *a far more excellent weight of glory.* 2 Cor. iv. 17. It weighs down all labour and sufferings in the way, so far, as that they are not once worth the speaking of in respect of it. It is the *hyperbole* καθ' ὑπερβολὴν εἰς ὑπερβολὴν. Other glory is over-spoken, but this Glory is over-glorious to be duly spoken: it exceeds and rises above all that can be spoken of it.

Eternal.] Oh, that adds much! Men would have more reason so to affect and pursue the glory of the present world, such as it is, if it were lasting, if it stayed with them when they have caught it, and they stayed with it to enjoy it. But how soon do they part! They pass away, and the glory passes away, both as smoke. Our life itself is as a vapour. And as for all the pomp and magnificence of those that have the greatest outward glory, and make the fairest show, it is but a show, a *pageant* that goes through the street, and is seen no more. But this hath length of days with it—*Eternal Glory.* Oh, a thought of that swallows up all the grandeur of the world, and the noise of reckoning years and ages. Had one man continued, from the Creation to the end of the world, at the top of earthly dignity and glory, admired by all, yet, at the end, everlasting oblivion being the close, what a nothing were it to *eternal glory!* But, alas! we cannot be brought to believe, and deeply to take the impression of eternity; and this is our undoing.

By Jesus Christ.] Your portion, while out of him, was eternal shame and misery, but *by* him, it is even all glory. And this hath in it likewise an evidence of the greatness of this glory; it can be no small estate, which the blood of the Son of God was let out to purchase.

His glory.] It is that which he gives, and gives as his choicest of all, to his chosen, his children. And if there be any thing here that hath delight or worth, in the things which he gives in common even to his enemies; if there be such a world and such a variety of good things for them that hate him, oh how excellent must those things be which he hath reserved for his friends, for those he loves, and causes to love him!

As it is his gift, so it is indeed himself; the beholding and enjoying of himself. This we cannot now conceive. But, oh, that blessed day when the soul shall be full of God, shall be satisfied and ravished with full vision! Should we not admire that such a condition is provided for man, wretched, sinful man? *Lord, what is man, that thou art mindful of him, and the son of man, that thou visitest him?* Psal. viii. 3. And is it provided for me, as wretched as any who are left and fallen short of this glory, a base worm taken out of the mire, and washed in the blood of Christ, and within awhile set to shine in glory without sin! Oh, the wonder of this! How should it excite us to praise, when we think of Such a One there, who will bring us up in the way to this crown! How will this hope sweeten the short sufferings of this life! And death itself, which is otherwise the bitterest in itself, is most of all sweetened by this, as being nearest it, and setting us into it. What though thou art poor, diseased, and despised here! Oh, consider what is there, how worthy the affection, worthy the earnest eye and fixed look of an heir of this glory! What can he either desire or fear, whose heart is thus deeply fixed? Who would refuse this other clause, *to suffer a while,* a little while, any thing outward or inward which he thinks fit? How soon shall all this be overpast, and then overpaid in the very entry, at the beginning of this glory that shall never end!

Ver. 11. To him be glory and dominion for ever and ever. Amen.

THEY know little of their own wants and emptiness, who are not much in prayer; and they know little of the greatness and goodness of God, who are not much in praises. The humble Christian hath a heart in some measure framed to both. He hath within him the best school-master, who teaches him how to pray, and how to praise, and makes him delight in the exercise of them both.

The Apostle, having added prayer to his doctrine, adds here, you see, praise to his prayer. *To him be glory and dominion for ever.*

The living praises of God spring from much holy affection, and that affection springs from a Divine light in the understanding. So says the Psalmist, *Sing ye praises with understanding,* or, *you that have understanding.* Psal. xlvii. 7. It is a spiritual knowledge of God, that sets the soul in tune for his praises, and therefore the most can bear no part in this song: they mistune it quite, through their ignorance of God, and unacquaintance with him. Praise is unseemly in the mouth of fools: they spoil and mistune it.

Observe, 1. The thing ascribed. 2. The term or endurance of it. The former is expressed in two words; *glory, and power. Glory,* that is, the shining forth of his dignity, the knowledge and acknowledgment of it by his creatures; that his excellency may be confessed and praised, his name exalted; that service and homage may be done to him. Which all add nothing to him, for how can that be? But as it is the duty of such creatures as he hath fitted for it, to render praise to him, so it is their happiness. All created things, indeed, declare and speak his glory: the heavens sound it forth, and the earth and sea resound and echo it back. But his reasonable creatures hath he peculiarly framed, both to take notice of his glory in all the rest, and to return it from and for all the rest, in a more express and lively way.

And in this lower world, it is Man alone that is made capable of observing the glory of God, and of offering him praises. He expresses it well, who calls man *the world's high priest;* all the creatures bring their oblations of praise to him, to offer up for them and for himself, for whose use and comfort they are made. The light and motion of the heavens, and all the variety of creatures below them, speak this to man: he that made us and you, and made us for you, is great, and wise, and worthy to be praised. And you are better able to say this than we; therefore praise him on our behalf and on your own. Oh! he is great and mighty, he is the Lord our Maker.

Power, here expresses not only ability, but authority and royal sovereignty; that, as he can do all things, he rules and governs all things, is King of all the World, Lord paramount. All hold their crowns of him, and *the shields of the earth belong unto God; he is greatly to be exalted.* Psal. xlvii. 9. He disposeth of states and kingdoms at his pleasure, establisheth or changeth, turns and overturns, as seems him good; and hath not only might, but right to do so. *He is the Most High, ruling in the kingdoms of the children of men and giving them to whomsoever he will,* Dan. iv. 32, pouring contempt upon princes when they contemn his power.

The Term of this glory is *for ever.* Even in the short life of man, men who are raised very high in place and popular esteem may, and often do, outlive their own glory. But the glory of God lasteth as long as himself, for he is unchangeable: his throne is *for ever,* and his wrath *for ever,* and his mercy *for ever;* and therefore his glory *for ever.*

Reflection 1. Is it not to be lamented, that he is so little glorified and praised? that the earth, being so full of his goodness, is so empty of his praise from them who enjoy and live upon it?

How far are the greatest part from making this their great work, to exalt God, and ascribe power and glory to his name! So far, that all their ways are his dishonour: they seek to advance and raise themselves, to serve their own lusts and pleasures, while they are altogether mindless of his glory. Yea, the Apostle's complaint holds good against us all; we are *seeking our own things, and none the things of the Lord Jesus Christ.* Phil. ii. 21. It is true, some exceptions there are; but, as his meaning is, they are so few, that they are, as it were, drowned and smothered in the crowd of self-seekers, so that they appear not. After all the judgments of God upon us, how do luxury and excess, uncleanness, and all kinds of profaneness, still outdare the very light of the Gospel, and the rule of holiness shining in it! Scarcely any thing is a matter of common shame and scorn, but the *power of godliness;* turning indeed our true glory into shame, and glorying in that which is indeed our shame. Holiness is not only our truest glory, but that wherein the ever-glorious God doth especially glory. He hath made known himself particularly by that name, *The holy God;* and the express style of his glorious praises uttered by *seraphims,* is, *Holy, holy, holy is the Lord of hosts: the whole earth is full of his glory.* Isa. vi. 3.

Instead of sanctifying and glorifying this holy Name, how doth the language of hell, oaths and curses, abound in our streets and houses! How is that blessed Name, which angels are blessing and praising, abused by base worms! Again, notwithstanding all the mercies multiplied upon us in this land, where are our praises, our songs of deliverance, our ascribing glory and power to our God, who hath prevented us with loving-kindness and tender mercies; hath removed the strokes of his hand, and made cities and villages populous again, that were left desolate without inhabitants?

Oh, why do we not stir up our hearts, and one another, to extol the name of our God, and say, *Give unto the Lord glory and strength; give unto the Lord the glory due unto his name?* Have we not seen the pride and glory of all flesh stained and abased? Were there ever affairs and times that more discovered the folly and weakness of men, and the wisdom and power of God? Oh that our hearts were set to magnify him, according to that word so often repeated in Psal. cvii., *Oh that men would praise the Lord for his goodness, for his wonderful works to the children of men!*

Reflection 2. But what wonder is it that the Lord loses the revenue of his praises at the hands of the common ungodly world, when even his own people fall so far behind it as usually they do? *The dead cannot praise him;* but that they whom he hath quickened by his Spirit, should yet be so surprised with deadness and dulness as to this exercise of exalting God, this is very strange. For help of this, take the three following directions.

Direct. I. We should seek after a fit temper, and labour to have our hearts brought to a due disposition for his praises. And in this view, [1.] See that they be spiritual. All spiritual services require that, but this service most, as being indeed the most spiritual of all. Affection to the things of this earth, draws down the soul, and makes it so low set, that it cannot rise to the height of a song of praise; and thus, if we observed ourselves, we should find, that when we let our hearts fall and entangle themselves in any inferior desires and delights, as they are unfitted generally for holy things, so, especially, for the praises of our holy God. Creature loves debase the soul, and turn it to earth, and praise is altogether heavenly.

[2.] Seek a heart purified from self-love, and possessed with the love of God. The heart which is ruled by its own interest is scarcely ever content, still subject to new disquiet. Self is a vexing thing, for all things do not readily suit our humours and wills, and the least touch that is wrong to a selfish mind distempers it, and disrelishes all the good things about it. A childish condition it is, if crossed but in a toy, to throw away all. Whence are our frequent frettings and grumblings, and why is it that we can drown a hundred high favours in one little displeasure, so that still our finger is upon that string, and there is more malcontent and repining for one little cross, than praises for all the mercies we have received? Is not this evidently from the self-love that abounds in us? Whereas, were the love of God predominant in us, we should love his doings and disposals, and bless his name in all. Whatsoever were his will, would, in that view, be amiable and sweet to us, however in itself harsh and unpleasant. Thus should we say in all: This is the will and the hand of my Father, who doth all things wisely and well; blessed be his name!

The soul thus framed, would praise in the deeps of troubles: not only in outward afflictions, but in the saddest inward condition, it would be still extolling God, and saying, However he deal with me, he is worthy to be loved and praised. He is great and holy, he is good and gracious; and whatsoever be his way and thoughts towards me, I wish him glory. If he will be pleased to give me light and refreshment, blessed be he; and if he will have me to be in darkness again, blessed be he, glory to his name! Yea, what though he should utterly reject me, is he not for that to be accounted infinitely merciful in the saving of others? Must he cease to be praiseworthy for my sake? If he condemn, yet he is to be praised, being merciful to so many others; yea, even in so dealing with me, he is to be praised, for in that he is just.

Thus would pure love reason for him, and render praise to him. But our ordinary way is most untoward and unbeseeming his creatures, even the best of them, much more such worms as we are; that things must rather be to our mind than his, and we must either have all our will, or else, for our part, he shall have none of his praises.

[3.] Labour for that which on these two will follow, a *fixed heart*. If it be refined from creature-love, and self-love, spirituality and love of God will fix it; and then shall it be fit to praise, which an unstable, uncomposed heart can never be, any more than an instrument can be harmonious and fit to play on, that hath loose pins, still slipping and letting down the strings, pins that never fasten. And thus are the most: they cannot fix to Divine thoughts, to consider God, to behold and admire his excellency and goodness, and his free love. Oh, that happy word of David, worthy to be twice repeated! When shall we say it? *O God, my heart is fixed:* well might he add, *I will sing and give praise.* Psal. lvii. 7. Oh that we would pray much that he would fix our hearts, and then, he having fixed them, we should praise him much.

Direct. II. If any due disposition be once attained for praises, then must the heart, so disposed, be set to study the matter of praises.

And, 1. Study the infinite excellency of God in himself; of which though we know little, yet this we know, and should consider it, that it is far beyond what all the creatures and all his works are able to testify of him; that he transcends all we can speak, or hear, or know of him. 2. Look on him in his works. Can we behold the vast heavens above, or the firm earth beneath us, or all the variety of his works in both, without holy wonder excited in us, and that stirring us up to sing praises? Oh his greatness, and might, and wisdom shining in these! *Lord, how manifest are thy works! In wisdom hast thou made them all.* Psal. civ. 24. But above all, that work, that marvel of his works, the sending of his Son forth of his bosom. This is the mystery which the Apostles do so much magnify in their writings, which is so much magnified in this Epistle, and which forms the chief incentive to the ascription of praise with which it closes. This praise looks particularly back to the style in the prayer, *The God of all grace, who hath called us to his eternal glory by Jesus Christ.* So many other mercies are not to be forgotten, but chiefly is he to be praised for that choicest of mercies. *To his glory, who hath called us to his glory.* Then, look through the work of saving his chosen, so redeemed by the blood of his Son. His maintaining his own work in them against all surrounding enemies and oppositions, the advancing of it in the midst of them, and even by means of those oppositions, and bringing them safe to glory; that *perfecting* and *establishment*, as in the foregoing words. It is this which so affects the Apostle in the very entry of this Epistle, that there he must break forth into praise: *Blessed be the God and Father of our Lord Jesus Christ, who, accord-*

ing to his abundant mercy, hath begotten us again unto a lively hope, by the resurrection of Jesus Christ from the dead, ch. i. ver. 3. He begins there in praise, and here he ends in it, and so encloses all within that divine circle. And as we should consider these things in general, so should we also reflect on his particular dealing with us, his good providence both in spirituals and temporals. Would we search, oh! what a surcharge of innumerable mercies should each of us find! And were we better acquainted with the Holy Scriptures, had we more our delight in them, they would acquaint us better with all these things, and give us light to see them, and warm our hearts, and excite them to his praises, who is the God of all our mercies.

Direct. III. The heart being somewhat disposed to praise, and then studying the matter of it, should be applied actually to render praise. And in order to this, we must be careful, 1. To aim at God in all, which is continued praise; to eye his glory in every thing, and chiefly to desire that, as our great end, that his name may be exalted. This is *the excellent way* indeed. Whereas most are either wholly for their self-ends, or often squinting out to them. That soul is most noble, which singly and fixedly aims at exalting God, and seeks to have this stamp on all it speaks, and does, and desires: all to the greater glory of my God. 2. To abound in the express and solemn return of praise this way. *To him be glory,* not a customary dead saying of it over, as is usual with us, but the heart offering it up. What is so pure and high as this exercise, the praises of the ever-glorious Deity? What is heaven but these? And were it not best, as we can, to begin it here, and long to be there, where it shall never end? *To him be glory and dominion for ever and ever.* Amen.

Ver. 12. By Silvanus, a faithful brother unto you, as I suppose, I have written briefly, exhorting, and testifying that this is the true grace of God wherein ye stand.

13. The church that is at Babylon, elected together with you, saluteth you; and so doth Marcus my son.

14. Greet ye one another with a kiss of charity. Peace be with you all that are in Christ Jesus. Amen.

THIS is a kind of postscript, and contains a testimony of the bearer, and the apostolic form of saluting. Withal, the Apostle expresses the measure of his writing, that it was *brief,* and the end of it, *that it was to testify the true grace of God.* And this is, indeed, the end of our preaching, and we ought each to seek it by the word, and by mutual exhortations; and sometimes a few words may avail much to this purpose, to our hearty establishment in the faith. And not only are we to believe, but to remember that we have the best of it; that there is truth in our hopes, and they shall not deceive us. They are no fancy, as the world thinks, *but the true grace of God;* yea, when all things else shall vanish, their truth shall most appear in their full accomplishment.

The entertainment and increase of Christian love, of due esteem one of another, and affection one to another, is no matter of empty compliment, but is the very stamp and badge of Jesus Christ upon his followers; it is, therefore, most carefully to be preserved entire, and unhappy are they that do by any means willingly break it. Oh, let us beware of doing so, and *follow peace,* even when it seems to fly from us !

This *peace* that is the portion of those in Christ, is indeed within them, and with God. But through him, it is likewise *one with another,* and in that notion it is to be desired and wished jointly with the other.

They that are in Christ are the only children and heirs of true peace. Others may dream of it, and have a false peace for a time, and wicked men may wish it to themselves and one another ; but it is a most vain hope, and will come to nought. But to wish it to them that are in Christ hath good ground ; for all solid peace is founded on him, and flows from him. *Now, the peace of God, which passeth all understanding, keep your hearts and minds, through Jesus Christ.* Amen.

Other Titles

by CalvaryPress

Stepping Heavenward -Elizabeth Prentiss

From Religion to Christ -Peter Jeffery

Thoughts for Young Men -J.C. Ryle

A Dying Man's Regrets -Adolphe Monod

More Love to Thee -George Lewis Prentiss

The Little Preacher -Elizabeth Prentiss

The Glory of the Church -Various Authors

From Forgiven to Forgiving -Jay Adams

The Person & Work of the Holy Spirit -B.B. Warfield

A Plea to Pray for Pastors -Gardiner Spring

A Tearful Farewell from a Faithful Pastor -E. Griffin

Heaven: A World of Love -Jonathan Edwards

You Know God's in Control -J.I. Packer

The History of Redemption -Jonathan Edwards

To Order or inquire about this ministry; call us toll-free at 1 800 789-8175 or write us at:

CalvaryPress

Box 805, Amityville, New York

The Publishing Mission of Calvary Press

Calvary Press is a publishing ministry completely owned and operated by Grace Reformed Baptist Church of Long Island, New York. We are firmly committed to bringing into print outstanding Christian literature that glorifies God and His Word and which is relevant to the crying needs of the church and the world at the close of the 20th century. We unashamedly stand upon the foundation stones of the Reformation: Scripture alone, Faith alone, Grace alone, Christ alone, and God's Glory alone! Our prayer for this ministry is found in two portions taken from the Psalms: "And let the beauty of the LORD our God be upon us, And establish the work of our hands; Yes, establish the work of our hands." (Psalm 90:17) and "Not unto us, O LORD, not unto us, but to Your name give glory." (Psalm 115:1).

A Special Word to Our Readers

Like similar ministries we are funded by a combination of the proceeds from the sale of our books and the generous financial support of God's people. Hopefully you have enjoyed this or one of our other books and have a burden to see solid Christian materials put into the hands of God's people all over our nation and world, —would you then consider supporting our ministry this year with a donation, and help make it possible to reach more people with the Gospel and solid teaching from God's Word. Your contributions are fully tax-deductible and will be put toward the various projects we have planned, our pressing need for equipment, and our growing staffing requirements. If the Lord leads you to lend a hand to our ministry would you please mail your donation to: "Calvary Press Donation", P.O. Box 805, Amityville, NY 11701. —Thank you for the support.